¿HABLA ESPAÑOL?

Second Edition

¿HABLA ESPAÑOL?

AN
INTRODUCTORY
COURSE

SECOND EDITION

EDWARD DAVID ALLEN
The Ohio State University

LYNN A. SANDSTEDT
University of Northern Colorado

BRENDA WEGMANN

TERESA MÉNDEZ-FAITH
Brandeis University

HOLT, RINEHART AND WINSTON

New York·Chicago·San Francisco·Atlanta·Dallas·Montreal·Toronto·London·Sydney

CONTRIBUTORS:

Naldo Lombardi
Servio Becerra, *University of Michigan*, Ann Arbor
Mary McVey Gill

Library of Congress Cataloging in Publication Data

Main entry under title:

¿Habla español?

First ed. (1976) by E. D. Allen, L. A. Sandstedt, and B. Wegmann.
Includes index.
1. Spanish language—Grammar—1950–
I. Allen, Edward David   II. Allen,
Edward David   ¿Habla español?
PC4112.H26 1980   468.2'421   80-23174
ISBN 0-03-057196-0

Text and cover design by Carmen M. Cavazos
Cover art: Mola from the San Blas Islands, Panama
    Courtesy: Tianguis Folk Art, N.Y.
Illustrations by Tom O'Sullivan
Credits for photographs appear at the end of this book.

TABLE OF CONTENTS

CAPÍTULO 22:
Valores morales y religiosos 407

PREFACE

The Second Edition of *¿HABLA ESPAÑOL? An Introductory Course* reflects the comments and suggestions of professors across the country who have used the original text with great success in their classrooms. In planning the revision, a comprehensive survey was sent out to both users of the text and other instructors of first-year Spanish courses. The book has been revised according to the responses to that survey. This text is designed to give the instructor as much freedom and flexibility as possible in creating his or her own course and to provide that combination of features which most participants in the survey requested. Special features of the book are: concise grammar explanations with abundant examples; mini-dialogues of two to ten lines illustrating grammatical structures in context and introducing only one new grammatical structure at a time; personalized questions to encourage real conversation in class; cultural notes on customs, points of interest and usage; a large variety of exercises and components to choose from, and optional activities and illustrated readings on Hispanic culture.

ORGANIZATION

This Second Edition consists of a preliminary lesson and 22 chapters, four review sections and ten illustrated readings. The preliminary lesson emphasizes pronunciation and presents classroom expressions, as well as simple vocabulary and structures to enable the students to introduce themselves. Each of the following 22 chapters is divided into three parts as follows:

   I.   *Explicación:* three to five grammar topics, each introduced by a mini-dialogue with English translation and accompanied by exercises ranging from very simple oral drills to more challenging work, including personalized questions and situational exercises

   II.   Main dialogue, followed by comprehension questions and cultural notes in English

   III.   *Actividades:* directed oral and written activities that combine and reinforce the grammar topics, vocabulary and culture of the chapter

Each chapter concludes with the chapter vocabulary list.

FLEXIBILITY

The chapters are organized so that the class can begin either with Part I, the *Explicación,* or Part II, the main dialogue. By beginning with the *Explicación,* the instructor can present the mini-dialogues first and thus introduce only one grammar point at a time within a meaningful context. Most users of the first edition preferred this approach, as the main dialogue serves as a logical culmination of the grammar and vocabulary presented in the lesson. On the other hand, by beginning with the main dialogue, the instructor can expose the students to all the grammatical structures of the chapter within a single, authentic and meaningful context before moving to the grammar section where each structure is taken up separately.

Class recitation of the oral substitution drills after each grammar topic is optional, as these drills are included in the laboratory manual and tape program. The personalized questions are also optional. These questions were written to be directed to the student by the instructor, but they can be modified in many ways to elicit different responses.

Each chapter is organized around a particular theme, as shown by the individual chapter titles. This theme is reflected in the topic of the dialogues, in the grammar examples and exercises, and in the activities. The chapter vocabularies have also been reorganized to group the lists according to the themes of the individual lessons. After every even-numbered chapter (except Chapter 22) there is an illustrated reading on Hispanic culture. The instructor may present these readings in any way he or she wants and use the text and the photographs as a springboard for a variety of classroom or home assignments for cultural enrichment. The students may be asked to prepare a short paragraph about one of the photographs, or a short report on the theme of the essay.

The four review sections (one each after Chapters 5, 11, 17, and 22) are designed to review key grammar points and provide review exercises which the students can do in class or at home as a self-test.

NEW TO THIS EDITION

In response to users' suggestions, the preterite and imperfect tenses are now presented in the first half of the text. In addition, the mini-dialogues have all been updated, revised and shortened to make them more interesting, livelier, and more focussed on the theme vocabulary.

The number and variety of exercises have been increased to offer the instructor greater choice and the student more practice. Situational exercises related to the chapter theme have been added to induce more active participation by the student.

The activities are now illustrated and better coordinated with the rest of the chapter. They now serve to reinforce the thematic vocabulary.

Finally, the main dialogue now appears at the end of each chapter to summarize the new grammar and vocabulary in context.

SUPPLEMENTARY MATERIALS

This text may be used in conjunction with any of the following components:
Manual de laboratorio and tape program. Each chapter of this manual corre-

sponds to the respective chapter in the text. Each laboratory session is approximately forty minutes and includes pronunciation exercises, a dramatic reading of some of the mini-dialogues and the main dialogue, listening comprehension questions, substitution drills from the main text, a dictation, and additional grammar exercises.

Cuaderno de ejercicios. Each chapter of this workbook corresponds to the respective chapter in the book and provides additional practice of the grammatical structures through a variety of written assignments. The workbook may be used as a self-study manual or it may be assigned to give students practice in writing or additional work in specific problem areas.

Manual del instructor. This Instructor's Manual provides suggestions for the teaching of this first-year Spanish course. Sample lesson plans, sample tests, a discussion of the various chapter elements, and a chapter-by-chapter guide are provided.

Readers. This program also offers three beginning level readers to give students additional reading practice. Any of the three readers may be introduced midway through the course.

Lecturas básicas: A Literary Reader, Second Edition, by Guillermo I. Castillo-Feliú and Edward J. Mullen, contains 10 easy-to-read stories by Spanish-speaking writers of Spain, Latin America, and the United States.

Lecturas básicas: A Civilization Reader, Second Edition, by Joaquín Valdés contains 12 essays that focus on historical events and modern life in each country or region of the Spanish-speaking world.

Lecturas básicas: A Cultural Reader, Second Edition, by Helen C. Agüera and Modesto M. Díaz, contains 10 readings that focus on contemporary lifestyles of Spanish-speaking people and their traditional social attitudes and values.

In each of these three books the reading selections are short, have been carefully annotated and are accompanied by appropriate illustrations. Each selection is followed by comprehension questions and exercises for vocabulary development.

ACKNOWLEDGMENTS

We would like to thank Inés Bergquist for her careful editing of the manuscript and many helpful suggestions. We would also like to thank Karen Misler of Holt, Rinehart and Winston for her constant support, advice, and diligence throughout the development and production of the project.

We are also grateful to the teachers, editors, and consultants who participated in the survey and who reviewed the material. Special thanks is due to the following reviewers whose comments, both positive and critical, were instrumental in the revision of this text:

Mark Accornero, *Cabrillo College*; Jack S. Bailey, *The University of Texas at El Paso*; Karen Breiner-Sanders, *Georgetown University*; Fe' Brittain, *Pima Community College*; R. Thomas Douglass, *The University of Iowa*; Pia Friedrich, *University of Washington*; John R. Garnett, *Miami-Dade Community College*; Joe R. González, *Sacramento City College*; Donna J. Gustafson, *San Jose State University*; Pamela Lee Guy, *Texas A & M University*; Hilda Losada, *Evergreen Valley College*; María Lafuente Rekowski, *Sacramento City College*; Katherine C. Richards, *Texas A & M University*; Harry Rosser, *Brandeis University*; Emily Spinelli, *The University of Michigan, Dearborn*; Alan Swietlicki, *The University of Missouri, Columbia*; Betty Weibezahl, *SUNY, College at Cortland*; and Leslie N. Wilson, *The Florida State University*.

¿HABLA ESPAÑOL?

Second Edition

Lección preliminar

LA SALA DE CLASE

Una sala de clase en la Universidad de Valencia

OBJECTIVES

In this preliminary lesson we introduce, discuss, and practice:

1. the sounds of Spanish, vowels and consonants
2. numbers 1–30
3. the Spanish alphabet, which has 30 letters rather than 26
4. word stress, or how to know which syllable of a word receives the emphasis
5. capitalization and punctuation in Spanish

You will also learn how to greet someone and introduce yourself, some useful polite expressions like *thank you* or *you're welcome*, and vocabulary and expressions related to the classroom.

PRESENTACIONES

Buenos días. Me llamo
Elvira García. ¿Cómo se
llama usted, señorita?

Y usted, señor,
¿cómo se llama?

Me llamo
Elena Ramírez.

Me llamo
Miguel Guzmán.

Mucho gusto, señorita.
Mucho gusto, señora García.

Buenos días,
señor Guzmán.

Preguntas

1. ¿Cómo se llama la profesora? (Se llama . . .) 2. ¿Cómo se llama la señorita? 3. ¿Cómo se llama el señor? 4. ¿Cómo se llama usted? (Me llamo . . .)

PRONUNCIATION: VOWELS

A. In general, Spanish vowels are short, clear, and tense. English speakers must avoid the tendency to lengthen them when they are stressed and to shorten them when they are unstressed. There are five simple vowel sounds, represented by the letters *a, e, i* (or *y*), *o* and *u*.

a   This vowel is similar in sound to the first vowel of *father*, but it is more open, tense, and shorter than that of English. The stressed syllables appear in bold type.

        A**de**la, **A**na, Cata**li**na, Marga**ri**ta

e   This vowel in most cases has a sound similar to the first vowel in the English word *ate*, but shorter and tenser.

        E**le**na, Fede**ri**co, Te**re**sa, Fe**li**pe

i, (y)   These letters are pronounced like the second vowel of *police*.

        Mi**guel**, Isa**bel**, Chris**ti**na, Fe**li**sa

o   The *o* is similar to the English *o* of *so* or *no*, except shorter.

        Paco, Al**fon**so, Ro**dol**fo, Ra**món**, An**to**nio, Teo**do**ro

u   The **u** is pronounced like the English *oo* in *cool* or *fool* (never the sound of *book* or of the *u* in *universal*).

        Su**sa**na, Ra**úl**, Je**sús**, **Úr**sula

B. Diphthongs

There are two weak vowels in Spanish, *i* and *u*, and three strong vowels, *a*, *e*, and *o*. Two strong vowels constitute two syllables, or sounds: **Le-al**. However, a combination of two weak vowels or of a weak and a strong vowel is a diphthong, a multiple vowel sound pronounced in the same syllable.

ia	Ali**cia**, Pa**tri**cia, San**tia**go
ua	Juan, Jua**ni**ta, E**duar**do
ie	Gabriel, **Die**go, Javier
ue	Con**sue**lo, Ma**nuel**
io	**Ma**rio, An**to**nio, **ra**dio, a**diós**
uo	an**ti**guo (*ancient*), **cuo**ta (*installment*)
iu	tri**un**fo (*triumph*), ciu**dad** (*city*)
ui (uy)	Luis, muy (*very*)
ai (ay)	**Jai**me, Rai**mun**do, hay (*there is*)
au	**Pau**la, Au**re**lio, Au**ro**ra
ei (ey)	rey (*king*), seis (*six*)
eu	Eu**ge**nio, Eu**ro**pa, feu**dal**
oi (oy)	hoy (*today*), es**toi**co (*stoic*)

LA SALA DE CLASE

El profesor:	Buenas tardes, estudiantes.
La clase:	Buenas tardes, profesor.
El profesor:	Repitan, por favor: la ventana.
La clase:	La ventana.
El profesor:	¿Qué es esto?
La clase:	Es la ventana.
El profesor:	Y esto, ¿qué es?
La clase:	Es el libro.
El profesor:	¡Muy bien! Y, ¿cómo se dice en español *door*?
La clase:	Se dice «puerta».
El profesor:	¡Excelente!

Preguntas

¿Cómo se dice en español . . . ?

a. desk
b. notebook
c. chalk
d. blackboard
e. table
f. chair
g. pencil

PRONUNCIATION: b, v, c, z, d, g, j, h, ll

b, v The letters *b* and *v* are pronounced in the same way. At the beginning of a word, they sound much like an English *b*, whereas in the middle of a word they have a sound somewhere between *b* and *v̱* in English.

Bogotá, Valencia, ventana, burro; Habana, Sevilla, Córdoba

c, z In Spanish America the letters *c* (before *e* and *i*) and *z* are pronounced like an English *s*.*

Alicia, Galicia, Cecilia, Zaragoza, tiza, La Paz

A *c* before *a, o, u,* or any consonant other than *h*, is pronounced like a *k*.

inca, coca, costa (*coast*), Cuzco, secreto, clase
But: chocolate, Chile, cha-cha-chá

d The letter *d* has two sounds. At the beginning of a word or after an *n* or *l*, it is somewhat like a *d* in English, but "softer."

día, don, Diego, Miranda, Matilde

In all other positions, it is similar to the *th* in the English word *then*.

Felicidad, Eduardo, Ricardo, pared, estudiante

g, j The *g* before *i* or *e*, and the *j*, are both pronounced approximately like an English *h*.

Jorge, Josefina, geología, Jalisco, ingeniería, región, página

The *g* before *a, o,* or *u* is pronounced approximately like the English *g* of *gate*. In the combinations *gue* and *gui* the *u* is not pronounced, and the *g* has the same English *g* sound.

amigo, amiga, gusto, Miguel, guitarra

In the combinations *gua* and *guo*, the *u* is pronounced like a *w* in English.

antiguo, Guatemala

h The Spanish *h* is silent.

Habana, Honduras, Hernández, hotel, Hugo

ll In most of the Spanish-speaking world, a double *l* (*ll*) is much like the English *y* of *yes*.

llama, Vallejo, Sevilla, Murillo

---

* In most parts of Spain a *c* before *e* or *i*, a *z* before *a, e, i, o,* or *u*, and a final *z* are pronounced like a *th* in the English word *thin*. This is a characteristic feature of the Castilian accent.

EXPRESIONES ÚTILES

Por favor. *Please.*
Muchas gracias. *Thank you.*
De nada. (No hay de qué.) *You're welcome.*
Perdón. *Excuse me (for something I've done—forgive me).*
Con permiso. *Excuse me (for something I'm about to do—pass in front of someone, eat something, etc.). With your permission.*

No sé. *I don't know.*
No comprendo. *I don't understand.*
Tengo una pregunta. *I have a question.*
¡Hola! ¿Qué tal? *Hello! How are things?*
¡Adiós! *Good-bye.*
¡Hasta luego! *See you later.*
¡Felicitaciones! *Congratulations!*

Una expresión apropiada

Give an appropriate Spanish expression for each of the following situations, using those above.

PRONUNCIATION: n, ñ, q, r, rr, x

n The *n* is usually pronounced like an *n* in English, except before certain consonants. Before *b, p* or *m* it is pronounced like an *m*.

en (*in*) Ma**dr**id, en Bogotá, en Panamá, inmi**gran**te

Before a *g* or a *k* sound or before a *j* (h sound), it represents a sound close to the English ending -*ng*.

banco, **tan**go, anara**nj**ado (*orange colored*), i**nglé**s

ñ   The sound of *ñ* is roughly equivalent to the English *ny* of *canyon*.

se**ñor**, ma**ñan**a, espa**ñol**

q   A *q* is always combined with a *u* in Spanish, and represents the sound *k*.

Quito, En**ri**que

r   There are two ways of pronouncing the single *r*. At the beginning of a word or after *l, n,* or *s,* it has the same sound as the *rr* (see below). Otherwise, it is close to a *tt (kitty, Betty)* or *dd (ladder)* in conversational American English.

Pat**ri**cia, El**vi**ra, To**rti**lla, Pi**la**r

rr   The *rr* sound is trilled, like a Scottish burr or a child imitating the sound of a motor. The *rr* sound is represented in two ways in writing: by a single *r* at the beginning of a word or after *l, n,* or *s,* and by the *rr*.

Rosa, **R**ita, **R**obe**r**to, **r**ico (*rich*) **ra**dio
En**ri**que, alrede**dor** (*around*), Is**ra**el
Perro (*dog*), as contrasted with **pero** (*but*)

x   The *x* has several different sounds in Spanish. Before a consonant, it is pronounced like an English *s.*

e**x**terno, **tex**to

Before a vowel it is like a *gs.*

e**x**amen, exis**ten**cia

In many words *x* used to have the sound of the Spanish *j.* In most of these words the spelling has been changed, but a few words still use the old spelling: **Mé**xico, Qui**x**ote, Oa**x**aca.

NUMBERS 1–30

0 cero		
1 uno (un, una)	11 once	21 veintiuno
2 dos	12 doce	(veinte y uno)
3 tres	13 trece	22 veintidós
4 cuatro	14 catorce	(veinte y dos)
5 cinco	15 quince	23 veintitrés
6 seis	16 dieciséis (diez y seis)	(veinte y tres)
7 siete	17 diecisiete (diez y siete)	24 veinticuatro
8 ocho	18 dieciocho (diez y ocho)	(veinte y cuatro)
9 nueve	19 diecinueve (diez y nueve)	25 veinticinco
10 diez	20 veinte	(veinte y cinco)

26 veintiséis	28 veintiocho	30 treinta
(veinte y seis)	(veinte y ocho)	
27 veintisiete	29 veintinueve	
(veinte y siete)	(veinte y nueve)	

The numbers 16 to 19 and 21 to 29 can be written in two ways, but they are usually written as one word. Notice the spelling changes and the use of the accent on numbers ending in *s*.

¿Cuántos libros hay aquí? –Veintiséis.	*How many books are there here?*
(Veinte y seis.)	*Twenty-six.*
¿Cuántos estudiantes hay?	*How many students are there?*
–Diecinueve. (Diez y nueve.)	*Nineteen.*

Ejercicios

A.   *Uno, dos, tres* . . . Count from 1 to 30, each student taking a turn.

B.   *Y ahora, de a dos.* Count to 30 by two's.

C.   *Preguntas*

   a. En la sala de clase, ¿cuántas paredes hay?
   b. ¿Cuántos libros hay?
   c. ¿Cuántos profesores hay?
   d. ¿Cuántos lápices hay en la mesa (en el escritorio)?
   e. ¿Hay diez ventanas? ¿diez puertas?
   f. ¿Cuántas páginas hay en esta lección preliminar?

THE SPANISH ALPHABET

a	(a)	j	(jota)	r	(ere)
b	(be)	k	(ka)	rr	(erre)
c	(ce)	l	(ele)	s	(ese)
ch	(che)	ll	(elle)	t	(te)
d	(de)	m	(eme)	u	(u)
e	(e)	n	(ene)	v	(ve or uve)
f	(efe)	ñ	(eñe)	w	(doble ve)
g	(ge)	o	(o)	x	(equis)
h	(hache)	p	(pe)	y	(i griega)
i	(i)	q	(cu)	z	(zeta)

There are 30 letters in the Spanish alphabet. The *ch*, *ll*, and *rr*, although they are two-letter groups, stand for only one sound and are considered as single letters.

Ejercicios

A. Spell the following words in Spanish.

1. mucho   3. guerrilla   5. tiza   7. favor
2. muy   4. quince   6. excelente   8. Juan

B. Now spell your name for the class.

PRONUNCIATION: WORD STRESS (EMPHASIS OF SYLLABLES)

1. Most Spanish words are divided into syllables after a vowel or diphthong; diphthongs are not divided. A single consonant (including *ch*, *ll*, and *rr*) between two vowels begins a new syllable.

co-mo	mu-cho	a-diós
cla-se	gra-cias	fe-li-ci-ta-cio-nes
Te-re-sa	pi-za-rra	au-to

2. Where there are two consonants between vowels, the syllable is usually divided between the consonants.

ex-ce-len-te	cua-der-no	Ca-li-for-nia
es-pa-ñol	u-ni-ver-sal	Jor-ge

3. Words ending in a vowel, *n*, or *s* are pronounced with the emphasis on the next-to-the-last syllable.

his-**to**-ria	**co**-mo	re-**pi**-tan
A-na	**bue**-nos	**cla**-ses

4. Words ending in a consonant other than *n* or *s* have the emphasis on the final syllable.

es-pa-**ñol**	fa-**vor**	pa-**pel**
se-**ñor**	us-**ted**	pro-fe-**sor**

5. Words whose pronunciation differs from the above two patterns have written accents. The emphasis falls on the syllable with the accent.

ca-fé	pá-gi-na	lá-piz
per-dón	Her-nán-dez	a-diós

6. In a combination of a strong vowel (**a**, **e**, or **o**) and a weak vowel (**i** or **u**) where the weak vowel is stressed, a written accent divides them into two syllables. (If the weak vowel is not stressed, the combination is a diphthong and is one syllable.)*

E-fra-ín	dí-a	fi-lo-so-fí-a

Ejercicio

Divide the following words into syllables. Then underline the stressed syllable in each word.

1. señorita	5. color	9. pared
2. escritorio	6. Sevilla	10. lección
3. América	7. elefante	
4. universidad	8. guerrilla	

CAPITALIZATION AND PUNCTUATION

A. Capitalization

1. Nouns and adjectives of nationality are not capitalized.

francés	*French (adj.)*	el francés	*the Frenchman*
español	*Spanish (adj.)*	el español	*the Spaniard*
inglés	*English (adj.)*	el inglés	*the Englishman*

2. Names of languages are not capitalized.

el francés	*French (language)*
el español	*Spanish (language)*
el inglés	*English (language)*

B. Punctuation

1. In writing questions or exclamations, an inverted question mark or exclamation mark precedes the sentence, in addition to the usual marks at the end.

¿Cómo se llama ella?	*What is her name?*
¡Felicitaciones!	*Congratulations!*

---

* Note that an accent is also used with a few words to distinguish between meanings: **sí** *yes,* **si** *if;* **él** *he, it,* **el** *the.*

2. A dash is used instead of quotation marks to indicate a change of speaker in a dialogue.

—¡Hola! ¿Qué tal?   *"Hello! How are you?"*
—Muy bien, gracias.   *"Very well, thank you."*

3. When quotation marks are used, they are written differently in Spanish than in English.

Francisco se llama también «Paco».   *Francisco is also called "Paco."*

ACTIVIDADES

Una Expresión Apropiada

Tell what the people in each of the following drawings might be saying in Spanish.

Palabras Revueltas

Unscramble the letters to find words that are classroom items.

Modelo: olbri **libro**

1. palzi
2. uercadon
3. ziat

4. lisal
5. ripraza

¡Bingo!

Play the game of bingo, with your instructor calling out the numbers. Each student makes a card like the one shown, filling in each square with a number (of course, each card should be different). As the instructor calls off the numbers, cross off any number called that appears on your card. The first student with three numbers in a row crossed off wins.

3	30	12
13	10	11
7	29	22

VOCABULARIO ACTIVO

Expresiones útiles

¡Adiós! *Good-bye.*
Buenos días. *Good morning. Good day.*
Buenas tardes. *Good afternoon.*
¿Cómo se dice . . . ? *How do you say . . . ?*
¿Cómo se llama . . . ? *What is the name of . . . ?*
Con permiso. *Excuse me (for something I'm about to do). With your permission.*
De nada. (No hay de qué.) *You're welcome.*
Es . . . *It's . . .*
¡Felicitaciones! *Congratulations!*
¡Hasta luego! *See you later.*
¡Hola! ¿Qué tal? *Hi. How are you?*
Me llamo . . . *My name is . . .*
Muchas gracias. *Thank you.*
Mucho gusto. *Glad to meet you.*
Muy bien. Excelente. *Very good. Excellent.*
No comprendo. *I don't understand.*
No sé. *I don't know.*
Perdón. *Excuse me.*
Por favor. *Please.*
¿Qué es esto? *What is this?*
Repitan. *Repeat.*
Se dice . . . *You say . . .*
Tengo una pregunta. *I have a question.*

En la sala de clase

el cuaderno *notebook*
el escritorio *desk*
el español *Spanish*
el estudiante *(male) student;* **la estudiante** *(female) student*
el francés *French*
el inglés *English*
el lápiz *pencil*
la lección *lesson*
el libro *book*
la mesa *table*
la página *page*
el papel *paper*
la pared *wall*
la pizarra *blackboard*
la pluma *pen*
el profesor *(male) professor;* **la profesora** *(female) professor*
la puerta *door*
la silla *chair*
la tiza *chalk*
la ventana *window*
el señor *man; sir; Mr.*
la señora *lady; ma'am; Mrs.*
la señorita *young lady; miss; Miss*
Sí *Yes*
No *No*
y *and*

CAPÍTULO 1

LA FAMILIA

El abuelo La abuela

La madre El padre

Los niños

El hijo La hija El esposo (de la hija)

OBJECTIVES

LANGUAGE: In this chapter we introduce, discuss, and practice:

1. subject pronouns (corresponding to *I, you*, etc.in English) and **estar,** a verb meaning *to be*
2. the present tense of regular verbs that end in **-ar**
3. articles and gender of nouns
4. the plural of nouns and articles
5. how to make Spanish sentences negative

You will also learn vocabulary related to the family and family life.

CULTURE: The dialogue takes place on a plane headed for La Paz, capital of Bolivia and highest capital city in the world.

EXPLICACIÓN

I. SUBJECT PRONOUNS AND PRESENT TENSE OF ESTAR

(1)	**Sr. Gómez:**	¡María! ¿Tú aquí? ¿Cómo *estás*?
(2)	**María:**	*Estoy* bien, gracias.
(3)	**Sr. Gómez:**	Y la familia, ¿cómo *está*?
(4)	**María:**	Papá y mamá *están* bien, pero el hermano de mamá *está* enfermo. Y ustedes, ¿cómo *están*?
(5)	**Sr. Gómez:**	Nosotros *estamos* bien, gracias.
(6)	**María:**	¡Qué suerte! Y . . . el hijo de doña Lola, ¿*está* en La Paz?
(7)	**Sr. Gómez:**	No, él *está* en Sucre, con el abuelo.
(8)	**María:**	¡Ah, qué bien! Bueno . . . adiós señor Gómez.
(9)	**Sr. Gómez:**	Adiós María.

1. ¿Cómo está María?   **2.** ¿Cómo está el hermano de la mamá de María?   **3.** ¿Dónde está el hijo de doña Lola?   **4.** ¿Dónde está usted en este momento?

A.   **Estar** *(to be)* is an infinitive verb form. It is conjugated by removing the **-ar** ending and adding other endings to the **est-** stem.

estar

Person		Singular			Plural		
1st	yo*	estoy	*I am*		nosotros nosotras	estamos	*we are*
2nd	tú	estás	*you are*		vosotros vosotras	estáis	*you are*
3rd	él ella usted	está	*he is* *she is* *you are*		ellos ellas ustedes	están	*they are* *you are*

(1) María! You (are) here? How are you? (2) I'm fine, thank you. (3) And the family, how are they? (4) Mom and Dad are fine, but Mother's brother is sick. And all of you, how are you? (5) We are fine, thank you. (6) What luck! And . . . doña Lola's son, is he in La Paz? (7) No, he is in Sucre with (his) grandfather. (8) Oh, how nice! Well . . . goodbye, Mr. Gómez. (9) Goodbye, María.

*Notice that **yo,** the first person singular subject pronoun, is not capitalized.

B. Subject pronouns are used far less frequently in Spanish than in English, since in Spanish the verb endings indicate the subject of the sentence. However, subject pronouns *are* used in Spanish, mainly to avoid confusion or for the sake of emphasis.

Estoy bien.	*I'm fine.* (statement of fact)
Yo estoy bien.	*I'm fine.* (emphatic)
Él está aquí. (Ella está aquí.)	*He is here. (She is here.)* (clarification)

C. There are several ways of saying *you* in Spanish. In general, **tú,** the familiar singular form, is used in speaking to friends, young children, and family members. It corresponds to "first-name basis" in English. The **usted** form is used in more formal situations, such as with older people or people in authority.

D. In most parts of Spain the plural of **tú** is **vosotros** (masculine), **vosotras** (feminine). However, in Latin America, where the **vosotros** form is not generally used, **ustedes** is the plural of both **tú** and **usted.***

E. **Usted** and **ustedes** are frequently abbreviated in written Spanish, as **Ud.** and **Uds.,** or **Vd.** and **Vds.**

Ud. está en el aeropuerto con don Fernando.	*You are in the airport with don Fernando.*
Vds. están en la farmacia con tía Eva.	*You are in the drugstore with Aunt Eva.*

F. The Spanish subject pronouns **él, ella, nosotros, nosotras, vosotros, vosotras, ellos,** and **ellas** show gender, either masculine or feminine. In speaking about two or more males, or about a mixture of males and females, the masculine forms **nosotros** and **ellos** are used. The feminine forms **nosotras** and **ellas** are used only to refer to two or more females.

Ellos (Hugo y José) están en Madrid con abuelo.	*They (Hugo and José) are in Madrid with Grandfather.*
Ellos (Juan y María) están aquí.	*They (Juan and María) are here.*
Ellas (Rita y Teresa) están en la universidad.	*They (Rita and Teresa) are at the university.*
Nosotros (Elena, Ricardo y yo) estamos en casa con los niños.	*We (Elena, Ricardo, and I) are at home with the children.*
Nosotras (María y Andrea) estamos en casa con mamá y papá.	*We (María and Andrea) are at home with Mom and Dad.*

*Since the **vosotros** form is not widely used, except in Spain, it is not practiced extensively in this book.

Ejercicios

A. Give the feminine form of the following subject pronouns.

1. él _____
2. nosotros _____
3. usted _____
4. vosotros _____

5. yo _____
6. ellos _____
7. tú _____
8. ustedes _____

B. Give the singular form of the following subject pronouns.

1. nosotros _____
2. ellos _____
3. vosotras _____

4. ustedes _____
5. ellas _____

C. Create new sentences, substituting the words in the list for those in italics. Change the verb form if necessary.

1. Aquí está *Roberto*.
   a. María   **b.** Teresa y José   **c.** yo   **d.** nosotros   **e.** tú

2. ¿Cómo está *el señor López*?
   a. Manuel y Alicia   **b.** tú   **c.** ustedes   **d.** la señorita Pérez   **e.** Juan y tú

D. Mrs. Ramos always likes to know where everyone is and how they are. Answer her questions with a subject pronoun, using **sí** (*yes*) as in the example.

Modelo: ¿Eva está en Guatemala?   **Sí, ella está en Guatemala.**

1. ¿Susana y Jorge están en Madrid?
2. ¿Mamá está en Los Ángeles?

3. ¿El hijo de doña Lola está en Sucre?
4. ¿Los abuelos de José están aquí?
5. ¿Las hermanas de María están en clase?
6. ¿Tú y Alicia están bien?
7. ¿La señora López está en el aeropuerto?
8. ¿Usted y los niños están en casa?

E. Complete each subject in column A with an appropriate ending from column B.

A	B
Usted	están en México
Tío Ricardo	estoy bien
Papá y yo	está en San Francisco
Cecilia y mamá	estás aquí
Tú y tu hermano	está muy enfermo
Yo	estamos en casa
La familia de Teresa	está con el abuelo de Pablo
Tú	estáis en España

Preguntas

1. ¿Cómo está usted? ¿Y la familia? **2.** ¿Está usted con amigos *(friends)*? **3.** ¿Está usted en la universidad? **4.** ¿Están ustedes en la clase de español? **5.** ¿Está aquí el profesor? **6.** ¿Están bien ustedes? Y yo, ¿estoy bien?

II. PRESENT TENSE OF REGULAR -AR VERBS

(1) **Teresa:** Tú *estudias* geografía, ¿verdad?
(2)   **Juan:** Sí, ahora *estudiamos* la formación de la tierra; por eso *busco* un libro sobre los volcanes.
(3) **Teresa:** ¿Y *hablan* ustedes de ecología?
(4)   **Juan:** Sí, el profesor Vega, el esposo de Clarita, *enseña* cómo *conservar* energía.
(5) **Teresa:** ¡Qué interesante! Ahora *deseo conservar* energía. Tú *llevas* los libros ¿bien?

1. ¿Quién estudia geografía? **2.** ¿Qué busca ahora? **3.** ¿Hablan mucho de ecología en la clase? **4.** ¿Quién desea conservar energía?

(1) You are studying geography, right? (2) Yes, now we are studying the formation of the earth; for that reason I am looking for a book on volcanoes. (3) And you talk about ecology? (4) Yes, professor Vega, Clarita's husband, teaches how to conserve energy. (5) How interesting! Now I want to conserve energy. You carry the books, okay?

A. Verbs that end in **-ar** in Spanish are referred to as **-ar** verbs, one of which is **estar**, which you just saw. **Estar** is an irregular **-ar** verb; that is, it has its own special forms. Most **-ar** verbs are conjugated by removing the infinitive ending **-ar** and replacing it with the endings, **-o, -as, -a, -amos, -áis, -an. Hablar,** *to speak*, is a regular **-ar** verb:

hablar *(to speak)*

yo	hablo	nosotros(-as)	hablamos
tú	hablas	vosotros(-as)	habláis
él ⎱		ellos ⎱	
ella ⎬ habla		ellas ⎬ hablan	
usted ⎰		ustedes ⎰	

Other regular **-ar** verbs are:

buscar	*to look for*	llegar	*to arrive*
desear	*to want*	llevar	*to carry, to take*
enseñar	*to teach*	necesitar	*to need*
hablar	*to talk, to speak*	tomar	*to take; to drink*
estudiar	*to study*	viajar	*to travel*

¿Llevas los libros?	*Are you carrying the books?*
El no desea viajar.	*He doesn't want to travel.*
El esposo de Graciela necesita un pasaporte.*	*Graciela's husband needs a passport.*
Nosotros también buscamos un hotel.	*We are also looking for a hotel.*

C. Notice that the present tense in Spanish can be rendered in several ways in English.

Hablo español.	*I speak Spanish.* *I do speak Spanish.* *I am speaking Spanish.*
¿Estudias francés?	*Do you study French?* *Are you studying French?*

The present tense is also often used in place of the future tense, to imply that the action will take place in the immediate future.

El hermano de Juan lleva el regalo.	*Juan's brother will take (is taking) the present.*
Los padres de Eva toman el avión.	*Eva's parents will take (are taking) the plane.*

*Note that **de** (*of*) is used for the possessive in Spanish.

D. Verbs of motion, such as **viajar** and **llegar,** require the preposition **a** before a noun that indicates a destination.

Ellos no viajan a Los Ángeles; viajan a Nueva York.   *They aren't traveling to Los Angeles; they're traveling to New York.*
Las dos hermanas viajan en avión.   *The two sisters are traveling by plane.*
El avión llega a Madrid.   *The plane arrives in Madrid.*
El avión llega hoy.   *The plane arrives today.*

Ejercicios

A.   Answer each question in the affirmative.

Modelo: Hablo español. ¿Y Roberto?   **Roberto también habla español.**

1. Estudio geografía. ¿Y los hijos de Carmen?
2. Busco un libro. ¿Y usted?
3. Enseño aquí. ¿Y el profesor Vega?
4. Llevo un regalo. ¿Y ustedes?
5. Necesito un lápiz. ¿Y tía Rosa?

B.   Change each sentence, substituting the words in the list for those in italics.
1. *Sofía* estudia francés.
   a. Antonio y yo   **b.** tú   **c.** los abuelos de Pedro   **d.** yo   **e.** usted
2. *Nosotros* deseamos conservar energía.
   a. papá y mamá   **b.** yo   **c.** abuelo   **d.** tú   **e.** ustedes

C.   Change the verbs and subjects to the plural.

1. Llego hoy.
2. Él habla mucho.
3. Ella estudia la formación de la tierra.
4. Usted busca un libro sobre ecología.
5. Necesitas estudiar.

D.   Complete the sentences with the appropriate form of the verb in parentheses.

1. (buscar) Nosotros _____ la clase de español.
2. (necesitar) El esposo de Juana _____ un diccionario.
3. (enseñar) El profesor _____ muy bien.
4. (hablar) Los estudiantes _____ en la clase.
5. (viajar) Paco y yo _____ a Madrid.
6. (llevar) Yo _____ los pasaportes.
7. (desear) Tú _____ hablar con los padres de Jaime.
8. (llegar) La esposa de Felipe _____ hoy.

E. Give the Spanish equivalent of the following sentences.

1. I study Spanish.
2. We are looking for a pencil.
3. Uncle John travels a lot.
4. You (*tú*) are carrying the present.

5. You (*usted*) need the book.
6. You (*ustedes*) conserve energy.
7. Grandpa wants to travel.
8. Mom and Dad arrive today.

Preguntas

1. ¿Estudia usted español? **2.** ¿Desea usted hablar bien español?   **3.** ¿Hablamos español ahora?   **4.** ¿Habla bien español el profesor?   **5.** ¿Desea usted viajar a México? ¿a España? ¿a Venezuela?   **6.** ¿Necesita pasaporte para viajar a México? ¿a Chile? ¿a Bolivia? **7.** Habla mucho el profesor? ¿y los estudiantes? (Sí, . . .)   **8.** ¿Necesitamos viajar por avión o por barco (*ship*) para llegar a España?   **9.** ¿Desean ustedes conservar energía? ¿hablar de ecología?

III. ARTICLES AND GENDER OF NOUNS

(1) **Tía Pepa:** ¿Qué guardas en *el* cuarto, Juanito?
(2) **Juanito:** Bueno . . . guardo *la* bicicleta, *una* calculadora, *el* televisor, *un* diccionario, *la* silla de tía Tula, *una* mesa . . .
(3) **Tía Pepa:** ¿Guardas también *un* elefante?
(4) **Juanito:** ¿*Un* elefante? ¡Qué ridículo! *El* elefante está en *la* sala.

1. ¿Qué guarda Juanito en el cuarto?   **2.** ¿Dónde está el elefante?

A. In Spanish all nouns are classified according to their gender—that is, according to whether they are masculine or feminine. This classification seldom corresponds to the sexual nature of the words themselves. When you learn a noun in Spanish it is important that you also learn its gender—that is, whether it is a masculine noun or a feminine noun.

B. Articles in Spanish are also masculine or feminine. The singular definite articles in Spanish are **el** (masculine) and **la** (feminine).

(1) What do you keep in (your) room, Juanito? (2) Well . . . I keep (my) bicycle, a calculator, the television set, a dictionary, Aunt Tula's chair, a table . . . (3) Do you also keep an elephant there? (4) An elephant? How ridiculous! The elephant is in the living room.

C. Most Spanish nouns ending in **-o** in the singular are masculine. Most nouns ending in **-a** in the singular are feminine.

el libro	*the book*	la familia	*the family*
el regalo	*the present*	la mesa	*the table*
el esposo	*the husband*	la esposa	*the wife*

D. With nouns that do not end in the singular **-o** or **-a,** it can be helpful to learn the singular definite article at the same time that you learn the noun itself.

el avión	*the airplane*	la nación	*the nation*
el viaje	*the trip*	la verdad	*the truth*
el pasaporte	*the passport*	la región	*the region*
el hombre	*the man*	la mujer	*the woman*

It is useful to remember that nouns ending in **-ción** and **-dad** are feminine.

E. The singular indefinite articles are **un** (masculine) and **una** (feminine):

un regalo	*a present*	una montaña	*a mountain*
un cuaderno	*a notebook*	una puerta	*a door*
un hotel	*a hotel*	una ciudad	*a city*

F. The gender of many nouns that refer to people can be changed by changing the noun ending.

el abuelo	*the grandfather*	la abuela	*the grandmother*
el primo	*the (male) cousin*	la prima	*the (female) cousin*
el señor	*the man*	la señora	*the lady*
el hijo	*the son*	la hija	*the daughter*
un niño	*a boy*	una niña	*a girl*
un amigo	*a (male) friend*	una amiga	*a (female) friend*
un tío	*an uncle*	una tía	*an aunt*
un hermano	*a brother*	una hermana	*a sister*
un sobrino	*a nephew*	una sobrina	*a niece*

However, for some nouns the ending does not change, and so the gender of the person the noun refers to is shown by the gender of the article.

un turista	*a (male) tourist*	una turista	*a (female) tourist*

G. The definite article is used with titles such as **señor, señora,** or **señorita** when you are talking or asking *about* an individual:

¿Cómo está el señor Martínez?	*How is Mr. Martínez?*
El doctor García está en la farmacia.	*Doctor García is in the drugstore.*
La señorita Vargas pasa diez días en Montevideo.	*Miss Vargas is spending ten days in Montevideo.*

But the definite article is not used with the titles when you are speaking directly *to* the person with the title.

Buenos días, señor Martínez.　　　*Good morning (Good day), Mr.*
　　　　　　　　　　　　　　　　　Martínez.

Sí, doctor García.　　　　　　　　*Yes, Dr. García.*

¿Cómo está usted, señorita Vargas?　*How are you, Miss Vargas?*

Ejercicios

A.　Create new sentences by replacing the words in italics with those in the list.

1.　¿Dónde está *el abuelo?*
   a. familia　**b.** hotel　**c.** ciudad　**d.** señor　**e.** hermana de Daniel

2.　Buscan *una silla.*
   a. libro　**b.** farmacia　**c.** tiza　**d.** regalo　**e.** lápiz

B.　Change each definite article in the following sentences to the appropriate indefinite article.

Modelo:　Necesito el pasaporte.　**Necesito un pasaporte.**

1.　Tía Mirta lleva el regalo.
2.　Hablamos con la profesora.
3.　Mamá busca la farmacia.
4.　Bárbara necesita la mesa.
5.　Estudio con el amigo de Tomás.

C.　Make sentences from the following elements. Provide the appropriate definite articles, as in the example.

Modelo:　esposa de Ernesto/hablar/con/señor　**La esposa de Ernesto habla con el señor.**

1.　niño/buscar/ regalo
2.　mamá de Anita/ viajar/ a/ ciudad
3.　hermano de Pedro/ necesitar/silla
4.　señora/ llevar/ libro
5.　profesor/ enseñar/ capítulo uno

D.　Give the Spanish equivalent of the following sentences.

1.　Mr. Gómez teaches geography.
2.　Dr. García, how is the boy?
3.　Mrs. Rodríguez is spending three days in Barcelona with a friend.
4.　How are you, Miss Vega?
5.　She travels to the city with the family.
6.　Professor Martínez wants to speak with the student.

IV. PLURAL OF NOUNS AND ARTICLES

En el aeropuerto

(1) **Agente:** Buenos *días. Los pasaportes,* por favor.
(2) **Ramón:** Aquí están.
(3) **Isabel:** Ramón, ¿dónde están *los regalos* para *las sobrinas de Consuelo?*
(4) **Ramón:** ¡Dios mío! ¡Están en el avión!

1. ¿Dónde están Isabel y Ramón?   **2.** ¿Necesita el agente los pasaportes?   **3.** ¿Lleva Ramón los pasaportes?   **4.** ¿Dónde están los regalos para las sobrinas de Consuelo?

A. The plural of most nouns ending in a vowel is formed by adding **-s.** The plural of most nouns ending in a consonant is formed by adding **-es.**

libro, libros	hotel, hoteles
pizarra, pizarras	ciudad, ciudades
padre, padres	región, regiones*
abuelo, abuelos	señor, señores

To form the plural of a noun that ends in **-z,** change the **z** to **c** and add **-es; lápiz, lápices.**

At the airport
(1) Good morning (Good day). Passports, please. (2) Here they are. (3) Ramón, where are the presents for Consuelo's nieces? (4) Good grief! They're on the plane!

*Note that there is no accent mark on **regiones**, since the accent falls on the next-to-the-last syllable.

B. The plural definite articles are **los** (masculine) and **las** (feminine).

Buscamos el hotel.   *We are looking for the hotel.*
Buscamos los hoteles.   *We are looking for the hotels.*
Necesitamos la mesa.   *We need the table.*
Necesitamos las mesas.   *We need the tables.*

C. The plural indefinite articles are **unos** (masculine) and **unas** (feminine). In Spanish the plural indefinite article is equivalent in meaning to the English *some* or *several.*

Tío Manuel lleva un cuaderno.   *Uncle Manuel is carrying a notebook.*
Tío Manuel lleva unos cuadernos.   *Uncle Manuel is carrying some notebooks.*

Ramón está con una amiga.   *Ramón is with a friend.*
Ramón está con unas amigas.   *Ramón is with several friends.*

Ejercicios

A. Change the nouns and articles to the plural.

1. Necesitan la mesa.
2. Busco un lápiz.
3. Tú llevas el pasaporte.
4. Susana habla con una amiga.
5. Viajamos con el profesor.
6. Estoy con una prima.
7. Buscan la farmacia.
8. Estudio con un sobrino de Antonio.

B. Sara's mother calls her as she is studying with a friend. Her mother is very curious about how her daughter is doing. Answer her mother's questions using the singular form of the nouns, as Sara would.

Modelo: ¿Estudias con uno o dos amigos? **Estudio con un amigo.**

1. ¿Enseñas una o dos clases de español?
2. ¿Estás en una o dos clases de literatura?
3. ¿Viajas en uno o dos aviones para llegar a España?
4. ¿Deseas llegar en uno o dos días?
5. ¿Necesitas viajar a una o dos ciudades?
6. ¿Deseas hablar con uno o dos profesores allí?

Preguntas

1. ¿Desea usted viajar a muchas ciudades de España? ¿de México? ¿de Perú? **2.** ¿Necesita usted uno o dos lápices? ¿libros? ¿cuadernos? **3.** ¿Necesita usted uno o dos pasaportes para viajar a Colombia? ¿a Vietnam? **4.** ¿Necesita usted uno(a) o dos amigos(as)? ¿esposos(as)?

V. NEGATION

(1)	**Madre:**	Entonces *no deseas* tomar la sopa ¿verdad Tato?
(2)	**Tato:**	¡No! ¡*No tomo* la sopa!
(3)	**Madre:**	Está bien, pero tú *no hablas* ¡tú gritas! ¡*no necesitas* gritar!
(4)	**Tato:**	Y tú *no escuchas.*
(5)	**Madre:**	Sí, escucho, hijo, pero . . . ¿deseas o *no deseas* tomar la sopa?

1. ¿Desea tomar la sopa Tato?   **2.** ¿Escucha la madre de Tato?

The most common way to make a Spanish sentence negative is to place the word **no** directly in front of the conjugated form of the verb.

Eduardo no estudia mucho.	*Eduardo doesn't study much.*
Juan no está aquí. ¡Qué lástima!	*Juan isn't here. Too bad!*
No escuchan.	*They aren't listening.*

Ejercicios

A. Change each sentence to the negative.

Modelo: Los niños están aquí. **Los niños no están aquí.**

1. El profesor está en la clase.
2. Abuela desea viajar a España.
3. Tú estás enfermo.
4. El hotel está en la ciudad.
5. Papá y yo escuchamos música.
6. Paco desea tomar la sopa.

B. Francisco goes to visit his friends, the Garcías, but when he arrives at their house they don't seem to be home. However, someone answers the door and the following conversation takes place between them. Answer Francisco's questions in the negative as the man he's talking to would.

Modelo: Francisco: ¿Los señores García? ¿están en casa?
El hombre: **No, los señores García no están en casa.**

1. Francisco: ¿Y el hijo de los señores? ¿está aquí?
   El hombre: _____

(1) Then you don't want to eat the soup, right Tato? (2) No! I won't eat the soup! (3) All right, but you aren't talking, you are yelling! You don't need to yell! (4) And you aren't listening. (5) Yes, I am listening, son, but . . . do you or don't you want to eat the soup?

2. Francisco: ¿Y las hijas? ¿estudian con las primas?
   El hombre: _____
3. Francisco: ¿Y los padres? ¿escuchan música?
   El hombre: _____
4. Francisco: ¿Usted enseña en la universidad?
   El hombre: _____
5. Francisco: ¿Usted también desea hablar con los señores?
   El hombre: _____
6. Francisco: La casa está muy oscura (*dark*). ¿Usted desea conservar energía?
   El hombre: _____. Yo deseo
   robar (*steal*).

Preguntas

1. ¿Estudia usted geología? ¿ecología? ¿historia? ¿inglés?   **2.** ¿Se llama usted Albert Einstein? ¿Indira Gandhi?   **3.** ¿Me llamo yo Pablo Picasso? ¿Elizabeth Taylor?   **4.** ¿Estamos en una farmacia? ¿en un hotel? ¿en Madrid?   **5.** ¿Está usted en la clase de francés? ¿de geografía?   **6.** ¿Madrid está en Chile? ¿en Bolivia?   **7.** ¿Necesitan ustedes un pasaporte para viajar a Michigan? ¿a Florida? ¿a Canadá?   **8.** ¿Enseña usted español? ¿Enseño yo francés?

LA PAZ: LA CAPITAL DE BOLIVIA⁽¹⁾

En un avión. Los señores⁽²⁾ *García, de Venezuela, viajan a La Paz a pasar dos semanas con la familia del señor García.*

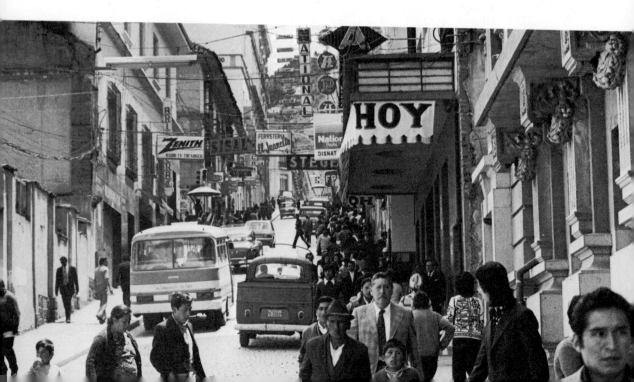

Madre:	En treinta minutos llegamos a La Paz. ¡Jesús[3], los pasaportes! ¡Ah!, están aquí. Tú llevas el regalo para doña Isabel ¿verdad?
Padre:	Sí, aquí está. Calma, por favor.
Pepito:	Mamá . . . ¿dónde está la casa de abuela y de tía Isabel?
Madre:	¿Cómo?[4] ¡Ah! . . . está en La Paz, hijo.
Pepito:	¿Y dónde está La Paz?
Padre:	Pepito, mamá está nerviosa y necesita descansar. Tú hablas con papá, ¿está bien? Y yo contesto todas las preguntas. Bueno, la ciudad de La Paz está en Bolivia.
Pepito:	¿Y dónde está Bolivia, papá?
Padre:	Bolivia está en Sudamérica.
Pepito:	¿Y dónde estamos nosotros ahora? ¿en Sudamérica o en un avión?
Padre:	Bueno, estamos en un avión y también estamos en Sudamérica.
Pepito:	¿Por qué?
Padre:	Porque . . . pues[5] . . . ¡porque sí! Pepito, ¿por qué no miras por la ventana? Yo necesito unos minutos de paz.
Pepito:	Pero La Paz está en Bolivia, papá.
Padre:	Uno . . . dos . . . tres . . . cuatro . . .
Pepito:	¿Y ahora hablamos de matemáticas?
Padre:	¡Señorita! (a la azafata). Señorita, por favor, ¿cuándo llegamos al aeropuerto?
Azafata:	Llegamos en dieciocho minutos, señor. ¿Está usted bien?

En el aeropuerto

Doña Isabel:	Hola, Catalina. ¿Cómo está usted? Y tú, Pepito, ¿cómo estás?
Pepito:	Bien, gracias, pero ¿dónde está papá?
Madre:	Está en la farmacia. No está bien. Busca un tranquilizante.
Doña Isabel:	¡Qué lástima! Está nervioso por el viaje ¿no?

semanas	*weeks*	**nerviosa**	*nervous*	**dónde**	*where*	**descansar**	*to rest*	**paz**	*peace*
azafata	*stewardess*	**cuándo**	*when*	**hola**	*hello*	**tranquilizante**	*tranquilizer*		

Ejercicio

Complete the sentences with the appropriate words from the dialogue:

1. Los señores García _____ a La Paz.
2. El padre lleva el _____ para doña Isabel.
3. Mamá _____ nerviosa y _____ descansar.
4. La ciudad de La Paz _____ en _____.
5. ¿Dónde _____ nosotros ahora?
6. ¿En Sudamérica o en _____ avión?
7. Pepito, ¿por qué no _____ por la _____?
8. Señorita, por favor, ¿cuándo _____ al aeropuerto?
9. (Papá) Está en la _____. _____ un tranquilizante.
10. ¡Qué _____! Está nervioso por _____ viaje ¿no?

NOTAS CULTURALES

1. La Paz: Even though the city of **Sucre** is officially considered Bolivia's legal capital, the seat of the national government was established in La Paz in 1898 and since then La Paz has functioned as the *de facto* capital of the country. The city lies in a deep, broad canyon at 11,735 ft. above sea level and is the world's highest capital. La Paz is 42 mi. southeast of Lake Titicaca, the world's highest lake navigable to large vessels (12,500 ft. above sea level).

2. The titles of address **señor (Sr.), señorita (Srta.),** and **señora (Sra.)** are used with last names and are roughly the equivalent of *Mr., Miss,* and *Mrs.* There is yet no equivalent of *Ms.,* though a few feminists have suggested **Sa.** When **señor** is used in the plural, it may refer to a couple (**los señores García** *Mr. and Mrs. García*).

Spanish also has two titles, **don** and **doña,** which are used only with first names. Originally titles of nobility, they are now used to show respect or deference to someone of higher professional or social position or to an older person. **Don** and **doña** are used when you are too intimate with someone to use **señor** or **señora,** but not intimate enough to be on a first-name basis.

3. Expressions such as **¡Jesús!,** and **¡Dios mío!** are commonly used in Spanish and are not regarded as blasphemous or coarse.

4. When a Spanish speaker does not hear or understand something, he or she usually indicates this by saying **¿Cómo?** where in English it is common to say *Huh?, What?,* or *Pardon me?*

5. Pues, bueno, and **este** are often used in Spanish when a person is momentarily at a loss for words. English speakers most often say *well, uh,* or *um* in these circumstances.

ACTIVIDADES

La Familia Sánchez: Tres generaciones

Using the labeled portraits of the Sánchez family, fill in the blanks with the appropriate Spanish words. You may wish to consult the *Vocabulario Activo* at the end of the chapter.

1. ¿Cómo se llama la esposa de Julio?. Ella se llama _____.
2. ¿Cómo se llaman los hijos de Julio?. Ellos se llaman _____ y _____.
3. Toño, el _____ de Susy, habla mucho.
4. Luz y Andrés, los _____ de Susy y Toño, llegan a la casa con regalos.
5. Irene y Julio, los _____ de Susy y Toño, buscan una aspirina para Josefina.

Situación

Study the following situation. Your teacher may call on you to act out one of the three roles. You may wish to consult the *Diálogo* or the *Vocabulario Activo* at the end of the chapter for assistance.

En el avión

Roberto and **María** are travelling by plane to La Paz. Roberto is nervous and María is calm. They talk for a while. Then one of them calls the stewardess. The stewardess asks them what they need. They answer. She says "Just a minute, please" *(un momento, por favor)*. She tells them that they are arriving at the airport in a few minutes. They say "Thank you."

VOCABULARIO ACTIVO

Verbos útiles

buscar *to look for, to search*
conservar (energía) *to save (energy)*
desear *to want*
enseñar *to teach*
escuchar *to listen to*
estar (bien, mal, enfermo) *to be (well, unwell, ill)*
estudiar *to study*
hablar *to talk, speak*
llegar *to arrive*
llevar *to carry; to take*
mirar *to look at*
necesitar *to need*
pasar *to pass, spend*
tomar *to take; to drink*
viajar *to travel*

La familia

el abuelo *grandfather;*
   la abuela *grandmother*
don, doña *titles of respect used with the first name of someone you know well*
el esposo *husband;* **la esposa** *wife*
el hermano *brother,* **la hermana** *sister*
el hijo *son;* **la hija** *daughter*
el hombre *man;* **la mujer** *wife*
el niño (la niña) *child*
el padre *father;* **la madre** *mother;*
   los padres *parents*
el primo (la prima) *cousin*
el sobrino *nephew;* **la sobrina** *niece*
el tío *uncle;* **la tía** *aunt*

Los viajes

el aeropuerto *airport*
el avión *airplane*

la capital *capital (city)*
la ciudad *city*
la farmacia *pharmacy*
el hotel *hotel*
el pasaporte *passport*
el regalo *gift*
la tierra *earth, land*
el viaje *trip*

Preposiciones

a *at, to*
con *with*
de *of, from*
en *in, on, at;* **en casa** *at home*
para *for, in order to*
por *by, for, through, because of;*
   por eso *for that reason*
sobre *about*

Otras palabras

ahora *now*
aquí *here*
¿Cómo . . . ? *How . . . ?*
¿Cómo? *What?*
hoy *today*
mucho *much; many; a lot*
muy *very*
pero *but*
¿Por qué? *Why?*
porque *because*
¡Qué bien! *Great!*
¡Qué interesante! *How interesting!*
¡Qué lástima! *What a shame!*
¡Qué suerte! *What luck!*
también *also, too*
la universidad *university*
la verdad *truth;* **¿verdad?** *right? true?*

¿DÓNDE ESTÁ . . . ?

¿Dónde está . . . la plaza de Mayo? Está enfrente de la Casa Rosada.

OBJECTIVES

LANGUAGE: In this chapter we introduce, discuss, and practice:

1. interrogative words and word order in questions—that is, how to form questions in Spanish

2. agreement and position of adjectives and shortened forms of some adjectives

3. the present tense of the verb **ser**, *to be*, and how to distinguish between the use of **ser** and the use of **estar**

4. the contractions **al** and **del**

5. the personal **a**, used before a direct object that refers to a person or persons

You will also learn how to ask directions, how to use words that indicate position or location (*on top of, under, left, right,* and so forth) and how to carry on a simple telephone conversation.

CULTURE: The dialogue takes place in Buenos Aires. You will learn something about the Argentinean people and the city of Buenos Aires.

EXPLICACIÓN

I. INTERROGATIVE WORDS AND WORD ORDER IN QUESTIONS

En el teléfono

(1)	**Señora Roca:**	*¡Hola . . . !*
(2)	**Miguel:**	Buenos días. *¿Está Laura en casa, por favor?*
(3)	**Señora Roca:**	Sí, está arriba. *¿De parte de quién?*
(4)	**Miguel:**	De Miguel.
(5)	**Sehnora Roca:**	¡Ah, Miguel!. Un momento, por favor.
(6)	**Laura:**	Hola . . . sí . . . *¿cómo estás, Miguel?*
(7)	**Miguel:**	Bien, gracias. *¿Estudias con Adela para el examen de mañana?* Yo estoy cerca de tu casa y . . .
(8)	**Laura:**	. . . y deseas estudiar con nosotras, *¿verdad?*
(9)	**Miguel:**	Sí. Llevo los libros, *¿no?*
(10)	**Laura:**	Por supuesto. Hasta luego.

1. ¿Quién desea hablar con Laura? **2.** ¿Dónde está Laura? **3.** ¿Cómo está Miguel? **4.** ¿Con quién estudia Laura? **5.** Miguel desea estudiar con Adela y Laura ¿verdad? **6.** Miguel lleva los libros ¿no? **7.** ¿Habla usted mucho por teléfono?

A. In English, questions that can be answered with a simple yes or no are generally signaled by an inversion of verb and subject: *Are you tired? Is the book new?* In Spanish, such questions can be posed in a number of ways.

¿Está el niño bien?
¿Está bien el niño? } *Is the boy well?*
¿El niño está bien?

On the telephone
(1) Hello! (2) Good Day. Is Laura at home, please? (3) Yes, she is up(stairs). Who's calling? (On behalf of whom?) (4) (of) Miguel. (5) Oh, Miguel! One moment, please. (6) Hi . . . yes . . . How are you, Miguel? (7) Fine, thank you. Are you studying with Adela for tomorrow's exam? I'm near your house and . . . (8) . . . and you want to study with us, right? (9) Yes. I'll bring the books, okay? (10) Of course. See you later.

In yes or no questions the voice must rise on the last word to make it clear that the speaker is asking a question, since otherwise the question could be taken as a statement of fact, particularly in the third example, where there is no inversion of subject and verb.

B. A statement can be made into a question by adding a "confirmation tag" at the end to elicit verification or denial of the information contained in the statement. Three common tags in Spanish are **¿de acuerdo?, ¿verdad?** and **¿no?** The latter is never used after a negative sentence.

Cenamos aquí, ¿de acuerdo?	*We'll have dinner here, okay?*
Ustedes no viajan a España, ¿verdad?	*You are not traveling to Spain, are you?*
Los chicos llegan hoy, ¿no?	*The boys are arriving today, right?*
Visitan el museo, ¿verdad?	*They're visiting the museum, aren't they?*

Notice that **¿de acuerdo?** *(okay?)* is used when some kind of action is proposed.

C. The word order for Spanish questions that elicit information is: interrogative word + verb + subject (if any) + remainder (if any). At the end of such questions the voice normally falls.

INFORMATION QUESTIONS

Interrogative Word	Verb	Subject	Remainder
¿Cómo (*how*) ¿Cuándo (*when*)	viajan	los señores	a México?
¿Qué (*what*)	buscan	los chicos?	
¿Por qué (*why*) ¿Quién (*who, singular*)	estudia		aquí?
¿Quiénes (*who, plural*)	estudian		aquí?
¿Cuánto(-a) (*how much*)	necesita	usted?	
¿Cuántos(-as) (*how many*)	están		en el avión?
¿Dónde (*where*)	están	los turistas?	
¿Adónde (*to where*)	viajan	las niñas?	
¿Cuál (*which*) ¿Cuáles (*which, plural*)	necesitan	ustedes	ahora?

D. Notice the written accents on interrogative words. **Quién cuál** and **cuánto** have plural forms; **cuánto** also has masculine and feminine forms.

Ejercicios

A. Use the following interrogatives to form the questions that correspond to the answers given. Follow the example.

Modelo: **¿Qué?**
Pablo busca el pasaporte.   **¿Qué busca Pablo?**

1. **¿Qué?**
   a. Los turistas visitan el museo.
   b. José estudia francés.
   c. María necesita un pasaporte.
2. **¿Quién? ¿Quiénes?**
   (a-c above)
3. **¿Con quién? ¿Con quiénes?**
   a. La señora Rodríguez está con los niños.
   b. Viajan con el profesor.
   c. Cenamos con los señores Pérez.
4. **¿Dónde? ¿Adónde?**
   a. Estela está en la universidad.
   b. Viajan a Madrid.
   c. Llegamos al hotel.
5. **¿Cuándo? ¿Cómo?**
   a. El avión llega ahora.
   b. Se llama Marta Hernández.
   c. Llegamos en unos minutos.
6. **¿Cuánto?**
   a. Susana desea visitar cuatro ciudades.
   b. Ellos pasan tres días en la capital.
   c. José necesita muchos lápices.
7. **¿Por qué?**
   a. No están aquí porque están de vacaciones.
   b. No mira televisión porque estudia para el examen.
   c. Busca un teléfono porque desea hablar con Teresa.

B. Ask for confirmation of the following statements by adding **¿no?**, **¿verdad?**, or **¿de acuerdo?**, as appropriate.

1. Necesitas el pasaporte.
2. Ustedes no hablan francés.
3. Ahora estudiamos para el examen.
4. Desean visitar la ciudad.

C. Complete the following dialogue between Pedro and Miguel with the appropriate interrogative words.

Miguel: Hola Pedro, ¿_____ estás?
Pedro: No muy bien, Miguel. ¿_____ es el examen de geografía?

Miguel:	Mañana, ¿_____?
Pedro:	Porque no estoy preparado. ¿_____ lecciones necesitamos estudiar?
Miguel:	Seis. ¿Deseas estudiar con nosotros?
Pedro:	¿Con _____ estudias?
Miguel:	Con Teresa y Adela.
Pedro:	¿_____ desean estudiar hoy?
Miguel:	Hoy deseamos estudiar España, Venezuela y Paraguay.
Pedro:	Paraguay . . . , ¿_____ está Paraguay?
Miguel:	En el centro de América del Sur.
Pedro:	¿Y _____ es la capital de España?
Miguel:	¡Madrid! . . . Pedro, tú necesitas estudiar mucho . . .

II. ADJECTIVES

(1) **Pepe:** Busco un buen restaurante *argentino*.

(2) **Marta:** Enfrente de la universidad está «La Casa *Argentina*», al lado del hospital.

(3) **Pepe:** ¿Preparan *buena* comida *típica* allí?

(4) **Marta:** Sí, preparan empanadas *sabrosas* y carne *asada excelente*.

(5) **Pepe:** ¿Y las bebidas?

(6) **Marta:** Allí tomas un vino *tinto delicioso*.

(7) **Pepe:** ¡*Estupendo*!

1. ¿Qué busca Pepe?   **2.** ¿Cómo se llama el restaurante?   **3.** ¿Dónde está?   **4.** ¿Preparan comida típica?   **5.** ¿Qué preparan en el restaurante?   **6.** ¿Toman vino en el restaurante?

A. Agreement of Adjectives

1. In Spanish, adjectives, like nouns, are (1) either masculine or feminine, and (2) either singular or plural. An adjective must agree both in *gender* and in *number* with the noun it modifies. The most common singular endings for adjectives are **-o** (masculine) and **-a** (feminine).

el muchacho bueno	*the good boy*
la muchacha buena	*the good girl*
un regalo bonito	*a pretty present*
una ciudad bonita	*a pretty city*

(1) I am looking for a good Argentean restaurant. (2) "The Argentean House" is in front of (opposite) the University, beside the hospital. (3) Do they fix good, typical food there? (4) Yes, they fix tasty *empanadas* (meat turnovers) and excellent roast beef. (5) And the drinks? (6) There you (can) drink a delicious red wine. (7) Great!

2. Adjectives of nationality that end in a consonant and adjectives that end in **-dor** are made feminine by adding **-a.***

un chico trabajador	*a hard-working boy*
una chica trabajadora	*a hard-working girl*
el profesor portugués	*the Portuguese professor*
la profesora portuguesa**	*the Portuguese professor*

3. Adjectives that don't end in **-o, -a,** or **-dor** are the same in the feminine as in the masculine.

la casa interesante	*the interesting house*
el museo interesante	*the interesting museum*
el hotel internacional	*the international hotel*
la agencia internacional	*the international agency*

4. To form the plural of an adjective that ends in a vowel, add an **-s.** To form the plural of an adjective that ends in a consonant, add **-es.**

el plato mexicano	*the Mexican dish*
los platos mexicanos	*the Mexican dishes*
la silla española	*the Spanish chair*
las sillas españolas	*the Spanish chairs*
el pasajero inglés	*the English passenger*
los pasajeros ingleses	*the English passengers*
la ciudad grande	*the big city*
las ciudades grandes	*the big cities*

B. Position of Adjectives

1. Most adjectives are descriptive—that is, they specify size, shape, color, type, nationality, and so forth. Descriptive adjectives usually follow the nouns they modify.

Preparan comida portuguesa.	*They're preparing Portuguese food.*
Hablan con un pasajero amable.	*They're talking to a friendly passenger.*

2. Adjectives that specify quantity usually precede the nouns they modify.

Las dos maletas están aquí.	*The two suitcases are here.*
Compran muchos regalos bonitos.	*They buy many pretty presents.*
Invitan a unas personas.	*They're inviting several people.*

3. **Bueno(-a)** may be placed before or after a noun.

Necesito una buena amiga.	*I need a good friend.*
Necesito una amiga buena.	

* Adjectives that end in **-ón, -án,** and **-in** are also made feminine by dropping the accent and adding **-a,** but there are few of these.

** Remember that the written accent on the last syllable of the masculine form will not be necessary after you change the adjective to the feminine.

C. Shortened Forms of Adjectives

    1. Certain adjectives, such as bueno (*good*) and uno (*one, a, an*) drop the final **-o** when they are used before a masculine singular noun.

Necesito un cuaderno nuevo.	*I need a new notebook.*
Él pregunta dónde hay un buen hotel.	*He asks where there is a good hotel.*

Such adjectives agree in gender and number as usual when they are used before singular feminine nouns and all plural nouns.

Ejercicios

A. Change the nouns from the masculine to the feminine.

1. un amigo inglés
2. un chico mexicano
3. el señor español
4. el niño inteligente
5. un muchacho trabajador

B. Change the nouns from the singular to the plural.

1. el plato típico
2. el viaje interesante
3. una ciudad grande
4. una casa bonita
5. un buen restaurante

C. Create new sentences, substituting the words in the list for those in italics.

¿Dónde está *el señor* mexicano?

1. profesores
2. pasajera
3. muchachas
4. museo
5. niñas
6. señora

D. Give the Spanish equivalent of the following sentences.

1. She visits interesting museums.
2. They are traveling to an Argentinean city.
3. Juan and María need a big house.
4. Mr. González is a good professor.
5. I'm studying with two hard-working girls.

Preguntas

1. ¿En qué restaurante preparan comida mexicana? **2.** ¿Prepara usted platos norteamericanos típicos? ¿mexicanos? ¿españoles? **3.** ¿Preparan buena comida en la cafetería de la universidad? **4.** ¿Viaja usted mucho? ¿Adónde viaja cuando está de vacaciones? **5.** ¿Compra usted muchos regalos? ¿muchos libros interesantes?

III. PRESENT TENSE OF **SER**; DISTINCTION BETWEEN **SER** AND **ESTAR**

---

(1)   **Julito:**   ¿De dónde *son* ustedes, señor Larkin?

(2) **Sr. Larkin:** La doctora Todd y yo *somos* de los Estados Unidos. Ella *es* del norte y yo *soy* del suroeste

(3)   **Julito:**   Usted habla bien el español.

(4) **Sr. Larkin:** Gracias, *eres* muy amable. Muchos norteamericanos del suroeste hablan español.

(5)   **Julito:**   ¿Y *están* de vacaciones en Buenos Aires?

(6) **Sr. Larkin:** *Estamos* aquí para asistir a una conferencia sobre ecología.

---

1. ¿De dónde es el señor Larkin?   **2.** ¿De dónde es la doctora Todd?   **3.** ¿Dónde están ahora?   **4.** ¿Para qué están allí?

A.   The present tense forms of **ser** (*to be*) are:

ser (*to be*)

yo	soy	nosotros(-as)	somos
tú	eres	vosotros(-as)	sois
él		ellos	
ella	es	ellas	son
usted		ustedes	

B.   **Ser** is used:

1. To link the subject to a noun or pronoun.

La Paz es la capital de Bolivia.	*La Paz is the capital of Bolivia.*
Silvia es italiana.	*Silvia is an Italian.*
Somos turistas.	*We're tourists.*
El señor García es profesor.	*Mr. García is a professor.*

Note that after **ser**, the indefinite article is not used with a profession or nationality (unless it is modified by an adjective, as you shall see later on in the book).

2. To indicate origin (where someone or something is from).

Soy de los Estados Unidos.	*I'm from the United States.*
¿De dónde es Cantinflas? Es de México.	*Where is Cantinflas from? He's from México.*

(1) Where are you (and Dr. Todd) from, Mr. Larkin? (2) Dr. Todd and I are from the United States. She is from the North and I'm from the Southwest. (3) You speak Spanish well. (4) Thank you, you are very nice. Many Northamericans from the Southwest speak Spanish. (5) And are you on vacation in Buenos Aires? (6) We're here to attend a conference on ecology.

3. To indicate where an event takes place.

El concierto es en la universidad.	*The concert is in the university.*
La ópera es en el Teatro Colón.	*The opera is in Columbus Theater.*
La exposición es en el museo.	*The exhibit is in the museum.*

4. With **de** to describe what something is made of.

¿Es de oro o de plata el reloj?	*Is the watch (made of) gold or silver?*
Las sillas son de madera.	*The chairs are wooden (made of wood).*

5. With **de** to indicate possession.

El examen es de Ricardo.	*The exam is Ricardo's.*
Las bicicletas son de Enrique y Pablo.	*The bicycles are Enrique and Pablo's.*

C. **Estar** is used:

1. To indicate location or position.

El hotel está cerca de la avenida Colón.	*The hotel is near Columbus Avenue.*
Nosotros estamos enfrente de la biblioteca.	*We are in front of the library.*
Están de vacaciones en Bogotá.	*They are on vacation in Bogotá.*
El hotel está a la izquierda, ¿verdad?	*The hotel is on the left, isn't it?*
—No, está a la derecha.	*—No, it's on the right.*

2. To indicate the condition of a person or thing at a particular time.

El aire está contaminado.	*The air is polluted.*
¿Cómo estás? Estoy bien, gracias.	*How are you? I'm fine, thanks.*
Nosotros estamos perdidos.	*We are lost.*

D. **Ser** and **estar** with adjectives

1. When an adjective expresses a quality or characteristic that you think of as *normal* or *characteristic* of the subject, use **ser.**

Marta es inteligente.	*Marta is intelligent.*
Las chicas son simpáticas.	*The girls are nice.*
Buenos Aires es una ciudad interesante y grande.	*Buenos Aires is an interesting and large city.*
Las residencias estudiantiles son muy modernas.	*The student residences are very modern.*

2. When an adjective expresses a quality or characteristic of the subject that appears to be the case at a particular time but that may or may not normally be true of the subject, use **estar.**

El señor Cano está perdido.	*Mr. Cano is lost.*
Marta está bonita hoy.	*Marta looks pretty today. (She may not always be pretty, but she looks pretty today.)*
Estás muy elegante, Susana.	*You look very elegant, Susana.*
Estamos contentos con la nueva casa.	*We're happy with the new house.*

Ejercicios

A. Professor Benítez is a specialist in foreign accents. Every time he meets someone, he wants to guess where he or she is from. Make questions he would ask, following the model.

Modelo: José/España **¿De dónde es José? ¿Es de España?**

1. Marta/Argentina
2. los señores Jones/los Estados Unidos
3. tú/Francia
4. usted/Puerto Rico
5. los turistas/Italia
6. ustedes/México

B. Answer in the affirmative, using the verb **ser.**

1. ¿Son de Bolivia los doctores?
2. ¿Es Randy estudiante de español?
3. ¿Somos inteligentes nosotros?
4. ¿Eres amiga de los Kennedy?
5. ¿Son de oro los relojes?
6. ¿Son venezolanas las pasajeras?
7. ¿Es de Paco el libro?
8. ¿Es el concierto en el Teatro Colón?

C. Complete the sentences, using **es** or **está,** as appropriate.

1. Ricardo _____ en Bogotá.
2. _____ estudiante de historia.
3. _____ de vacaciones.
4. Marta no _____ aquí.
5. _____ un hotel grande.
6. La mesa no _____ de madera.
7. _____ norteamericano.
8. Ella _____ bien.
9. _____ inteligente.
10. _____ muy elegante hoy.
11. ¿Dónde _____ el libro de Ernesto?
12. ¿De dónde _____ Eliana?

D. Complete the following paragraph, using the appropriate form of **ser** or **estar.**

En este momento yo _____ en clase. Pepito _____ en casa porque no _____
bien. Él y yo _____ hermanos; _____ solos (*alone*) porque papá y mamá _____
de vacaciones en Buenos Aires. Ellos _____ en un hotel muy grande. Mamá
_____ muy contenta. Ella comenta en una carta: «La ciudad _____ muy bonita,
pero el aire _____ muy contaminado. El hotel _____ excelente. A la izquierda
del hotel _____ la agencia de viajes ya la derecha _____ la casa de los abuelos
de Lucía. Ahora nosotros _____ en un restaurante en la avenida '9 de Julio'. Hoy
deseamos visitar el Teatro Colón; _____ muy famoso, y _____ cerca de aquí.»
Papá y Mamá _____ contentos en Buenos Aires. _____ un viaje interesante,
¿verdad?

Preguntas

1. ¿Es usted norteamericano(-a)? ¿Es de Nueva York? ¿de California? ¿De dónde es?
2. ¿Es usted bueno(-a) o malo(-a)? ¿trabajador(-a) o perezoso (-a) (*lazy*)? **3.** ¿Son brillantes los estudiantes aquí? ¿y los profesores? **4.** ¿Es de usted el libro de español? ¿Es
interesante o aburrido (*boring*)? **5.** ¿Es de usted el reloj? ¿Es de oro? ¿Es un buen reloj? **6.** ¿Es usted doctor? ¿matemático? ¿sociólogo? **7.** ¿Cómo está el aire aquí? ¿contaminado o puro? **8.** ¿Está la universidad cerca de una agencia de viajes?

IV. CONTRACTIONS AL AND DEL

(1) **Señor García:** Por favor, señor, ¿dónde está el restaurante
«La Estancia»? ¿Está cerca o lejos?
(2) **Un señor:** Está allí a la izquierda, *al* lado *del* Hotel
Continental.

1. ¿Está el restaurante a la izquierda o a la derecha? **2.** ¿Está el restaurante cerca?
3. ¿Está al lado del teatro o al lado del hotel? **4.** El señor busca el restaurante «Rancho
del Norte», ¿verdad?

A. When the preposition **a** and the masculine definite article **el** occur together,
they are combined to form **al.**

Las chicas llegan al teatro. *The girls arrive at the theater.*

---

(1) Please, sir. Where is the restaurant "La Estancia"? Is it nearby or far
away? (2) It's there on the left, beside the Continental Hotel.

B. When the preposition **de** and the masculine definite article **el** occur together, they are combined to form **del**.

Los señores Castillo están lejos del museo.

Mr. and Mrs. Castillo are far from the museum.

These two forms, **al** and **del,** are the only contractions used in Spanish.

Ejercicios

A. Create new sentences, substituting the words in the list for those in italics.

1. Las chicas llegan *al hotel*.
   a. Perú **b.** farmacia **c.** restaurante **d.** ciudad **e.** museo
2. El hotel está cerca *del hospital*.
   a. aeropuerto **b.** teatro **c.** agencia **d.** universidad **e.** capital

B. Form sentences for each group of three words, using them in the order given.

Modelo: hotel/izquierda/aeropuerto **El hotel está a la izquierda del aeropuerto.**

1. restaurante/lado/escuela
2. hospital/izquierda/farmacia
3. universidad/enfrente/teatro
4. museo/derecha/agencia
5. aeropuerto/lejos/ciudad

C. Complete the sentences, using **del, de los, de la, de las, al, a los, a la,** or **a las,** as appropriate.

1. El libro es _____ profesor.
2. Ellos llegan _____ hotel.
3. Los señores Gutiérrez viajan _____ capital.
4. El auto es _____ amigos de Ana.
5. Las bibliotecas están cerca _____ universidades.
6. Llevan el regalo _____ niñas.

Preguntas

1. ¿Desea usted viajar a la ciudad de México? ¿al Perú? **2.** ¿Lleva usted un pasaporte cuando viaja al Canadá? ¿a la Argentina? ¿a Texas? **3.** En la clase de español, ¿está usted cerca o lejos de la puerta? ¿Quién está a la derecha de usted? ¿a la izquierda? **4.** ¿Está la universidad lejos o cerca del museo? ¿del aeropuerto? ¿de las residencias estudiantiles?

V. THE PERSONAL A

---

(1) **Eduardo:** Busco *a* María.

(2) **Julia:** Está en la universidad, Eduardo. Busca un libro para la clase de español.

---

1. ¿A quién busca Eduardo?   **2.** ¿Dónde está María?   **3.** ¿Qué busca María?

A personal **a** must precede a direct object that refers to a person or persons.

Juan mira a la chica.	*Juan is looking at the girl.*
Teresa visita a los señores Navarro.	*Teresa is visiting Mr. and Mrs. Navarro.*
Elena llama a un pasajero.	*Elena calls (beckons) a passenger.*

But

Felipe mira la pizarra	*Felipe is looking at the blackboard.*
Visitamos el museo de arte.	*We're visiting the art museum.*

Ejercicios

A.   Complete the sentences with the personal **a** when needed.

1. Buscamos _____ la doctora.
2. Felipe mira _____ los niños.
3. Deseo comprar _____ una casa grande.
4. ¿Qué preguntas _____ la profesora?
5. ¿Por qué no llaman _____ un taxi?
6. Ahora usted llama _____ un amigo de Pablo, ¿no?

B.   Give the Spanish equivalent of the following sentences.

1. Juan looks at Adela.
2. They are looking for a good restaurant.
3. The student visits the museum.
4. I want to visit Mr. Flores.
5. Mr. Álvarez is calling the passengers now.

Preguntas

1. ¿Visita usted a unos amigos hoy?   **2.** ¿Mira usted a veces (*sometimes*) al presidente en la televisión?   **3.** ¿Necesita usted a veces al (a la) profesor(-a)?   **4.** ¿Llama usted a un (-a) amigo(-a) hoy?   **5.** ¿Visita usted mucho al doctor? ¿al dentista? ¿al (a la) profesor(-a) de español?

(1) I'm looking for María. (2) She's at the university, Eduardo. She's looking for a book for Spanish class.

BIENVENIDOS AL PARÍS DE SUDAMÉRICA

En un autobús. El señor y la señora Smith son ingleses y están de vacaciones en Buenos Aires. Buscan un museo de historia natural.

El señor Smith:	¡Dios!, el tráfico está horrible y el aire está contaminado.
La señora Smith:	Es el precio del progreso. Pero la ciudad es bonita ¿no?
El señor Smith:	Sí, pero es muy grande. Estoy perdido . . . ¿Cómo llegamos al museo?
La señora Smith:	Los dos estamos perdidos. ¿Por qué no preguntas?
El señor Smith:	Buena idea. *(Habla a un pasajero).* Por favor . . . ¿Dónde está el Museo de La Plata?[1]
El pasajero:	Está lejos. Ustedes no son porteños,[2] ¿verdad?
La señora Smith:	No, somos ingleses.
El pasajero:	¡Ah!, son de Inglaterra. Pues . . . bienvenidos al París de Sudamérica. ¿Para qué desean visitar el museo?

La señora Smith:	Para mirar las exposiciones sobre los animales[3] del país, sobre fósiles, sobre la cultura de los indios, y sobre . . .
El pasajero:	Un momento, por favor. Me llamo Emilio Tamborini[4] y soy agente de viajes. Por casualidad, estamos enfrente de la agencia *Viajes Tamborini*. ¿Por qué no bajamos?
El señor Smith:	¿Para visitar el museo?
El pasajero:	No. Pero es posible visitar una estancia, visitar a los gauchos[5] y . . .
La señora Smith:	Gracias, señor. Otro día, quizás.
El pasajero:	Bueno, adiós.

El señor Tamborini baja del autobús. Los señores Smith no bajan.

El señor Smith:	Otra vez estamos perdidos. ¿Por qué no preguntas?
La señora Smith:	Buena idea. *(A un pasajero).* Por favor . . . dónde está el Museo de La Plata?
El pasajero:	Está lejos. Ustedes no son porteños ¿verdad?

por casualidad *it just so happens*   **indios** *Indians*   **estancia** *cattle ranch*

Preguntas

1. ¿Dónde están los señores Smith? **2.** ¿De dónde son ellos? **3.** ¿Qué buscan? **4.** ¿A quién pregunta el señor Smith dónde está el museo? **5.** ¿Para qué desean visitar el museo? **6.** ¿Cómo se llama el pasajero? **7.** ¿Es profesor el señor Tamborini? **8.** ¿Adónde desea llevar él a los señores Smith? **9.** Al final ¿llegan al museo? **10.** ¿Visita usted los museos con frecuencia? **11.** ¿Para qué visitamos los museos?

NOTAS CULTURALES

1. The **Museo de Historia Natural,** known also as the **Museo de La Plata,** is in the city of La Plata, about 40 miles from Buenos Aires. It is a famous museum of natural history, science, anthropology, and ethnology.

2. Porteño (literally, *port-dweller*) is the usual term given to someone who lives in the city of Buenos Aires, Argentina's capital and main port on the Río de La Plata. In general **porteños** are sophisticated and proud people who frequently refer to their city as the "Paris of South America."

3. Because of the variety of its terrain, Argentina has a number of unusual animals, like the **jaguar** (jaguar), the **cóndor,** the largest bird of flight, and the **carpincho,** the largest living rodent, which sometimes attains a weight of 100 pounds and in some parts of South America is hunted by the natives for food.

4. If Emilio Tamborini sounds more Italian than Spanish to you, you are correct. In fact, a large number of Argentineans are of Italian descent. (A glance at the capital's phone book would confirm this.) The British, French, and Germans have also contributed to Argentina's population.

5. The **gaucho,** or Argentine cowboy, is now more a legendary figure than a real one. In the early 1800s, thousands of these men led a nomadic life on the pampas (dry grasslands) living off the wild herds of cattle and horses which had descended from those of the Spanish conquistadors. The word is also used for the descendents of the original **gauchos** who now work as ranchhands on the large **estancias** (Argentine ranches) and preserve some of the old traditions.

ACTIVIDADES

En la clase

Answer the following questions according to the illustration.

1. ¿Dónde está la puerta, a la derecha o a la izquierda del profesor?
2. ¿Dónde está el libro, arriba o abajo del escritorio?
3. ¿Está el profesor cerca o lejos de la ventana?
4. ¿Cómo se llama el/la estudiante que está al lado de Pepe?
5. ¿Cómo se llama el/la estudiante que está enfrente del escritorio?
6. La ventana está detrás de la clase, ¿verdad?

Entrevista

Ask a classmate the following questions. Then report the information to the class.

1. ¿Preparas comida mexicana?
2. ¿Tomas vino tinto o blanco?
3. ¿Eres de Buenos Aires? ¿De dónde eres?
4. ¿Dónde estás ahora?
5. ¿Eres estudiante en la Universidad de Buenos Aires?
6. ¿Estudias en casa o en la biblioteca?

Situación

Study the following "situación". Your teacher may call on you to act out one of the three roles. You may wish to consult the *Diálogo* or the *Vocabulario Activo* at the end of the chapter for assistance.

En el autobús

Two tourists are on a bus in Buenos Aires. They are talking about the city. They ask a passenger where the Museum of Natural History is. He/She tells them it is interesting but very far away. He/She asks them several questions: what their names are, where they are from, etc. Then the passenger gets off the bus. All three say goodbye to each other.

VOCABULARIO ACTIVO

Verbos útiles

asistir a   to attend
bajar de   to get off
cenar   to have supper, eat dinner
criticar   to criticize
estar de vacaciones   to be on vacation
invitar   to invite
llamar   to call; **llamar por teléfono**   to telephone
preguntar   to ask
ser   to be
visitar   to visit

Posiciones

abajo (de)   below, underneath
al lado de   beside
allí   there

arriba (de)   above, over
cerca de   near
detrás de   behind
enfrente de   in front of
lejos de   far from
a la derecha   on the right
a la izquierda   on the left
el este   east
el norte   north
el oeste   west
el sur   south

Adjetivos

amable   nice, friendly
argentino(a)   Argentinean
bonito(a)   pretty
bueno(a)   good, fine; **bueno**   well. Okay.

contaminado(a) *polluted*
contento(a) *content, happy*
elegante *elegant*
famoso(a) *famous*
grande (gran before a masculine
    singular noun) *big, tall; great*
inteligente *intelligent*
internacional *international*
italiano(a) *Italian*
mexicano(a) *Mexican*
moderno(a) *modern*
norteamericano(a) *North American*
perdido(a) *lost*
portugués, (portuguesa) *Portuguese*
simpático(a) *nice, congenial*
típico(a) *typical*
trabajador(a) *hard-working*

Interrogativos

¿adónde? *(to) where?*
¿cuál(es)? *which? which ones?*
¿cuándo? *when?*
¿dónde? *where?*
¿qué? *what?*
¿quién(es)? *who, whom?*

Sustantivos

la agencia *agency*
el, la agente de viajes *travel agent*
el aire *air*

el autobús *bus*
la avenida *avenue*
la biblioteca *library*
la casa *house*
el concierto *concert*
la conferencia *lecture*
el chico *boy;* **la chica** *girl*
el examen *test, exam*
la exposición *exhibition*
la madera *wood*
la maleta *suitcase*
el museo *museum*
la ópera *opera*
el oro *gold*
el país *country*
el pasajero (la pasajera) *passenger*
la persona *person*
la plata *silver*
el plato *dish*
el precio *price*
el reloj *watch*
el teatro *theater*
el, la turista *tourist*

a veces *at times*
¡Dios mío! *My goodness!*
mañana *tomorrow*
otro(a) *other, another;* **otra vez** *again,*
    once more
quizás *perhaps*
siempre *always*
todo *everything*

El Mundo Hispánico

¿Desea usted hablar español y pasar unas semanas estupendas? Bueno, un viaje a tierras hispánicas es una idea excelente. ¿No es posible ahora? ¡Qué lástima!; pero siempre es posible viajar con la imaginación, ¿no? . . .

Primero llegamos a México, la gran nación al sur de los Estados Unidos. Observamos dos *sierras* importantes y una gran *meseta* donde está la capital, México, una ciudad grande, moderna, con muchos parques y bonitos museos. En la costa y en la península de Yucatán (donde está la ciudad de Mérida) el clima es tropical. En todas partes *hallamos gente simpática* y *comida* deliciosa pero *picante*.

mountain ranges / plateau

we find / nice people / food / hot (spicy)

ESTADOS UNIDOS

GOLFO DE MÉXICO

Monterrey

La Paz

Guadalajara

Jalapa

MÉXICO D.F.

Mérida

Península de Yucatán

OCÉANO PACÍFICO

¿O desea usted visitar *el Caribe?* En tres de las islas del Caribe la   the Caribbean
gente habla español: en Cuba, en Puerto Rico y en la República
Dominicana. Allí el clima es muy bueno y el océano muy *azul.*   blue

Al sur de México está América Central. Es una región tropical con
muchas *montañas* y volcanes activos. En Guatemala, El Salvador,   mountains
Honduras, Nicaragua, Costa Rica y Panamá, las seis *pequeñas* re-   small
públicas de América Central, la gente habla español. Exportan pro-
ductos importantes *como* el *café* y las bananas o los plátanos.   like, such as / coffee

Llegamos *luego* a los nueve *países* hispanos de la América del Sur: Venezuela, Colombia y el Ecuador en el norte; el Perú, Bolivia y el Paraguay en el centro; Chile, la Argentina y el Uruguay en el sur. El Brasil y las Guayanas no son países hispanos. En el oeste, los Andes dominan el continente.

then / countries

Es un mundo exótico de animales *extraños* y grandes contrastes geográficos. Aquí es posible visitar ruinas de civilizaciones muy *antiguas* y también ciudades muy modernas y cosmopolitas.

strange
ancient

Finalmente, cruzamos el océano Atlántico y llegamos a España que forma, con Portugal, la Península Ibérica.

finally / we cross

España es un país de regiones muy diferentes. En el *noroeste* y en la costa del Mediterráneo, el clima es ideal, muy moderado. La capital, Madrid, está en la meseta central. Aquí las temperaturas son extremas. En el sur está Andalucía, una región muy fértil, famosa por sus históricas ciudades y la música *flamenca*.

northwest

Y ahora, ¿no desea usted visitar el mundo hispánico?

Flamenco (Andalusian gypsy music or dance)

Preguntas

1. ¿Cómo se llama la gran nación al sur de los Estados Unidos?   2. ¿Cómo es la capital de la nación? ¿Cómo es la comida?   3. ¿Cuáles son las tres islas del Caribe donde la gente habla español?   4. ¿Cuántas repúblicas hispanas forman América Central? ¿Qué productos importantes exportan?   5. ¿Qué países hispanos están en el norte de América del Sur? ¿En el centro? ¿Y en el sur?   6. ¿Dónde están las montañas que dominan el continente? ¿Cómo se llaman?   7. ¿Qué contrastes observamos en América del Sur?   8. ¿Cuáles son los dos países que forman la península Ibérica?   9. ¿Dónde está la capital de España y cómo se llama?   10. ¿Por qué es famosa Andalucía?

CAPÍTULO 3

ESTUDIOS UNIVERSITARIOS

Estudiantes en la Universidad Nacional Autónoma de México

OBJECTIVES

LANGUAGE: In this chapter we introduce, discuss, and practice:

1. the present tense of regular verbs that end in **-er** and **-ir**
2. demonstrative adjectives and pronouns (corresponding to *this, that, these, those*)
3. the present tense of the irregular verb **tener**, *to have*
4. cardinal numbers 31–100
5. how to tell time in Spanish

You will also learn vocabulary related to fields of study or academic subjects, as well as expressions that mark the passing of time: *month, year*, and so on.

CULTURE: The dialogue takes place in Mexico City, in the National Museum of Anthropology. You will learn something about the history and peoples of Mexico, the Indian influences, and the ethnic background of the population.

EXPLICACIÓN

I. THE PRESENT TENSE OF REGULAR -ER AND -IR VERBS

(1) **Juan:** *Lees* y *escribes* mucho, Luisa. ¿Qué *lees* ahora?

(2) **Luisa:** En este momento *leo* un libro de filosofía y *escribo* notas para una composición.

(3) **Juan:** No *comprendo*. *Vivimos* en el siglo veinte. *Debemos* leer libros prácticos, *aprender* matemáticas, computación, ingeniería, física.

(4) **Luisa:** Juan, tú no *debes* despreciar la filosofía. En la filosofía *descubrimos* « la verdad en la vida y la vida en la verdad ».

(5) **Juan:** *Creo* que los filósofos *comprenden* el pasado, pero tú *debes* estudiar para el futuro.

1. ¿Lee mucho Luisa? ¿Qué lee ahora? **2.** ¿Qué escribe Luisa? **3.** ¿Qué cree Juan que debemos leer? **4.** ¿Qué cree Juan que debemos aprender? **5.** ¿Qué descubrimos en la filosofía? **6.** ¿Con quién está usted de acuerdo (*in agreement*): con Juan o con Luisa? ¿por qué?

(1) You are reading and writing a lot, Luisa. What are you reading now? (2) Right now (at this moment) I am reading a philosophy book and I am writing (taking) notes for a composition. (3) I don't understand. We live in the twentieth century. We should read practical books, learn mathematics, computation, engineering, physics. (4) Juan, you shouldn't look down on philosophy. In philosophy we discover "the truth in life and the life in truth" (a well-known phrase of the Spanish philosopher Miguel de Unamuno, (1864–1936). (5) I think that philosophers understand the past, but you should study for the future.

A. Spanish verbs with infinitives ending in **-er** are referred to as second-conjugation, or **-er**, verbs. To conjugate a regular **-er** verb in the present tense, replace the infinitive ending **-er** by the endings **-o, -es, -e, -emos, -éis, -en:**

comer	(to eat)		
yo	como	nosotros(-as)	comemos
tú	comes	vosotros(-as)	coméis
él		ellos	
ella	come	ellas	comen
usted		ustedes	

¿Qué comes?　　　　　　　　　What are you eating?
—Como unas enchiladas.　　　　—I'm eating some enchiladas

B. Other verbs conjugated like **comer** are:

aprender *to learn*　　　　　　**creer** *to believe, to think*
beber *to drink*　　　　　　　**deber** *should, ought to*
comprender *to understand*　　**leer** *to read*

Marcelo bebe mucho café.　　　　Marcelo drinks a lot of coffee.
Laura y yo creemos que la clase es　　Laura and I think the class is boring.
　aburrida.
Debo leer un libro de ciencias　　I should read a book on political science
　políticas esta semana pero no está　　this weekend, but it's not in the
　en la biblioteca.　　　　　　　　library.

C. Verbs with infinitives ending in **-ir** (third-conjugation verbs) are conjugated by removing the **-ir** and adding these endings to the stem: **-o, -es, -e, -imos, -ís, -en:**

vivir	(to live)		
yo	vivo	nosotros(-as-	vivimos
tú	vives	vosotros(-as)	vivís
él		ellos	
ella	vive	ellas	viven
usted		ustedes	

¿Dónde viven ustedes? —Vivimos en　　Where do you live? —We live on
　la calle Cabrillo.　　　　　　　　Cabrillo Street.

As you can see, the endings for **-ir** verbs are the same as for **-er** verbs except the **nosotros** and **vosotros** forms.

D. Other verbs conjugated like **vivir** are:

abrir *to open*　　　　　　　　**escribir** *to write*
describir *to describe*　　　　　**recibir** *to receive, get*

¿Abres la ventana?	*Are you opening the window?*
Escribe un libro de historia. Describe a los políticos de Sudamérica.	*He's writing a history book. It describes the politicians of South America.*
¿Reciben ustedes muchas cartas?	*Do you get many letters?*
¿Dónde vive usted?	*Where do you live?*
Todavía vivo en la calle Séptima.	*I still live on Seventh Street.*

Ejercicios

A. Create new sentences, substituting the words in the list for those in italics.

1. *Él* aprende matemáticas.
    a. yo **b.** tú **c.** ustedes **d.** Mario y yo **e.** ellas

2. *Yo* escribo una composición.
    a. usted **b.** Marta **c.** nosotros **d.** Pablo y José **e.** tú

B. Complete the following sentences with the appropriate form of the verb in parentheses.

1. (vivir) Anita _____ en California.
2. (leer) Federico _____ un libro de física.
3. (deber) Tú _____ ir a la biblioteca, ¿no?
4. (escribir) ¿A quién _____ usted?
5. (comprender) Nosotros _____ español.
6. (aprender) ¿Qué _____ ustedes en la clase de computación?
7. (creer) ¿_____ ellos que los filósofos comprenden el pasado?
8. (abrir) Ahora yo _____ la puerta, ¿de acuerdo?
9. (recibir) ¿_____ ustedes muchas cartas?
10. (beber) Yo _____ mucho café cuando estudio.

C. Select an appropriate sentence ending from the column on the right for each verb in the column on the left.

1. Leen	la librería
2. Creo que	matemáticas y computación
3. Viven	una composición para la clase de
4. Debemos	español
5. Escribes	un libro de filosofía
6. Aprende	estudiar mucho
	él es de Venezuela
	en México
	el profesor de ingeniería

Preguntas

1. ¿Lee usted muchos libros? **2.** ¿Aprende usted mucho en la universidad? **3.** ¿Qué aprendemos en la clase de español ahora? **4.** ¿Come usted en la cafetería de la universidad? **5.** ¿Escribe usted muchas cartas? ¿muchas composiciones? **6.** ¿Recibe usted muchas cartas? ¿de quién? ¿de dónde?   7. ¿Vive usted cerca o lejos de la universidad? ¿de la biblioteca? ¿de una buena librería?   8. ¿En qué ciudad vivimos? ¿en qué estado?

II. DEMONSTRATIVE ADJECTIVES AND PRONOUNS

(1) **Ana:** ¿En qué restaurante comemos?

(2) **Oscar:** ¿En *este* restaurante francés, aquí al lado de la Escuela de Ciencias Sociales?

(3) **Ana:** No, no deseo comida francesa *esta* noche.

(4) **Oscar:** Bueno. ¿Y en *ese* italiano que siempre está lleno de estudiantes de psicología?

(5) **Ana:** Creo que *ese* no es bueno.

(6) **Oscar:** De acuerdo. ¿Y en *aquel* restaurante alemán que está detrás de la Facultad de Medicina?

(7) **Ana:** Pero *aquél* está lejos.

(8) **Oscar:** Pues... ¿y en *aquella* cafetería que está en la Avenida Juárez?

(9) **Ana:** En *aquélla* la comida es cara ¿no?

(10) **Oscar:** ¡Ay, ay! ¿Por qué no comemos en casa?

1. ¿Dónde está el restaurante francés?   **2.** ¿Por qué Ana no desea comer en éste?   **3.** ¿Cree Ana que el restaurante italiano es bueno?   **4.** ¿Dónde está el restaurante alemán? ¿está aquél muy lejos?   **5.** ¿Cómo es la comida en la cafetería?   **6.** ¿Dónde desea comer Oscar?

(1) What restaurant shall we eat in? (2) In this French restaurant here next to the School of Social Science? (3) No, I don't want French food this evening. (4) Okay. And in that Italian one that's always full of psychology students? (5) I think that that one isn't good. (6) All right. And in that German restaurant that's behind the Medical School? (7) But that one is far away. (8) Well . . . and at the cafeteria that is on Juarez Avenue? (9) The food in that one is expensive, isn't it? (10) Good grief! Why don't we eat at home?

A. Demonstrative Adjectives

1. Demonstrative adjectives are used to point out or indicate a particular person or object. They precede the nouns they modify and agree with them in gender and number.

DEMONSTRATIVE ADJECTIVES

	Singular			*Plural*	
masculine	este	*this*	estos	*these*	
feminine	esta		estas		
masculine	ese	*that*	esos	*those*	
feminine	esa		esas		
masculine	aquel	*that ... over there*	aquellos	*those ... over there*	
feminine	aquella		aquellas		

¿Siempre comes en este restaurante?	*Do you always eat in this restaurant?*
Esta arquitectura es una maravilla.	*This architecture is a wonder.*
... la física, la biología y la química— estas tres materias son muy difíciles.	*. . . physics, biology, and chemistry— these three subjects are very difficult.*
¿Ese libro? Es muy caro.	*That book? It's very expensive.*
Esos señores son políticos.	*Those men are politicians.*
Llevo aquel reloj, por favor.	*I'll take that watch, please.*
Aquella señora es la presidente.	*That woman (over there) is the president.*

2. Both **ese** and **aquel** correspond to *that* in English. **Ese, esa, esos,** and **esas** are used to indicate persons or objects located fairly close to the person addressed. **Aquel, aquella, aquellos,** and **aquellas** are used to indicate persons or objects that are remote or distant from both the speaker and the person spoken to.

B. Demonstrative Pronouns

1. Demonstrative pronouns in Spanish have the same form as demonstrative adjectives, except that the pronouns have written accents. They agree in gender and number with the noun they replace.

¿Éste? Es un libro de filosofía.	*This? It's a philosophy book.*
Ésta es la idea de Paco.	*This is Paco's idea.*
Éstos son calendarios.	*These are calendars.*
¿Ése? Es un estudiante francés, y ésa es alemana.	*That one? He's a French student, and that one is German.*
¿Qué son ésos? Son cuadernos.	*What are those? They're notebooks.*
¿Hablas de aquél o de aquélla?	*Are you talking about that one (masculine) or that one (feminine)?*

¿Quiénes son aquellas chicas?
—¿Aquéllas? Son amigas
de Magdalena.

Who are those girls?
—Those (over there)? They're
friends of Magdalena's.

2. There are three neuter demonstrative pronouns in Spanish: **esto** *(this)*, **eso**
(that) and **aquello** *(that—distant)*. They are used to refer to statements, abstract ideas, or something that has not been identified. There are no plural
forms, and they do not take a written accent.

¿Qué aprendemos de todo esto?
¿Qué es eso?
Todo aquello es la estancia de
don Fernando.

What do we learn from all this?
What's that (thing, situation, etc.)?
All that (remote, distant) is Don
Fernando's ranch.

Ejercicios

A. Create new sentences, substituting the words in the list for those in italics.

1. Ahora abren ese *libro.*
   a. regalos **b.** diccionario **c.** farmacia **d.** puertas **e.** cafetería
2. Hablo con este *señor.*
   a. chica **b.** profesores **c.** personas **d.** doctor **e.** niños
3. Aquella *biblioteca* es buena.
   a. hotel **b.** restaurantes **c.** diccionario **d.** universidad **e.** cafetería

B. Change the nouns to the feminine, and make the adjectives agree.

1. Este chico es muy trabajador.
2. Ese niño es bueno.
3. Ésos señores son norteamericanos.
4. Aquel muchacho es estudiante.
5. Estos chilenos son amigos de Luis.

C. Change the nouns to the plural, and make the adjectives agree.

1. Este restaurante es caro.
2. Esta comida es típica.
3. Aquella chica es muy simpática.
4. Ese hotel es horrible.
5. Esa persona es famosa.

D. Replace the following noun phrases with pronouns.

Modelo: esa noche **ésa**

1. esos conciertos
2. esta cafetería
3. aquel hombre
4. esas sillas

5. este calendario
6. estos políticos
7. ese estudiante
8. aquellas casas

E.   Give the Spanish equivalent of the following sentences.

1. That man (over there) is from Bolivia.
2. These students are learning French and Spanish.
3. That girl lives far from the university.
4. This chapter is not difficult.
5. That politician wishes to visit this city.

Preguntas

1. ¿Es cara la comida en este país? ¿en esta ciudad? ¿en la cafetería de esta universidad? **2.** ¿Estudia mucho esa chica (que está al lado de usted)? ¿ésta? ¿aquélla? **3.** ¿Cómo se llama este muchacho (que está cerca del profesor o de la profesora)? ¿ése? ¿aquél? **4.** ¿Qué es esto? (Es un libro.) ¿eso? ¿aquello? **5.** ¿Estudia usted matemáticas? ¿historia? ¿francés? ¿italiano? ¿literatura? ¿geografía?

III. PRESENT INDICATIVE OF TENER

(1)	**Bárbara:**	¿*Tienes* tiempo para estudiar español esta tarde?
(2)	**Dora:**	No, no *tengo* tiempo. Roberto y yo *tenemos* otros planes: visitar el Museo de Historia Natural.
(3)	**Bárbara:**	¿Pero y el examen de inglés que *tienen* mañana?
(4)	**Dora:**	No *tiene* importancia. El inglés es fácil, y con Roberto aprendo más.
(5)	**Bárbara:**	Comprendo. La escuela de la vida ¿no?

1. ¿Tiene Dora tiempo para estudiar español con Bárbara? **2.** ¿Qué planes tienen Dora y Roberto? **3.** ¿Por qué no tiene importancia para Dora el examen de inglés?

The verb **tener** is irregular.

tener	*(to have)*
Singular	**Plural**
tengo	tenemos
tienes	tenéis
tiene	tienen

No tengo mucho tiempo.	*I don't have much time.*
¿Tenemos tiempo para comer?	*Do we have time to eat?*
¿Qué tienes allí?	*What do you have there?*

---

(1) Do you have time to study Spanish this afternoon? (2) No, I don't have time. Roberto and I have other plans: to visit the Museum of Natural History. (3) But, the English test that you have tomorrow? (4) It's not important. English is easy, and with Roberto I learn more. (5) I understand. The school of life, right?

Un mestizo tiene sangre india.
Los señores Gómez tienen muchos
  libros sobre medicina.

A mestizo has Indian blood.
Mr. and Mrs. Gómez have a lot of books
  about medicine.

Ejercicios

A. Fill in the blanks with the appropriate form of **tener.**

1. Yo _____ un diccionario.
2. Ana y María _____ una clase de biología ahora.
3. Nosotros _____ un examen muy difícil mañana.
4. ¿_____ usted un lápiz?
5. Tú _____ sangre india, ¿no?
6. El profesor _____ muchos amigos mexicanos.
7. ¿_____ tiempo ustedes para estudiar la lección?
8. Creo que Rolando _____ dos libros sobre literatura inglesa.

B. Create ten sentences using the following material. Use each subject pronoun twice.

él	tenemos	un examen de filosofía hoy
yo	tienen	una amiga estupenda
ustedes	tiene	un libro de historia de América
tú	tengo	una estancia muy grande
nosotros	tienes	dos clases de psicología
		tiempo de llamar a Susana
		muchas ideas aburridas
		sangre india
		un reloj de oro
		una hermana doctora

Preguntas

1. ¿Tiene la universidad una buena biblioteca? **2.** ¿Tienen programas en español en la televisión aquí? **3.** ¿Tiene usted una clase de francés? ¿de matemáticas? ¿de biología? ¿de literatura? ¿son fáciles o difíciles? **4.** ¿Tiene usted amigos latinoamericanos? ¿españoles? **5.** ¿Tenemos muchos estudiantes brillantes en la clase? ¿en esta universidad? **6.** ¿Tiene usted sangre india? ¿africana? ¿oriental? ¿europea? **7.** ¿Tiene usted ideas originales? ¿brillantes?

IV. CARDINAL NUMBERS 31–100

En la librería

(1) **Estudiante:** Señorita, necesito un libro sobre la civilización azteca.
(2) **Señorita:** Este libro es muy bueno. ¿Es usted estudiante?
(3) **Estudiante:** Sí. ¿Qué precio tiene, por favor?

(4)	**Señorita:**	*Ochenta* pesos.	
(5)	**Estudiante:**	¿Y el precio de ése?	
(6)	**Señorita:**	*Sesenta y cinco.*	
(7)	**Estudiante:**	¿Y aquél allí?	
(8)	**Señorita:**	*Cincuenta y cinco.*	
(9)	**Estudiante:**	Bueno, gracias. Llevo aquél.	

1. ¿Dónde está el estudiante? **2.** ¿Qué necesita el estudiante? **3.** ¿Qué precio tiene el libro que lleva?

31	treinta y uno(-a)	39	treinta y nueve
32	treinta y dos	40	cuarenta
33	treinta y tres	50	cincuenta
34	treinta y cuatro	60	sesenta
35	treinta y cinco	70	setenta
36	treinta y seis	80	ochenta
37	treinta y siete	90	noventa
38	treinta y ocho	100	cien (ciento)

A. While the numbers *sixteen* to *nineteen* and *twenty-one* to *twenty-nine* are usually written as one word in Spanish, notice that subsequent numbers are always written in the long form: **treinta y uno.**

veintidós muchachas	*twenty-two girls*
treinta y dos minutos	*thirty-two minutes*
cuarenta y una ciudades	*forty-one cities*
noventa y nueve hoteles	*ninety-nine hotels*

B. **Ciento** is shortened to **cien** before a noun.

cien chicos	*one hundred boys*
cien chicas	*one hundred girls*

C. With the exception of **uno (un, una)** and numbers ending in **-uno,** numbers do not show gender agreement with the nouns they modify. **Uno** and numbers that end in **-uno** are changed to **un (-ún)** before a masculine noun and to **una** before a feminine noun. Notice the accent on numbers ending in **-ún.**

ocho niñas	*eight girls*
treinta hombres	*thirty men*
veintiún aviones	*twenty-one planes*

In the bookstore

(1) Miss, I need a book on the Aztec civilization. (2) This book is very good. Are you a student? (3) Yes. How much is it, please? (4) Eighty pesos. (5) And that one, how much is that? (6) Sixty-five. (7) And that one over there? (8) Fifty-five. (9) Okay, thank you. I'll take that one over there.

veintiuna mujeres	*twenty-one women*
cuarenta y un pasajeros	*forty-one passengers*
sesenta y una ciudades	*sixty-one cities*

Ejercicios

A. Read in Spanish.

1. 31   3. 93   5. 67   7. 100   9. 44
2. 58   4. 85   6. 92   8. 79   10. 86

B. Write out each of the following numbers.

1. 70 países   6. 31 ciudades
2. 81 libros   7. 55 indios
3. 42 personas   8. 90 horas
4. 56 casas   9. 41 amigas
5. 65 minutos   10. 100 estudiantes

C. (*En la librería*) Imagine that you are in a bookstore and a clerk is quoting prices of various books to you, in pesos. Read aloud the lowest price in each group of three.

1. treinta y tres pesos   3. ochenta y siete pesos
   cincuenta pesos   treinta y seis pesos
   cuarenta pesos   cuarenta y nueve pesos
2. setenta pesos   4. noventa y dos pesos
   ochenta pesos   setenta pesos
   sesenta pesos   sesenta y cinco pesos

V. TELLING TIME

ES LA UNA.

ES LA UNA Y CUARTO (QUINCE).

ES LA UNA Y MEDIA (TREINTA).

SON LAS DOS MENOS VEINTE DE LA TARDE.

SON LAS DOS MENOS CUARTO DE LA MAÑANA.

SON LAS DOS EN PUNTO DE LA TARDE.

A. To tell time in Spanish, use a third person form of **ser** (**es** for *one o'clock* and **son** for all other hours) plus the feminine form of the definite article (**la** for *one* and **las** for all others) plus the hour.

¿Qué hora es?   *What time is it?*
Es la una.   *It's 1:00 (one o'clock).*
Son las once.   *It's 11:00.*
Son las once en punto.   *It's 11:00 on the dot.*

B. To express the time between the hour and the half hour, add the number of minutes to the hour by using **y.**

Es la una y veinte.   *It's 1:20.*
Son las seis y diez.   *It's 6:10.*
Son las ocho y cinco.   *It's 8:05.*

C. To express the time between the half hour and the next hour, subtract the number of minutes from the next hour by using **menos** (*less*).

Es la una menos veinte.   *It's twenty to 1:00.*
Son las tres menos diez.   *It's ten to 3:00.*
Son las cuatro menos veinticinco. *It's 3:35.*

D. A quarter past the hour and a quarter till the next hour is expressed by either **cuarto** or **quince.** Half past the hour is expressed by **media** or **treinta.**

Son las cinco y cuarto (cinco y   *It's 5:15.*
  quince).
Es la una menos cuarto (la una menos *It's a quarter to 1:00.*
  quince).
Son casi las diez y media (las diez y *It's almost 10:30.*
  treinta).
¿A qué hora llega? Llega a las dos y   *At what time is he arriving? He's*
  cuarto.   *arriving at 2:15.*
Debo estar allí a las diez y media.   *I ought to be there at 10:30.*

Note the use of the preposition **a** in the last two examples.

E. **De la mañana** is used for A.M., and **de la tarde** or **de la noche** for P.M. **De la tarde** is generally used up until about 7:00 P.M.

¡Qué problema! José llega al   *What a problem! José is arriving at the*
  aeropuerto a las tres de la mañana.   *airport at 3:00 A.M.*
En España cenamos a las diez de la   *In Spain we eat at 10:00 P.M.*
  noche.
Tengo una clase de ciencias de   *I have a computer science class at*
  computación a las cuatro de la   *4:00 P.M.*
  tarde.

Ejercicios

A. Give the time on each clock in Spanish, answering, in each case, **¿Qué hora es?**

B. Create new sentences, substituting the phrases in the list, translated into Spanish, for the phrase in italics.

El avión llega *a las dos y media de la tarde.*

1. at 6:30 P.M.
2. at 8:45 A.M.
3. at 10:15 P.M.
4. at 9:30 A.M.
5. at 7:45 A.M.

C. Give the Spanish equivalent of the following sentences.

1. I have a class at seven-thirty in the morning.
2. The concert is at eight fifteen in the evening.
3. The plane arrives at three twenty-five in the afternoon.
4. We have a difficult exam at three in the afternoon.
5. At what time does the library open?

Preguntas

1. ¿Qué hora es ahora?   **2.** ¿A qué hora llega usted a la universidad?   **3.** ¿A qué hora estamos en la clase de español?   **4.** ¿A qué hora cena usted? ¿mira televisión? ¿estudia español?   **5.** ¿A qué hora llega usted a casa?

EL MUSEO NACIONAL DE ANTROPOLOGÍA [1]

Bob, un joven de Nueva York, está en el Museo Nacional de Antropología [1] de la ciudad de México con Paco, un amigo mexicano.

Paco: ¿Todavía crees que los buenos museos están todos en Nueva York?

Bob: Bueno… allá tenemos unos treinta y cinco o cuarenta. Pero admito que éste es una maravilla de arquitectura.

Paco: Además, aquí es posible aprender mucho sobre las civilizaciones indias del pasado. [2]

Bob: ¿Estudian ustedes la historia de las civilizaciones indígenas en la universidad?

Paco: ¡Claro! Mi hermana es profesora de Civilización Azteca y tiene muchos estudiantes en ese curso.

Entran a otra sala

Bob: ¡Hombre! Aquél debe ser el famoso calendario azteca. [3] ¡Es estupendo!

Paco: Y es un calendario bastante exacto. El año azteca tiene dieciocho meses de veinte días, y cinco días extra.

Bob: Ahora que hablas del tiempo, ¿qué hora es?

Paco: Son las doce y media. Es hora de comer. ¿Qué decidimos?

Bob: Creo que debemos comer tacos [4] en honor de Cinteotl, el dios del maíz.

Paco: Tú aprendes pronto, gringo. [5]

Bob: Verdad. Todos los neoyorquinos somos inteligentes.

Paco: ¡Y modestos!

admito *I admit*   **maravilla** *marvel*   **sala** *room*   **¡Hombre!** *Hey!*   **en honor de** *in honor of*   **dios del maíz** *god of corn*

Preguntas

1. ¿Dónde están los dos amigos? **2.** ¿Quién cree que los buenos museos están todos en Nueva York? **3.** ¿Qué estudia Paco en la universidad? **4.** ¿Es bastante exacto el calendario azteca? **5.** ¿Cuántos meses tiene el año azteca? **6.** ¿Quién es Cinteotl? **7.** ¿Come usted tacos? ¿dónde? **8.** ¿Qué opinión tiene usted de los restaurantes de esta ciudad?

NOTAS CULTURALES

1. The Museum of Anthropology and History of Mexico City is an immense structure covered by the largest suspended roof in the world. Plants and fountains give a cool and pleasant look to the modernistic style of its halls and courts.

2. While the Museum of Anthropology has exhibits from all over the world, the largest part of the museum contains artifacts from Mexico itself and concentrates on the many and varied Indian cultures which successively inhabited its regions.

3. The Aztec calendar stone, or **Piedra del Sol,** is a large carved stone from sixteenth century Aztec culture. The year consisted of 365 days divided into 18 months, each with 20 days and five extra days, considered unlucky and dangerous.

4. Tacos, like many Mexican foods, are made with tortillas, flat corn cakes, which are cooked and filled with meat, cheese, beans or other vegetables and sauces. Corn has been the staple of the Mexican diet from as far back as history and mythology record.

5. Gringo (-a) is a sometimes pejorative term for a foreigner, mainly for a person from the United States or England. Here, of course, the word is used with affection.

ACTIVIDADES

En la librería _____

Elisa is trying to find a present for Ricardo. Help her to select one by circling the correct word.

1. Elisa: ¿Cuál es el precio de *(este—ese—aquel)* libro de física?
2. Dependiente *(Clerk)*: Sesenta pesos. Pero ¿por qué no lleva *(esta—esa—aquella)* colección de libros de arquitectura?
3. Elisa: No, Ricardo no estudia para arquitecto. ¿Son interesantes *(estos—esos—aquellos)* libros de química?
4. Dependiente: No, *(éstos—ésos—aquéllos)* son aburridos. Pero *(estas—esas—aquellas)* novelas italianas son interesantes.
5. Elisa: ¿Cuáles? ¿*(éstas—ésas—aquéllas)* que están arriba de los libros de historia?. ¡Ah!, no. Ricardo no lee literatura.
6. Dependiente: Y... ¿por qué no lleva *(estas—esas—aquellas)* historietas *(comics)* del Pato Donaldo?
7. Elisa: ¡Claro!, *(éstas—ésas—aquéllas)* son perfectas!

Entrevista

Ask a classmate the following questions, then report the information you have gathered to the class.

1. ¿Para qué estudias? ¿para médico?
2. ¿Crees que es importante o no es importante estudiar filosofía?
3. ¿Qué libros lees ahora?
4. ¿Qué curso tienes a las dos de la tarde?
5. ¿Estás interesado(-a) en la antropología?
6. ¿A qué hora llegas a la universidad?
7. ¿A qué hora tienes clases?

Situación

En el museo

Two students are in the Anthropology Museum in Mexico City. One student says that this museum is very good. It is an architectural marvel. It has many exhibits on anthropology and on the Indians. It is interesting to learn about the civilizations of the past. The other student says that it is interesting but it is not important. We live in the twentieth century (**en el siglo veinte**). We should study practical subjects (**materias prácticas**). He mentions several of these subjects. A lady who is passing by interrupts them to ask "Where is the Aztec calendar stone?" She says she is American and does not speak Spanish well. They tell her (in very slow, clear Spanish) that that exhibit is far away in room 16 (**la sala 16**) and it is wonderful. She says "Thank you" and "Goodbye."

VOCABULARIO ACTIVO

Verbos útiles

abrir   to open
aprender   to learn
beber   to drink
comer   to eat
comprender   to understand
creer   to believe, think
deber   should, ought to
decidir   to decide
describir   to describe
descubrir   to discover
escribir   to write
existir   to exist
leer   to read
recibir   to receive
tener   to have
vivir   to live

Estudios universitarios

la antropología   anthropology
la arquitectura   architecture
la biología   biology
las ciencias de computación   computer sciences
las ciencias sociales   social sciences
las ciencias políticas   political sciences
la composición   composition, theme
la filosofía   philosophy
la física   physics
la ingeniería   engineering
la literatura   literature
las matemáticas   mathematics
la medicina   medicine
la psicología   psychology
la química   chemistry

La hora / el tiempo

el año *year*
el calendario *calendar*
el día *day*
en punto *on the dot*
el futuro *future*
la hora *hour*
hoy en día *nowadays*
el mes *month*
el minuto *minute*
el momento *moment*
el pasado *past*
por la mañana *in the morning;* **por la**
　tarde *in the afternoon;* **por la**
　noche *at night*
¿Qué hora es? *What time is it?*
la semana *week*
Son las dos y media (cuarto). Son las
　dos menos cuarto. *It's 2:30 (2:15).*
　It's 1:45.
el tiempo *time (in a general sense)*

Adjetivos

aburrido(a) *boring*
alemán (alemana) *German*
blanco(a) *white*
caro(a) *expensive*
difícil *difficult*
estupendo(a) *great*
exacto(a) *exact*

fácil *easy*
indio(a) *Indian*
joven *young*
lleno(a) de *filled with*
mestizo(a) *Indian and European*
modesto(a) *modest*
orgulloso(a) *proud*

Otras palabras útiles

además *besides, moreover*
bastante *rather; enough*
la carta *letter*
casi *almost*
la clase (media, alta) *(middle, upper)*
　class
entonces *well; then*
la escuela *school*
el gobierno *government*
la idea *idea*
la librería *bookstore*
la mayoría *majority*
el, la política-o *politician*
el, la presidente *president*
el problema *problem*
pronto *soon*
la sangre *blood*
todavía *still, yet*
la vida *life*

CAPÍTULO 4

LA NATURALEZA

Las montañas (*mountains*), el sol (*sun*), el cielo (*sky*), el lago (*lake*)... ¡Qué belleza (*beauty*)!

OBJECTIVES

LANGUAGE: In this chapter we introduce, discuss, and practice:

1. the present tense of the irregular verbs **ir,** *to go,* and **hacer,** *to make or do*
2. weather expressions and some idioms that use **tener**
3. ordinal numbers (*first, second, third,* and so on)
4. dates (days of the week and months of the year)

You will also learn vocabulary related to the seasons and the out-of-doors.

CULTURE: The dialogue takes place in Santiago, Chile, in July, when it is winter. You will learn something about some Chilean customs.

EXPLICACIÓN

I. THE IRREGULAR VERBS **IR** AND **HACER**

(1)	**César:**	¿*Vas* de vacaciones a las montañas este año?
(2)	**Néstor:**	No, *voy* a la costa del Pacífico.
(3)	**César:**	También *va* Pablo, el muchacho que *hace* cerámica ¿no?
(4)	**Néstor:**	Sí, *vamos* a estar allí tres semanas.
(5)	**César:**	¿Y *van* en auto?
(6)	**Néstor:**	No, *vamos* en autobús. Tú y Lucio ¿qué *hacen*?
(7)	**César:**	Lucio y yo *hacemos* la comida para ayudar en casa.
(8)	**Néstor:**	¿Por qué no *van* al mar con nosotros? Allá *hacemos* deportes, *vamos* a la playa y pescamos en el río.
(9)	**César:**	¿Y quién *hace* la comida?
(10)	**Néstor:**	¡Ustedes, por supuesto! Detesto cocinar!

1. ¿Adónde va Néstor este año? ¿Con quién va?   **2.** ¿Cuánto tiempo van a estar allí?
3. ¿Cómo van?   **4.** ¿Qué hacen Lucio y César para ayudar en la casa?   **5.** ¿Qué hacen los muchachos cuando están cerca del mar?   **6.** ¿Quién va a hacer la comida allí?
7. ¿Adónde va usted de vacaciones?

A.   The present-tense forms of the irregular verb **ir** are:

ir   *(to go)*

Singular	Plural
voy	vamos
vas	vais
va	van

¿Vas de vacaciones este invierno?	*Are you going on vacation this winter?*
¿Vamos en auto o en autobús?	*Are we going by car or bus?*

---

(1) Are you going on vacation to the mountains this year? (2) No, I'm going to the Pacific coast. (3) Pablo, the boy who makes ceramics, is going too, isn't he? (4) Yes, we are going to be there (for) three weeks. (5) And are you going by car? (6) No, we are going by bus. What are you and Lucio doing? (7) Lucio and I make the meals to help out at home. (8) Why don't you come to the ocean with us? We'll participate in sports, we'll go to the beach and fish in the river. (9) And who's making the meals? (10) You, of course. I hate cooking.

B. Like other verbs of motion, the verb **ir** is usually followed by the preposition **a** when a destination is mentioned.

Voy a la playa todos los días en el verano.	*I go to the beach every day in the summer.*
Enrique va a Acapulco.	*Enrique is going to Acapulco.*
Paco y Anita van al café.	*Paco and Anita are going to the café.*

C. The verb **ir** is also followed by the preposition **a** before an infinitive. The **ir a** + *infinitive* construction is often used in place of the future tense to express an action or event that is going to take place.

Voy a esquiar en las montañas que están cerca de Bariloche.	*I'm going to ski in the mountains that are near Bariloche.*
Va a ser un concierto excelente.	*It's going to be an excellent concert.*
Vamos a ir de vacaciones en la primavera.	*We're going to take a vacation in the spring.*

D. The present-forms of **hacer,** which is also irregular, are:

hacer *(to do, make)*

hago	hacemos
haces	hacéis
hace	hacen

Hago ejercicios todos los días.	*I do exercises every day.*
Ellos hacen la cena y nosotros hacemos el café.	*They're making the dinner and we're making the coffee.*

Ejercicios

A. Create new sentences, substituting the words in the list for those in italics.

1. *José* va a Acapulco.
   a. Elena y Paco **b.** yo **c.** nosotros **d.** el profesor **e.** tú
2. *Estela y Juanita* van a ir a la playa mañana.
   a. Roberto **b.** nosotros **c.** la señora Rodríguez **d.** tú **e.** yo
3. *Yo* hago deportes.
   a. ustedes **b.** tú **c.** papá **d.** Irene y yo **e.** los muchachos

B. Complete each sentence with the correct present tense form of **ir.**

1. Rafael y yo _____ a pescar al lago.
2. Ellos _____ a pasar el invierno en Puerto Rico.
3. Felipe _____ a ir a las montañas.
4. Yo _____ a viajar por Sudamérica.
5. ¿_____ tú de vacaciones a Viña del Mar?
6. ¿_____ usted a Guatemala en auto o en avión?

C. It's Saturday afternoon and Jorge is trying to find someone to go to the beach with him. He's out of luck, however. To find out why, complete the questions in his dialogue with Paco, using the appropriate form of **hacer.**

Jorge: ¿Qué _____ Pedro hoy?
Paco: Él estudia para un examen.
Jorge: ¿Qué _____ tú?
Paco: Yo voy a las montañas con Lolita.
Jorge: ¿Qué _____ Juan y Sonia?
Paco: Ellos pasan el día en el campo.
Jorge: ¿Qué _____ Ana?
Paco: Ella va a casa de unos tíos que viven cerca del mar.
Jorge: Y entonces, ¿qué _____ yo?
Paco: Pues vas a la playa solo (*alone*) o no vas allí hoy...

D. Using **ir a** + infinitive, answer the questions to indicate that the subjects are going to do these things soon.

Modelo: ¿Estudian ustedes ahora? **No, vamos a estudiar mañana.**

1. ¿Pescas ahora?
2. ¿Hacen ellos ejercicios ahora?
3. ¿Abre ella el regalo ahora?
4. ¿Esquían los niños ahora?
5. ¿Van ustedes de vacaciones ahora?

Preguntas

1. ¿Adónde va usted de vacaciones este año? **2.** ¿Va con un(a) amigo(a)? **3.** ¿Cómo va(n) a viajar? ¿en auto? ¿en avión? **4.** ¿Va usted mucho a la playa? ¿a las montañas? **5.** ¿Qué hace usted esta noche? ¿este invierno? ¿en las vacaciones? **6.** ¿Hace usted ejercicios en este momento? ¿Qué hace usted? **7.** ¿Qué desea hacer usted ahora? ¿Por qué?

II. HACE WITH WEATHER EXPRESSIONS; IDIOMS WITH TENER

---

(1)	**Dina:**	*¡Qué calor hace!* Voy a abrir la ventana.
(2)	**Damián:**	¿Calor? Yo *tengo frío.* El cielo está nublado.
(3)	**Dina:**	Pero yo *tengo calor.* Necesito aire.
(4)	**Damián:**	*¡Hace frío!* Estamos en otoño.
(5)	**Dina:**	Abuela, ¿crees que *hace frío o calor* hoy?
(6)	**Abuela:**	¿Frío? ¿Calor? *¡Hace un tiempo magnífico!*

---

1. ¿Quién tiene frío? **2.** ¿Quién tiene calor? **3.** ¿Quién va a abrir la ventana? **4.** ¿Quién necesita aire? **5.** ¿Cree la abuela que hace frío o calor?

A. The third person singular of the verb **hacer** (*to make or do*), **hace,** is used with certain nouns to make statements about the weather.

Hace frío en el invierno.	*It's cold in the winter.*
Siempre hace buen tiempo en la primavera.	*It's always nice weather in the spring.*
Hace viento en el otoño.	*It's windy in the fall.*
Hace sol en las montañas.	*It's sunny in the mountains.*
Hace calor en el verano pero ahora hace fresco.	*It's warm (hot) in the summer but now it's cool.*
¿Qué tiempo hace?	*How's the weather?*

B. Note that **mucho** (*very*) is used in many expressions about the weather to mean *very.* **Mucho(s)** generally means *much, many,* or *a lot.*

Hace mucho frío.	*It's very cold.*
Hace mucho viento.	*It's very windy.*
Hace mucho calor.	*It's very hot.*
Hace mucho sol.	*It's very sunny.*

C. The idiomatic expression **tener frío** means *to be cold,* while **tener calor** means *to be warm (hot).*

Tenemos calor. ¡Vamos a la playa!	*We're warm (hot). Let's go to the beach!*
¿Tienes frío?	*Are you cold?*

---

(1) How warm it is! I'm going to open the window. (2) Warm? I'm cold. The sky is cloudy. (3) But I'm warm. I need air. (4) It's cold! It's autumn. (5) Grandmother, do you think it's cold or warm today? (6) Cold? Warm? It's magnificent weather!

Ejercicios

A. Create questions to which the following would be possible answers.

Modelo: Hace mucho calor hoy. **¿Qué tiempo hace hoy?**

1. Hace buen tiempo aquí.
2. Hace mucho frío ahora.
3. Hace calor en el verano.
4. Hace viento en las montañas.
5. Donde yo vivo, siempre hace sol.

B. Answer the following questions using the correct form of **tener frío** or **tener calor,** as appropriate.

Modelo: ¿Por qué abres las puertas? **Porque tengo calor.**

1. ¿Por qué buscan ustedes una chaqueta (*jacket*)?
2. ¿Por qué toma ella un té frío?
3. ¿Por qué va usted a la playa?
4. ¿Por qué abren ellos las ventanas?
5. ¿Por qué desea usted tomar un chocolate caliente (*hot*)?

C. Give the Spanish equivalent of the following sentences:

1. It's windy in the fall.
2. In the spring, the weather is nice.
3. It's cold in the mountains.
4. What's the weather like today?
5. It's warm in the summer.
6. Are you (**tú**) cold today?
7. I am very warm now.
8. Today the weather is magnificent.

Preguntas

1. ¿Hace frío hoy? ¿fresco? ¿calor? **2.** ¿Hace frío aquí en la clase? ¿fresco? ¿calor? **3.** ¿Qué tiempo hace en el invierno? ¿en la primavera? ¿en el otoño? ¿en el verano? **4.** ¿Qué tiempo hace en Santiago de Chile ahora? ¿en Vancouver? ¿en Cuba? ¿en España? ¿aquí? **5.** ¿En qué estación hace mucho sol aquí? ¿viento? **6.** ¿Tiene usted frío ahora? ¿calor?

III. ORDINAL NUMBERS FIRST TO TENTH

En el Hotel Multivistas

(1)   **Sr. Ochoa:**   ¿Qué precios tienen los cuartos?
(2)   **Recepcionista:**   Bueno, depende. En el *primer* piso* y en el

---

* **el primer piso:** *the first floor.* However, in Spanish-speaking countries and most European countries, the ground floor is not considered the first floor, so **el primer piso** really refers to what we call the second floor, **el segundo piso** to what we call the third floor, etc. (In Spanish, the ground floor is called **la planta baja**.)

		segundo, noventa y cinco pesos. Tienen vista al océano.
(3)	**Sr. Ochoa:**	¿Y en el *tercero*?
(4)	**Recepcionista:**	En el *tercer* piso y en el *cuarto,* setenta y cinco. Tienen vista al campo.
(5)	**Sr. Ochoa:**	¿Y en el *quinto* piso?
(6)	**Recepcionista:**	En el *quinto* y en el *sexto,* sesenta y cinco. Tienen vista a la isla.
(7)	**Sr. Ochoa:**	Gracias. Creo que ustedes necesitan un piso más, con vista a mi estado económico.

1. ¿Qué precio tiene un cuarto en el primer piso o en el segundo? **2.** ¿Qué vista tienen estos cuartos? **3.** ¿Qué precio tiene un cuarto en el tercero o en el cuarto piso? **4.** ¿Qué vista tienen estos cuartos? **5.** ¿Qué precio tiene un cuarto en el quinto o en el sexto piso? **6.** ¿Qué vista tienen estos cuartos? **7.** ¿Qué cree el señor Ochoa que necesita el hotel?

A. The ordinal numbers *first* to *tenth* in Spanish are:

primero (-a)	*first*	sexto (-a)	*sixth*
segundo (-a)	*second*	séptimo (-a)	*seventh*
tercero (-a)	*third*	octavo (-a)	*eighth*
cuarto (-a)	*fourth*	noveno (-a)	*ninth*
quinto (-a)	*fifth*	décimo (-a)	*tenth*

B. Ordinal numbers agree in number and gender with the nouns they modify.

Voy a viajar en segunda clase.	*I'm going to travel second class.*
Los primeros días de la primavera son una belleza.	*The first days of spring are beautiful (a beauty).*
¡Ésta es la décima vez!	*This is the tenth time!*

C. The final **-o** of **primero** and **tercero** is dropped before a masculine singular noun.

Voy a tomar el primer autobús.	*I'm going to take the first bus.*
Es el tercer libro a la derecha.	*It's the third book on the right.*

In the Multi-view Hotel
(1) How much do the rooms cost? (2) Well, it depends. On the first* and second floors, ninety-five pesos. They have a view of the ocean. (3) And on the third? (4) On the third and fourth floors, seventy-five. They have a view of the countryside. (5) And on the fifth floor? (6) On the fifth and sixth, sixty-five. They have a view of the island. (7) Thank you. I think you need one more floor, with a view toward my economic condition.

Tengo que estar en Toledo durante la
tercera semana de este mes.

*I have to be in Toledo during the third
week of this month.*

Ejercicio

Fill in the blanks with the ordinal number (translated into Spanish) indicated in parentheses.

1. (tenth) Es la ＿＿＿＿＿＿ vez que visito Chile.
2. (sixth) Van en el ＿＿＿＿＿＿ auto.
3. (fifth) Es la ＿＿＿＿＿＿ puerta a la izquierda.
4. (third) Es el ＿＿＿＿＿＿ día de la semana.
5. (second) Hoy es el ＿＿＿＿＿＿ día del mes.
6. (first) Ésta es mi ＿＿＿＿＿＿ clase de español.
7. (fourth) Los señores Menéndez viven en el ＿＿＿＿＿＿ piso.
8. (ninth) Aquélla es la ＿＿＿＿＿＿ avenida.
9. (eighth) Uruguay es el ＿＿＿＿＿＿ país que visitamos este verano.
10. (seventh) Ernesto es el ＿＿＿＿＿＿ hijo de esa señora.

Preguntas

1. ¿Vive usted en una planta baja? ¿en un primer piso? ¿en un segundo piso? ¿En qué piso vive usted?   **2.** ¿Es ésta la primera vez que usted estudia español? ¿la segunda vez?   **3.** ¿Es éste el primer año que usted está aquí? ¿el segundo? ¿el tercero? ¿el cuarto?   **4.** Cuando usted viaja en avión, ¿viaja en primera clase? ¿en clase turística?

IV. DATES

(1) **Matías:** ¿Qué día es hoy? ¿es *el treinta de octubre*?
(2) **Estela:** No, hoy es *el primero de noviembre.*
(3) **Matías:** ¿Y cuál es el primer día de verano? ¿es *el veintiuno o el veintidós de diciembre*?
(4) **Estela:** Este año es *el veintitrés.*
(5) **Matías:** ¿Es un *miércoles* o un *jueves*?
(6) **Estela:** Es un *domingo*. Matías ¿en qué mundo vives?
(7) **Matías:** Pues, en este mundo y en el siglo veinte. Pero no tengo memoria para las fechas.

(1) What day is it today? Is it the thirtieth of October? (2) No, today is the first of November. (3) And what is the first day of summer? Is it the twenty-first or the twenty-second of December? (4) This year it's the twenty-third. (5) Is it a Wednesday or a Thursday? (6) It's a Sunday. Matías, what world do you live in? (7) Well, in this world and in the twentieth century. But I don't have a memory for dates.

1. ¿Qué día es (en el diálogo)?   **2.** ¿Cuál es el primer día de verano allí?   **3.** ¿Dónde vive Matías?   **4.** ¿Qué problema tiene? ¿Qué necesita él?

A. The days of the week in Spanish are all masculine. They are not capitalized.

Los días de la semana:

domingo	*Sunday*	jueves	*Thursday*
lunes	*Monday*	viernes	*Friday*
martes	*Tuesday*	sábado	*Saturday*
miércoles	*Wednesday*		

B. The definite article is almost always used with the days of the week as the equivalent of *on*, when *on* could be used in English.

Hoy es jueves.	*Today is Thursday.*
Ella llega el martes.	*She's arriving (on) Tuesday.*
Voy de vacaciones el viernes.	*I am going on vacation on Friday.*

C. The plurals of **sábado** and **domingo** are formed by adding **-s: los sábados, los domingos.** The plurals of the other days are formed simply with the use of the plural article **los.**

Vamos al parque los domingos.	*We go to the park on Sundays.*
Estoy en la universidad los martes y los jueves.	*I'm at the university on Tuesdays and Thursdays.*
Teresa siempre está en casa los miércoles.	*Teresa is always home on Wednesdays.*

D. The months of the year in Spanish are all masculine and are not capitalized.

Los meses del año:

enero	*January*	julio	*July*
febrero	*February*	agosto	*August*
marzo	*March*	septiembre	*September*
abril	*April*	octubre	*October*
mayo	*May*	noviembre	*November*
junio	*June*	diciembre	*December*

E. With one exception, *the first* (**el primero**), cardinal numbers are used to express dates.

Van al concierto el primero de septiembre.	*They're going to the concert on September 1st.*
Viajan a España el 10 de mayo (el diez de mayo).	*They are traveling to Spain on May 10th.*

Hoy es el 27 de febrero (el veintisiete de febrero).	*Today is February 27th.*
Llegamos el lunes, cuatro de noviembre.*	*We're arriving on Monday, November 4th.**
¿Qué día es hoy? Hoy es jueves, veintitrés de octubre.	*What day is today? Today is Thursday, October 23rd.*

Ejercicios

A. Give the following dates in Spanish.

1. Friday, April 3rd.
2. Monday, May 21st.
3. Wednesday, November 17th.
4. Sunday, August 5th.
5. Tuesday, January 6th.
6. Thursday, December 7th.
7. Saturday, March 1st.
8. Wednesday, September 30th.

B. Write the dates of the following holidays in Spanish.

Modelo: Navidad (*Christmas*) **el veinticinco de diciembre**

1. Día de Año Nuevo (*New Year's Day*)
2. Día de la Raza (*Columbus Day*)
3. Día de los Reyes Magos (*Epiphany*, January 6th)
4. Nochebuena (*Christmas Eve*)
5. Día de los Muertos (*All Souls' Day*, November 2nd)
6. Día de las Américas (*Pan American Day*, April 14th)

C. Give the Spanish equivalent of the following sentences.
1. Do you (**tú**) want to travel on Tuesday the 13th?**
2. We are arriving on Wednesday, June 27th.
3. I am going to be in the country on Sunday, February 3rd.
4. Is Peter going to the mountain on Thursday, March 21st?
5. Mr. and Mrs. Becerra are always home on Saturdays.

Preguntas

1. ¿Qué día es hoy? 2. ¿Qué día es mañana? 3. ¿Cuándo es el cumpleaños (*birthday*) de Washington? ¿de Lincoln? ¿de usted? 4. ¿Cuáles son los meses del invierno? ¿de la primavera? ¿del otoño? ¿del verano? 5. ¿En qué mes(es) hace mucho frío aquí? ¿calor? ¿sol? ¿viento?

---

* The definite article **el** is not repeated after the day of the week.

** In Hispanic countries Tuesday the 13th, like Friday the 13th in the U.S. and Canada, is considered unlucky.

UN PAÍS DE INMIGRANTES

Isabel, una estudiante de Canadá, pasa las vacaciones de verano en Santiago con una familia chilena. Va en auto con los dos hijos de la familia.

Isabel: ¡Caramba! Tengo mucho frío.

Sarita: Por supuesto, hace frío porque es el primero de julio. ¿Qué tiempo hace ahora en Vancouver?

Isabel: Hace calor. Los domingos, todo el mundo va a la playa.

Jorge: ¡Qué gracioso! En Chile vamos a la playa en diciembre, enero y febrero[1]. O vamos a los lagos.

Isabel: En esos meses tenemos mucha nieve allá. ¿Y esquían ustedes ahora?

Sarita: Claro, pues es invierno. Las montañas están cerca.

Isabel: ¡Dios mío! Aquí hacen todo al revés.

Jorge: Aquí somos normales; ustedes hacen todo al revés.

Sarita: ¿Van a discutir toda la tarde? ¿Por qué no vamos de compras? Creo que vamos a tener lluvia y es mejor estar en las tiendas.

Isabel: Bueno, ¿adónde vamos? ¿al otro lado del río?

Sarita: A la Alameda, una avenida que está en el centro. En realidad el nombre es Avenida O'Higgins[2] en honor del héroe nacional de Chile.

Isabel: O'Higgins . . . ¿estás segura? ¿no es de Irlanda?

Sarita: ¡Qué va!, Chile es un país de inmigrantes, como el Canadá. Aquí vive gente de origen inglés, español, alemán...

Jorge: ¡Alemán! Tengo una idea. ¿Por qué no vamos al Salón de Té Alemán para tomar once[3]?

Isabel: Bueno, a las cinco, como Dios manda.

pues *since*   **al revés** *backwards*   **discutir** *argue*   **como Dios manda** *the proper way*

Preguntas

1. ¿Dónde pasa Isabel las vacaciones de verano?   **2.** ¿Qué tiempo hace en Chile en julio?   **3.** ¿Hace frío en Vancouver en el verano?   **4.** ¿Cuándo van a la playa en Chile?   **5.** ¿Qué es la Alameda?   **6.** ¿Cuál es, en realidad, el nombre de la Alameda?   **7.** ¿Es Chile un país de inmigrantes?   **8.** ¿A qué hora toman la merienda? ¿qué toman?   **9.** ¿Va usted a la playa en el verano?   **10.** ¿Qué merienda toma usted generalmente? ¿café? ¿té? ¿chocolate?

NOTAS CULTURALES

1. Note that the seasons are reversed in the Northern and Southern hemispheres.

2. Bernardo O'Higgins is the hero of Chile's war of independence against Spain (1814–1818). His mother was a Chilean, his father an Irish immigrant who began as a traveling peddler in Ireland, moved to Spain, and was later appointed viceroy of Peru by the Spanish government. (This was a most unusual case in socially rigid, colonial Spanish America.) A brilliant and daring general during the war, O'Higgins served afterwards as the first leader of the government of Chile.

3. Chileans and many other Latin Americans pause in the late afternoon for a **merienda,** a snack usually including biscuits, cookies or pastry accompanied by tea, coffee, or a soft drink. In most countries, at about four or five in the afternoon, people say that it's time to **tomar el té.** In Chile, however, one frequently hears **tomar once.** This is said to have derived from the euphemism used by Chilean men in colonial times when they would leave the women with their teapots and go out to have a brandy **(aguardiente).** Fearing to offend refined sensibilities, the men would say they were going out to "take (drink) eleven." (There are eleven letters in **aguardiente.**)

ACTIVIDADES

De vacaciones

Looking at the illustration, answer the following questions.

1. ¿Qué tiempo hace en la playa?
2. ¿Qué tiempo hace en las montañas?
3. ¿Quién va a tener frío, Lola o Tito?
4. ¿Quién tiene problemas con el viento?
5. ¿Está nublado el cielo cerca del mar?
6. ¿Qué cree usted que Lola hace ahora? ¿va a clase? ¿toma sol?
7. ¿Qué hace Tito? ¿va a clase? ¿escribe un poema? ¿observa los árboles?
8. ¿Adónde va usted de vacaciones este verano? ¿va al mar? ¿a las montañas? ¿por qué?

Entrevista

Ask a classmate the following questions. Then report the information to the class.

1. ¿De qué origen eres? ¿inglés? ¿italiano? ¿alemán? ¿francés? ¿africano? ¿chino? ¿japonés? ¿indio? ¿español? ¿mexicano? ¿cubano?
2. ¿Dónde vive tu familia?
3. ¿Cuál es la fecha de tu cumpleaños?
4. ¿Tienes un día favorito de la semana? ¿Por qué?

Situación

Study the following "situación." Your teacher may call on you to act out one of the three roles. You may wish to consult the *Diálogo*, the mini-dialogues, or the *Vocabulario Activo* at the end of the chapter for assistance.

<u>¿Adónde vamos?</u>

Three students are talking about where they are going on vacation. Each one is going to a different place. They talk about what the weather is going to be like and how they are going to get to their vacation spot. Then one student has an idea: why not go to a restaurant to have tea?

VOCABULARIO ACTIVO

Verbos útiles

ayudar *to help*
esquiar *to ski*
hacer *to make or do;*
   hacer deportes *to play sports;*
   hacer ejercicios *to do exercises*
ir *to go;* **ir a** + *inf.* *to be going to* + *inf;*
   ir de compras *to go shopping;*

ir de vacaciones *to go on vacation;*
ir en auto (autobús, avión) *to go by car (bus, plane)*
pescar *to fish*

El tiempo

¿Qué tiempo hace? *What's the weather like?*

Hace buen tiempo.   *The weather is nice.*
**Hace calor (fresco, frío, sol,
    viento).**   *The weather is warm (cool,
    cold, sunny, windy).*
Está nublado.   *It's cloudy.*
tener calor (frío)   *to be warm (cold) (of a
    person)*

La naturaleza

la belleza   *beauty*
el campo   *country; field*
el cielo   *sky*
la costa   *coast*
la isla   *island*
el lago   *lake*
el mar   *sea*
la montaña   *mountain*
el océano   *ocean*
la playa   *beach*
el río   *river*
la vista   *view*

Las estaciones del año

la primavera   *spring*
el verano   *summer*
el otoño   *fall*
el invierno   *winter*

Los días de la semana

lunes   *Monday*
martes   *Tuesday*
miércoles   *Wednesday*
jueves   *Thursday*
viernes   *Friday*
sábado   *Saturday*
domingo   *Sunday*

Los meses del año

enero   *January*
febrero   *February*
marzo   *March*
abril   *April*
mayo   *May*
junio   *June*
julio   *July*
agosto   *August*
septiembre   *September*
octubre   *October*
noviembre   *November*
diciembre   *December*

Expresiones útiles

¡Caramba!   *Good grief!*
¡Claro!   *Of course!*
en realidad   *in reality, really*
¿Está usted seguro?   *Are you sure?*
por supuesto   *of course, naturally*
¡Qué gracioso!   *How funny!*
¡Qué va!   *Oh come on!*
todo el mundo   *everyone*
todos los días   *every day;*
    todas las semanas   *every week*

Otras palabras útiles

la cena   *dinner, supper*
el centro   *downtown; center*
la comida   *food*
el cuarto   *room*
la fecha   *date*
el, la inmigrante   *immigrant*
junto (a)   *together*
el mundo   *world*
el nombre   *name*
el origen   *origin*
el piso   *floor, story*
la vez   *time, instance*

La Gente

Pero, ¿es posible? ¿Es española esa chica *rubia* de *ojos* azules? Sí, señor.

En Galicia, una región del noroeste de España, la gente es de origen céltico, como los *irlandeses* y *escoceses*. En casa hablan *gallego*, una *lengua* similar al portugués, y en las *fiestas tocan gaitas*. Tenemos que ir a Andalucía, en el sur, para encontrar al español de *piel oscura* y de *pelo* y ojos negros.

Vemos así que la gente y la cultura de España, como la geografía, son muy variadas. La historia española explica esta *mezcla* de razas y culturas. Todavía hoy coexisten en el país tipos humanos muy variados y cuatro lenguas diferentes: el español, la lengua oficial; el gallego; el catalán, una lengua romance del *nordeste;* y el vasco, una lengua antigua de las provincias del norte.

¿Y si cruzamos el Atlántico? Pues, también descubrimos una gran variedad. En *lugares* como México, *por ejemplo*, gran parte de la gente es mestiza, producto de la mezcla entre indios y españoles. Están muy orgullosos de esa *herencia* india.

blonde / eyes

Irish / Scots / Galician
tongue / celebrations /
  they play bagpipes
skin / dark
hair

mixture

northeast

places / for example

heritage

En otras partes de Hispanoamérica, como en Bolivia y Guatemala, los indios forman *la mayor parte* de la población y muchos viven en pequeños pueblos de las montañas, separados de la vida moderna de las ciudades.   the majority

En países como la Argentina y el Uruguay casi *todo el mundo* es de   everybody
origen europeo: español, italiano, francés, inglés, alemán, polaco, etcétera. En Chile también predominan los europeos, *aunque* parte   although
de la población tiene *cierta* mezcla india.   a certain

Por fin, en el Caribe, la influencia africana es muy importante. Como es evidente, el mundo hispánico es un mundo muy variado.

Preguntas

1. ¿De qué origen es la gente de Galicia?   2. ¿Vemos en España una sola cultura o varias? ¿Qué cosa explica esto?   3. ¿Cuántas lenguas hablan en España? ¿Cuáles son?   4. ¿Cómo es la gente en lugares como México? ¿De qué están orgullosos?   5. ¿Dónde forman los indios la mayor parte de la población?   6. ¿En qué países hay más gente de origen europeo? ¿Cuáles son los principales grupos europeos representados allí?   7. ¿Qué influencia es importante en el Caribe?

CAPÍTULO 5

LA CIUDAD

OBJECTIVES

LANGUAGE: In this chapter we introduce, discuss, and practice:
1. **e** to **ie** stem-changing verbs
2. the expression **hay** (*there is, there are*)
3. three verbal structures that express obligation: **tener que, deber,** and **hay que**
4. possessive adjectives
5. direct object pronouns

You will also learn words and expressions related to the city and be able to talk about the advantages and disadvantages of city life.

CULTURE: The dialogue takes place in the city of New York, where two Puerto Ricans compare life in New York with life in Puerto Rico.

EXPLICACIÓN

I. STEM-CHANGING VERBS E TO IE

En el cine

(1)	**Ana:**	Margarita, *¿quieres* una coca-cola, un café o...?
(2)	**Margarita:**	Una coca, por favor. ¿Y tú?
(3)	**Ana:**	Yo *prefiero* café. *¿Quieres* esperar aquí?
(4)	**Margarita:**	*Prefiero* entrar.
(5)	**Margarita:**	Ana, la película *empieza*. Pero estas señoras hablan y hablan.
(6)	**Ana:**	Perdón, señora. ¡Es imposible entender!
(7)	**Señora:**	¿Cómo? ¿Usted no *entiende*? Señorita, ¡ésta es una conversación privada!

1. ¿Qué quiere Margarita, un café o una coca? **2.** ¿Qué prefiere Ana? **3.** ¿Por qué no entienden la película Ana y Margarita? **4.** ¿Cómo es la conversación de las señoras? **5.** ¿Qué clase de películas prefiere usted: las cómicas, las dramáticas o las de ciencia-ficción?

A. There are certain groups of Spanish verbs known as stem-changing verbs. These verbs have regular endings, but show a change in the stem when the stem is stressed. In the following verbs the **e** of the stem is changed to **ie**.

pensar *(to think)*		entender *(to understand)*		preferir *(to prefer)*	
pienso	pensamos	entiendo	entendemos	prefiero	preferimos
piensas	pensáis	entiendes	entendéis	prefieres	preferís
piensa	piensan	entiende	entienden	prefiere	prefieren

In the first- and second-person plural forms the stress does not fall on the stem and so the stem vowel **e** does not change.

At the movie theater
(1) Margaret, do you want a coke, coffee or . . . (2) A coke, please. And you? (3) I prefer coffee. Do you want to wait here? (4) I prefer to go in. (5) Ana, the film is beginning. But these ladies are talking and talking. (6) Excuse me, ma'am. It's impossible to hear (understand)! (7) What? You can't hear? Miss, this is a private conversation!

B. Other **e** to **ie** stem-changing verbs are:

empezar *to begin*   querer *to want*
perder *to lose*

No entiendo la conversación.	*I don't understand the conversation.*
Empiezas mañana.	*You begin tomorrow.*
Juan no quiere aceptar un trabajo en ese lugar.	*Juan doesn't want to accept a job in that place.*
Pienso vender mi auto.	*I'm thinking of selling my car.*
A veces pienso en ella.*	*Sometimes I think of her.*
¿Entiende usted el formulario?	*Do you understand the form?*
Preferimos regresar temprano.	*We prefer to return early.*
Prefiero trabajar en la oficina, no en casa.	*I prefer to work at the office, not at home.*
Ellos siempre pierden dinero.	*They always lose money.*

Ejercicios

A.   Create new sentences, substituting the words in the list for those in italics.

1. *Yo* prefiero vivir en Puerto Rico.
   a. tú **b.** nosotros **c.** Carlos y usted **d.** Ana y Luis **e.** mamá

2. *Nosotros* queremos empezar.
   a. Juan **b.** tú **c.** usted **d.** yo **e.** los chicos

3. ¿Piensa ir *usted* a la oficina?
   a. ellos **b.** la profesora **c.** los señores Ramos **d.** tú **e.** ustedes

B.   Change the italicized words from the singular to the plural or vice versa, and make any other necessary changes.
1. *Él* quiere trabajar.
2. ¿Entiende *usted* a la señora?
3. *Ellas* quieren regresar el sábado.
4. *Los muchachos* siempre pierden dinero.
5. *Esa clase* empieza mañana.
6. *Nosotros* pensamos cenar tarde, ¿y ustedes?
7. *Prefiero* ir a la playa ahora.
8. ¿Entiendes *tú* la película?

C.   Complete each sentence with the appropriate form of the verb in parentheses.

1. (querer) Nosotros _____ visitar la ciudad.
2. (perder) Yo no _____ el tiempo con esos formularios.
3. (preferir) Carlos _____ trabajar en casa hoy.

*****Pensar** takes the preposition **en** when it means *to think of or about*; it takes **de** to mean *to think of* in the sense of *to have an opinion (of someone or something)*.

4. (empezar) ¿A qué hora _____ la película?
5. (pensar) ¿_____ usted aceptar ese trabajo?
6. (preferir) Tú _____ el cine italiano, ¿no?
7. (entender) ¿_____ ustedes al profesor?

D. Complete the sentences using **de** or **en** as appropriate.

1. Papá siempre piensa _____ los problemas de la oficina.
2. ¿Qué piensas _____ la esposa de Bernardo?
3. ¿Piensas a veces _____ el pasado?
4. Ustedes no piensan eso _____ el presidente, ¿no?
5. Creo que tú piensas _____ el examen de mañana, ¿no?
6. ¿Qué piensan ustedes _____ este libro?

Preguntas

1. ¿Entiende usted español? ¿mucho o poco? 2. ¿A qué hora empieza usted a estudiar? 3. ¿Prefiere usted café o té? ¿vino o cerveza (*beer*)? 4. ¿Prefiere usted vivir en una ciudad grande o en una región rural? ¿Por qué? 5. ¿Prefiere usted viajar en auto, en autobús o en avión? 6. ¿Qué piensa hacer usted esta noche? ¿mañana? ¿el domingo? ¿en las vacaciones?

II. HAY

(1) **Miguel:** Silvia, busco un apartamento en este edificio.
(2) **Silvia:** ¿Por qué no vives en el barrio San Ignacio? Está cerca del centro.
(3) **Miguel:** Prefiero estar aquí cerca de la universidad. Allí *hay* robos, basura, drogas . . .
(4) **Silvia:** Es verdad. En las ciudades grandes *hay* problemas. Pero también *hay* tiendas, museos, cines. La vida es interesante.
(5) **Miguel:** ¡Y corta!

1. ¿Qué busca Miguel? 2. ¿Dónde está el barrio San Ignacio? 3. ¿Quiere Miguel vivir allí? ¿Por qué? 4. ¿Hay problemas en las ciudades grandes? 5. ¿Hay también lugares interesantes en ellas?

(1) Silvia, I'm looking for an apartment in this building. (2) Why don't you live in the San Ignacio neighborhood? It's close to the downtown section. (3) I prefer to be here, near the university. There there are robberies, garbage, drugs . . . (4) That's true. In big cities there are problems. But there are also stores, museums, movie theaters. Life is interesting. (5) And short!

Hay means both *there is* and *there are*. It has no subject.

No hay empleo aquí.	*There are no jobs (there is no employment) here.*
En mi barrio hay un edificio nuevo de cuarenta pisos.	*In my neighborhood there's a new building with forty stories.*
Hay mucha gente amable en esta clase.*	*There are a lot of nice people in this class.*
Aquí hay buenas obras de teatro.	*There are good plays here.*

Ejercicios

A. Answer the following questions using **hay**. Answer in the affirmative or negative, as appropriate.

Modelo: ¿Hay niños en esta clase? **No, no hay niños en esta clase.**

1. ¿Hay muchos estudiantes en esta universidad?
2. ¿Hay muchos apartamentos cerca de aquí?
3. ¿Hay mucho tráfico en esta ciudad?
4. ¿Hay un estudiante boliviano en esta clase?
5. ¿Hay un barrio puertorriqueño en esta región?

B. Give the Spanish equivalent of the following sentences.

1. Is there a form on the table?
2. Are there many robberies in New York City?
3. Are there many offices downtown?
4. There are no jobs in San Francisco now.
5. There are many immigrants in this country.
6. Is there a theater on 10th Avenue?

*Note that **la gente,** *people,* is singular in Spanish: **La gente de Paraguay es bilingüe; habla español y guaraní, una lengua india.** *The people of Paraguay are bilingual; they speak Spanish and Guaraní, an Indian language.*

Preguntas

1. ¿Hay muchos problemas en las ciudades grandes? ¿Qué problemas? **2.** ¿Hay muchos robos en el barrio donde usted vive? ¿mucha basura? **3.** ¿Hay problemas de drogas en esta universidad? ¿en esta ciudad? ¿en Los Ángeles? **4.** ¿Hay estudiantes brillantes en esta clase? ¿trabajadores? ¿perezosos (*lazy*)? **5.** ¿Hay películas buenas aquí? ¿conciertos? ¿obras de teatro? **6.** ¿Hay muchas actividades culturales donde usted vive? ¿Qué actividades?

III. EXPRESSIONS OF OBLIGATION: TENER QUE, DEBER, HAY QUE

En casa de los Sánchez.

(1)	**Sra. Sánchez:**	Pedro, no *debes* llegar tarde a la escuela.
(2)	**Pedro:**	Pero mamá . . . no *tengo que* ir.
(3)	**Sra. Sánchez:**	¿Cómo? ¡Claro que *tienes que* ir! ¡Si no estás listo en diez minutos, vas a perder el autobús!
(4)	**Pedro:**	Pero mamá . . . hoy no *hay que* ir a la escuela. ¡Es sábado!

1. ¿Quién no debe llegar tarde a la escuela? **2.** ¿Tiene que ir a la escuela Pedro? **3.** ¿Cuándo tiene que estar listo Pedro? **4.** ¿Hay que ir a la escuela los sábados?

A. **Tener que** plus infinitive is a common expression of obligation or compulsion meaning *to have to* or *must*. It is a personal expression in that it refers specifically to the individual or individuals who must carry out the action stated.

Tengo que usar el auto.	*I have to use the car.*
¡Tenemos que prohibir la discriminación!	*We have to (must) prohibit discrimination!*
Tienen que empezar ahora.	*They have to (must) begin now.*

B. **Deber** plus infinitive is another common personal expression of duty or obligation, but it does not convey so strong a sense of compulsion or obligation as **tener que**.

Debo ir al correo.	*I should (must, ought to) go to the post office.*

At the Sánchez's house.
(1) Pedro, you mustn't be late for school. (2) But Mama . . . I don't have to go. (3) What? Of course you have to go! If you aren't ready in ten minutes, you are going to miss the bus! (4) But Mama . . . Today we don't have to go (there is no need to go) to school. It's Saturday!

| Debes buscar empleo. | You should (must, ought to) look for employment. |
| No deben hablar así. | You shouldn't talk like that. |

C. **Deber** may also indicate probability or likelihood.

| Debe ser la una. | It must be (probably is) one o'clock. |
| Las tiendas deben estar cerradas hoy. | The stores are probably closed today. |

D. **Hay que** plus infinitive is an impersonal expression of obligation or compulsion meaning *one has to, one must,* or *it is necessary to.*

| Hay que conservar energía. | One (you, we, anybody) should conserve energy. |
| Ahora hay que trabajar. | Now we (one, anybody) must work. |

Ejercicios

A. Answer the questions in the negative, using the appropriate form of **tener que.**

Modelo: ¿Empieza usted el martes? **No, tengo que empezar ahora.**

1. ¿Van ustedes al correo el lunes?
2. ¿Regresas tú el miércoles?
3. ¿Estudian ellos el sábado?
4. ¿Busca usted empleo el jueves?
5. ¿Trabajas tú el domingo?

B. Create questions to which the following would be possible answers.

Modelo: Sí, debo aceptar ese trabajo. **¿Debes aceptar ese trabajo?**

1. Sí, debemos invitar a Enrique.
2. No, no debes vender esta casa.
3. Sí, deben prohibir la discriminación.
4. No, no debo llegar tarde a clase.
5. Sí, debe estudiar esta noche.

C. Amalia and Eduardo, two philosophy students, like to talk about the big issues in life. Complete the dialogue between them, answering Amalia's questions in the affirmative, as Eduardo would. Use the expression **hay que** + infinitive in your answers.

Modelo: Amalia: ¿Es necesario pensar para entender?
Eduardo: **Sí, hay que pensar para entender.**

1. Amalia: ¿Es necesario trabajar para vivir?
   Eduardo: _____
2. Amalia: ¿Es necesario escuchar para comprender?
   Eduardo: _____

3. Amalia: ¿Es necesario estudiar para aprender?
   Eduardo: _____

4. Amalia: ¿Es necesario comer para existir?
   Eduardo: _____

5. Amalia: ¿Es necesario ver para creer?
   Eduardo: _____

D. Give the Spanish equivalent of the following sentences.

1. I should study tonight.
2. José has to be there at five o'clock.
3. They have to work at night.
4. Teresa is probably in the office.
5. They ought to start the work on Monday.
6. It must be nine o'clock.
7. One must (should) accept the truth.

Preguntas

1. ¿Deben ustedes llegar tarde a clase?   **2.** ¿Tiene usted que estudiar mucho esta noche?   **3.** ¿Qué tiene que estudiar?   **4.** ¿Debemos hablar español en esta clase? ¿en la clase de francés?   **5.** ¿Tiene usted que buscar empleo ahora? ¿en diciembre? ¿en las vacaciones?   **6.** ¿Hay que ir a la universidad el sábado? ¿el lunes?   **7.** ¿Qué hay que hacer para buscar un apartamento? ¿para pasar los exámenes?

IV. POSSESSIVE ADJECTIVES

En la escuela

(1) **Sr. Morales:** ¿Cómo van *mis* hijos en *sus* estudios, profesor?
(2) **Profesor:** Realmente no muy bien. Ricardo . . .
(3) **Sr. Morales:** Pero, ¿qué pasa con Ricardo? ¿No hace *sus* deberes?
(4) **Profesor:** *Su* hijo no estudia mucho. Él es inteligente, pero *su* última composición sobre la lucha entre los conquistadores y los aztecas no es buena.
(5) **Sr. Morales:** Entiendo, pero es *mi* culpa. En *nuestra* casa hablamos poco de basquetbol.

(1) How are my children doing in their studies, professor? (2) In reality, not too well. Ricardo . . . (3) But what's the matter with Ricardo? Doesn't he do his homework? (4) Your son doesn't study much. He is intelligent, but his last composition about the struggle (competition) between the conquistadors and the Aztecs isn't good. (5) I understand, but it's my fault. In our house we don't talk much about basketball.

1. ¿Cómo van los hijos del señor Morales en sus estudios?   **2.** ¿Estudia sus lecciones Ricardo?   **3.** ¿Es buena su última composición?   **4.** ¿Por qué cree el señor Morales que es su culpa?

UNIVERSIDAD NACIONAL AUTONOMA DE MEXICO DIRECCION DE CURSOS TEMPORALES	NATIONAL UNIVERSITY OF MEXICO TEMPORARY COURSES	UNIVERSITE NATIONALE DE MEXICO COURS TEMPORAIRES
	VALDÉS BLANCO, MARÍA	
NOMBRE DEL ALUMNO	Student's Name	Nom et prénom de l'étudiant(e)
	EL VERANO DE 1980	
GRADO Degree Grade	SEMESTRE O JORNADA Semester or Session	Semestre ou Journée

A. Possessive adjectives are placed in front of the nouns they modify (the items possessed) and agree with them in number and gender. They do not agree with the possessor.

POSSESSIVE ADJECTIVES

Singular Possession		*Plural Possession*	
mi abuelo	*my grandfather*	mis regalos	*my presents*
mi abuela	*my grandmother*	mis maletas	*my suitcases*
tu abuelo	*your grandfather*	tus regalos	*your presents*
tu abuela	*your grandmother*	tus maletas	*your suitcases*
nuestro abuelo	*our grandfather*	nuestros regalos	*our presents*
nuestra abuela	*our grandmother*	nuestras maletas	*our suitcases*
vuestro abuelo	*your grandfather*	vuestros regalos	*your presents*
vuestra abuela	*your grandmother*	vuestras maletas	*your suitcases*
su abuelo	*his, her, your, their grandfather*	sus regalos	*his, her, your, their presents*
su abuela	*his, her, your, their grandmother*	sus maletas	*his, her, your, their suitcases*

Mis hermanas viven en San Juan.	*My sisters live in San Juan.*
Tu esposa trabaja en Brooklyn, ¿verdad?	*Your wife works in Brooklyn, doesn't she?*
¿Su hijo es ingeniero?	*His (her, your, their) son is an engineer?*
Sus empleos anteriores son muy interesantes, señor.	*Your previous jobs are very interesting, sir.*
Nuestra oficina está cerca del correo.	*Our office is near the post office.*
Nuestros formularios están aquí.	*Our forms are here.*

B. **Nuestro (-a)** and **vuestro (-a)** are the only possessive adjectives that show gender as well as number. All other possessive adjectives show number only.

C. Because **su** and **sus** have several potential meanings *(his, her, your, their)*, some-
    times for the sake of clarity it is better to use the following construction to
    show possession:

definite article + noun + **de**	**él** **ella** **usted** **ellos** **ellas** **ustedes**

Su madre es dentista.
La madre de ella es dentista. } *Her mother is a dentist.*

Ejercicios

A. Ricardo's grandfather doesn't hear too well, and everything has to be repeated twice
    for him. Give Ricardo's responses to his grandfather's questions, following the
    model.

Modelo: El abuelo: ¿Vamos a la casa de Estela?
             Ricardo: **Sí, vamos a la casa de Estela. Sí, vamos a su casa.**

1. ¿Regresamos a la escuela de los niños?
2. ¿Vendemos los libros de María?
3. ¿Tenemos el reloj de Carlos?
4. ¿Estamos en la oficina del doctor?
5. ¿Comemos con los hijos de Isabel?

B. Ana's little sister, Juanita, is very assertive. Every time Ana refers to something as
    hers, Juanita corrects her. Give Juanita's comments to her sister, following the model.

Modelos: Ana: Mi casa . . .
             Juanita: **No es tu casa; es nuestra casa.**

1. Mi madre . . .   4. Mi barrio . . .
2. Mi auto . . .   5. Mi abuela . . .
3. Mis amigas . . .   6. Mis hermanos . . .

C. Give the Spanish equivalent of the following sentences.

1. His grandfather is Spanish.
2. We want to sell our books.
3. She's thinking about her mother.
4. Your friends are here, Sr. Gómez.
5. My grandparents live in San Juan.
6. There are no robberies in our neighborhood.
7. Their children have to work on Saturday.
8. Your father is at his office, Paquito.

Preguntas

1. ¿Tiene usted hermanos? ¿Cuántos? ¿Cómo se llaman sus hermanos?   2. ¿Cómo se llama su madre? ¿su padre?   3. ¿Viven sus abuelos? ¿Cuántos hijos tienen ellos? ¿Dónde viven?   4. ¿Dónde trabajan sus padres?   5. ¿Tiene usted muchos amigos? ¿Cómo se llama su amigo (-a) favorito (-a)?   6. ¿Es grande o pequeña nuestra universidad? ¿nuestra clase?   7. ¿Cómo se llama su profesor (-a) de español? ¿de matemáticas?

V. DIRECT OBJECT PRONOUNS

(1)	**Ofelia:**	¡Julián! ¿*Me* escuchas?
(2)	**Julián:**	Sí, *te* escucho . . . aquí estoy, en la cuadra de nuestra casa . . . miro nuestra esquina, el puente, la gente . . .
(3)	**Ofelia:**	¡Julián! No estamos en San Juan.
(4)	**Julián:**	. . . y el edificio del correo . . . *lo* tengo delante de mis ojos . . .
(5)	**Ofelia:**	¿Los ojos? Pues, *los* tiene cerrados.
(6)	**Julián:**	. . . y las luces de la calle . . . casi las toco . . .
(7)	**Ofelia:**	¡Es la luz de la lámpara, hombre! Estamos en Nueva York. Siempre el mismo sueño. *Lo* tienes todas las noches.

1. ¿Escucha Julián a Ofelia?   2. ¿Qué ve Julián?   3. ¿Ve él las luces de la calle?
4. ¿Dónde están Julián y Ofelia realmente?

A. Direct object pronouns replace the direct object of a sentence and receive the direct action of the verb. For instance, in the sentence *I have it* (the book), the direct object pronoun is *it*.

DIRECT OBJECT PRONOUNS

	Singular		Plural
me	*me*	nos	*us*
te	*you* (tú)	os	*you* (vosotros)
lo	*him, it, you* (usted)	los	*them, you* (ustedes)
la	*her, it, you* (usted)	las	*them, you* (ustedes)

(1) Julián! Are you listening to me? (2) Yes, I am listening to you . . . I am here, on our block (on the block of our home) . . . I see our corner, the bridge, the people . . . (3) Julián! We're not in San Juan. (4) . . . and the Post Office building . . . I have it right before my eyes . . . (5) Your eyes? Well, you have them closed. (6) . . . and the street lights . . . I can almost touch them . . . (7) It's the light from the lamp, man! We're in New York. Always the same dream. You have it every night.

B. **Lo** and **la** are the direct object pronouns which correspond to the subject pronouns **él, ella** and **usted. Lo** is used to refer to a person or thing of masculine gender, and **la** is used to refer to a person or thing of feminine gender. **Lo** is also used to refer to actions or situations.*

¿El autobús? Sí, tengo que tomarlo.	*The bus? Yes, I have to take it.*
¿La carta? La llevo al correo.	*The letter? I'm taking it to the post office.*
No lo entiendo a usted, señor.	*I don't understand you, sir.*
¡No lo creo!	*I don't believe it!*

C. **Los** and **las** are the direct object pronouns which correspond to the subject pronouns **ellos, ellas** and **ustedes. Los** is used to refer to people or things of masculine gender, and **las** is used to refer to people or things of feminine gender. **Los** is used to refer to groups where the genders are mixed.

¿Esos lugares? Los voy a visitar pronto.	*Those places? I'm going to visit them soon.*
¿Las bicicletas? Las usamos mucho.	*The bicycles? We use them a lot.*
¿Esa casa y ese apartamento? Ellos los venden.	*That house and that apartment? They're selling them.*

D. **Te,** which corresponds to the subject pronoun **tú,** is used when referring to family, friends, and children. In Latin America the plural of **te** is **los** or **las.** In most areas of Spain, the plural of **te** is **os** which corresponds to the subject pronoun **vosotros (-as).**

Te necesito ahora.	*I need you now.*
Te buscan en el restaurante.	*They are looking for you in the restaurant.*
Os llamo mañana.	*I'll call you (both, all) tomorrow.*

E. Direct object pronouns are placed directly before a conjugated verb form.

¿Me esperas?	*Will you wait for me?*
José no lo tiene.	*José does not have it.*
Nos miran ahora.	*They are looking at us now.*

F. Direct object pronouns are placed after an infinitive and are attached to it.

Es imposible describirlo.	*It is impossible to describe it.*
¿La puerta? No tengo que cerrarla.	*The door? I don't have to close it.*
Vamos a visitarte mañana.	*We are going to visit you tomorrow.*

* In Spain it is common practice to use **le (les)** instead of **lo (los)** as the masculine direct object pronoun to refer to a man (men) and to use **lo (los)** to refer to things. However, this distinction is not observed in Latin America.

However, if the infinitive is part of a verb construction, the direct object pronoun can either be attached to the infinitive, as above, or it can be placed in front of the entire verb construction. In spoken Spanish the latter position is more common.

¿Mi programa favorito? Lo voy a mirar ahora. Voy a mirarlo ahora.

My favorite program? I'm going to watch it now.

Ejercicios

A. Answer the questions in the negative, using direct object pronouns.

Modelo: ¿Quieres el reloj?   **¿El reloj? No, no lo quiero.**

1. ¿Quieres el programa?
2. ¿Quieres la bicicleta?
3. ¿Quieres los formularios?
4. ¿Quieres el dinero?
5. ¿Quieres las plumas?
6. ¿Quieres las cartas?

B. Change the sentences, attaching the direct object pronoun to the infinitive.

Modelo: La voy a llamar.   **Voy a llamarla.**

1. Me va a visitar.
2. No lo van a aceptar.
3. Nos van a entender.
4. ¿Por qué los vas a vender?
5. ¿Quién te va a querer?
6. Susana las va a abrir.

C. Restate the sentences, replacing the direct object with the corresponding pronoun.

Modelo: José necesita ese empleo.   **José lo necesita.**

1. Elvira hace la comida.
2. No venden esas drogas.
3. ¿Abres las ventanas?
4. Quiero su número de teléfono.
5. No necesitamos a los chicos.
6. ¿Mira usted el avión?
7. Buscamos una buena tienda.
8. ¿Entienden los formularios?

D. Answer the questions in the affirmative, using the direct object pronoun.

Modelo: a. ¿Te busca Enrique?   **Sí, Enrique me busca.**

1. ¿Te necesitan los chicos?
2. ¿Me entiendes tú?
3. ¿Nos llama usted mañana?
4. ¿La visita usted el martes?

5. ¿Te quiere Anita?

6. ¿Lo usan ustedes?

Modelo: b. ¿Tienes que llevar a los niños? **Sí, tengo que llevarlos.**

1. ¿Quieres hacer la cena?
2. ¿Va a buscar los formularios?
3. ¿Necesita usted estudiar las lecciones?
4. ¿Vas a llevar las cartas al correo?
5. ¿Piensa vender su casa José?
6. ¿Deben tomar ese autobús?

Preguntas

1. ¿Necesita usted un auto? ¿Por qué lo necesita? **2.** ¿Tiene usted una bicicleta? ¿La usa mucho? ¿Dónde la lleva? **3.** ¿Busca usted un buen empleo? ¿Dónde? **4.** ¿Cuáles son sus programas favoritos? ¿Cuándo los mira usted? **5.** ¿Estudia usted las lecciones de español de noche? ¿de tarde? ¿de día? **6.** ¿Llama usted a sus amigos por teléfono? ¿Los llama de noche o prefiere llamarlos de tarde?

LOS PUERTORRIQUEÑOS

Dos puertorriqueños están en la Oficina de Empleos del Edificio Municipal de Nueva York. Uno de ellos lleva en la mano un formulario de empleo.

Rafael: ¡Carlos! ¿Qué haces aquí?

Carlos: Soy superintendente aquí ¿y tú?

Rafael: Busco empleo. Pero este formulario es difícil y no lo entiendo.

Carlos: Yo te ayudo. Primero tienes que escribir tu nombre y apellido.

Rafael: Bueno. Los escribo en esta línea. Escribo Rafael Álvarez Balboa. [1]

Carlos: ¡No m'ijo! [2] Aquí prefieren nombres cortos. Mejor escribes Ralph Álvarez.

Rafael: Pero ése no es mi nombre.

Carlos: Sin embargo, es mejor así. ¿O no quieres el trabajo?

Rafael: Realmente . . . ahora pienso que no lo quiero. Además, hay que ser norteamericano para trabajar acá.

Carlos: Estás equivocado. Hay leyes que prohiben la discriminación. ¿Las quieres leer?

Rafael: No ahora. Pero . . . las mejores oportunidades . . .

Carlos: Sí, las tienen los otros. Eso pasa a veces. Pero ¿tú prefieres la Isla [3] y no este lugar?

Rafael: ¡Claro! Y mi esposa también. Puerto Rico es nuestra patria. Queremos regresar ¿me entiendes?

Carlos: Sí, pero yo prefiero vivir aquí. De todas maneras, buena suerte. Mis saludos a tu esposa.

Rafael: Gracias por tus buenos deseos. Hasta pronto.

---

en la mano *in his hand* **apellido** *last name* **línea** *line* **mejor** *better*
sin embargo *however* **acá** *here* **equivocado** *wrong* **patria** *homeland*
saludos *greetings* **deseos** *wishes* **superintendente** *supervisor*

Preguntas

1. ¿Qué lleva uno de los puertorriqueños en la mano? **2.** ¿Qué buscan Carlos y Rafael? **3.** ¿Entiende Rafael el formulario? **4.** ¿Cuál es el nombre corto que Carlos prefiere? **5.** ¿Hay leyes que prohiben la discriminación? **6.** ¿Qué prefieren Rafael y su esposa: Nueva York o la Isla? **7.** ¿Prefiere usted vivir en Nueva York o en Puerto Rico? **8.** Y usted ¿qué tiene que hacer para obtener (*obtain*) un buen trabajo?

NOTAS CULTURALES

1. Most people of Spanish descent use both their father's and mother's surnames (**apellidos**), sometimes separating them by **y**. The father's name is customarily put first. Consequently the mother, father, and children of the same family have different last names.

2. M'ijo is short for **mi hijo** (*my son*) and denotes friendship or empathy with the person addressed. (**M'ija** is used when speaking to a girl or woman.)

3. Many Puerto Ricans refer to their homeland as **la Isla del Encanto** (*the Isle of Enchantment*) or simply as **la Isla**. Because of its natural beauty, agreeable climate, and Hispanic atmosphere, most Puerto Ricans who leave to find work long to return. Since Puerto Rico is an **estado libre asociado** (United States commonwealth), its inhabitants are U.S. citizens, and there is no visa required for entry.

¿Perdido en la Ciudad Feliz?

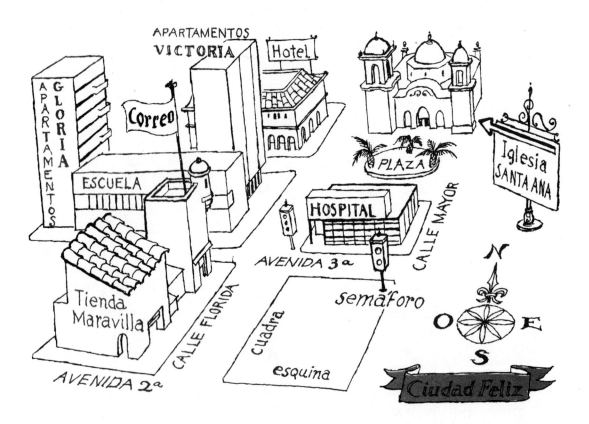

a- Usted quiere visitar a su amiga Elsa. Usted va en auto por la Avenida 2ª hacia el oeste. Tiene que doblar a la derecha cuando llega a la calle Florida. Al final de la primera cuadra, cruza la Avenida 3ª. A su derecha está el hospital y a su izquierda está la escuela. Al final de esta cuadra, a la izquierda, está el edificio donde vive Elsa. ¿En qué edificio vive Elsa?

b- Usted toma el autobús 17 en la plaza que está delante de la Iglesia de Santa Ana. El autobús va por la calle Mayor hacia el sur. En la primera esquina el autobús debe esperar porque hay luz roja. Cuando tiene luz verde, el autobús dobla a la derecha por la Avenida 3ª. Continúa una cuadra y en la esquina dobla a la izquierda. Pasa enfrente del edificio de Correo y usted baja en la esquina. ¿Dónde está usted?

hacia *towards*   **doblar** *to turn*   **cruzar** *to cross*

Entrevista

Ask a classmate the following questions. Then report the information to the class.

1. ¿Tienes empleo? ¿Buscas empleo?
2. ¿Trabajas en una oficina? ¿En una tienda?
3. ¿Ganas (*do you earn*) mucho dinero?
4. ¿Prefieres vivir en una casa o en un apartamento? ¿Por qué?
5. ¿Prefieres vivir en una ciudad grande?
6. ¿Cuál es tu ciudad preferida? ¿Por qué?
7. ¿Hay problemas en tu barrio? ¿Cuáles?

Situación

En la Oficina de Empleos

Two friends, **Carlos** and **Alberto,** meet in an employment office. Carlos doesn't understand the application form and Alberto helps him to fill it out. Alberto says that really (*en realidad*) he does not want to work in the big city, but that he has to earn some money now for his family. He tells his friend why he does not want to live in the city. Alberto says that he does not understand him because he thinks the city is wonderful. The secretary comes in and asks the two men if they have their forms and if they want their interview now. Carlos says yes he does, but Alberto says that he doesn't. He then says thank you and goodbye.

VOCABULARIO ACTIVO

Verbos útiles

aceptar *to accept*
cerrar (ie) *to close*
empezar (ie) *to begin, start*
entender (ie) *to understand; to hear*
esperar *to wait for; to hope*
hay *there is or there are;* **hay que** + *inf.*
  one must + *inf.*

pensar (ie) *to think;* **pensar de** *to think about (have an opinion);* **pensar en** *to think about (reflect on)*
perder (ie) *to lose; to miss (train, plane, etc.)*
preferir (ie) *to prefer*
prohibir *to prohibit, forbid*
querer (ie) *to want; to love or like*
regresar *to return, go back*

tener que + inf. *to have to* + inf.
trabajar *to work*
usar *to use*
vender *to sell*

La ciudad

el apartamento *apartment*
el barrio *neighborhood, community*
la basura *garbage*
la calle *street*
el cine *movie theater*
el correo *post office; mail*
la cuadra *(city) block*
el dinero *money*
la droga *drug*
el edificio *building*
el empleo *employment*
la esquina *corner*
el formulario *form*
la gente *people*
la iglesia *church*
la ley *law*
el lugar *place*
la luz *light; spotlight*
la obra de teatro *play*
la oficina *office*
la película *film*

la plaza *square, plaza*
el puente *bridge*
el robo *theft, robbery*
la tienda *store*
el trabajo *work*

Otras palabras útiles

anterior *former*
a veces *sometimes*
la bicicleta *bicycle*
cerrado (a) *closed*
corto (a) *short*
la culpa *guilt*
de todas maneras *anyhow, anyway*
los deberes *homework*
Hasta pronto *See you soon*
el, la ingeniera (o) *engineer*
listo (a) *ready*
mismo (a) *same*
el ojo *eye*
la oportunidad *opportunity*
el programa *program*
realmente *really*
el sueño *dream*
tarde *late*
temprano *early*
último (a) *most recent, latest*

PRIMER REPASO

I. THE PRESENT TENSE

A. Review the following Spanish verbs in the present tense.

   1. Regular **-ar** verbs **(llegar): llego, llegas, llega, llegamos, llegáis, llegan**
   2. Regular **-er** verbs **(creer): creo, crees, cree, creemos, creéis, creen**
   3. Regular **-ir** verbs **(existir): existo, existes, existe, existimos, existís, existen**
   4. Stem-changing **e** to **ie** verbs **(empezar): empiezo, empiezas, empieza, empezamos, empezáis, empiezan**
   5. Irregular verbs:
      a. **ser: soy, eres, es, somos, sois, son**
      b. **estar: estoy, estás, está, estamos, estáis, están**
      c. **tener: tengo, tienes, tiene, tenemos, tenéis, tienen**
      d. **ir: voy, vas, va, vamos, vais, van**
      e. **hacer: hago, haces, hace, hacemos, hacéis, hacen**

B. Complete the following sentences with the present tense of the verb in parentheses.

   1. Yo (estar) _____ contento porque tú (estar) _____ aquí.
   2. Los señores García (buscar) _____ a su prima, Isabel.
   3. Ahora tú (escuchar) _____ y yo (hablar) _____.
   4. ¿Qué (creer) _____ usted? ¿Que yo (ser) _____ idiota?
   5. Nosotros (deber) _____ conservar energía.
   6. Los agentes (querer) _____ los pasaportes.
   7. Yo (pensar) _____ que Portugal (ser) _____ un país importante.
   8. Yo (tener) _____ dos semanas de vacaciones. ¿Cuántas (tener) _____ tú?
   9. Yo (ir) _____ a Venezuela este verano.
   10. ¿Qué (tener) _____ que hacer nosotros?
   11. Mis padres (ir) _____ en avión pero mis amigos y yo (ir) _____ en auto.
   12. Adela (vivir) _____ en Buenos Aires, pero ahora (estar) _____ en Caracas con unos amigos.
   13. Luis y Ramona (ser) _____ de España, ¿no?
   14. ¿(ir) _____ usted mucho a la biblioteca?
   15. Rogelio (estudiar) _____ medicina porque (querer) _____ ser doctor como su papá.
   16. ¿Qué tiempo _____ (hacer)?
   17. Yo _____ (hacer) ejercicios todos los días.

II. THE VERBS **SER** AND **ESTAR**

A. **Ser** is used: to link a subject and a noun **(es italiana, son hermanos)**; with **de** to indicate origin **(de Nueva York)** or what something is made of **(de oro)**; to tell where an event takes place **(en el Teatro Colón)**; and with **de** to indicate possession **(de Luis)**. It is also used with adjectives **(inteligente)** to indicate qualities which we consider to be normal or characteristic of the nouns they modify.

    Estar is used to indicate: location or position **(cerca de la plaza)** and condition **(bien)**. It is also used with adjectives **(contento, perdido)** to indicate either a change or the result of a previous action.

B. Complete the following narration with an appropriate form of **ser** or **estar**. In each case, state why you have chosen **ser** or **estar**.

Vivo con Felipe en un apartamento que _____ muy cerca de la universidad. Felipe y yo _____ buenos amigos y los dos _____ contentos de vivir juntos. Él _____ estudiante de primer año y yo _____ estudiante de segundo año, pero los dos _____ en la misma clase de biología. Felipe no _____ norteamericano. Él _____ argentino pero no _____ de Buenos Aires; _____ de Córdoba, otra ciudad importante. Córdoba _____ en el interior de la Argentina. Felipe _____ un chico muy inteligente y simpático. Esta noche él y yo queremos ir a una cena que _____ en casa de una amiga, pero Felipe _____ un poco enfermo. Si él no _____ bien esta noche, no va a ir a la cena porque va a tener que ir al doctor.

III. ADJECTIVES

A. Adjectives agree in gender and number with the nouns they modify.

    1. The possessive adjectives are: **mi(-s), tu(-s), su(-s), nuestro(-a, -os, -as), vuestro(-a, -os, -as)**, and **su(-s)**. They precede the nouns they modify.

    2. The demonstrative adjectives are: **este, esta, estos, estas** *(this, these);* **ese, esa, esos, esas** *(that, those—near you);* **aquel, aquella, aquellos, aquellas** *(that, those—over there).* They also precede the nouns they modify.

B. Complete the sentences with the appropriate possessive or demonstrative adjective, as indicated by the cue in parentheses.

    1. ¿Dónde está _____ pasaporte? (my)
    2. _____ ideas son brillantes. (your, familiar)
    3. ¿Cuándo empiezan _____ vacaciones? (their)
    4. _____ agente de viajes es Fernando Olivera. (our)
    5. _____ familia está en Puerto Rico. (your, formal)

1. ¿Hay muchos teatros en _____ ciudad? (this)
2. ¿Son ricos _____ señores? (those, over there)
3. _____ libro es de Manuel. (this)
4. No entiendo _____ formularios. (those, by you)
5. _____ chica es chilena. (that, by you)

IV. SUBJECT AND DIRECT OBJECT PRONOUNS

A.   Review the following chart of subject and direct object pronouns.

SUBJECT PRONOUNS	DIRECT OBJECT PRONOUNS
yo	me
tú	te
él, ella, usted	lo la
nosotros(-as)	nos
vosotros(-as)	os
ellos, ellas, ustedes	los las

1. Subject pronouns generally tell who carries out the action expressed by a verb: **Ustedes van a Puerto Rico, ¿no?**
2. Direct object pronouns tell who or what receives the action expressed by a verb: **Juan critica mucho al gobierno. Juan lo critica mucho.**

B.   Answer the following questions in the affirmative, replacing the words in italics with the appropriate direct object pronoun.

Modelo: ¿Tienes *las maletas?*   **Sí, las tengo.**

1. ¿Vas a estudiar *la lección* esta noche?
2. ¿Tienen ustedes *los pasaportes?*
3. ¿*Me* quiere Ramón?
4. ¿Va a escribir usted *una carta?*
5. ¿Quieren ustedes *mi número de teléfono?*
6. ¿*Te* lleva al concierto Raquel?
7. ¿Buscas *a las muchachas?*
8. ¿Pasan *el verano* en la playa?
9. ¿Cierran *el museo* a las cinco?
10. ¿Quieres llenar *los formularios* ahora?

V. QUESTIONS FOR CONVERSATION

1. ¿Qué hora es? ¿A qué hora llega usted a la universidad? ¿A qué hora llega a su casa?
2. ¿Qué tiempo hace hoy? ¿En qué meses hace buen tiempo? ¿En qué meses hace mal tiempo?   **3.** ¿Qué día es hoy? ¿Cuál es una fecha importante para usted? ¿Por qué? ¿Cuándo es el día de la independencia de su país?   **4.** ¿En qué piso de este edificio estamos ahora? ¿Cuántos pisos hay? ¿Cuántos pisos tiene el edificio donde usted vive? **5.** ¿Cuántos estados hay en los Estados Unidos? ¿Cuáles quiere usted visitar? De los países latinos, ¿cuáles quiere usted visitar?   **6.** ¿Qué tiene usted que hacer todos los días? ¿Hay que hacer muchas cosas desagradables (*unpleasant*) en la vida? ¿Por ejemplo?   **7.** ¿Debe usted practicar español? ¿Hay que ir al laboratorio de lenguas? ¿Con quién practica usted español? ¿Qué día(s) va usted al laboratorio?

VI. SUPPLEMENTARY TRANSLATION EXERCISE

A.   Review the following words and expressions.

asistir a   *to attend*
bajar de   *to get off*
buscar   *to look for*
deber + infinitive   *should, ought to*

hay que + infinitive   *one has to, it's necessary*
para + infinitive   *in order to*

estar de vacaciones   *to be on vacation*
esto, eso, aquello   *this (thing, stuff), that*
hacer calor   *to be warm, hot (outside)*

pensar + infinitive   *to plan to (on)*
por   *because of*
tener que + infinitive   *must, to have to*

B.   Give the Spanish equivalent of the following sentences.
1. When it's very hot, everyone goes to the beach.   **2.** Poor María Luisa! She's nervous because of the trip, isn't she?   **3.** Three men get off the bus and look for the agency "Tamborini Travels".   **4.** In order to live in this neighborhood, it's necessary to be rich.   **5.** They're looking for a job but they don't understand that application form.   **6.** All that belongs to Isabel Magaña.   **7.** But Mom, we don't have to go to school today. It's Sunday.   **8.** Do you plan on leaving early?

CENTROAMÉRICA Y EL CARIBE

1 Un mercado indio en Chichicastenango, Guatemala
2 Las dos caras de San Juan, Puerto Rico
3 Una estudiante cubana

MÉXICO

4 Las Hadas, Manzanillo
5 El día de los muertos en Patzcuaro
6 Una catedral en Queretaro

7   Las ruinas mayas de Tulum
8   Una india de Oaxaca
9   La Ciudad Satélite de México, D. F.

10

11

12

13

14

10 Un festival en el Lago Titicaca, Bolivia
11 La capital en Caracas, Venezuela
12 Un centro de Quito, Ecuador
13 Mar del Plata, centro turístico en el Atlántico, Argentina
14 Las famosas ruinas de Machu Picchu, Perú

ESPAÑA

15

16

17

18

EL ARTE

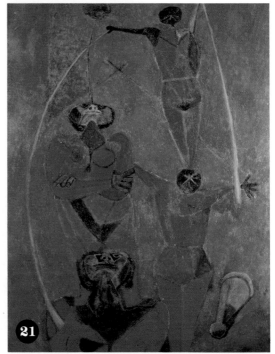

19 Velázquez, Diego Rodríguez de Silva y (1599–1660). Portrait of Juan de Pareja. Dated 1650.
20 Goya, Francisco de (1746–1828). Majas on a Balcony.
21 Tamayo, Rufino. Acrobats. Signed and dated 0-'47.

ALIMENTOS

bananas

leche

mantequilla

huevos

¡Plátanos (bananas)! ¡Mantequilla! ¡Huevos! ¡Leche!...... ¡Um!... ¡qué banquete!

OBJECTIVES

LANGUAGE: In this chapter we introduce, discuss, and practice:

1. stem-changing verbs **o** to **ue** and **u** to **ue**
2. indirect object pronouns
3. the present tense of **dar,** *to give,* and **ver,** *to see,* and idioms with these verbs
4. the present tense of the verb **gustar,** *to please,* used in expressing likes and dislikes

5. prepositional object pronouns—that is, pronouns used after a preposition

You will also learn vocabulary related to food and meals.

CULTURE: The dialogue takes place in Los Angeles, where some students are talking about life for the Mexican-American in the United States. You will learn some Mexican-American words and expressions.

EXPLICACIÓN

I. STEM CHANGING VERBS:
O TO **UE**, U TO **UE**

En el hotel. Joaquín habla con el gerente.

(1) **Joaquín:** Por favor, ¿cuánto *cuesta* un cuarto para dos?

(2) **Gerente:** Ochenta pesos, con desayuno continental, es decir café con leche, tostadas, mantequilla y mermelada.

(3) **Joaquín:** Está bien. *¿Puedo* reservar un cuarto doble?

(4) **Gerente:** Cómo no. ¿Por cuántas noches?

(5) **Joaquín:** Sólo una. Mañana temprano *volvemos* a Asunción.

(6) **Gerente:** *Vuelven* mañana temprano ¿eh? La recepcionista *puede* despertarlos.

(7) **Joaquín:** No es necesario. *Duermo* como un gato. Todas las mañanas abro los ojos a las seis en punto.

(8) **Gerente:** En ese caso ¿*puede* usted despertar a la recepcionista, por favor?

At the hotel. Joaquín is speaking to the manager.
(1) Please, how much does a room for two cost? (2) Eighty pesos with continental breakfast, that is coffee with hot milk, toast, butter and marmalade. (3) All right. May I reserve a double room? (4) Of course. For how many nights? (5) Only one. Early tomorrow we return to Asunción. (6) You return tomorrow, eh? The receptionist can wake you up. (7) It's not necessary. I sleep like a cat. Every morning I open (my) eyes at six on the dot. (8) In that case, can you wake up the receptionist, please?

1. ¿Cuánto cuesta un cuarto para dos en el hotel? 2. ¿Qué puede comer Joaquín si toma el desayuno continental? 3. ¿Adónde vuelve Joaquín en la mañana? 4. ¿Quién puede despertarlo, si él quiere? 5. ¿Cómo duerme Joaquín? 6. ¿A qué hora de la mañana abre los ojos todos los días? 7. ¿A qué hora de la mañana puede usted abrir los ojos?

A. Certain Spanish verbs show a stem change from **o** to **ue** when the stem is stressed. This change does not occur in the first and second person plural forms because the stress does not fall on the stem.

recordar (to remember)		volver (to return)		dormir (to sleep)	
recuerdo	recordamos	vuelvo	volvemos	duermo	dormimos
recuerdas	recordáis	vuelves	volvéis	duermes	dormís
recuerda	recuerdan	vuelve	vuelven	duerme	duermen

B. Other **o** to **ue** stem-changing verbs are:

almorzar	*to have lunch*	encontrar	*to find*
costar	*to cost*	poder	*to be able to*

¿Recuerdas la cena de los Hernández? *Do you remember the Hernández' dinner?*

No encuentro el arroz aquí. *I don't find the rice here.*

¿Con quién almuerza usted hoy? *With whom are you having lunch today?*

Podemos comprar naranjas y manzanas en esta tienda de comestibles. *We can buy oranges and apples in this grocery store.*

Vuelven a Texas el jueves. *They are returning to Texas on Thursday.*

¿Cuánto cuestan los plátanos? *How much do the bananas cost?*

Elvira siempre duerme bien en las montañas. *Elvira always sleeps well in the mountains.*

C. In the verb **jugar** the stem change is from **u** to **ue**.

jugar (to play)	
juego	jugamos
juegas	jugáis
juega	juegan

Juego al tenis. *I play tennis.*

Paco y Miguelito juegan en el patio. *Paco and Miguelito are playing on the patio.*

Before the name of a sport or game, **jugar** usually takes the preposition **a,** as in the example above.

Ejercicios

A. Create new sentences, substituting the words in the list for those in italics.

1. *Nosotros* podemos hacer el desayuno.
   a. mi esposo b. yo c. Juan y Alicia d. usted e. tú
2. Mañana *ellos* vuelven a Asunción.
   a. los señores Méndez b. tú c. Ernesto y yo d. usted e. yo
3. *Mis padres* juegan al tenis.
   a. tú b. nosotros c. tú y tus amigos d. yo e. el gerente

B. Restate, changing the verbs to the plural.

Modelo: No vuelvo temprano. **No volvemos temprano.**

1. Duermo como un gato.
2. Almuerzo a las doce.
3. No puedo ir a Antigua.
4. Recuerdo a esa chica.
5. No encuentro el café.

C. Restate, changing the verbs to the singular.

Modelo: Recordamos a tío Carlos. **Recuerdo a tío Carlos.**

1. Jugamos al basquetbol.
2. No encontramos la mantequilla.
3. Volvemos a las seis.
4. No podemos encontrar la leche.
5. Dormimos mucho.

D. Complete each sentence with the appropriate form of each verb in parentheses.

1. (poder) Nosotros _____ preparar la cena.
2. (volver) La recepcionista _____ a las siete.
3. (recordar) ¿No _____ (tú) su número de teléfono?
4. (almorzar) Yo no _____ en el hotel.
5. (costar) ¿Cuánto _____ la comida en este restaurante?
6. (encontrar) Nosotros _____ las manzanas aquí.
7. (dormir) ¿A qué hora _____ los niños?
8. (jugar) Joaquín y yo no _____ al tenis, ¿y ustedes?

Preguntas

1. ¿Cuánto cuesta una libra (*pound*) de arroz? ¿de café? ¿de manzanas? ¿de plátanos?
2. ¿Vuelve usted temprano o tarde de la universidad? ¿A qué hora vuelve generalmente? 3. ¿Duerme usted bien por la noche? ¿por la tarde? 4. ¿Juega usted al tenis? ¿al basquetbol? 5. ¿Dónde almuerza usted? ¿Almuerza usted tarde o temprano? 6. ¿Puede usted preparar una comida (*meal*) mexicana? ¿un desayuno continental?

II. INDIRECT OBJECT PRONOUNS

(1)	**Sra. Pérez:**	*Te* quiero hablar, Marta. Hoy debes escribir*le* una carta a tu abuela.
(2)	**Marta:**	¡Ay, mamá! Ahora no *le* quiero escribir.
(3)	**Sra. Pérez:**	Si *le* escribes la carta, *te* compro dulces.
(4)	**Marta:**	¿Vas a comprar*me* dulces? Bueno, ¿dónde hay un lápiz?

1. ¿A quién tiene que escribir Marta?   **2.** ¿Quiere la niña escribir la carta?   **3.** Si Marta le escribe a su abuela, ¿qué va a comprarle su mamá?

A. Indirect object pronouns receive the action of the verb indirectly. That is, they indicate to *whom* or *for whom* something is done, said, made, or whatever. For instance, in the sentence *I am buying you a present, you* is an indirect object pronoun.

B. Except for the third-person singular and plural forms, the indirect object pronouns are the same as the direct object pronouns.

INDIRECT OBJECT PRONOUNS

Singular	*Plural*
me *(to, for) me*	nos *(to, for) us*
te *(to, for) you*	os *(to, for) you*
le *(to, for) you, him, her, it*	les *(to, for) you, them*

¿Me hablas?	*Are you speaking to me?*
Les quiero escribir.	*I want to write to them.*
Quieren contarte la historia.	*They want to tell you the story.*

C. Indirect object pronouns follow the same rules for placement as do direct object pronouns; that is, they precede a conjugated verb form or they can come after and be attached to an infinitive.

Te queremos vender ese libro. }	*We want to sell you that book.*
Queremos venderte ese libro. }	
¿Les debo comprar chocolates? }	*Should I buy them some chocolates?*
¿Debo comprarles chocolates? }	

---

(1) I want to talk to you, Marta. You have to write a letter to your grandmother today. (2) Oh, Mom! I don't want to write to her now. (3) If you write the letter to her, I'll buy you candy. (6) You're going to buy me candy? Okay, where is a pencil?

D. Ordinarily it is clear from the context what or whom the indirect object pronoun refers to. Occasionally, however, a prepositional phrase (**a él, a usted,** and the like) is used or is necessary for emphasis or clarity.

$$\text{Le hablo a} \begin{cases} \textbf{él} \\ \textbf{ella} \\ \textbf{usted} \end{cases} \qquad \text{Les hablo a} \begin{cases} \textbf{ellos} \\ \textbf{ellas} \\ \textbf{ustedes} \end{cases}$$

E. In Spanish the indirect object pronoun is customarily included in the sentence even when the indirect object noun is also expressed.

Juan le cuenta la historia a María.   *Juan is telling the story to María.*
Les preparamos la sopa a los niños.   *We are preparing the soup for the children.*

Ejercicios

A. Answer each of the following questions in the affirmative.

Modelos: ¿Me escriben ustedes?   **Sí, nosotros te (le) escribimos.**
¿Les preparan ellos la cena?   **Sí, ellos nos preparan la cena.**

1. ¿Nos habla usted?
2. ¿Te hace ella el almuerzo?
3. ¿Les cuesta mucho el hotel?
4. ¿Me preguntas el número de Ana?
5. ¿Nos preparan ustedes la comida?
6. ¿Le compra dulces su mamá?

B. Make sentences, replacing the indirect objects given with indirect object pronouns, following the models.

Modelos: Silvia / hablar / al doctor.   **Silvia le habla.**
Los Pérez / leer el libro / a nosotros.   **Los Pérez nos leen el libro.**

1. Este almuerzo / costar cien pesos / a los muchachos
2. Mamá / preparar el desayuno / a nosotros
3. Ellos / comprar un dulce / a Pedrito
4. Yo / hablar de mis amigos / a ustedes
5. Tú / hacer la sopa / a nosotros

C. Complete the sentences with the indirect object pronouns indicated in parentheses.

Modelo: (to them) _____Les_____ tiene que decir la verdad.

1. (to you, pl.) _____ quiero preparar unas tostadas.
2. (to me) _____ preguntan dónde vivo.
3. (to him) _____ leen una historia muy interesante.
4. (to you) _____ compra dulces y chocolate.
5. (to you, *tú* form) _____ habla por teléfono.

6. (to them) ＿＿＿＿＿ llevamos arroz y café.
7. (to her) ＿＿＿＿＿ piensan hacer una fiesta.
8. (to us) ＿＿＿＿＿ cuestan quince pesos.

D.　Give the Spanish equivalent of the following sentences.

1. We write to her.
2. Rice doesn't cost him much.
3. He believes you.
4. They ask me why.

5. You should prepare breakfast for them.
6. He writes to us.
7. He speaks to you (*tú* form) a lot.
8. I read to you (pl.) in Spanish.

Preguntas

1. ¿Les escribe cartas a sus padres? ¿Les escribe mucho? **2.** ¿Habla mucho con sus padres? ¿con sus amigos? **3.** ¿Les habla por teléfono a sus abuelos? ¿a sus primos? **4.** ¿Quién le prepara a usted la cena? ¿el almuerzo? ¿el desayuno? **5.** ¿Me escribe usted cartas todos los días? ¿Me hace la comida?

III. THE PRESENT TENSE OF **DAR** AND **VER**

(1) **Madre:** *Veo* que quieres comer... ¿Qué te *doy?*... ¿naranjas? ¿un pedazo de torta? ¿queso y galletas?

(2) **Carlos:** Queso y galletas, por favor. Pero pronto porque voy al cine.

(3) **Madre:** ¿Vas con Susana y Naldo?

(4) **Carlos:** No, voy solo. Ellos *ven* la película mañana. Hoy no pueden.

(5) **Madre:** Bueno, ¿y qué te *doy* para beber? ¿leche caliente?

(6) **Carlos:** El queso me *da* sed, pero la leche caliente me *da* sueño. Mejor me *das* té.

(7) **Madre:** ¡Qué trabajo me *das!*

1. ¿Qué tiene la madre para dar a su hijo? **2.** ¿Qué le pide Carlos? **3.** ¿Adónde quiere ir después? **4.** ¿Por qué no quiere tomar leche caliente? **5.** ¿Qué toma, al final?

(1) I see that you want (something) to eat. What shall I give you (to eat)? . . . oranges? a piece of cake? cheese and crackers? (2) Cheese and crackers, please. But soon because I'm going to the movies. (3) Are you going with Susana and Naldo? (4) No, I am going alone. They are going to see the film tomorrow. Today they can't. (5) Well, and what shall I give you to drink? hot milk? (6) Cheese makes me thirsty, but hot milk makes me sleepy. Better give me tea. (7) What trouble you give (cause) me!

A. The verb **dar** (*to give*) has an irregular first-person singular form, **doy.**

dar

doy	damos
das	dais
da	dan

Dar is used in a number of idiomatic expressions, such as:

darle hambre (sed, sueño) a alguien	*to make someone hungry (thirsty, sleepy)*
darle las gracias a alguien	*to thank someone*
dar un paseo	*to take a walk*
¡Qué hambre me da esa torta!	*How hungry that cake is making me!*
El vino nos da mucho sueño.	*The wine is making us sleepy.*
Vamos a dar un paseo por la plaza.	*Let's take a walk around the plaza.*
Los García nos dan las gracias por el almuerzo.	*The Garcías thank us for the lunch.*

B. The verb **ver** (*to see*) is also irregular in the first person.

ver

veo	vemos
ves	veis
ve	ven

No veo el azúcar en la mesa.	*I don't see the sugar on the table.*
¿Ves el arroz aquí?	*Do you see the rice here?*

Ejercicios

A. Create new sentences, substituting the words in the list for those in italics.

1. *Nosotros* damos un paseo en auto.
   a. usted b. Rolando y Diana c. yo d. ustedes e. tú
2. *Ella* no los ve.
   a. yo b. mis padres c. tú d. Enrique y yo e. usted

B. Restate, changing the verbs to the plural.

1. Siempre les doy café y torta a mis amigos.
2. ¿Ves mi libro de español aquí?
3. Ella da un concierto esta tarde.
4. No veo la mantequilla en la mesa.
5. ¿Le das el auto a Tomás?
6. Usted no ve a sus padres esta semana, ¿verdad?

C. Complete each sentence with the correct form of **dar** or **ver.**

1. Nosotros no _____ a Margarita aquí.
2. ¿Por qué le _____ usted esos dulces al niño?

3. Paco _____ que su hermana lo necesita.

4. Yo no _____ plátanos en este esta tienda.

5. Mi esposo y yo les _____ las gracias por la invitación.

6. ¿A qué hora le _____ tú el desayuno a Teresita?

7. Los Gómez _____ una fiesta para su hija.

8. ¿_____ tú el arroz aquí?

Preguntas

1. ¿Ve usted televisión? ¿Qué programas ve usted? **2.** ¿Ven sus padres los mismos (*same*) programas? ¿sus amigos? **3.** ¿Qué películas ve usted cuando va al cine? **4.** ¿Cuándo ve usted a sus padres? ¿a sus amigos? **5.** Cuando un amigo o una amiga necesita dinero, ¿le da usted unos pesos o prefiere no darle? **6.** ¿Le da a usted hambre ver una comida deliciosa? **7.** ¿Quiere usted dar un paseo por la clase ahora? ¿por la universidad? ¿por la calle?

IV. THE PRESENT TENSE OF GUSTAR

(1) **Carlos:** Umm . . . ¡Qué aroma! *Me encantan* los huevos con jamón que preparas.

(2) **Inés:** ¿De veras *te gustan*?

(3) **Carlos:** Sí, *me gustan* mucho, y también *me gusta* esa sopa de verduras . . . ¡y ese pan dulce! . . . *me fascina*.

(4) **Inés:** Veo que *te gustan* todos estos platos.

(5) **Carlos:** *Me gusta* mucho comer estas cosas.

(6) **Inés:** A Esteban y a mí también *nos gustan* estas cosas. Y además, *nos gusta* almorzar solos.

(1) Mm. . . what an aroma! I love the ham and eggs you prepare. (2) You really like them? (3) Yes, I like them a lot and I also like that vegetable soup. . . and sweet bread! I adore it. (4) I see that you like all these dishes. (5) I like eating these things a lot. (6) Esteban and I like eating these things too. Besides, we like eating lunch alone.

1. ¿Le gustan a Carlos los huevos con jamón que Inés prepara? 2. ¿Y le gusta la sopa de verduras? 3. ¿Se da cuenta Inés de que a él le gustan estos platos? 4. ¿Les gustan a Inés y a Esteban? 5. ¿Qué otra cosa les gusta a Inés y a Esteban?

A. **Gustar** means *to please* or *to be pleasing*. **Gustar** can be used to express the equivalent of the English expression *to like*. However, in Spanish the person, thing or idea that is pleasing (pleases) is the *subject* of the sentence. **Gustar** is usually used in the third-person singular or plural, depending on whether the subject is singular or plural. An indirect object pronoun is used with it.

Me gusta esta bebida.

I like this beverage. (This beverage pleases me.)

¿Te gustan las verduras?

Do you like vegetables? (Are vegetables pleasing to you?)

Le gusta la cerveza alemana.
Nos gustan mucho los dulces.

He (she, you) likes German beer.
We like sweets a lot.

B. The prepositional phrase **a** + noun or pronoun is often used or is necessary for emphasis or clarity. It is usually placed at the beginning of the sentence.

A Fernando le gusta el chocolate con nueces.

Fernando likes chocolate with nuts.

A los hispanos les gusta el café con leche.

Hispanic people like coffee and milk.

A usted le gustan los vinos buenos. ¿no?

You like good wines, don't you?

C. If what is liked (or what is pleasing) is an action in the infinitive, the third person singular of **gustar** is used.

No me gusta estar a dieta.
A María le gusta mucho comer carne.

I don't like to be on a diet.
María likes to eat meat very much.

D. Other verbs that function like **gustar** include **fascinar, encantar,** and **importar.**

Me encanta cocinar.

I love to cook (it delights or enchants me).

Me fascinan los juegos de toda clase.
No nos importa el dinero.

Games of all sorts fascinate me.
Money isn't important (doesn't matter) to us.

Ejercicios

A. Create new sentences, substituting the words in the list for those in italics.

1. No me gusta *este arroz.*
   a. las naranjas   b. esta cena   c. la leche   d. esos vinos   e. comer mucho
2. *A Eduardo* le gusta cocinar.
   a. a nosotros   b. a Conchita   c. a ellos   d. a Juan y a Rita   e. a ustedes

B.   Eduardo is a very fussy eater. Every time his mother asks him why he doesn't eat or drink something, he answers that he doesn't like it. Give Eduardo's answer, following the model.

Modelo: ¿Por qué no comes las tostadas?   **¡No me gustan las tostadas!**

1. ¿Por qué no comes las verduras?
2. ¿Por qué no tomas el café con leche?
3. ¿Por qué no comes los plátanos?
4. ¿Por qué no tomas la sopa?
5. ¿Por qué no comes las manzanas?

C.   Make a question asking whether or not your friend likes the following:

Modelo: el chocolate con nueces   **¿Te gusta el chocolate con nueces?**

1. la carne
2. las naranjas
3. viajar
4. las películas españolas
5. cocinar

D.   Complete the following sentences with one or more nouns or with an infinitive, as shown in the examples.

Modelo: A José le gusta(n) mucho . . .   **A José le gusta mucho viajar.**
A José le gustan mucho los vinos buenos.

1. No me gusta(n) . . .
2. ¿Te gusta(n) mucho . . . ?
3. A nosotros no nos importa(n) . . .
4. ¿Les encanta(n) . . . ?
5. A mis padres les fascina(n) . . .
6. A los jóvenes de hoy les gusta(n)

E.   Give the Spanish equivalent of the following sentences.

1. I like this coffee.
2. Paco doesn't like tacos.
3. It doesn't matter to me.
4. This city fascinates me.
5. We like these fruits very much.
6. Do you (*tú* form) like Mexican food?
7. They don't like to play tennis.
8. Does she like chocolates?

Preguntas

1. ¿Le gusta ir al cine? ¿cocinar?   2. ¿Le importa la política?   3. ¿Le encantan los dulces? ¿las manzanas? ¿las naranjas?   4. ¿Le importa mucho el dinero? ¿Les importa mucho a sus padres? ¿a sus amigos?   5. ¿Le importan mucho sus notas? ¿sus estudios? ¿Por qué

sí o por qué no? **6.** ¿Le gusta la comida francesa? ¿mexicana? ¿española? ¿Cuál le gusta más? **7.** ¿Le gustan los vinos buenos? ¿Le gusta la cerveza?

V. PREPOSITIONAL OBJECT PRONOUNS

En la tienda de comestibles.

(1)	**Nicanor:**	Me encanta hacer las compras *contigo*.
(2)	**Valentina:**	*A mí* también me gusta. ¿Qué llevamos? A ver... pan, plátanos, chocolate, nueces, arroz, huevos... ¿estas manzanas son *para ti*?
(3)	**Nicanor:**	Sí, son *para mí*. ¿Dónde están las cervezas?
(4)	**Valentina:**	Detrás *de ti*. Ahora necesito comprar sacarina.
(5)	**Nicanor:**	¿Sacarina?
(6)	**Valentina:**	¡Claro! Siempre la llevo *conmigo* porque estoy a dieta.

1. ¿Dónde están Nicanor y Valentina? **2.** ¿A Nicanor le gusta hacer compras con ella? **3.** Y a Valentina ¿le gusta hacer compras con él? **4.** ¿Qué llevan ahora? **5.** ¿Qué necesita comprar Valentina? ¿Por qué?

A. Pronouns used as objects of prepositions in Spanish are:

SINGULAR		PLURAL	
mí	*me, myself*	nosotros(-as)	*us, ourselves*
ti	*you (fam.), yourself*	vosotros(-as)	*you (fam.), yourselves*
usted	*you*	ustedes	*you*
él	*him*	ellos	*them*
ella	*her*	ellas	*them*

B. Prepositional pronouns always follow a preposition and have the same forms as subject pronouns, except for **mí** and **ti**.

Tengo un regalo para ella.	*I have a gift for her.*
Ella no quiere salir sin ti.	*She does not want to leave without you.*
A mí me gusta trabajar en el jardín.	*I like to work in the garden.*

At the grocery store.
(1) I love going shopping with you. (2) I like it too. What shall we take? Let's see... bread, bananas, chocolate, nuts, rice, eggs... these apples are for you? (3) Yes, they're for me. Where are the beers? (4) Behind you. Now I need to buy saccharine. (5) Saccharine? (6) Of course! I always carry it with me because I'm on a diet.

C. The preposition **con** combines with **mí** to form **conmigo** and with **ti** to form **contigo.**

Ellos van conmigo a Europa. *They are going with me to Europe.*
Ella quiere estudiar contigo. *She wants to study with you.*

D. The subject pronouns **yo** and **tú** are used instead of **mí** and **ti** after the prepositions **entre, excepto,** and **según.**

Entre tú y yo, . . . *Between you and me, . . .*
Todos almorzaron excepto yo. *Everyone ate lunch except me.*
Según tú, ¿cuesta mucho cenar en ese *In your opinion, does it cost a lot to eat*
restaurante? *dinner at that restaurant?*

Ejercicios

A. Complete the following sentences with the prepositional forms of the pronouns given in parentheses.

Modelo: Ustedes pueden ir con ____migo____ (yo).

1. Va al restaurante con _____ (ella).
2. Te llamamos por teléfono a _____ (tú).
3. Almorzamos con _____ (tú).
4. El café con leche es para _____ (nosotros).
5. ¿Me vas a dar el dinero a _____ (yo)?
6. No cena sin _____ (él).

B. Restate, changing the preposition **sin** to **con** and making any other necessary changes.

1. Hoy almuerzo sin ti.
2. ¿Puedes vivir sin mí?
3. Cenamos todos los días sin él.
4. ¿Juegan ellos sin ustedes?

C. Mrs. Ybarra has a tendency to react incredulously to every comment her son Alberto makes. Make questions she would ask, following the model.

Modelo: Alberto: Silvia me prepara el desayuno.
La Sra. Ybarra: **¿Te prepara el desayuno a ti?**

1. Los Gutiérrez me invitan a cenar.
2. Le doy cien pesos a Ramón.
3. Pedro nos quiere ver hoy.
4. Mis amigos te recuerdan.
5. Anita me quiere mucho.
6. A ellos les gusta comer arroz.

D. Give the Spanish equivalent of the following sentences.
   1. This tea is for you (*tú* form).
   2. They are having supper with me.
   3. Are these apples for her?
   4. According to them, this restaurant is excellent.
   5. We are playing without you (*usted* form).
   6. These pieces of toast are for me.

Preguntas

1. ¿A usted le gusta tomar café con leche? ¿Le gustan también las tostadas?   **2.** ¿Con quién le gusta ir de compras?   **3.** ¿Le gusta cenar con sus amigos o prefiere cenar solo? **4.** ¿Juega usted al tenis conmigo? ¿con un(a) amigo(a)?   **5.** ¿Le da usted regalos a su papá? ¿a su mamá? ¿Les da regalos a sus amigos?

EN EL BARRIO CHICANO

En el apartamento de Andrea, en Los Ángeles

Andrea: ¿Qué piensan ustedes de la campaña política?
Jacinto: Bueno… el candidato Díaz promete muchas cosas a los chicanos.[1] Pero a mí, él no me gusta, no me convencen sus palabras.
Elvira: Recuerdo las elecciones pasadas. Promesas… y luego nada. Además, veo que Díaz no encuentra soluciones para nosotros, y su programa no resuelve problemas urgentes como el desempleo y la instrucción primaria.

Jacinto: Estoy de acuerdo contigo, Elvira. Los niños no pueden estudiar porque no hablan bien inglés. Necesitan programas bilingües.

Elvira: Pero esos programas cuestan mucho. Estamos en los Estados Unidos y acá hablan inglés, ¿no?

Andrea: Sí, pero el idioma español también es importante. Es una cuestión de orgullo de raza.[2]

Elvira: Pero no es bueno vivir separados del resto del país. Tú, Manuel ¿qué crees? ¡eh, carnal![3] ¿duermes?

Manuel: No duermo. Pienso que el hambre es un problema importante. A propósito, ¿no les da hambre ahora que hablamos del tema?

Jacinto: ¡De veras, son las dos de la tarde! Chicas ¿qué nos van a dar de comer?

Andrea: ¿Qué te parece esto, Elvira? La cocina está allí. En el refrigerador hay huevos, leche, pan, fruta y vino. ¿Por qué tenemos que darles de comer nosotras? Pueden cocinar ustedes. ¿O no les gusta cocinar?

Elvira: Creo que estos muchachos necesitan unas lecciones sobre la igualdad de los sexos y tal vez algún libro de recetas.

Andrea: Aquí hay uno. Ahora mismo les doy el libro a estos dos muchachos. A ver qué sorpresa nos preparan. Y nosotras, Elvira, ¿por qué no vamos a dar un paseo por el centro?

campaña *campaign*   **promete** *promises*   **convencer** *to convince*   **y luego nada** *and then nothing*   **desempleo** *unemployment*   **instrucción primaria** *elementary education*   **cuestión** *matter*   **orgullo** *pride*   **separados** *apart*   **A propósito** *By the way*   **dar de comer** *feed*   **igualdad** *equality*   **sorpresa** *surprise*

Preguntas

1. ¿Le gusta el candidato Díaz a Jacinto?   **2.** ¿Qué recuerda Elvira de las elecciones pasadas? Según ella, ¿cuáles son los problemas urgentes que Díaz no resuelve?   **3.** ¿Qué necesitan en las escuelas los estudiantes? ¿qué piensa Elvira de ésto? ¿Y qué opina usted?   **4.** ¿Qué piensa Manuel?   **5.** ¿Qué quieren Manuel y Jacinto?   **6.** ¿Qué hay en el refrigerador?   **7.** Según Elvira, ¿qué necesita Jacinto?   **8.** ¿Le gusta cocinar a usted? ¿Qué les prepara a sus amigos cuando los invita a cenar?

NOTAS CULTURALES

1. The term **chicano** refers to the people and culture of Mexican-American heritage. Not all people of Mexican-American ancestry call themselves **chicano;** some prefer the term **méxico-americano.**

2. The term **la raza** (*the race*) is used by many Spanish Americans to refer to all people of Hispanic origin and is sometimes extended to include American Indians. The day set aside to celebrate the discovery of the Americas (Columbus Day) is referred to by Spanish-speaking people as **El día de la Raza.**

3. Carnal is used frequently in informal conversation by Chicanos as "my friend". The term is probably derived from **hermano carnal,** which means blood brother. **Mano** (from **hermano**) has approximately the same meaning when used by Mexicans. Similar terms of affection are common in other parts of the Hispanic world, notably **chico** used by Cubans and **ché** by Argentineans and Paraguayans. These terms are employed only among people addressing each other in the **tú** form.

ACTIVIDADES

Los alimentos

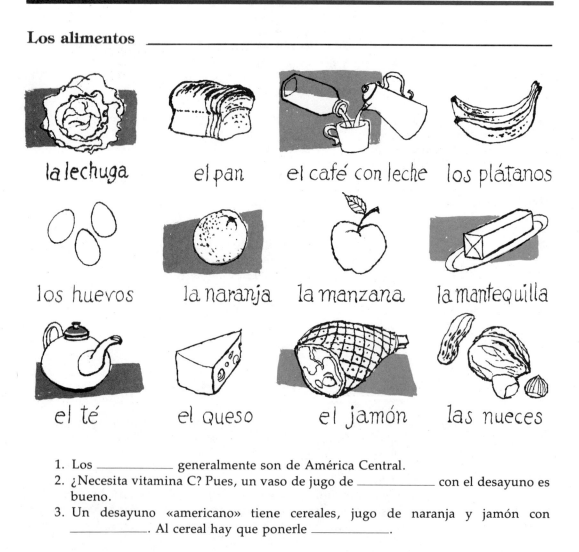

la lechuga   el pan   el café con leche   los plátanos

los huevos   la naranja   la manzana   la mantequilla

el té   el queso   el jamón   las nueces

1. Los _____ generalmente son de América Central.
2. ¿Necesita vitamina C? Pues, un vaso de jugo de _____ con el desayuno es bueno.
3. Un desayuno «americano» tiene cereales, jugo de naranja y jamón con _____. Al cereal hay que ponerle _____.

4. Un sandwiche se prepara con dos rebanadas (*slices*) de _____, jamón y, a veces, _____.

5. En la Biblia, Eva le da a Adán una _____, y así empiezan los problemas del mundo.

Entrevista _____

Ask a classmate the following questions. Then report the information to the class.

1. ¿Dónde vas a almorzar mañana?
2. ¿Te gusta el café o prefieres el té?
3. ¿A qué hora te da hambre por la mañana?
4. ¿Puedes preparar tu desayuno por la mañana?
5. ¿Preparas la comida sólo para ti?
6. ¿Les compras alimentos a tus compañeros (a tus padres)?

La compra de la semana _____

Using the illustrated vocabulary list as a guide, write out in Spanish a possible shopping list for the week's groceries. The following expressions may be of use:

paquete	*package*
libra/media libra	*pound/half a pound*
docena/media docena	*dozen/half a dozen*
galón/medio galón	*gallon/half gallon*

Situación _____

En el apartamento de Mateo

Mateo, Ofelia, and Susana are in Mateo's apartment. They are talking about the elections and the new candidate Juana Vargas. Mateo and Ofelia like Juana Vargas because she wants bilingual programs in the schools. But Susana does not agree; she does not like Vargas. She likes the candidate Carlos García who promises many jobs for Chicanos. Ofelia says she is getting hungry. Mateo tells the girls what there is in the refrigerator and asks what they prefer to eat. They tell him what they want and all three go to the kitchen to prepare it.

VOCABULARIO ACTIVO

Verbos útiles

almorzar (ue)   *to have lunch*
cocinar   *to cook*
comprar   *to buy*
contar (ue)   *to tell, recount (story, joke)*
costar (ue)   *to cost*

dar   *to give;* **dar un paseo**   *to take a walk;* **darle las gracias a alguien**   *to thank someone;* **darle hambre (sed, sueño) a alguien**   *to make someone hungry (thirsty, sleepy)*
despertar (ie)   *to wake (someone) up*
dormir (ue)   *to sleep*

encantar *to fascinate;* **Me encanta . . .** *I love . . .*

encontrar (ue) *to find, encounter*

fascinar *to fascinate*

gustar *to please, be pleasing to;* **Me gusta . . .** *I like . . .*

importar *to be important, matter;* **No importa el dinero.** *Money doesn't matter.*

jugar (ue) (a) *to play*

poder (ue) *to be able; can*

preparar *to prepare*

recordar (ue) *to remember*

reservar *to reserve*

resolver (ue) *to solve*

ver *to see*

volver (ue) *to return, come back, go back*

Los alimentos

el alimento *food, nourishment*

el almuerzo *lunch, large mid-day meal*

el arroz *rice*

el azúcar *sugar*

la bebida *beverage*

el café *coffee*

caliente *hot (temperature)*

la carne *meat*

la cerveza *beer*

la cocina *cuisine; kitchen*

los comestibles *groceries*

el chocolate *chocolate*

el desayuno *breakfast;* **tomar el desayuno** *to have breakfast*

la dieta *diet;* **estar a dieta** *to be on a diet*

el dulce *sweet, candy*

la fruta *fruit*

la galleta *cracker, cookie*

el huevo *egg*

el jamón *ham*

la leche *milk*

la lechuga *lettuce*

la mantequilla *butter*

la manzana *apple*

la mermelada *jam, marmalade*

la naranja *orange*

la nuez *nut, walnut*

el pan *bread, loaf of bread*

el plátano *banana*

el queso *cheese*

la receta *recipe*

la sopa *soup*

el té *tea*

la torta *cake*

la tostada *piece of toast*

la verdura *vegetable*

el vino *wine*

Otras palabras útiles

al aire libre *in the open air*

bilingüe *bilingual*

¡Cómo no! *Of course!*

conmigo *with me;* **contigo** *with you (tú)*

¿De veras? *Really?*

entre *between; among*

el estado *state;* **Estados Unidos** *United States*

excepto *except*

la foto(grafía) *the photo(graph)*

el gato *cat*

el gerente *manager*

el idioma *language*

el jardín *garden*

el programa *program*

la promesa *promise*

la recepcionista *receptionist*

según *according to*

sólo *only*

solo(a) *alone*

el tema *topic, theme*

Los Hispanos de Los Estados Unidos

¿Por qué encontramos *letreros* como éstos en tiendas de Nueva York, Chicago, Los Ángeles, o San Francisco? La *respuesta* está en los doce millones de hispanos que viven en los Estados Unidos (*sin mencionar* los varios millones de inmigrantes ilegales). Hay tres grupos principales: los méxico-americanos, los puertorriqueños y los cubanos. Hoy día viven en este país *unos* siete millones de méxico-americanos, dos millones de puertorriqueños y casi un millón de cubanos. *La mayor parte* de la población de Miami es de origen cubano; en Nueva York viven *más* puertorriqueños que en San Juan, la capital de Puerto Rico.

signs
answer
without
mentioning

about

greater part
more

La presencia hispana en el territorio del *suroeste* de los Estados Unidos es *muy anterior* a la presencia anglosajona. Nombres de estados como Nevada y Colorado, y de ciudades como San Francisco y Las Vegas, reflejan su origen hispano. La Misión de Santa Bárbara (en la fotografía) *fue fundada* por padres españoles en 1786.

southwest
much earlier than

was founded

Con la victoria militar de 1848, los Estados Unidos *ganan a* México   **win from**
el territorio que hoy forma el suroeste norteamericano. Muchos habitantes de esta región son descendientes de los primeros coloni-
zadores españoles; otros son trabajadores mexicanos que vienen a
este país a trabajar en el campo. Casi siempre el trabajo es *duro* y   **hard**
los salarios son muy bajos.

Por suerte, hoy la situación empieza a cambiar. En años recientes,   **Fortunately**
grupos de méxico-americanos insisten en obtener sus *derechos.* Los   **rights**
jóvenes están orgullosos de su identidad. Ahora muchas escuelas del
suroeste tienen programas bilingües, y los «chicanos» empiezan a
ocupar *puestos* importantes en el gobierno.   **posts, positions**

La historia de los puertorriqueños en los Estados Unidos empieza

con la victoria norteamericana en la *guerra* de 1898 contra España;   **war**
desde entonces, la isla de Puerto Rico es territorio de los Estados Uni-   **since then**
dos. Hoy, los puertorriqueños son *ciudadanos* de los Estados Unidos.   **citizens**
Como en el caso de los mexicanos, muchos salen de su *patria* para   **homeland**
buscar trabajo en Nueva York o en otras ciudades.

Los cubanos están aquí como exilados políticos del régimen so-
cialista-comunista de Fidel Castro. Aunque están en todos los estados, una gran mayoría vive en Miami. Allí tienen un barrio muy
próspero.

Preguntas

1. ¿Cuántos millones de hispanos viven en los Estados Unidos?   2. ¿Cuáles son los tres
grupos principales?   3. En el suroeste de los Estados Unidos, ¿la presencia hispana es
anterior o posterior a la anglosajona?   4. ¿Qué estados y ciudades recuerda usted con
nombres españoles?   5. ¿Cuándo ganan los Estados Unidos los territorios que hoy forman el suroeste norteamericano?   6. ¿De quiénes son descendientes muchos habitantes
de estos estados?   7. ¿Cómo empieza a cambiar la situación de los méxico-americanos?
8. ¿Desde cuándo Puerto Rico es parte del territorio de los Estados Unidos?   9. ¿Por qué
entran sin problemas a los Estados Unidos los puertorriqueños?   10. ¿Dónde viven muchos cubano-americanos?

Capítulo 7

DIVERSIONES

OBJECTIVES

LANGUAGE: In this chapter we introduce, discuss, and practice:

1. stem-changing verbs **e** to **i**
2. the verbs **pedir** and **preguntar,** which can both mean *to ask* but have different uses
3. sentences that have both direct and indirect objects
4. the verbs **saber** and **conocer,** which can both mean *to know* but are used to convey different meanings

You will also learn vocabulary related to amusements and pastimes and to music.

CULTURE: The dialogue takes place in Guadalajara, Mexico, where a group of mariachi musicians are serenading some young people. You will read something about Mexican music and dance.

EXPLICACIÓN

I. STEM-CHANGING VERBS E to I

(1) **Elisa:** ¡Ay, qué problemas con Gustavo! Te *pido* ayuda porque tus consejos siempre me *sirven*.

(2) **Elma:** Te *sigue* a todas partes ¿verdad?

(3) **Elisa:** No, pero todos los días me llama por teléfono para ver si estoy en casa. *Dice* que no le soy fiel.

(4) **Elma:** ¡Qué insolencia! Y tú ¿qué le *dices*?

(5) **Elisa:** Le *digo* que eso me molesta, pero ¿qué hago?

(6) **Elma:** ¿Por qué no lo llamas todas las noches tú, para ver si él va de paseo?

(7) **Elisa:** No puedo. Si estoy en casa todas las noches ¿cuándo voy a bailar con Jaime o con Miguel?

1. ¿Por qué le pide Elisa ayuda a su amiga? **2.** ¿Es que Gustavo la sigue a todas partes? **3.** ¿Por qué la llama todos los días? **4.** ¿Qué dice Gustavo de ella? ¿es verdad? **5.** ¿Qué dice usted de la actitud de Elisa?

A. Certain **-ir** verbs show a stem change from **e** to **i** when the stem syllable is stressed.

pedir *(to ask for)*		**seguir** *(to continue, to follow)*		**servir** *(to serve)*	
pido	pedimos	sigo	seguimos	sirvo	servimos
pides	pedís	sigues	seguís	sirves	servís
pide	piden	sigue	siguen	sirve	sirven

Les pido ayuda.   *I'm asking them for help.*
Seguimos a los niños.   *We're following the children.*

---

(1) Oh, what problems with Gustavo! I'm asking you for help because your advice always helps me. (2) He follows you everywhere, right? (3) No, but everyday he calls me on the telephone to see if I'm home. He says I'm not faithful to him. (4) What insolence! And what do you tell him? (5) I tell him that (that) bothers me, but what shall I do? (6) Why don't you call him every night, to see if he goes out (on the town)? (7) I can't. If I'm home every night, when will I go dancing with Jaime or Miguel?

El camarero nos sirve el desayuno. *The waiter is serving us breakfast.*
Rafael sigue cuatro cursos. *Rafael is taking four courses.*

decir *(to say, tell)*	
digo	decimos
dices	decís
dice	dicen

Te digo la verdad. —Ya te creo. *I'm telling you the truth. —I believe you.*

¿Tu novio dice mentiras? ¡Qué barbaridad! *Your boyfriend tells lies? Good grief!*

Cecilia dice que no puede ir a la playa con nosotros este fin de semana. *Cecilia says (that) she can't come to the beach with us this weekend.*

Ejercicios

A. Create new sentences, substituting the words in the list for those in italics.
1. *Ella* pide café.
   a. tú **b.** nosotros **c.** yo **d.** Miguel y José **e.** ustedes
2. *Roberto* les dice la verdad.
   a. yo **b.** ellas **c.** Conchita y yo **d.** tú **e.** mi amigo
3. ¿Sigues *tú* muchos cursos?
   a. tu hermano **b.** Ana y su novio **c.** usted **d.** nosotros **e.** tú y Pedro
4. *El camarero* sirve la comida.
   a. usted **b.** nosotros **c.** yo **d.** Teresa y Ramón **e.** tú

B. Restate, changing the verbs to the plural.
1. Les sirvo el té.
2. Te pido un favor.
3. ¿Me sigue al restaurante?
4. ¿Qué digo ahora?
5. Mi hijo me pide dinero.

C. Give one appropriate question for each one of the following answers.

Modelo: Sí, seguimos dos cursos aquí. **¿Siguen dos cursos aquí?**
Pido un café. **¿Qué pide usted?**

1. No, no le decimos la verdad.
2. Mi hermano sirve la cena hoy.
3. Sí, ella siempre me pide consejos.
4. No, yo no digo mentiras.
5. Piden ayuda a sus padres.
6. Sigo español, historia y matemáticas.

Preguntas

1. ¿Cuál es su restaurante favorito? ¿Qué platos sirven allí? ¿Qué pide usted generalmente? **2.** ¿Sirven cerveza en la cafetería de la universidad? ¿vino? ¿café? ¿té? **3.** ¿Les pide usted favores a sus padres? ¿a sus amigos? **4.** ¿Dice usted siempre la verdad? ¿A quién(es) no le(s) dice usted siempre la verdad? **5.** ¿Cuántos cursos sigue usted este semestre? ¿Son interesantes o aburridos?

II. PEDIR AND PREGUNTAR

(1)	**José:**	Papá, necesito dinero.
(2)	**Señor Ortega:**	¿Otra vez? ¿Por qué no le *preguntas* a tu mamá dónde está su bolso?
(3)	**José:**	Mamá no está en casa; está en el cine.
(4)	**Señor Ortega:**	¡Caramba! Los niños de hoy no tienen idea del valor de un peso.
(5)	**José:**	Sí, papá, yo la tengo. Por eso te *pido* diez.

1. ¿Qué quiere el niño? **2.** ¿A quién puede preguntar dónde está su bolso? **3.** ¿Quién no está? **4.** ¿Qué cree el papá? **5.** ¿Cuántos pesos pide el niño?

Pedir means to ask for something, to request (someone) to do something. **Preguntar** means to ask a question.

Pedimos la cena.	*We're ordering (asking for) dinner.*
Me piden un favor.	*They're asking me for a favor.*
Hay que pedirle permiso al abuelo.	*We have to ask grandfather for permission.*
Me preguntan dónde está la discoteca.	*They ask me where the discotheque is.*
¿Por qué no le preguntas al policía?	*Why don't you ask the policeman?*

Ejercicios

A. Complete each sentence with the correct form of **pedir** or **preguntar**

1. José me _____ treinta pesos.
2. Concha le _____ a su novio dónde va a ser la fiesta.
3. Generalmente yo les _____ consejos a mis padres.

---

(1) Dad, I need money. (2) Again? Why don't you ask your mother where her purse is? (3) Mom isn't home, she is in the movie theater. (4) Good grief! The children of today don't have any idea of the value of a peso. (5) Dad, I do. That's why I'm asking you for ten.

4. Ella te quiere _____ cuándo es el concierto.
5. ¿Por qué no le _____ nosotros si piensa ver esa película?
6. ¿Qué _____ ustedes? ¿cerveza o vino?
7. Susana me _____ si me gusta bailar tangos.
8. ¿Le _____ tú ese favor a Pablo?

B. Give the Spanish equivalent of the following sentences.

1. Juan is asking if Rita is home.
2. My friends are asking me for a favor.
3. Are we ordering three beers?
4. Why are they asking that?
5. She is going to ask him for advice.

Preguntas

1. Cuando usted baila con una persona que le gusta, ¿le pregunta usted su nombre? ¿dónde vive? ¿su número de teléfono? ¿Qué más le pregunta usted? 2. Si usted quiere usar el auto de su papá, ¿tiene que pedirle permiso a él? 3. ¿Les pide usted consejos a sus padres? ¿a sus amigos? 4. Si usted necesita encontrar una calle, ¿pregunta a un policía dónde está?

III. DIRECT AND INDIRECT OBJECT PRONOUNS IN THE SAME SENTENCE

(1)	**Arturo:**	¿Recuerdas la canción «Guantanamera»? Es parte de un poema del poeta cubano José Martí.
(2)	**Josefina:**	Los versos los recuerdo de memoria, pero no recuerdo la música. *¿Me la* puedes tocar en la guitarra?
(3)	**Arturo:**	¿La guitarra? . . . la tiene Camilo. *Se la* doy los sábados porque toca en la orquesta.

1. ¿De quién son los versos de la canción «Guantanamera»? 2. ¿Los recuerda Josefina? 3. ¿Recuerda ella la música? 4. ¿Por qué no se la puede tocar Arturo en la guitarra?

(1) Do you remember the song "Guantanamera"? It's part of a poem by the Cuban poet José Martí. (2) The lines (of poetry) I remember (them) by heart, but I don't remember the music. Can you play it for me on the guitar? (3) The guitar? . . . Camilo has it. I give it to him every Saturday because he plays in the orchestra.

A. When an indirect and a direct object pronoun are used in the same sentence, the indirect object pronoun is always placed immediately before the direct object pronoun. The two object pronouns (indirect-direct) both precede a conjugated form of the verb.

Te doy la dirección   *I'll give you the address.*
Te la doy.   *I'll give it to you.*

B. The object pronouns can also be attached to an infinitive (with the indirect object preceding the direct object). Note that when two object pronouns are attached to the infinitive, an accent is required over the last syllable of the infinitive.

Voy a pedirte un consejo.   *I am going to ask you for some advice.*
Voy a pedírtelo ⎫
Te lo voy a pedir. ⎭   *I am going to ask you for it.*

C. If a third person indirect object pronoun (**le, les**) is used in conjunction with a third person direct object pronoun (**lo, la, los, las**), the indirect object pronoun is replaced by **se.** The various meanings of **se** may be clarified by adding to the sentence: **a él, a ella, a usted, a ellos, a ellas, a ustedes.**

Elena les cuenta el chiste (a ellos).   *Elena tells them the joke.*
Elena se lo cuenta (a ellos).   *Elena tells it to them.*
El camarero le sirve la cerveza (a ella).   *The waiter is serving her the beer.*
El camarero se la sirve (a ella).   *The waiter is serving it to her.*
Yo le canto unas canciones tristes (a usted). *I will sing you some sad songs.*
Yo se las canto (a usted).   *I will sing them to you.*

Ejercicios

A.   Answer the questions according to the examples.

Modelo: ¿A quién le das la carta?   **Se la doy a Marta.**

1. ¿A quién le das el dinero?
2. ¿A quién le dices la verdad?
3. ¿A quién le pides esos favores?
4. ¿A quién le sirves la cerveza?
5. ¿A quién le cantas esas canciones?

Modelo: ¿Cuándo te van a dar el auto?   **Me lo van a dar ahora.**

1. ¿Cuándo te van a servir la comida?
2. ¿Cuándo te van a decir el secreto?
3. ¿Cuándo te van a dar sus direcciones?
4. ¿Cuándo te van a pedir los cien pesos?
5. ¿Cuándo te van a leer el poema?

B.   Create sentences starting with **Le(s) doy** and using the nouns listed. Then replace the nouns with the appropriate object pronouns.

Modelo: el lápiz / a José   **Le doy el lápiz a José. Se lo doy.**

1. la guitarra / a María
2. el dinero / al camarero
3. los regalos / a los niños
4. las cartas / a usted
5. el examen / a la profesora
6. el bolso / a la joven
7. las gracias / a los músicos
8. los diez pesos / a las muchachas

C.   Replace the nouns with the appropriate object pronouns, following the models.

Modelo: Mi papá me compra un auto. **Me lo compra.**
   Ellos nos cantan una canción triste.   **Ellos nos la cantan.**

1. Ricardo me pide permiso.
2. ¿Por qué no les das los regalos?
3. Te vendo mi auto por cinco mil pesos.
4. Allí siempre te dan café ¿no?
5. ¿Cuándo me vas a decir tu secreto?
6. ¿Nos sirve las cervezas ahora?
7. Mañana le voy a pedir un favor a Susana.
8. ¿Quién te escribe esos poemas?

D. José wants to borrow his father's car to take his girlfriend to a party. He promises his Dad everything so that he can have the car for the day. Following the model, supply his answers to the questions his father asks him.

Modelo: ¿Me vas a pedir el auto mañana? **No, no te lo voy a pedir mañana.**
¿Nos vas a decir siempre la verdad? **Sí, se la voy a decir siempre.**

1. ¿Les vas a servir el desayuno a tus hermanos?   Sí, _____
2. ¿Le vas a dar problemas a tu madre?   No, _____
3. ¿Me vas a llevar las cartas a la oficina?   Sí, _____
4. ¿Nos vas a pedir dinero todos los días?   No, _____
5. ¿Nos vas a hacer el almuerzo?   Sí, _____
6. ¿Le vas a decir mentiras a tu novia?   No, _____

Preguntas

1. ¿Puede usted bailar el cha cha chá? ¿la rumba? ¿el tango? ¿Nos lo (los la) quiere enseñar? **2.** ¿Toca usted un instrumento musical? ¿el piano? ¿la guitarra? ¿el violín? ¿Quién se lo (la) enseña? **3.** ¿Escucha usted canciones en español? ¿Las puede entender? **4.** ¿Tiene usted cincuenta dólares? ¿Me los quiere dar? ¿Por qué? **5.** ¿Pide usted a veces dinero a sus amigos? ¿Se lo dan? ¿Les pide consejos? ¿Se los dan? ¿Los sigue usted?

IV. SABER vs. CONOCER

(1) **Alfredo:** *¿Sabes* bailar la cumbia, María?

(2)   **María:** Sí, y también *sé* bailar el tango.

(3) **Alfredo:** Entonces, me lo puedes enseñar. *Conozco* una buena discoteca donde podemos ir el sábado. ¿O tú prefieres ir a un concierto?

(4)   **María:** *¿Sabes?* . . . el sábado voy a una fiesta con Esteban Ramírez. ¿Lo *conoces*?

(5) **Alfredo:** Creo que sí. ¿Es ese pescado frío y aburrido?

(6)   **María:** ¡Pero, Alfredo! Esteban es muy simpático. *Conoce* a todo el mundo y *sabe* hacer muchas cosas.

(7) **Alfredo:** ¿Simpático? La gente que lo *conoce* dice que es un Don Juan.

(8)   **María:** Alfredo . . . tú estás celoso . . .

(1) Do you know how to dance the cumbia, María? (2) Yes, and I also know how to dance the tango. (3) Then, you can teach it to me. I know a good Disco where we can go on Saturday. Or do you prefer to go to a concert? (4) You know (what)? On Saturday I'm going to a party with Esteban Ramírez. Do you know him? (5) I think so. Is he that cold, boring dope (fish)? (6) But, Alfredo! Esteban is very charming. He knows everybody and knows how to do many things. (7) Charming? People who know him say he's a Don Juan. (8) Alfred . . . you're jealous . . .

1. ¿Sabe María bailar la cumbia o el tango? **2.** ¿Por qué no puede ir con Alfredo a la discoteca el sábado? **3.** ¿Conoce Alfredo a Esteban Ramírez? ¿Qué piensa de él? **4.** ¿Qué dice María de Esteban? **5.** ¿Por qué habla mal Alfredo de Esteban?

A. The verbs **saber** and **conocer** are irregular in the first person singular.

saber *(to know, know how to)*		**conocer** *(to know, be acquainted with)*	
sé	sabemos	**conozco**	conocemos
sabes	sabéis	conoces	conocéis
sabe	saben	conoce	conocen

B. **Saber** means to have knowledge of facts or information about something or someone. **Conocer** means to know or to be acquainted with a person, place, or thing. Note that **conocer** takes a personal **a** before a direct object that refers to a person or group of persons.

Conozco a Conchita pero no sé donde está.
I know (am acquainted with) Conchita but I don't know (have information about) where she is.

Sé jugar al tenis pero no conozco este club.
I know how to (I can) play tennis but I don't know (I'm not familiar with) this club.

Conocemos un chiste muy divertido, pero yo no sé contarlo bien.
We know a very amusing joke, but I don't know how to tell it well.

Ejercicios

A. Create new sentences, substituting the words in the list for those in italics.

1. *Tú* sabes bailar la rumba y el cha cha chá.
   a. el muchacho **b.** Tito y yo **c.** ustedes **d.** tus amigos **e.** yo

2. *Elena* conoce un buen restaurante.
   a. nosotros **b.** yo **c.** mis padres **d.** tú **e.** usted

B. Complete the sentences with the correct form of **saber** or **conocer**.

1. Yo _____ al novio de Marisa.
2. Ustedes _____ que Paco canta muy bien, ¿no?
3. José no _____ bailar.
4. Elena _____ a todo el mundo.
5. Yo _____ tocar la guitarra.
6. ¿_____ usted al camarero que trabaja aquí?
7. Nosotros _____ jugar al tenis.
8. Tú _____ a mi padre, ¿verdad?

C. Complete the following dialogue with the appropriate form of **saber** or **conocer**.

Jorge: ¿_____ tú bailar el tango?
Mirta: No, pero _____ bailar la samba y el cha cha chá.
Jorge: ¿_____ a Ana Rodríguez?
Mirta: Sí, la _____. Ana y yo somos muy buenas amigas.
Jorge: ¿_____ si ella tiene novio?
Mirta: Sí, ella tiene novio. Se llama Rubén ¡y es muy celoso!
Jorge: ¿Rubén Gutiérrez?
Mirta: ¡Sí! ¿Lo _____?
Jorge: ¡Claro! Rubén y yo vivimos en el mismo apartamento.
Mirta: ¿Sí? ¿_____que Rubén va a enseñarme a bailar el tango?
Jorge: ¡Y Ana me va a enseñar a mí el cha cha chá! Pero tengo una idea . . . Ana y
        Rubén _____ bailar muy bien, pero en realidad no los necesitamos.
        Tú quieres _____ bailar el tango. ¡Pues yo te lo puedo enseñar!
Mirta: Y tú no _____ bailar el cha cha chá. ¡Por eso yo te lo puedo enseñar!
        Después de las lecciones tú y yo vamos a _____ bailar un nuevo
        ritmo (*rhythm*) latino.
Jorge: . . . y también tú y yo nos vamos a _____ muy bien, ¿no?

D. Give the Spanish equivalent of the following sentences.

1. I know her; she plays in the orchestra.
2. Do you know how to speak Spanish?
3. Do you (*tú*) know this city well?
4. We know everyone here.
5. I don't know if you (*tú*) know where they serve good beer.
6. Does he know that Mary knows his sister?

Preguntas

1. ¿Sabe usted cómo se llama la capital de España? ¿de Chile? ¿de la Argentina? ¿de México? **2.** ¿Sabe usted cantar «Guantanamera»? ¿otra canción latinoamericana o española? **3.** ¿Conoce usted a muchos latinoamericanos? ¿españoles? **4.** ¿Conoce usted a un jugador (*player*) de béisbol de origen hispano? ¿a un jugador de tenis? **5.** ¿Sabe usted el nombre de una o dos (*o más*) personas famosas de origen hispano? **6.** ¿Conoce usted México? ¿España? ¿Venezuela? ¿Qué países conoce usted?

EN LA PLAZA DE LOS MARIACHIS

Tres amigos, estudiantes de la Universidad de Guadalajara.[1]

Tomás   ¿Qué pedimos? ¿Tequila?
Conchita: No. Prefiero una cerveza. ¿Y tú, Elena?
Elena: Yo también.

Tomás: ¡Camarero! Tres cervezas, por favor.

Conchita: Quiero pedirles un consejo.

Tomás: ¡Cómo no! Te lo damos gratis.

Elena: ¿Otra pelea con Enrique?

Conchita: Sí, otra vez.

Elena: Pues, te digo la verdad . . . creo que Enrique es estupendo para novio, pero debe ser horrible para marido.

Conchita: ¿Por qué?

Elena: Sabe bailar muy bien. Conoce a todo el mundo. Es inteligente y guapo. Pero no te es fiel.

Conchita: Sí, Lo sé, es un Tenorio.[2]

Tomás: Y, al mismo tiempo, es celoso ¿no?

Conchita: ¡Claro! Me llama todos los días.

Elena: Para saber si estás en casa y preguntarte qué haces ¿verdad?

Conchita: Y tu novio ¿no te llama?

Elena: No, Alberto sigue muchos cursos y está muy ocupado con sus estudios de música. En realidad, es un poco frío y aburrido, pero siempre me dice la verdad.

Tomás: Aquí llegan los mariachis.

Conchita: ¡Ay, los conozco! Son amigos de Enrique.

Los mariachis: Buenas tardes, señoras y señores. Vamos a cantarle una canción especial a la señorita Conchita González, de parte de un admirador secreto:

Dicen que no tengo duelo, llorona,
porque no me ven llorar.
Hay muertos que no hacen ruido, llorona,
y es más triste su pesar.[3]

Conchita: ¡Qué emoción! A pesar de sus defectos, Enrique sabe hacerme feliz.
Tomás: Y también infeliz.
Elena: Pues, así es el amor.

---

al mismo tiempo *at the same time*   **admirador** *admirer*   **a pesar de** *in spite of*

Preguntas

1. ¿Qué piden los estudiantes? **2.** ¿Qué quiere Conchita pedir a sus amigos? ¿Se lo dan gratis? **3.** ¿Por qué Enrique es estupendo para novio? **4.** ¿Le es fiel Enrique a Conchita? ¿Es celoso? **5.** ¿Llama Enrique a Conchita todos los días? ¿para qué? **6.** ¿Por qué no llama Alberto a Elena todos los días? **7.** ¿Quiénes llegan? **8.** ¿De quién son amigos los mariachis? **9.** ¿Quién es el admirador secreto? **10.** ¿Qué opina usted: nos hace felices el amor?

NOTAS CULTURALES

1. Guadalajara is Mexico's second largest city, with a population of over one and a half million. The **mariachis** originated in Guadalajara. They are brightly-costumed, strolling musicians who sing and play string instruments and trumpets. They play typical Mexican music, including the **ranchera,** usually a sad complaint of unrequited love. They may be hired for parties, serenades, or simply for a song or two. The name **mariachi** is derived from the French word for *wedding* and dates back to Emperor Maximilian's brief reign in Mexico in the 19th century. These musicians were frequently employed then to entertain at marriage feasts.

2. Un Tenorio is a lady-killer, a man who runs after women. The name comes from that of the hero of a seventeenth-century Spanish play, **El burlador de Sevilla** *(The Seducer of Seville),* by Tirso de Molina, a work which served as the basis of later works by several authors: the Spanish romantic poet Zorrilla, the French playwright Molière, the English poet Lord Byron, and many others. The hero's complete name is **don Juan Tenorio.** Many Spanish-speaking people use his last name as a synonym for this type of man, while English-speaking people speak of a *Don Juan.*

> *They say I'm not in sorrow,* **llorona,**
> *because they don't see me weep.*
> *There are dead people who make no noise,* **llorona,**
> *and more sorrowful is their pain.*

This song, «**La llorona**» (*"The Crying Woman"*), is very old and popular. Some verses seem to symbolize the fall to the Spaniards of the great Indian civilizations of the past.

ACTIVIDADES

La fiesta de Margarita

¿Qué pasa en la fiesta?

Use your imagination to describe in Spanish what is happening at Margarita's party with as many details as possible.

Entrevista

Ask a classmate the following questions. Then report the information to the class.

1. ¿Sabes bailar bien? ¿cantar? ¿tocar la guitarra?
2. ¿Conoces una buena discoteca?
3. ¿Qué haces en las fiestas?
4. ¿Te gustan las fiestas grandes o pequeñas? ¿Por qué?
5. ¿Tienes novio(a)? ¿Te sigue a todas partes? ¿Te llama mucho?
6. ¿Conoces a algún Tenorio? ¿Qué piensas de él?

Situación

Conchita and Guillermo are in a café talking about their favorite films. The waiter comes and asks them what they want to order. They order beer, bread, and cheese. The waiter replies that he will serve them right away (**en seguida**). Conchita and Guillermo then talk about what they like to do on the weekends (for example dance at the discotheque, sing, watch television, go to movies, play a musical instrument, listen to records, tapes, the radio (**la radio**), chat with friends, etc.). Then Conchita says that the **mariachis** are coming. Guillermo says yes, he sees them and knows them well. One is Pedro, the former boyfriend (**novio anterior**) of Conchita.

VOCABULARIO ACTIVO

Verbos útiles

bailar   *to dance*
cantar   *to sing*
conocer (zc)   *to be acquainted with, know*
decir (i)   *to say, tell*
ir de paseo   *to take a walk; go out*
molestar   *to bother, annoy, trouble*
pedir (i)   *to ask for; to order*
saber   *to know, have knowledge of; to be able to (do something)*
seguir (i)   *to follow, continue;* **seguir un curso**   *to take a course*
servir (i)   *to serve*
tocar   *to play (music)*

Diversiones

la canción   *song*
el chiste   *joke*
la discoteca   *discotheque*
la guitarra   *guitar*
la música   *music*
la orquesta   *orchestra*

Otras palabras útiles

el amor   *love*
Así es . . .   *That's . . .*
la ayuda   *help*

el bolso   *purse, handbag*
el camarero   *waiter*
celoso(a)   *jealous*
el consejo   *advice, piece of advice;* **dar consejos**   *to give advice*
divertido   *amusing, enjoyable*
feliz   *happy;* **infeliz**   *unhappy*
fiel   *faithful;* **infiel**   *unfaithful*
fin de semana   *weekend*
gratis   *free of charge, gratis*
guapo(a)   *handsome, good-looking*
el marido   *husband*
la mentira   *lie*
el novio   *boyfriend;* **la novia**   *girlfriend*
ocupado(a)   *busy*
la parte   *part;* **de parte de**   *on the part of, from;* **todas partes**   *everywhere*
la pelea   *argument, disagreement*
el permiso   *permission*
el policía   *policeman;* **la policía**   *policewoman or police station*
el poema   *poem*
el poeta (la poetisa)   *poet*
¡Qué barbaridad!   *Good grief!*
¡Qué emoción!   *How exciting!*
secreto(a)   *secret*
triste   *sad*
el valor   *value*
el verso   *verse*

CAPÍTULO 8

PRENDAS DE VESTIR

Sombrero

blusa amarilla

camisa blanca

chaqueta negra

falda azul

Pantalón negro

zapatos blancos

OBJECTIVES

LANGUAGE: In this chapter we introduce, discuss, and practice:

1. reflexive verbs and pronouns–that is, verbs that indicate an action that reflects back to the subject, such as *I enjoy myself,* or *the children dress themselves*
2. the reciprocal reflexive, which expresses a reciprocal action on the part of two or more people (*they write to each other, we see each other*)
3. some idiomatic expressions that use the verb **tener**
4. the relative pronouns **que, quien,** and **cuyo**

You will also learn vocabulary related to clothing and fashion.

CULTURE: The dialogue takes place in Barcelona, Spain, where some students are listening to a **tuna** (a group of students who sing and play the guitar).

EXPLICACIÓN

I. THE REFLEXIVE

(1) **Aldo:** Ese traje gris es el que vas a usar para la fiesta ¿verdad?

(2) **José:** No voy a la fiesta; voy a quedar*me* en casa. No *me* divierto en las fiestas.

(3) **Aldo:** Pero José . . . siempre *nos* divertimos mucho, bailamos, hablamos con la gente . . .

(4) **José:** No bailo y no me gusta hablar. Voy a acostar*me* temprano y mañana *me* voy a levantar a las siete.

(5) **Aldo:** ¿*Te* levantas a las siete los domingos? ¡A esa hora, nosotros *nos* acostamos!

1. ¿Va a la fiesta José o se queda en casa? ¿Por qué? **2.** ¿Qué hacen Aldo y sus amigos en las fiestas? **3.** ¿Qué va a hacer José? **4.** ¿A qué hora se levanta José los domingos? **5.** En general ¿qué hace usted a las siete de la mañana los domingos? ¿Se levanta o se acuesta?

A. In a reflexive construction the action of the verb reflects back to and acts upon the subject of the sentence. Examples of the reflexive in English are: *I enjoy myself, the child dresses himself, they seat themselves without waiting.*

REFLEXIVE PRONOUNS			
Singular		*Plural*	
me	*myself*	nos	*ourselves*
te	*yourself*	os	*yourselves*
se	*himself* / *herself* / *yourself* / *itself*	se	*themselves* / *yourselves*

(1) That grey suit is the one you're going to wear for the party, right? (2) I'm not going to the party; I'm going to stay at home. I don't enjoy myself at parties. (3) But, José . . . we always enjoy ourselves, we dance, we talk with people . . . (4) I don't dance and I don't like talking. I'm going to go to bed early and tomorrow I'm getting up at seven o'clock. (5) You get up at seven on Sundays? At that time we go to bed!

Except for the third person **se** (singular and plural) reflexive pronouns have the same forms as direct and indirect object pronouns.

B. Reflexive verbs in Spanish are conjugated with the reflexive pronouns. The pronoun **se** attached to an infinitive indicates that the verb is reflexive.

levantarse *(to get up)*	
me levanto	nos levantamos
te levantas	os levantáis
se levanta	se levantan

C. The following are reflexive verbs. Stem changes are indicated in parentheses.

acostarse (ue)	*to go to bed*	llamarse	*to be named (call oneself)*
acostumbrarse	*to get used to*	probarse (ue)	*to try on*
despertarse (ie)	*to wake up*	quedarse	*to remain, stay*
divertirse (ie)	*to enjoy oneself*	quitarse	*to take off (clothing)*
irse	*to leave*		
lavarse	*to wash*	sentarse (ie)	*to sit down*
despertarse (ie)	*to wake up*	vestirse (i)	*to get dressed*

D. Like indirect and direct object pronouns, reflexive pronouns precede a conjugated form of the verb.

¿Te pruebas la chaqueta anaranjada?	*Will you try on the orange jacket?*
¿Nos sentamos aquí?	*Shall we sit here?*
Me divierto mucho en las fiestas.	*I enjoy myself a lot at parties.*
Entonces, me voy.	*Then I'm leaving.*

E. Reflexive pronouns may also follow and be attached to an infinitive.

¿No vas a quedarte? ⎱ ¿No te vas a quedar? ⎰	*Aren't you going to stay?*
Van a quitarse el abrigo. ⎱ Se van a quitar el abrigo. ⎰	*They're going to take off their coats.**

F. In a sentence with both a reflexive and a direct object pronoun, the reflexive pronoun precedes the direct object pronoun.

Se lava la cara.	*She washes her face.*
Se la lava.	*She washes it.*
¿Te quitas los zapatos?	*Are you taking off your shoes?*
¿Te los quitas?	*Are you taking them off?*

* Note that **el abrigo,** the singular, is used, since it is assumed that each person takes off one coat.

G. Most reflexive verbs are also used non-reflexively. In some cases the use of the reflexive pronoun changes the meaning of the verb.

Se llama Conchita.	Her name is Conchita (she calls herself Conchita). (reflexive)
José llama a Conchita.	José calls Conchita. (non-reflexive)
Me voy ahora.	I'm leaving now. (reflexive)
Voy ahora.	I'm going now. (non-reflexive)
Nos despertamos temprano todos los días.	We wake up early every day. (reflexive)
Despertamos a José a las siete.	We wake José up at seven. (non-reflexive)
Los niños se acuestan temprano.	The children go to bed early. (reflexive)
Los acostamos temprano.	We put them to bed early. (non-reflexive)

Ejercicios

A. Create new sentences, substituting the words in the list for those in italics.

1. *Ellos* se visten para la fiesta.
   a. Rogelio y yo **b.** tú **c.** ustedes **d.** Jorge **e.** yo

2. *Anita* debe quitarse los zapatos.
   a. yo **b.** los niños **c.** usted **d.** tú **e.** nosotros

3. *Carlos y yo* siempre nos levantamos tarde.
   a. mi hermana **b.** los Gutiérrez **c.** yo **d.** ustedes **e.** tú

B. Restate, changing the verbs from the plural to the singular.

1. ¿Nos sentamos aquí?
2. Se acuestan muy tarde.
3. ¿Cómo se llaman ellos?
4. Nos vamos a las siete.
5. Ustedes se van a quitar el abrigo, ¿no?

C. Restate, changing the verbs from the singular to the plural.

1. Me voy a probar el vestido anaranjado.
2. ¿Ya te acuestas?
3. Ella piensa divertirse mucho.
4. No me acostumbro a levantarme temprano.
5. ¿Se va a quedar aquí?

D. Fill the blanks with the correct form of the most appropriate verb in parentheses.

Modelo: Nosotros ____**vamos**____ (ir / irse) de compras los sábados.

1. María _____ (vestir / vestirse) para ir al baile.
2. En general, yo _____ (acostar / acostarse) a mi hijo temprano.

3. ¿A qué hora _____ (levantar / levantarse) tú?
4. Ustedes _____ (divertir / divertirse) en esta clase, ¿no?
5. Jorge prefiere _____ (quedar / quedarse) en casa esta noche.
6. Nosotros _____ (lavar / lavarse) el auto todos los viernes.
7. ¿Cuándo vas a _____ (llamar / llamarse) a Susana?
8. Ahora él debe _____ (ir / irse) porque es muy tarde.

E. Give the Spanish equivalent of the following sentences.

1. I always get up early.
2. When do you go to bed?
3. He calls her every day.
4. We are going to enjoy ourselves at the concert tomorrow.
5. They try on the shoes.
6. She puts them to bed at eight.

Preguntas

1. ¿A qué hora se despierta usted? ¿Y a qué hora se acuesta?   **2.** ¿A qué hora se levanta usted los lunes? ¿los sábados?   **3.** ¿Se divierte usted en las fiestas?   **4.** ¿Va a quedarse en casa esta noche? ¿mañana? ¿este fin de semana?   **5.** ¿Qué hace usted después de despertarse? ¿antes de acostarse?

II. THE RECIPROCAL REFLEXIVE

(1)	**Lola:**	¿Cómo es tu nueva obra de teatro «Tragedia de Amor»? Tengo que diseñar los vestidos para la actriz.
(2)	**Ángel:**	Pues, te la cuento en pocas palabras: primer acto, el hombre y la mujer *se conocen, se quieren, se besan* Segundo acto, no *se comprenden*, no *se hablan*, no *se miran*. Tercer acto . . .
(3)	**Lola:**	Sí, lo adivino: *se gritan, se insultan, se rompen* la ropa, *se matan*. ¡Fin!

1. ¿Cómo se llama la nueva pieza teatral de Ángel?   **2.** ¿Qué pasa (what happens) en el primer acto?   **3.** ¿Y en el segundo?   **4.** ¿Qué hacen en el acto final?

(1) What's your new play "Tragedy of Love" like? I have to design the dresses for the actress. (2) Well, I'll tell you (it) in a few words: first act, the man and the woman meet each other, love each other, kiss each other. Second act, they don't understand each other, they don't talk to each other, they don't look at each other. Third act . . . (3) Yes, I (can) guess: they shout at each other, they insult each other, they tear each other's clothes, they kill each other. The End!

The reflexive pronouns **nos** and **se** may be used with a first or third person plural verb form, respectively, in order to express a reciprocal action. This construction corresponds to the English *each other, one another.*

Se confiesan su amor.	*They confess their love to each other.*
Todos se miran.	*They all look at one another.*
Ya nos entendemos.	*We understand each other now.*
No nos vemos mucho.	*We don't see each other often.*

Ejercicios

A. **Progresión amorosa o «Historia de un amor recíproco.»** To follow Juan and Juanita's love story, complete the puzzle below using the reciprocal reflexive as in the example. The ending of the story will appear in the column marked **Final.** (Allow for a blank between words.)

Modelo: (querer) **Juan y Juanita** s e q u i e r e n **mucho.**

1. (conocer)   Un día él y ella _____ en un baile.
2. (ver)   Otro día _____ en una fiesta.
3. (confesar)   Esa noche _____ su amor.
4. (amar)   Después _____ cada día más.
5. (hablar)   Todos los días _____ por teléfono y
   (ayudar)   _____ siempre.
6. (entender)   Los dos _____ muy bien.

B. Rewrite the story above changing "Juan y Juanita" to "Juan y yo". Include the ending.

Modelo: (querer) **Juan y yo** <u>n o s   q u e r e m o s</u> **mucho.**

1. _____
2. _____
3. _____
4. _____
5. _____
6. _____
7. **Final** _____

Preguntas

1. ¿Nos vemos aquí los domingos? ¿los lunes? ¿los jueves?   2. ¿Se ayudan usted y sus amigos? ¿Se dicen sus problemas?   3. ¿Se entienden usted y su novio(a)? ¿Se necesitan? ¿Se hablan mucho por teléfono?

III. IDIOMATIC EXPRESSIONS WITH **TENER**

En el consultorio del médico:

(1) **El médico:** *¿Cuántos años tiene* usted, señor García?
(2) **Sr. García:** Tengo ochenta y ocho años.
(3) **El médico:** ¿Y por qué está hoy aquí?
(4) **Sr. García:** Porque *tengo sueño* durante el día, y *no tengo ganas* de comer. Además, *tengo* mucha *sed.*
(5) **El médico:** ¿Puede quitarse el abrigo y la camisa? Voy a examinarlo.
(6) **El médico:** Bueno . . . usted está bien, pero debe *tener cuidado* con la bebida. En general, su salud es excelente.
(7) **Sr. García:** ¡Qué *suerte tengo!* Voy a morir sano.

1. ¿Cuántos años tiene el señor García?   2. ¿Qué problemas tiene?   3. ¿Con qué debe tener cuidado?   4. ¿Por qué tiene suerte el señor García?

At the doctor's office:
(1) How old are you, Mr. García? (2) I'm eighty-eight years old. (3) And why are you here today? (4) Because I'm sleepy during the day, and I don't feel like eating. Besides, I'm very thirsty. (5) Can you take off your coat and shirt? I'm going to examine you. (6) Well . . . you are fine, but you should be careful about drinking (alcohol). In general, your health is excellent. (7) How lucky I am! I'm going to die healthy.

A. There are many expressions in Spanish that use the verb **tener.**

tener ganas de	*to feel like to*
tener . . . años	*to be . . . years old*
tener prisa	*to be in a hurry*
Tenemos prisa. Vamos de compras.	*We are in a hurry. We are going shopping.*
Tengo ganas de comprar una falda negra y una blusa roja.	*I feel like buying a black skirt and a red blouse.*
Marisa tiene diez años. ¿Y Jorge?	*Marisa is ten years old. And Jorge?*

B. The construction **tener** + a noun can often be rendered in English by the verb *to be* + an adjective.

tener		to be	
	cuidado		*careful*
	razón		*right*
	sueño		*sleepy*
	hambre		*hungry*
	sed		*thirsty*
	suerte		*lucky*

C. In other instances **tener** is equivalent to *to have,* but note that the indefinite article is not used in Spanish in these cases.

tener dolor de cabeza, de estómago	*to have a headache, a stomach ache*
tener fiebre	*to have a fever*

Ejercicios

A. Fill the blanks with the most appropriate expression from the list below.

tener frío	tener razón
tener sueño	tener cuidado
tener sed	tener . . . años
tener ganas de	tener calor

1. El niño no duerme porque no _____.
2. Yo _____ quitarme el abrigo porque _____.
3. Papá _____. Hoy es el 12 de mayo.
4. El doctor dice que tú debes _____ con la bebida.
5. Susanita es muy grande. ¿Cuántos _____ ella?
6. ¿Por qué no piden cerveza si _____?
7. Nosotros vamos a llevar el abrigo porque _____.

B. Give the Spanish equivalent of the following sentences.

1. You (*ustedes*) are right. Juan is twenty years old.
2. I'm cold because it's very cold here.

3. He is hungry and she is thirsty.
4. You (*tú*) are always sleepy because you have to get up early.
5. We feel like going shopping today.

Preguntas

1. ¿Cuántos años tiene usted? ¿su mamá? ¿su papá? ¿su hermano(a)? **2.** ¿Tiene hambre ahora? ¿sed? **3.** ¿Tiene usted dolor de cabeza cuando estudia mucho? ¿cuando escribe una composición? **4.** ¿Tiene usted sueño? ¿calor? ¿frío? **5.** ¿Tiene usted ganas de ir al cine? ¿de ir a su casa?

IV. RELATIVE PRONOUNS **QUE, QUIEN, CUYO**

GRAN LIQUIDACIÓN DE TIENDAS «LA ELEGANCIA»

Impermeables y sombreros para aquéllas a *quienes* les importa vestirse bien.

Blusas y faldas *cuyo* corte es sinónimo de distinción.

Zapatos, sandalias, y botas en diferentes tonos de marrón—el color *que* está de moda.

1. Según el anuncio (*ad*), ¿para quiénes son los impermeables que están en liquidación? **2.** ¿Qué tipo de blusas hay en la tienda? **3.** ¿Qué tipo de zapatos tienen?

A. **Que** is the most commonly-used equivalent for *that, which, who,* or *whom,* when referring to either persons or things.

Ese vestido violeta que me gusta es un poco caro.	*That purple dress (that) I like is a bit expensive.*
Éstos son los calcetines de que hablo.	*These are the socks (which) I'm talking about.*
El hombre que lleva la camisa azul y amarilla es mi primo.	*The man who is wearing the blue and yellow shirt is my cousin.*
¿Quién es la mujer que abre el paraguas dentro de la casa?	*Who is the woman (who is) opening the umbrella inside the house?*

Frequently the relative pronoun (*that, which, who*) is omitted in English, but in Spanish it is always used.

Big Sale at "La Elegancia" stores
Raincoats and hats for those to whom dressing well is important.
Blouses and skirts whose cut is synonymous with distinction.
Shoes, sandals, and boots in various shades of brown—the color that is fashionable.

B. **Quien** (**quienes** in the plural) refers only to people. It is usually used as the object of a preposition. When used as an indirect object, **quien** (**quienes**) must be preceded by the preposition **a**.

Es el ingeniero de quien tú me
  hablas, ¿verdad?
Ésos son los amigos con quienes
  cenamos esta noche.
Ésta es la chica a quien le importa
  mucho la moda.

*He's the engineer you are telling me
  about, right?*
*Those are the friends we are having
  dinner with tonight.*
*This is the girl who cares very much
  about fashion.*

C. **Cuyo** means *whose* or *of which*. It agrees with the noun it modifies, not the possessor.

Adriana es la señora cuyo esposo
  siempre lleva una corbata verde.
El senor Blanco es el señor cuya hija
  trabaja en esta tienda.
Es la ciudad cuyo nombre nunca
  recuerdo.

*Adriana is the woman whose husband
  always wears a green tie.*
*Mr. Blanco is the man whose daughter
  works in this store.*
*It's the city the name of which I never
  remember.*

Ejercicios

A. Complete each of the following sentences with **que, quien(es)**, or a form of **cuyo**.

1. Éste es el vestido _____ quiero comprar
2. ¿Dónde están los calcetines _____ necesitas?
3. Aquí vive la chica _____ padres son amigos de mi tía.
4. ¿A qué hora vuelve la persona con _____ tenemos que hablar?
5. Carmen y Enrique son los amigos a _____ siempre recuerdas, ¿no?
6. ¿Sabe cuánto cuesta el abrigo violeta _____ me gusta? . . . ¡Mil dólares!

B. Circle the relative pronoun which best completes each of the following sentences.

Modelo: Allí viene el profesor de (que, (quien,) cuyo) siempre te hablo.

1. ¿Es ésta la camisa marrón (quien, cuya, que) usted quiere comprar?
2. Conocemos a unos estudiantes (quienes, que, cuyos) saben bailar el tango.
3. José Martí es el poeta (cuya, que, cuyo) poema «Domingo triste» me fascina.
4. ¿Cuándo llegan los pasajeros con (que, quienes, quien) vamos a viajar?
5. No veo la blusa azul y verde de (cuya, quien, que) ustedes hablan.

C. Give the Spanish equivalent of the following sentences.

1. Those are the shoes I want to buy.
2. The woman I am talking about is going to stay here tonight.
3. Mr. Rodríguez is the man whose sister is a doctor.
4. That yellow shirt that he likes is very expensive.

5. The person you (*tú*) see there is Amalia's husband.

6. They are the students whose teacher is leaving this week.

Preguntas

1. ¿Cuál es el color de ojos que más le gusta? ¿Tiene usted ese color de ojos? **2.** ¿Qué debe hacer una persona que tiene dolor de cabeza? ¿que tiene fiebre? **3.** ¿Cómo se llama la ropa que uno lleva cuando hace frío? **4.** ¿Habló usted con alguien anoche? ¿Dónde vive la persona con quien habló? **5.** ¿Cómo se llama el actor o la actriz a quien usted más admira? ¿Por qué? ¿el escritor o la escritora cuyas obras a usted le gusta leer?

LAS RAMBLAS

Dos muchachos españoles y dos muchachas norteamericanas están de paseo por las Ramblas de Barcelona.[1]

Hugo:	¿Nos sentamos aquí?
Sharon:	Bueno. ¿Qué tienen ganas de tomar?
Hugo:	¿Les gusta la sangría?[2]
Patsy:	Me encanta la sangría cuando tengo sed.
	Llega Omar
Omar:	¡Hola, guapas! ¡Qué vestidos tan elegantes! Voy a sentarme aquí para poder mirarlas.
Hugo:	Hay que tener cuidado, Patsy. Omar es el muchacho de quien te hablé. Siempre dice piropos.[3]
Patsy:	Entonces, me levanto y me voy.
Sharon:	¡Bah!, no es para tanto. Omar es inofensivo.
Patsy:	Bueno, me quedo entonces. Pero no puedo acostumbrarme a los piropos.
Sharon:	A veces son simpáticos. ¡Ay, qué suerte! ¡Ahora llega la tuna![4]
La tuna:	«Me gustan todas, me gustan todas, me gustan todas en general. Pero esa rubia, pero esa rubia, pero esa rubia me gusta más».

Sharon:	Me fascina esa música, pero ¿por qué no se quitan las capas? Deben tener calor con esa ropa tan pesada.
Omar:	¿Crees que debajo llevan más ropa?
Hugo:	¡Claro que sí! Pero creo que no llevan corbata, como tú. ¿Más sangría?
Patsy:	No, gracias, tengo que conducir.
Omar:	No tienes que preocuparte, preciosa. Puedo llevarte a tu casa.
Patsy:	Por eso me preocupo.
Sharon:	Bueno, chicos, basta de discusiones. Tenemos que irnos porque es tarde. Pero nosotras nos vemos mañana en el desfile de modas ¿verdad Patsy?
Omar:	Ustedes no necesitan vestirse a la moda para ser hermosas.
Patsy:	¿Crees, Sharon, que hay remedio para esta manía?
Sharon:	Creo que es incurable.

no es para tanto *it isn't that important*   **capas** *capes*   **pesada** *heavy*   **desfile** *show*
manía *mania, madness*

Preguntas

1. ¿Dónde están las muchachas norteamericanas y los muchachos españoles?   **2.** ¿Tienen hambre o sed? ¿Qué piden?   **3.** ¿Quién dice siempre piropos?   **4.** ¿Por qué se levanta Patsy?   **5.** ¿A qué no puede acostumbrarse ella?   **6.** ¿Quiénes llegan a cantar?   **7.** ¿Cree Hugo que llevan camisa y pantalón debajo de las capas?   **8.** ¿Por qué no acepta más sangría Patsy?   **9.** ¿Quiénes van a verse en el desfile de modas?   **10.** ¿Qué piensa usted de la costumbre de decir piropos?

NOTAS CULTURALES

1. The main axis of the old section of Barcelona is formed by **Las Ramblas,** a series of wide, tree-lined avenues. Las Ramblas, a favorite promenade renowned for its charm, has seats beneath the trees along both sides and many stalls where birds and flowers are sold. There are also many cafés along the sidewalks.

2. Sangría is a traditional Spanish punch made of red wine, lemon and other fruit juices, sugar, and sometimes a shot of cognac.

3. Piropos are elaborate compliments made by men to women, often to women passing by on the street. Some Spaniards consider it an art to be able to instantly devise a piropo appropriate to a particular occasion. This is a time-honored custom and is usually not taken as harmful or offensive.

4. The **tunas** are groups of students who sing and play guitars and other instruments, usually receiving some recompense from bystanders. This is a tradition which goes back to the Middle Ages, when many a poor scholar did indeed have to sing for his supper. Nowadays, each school within a university generally has its own tuna. Sometimes the students stroll through the streets at night, dressed in academic gowns, and serenade their girlfriends. Often the girlfriends toss down ribbons to them to wear on their robes.

ACTIVIDADES

En la Tienda «La Elegancia»

The clerk at Tienda ''La Elegancia'' is trying to encourage customers to buy some clothing. Complete the sentences he might say with the names of the appropriate items.

1. ¿Se queda usted en casa porque llueve (*it rains*)? ¿Por qué no se compra un _____ y un _____?
2. ¿Hace mucho sol? Usted necesita un _____.

Prendas de vestir   **155**

3. Para ir a un restaurante elegante, señor, debe usar _____ y _____.
4. Para el frío del invierno usted necesita este _____ y estas _____.
5. Para una fiesta, señorita, puede comprarse una _____ larga o un _____ elegante.
6. No señor, ésas son blusas para señoras; pero acá hay algunas _____ para usted.

Entrevista

Ask a classmate the following questions. Then report the information to the class.

1. Tú y tus amigos ¿se ven mucho?
2. ¿Vas a quedarte en casa esta noche?
3. ¿A qué hora te acuestas los sábados?
4. ¿A qué hora te levantas los domingos?
5. ¿Tienes hambre ahora? ¿Sueño? ¿Sed?
6. ¿Tienes dolor de cabeza durante los exámenes?

Situación

En un café al aire libre

Two young women, Sandy, an American, and Pilar, a Spaniard, are seated at an open-air cafe in Madrid. They call the waiter and give him their order, and then begin discussing fashions. Alberto and Javier, who study at the University with Pilar, walk by. They stop to chat and Javier begins saying **piropos** to Sandy. She becomes upset and says she does not like **piropos** and cannot become accustomed to them. The others begin discussing the custom. Javier says it is pleasant and harmless, but Pilar and Alberto claim it is old-fashioned **(anticuado)** and that modern young people do not do it. They end up agreeing to go together that evening to a concert being given by several **tunas** from the University.

VOCABULARIO ACTIVO

Verbos útiles

acostar (ue) *to put to bed;* **acostarse** *to go to bed*
acostumbrarse *to get used to*
besar *to kiss*
confesar(ie) *to confess*
despertarse(ie) *to wake up*
divertir(i) *to amuse, entertain;* **divertirse** *to enjoy oneself, have a good time*

examinar *to examine*
gritar *to shout, yell*
insultar *to insult*
irse *to go away*
lavar *to wash;* **lavarse** *to wash oneself*
levantar *to raise;* **levantarse** *to get up, stand up*
llamarse *to be called*
matar *to kill*
morir(ue) *to die*

pasar *to happen;* **¿Qué pasa?** *What happens?*

quedar *to be left, remain;* **quedarse** *to stay*

quitarse *to take off*

sentarse(ie) *to sit down, be seated*

vestir(i) *to dress;* **vestirse** *to get dressed*

Modismos con el verbo tener

tener . . . años *to be . . . years old;* **¿Cuántos años tienes?** *How old are you?*

tener cuidado *to be careful*

tener dolor de cabeza (estómago) *to have a headache (stomach ache)*

tener fiebre *to have a fever*

tener ganas de + inf. *to feel like + pres. part*

tener hambre *to be hungry*

tener prisa *to be in a hurry*

tener razón *to be right*

tener sed *to be thirsty*

tener sueño *to be sleepy*

tener suerte *to be lucky*

La ropa

el abrigo *coat (winter coat)*

la blusa *blouse*

la bota *boot*

el calcetín *sock*

la camisa *shirt*

la corbata *tie*

el corte *cut (style)*

la chaqueta *jacket*

la falda *skirt*

el impermeable *raincoat*

la moda *fashion*

el pantalón *pair of pants;* **los pantalones** *pants*

el paraguas *umbrella*

prendas de vestir *garments*

la ropa *clothing*

la sandalia *sandal*

el sombrero *hat*

el traje *suit; outfit*

el vestido *dress*

el zapato *shoe*

Los colores

amarillo(a) *yellow*

anaranjado(a) *orange*

azul *blue*

gris *grey*

marrón *brown*

negro(a) *black*

rojo(a) *red*

verde *green*

violeta *purple*

Otras palabras útiles

Basta de . . . *Enough . . .*

cuyo *whose, of which*

inofensivo(a) *harmless*

la liquidación *sale, liquidation*

más *more*

nuevo(a) *new*

poco(a) (adj) *few*

que *that, which, who, whom*

quien *who, whom*

el remedio *cure, remedy*

rubio(a) *blond*

la salud *health*

sano(a) *healthy*

La Música

En España hay una gran variedad de música y bailes folklóricos. Estos jóvenes son de Cataluña y bailan la sardana, baile típico de esa región noreste. La sardana es un baile muy antiguo y *refleja*, como muchos otros bailes regionales, características culturales particulares y el amor que la gente *siente* por su región. Cada región de España tiene su música y baile característicos. Puede ser la muñeira melancólica de Galicia, la jota rápida de Aragón o el zortzico vasco. La gente del lugar conoce su baile y sabe bailarlo con gusto, especialmente en las fiestas. Un baile famoso es el flamenco de Andalucía.

reflect

feel

Es un baile muy sensual, acompañado de voz, guitarra y *castañuelas*. castanets
Tradicionalmente, los *gitanos* son los maestros del flamenco. gypsies

También es rico y variado el folklore de Hispanoamérica. Aquí la
música y los bailes reflejan una combinación de elementos indígenas, españoles y, a veces, africanos. En general, los instrumentos
musicales de *cuerda* son de origen español, los de viento de origen string
indio, y los de percusión de origen africano. Instrumentos típicos
hispanoamericanos son, por ejemplo, el *arpa paraguaya*, las diferen- Paraguayan harp
tes *flautas* indígenas en la región de los Andes (la quena en el Perú flutes
o la zampoña en Bolivia); las guitarras y sus diversas variantes como
el *charango* en la región *andina*, la *vihuela* en el Río de la Plata y el guitar made from shell
guitarrón de México.   of an armadillo /
  Andean / an early
  guitar
large guitar

El papel que en los tiempos medievales tienen los *juglares* y tro- minstrels
vadores en España corresponde hoy día a los *payadores* de la Argen- Gaucho singers
tina y del Uruguay aunque ya quedan pocos. El payador canta
melodías tristes sobre la vida solitaria del gaucho y sobre sus desi-
lusiones amorosas, o improvisa canciones que acompaña con la guitarra. Muy populares son las payadas o *competencias* entre dos pa- competitions
yadores que *se turnan*. Cada uno canta, *improvisando la letra*. Muchas take turns / improvising
veces, los espectadores dan los *temas* y los payadores tienen que   lyrics / themes, subjects
componer canciones sobre ellos. La competencia puede *durar* horas last
o días.

Vemos en la fotografía a unos artistas del famoso Ballet Folklórico de México. Pero la música mexicana no es la única que busca su inspiración en el folklore. Así, por ejemplo, las melodías tristes de la quena andina, los sonoros ritmos del Caribe y muchos otros temas y tradiciones indígenas *influyen* en la música *actual* de toda Hispanoamérica. *Actualmente*, gente de *todo el mundo* conoce y baila ritmos típicos hispanoamericanos como el tango, la samba, la rumba, el mambo o el cha-cha-chá.

have influence / of the present
Nowadays / the whole world

Preguntas

1. ¿Cómo se llama el baile típico de Cataluña?
2. ¿De dónde son la muñeira, la jota y el zortzico?
3. ¿En qué lugar de España bailan el flamenco?
4. ¿Cuál es la combinación de elementos que está presente en la música de Hispanoamérica?
5. ¿Cuáles son algunos de los instrumentos típicos de Hispanoamérica?
6. ¿Dónde hay payadores? ¿Qué hacen?
7. ¿Dónde busca inspiración la música latinoamericana?
8. ¿Cómo se llaman algunos de los ritmos típicos de Latinoamérica?
9. ¿Conoce a algún músico o cantante hispanoamericano?

CAPÍTULO 9

DEPORTES

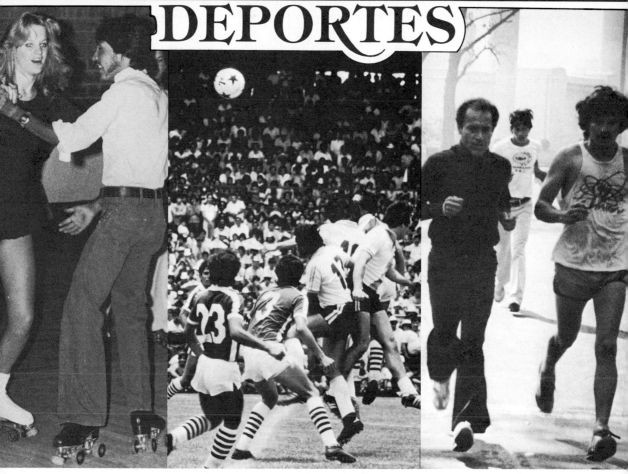

¿Vamos a . . . patinar, jugar al fútbol, correr?

OBJECTIVES

LANGUAGE: In this chapter we introduce, discuss, and practice:
1. a past tense, the preterite, of regular and stem-changing verbs
2. the formation and use of adverbs that end in **-mente**
3. comparisons of equality (*as . . . as*)
4. comparisons of inequality (*more or less . . . than*) and the superlative (*the most or least . . .*)

You will also learn vocabulary related to sporting events.

CULTURE: The dialogue takes place in Santander, Spain, where two couples are discussing jai alai, soccer, and bullfighting, three very popular sports in the Hispanic world.

EXPLICACIÓN

I. THE PRETERITE OF REGULAR VERBS (AND STEM-CHANGING VERBS)

(1)	**Eva:**	Te *llamé* anoche, Alfonso, pero no *contestaste*.
(2)	**Alfonso:**	*Asistí* a un partido de jai alai* con Elena.
(3)	**Eva:**	¿Les *gustó*?
(4)	**Alfonso:**	Sí, mucho. Pedro Ramos y Paco González *jugaron* muy bien.
(5)	**Eva:**	¿*Ganaste* dinero?
(6)	**Alfonso:**	*Perdí* treinta pesos, pero Elena *ganó* cuarenta. Así que *ganamos* diez. Y *nos divertimos mucho*.

1. ¿A quién llamó Eva?   **2.** ¿Contestó él el teléfono?   **3.** ¿A qué asistieron Elena y Alfonso?   **4.** ¿Les gustó el partido?   **5.** ¿Quiénes jugaron bien?   **6.** ¿Ganó Alfonso dinero? ¿Y Elena?   **7.** ¿Asistió usted a un partido de jai alai alguna vez?

A. The preterite tense is used to relate actions or events that occurred and were completed at a specific time or within a definite period in the past. The preterite tense of regular **-ar** verbs is formed by adding the endings **-é, -aste, -ó, -amos, -asteis, -aron** to the stem.

comprar	
compr**é**	compr**amos**
compr**aste**	compr**asteis**
compr**ó**	compr**aron**

Tres jugadores importantes no participaron en el partido de ayer.

Three important players did not participate in yesterday's game.

---

(1) I called you last night, Alfonso, but you didn't answer. (2) I went to a jai alai game with Elena. (3) Did you like it? (4) Yes, very much. Pedro Ramos and Paco González played very well. (5) Did you win money? (6) I lost thirty pesos, but Elena won forty. So we won ten. And we had a very good time.

* See **Notas culturales** page 175

B. The preterite tense of regular **-er** and **-ir** verbs is formed by adding the endings **-í, -iste, -ió, -imos, -isteis, -ieron** to the stem.

correr		escribir	
corrí	corrimos	escribí	escribimos
corriste	corristeis	escribiste	escribisteis
corrió	corrieron	escribió	escribieron

Aprendí a jugar al basquetbol.   *I learned how to play basketball.*
Escribieron un artículo sobre el   *They wrote an article about the team.*
  equipo.

C. While the preterite forms of stem-changing **-ar** and **-er** verbs are all regular (**pensé, volví**), stem-changing **-ir** verbs show a change in the third persons singular and plural of the preterite tense. The stem change is from **e** to **i** or **o** to **u**.

pedir		dormir		volver	
pedí	pedimos	dormí	dormimos	volví	volvimos
pediste	pedisteis	dormiste	dormisteis	volviste	volvisteis
pidió	pidieron	durmió	durmieron	volvió	volvieron

Other verbs that are conjugated like **pedir** are: **divertirse, seguir, servir,** and **preferir. Morir** is conjugated like **dormir.**

Alfredo siguió tres cursos el semestre   *Alfredo took three courses last semester.*
  pasado.
Murieron tres toreros el año pasado   *Three bullfighters died last year in the*
  en las corridas de toros.   *bullfights.*

D. A number of verbs have a spelling change in the first person singular of the preterite tense. Verbs ending in **-gar, -car,** and **-zar** have the following spelling changes, respectively: **g** to **gu, c** to **qu,** and **z** to **c**. These changes are required to preserve the sound of the last syllable of the infinitive.

llegar		tocar		empezar	
llegué	llegamos	toqué	tocamos	empecé	empezamos
llegaste	llegasteis	tocaste	tocasteis	empezaste	empezasteis
llegó	llegaron	tocó	tocaron	empezó	empezaron

Te busqué anoche en el partido de   *I looked for you last night at the soccer*
  fútbol.   *game.*
Llegué a las ocho ayer.   *I arrived at eight o'clock yesterday.*

E. Verbs such as **creer** and **leer** show an orthographic change in the third-persons singular and plural: **creyó, creyeron; leyó, leyeron**. The other forms are regular. This change is made because an **i** between two vowels becomes a **y**.

Leyó que el béisbol es un deporte muy popular en Centroamérica y México.	*He read that baseball is a very popular sport in Central America and Mexico.*

Ejercicios

A. Create new sentences, substituting the words in the list for those in italics.

1. *Ana* buscó al jugador y lo encontró.
   a. yo **b.** tú **c.** nosotros **d.** mi hermano **e.** ustedes
2. Anoche *Paco y yo* asistimos a un partido de fútbol.
   a. Silvia **b.** tus padres **c.** tú **d.** los García **e.** yo
3. *Tú* pediste café, ¿no?
   a. el jugador **b.** papá y yo **c.** ustedes **d.** yo **e.** los Méndez
4. ¿Durmió *usted* bien anoche?
   a. ella **b.** tú **c.** ustedes **d.** nosotros **e.** Ana y Antonio
5. ¿A qué hora llegaron *ustedes* ayer?
   a. tú **b.** los jugadores **c.** yo **d.** usted **e.** Juan y yo

B. Restate, changing the verbs to the preterite.

1. Ella gana cien pesos.
2. Paco sigue un curso de inglés.
3. Empiezo a estudiar a las diez.
4. ¿Juegan ustedes al tenis?
5. Hablamos de la corrida de toro
6. ¿Cuántos cursos sigues?
7. El torero vuelve en unos minutos.
8. ¿Se divierte Patricia en la fiesta?
9. Comemos en casa de los Pérez.
10. Yo toco el piano y Mario canta.
11. Ellos prefieren ir al cine.
12. ¿Te gusta el vino que tomas?

C. Make appropriate questions to complete the following dialogue.

Modelo: Tito: **—¿Asististe al partido o lo miraste por televisión?**
Luis: **—Asistí al partido.**

Tito: — _____
Luis: —El partido empezó a las dos.
Tito: — _____
Luis: —Sí, mis padres también asistieron al partido.
Tito: — _____
Luis: —¡Sí, les gustó muchísimo!
Tito: — _____
Luis: —No, no dormí mucho anoche.
Tito: — _____
Luis: —Porque estudié unas horas para el examen de hoy.
Tito: — _____
Luis: —No, escribí un examen horrible...
Tito: — _____
Luis: —Estudié poco porque preferí ver el partido.

D. Give the Spanish equivalent of the following sentences.

1. She asked for cold beer.
2. Who did you talk to last night?
3. They wrote an article about basketball.
4. He called Mary but she didn't answer.
5. Did you (*tú*) have a good time at the movies?
6. The players returned from Asunción yesterday.
7. The team played very well.
8. How many courses did you take last semester?

Preguntas

1. ¿A qué hora cenó usted anoche? **2.** ¿Miró la televisión? ¿Qué programa(s) miró? **3.** ¿Habló con un(a) amigo(a) por teléfono? ¿De qué hablaron? **4.** ¿Leyó un libro o una revista (*magazine*) interesante? ¿Cuál? **5.** ¿Escribió cartas? ¿a quién(es)? **6.** ¿Durmió bien anoche? ¿Cuántas horas durmió? **7.** ¿Llegó tarde a clase? ¿A qué hora llegó aquí?

II. FORMATION AND USE OF ADVERBS IN -MENTE

Un profesor y un estudiante observan cuidadosamente el cielo.

(1) **Estudiante:** ¡Qué suerte! Mañana vamos a poder ir a nadar. Ahora estoy *completamente* seguro de que vamos a tener buen tiempo.

(2) **Profesor:** Y yo estoy *absolutamente* seguro de que mañana va a llover.

(3) **Estudiante:** *¿Realmente?* ¿Cómo puede estar usted *totalmente* seguro?

(4) **Profesor:** Porque hoy me duelen *terriblemente* los huesos.

1. ¿Por qué está contento el estudiante? **2.** ¿De qué está absolutamente seguro el profesor? **3.** ¿Cómo puede estar totalmente seguro?

A. Most adverbs in Spanish are derived from the feminine form of an adjective plus the suffix **-mente**.

lento → lenta	→ lentamente *slowly*
preciso → precisa	→ precisamente *precisely*
rápido → rápida	→ rápidamente *rapidly*

A professor and a student are carefully observing the sky.
(1) What luck! Tomorrow we're going to be able to go swimming. Now I'm completely sure that we're going to have good weather. (2) And I'm absolutely sure that tomorrow it's going to rain. (3) Really? How can you be completely sure? (4) Because today my bones ache terribly.

Those adjectives that are not simple add **-mente**.

fácil	→ fácilmente *easily*
probable	→ probablemente *probably*
feliz	→ felizmente *happily*

B. An adverb modifying a verb usually follows it directly or is placed as close to it as possible.

Nadaron cuidadosamente hacia la isla.	*They swam carefully toward the island.*
Vamos directamente al partido de tenis.	*We're going directly to the tennis match.*

C. An adverb modifying an adjective usually precedes it.

La carrera de automóviles es un deporte verdaderamente peligroso.	*Automobile racing is a truly dangerous sport.*

D. When there are two or more adverbs in a series, the **-mente** ending is used only with the final adverb.

El profesor explica la lección lenta y claramente.	*The professor explains the lesson slowly and carefully.*
Los aficionados gritaron alegre y entusiastamente.	*The fans yelled happily and enthusiastically.*

Ejercicios

A. Make adverbs from the following adjectives.

1. total	2. absoluto	3. preciso	4. directo	5. posible
6. rápido	7. general	8. verdadero	9. amable	10. completo

B. Create new sentences substituting the appropriate adverb for the words in italics.

Modelo: Lo observaron *de manera clara.* **Lo observaron claramente.**

1. *En realidad* jugaron muy bien.
2. Me lo pidió *de manera especial.*
3. *En general,* ¿qué haces los sábados?
4. ¿Por qué no me llamaron *de inmediato?*
5. ¿Lo aprendiste *por completo?*
6. ¿Juegan al fútbol *de manera regular?*

C. Answer the following questions using the adverbial form of the adjective(s) in parentheses.

Modelos: ¿Cómo jugaron? (horrible) **Jugamos horriblemente.**

¿Cómo lo explicaron? (rápido, claro) **Lo explicamos rápida y claramente.**

1. ¿Cómo nadaron? (cuidadoso, lento)
2. ¿Cómo comieron? (lento)
3. ¿Cómo llegaron? (fácil)
4. ¿Cómo lo leyeron? (correcto, rápido)
5. ¿Cómo volvieron? (alegre)
6. ¿Cómo durmieron? (terrible)

Preguntas

1. ¿Habla usted correctamente el español? ¿el inglés? **2.** ¿Qué hace usted generalmente a las once de la noche? **3.** ¿Qué deporte(s) practica usted regularmente? **4.** ¿Sabe usted nadar? ¿Nada usted lentamente? ¿rápidamente? **5.** ¿Cómo está usted físicamente? ¿académicamente? ¿sicológicamente?

III. COMPARISONS OF EQUALITY (ADJECTIVES AND ADVERBS)

En un gimnasio.

(1) **Teresa:** ¿Por qué buscas otro apartamento?

(2) **Bárbara:** No quiero pagar *tanto como* pago ahora. Además, el apartamento que tengo es muy pequeño. Cuando vienen tres personas, ¡una tiene que sentarse en el corredor!

(3) **Teresa:** No es *tan pequeño como* mi cuarto. Allí, cuando entra el sol, ¡tengo que irme yo!

1. ¿Por qué busca Bárbara otro apartamento? **2.** ¿Es su apartamento muy pequeño? **3.** ¿Es tan pequeño como el cuarto de Teresa?

A. Comparisons of equality are formed by using **tan . . . como** and **tanto (-a, -os, -as) . . . como.**

Juana es tan alta como Pablo.	*Juana is as tall as Pablo.*
No hay tantos espectadores hoy como ayer.	*There are not as many spectators today as yesterday.*

In a gymnasium.
(1) Why are you looking for another apartment? (2) I don't want to pay as much as I pay now. Besides, the apartment (that) I have is very small. When three people come in, one has to sit in the hall! (3) It's not as small as my room. There, when the sun comes in, I have to leave!

Él hace tanto ejercicio como yo.   *He does as much exercise as I do.*
No llovió tanto este año como el año   *It didn't rain as much this year as last*
  pasado.   *year.*

Tan is used before an adjective. Before a noun, **tanto (-a, -os, -as)** is used.
Tanto como means *as much as.*

B. **Tan** can also mean *so:* **¡Es tan inteligente!**

Ejercicios

A. Create new sentences, substituting the words in the list for those in italics.

1. Silvana asistió a tantos *partidos* como Sergio.
    a. conciertos **b.** clases **c.** bailes **d.** fiestas **e.** espectáculos
2. Estos jugadores tienen tanta *suerte* como aquéllos.
    a. dinero **b.** sed **c.** cuidado **d.** hambre **e.** calor
3. *Rubén* es tan pequeño como Alfonso.
    a. Luisa **b.** tus amigos **c.** esas personas **d.** Tito y Mirta **e.** Juan

B. Make sentences in the present using the comparative of equality, as in the examples.

Modelos: Carlos/ganar/dinero/Luis **Carlos gana tanto dinero como Luis.**
            Ellas/ser/celoso/ellos **Ellas son tan celosas como ellos.**

1. María/ser/simpático/su hermana
2. Los Gutiérrez/tener/suerte/nosotros
3. Tú/seguir/cursos/yo
4. Esos muchachos/ser/frío/Roberto

5. Usted/conocer/ciudades/su esposo
6. Jaime/ser/aburrido/Antonio
7. Este equipo/perder/partidos/aquel otro
8. Anita y Teresita/ser/pequeño/tus hijas
9. Nosotros/bailar/horas/ustedes
10. Estos ejercicios/ser/interesante/los otros

Preguntas

1. ¿Le gusta a usted el tenis tanto como el basquetbol? ¿el béisbol tanto como el fútbol? **2.** ¿Sigue usted tantos cursos ahora como el semestre pasado? ¿Estudia usted tanto? ¿Trabaja tanto? **3.** ¿Asiste usted a tantos partidos este año como el año pasado? **4.** ¿Tiene usted tiempo de ver tantas películas por semana como en el pasado? ¿de ir a tantos conciertos? ¿de leer tantas novelas? **5.** ¿Tiene usted tantos amigos como amigas? **6.** ¿Participa usted en tantas actividades culturales como sus amigos? ¿en tantos deportes?

IV. COMPARISONS OF INEQUALITY AND THE SUPERLATIVE

(1)	**Adela:**	Eduardo, ¿son mis ojos *más brillantes que* el sol?
(2)	**Eduardo:**	Sí, Adela, son *brillantísimos*.
(3)	**Adela:**	Y soy *la mejor* jugadora del equipo, ¿verdad?
(4)	**Eduardo:**	Claro, Adela, *la mejor*.
(5)	**Adela:**	¿Y soy *la muchacha más inteligente y menos vanidosa* que conoces?
(6)	**Eduardo:**	¡Por supuesto!
(7)	**Adela:**	Ah, Eduardo, ¡sólo tú puedes decir cosas tan lindas!

1. Según Eduardo, ¿quién tiene ojos más brillantes que el sol? **2.** ¿Y quién es la mejor jugadora del equipo? **3.** ¿Quién es la chica más inteligente y menos vanidosa que conoce Eduardo, según él?

A. Comparisons of Inequality

1. In Spanish, comparisons of inequality are expressed with **más** (*more*) . . . **que** or **menos** (*less*) . . . **que**. *More than* is expressed as **más que,** and *less than* is **menos que.**

---

(1) Eduardo, are my eyes brighter than the sun? (2) Yes, Adela, they're very bright. (3) And I'm the best player on the team, right? (4) Of course, Adela, the best. (5) And am I the most intelligent and least vain girl that you know? (6) Of course! (7) Oh, Eduardo! Only you can say such beautiful things!

Es un deporte más emocionante que el fútbol.	*It's a more exciting sport than soccer.*
Juan corre más rápidamente que los otros jugadores.	*Juan runs faster than the other players.*
Siempre tengo menos dinero que él.	*I always have less money than he does.*
Esta raqueta de tenis es menos cara que la otra.	*This tennis racquet is less expensive than the other one.*
Solamente Luis ganó más que nosotros.	*Only Luis won more than we did.*
Llovió menos hoy que ayer.	*It rained less today than yesterday.*

2. Before a number, **de** is used instead of **que** to mean *than*.*

Parecieron más de diez minutos.	*It seemed like more than ten minutes.*
Menos de cincuenta aficionados asistieron.	*Fewer than fifty fans attended.*

B. The Superlative

1. The superlative (*the most, the least . . .*) is formed by placing a definite article before the comparative.

un jugador importante	*an important player*
un jugador más importante	*a more important player*
el jugador más importante del equipo	*the most important player on the team*
Esteban es el más (menos) trabajador de la familia.	*Esteban is the most (least) hard-working in the family.*
Julia nadó más rápidamente.	*Julia swam the fastest.*
¿Quién perdió más (menos)?	*Who lost the most (the least)?*

Notice that **de** is used after a superlative to express the English *in* or *of*: **Ella es la mujer más atlética del grupo.** *She's the most athletic woman of the group.* Notice also that the noun is not always expressed: **Ella es la más atlética del grupo.** *She's the most athletic (one) of the group.*

2. While the superlative of adverbs does not require a definite article, as seen above, superlative adverbs followed by a phrase expressing possibility are preceded by **lo.**

José quiere saber el resultado del partido lo más pronto posible.	*José wants to know the score of the game as soon as possible.*
Lisa explica la lección lo más claramente que puede.	*Lisa is explaining the lesson as clearly as she can.*

---

* However, in a negative sentence, **que** can be used with the meaning of *only*: **No tengo más que diez centavos.** *I have only ten cents.*

C. Irregular Comparative and Superlative Forms

Adjective	Comparative	Superlative
bueno *good*	mejor *better*	el mejor *best*
malo *bad*	peor *worse*	el peor *worst*
pequeño *small*	menor (más pequeño) *younger (smaller)*	el menor (el más pequeño) *youngest (smallest)*
grande *big*	mayor (más grande) *older (bigger)*	el mayor (el más grande) *older (biggest)*

Adverb	Comparative	Superlative
bien *well*	mejor *better*	mejor *best*
mal *badly*	peor *worse*	peor *worst*

The comparative adjectives **mejor, peor, menor,** and **mayor** have the same forms in the feminine as in the masculine; the plurals are formed by adding **-es.**

Josefina es la mejor jugadora de vólibol de la escuela, pero es la peor estudiante de la clase de sociología.	*Josefina is the best volleyball player in the school, but she's the worst student in the sociology class.*
¿Cómo se llama el chico que nadó mejor?	*What is the name of the boy who swam the best?*
¿Dónde están las mejores tiendas?	*Where are the best stores?*

Note that **menor** and **mayor,** which usually follow the nouns they modify, are often used with people to refer to age (*younger, older*). When referring to physical size, bigger is usually expressed by **más grande** and smaller is expressed by **más pequeño.**

Paco y Pancho son menores que Felipe, pero Felipe es más pequeño.	*Paco and Pancho are younger than Felipe, but Philip is smaller.*
Adriana es mi hermana mayor; Silvia y Marta son mis hermanas menores.	*Adriana is my older sister; Silvia and Marta are my younger sisters.*

D. The Absolute Superlative

1. One way to express the superlative quality of an adjective is to use **muy** (*very*): **La casa es muy grande.** A second way is to add **ísimo (-ísima, -ísimos, -ísimas)** to the adjective. The **-ísimo(a)** ending is the absolute superlative, much stronger than **muy** plus the adjective. If the adjective ends in a vowel, drop the final vowel before adding the **-ísimo** ending.

Estos vasos son carísimos.	*These (drinking) glasses are very expensive.*
Ese atleta es fuertísimo.	*That athlete is very strong.*

2. The **-ísimo** ending can also be added to an adverb.

> Ese matrimonio llegó tardísimo.   *That couple arrived very late.*
> Hoy practicaron poquísimo.*   *Today they practiced very little.*

3. **Muchísimo(-a, -os, -as)** is used to express *very much* or *very many*.

> Hay muchísimas personas que   *There are very many people who come*
> vienen aquí a esquiar.   *here to ski.*
> ¿Te duele mucho la cabeza?   *Does your head ache much? —Very*
> —¡Muchísimo!   *much!*

Ejercicios

A. Complete the sentences by choosing the correct word or phrase in parentheses.

1. Babe Ruth es (más, menos) famoso que Juan Pérez.
2. Un equipo de béisbol tiene (más de, más que) tres jugadores.
3. Luis perdió cincuenta pesos. Mi papá perdió diez pesos. Luis perdió (más de, más que) mi papá.
4. El océano Pacífico es el océano (mayor, más grande) del mundo.
5. Es el deporte más popular (en, de) este país.

B. Restate the sentences below, following the examples.

Modelos: Estos apartamentos son carísimos.   **Estos apartamentos son muy caros.**
           El gimnasio es muy pequeño.   **El gimnasio es pequeñísimo.**

1. Este café es fuertísimo.
2. La corrida de toros es un deporte muy violento.
3. El partido de tenis empezó muy tarde.
4. Participamos en un juego interesantísimo.
5. El semestre pasado seguí un curso muy difícil.

C. Following the example, create sentences by adding the appropriate comparative.

Modelo: Millard Fillmore/ser/famoso/Abraham Lincoln   **Millard Fillmore es menos famoso que Abraham Lincoln.**

1. un equipo de fútbol/tener/70 jugadores
2. Argentina/ser/grande/Nicaragua
3. un día/tener/25 horas
4. un auto/ser/caro/una bicicleta
5. febrero/tener/días/diciembre

---

* The *c* of **poco** is changed to *qu* to preserve the /k/ sound.

D. Give the Spanish equivalent of the following sentences.

1. This is the most important game of the year.
2. Tomás is a good player, but he is not the best.
3. She is the best friend I have.
4. Paco is less vain than Pedro.
5. Adela is our youngest sister, but she is the tallest.
6. Mexico is bigger than Guatemala.
7. Last week he won less than seventy pesos.
8. He's the worst athlete in the world.
9. Alicia is the girl who swims the fastest.
10. Naldo and Ramón are the two students who ran the slowest.

Preguntas

1. ¿Quién es el mejor jugador de fútbol de los Estados Unidos? ¿de béisbol? ¿de tenis? ¿de basquetbol? **2.** ¿Cuál es el deporte más popular de los Estados Unidos? ¿de América del Sur? ¿del mundo? **3.** ¿Cuál es el deporte más violento que usted conoce? ¿el menos violento? ¿el más aburrido? ¿el menos aburrido? **4.** ¿Cuál es el país más grande de América del Sur? ¿el más pequeño? **5.** ¿Tiene usted un hermano o una hermana mayor? ¿menor? **6.** ¿Es usted el (la) más pequeño(a) de su familia? ¿el (la) menor? **7.** ¿Vive usted en un apartamento grandísimo? ¿pequeñísimo? ¿carísimo? **8.** ¿Tiene usted muchísimo que estudiar esta noche? ¿este fin de semana?

LOS DEPORTES

Dos matrimonios están en un café de Santander, a las siete de la tarde.[1]

Sr. Blanco:	Buenas tardes. ¿Ya pidieron?
Sr. Moreno:	Sí, pedimos jerez [2] para todos.
Sr. Blanco:	¡Vamos! ¿No recordaste que mi señora no toma bebidas tan fuertes como el jerez? ¿Verdad, María?
Sra. Blanco:	Pues, yo . . . solamente . . .
Sr. Blanco:	¡Camarero! Un vino de Málaga y un vaso de agua para la señora, por favor.[3]
Camarero:	Se lo sirvo inmediatamente, señor.
Sr. Moreno:	Bueno, ¿y qué hay de nuevo?
Sr. Blanco:	Anoche asistimos a un partido de jai alai.[4]
Sr. Moreno:	¿Y te gustó?
Sr. Blanco:	Me gustó muchísimo. Participaron los equipos más populares de España. El mejor jugador es Pardo. Empezó muy bien. Ganó doce puntos seguidos.
Sr. Moreno:	¡Qué bien! ¿Y siguió así?
Sr. Blanco:	No. Después jugó muy mal.
Sr. Moreno:	¡Ah! Triunfó el otro equipo. Y tú ¿perdiste dinero?

Sr. Blanco:	Perdí ochenta pesetas, pero me divertí.[5]
Sra. Moreno:	¿Y tú, María? ¿te divertiste también?
Sra. Blanco:	Pues, yo . . . verdaderamente . . .
Sr. Blanco:	¡Claro que se divirtió! Y no le importó el resultado.
Sra. Moreno:	Francamente, yo prefiero la corrida de toros. Es más emocionante que el jai alai, o el fútbol.
Sr. Moreno:	Y menos violento.
Sr. Blanco:	¡Qué idea más ridícula! En las corridas siempre hay un muerto.
Sr. Moreno:	Sí, pero es el toro el que muere.
Sr. Blanco:	Pero el verano pasado murió un torero.
Sra. Moreno:	¿Y no se hirieron veinte futbolistas?
Sr. Blanco:	Sí, pero . . . ¡La corrida es un deporte violentísimo!
Sr. Moreno:	¡Civilizadísimo!
Sra. Blanco:	¿Qué les parece? ¿Hablamos de otra cosa?
Sr. Blanco:	Acertadísima tu intervención. ¿De qué hablamos?
Sra. Blanco:	Pues . . . concretamente . . .

seguidos *in a row*   **Francamente** *Frankly*   **muerto** *dead*   **se hirieron** *were wounded*
civilizado *civilized*   **acertadísima** *very timely*   **concretamente** *actually*

Preguntas

1. ¿Dónde están los dos matrimonios?   2. Según el señor Blanco, ¿toma su señora be-bidas tan fuertes como el jerez?   3. ¿A qué asistieron los señores Blanco?   4. ¿Quiénes participaron en el partido?   5. ¿Quién ganó doce puntos seguidos?   6. ¿Ganó dinero el señor Blanco?   7. ¿Se divirtió él? ¿Y su señora?   8. ¿Qué deporte le gusta a la señora Moreno?   9. ¿Cree la señora Moreno que la corrida de toros es más violenta que el fútbol? ¿Qué cree usted?

NOTAS CULTURALES

1. Between the hours of about 6:00–8:00 P.M., it is customary in Spain to go out to bars and restaurants for snacks (tapas) to help tide one over until the 9:00 or 10:00 P.M. supper hour. A few simple tapas, such as olives or sausage, usually come free when you buy a drink; many places also feature a varied and elab-orate selection for a price. The town of Santander, where the dialogue takes place, is an important seaport in the North of Spain.

2. El jerez (*sherry*) comes from the South of Spain and takes its name from the town of Jerez de la Frontera (*sherry* is an English corruption of the word jerez). Its production and exportation have been largely in the hands of several fam-ilies of English descent.

3. Vino de Málaga is a sweet, heavy wine from the South of Spain, with a reputation as a "lady's wine."

4. Jai alai, or la pelota vasca (*Basque ball*), is a fast and strenuous game origi-nated by the Basque people and now popular in Spain, Mexico, Cuba, and, to a lesser extent, in some other Hispanic countries and in certain parts of the United States. It is usually played in a rectangular court called a frontón, with spectators seated on one side, which has a protective screen, and walls on the other three sides. The ball is thrown against the walls with the aid of curved baskets attached to the players' hands. One or two players are on each team. The extremely high velocity often attained by the ball makes the game some-what dangerous.

5. It is common to bet money on jai alai games.

ACTIVIDADES

Deportes y opiniones

el basquetbol   el vólibol   el béisbol   el tenis

el fútbol   el fútbol americano   la natación

el esquí   las carreras (el correr)   el atletismo

1. _____ no es tan peligroso como _____, ¿verdad?
2. Me gusta más _____ que _____ porque es más interesante.
3. _____ es menos difícil que _____.
4. Un equipo de _____ tiene menos de 12 jugadores.
5. Un jugador de _____ debe correr más rápidamente que un jugador de _____.
6. En los Estados Unidos, _____ es popularísimo(a), ahora.

Entrevista

Ask a classmate the following questions. Then report the information to the class.

1. ¿Asististe a un partido de fútbol recientemente?
2. ¿Hiciste yoga la semana pasada?
3. ¿Eres el mejor jugador (la mejor jugadora) de béisbol del mundo? ¿El (la) peor?
4. ¿Corres o haces ejercicio todos los días?
5. ¿Crees que en los Juegos Olímpicos participan los mejores atletas del mundo?
6. ¿Qué deporte te gusta más? ¿Lo practicas o sólo eres espectador(a)?

Situación

Después del partido de fútbol

Marta and **Jorge** are talking about the soccer match they have just seen. **Marta:** Pardo played better than García today. **Jorge:** "Baloney" (*Tonterías*). Pardo played much worse than García. He really thinks that Pardo is the worst player of the team. At that moment, their friend **Emilio** comes up and asks "What's new?". **Marta** says they enjoyed themselves at (*en*) the match. She thinks that soccer is the most interesting sport of all (*de todos*). **Emilio** says he prefers tennis and he thinks soccer is very boring and very violent. **Marta** says no, it is very interesting and very civilized. **Jorge** says that he has a very civilized idea: Why don't they go have a beer?

VOCABULARIO ACTIVO

Verbos útiles

contestar *to answer*
correr *to run*
doler(ue) *to ache, hurt;* **Me duele la cabeza.** *My head aches.*
entrar *to enter, come in*
explicar *to explain*
ganar *to win; to earn*
llover(ue) *to rain*
nadar *to swim*
observar *to observe*
pagar *to pay*
parecer *to seem;* **¿Qué les parece?** *What do you think?*
practicar *to practice*
participar *to participate*
triunfar *to win, triumph*

Los deportes

el aficionado (la aficionada) *fan*
el, la atleta *athlete;* **atlético(a)** *athletic*
el atletismo *athletics*
el basquetbol *basketball*
el béisbol *baseball*
la carrera *race*
la corrida de toros *bullfight*
el deporte *sport*
emocionante *exciting*

el equipo *team*
el espectador (la espectadora) *spectator*
el esquí *skiing*
fuerte *strong*
el fútbol *soccer;* **el fútbol americano** *football*
el gimnasio *gymnasium*
el jai alai *jai alai*
el jugador (la jugadora) *player*
la natación *swimming*
el partido *match, game*
peligroso(a) *dangerous*
popular *popular*
el punto *point*
la raqueta *racket*
el resultado *score*
el tenis *tennis*
el, la torera(o) *bullfighter*
el toro *bull*
violento(a) *violent*
el vólibol *volleyball*

Adverbios que terminan en -mente

absolutamente *absolutely*
alegremente *happily*
claramente *clearly*
completamente *completely*
correctamente *correctly*
cuidadosamente *carefully*

directamente *directly*
entusiastamente *entusiastically*
fácilmente *easily*
felizmente *happily*
generalmente *generally*
inmediatamente *immediately*
lentamente *slowly*
precisamente *precisely*
probablemente *probably*
rápidamente *rapidly*
realmente *really*
solamente *only*
terriblemente *terribly*
totalmente *totally*
verdaderamente *truly*

Otras palabras útiles

agua *water*
alto(a) *tall*

anoche *last night*
ayer *yesterday*
la cosa *thing*
lindo(a) *pretty, handsome*
más *more*
el matrimonio *married couple*
mayor *older;* el (la) mayor *oldest*
mejor *better;* el (la) mejor *best*
menor *younger;* el (la) menor *youngest*
menos *less*
peor *worse;* el (la) peor *worst*
pequeño(a) *small, little*
pobre *poor*
¿Qué hay de nuevo? *What's new?*
¡Qué idea más ridícula! *What a ridiculous idea!*
sincero(a) *sincere*
tan, tanto *so much, so many*
vanidoso(a) *vain*
el vaso *glass*

CAPÍTULO 10

A LA MESA

bistec

paella

ensalada

flan

sopa de pollo

arroz con pollo

pollo asado

—A ti te gusta el pollo, ¿verdad, Matilde?   —¿Cómo lo sabes?

OBJECTIVES

LANGUAGE: In this chapter we introduce, discuss, and practice:

1. the present tense of other irregular verbs: **oír,** *to hear,* **poner,** *to put or place,* **salir,** *to leave or go out,* **traer,** *to bring,* and **venir,** *to come*
2. the preterite tense of irregular verbs
3. affirmative and negative words (such as *someone, no one, something, nothing,* and so forth)

You will also learn vocabulary related to restaurants and typical Hispanic dishes.

CULTURE: The dialogue takes place in Sevilla, Spain, where some young people are visiting the famous Giralda, tower of the cathedral. You'll learn something about the history of that area and the various cultures that have influenced it.

EXPLICACIÓN

I. MORE IRREGULAR VERBS IN THE PRESENT TENSE (OÍR, SALIR, TRAER, PONER, VENIR)

(1) **Camarero:** *¿Pongo* aquí la sopa, señora?

(2) **Consuelo:** Sí. Y ¿nos puede *traer* dos tortillas, por favor?

(3) **Camarero:** En seguida se las *traigo*.

(4) **Consuelo:** ¿Cuánto tiempo vas a estar de visita en Sevilla, María?

(5) **María:** *Salgo* para Buenos Aires el viernes.

(6) **Consuelo:** Entonces, ¿quieres ver la ciudad conmigo?

(7) **María:** Cómo no, encantada. ¿Por qué no *salimos* mañana?

(8) **Consuelo:** De acuerdo. *Vengo* a buscarte aquí a las nueve.

(9) **Camarero:** Perdón, señora, pero no *oigo* bien. ¿Me dijo tortillas o natillas?

(10) **Consuelo:** Pues . . . las dos cosas; y la cuenta, por favor.

1. ¿Qué pone el camarero en la mesa? **2.** ¿Cuándo sale María para Buenos Aires? **3.** ¿A qué hora van a salir María y Consuelo para ver Sevilla? **4.** ¿Oye bien el camarero? **5.** ¿A qué hora viene usted a la universidad los lunes?

A. Several Spanish verbs take an **-ig-** or a **-g-** in the first person singular of the present tense. **Hacer,** presented in Chapter 4, is one such verb. Others are:

traer *(to bring)*		**oír** *(to hear)*	
traigo	traemos	oigo	oímos
traes	traéis	oyes	oís
trae	traen	oye	oyen

---

(1) Shall I put the soup here, madam? (2) Yes. And can you bring us two omelettes, please? (3) I'll bring them for you right away. (4) How long are you going to visit Sevilla, María? (5) I leave for Buenos Aires on Friday. (6) Then, do you want to see the city with me? (7) Of course, delighted. Why don't we go out tomorrow? (8) Okay, I'll come to get you here at nine o'clock. (9) Excuse me, madam. But I don't hear well. Did you say *tortillas* (omelettes) or *natillas* (custard) to me? (10) Well . . . both; and the check, please.

pone *(to put, place)*		**venir** *(to come)*	
pongo	ponemos	vengo	venimos
pones	ponéis	vienes	venís
pone	ponen	viene	vienen

salir *(to leave, go out)*	
salgo	salimos
sales	salís
sale	salen

¿Oyes música?	*Do you hear music?*
¿Pongo las gaseosas aquí, señor?	*Shall I put the soft drinks here, sir?*
Salgo temprano para Barcelona.	*I leave (I'm leaving) early for Barcelona.*
Enrique trae las frutas, y Susana trae la ensalada.	*Enrique is bringing the fruit and Susana is bringing the salad.*
¿Vienes al mercado conmigo?	*Are you coming to the market with me?*

B. When **poner** is used reflexively (**ponerse**), it can mean *to become* (*get*) or *to put on.*

Siempre me pongo nervioso durante los exámenes.	*I always get nervous during exams.*
José se pone el sombrero.	*José puts on his hat.*

Poner la mesa means *to set the table.*

¿Ya pones la mesa?	*You're already setting the table?*

C. Note that **oír** takes a **y** between the stem and the ending in the second and third person singular and the third person plural forms. There is a written accent mark on the **i** of the first and second person plural forms.

D. **Venir** is an **e** to **ie** stem-changing verb. It is conjugated like **tener,** presented in Chapter 3.

Ejercicios

A. Create new sentences, substituting the words in the list for those in italics.

1. *Tú* traes la sopa, ¿no?
   a. ustedes **b.** yo **c.** Ricardo **d.** Celia y yo **e.** los muchachos
2. Generalmente *ella* sale a las seis.
   a. Susana y su marido **b.** tú **c.** nosotros **d.** usted **e.** yo
3. ¿Qué oigo *yo* en este momento?
   a. tú **b.** los Pérez **c.** Luis y Ana **d.** Pablo y yo **e.** Marcelo

4. *Mis padres* siempre vienen a este restaurante.
   a. yo **b.** Eliana **c.** tú **d.** nosotros **e.** tú y Marta.

5. ¿Por qué pone *usted* la mesa tan temprano?
   a. él **b.** ustedes **c.** tú **d.** yo **e.** ellas

B. Restate, changing the verbs to the singular.

1. ¿Dónde ponemos las tortillas?
2. Esos señores no oyen bien.
3. Venimos muy tarde, ¿no?
4. ¿Cuándo traemos la ensalada?
5. Aquí no oímos la música.

C. Following the example, give an appropriate question for each of the answers given.

Modelo: Jorge y su novia traen las gaseosas. **¿Quién trae las gaseosas?**

1. Sí, oímos a Delia.
2. No, salgo con mis amigas.
3. El camarero trae la cuenta.
4. Ellos vienen al mercado.
5. Ahora ponemos la mesa para el desayuno.

Preguntas

1. ¿A qué hora viene usted a la clase de español? ¿A qué hora sale? **2.** ¿Sale usted los fines de semana? ¿Sale usted solo(a) o con amigos? **3.** ¿Oye usted música cuando estudia? ¿cuando almuerza o cena? **4.** ¿Trae usted su almuerzo a la universidad o prefiere comprarlo en la cafetería? **5.** ¿Le pone usted leche a su café? ¿azúcar? ¿sacarina?

II. PRETERITE OF IRREGULAR VERBS

(1) **Tomás:** ¿Qué *hiciste* anoche, Hilda?

(2) **Hilda:** *Fui* al restaurante «La Cazuela». Fernando *quiso* ir también, pero no *pudo*.

(3) **Tomás:** Y ¿con quién *fuiste*?

(4) **Hilda:** *Fui* con Ramona. También *fueron* unos amigos de ella. *Pedí* paella. ¡Qué rica!. Es un plato que tiene arroz, pescado, camarones y otros mariscos.

(5) **Tomás:** Y Ramona ¿qué *pidió*?

(6) **Hilda:** Primero, gazpacho andaluz, que es una sopa fría de tomates, pepinos, cebolla y pimientos. Después *pidió* un bistec, que el camarero le *trajo* con una ensalada.

(7) **Tomás:** Y el postre. ¿cómo *estuvo*?

(8) **Hilda:** Muy sabroso. Nos *dieron* flan.

(9) **Tomás:** *Tuviste* que abandonar la dieta, entonces.

(10) **Hilda:** No del todo. *Supe* cuidarme. No le *puse* azúcar al café.

---

1. ¿Qué hizo Hilda anoche? **2.** ¿Quién quiso ir pero no pudo? **3.** ¿Qué es paella? **4.** ¿Qué pidió Ramona? **5.** ¿Cómo estuvo el postre que les dieron? **6.** ¿Tuvo que abandonar la dieta Hilda?

A. There are a number of verbs in Spanish that have irregular preterite-tense forms, both stems and endings. These forms do not have written accents.

INFINITIVE	PRETERITE STEM	PRETERITE ENDINGS
hacer	hic-	
querer	quis-	
venir	vin-	-e
		-iste
poder	pud-	-o
poner	pus-	-imos
saber	sup-	-isteis
		-ieron
estar	estuv-	
tener	tuv-	

The endings in the chart are attached to form the preterite of all of the verbs listed. There is only one spelling change, in the third person singular of **hacer, hizo,** which involves a change from *c* to *z* to retain the sound of the infinitive.

Paco hizo un omelet con tres huevos, queso, una cebolla y un poco de sal.	*Paco made an omelette with three eggs, some cheese, an onion, and a little salt.*
Luisa no pudo mostrarme la ciudad.	*Luisa couldn't show me the city.*

---

(1) What did you do last night, Hilda? (2) I went to the restaurant "La Cazuela." Fernando wanted to go too, but couldn't. (3) Who did you go with? (4) I went with Ramona. Some friends of hers went too. I ordered paella. What a treat! It's a dish that has rice, fish, shrimp, and other seafood. (5) What did Ramona order? (6) First *gazpacho andaluz*, which is a cold soup of tomatoes, cucumbers, onions and peppers. Aferwards, she ordered a steak which the waiter brought her with a salad. (7) And how was the dessert? (8) Very good (delicious). They gave us *flan* (custard with carmel sauce). (9) You had to abandon your diet, then. (10) Not completely. I learned how (made sure) to be careful. I didn't put sugar in my coffee.

Tuve un accidente de automóvil la
semana pasada.

I had an automobile accident last week.

¿Estuviste en el parque hasta las seis?

You were in the park until six o'clock?

El camarero puso las servilletas en la
mesa.

*The waiter put the napkins on the
table.*

B. The preterite forms of **decir** and **traer** are also irregular.

decir		traer	
dije	dijimos	traje	trajimos
dijiste	dijisteis	trajiste	trajisteis
dijo	dijeron	trajo	trajeron

Notice that the third person plural ending is **-jeron**, rather than **-ieron**.

Dijeron que lo vieron durante las
vacaciones.

*They said they saw him during
vacation.*

¿Qué trajeron ustedes? —Un rico flan.

What did you bring? —A delicious flan.

C. **Ir** and **ser** have the same forms in the preterite tense.

ir, ser	
fui	fuimos
fuiste	fuisteis
fue	fueron

Fuimos allí anoche a comer arroz con
pollo.

*We went there last night to eat rice with
chicken.*

D. **Dar** is irregular in the preterite in that it requires the preterite endings for
regular **-er** and **-ir** verbs rather than the endings for **-ar** verbs.

dar	
di	dimos
diste	disteis
dio	dieron

Me imagino que te di el dinero para
los comestibles.

*I suppose I gave you the money for the
groceries.*

Ejercicios

A. Create new sentences, substituting the words in the list for those in italics.

1. *Fernando* no quiso almorzar.
    a. yo **b.** los jugadores **c.** tú **d.** nosotros **e.** ustedes

2. *Yo* tuve ganas de pedir paella.
   a. tú **b.** Susana **c.** el Señor García **d.** nosotros **e.** mis padres
3. *Alejandro* no estuvo en la fiesta anoche.
   a. usted **b.** yo **c.** Julia **d.** tú **e.** los señores Gómez
4. *María y yo* hicimos un postre delicioso.
   a. los muchachos **b.** tú **c.** yo **d.** Miguel **e.** Teresa y yo
5. Ayer *ustedes* fueron a un restaurante español muy caro.
   a. nosotros **b.** tu profesora **c.** yo **d.** las muchachas **e.** tú

B. Restate, changing the verbs from the present tense to the preterite.

1. Guillermo no puede oír el partido.
2. ¿Traes el vino y el pan?
3. Ma da bastante dinero.
4. Tenemos ganas de cenar temprano.
5. Los señores Pérez vienen de Barcelona el lunes.
6. José va a ese restaurante todos los sábados.
7. Dicen que sus hijos hacen la comida.
8. ¿Dónde ponemos las bebidas?

C. Restate the following paragraph, changing the verbs from the present tense to the preterite.

Esta semana voy a Sevilla. Salgo el miércoles a las dos de la tarde y llego dos horas después. En el aeropuerto me esperan unos amigos y paso la noche en casa de ellos. El jueves vamos a visitar las ruinas de Itálica, una antigua (*ancient*) ciudad romana. Allí tengo la oportunidad de aprender muchas cosas interesantes sobre la historia española. Volvemos a Sevilla a las diez de la noche y cenamos. Al otro día, el viernes, doy un paseo por la ciudad y esa misma noche vuelvo a casa. ¡Es un viaje magnífico!

D. Give the Spanish equivalent of the following sentences.

1. Ana brought me some eggs.
2. We came here last week.
3. Yesterday we had to eat late.
4. Catalina was at the airport at six o'clock.
5. They told her the truth.
6. Did you (*tú*) do this?

Preguntas

1. ¿Fue usted a un partido de fútbol ayer? ¿de béisbol? ¿Fue solo o con amigos? **2.** ¿Dónde estuvo ayer a las dos de la tarde? ¿a las nueve de la noche? **3.** ¿Comió usted recientemente en un restaurante? ¿dónde? ¿Qué pidió? **4.** ¿Fue usted a un restaurante español o latinoamericano? ¿Pudo usted pedir en español? **5.** ¿Qué hizo usted el fin de semana pasado? **6.** ¿Tuvo usted la oportunidad de visitar a sus padres últimamente? ¿a su novio(a)?

III. AFFIRMATIVE AND NEGATIVE WORDS

(1) **Rafael:** ¿Qué vas a desayunar?

(2) **Ellen:** Voy a pedir huevos fritos con jamón. *Alguien* me dijo que un buen desayuno es necesario para la salud.

(3) **Rafael:** Yo *nunca* como mucho en el desayuno: *ni* huevos revueltos, *ni* salchichas; sólo café con leche y pan tostado con mantequilla.

(4) **Ellen:** ¡Eres un hispano típico! Pero debes comer *algo* más. ¿No quieres *algún* jugo?

(5) **Rafael:** No, gracias, no quiero *nada*.

(6) **Ellen:** ¿*Tampoco* quieres un coctel de frutas?

(7) **Rafael:** No, *tampoco*. *Nunca* como mucho porque tú sabes que nuestro almuerzo es abundante.

(8) **Ellen:** Sí, es verdad. Creo que voy a aumentar *algunos* kilos aquí, pero… «estómago lleno, corazón contento».

---

1. ¿Qué va a desayunar Ellen? **2.** ¿Come mucho Rafael en el desayuno? **3.** ¿Qué piensa de eso Ellen? **4.** ¿Quiere Rafael un jugo o un coctel de frutas? **5.** ¿Por qué nunca come mucho?

Affirmative Words	Negative Words
sí *yes*	no *no*
alguien *someone, anyone*	nadie *no one, not anyone*
algo *something*	nada *nothing, not anything*
algún, alguno(-s), alguna(-s) *some, any*	ningún, ninguno(-s), ninguna(-s) *none, not any, no, neither (of them)*
también *also*	tampoco *not either, neither*
siempre *always*	nunca, jamás *never, not ever*
o...o *either . . . or*	ni...ni *neither . . . nor*

---

(1) What are you going to have for breakfast? (2) I'm going to order fried eggs with ham. Someone told me a good breakfast is necessary for (your) health. (3) I never eat much for breakfast: neither scrambled eggs nor sausages; only coffee with milk and toast with butter. (4) You're a typical Spanish person! But you should eat something more. Don't you want some juice? (5) No, thank you. I don't want anything. (6) You don't want a fruit cocktail either? (7) No, not that either. I never eat much because you know our lunch is large. (8) Yes, it's true. I think I'm going to gain a few kilos* here, but . . . "full stomach, happy heart."

---

* A **kilo** is short for **kilogramo,** 2.2 pounds. The metric system is used throughout the Spanish-speaking world.

A. The negative words **nadie, nada, ninguno, tampoco** and **nunca** can be placed either before or after the verb.

No lo pudo probar tampoco.⎫
Tampoco lo pudo probar. ⎭   *He (she) couldn't try it either.*

No le trajimos nada.⎫
Nada le trajimos. ⎭   *We didn't bring him (her) anything.*

No uso nunca pimienta.⎫
Nunca uso pimienta. ⎭   *I never use pepper.*

Notice that **no** precedes the verb when some other negative word follows the verb. **No** is omitted when the negative word precedes the verb.

B. **Alguno** and **ninguno** can refer either to people or things, while **alguien** and **nadie** refer only to people. **Alguno** and **ninguno** usually refer to certain members or elements of a group that the speaker or writer has in mind. Before a masculine singular noun, **alguno** becomes **algún** and **ninguno** becomes **ningún**.

Aquí nadie come tomates.	*No one here eats tomatoes.*
Ninguno de ellos sabe cocinar pescado.	*Neither of them knows how to cook fish.*
¿Hay alguien aquí?	*Is there anyone here?*
¿Hay algunos estudiantes de nuestra clase aquí?	*Are there some students from our class here?*
¿No quiere algún postre?	*Don't you want some dessert?*
No tengo ningún cuchillo grande de cocina.	*I don't have any large kitchen knives.**

* Note that the singular noun **cuchillo** is used for the plural *knives* in English.

The personal **a** is used with the pronouns **alguien, nadie** and with **alguno** and **ninguno** when they refer to people in the same way that it is used with nouns or other pronouns.

¿Busca usted a algunos amigos de Enrique? *Are you looking for some friends of Enrique's?*

No se lo voy a decir a nadie. *I'm not going to tell it to anyone.*

C. Several negatives can be used in the same sentence.

¡No dio nada a nadie, nunca! *He never gave anything to anyone, ever!*

D. *Either . . . or* is expressed with **o . . . o.** *Neither . . . nor* is expressed with **ni . . . ni,** which takes the plural form of a verb when used with the subject.

Josefina busca o una cuchara o un tenedor. *Josefina is looking for either a spoon or a fork.*

Ni los camarones ni los mariscos valen tanto. *Neither shrimp nor seafood is worth that much.*

Ejercicios

A. Change the negative constructions in the following sentences, as indicated in the example.

Modelo: Yo nunca desayuno antes de las ocho. **Yo no desayuno nunca antes de las ocho.**

1. Jamás salgo sin dinero.
2. Ellas nunca prueban el postre.
3. ¿Tampoco fueron ustedes?

4. Ni Rita ni su esposo comen tomates.
5. Ninguno de los muchachos quiere ir allí.
6. ¿Nunca fuiste a ese restaurante?
7. A nadie le gusta ese vino.
8. Realmente nada le duele, ¿verdad?

B. Change the following sentences to the negative.

Modelo: ¿Alguien trajo paella? **¿Nadie trajo paella?**

1. Pepe quiere preguntar algo.
2. Pensamos ir a algún restaurante español.
3. ¿También pidieron sopa?
4. Ellos siempre comen pescado los viernes.
5. Voy a preparar o carne asada o arroz con pollo.

C. When Guillermo calls Eliana, she is in a negative mood and this causes a fight. Complete the dialogue by giving Eliana's responses in the negative, as in the example.

Modelo: Guillermo: Hola, Eliana. ¿me llamó alguien? **No, no te llamó nadie.**

Guillermo: ¿Fue alguien contigo al doctor?
Eliana: No, _____
Guillermo: ¿Hay algún problema?
Eliana: No, _____
Guillermo: ¿Te pasa algo?
Eliana: No, _____
Guillermo: ¿Quieres salir a cenar o a bailar?
Eliana: No, _____
Guillermo: ¿No quieres ir al cine tampoco?
Eliana: No, _____
Guillermo: ¡Pero, Eliana!, ¿siempre gritas así?
Eliana: No, _____
            ¡... Perdón, Guillermo...!; ya no estoy enojada *(angry)* ¿Porqué no salimos esta noche? . . .

D. Give the Spanish equivalent of the following sentences.

1. Somebody put those sausages there.
2. I have never eaten such a delicious gazpacho as this one.
3. She didn't bring anything here.
4. Neither Enrique nor Lucinda is on a diet.
5. I'm going to ask for either fish or chicken.
6. I never want to see them again.
7. Do you need something? Yes, a spoon.
8. No one bought either knives or forks.
9. They also want to order (ask for) some omelettes and custard.
10. Did any of your friends go to the party last night?

```
BACALAÍTOS                                    24 bacalaítos
    ½ libra de bacalao      ½ cucharadita de polvo de
    2 tazas de harina          hornear
    2 tazas de agua         2 ajos machacados
    ½ cucharadita de sal    Manteca
```

Ponga el bacalao en remojo por algunas horas. Quite las espi-
nas y el pellejo. Corte en pedazos pequeños. Mezcle la harina
con el polvo de hornear, añada el bacalao, los ajos y el agua.
Si es necesario añada sal. Fría por cucharadas en manteca
abundante. Escurra sobre papel absorbente.

Preguntas

1. ¿A qué hora desayuna usted generalmente? ¿Qué desayuna usted?   **2.** ¿Conoce usted
algún restaurante español? ¿Sirven allí alguna comida típica? ¿Qué sirven?   **3.** ¿Invitó
usted a alguien a su casa para cenar recientemente? ¿Qué cenaron? ¿Sirvió usted algún
postre? ¿qué postre?   **4.** ¿Fue usted a comer a casa de algún amigo o de alguna amiga la
semana pasada? ¿Le sirvieron algo especial? ¿sabroso?   **6.** Cuando usted hace una fiesta
en su casa, ¿qué platos prepara usted? ¿Traen sus amigos algo? ¿Qué traen?

EN LA GIRALDA

Claudio, un joven de Sevilla, acompaña a unos amigos que están de visita a la Giralda,[1] *que es
la torre de la catedral.*

Esteban:	¡Por fin! ¡Qué subida más larga! Me dio un hambre terrible.
Claudio:	Pero valió la pena ¿no?. No hay ninguna vista de Sevilla como ésta.
Luisa:	Desde acá veo el Barrio de Santa Cruz.[2] Anoche fuimos allí a ver baile flamenco.
Esteban:	Y comimos un cocido y una cazuela como nunca probé antes.
Luisa:	¿Quién hizo esta torre, Claudio?
Claudio:	La empezó un jefe árabe en el siglo doce, y la terminó su sucesor, Almanzor.
Esteban:	¿Por qué no vamos a almorzar y venimos a la tarde? Sueño con unos ricos mariscos.
Luisa:	Te pones pesado, hombre. Claudio, me imagino que esta torre fue un sitio ideal para esperar el ataque del enemigo.
Claudio:	Y el enemigo vino. Fue el rey Fernando III, a quien llamaron «El Santo».[3] Tuve oportunidad de verlo el año pasado.

Esteban: ¿Oigo bien o el hambre me impide oír? ¿No vivió en el siglo trece?

Claudio: Oyes bien. Dije que lo vi el año pasado. Estuve en la catedral[(4)] el día de su fiesta, cuando abren la tumba. Su cadáver no muestra ninguna señal de descomposición. Es un milagro.

Luisa: Sí, alguien me dijo eso y no lo quise creer.

Esteban: Y ustedes no quieren creer que en el hotel no me dieron desayuno. No pude comer ni un chocolate ni tampoco una galleta.

Claudio: Veo que Esteban tiene ganas de ver un panorama de servilletas blancas, cucharas, cuchillos y tenedores.

Esteban: ¡Sí! Y con montañas de carne asada, campos de arroz con pollo, ríos de vino y océanos de helado de vainilla.

Luisa: Entonces, mejor nos vamos a comer.

Esteban: ¡Bueno, éste es el milagro! Y mañana no salgo a pasear antes de tomar un buen desayuno.

---

ataque *attack*   **impide** *prevents*   **su fiesta** *his feast-day*   **tumba** *tomb*   **señal** *sign*
descomposición *decay*   **milagro** *miracle*

Preguntas

1. ¿Qué es la Giralda?   **2.** ¿Qué pudieron ver los jóvenes desde allí?   **3.** ¿Para qué fueron los estudiantes al Barrio de Santa Cruz?   **4.** ¿Qué comieron allí?   **5.** ¿Quiénes hicieron la torre? ¿cuándo?   **5.** ¿Quién vino a atacar a los árabes?   **7.** ¿Qué milagro vio Claudio el año anterior?   **8.** En el hotel, ¿le dieron a Esteban algo para el desayuno?   **9.** ¿Cuál es la «vista» que Esteban tiene ganas de ver?   **10.** ¿Cree usted que ocurren milagros hoy en día?

NOTAS CULTURALES

1. La Giralda, the exquisite tower of the cathedral of Seville, is a popular landmark which can be seen from almost any part of the city. The bottom section was the minaret of the sumptuous mosque built by the Moslem rulers of southern Spain in the 1100s and later demolished by the Christians. The top section, called the Triumph of Faith, was added by the Christian rulers during the Renaissance. The pinnacle turns around in the wind and so has given rise to the popular name of the tower, **la Giralda** (*the Weather Vane*). To see a spectacular view of Seville, the visitor must climb a winding ramp up to the top of the 250-foot tower.

2. The Santa Cruz district, the old Jewish section of the city **(la Judería),** has narrow streets, flower-filled patios, and quaint and colorful houses. Several places there feature flamenco dancing and guitar music.

3. King Ferdinand III of Castilla y Leon, called **el Santo** (*the Saint*) because he was later canonized by the Catholic Church, captured Seville from the Moslems in 1248.

4. The Cathedral of Seville is a beautiful example of Spanish gothic architecture and a treasure-house of gold, silver and jeweled artifacts and historical documents. It is the third largest cathedral in the world (after St. Peter's in Rome and St. Paul's in London).

ACTIVIDADES

En el Restaurante «La Cazuela»

Restaurante La Cazuela
Menú Bilingüe

Entrades	**Hors d'oeuvres**	**Postres**	**Desserts**
Gazpacho	Gazpacho (cold soup)	Flan	Custard with caramel sauce
Sopa de verduras	Vegetable soup	Torta	Cake
Ensalada de atún	Tuna salad	Fruta fresca	Fresh fruit
Papas fritas	French fries	Helado	Ice cream
Platos del día	**Today's specialties**	**Bebidas**	**Beverages**
Paella	Paella (rice, seafood, vegetables)	Vino	Wine
		Cerveza	Beer
Arroz con pollo	Chicken with rice	Gaseosas	Soft drinks
Tortilla	Omelette	Leche	Milk
Hamburguesas	Hamburguers	Agua mineral	Mineral water
Bistec	Steak	Café/té	Coffee/tea

¡Buen provecho!

La última vez que estuvimos de vacaciones en España, fuimos al Restaurante «La Cazuela». Javier, que nunca quiere comer nada nuevo, pidió _____ y _____, y para beber _____. A mí me gustan las comidas nuevas y por eso pedí _____ y _____, y para beber _____. De postre, el camarero le trajo a Javier _____ y a mí me trajo _____. Toda la comida estuvo riquísima.

Entrevista

Ask a classmate the following questions. Then report the information to the class.

1. ¿Qué comiste anoche?
2. ¿Estuviste en algún restaurante ayer?

3. ¿Comiste comida española alguna vez? ¿Te gustó?
4. ¿Traes algo para comer a la universidad?
5. ¿Fuiste a comer a la casa de alguien la semana pasada? ¿Qué te dieron de postre?

Crucigrama

Change each verb to the preterite tense and fill in the squares.

Across
1. es/va
2. tienes
7. puede
8. hace
9. son/van

Down
1. soy/voy
2. trae
3. viene
4. estoy
5. dice
6. damos

Situación

En el restaurante

Esteban, Claudio, and Luisa are in the Restaurante "La Cazuela" (menu, *page 192*). The waiter comes and asks each one what he or she wants as an hors d'œuvre, as a main course and for a drink. Esteban says he came here last week and saw flamenco dancing. Luisa says she never goes to see flamenco dancing because she does not like it. Claudio says he does not like it either. The waiter returns and serves them and asks what they want for dessert. They all order different desserts and coffee or tea. Luisa says that someone told her that tonight a good guitarist is going to play. The waiter says no, that tonight they are going to see a wonderful show (*espectáculo*) of flamenco music!

VOCABULARIO ACTIVO

Verbos útiles

abandonar *to abandon*
aumentar (de peso) *to gain (weight)*

cuidar *to take care of, be careful*
desayunar *to have breakfast*
estar de visita *to visit*

imaginarse *to imagine*
mostrar(ue) *to show, demonstrate*
oír *to hear*
poner *to put, place, set down;* **poner la mesa** *to set the table;* **ponerse** *to try on;* **ponerse + adj.** *to become + adj.*
probar(ue) *to taste, try*
salir *to leave, go out*
soñar con *to dream about*
tener la oportunidad de *to have the opportunity to*
traer *to bring*
valer *to be worth;* **valer la pena** *to be worthwhile*
venir *to come*

Las comidas

asado(a) *roasted, barbecued*
abundante *abundant, ample*
el bistec *(beef) steak*
el camarón *shrimp*
la cazuela *stew; earthen pot in which the stew is cooked*
la cebolla *onion*
el cocido *stew*
la cuchara *spoon*
el cuchillo *knife*
la ensalada *salad*
el flan *flan, custard with caramel sauce*
frito(a) *fried*
la gaseosa *soft drink (carbonated)*
el gazpacho *cold tomato and vegetable soup*
la hamburguesa *hamburger*
el helado *ice cream*
el jugo *juice*
el marisco *shellfish*
el mercado *market*
la natilla *custard*
la paella *dish with rice, seafood, chicken, and other meats seasoned with saffron*
el pepino *cucumber*
el pescado *fish*
la pimienta *pepper (spice)*

el pimiento *pepper (red, green, or chili pepper)*
el pollo *chicken*
el postre *dessert*
revuelto(a) *scrambled*
rico(a) *delicious*
sabroso(a) *delicious*
la sal *salt*
la salchicha *sausage*
la servilleta *napkin*
el tenedor *fork*
el tomate *tomato*
la tortilla *tortilla (corn pancake of Central American origin) or omelette*

Otras palabras útiles

árabe *Arab*
¡Buen provecho! *Happy eating!; Enjoy your food!*
la catedral *cathedral*
el corazón *heart*
la cuenta *bill*
desde *from, since*
durante *during*
en seguida *at once, immediately*
encantado(a) *delighted*
el enemigo (la enemiga) *enemy*
el, la jefe *chief, leader; boss*
el kilo(gramo) *kilogram*
pesado(a) *boring, heavy*
por fin *finally*
el rey *king*
el sitio *place, site, spot*
la subida *climb*
la torre *tower*
algo *something*
alguien *someone, anyone*
algún, alguno(a) *some, any*
nada *nothing, not anything*
nadie *no one, not anyone*
ni . . . ni *neither . . . nor*
ningún, ninguno(a) *none, not any, no, neither (of them)*
nunca, jamás *never, not ever*
o . . . o *either . . . or*
tampoco *not either, neither*

Los Deportes

En el mundo hispánico de hoy hay un gran entusiasmo por los deportes. La gente de hoy pasa gran parte del día en estado de tensión. Pero en los deportes encuentra momentos de *placer* y una manera agradable *de evadir*, por unas horas, responsabilidades y preocupaciones. — pleasure / of escaping (from)

El basquetbol, *el boxeo,* la natación, el tenis, las carreras de automóviles y de *caballos*, y muchos otros deportes son populares en los países hispanos. Hoy día hay equipos femeninos en casi todos los deportes. Sin embargo, el vólibol siempre fue uno de los deportes más populares entre las mujeres. — boxing / horses

El béisbol es uno de los deportes favoritos en América Central, México, Venezuela y las islas del Caribe. Otro deporte favorito es el *ciclismo.* En todos los países hispanos son muy populares las carreras de bicicleta. — cycling

El fútbol es el deporte más popular del mundo hispánico. El fútbol de España y de América Latina se llama *soccer* en inglés. Hay que *patear* la pelota sin tocarla con las manos. Cada equipo tiene once jugadores. En Europa juegan al fútbol tanto como en el mundo hispano y los campeonatos mundiales son tan *emocionantes* e importantes que muchas veces obreros y jefes *dejan de trabajar* para escuchar el partido por radio o verlo por televisión. — to kick / exciting / stop working

Otro deporte bien conocido en el mundo hispánico es la pelota *vasca* o jai alai. Este juego se originó en las provincias vascas, al norte de España, pero ahora es popular en todo el territorio español y también en México, Cuba, otros países hispanoamericanos, y en partes de los Estados Unidos. En general, juegan en un *frontón* que tiene tres paredes y un cuarto *lado abierto* al público. Los jugadores usan *cestas* especiales para *lanzar* la pelota contra la pared. La pelota adquiere gran velocidad y por eso el jai alai es uno de los deportes más peligrosos del mundo.

También son populares *la caza, la pesca, los paseos en bote, y las caminatas por los bosques.* Todos los años, los *picos nevados* de España y Sudamérica atraen a innumerables aficionados al esquí y al *alpinismo.* En esos países, como en otras partes del mundo, la gente de la ciudad *aprovecha* sus vacaciones o los fines de semana para integrarse, *por lo menos* temporalmente, al mundo natural.

(Glosas al margen:) Basque / rectangular court / side open / baskets /to throw / hunting / fishing / boating / walks in the forests / snow-covered peaks / mountain-climbing / utilize / at least

Preguntas

1. ¿Cuáles son algunos de los deportes populares en los países hispanos? 2. ¿Cuál fue siempre uno de los deportes preferidos entre las mujeres? 3. ¿Cuáles son los deportes favoritos de América Central, México y Venezuela? 4. ¿Qué diferencia hay entre el fútbol y el fútbol americano? 5. ¿Dónde se originó el jai alai? ¿Dónde lo juegan ahora? 6. ¿Cómo es el lugar donde juegan este deporte? ¿Por qué es muy peligroso? 7. ¿Cuáles son los deportes que invita a practicar la naturaleza del mundo hispánico? 8. ¿Qué deportes practica usted?

NOVIOS Y AMIGOS

llevarse bien

enamorarse de

casarse

tener celos

OBJECTIVES

LANGUAGE: In this chapter we introduce, discuss, and practice:

1. another past tense, the imperfect
2. how to know when to use the imperfect and when to use the preterite
3. certain verbs that show a change in meaning depending on whether they are used in the imperfect or preterite

You will also learn vocabulary related to friends and **novios** (*sweethearts*).

CULTURE: The dialogue takes place in Toledo, Spain. You will learn something about the history of that famous city, home of the sixteenth-century artist El Greco, and about various cultural influences in Spain (Jewish, Arab, and Christian).

EXPLICACIÓN

I. IMPERFECT TENSE OF REGULAR AND IRREGULAR VERBS

(1)	**Ramón:**	*¿Sabías* que el semestre pasado Olga *trabajaba, estudiaba* y, al mismo tiempo *iba* a todas las conferencias?
(2)	**Pedro:**	¿En serio? Entonces, ¿cómo *obtenía* tan buenas notas? *Era* la mejor de su curso.
(3)	**Ramón:**	Porque sabía organizarse: *trabajaba* por la mañana, *asistía* a clases por la tarde y *estudiaba* por la noche.
(4)	**Pedro:**	¿Y qué *hacía* los fines de semana?
(5)	**Ramón:**	*Practicaba* deportes, *veía* televisión y *salía* con sus amigos.
(6)	**Pedro:**	¡Qué muchacha más admirable! Ustedes *se llevaban* muy bien, pero ¿por qué *rompiste* con ella?
(7)	**Ramón:**	¡Porque no le *quedaba* tiempo para tener novio!

1. ¿Qué hacía Olga el semestre pasado?   **2.** ¿Obtenía buenas o malas notas?   **3.** ¿Quién era la mejor de su curso?   **4.** ¿Cuándo estudiaba? ¿Cuándo trabajaba?   **5.** ¿Qué hacía los fines de semana?   **6.** ¿Por qué rompió Ramón con Olga?   **7.** ¿Cree usted que es posible trabajar, salir con amigos y obtener buenas notas? ¿Cómo?

A.   The imperfect tense of regular **-ar** verbs is formed by adding the endings **-aba, -abas, -aba, -ábamos, -abais,** and **-aban** to the stem of the infinitive.

hablar

habl**aba**	habl**ábamos**
habl**abas**	habl**abais**
habl**aba**	habl**aban**

(1) Did you know that last semester Olga was working, studying, and at the same time she was going to all the lectures? (2) Seriously? Then, how did she get such good marks? She was the best in her course. (3) Because she knew how to organize herself: she worked in the morning, attended classes in the afternoon and studied at night. (4) And what did she do on weekends? (5) She played sports, watched television and went out with her friends. (6) What a girl! You got along very well, but, why did you break up with her? (7) Because she had no time left for having a boyfriend!

B. To form the imperfect of regular **-er** or **-ir** verbs, the endings **-ía, -ías, -ía, -íamos, -íais,** and **-ían** are added to the stem.

comer		vivir	
comía	comíamos	vivía	vivíamos
comías	comíais	vivías	viví ais
comía	comían	vivía	vivían

C. There are only three verbs that are irregular in the imperfect: **ir, ser,** and **ver.**

ir		ser		ver	
iba	íbamos	era	éramos	veía	veíamos
ibas	ibais	eras	erais	veías	veíais
iba	iban	era	eran	veía	veían

D. The imperfect tense is used:

1. To express customary or repeated past actions.

Abrazaba a sus padres siempre que los veía.	*She used to hug her parents every time she saw them.*
Ellos me visitaban todos los veranos.	*They visited me every summer.*
Jugábamos tenis con el matrimonio Barrios todos los viernes.	*We played tennis with the Barrios' every Friday.*

2. To express progressive past actions.

Hablábamos con nuestros amigos.	*We were talking with our friends.*
Papá leía el periódico mientras mamá hacía la cena.	*Papa was reading the newspaper while mama made dinner.*
Íbamos a la boda.	*We were going to the wedding.*

3. To describe a situation or condition that existed for a prolonged period of time.

Marisa trabajaba más el semestre pasado.	*Marisa was working harder last semester.*
Pablo siempre llevaba un anillo de oro.	*Pablo always wore a gold ring.*
Engañaba a su novia.	*He was deceiving his girlfriend.*
Había mucho sol.*	*It was very sunny.*

4. To express the time of day in the past or the age of people or things.

Eran las ocho de la mañana.	*It was eight o'clock in the morning.*
Pablo Picasso tenía sesenta años en 1941.	*Pablo Picasso was sixty years old in 1941.*

* **Había** is the imperfect form of **hay,** presented in Chapter 5.

5. In addition, the imperfect is generally used to describe mental or emotional states.

Jorge amaba a Lisa; estaban muy felices y querían casarse.	*Jorge loved Lisa; they were very happy and they wanted to get married.*
Yo pensaba que Ana era más cariñosa.	*I thought that Ana was more affectionate.*
Cuando eras soltero, Enrique, ¿estabas más contento?	*When you were single, Enrique, were you happier?*
Adela tenía celos de su hermana.	*Adela was jealous of her sister.*

E. There are several possible translations of the imperfect in English.

Ellos estudiaban juntos. {
They used to study together.
They were studying together.
They studied together (often, from time to time).

F. Because the first- and third-person singular imperfect forms are identical, subject pronouns are used more frequently with them for clarity.

Yo sabía que ella cambiaba de opinión con frecuencia.	*I knew she changed her mind (opinions) frequently.*
Yo estaba segura que él ignoraba el plan.	*I was sure that he didn't know about the plan.*

Ejercicios

A. Create new sentences, substituting the words in the list for those in italics.

1. *Él* estudiaba los domingos.
   a. yo **b.** Luis y su novia **c.** nosotros **d.** tú **e.** ustedes
2. *Nosotros* teníamos veinte años entonces.
   a. Guillermo **b.** yo **c.** usted **d.** Teresa y Antonio **e.** tú
3. *Nosotros* íbamos todos los días a la playa.
   a. ella **b.** yo **c.** Daniel y mi hermano **d.** tú **e.** usted
4. *Ellas* eran muy cariñosas.
   a. Anita **b.** tú **c.** papá y mamá **d.** yo **e.** nosotros
5. *Él* la veía cuando iba a la ciudad.
   a. Elena. **b.** yo **c.** ustedes **d.** Juan y yo **e.** tú

B. Restate, changing the verbs to the imperfect.

1. Yo nunca desayuno mucho.
2. ¿Le escribes a tu novia todos los días?
3. Piensan ir de vacaciones a Sevilla.
4. ¿No te gusta bailar?
5. Nos divertimos mucho los fines de semana.

6. Nadie quiere ir a la playa.
7. Ella siempre obtiene buenas notas.
8. ¿A qué hora salen de clase?

C. Replace the nouns in italics with the words from the list, and make all necessary changes.

El señor García era rico. Iba al *teatro* todos los días. Allí veía a sus *amigos*.

1. Nosotros/ciudad/primos
2. Yo/cine/novia
3. Tú/centro/amigas
4. La señorita Gómez/cafetería/novio
5. El tío de Pepe/hospital/médico

II. THE IMPERFECT VS. THE PRETERITE

A. The imperfect emphasizes duration of time; the speaker or writer has put himself or herself back in time and describes a scene taking place over an indefinite time period. The preterite, on the other hand, reports a past completed action or event; often, there is some specific indication as to when the action began or ended.

Todas las mañanas Pedro besaba a su mujer antes de ir a la oficina.	*Every morning Pedro kissed his wife before going to the office.*
Pedro besó a su mujer y se fue.	*Pedro kissed his wife and left.*
Estudiaba mucho el año pasado.	*I studied a lot last year.*
Empecé a estudiar a las ocho.	*I began to study at eight o'clock.*
Compré las joyas.	*I bought the jewels.*
Compraba las joyas.	*I was buying the jewels.*
Siempre salía con él los viernes.	*I always went out with him on Fridays.*
Salí con él el viernes pasado.	*I went out with him last Friday.*

B. Often the preterite and imperfect are used in the same sentence to report that an action that was in progress in the past (expressed with the imperfect) was interrupted by another action or event (expressed with the preterite).

Paco miraba la televisión cuando Teresa lo llamó.	*Paco was watching television when Teresa called him.*
Encontré el anillo que buscaba.	*I found the ring I was looking for.*
Mirabel tenía veinticinco años cuando se enamoró de Eduardo.	*Mirable was twenty-five years old when she fell in love with Eduardo.*
Había demasiada niebla y no pudimos salir a tiempo.	*There was too much fog and we couldn't leave on time.*
Rompió con el chico con quien salía.	*She broke up with the guy she was going out with.*

Ejercicios

A. Form sentences in the preterite or imperfect, as appropriate. Provide the definite article when necessary.

Modelos: tía de Sonia/comer/pescado/viernes **La tía de Sonia comía pescado los viernes.**
usted/hablar/con/doctora/a/diez **Usted habló con la doctora a las diez.**

1. ¿dónde/vivir/señores Rojas/antes?
2. yo/romper/con/mi novio/semana pasada
3. niñas y yo/siempre/almorzar/a/una
4. ¿cuántos años/tener/José/año pasado?
5. padres de Roberto/asistir/a/boda/anoche
6. tú/hablar/con/profesora/todos/días
7. amiga de Paco/casarse/viernes/por/noche
8. ¿a qué hora/llegar/ustedes/a/clase de español/ayer?

B. Complete each passage with the appropriate preterite or imperfect form of the verb in parentheses.

1. Nosotros (llegar) _____ tarde a la boda porque no (saber) _____ cómo llegar al lugar y (tener) _____ que preguntar.
2. Mario (obtener) _____ la nota que (desear) _____, pero Isabel (recibir) _____ una mala nota porque (estudiar) _____ muy poco.
3. Anoche fui a una fiesta y (bailar) _____ toda la noche. (haber) _____ mucha gente en un apartamento muy pequeño, pero mis amigos y yo (divertirse) _____ muchísimo.
4. Lucía no (encontrar) _____ los libros que (buscar) _____ y por eso no (escribir) _____ la composición que su profesor le (pedir) _____.

C. Change the following passage to the past tense, using forms of the imperfect and preterite as appropriate.

El misterioso robo de los regalos de boda

Es una noche de invierno. Susana y su esposo Jaime duermen. Hoy ellos cumplen (*have*) exactamente un mes de casados. La sala (*living room*) todavía está llena de sus regalos de boda que incluyen muchas joyas. Susana y Jaime piensan guardar esos regalos en otro sitio porque en la sala no están bien. Cualquier persona puede robarlos.

A las doce en punto alguien entra en la casa. Es el hombre a quien la policía busca desde el sábado. Va directamente a la sala. Abre la puerta con mucho cuidado y sus ojos brillan de alegría. Allí ve los regalos de Susana y Jaime. El hombre hace cuatro viajes para poder llevarse todos los regalos. Nadie lo escucha cuando entra y nadie lo ve cuando finalmente se va. Cuando Jaime y Susana se despiertan y bajan para guardar los regalos, éstos ya no están allí. A pesar de todo, Jaime y Susana no están muy tristes porque las joyas más importantes, los anillos de boda, todavía los tienen.

D. Give the Spanish equivalent of the following sentences.

1. Those rings cost too much and I didn't buy them.
2. They were learning to play the guitar.
3. She used to live in Los Angeles.
4. Eduardo and Beatriz got married last Saturday.
5. Eduardo and Beatriz used to see each other on Saturdays.
6. What did you (*tú*) used to do on weekends?
7. What did you (*tú*) do last weekend?
8. We always ate late when my husband worked at the university.

Preguntas

1. ¿Trabajaba o estudiaba usted el año pasado? ¿Y anoche trabajó o estudió? 2. ¿Qué hacía usted los fines de semana? ¿Qué hizo el fin de semana pasado? 3. ¿Estaba usted muy ocupado(a) con sus estudios el semestre pasado? 4. ¿Tenía usted tiempo para novios(as)? 5. ¿Iba usted mucho al cine cuando estaba en la escuela secundaria? ¿cuándo era niño(a)? 6. ¿Veía usted mucho a sus amigos el año pasado? ¿a su novio(a)? 7. Cuando usted estaba en la escuela secundaria, ¿cómo eran sus cursos? ¿Cuál era el curso que más le gustaba? ¿por qué?

III. CONTRASTIVE MEANINGS OF CERTAIN VERBS IN THE IMPERFECT AND PRETERITE

(1) **Susana:**   ¡Hola, Marta! ¡Hola, Ron!
(2) **Marta:**   ¡Qué sorpresa, Susana! ¿Ya *conocías* a Ron?
(3) **Susana:**   Sí, lo *conocí* anoche en el baile. ¿*Sabías* que Ron bailó toda la noche?

(4)   **Ron:**   Sí, me acosté a las seis de la mañana, pero no *pude* dormir.

(5)   **Marta:**   Veo que se divirtieron mucho. Yo *quise* ir pero tenía un dolor de cabeza terrible. Pero esta noche . . .

(6)   **Susana:**   . . . vienes a mi fiesta, ¿verdad?

(7)   **Ron:**   ¡Otro baile! Pero, ¿cuándo duermen ustedes, los latinos?

---

1. ¿Cuándo conoció Susana a Ron? ¿Dónde lo conoció?   2. ¿Quién bailó toda la noche en el baile?   3. ¿A qué hora se acostó Ron? ¿Pudo dormir?   4. ¿Quién tenía dolor de cabeza?   5. ¿A qué fiesta pensaba ir Marta esa noche?   6. ¿Creía Ron que los latinos dormían mucho?

Several verbs in Spanish have different meanings in the imperfect than they have in the preterite. Among them are **poder, querer, saber,** and **conocer.** Compare the following sentences:

Juan no podía hacerlo.	*Juan could not do it (was not able, did not have the ability).*
Juan no pudo hacerlo.	*Juan could not do it (tried and failed).*
Marta no quería divorciarse.	*Marta did not want to get a divorce (did not have the desire).*
Marta no quiso divorciarse.	*Marta did not want to get a divorce (she refused to).*
Sabía que su esposo la engañaba.	*She knew her husband was deceiving her.*
Supo que su esposo la engañaba.	*She found out her husband was deceiving her.*
Ellos conocían a María.	*They knew (were acquainted with) María.*
Ellos conocieron a María.	*They met María (for the first time).*

Ejercicios

A.   Create new sentences, substituting the words in the list for those in italics.

1. *Juan* supo que su hermana iba a divorciarse.
    a. nosotros   **b.** yo   **c.** ustedes   **d.** Victoria   **e.** tú

---

(1) Hi, Marta! Hi, Ron! (2) What a surprise, Susana! Did you know Ron already? (3) Yes, I met him last night at the dance. Did you know that Ron danced the whole night? (4) Yes, I went to bed at six a.m. but couldn't sleep. (5) I see you had a good time. I wanted to go but I had a terrible headache. But tonight . . . (6) . . . you're coming to my party, aren't you? (7) Another dance! But when do you Latins sleep?

2. *Ramón y Lisa* conocieron a Cecilia en Acapulco.
    a. tú **b.** usted **c.** mi esposo y yo **d.** los Rojas **e.** yo

3. *Marta* quería ir al concierto pero no pudo.
    a. yo **b.** Rubén y yo **c.** ustedes **d.** tú **e.** Eduardo

B. Complete the following passage with the correct imperfect or preterite forms of the verbs in parentheses.

El Greco (1541–1614)

El nombre real del famoso pintor (*painter*) conocido como (*known as*) el Greco _____ (ser) Domenikos Theotokópoulos. _____ (ser) de Grecia. Cuando _____ (tener) aproximadamente veinte años _____ (ir) a Italia para estudiar arte. Allí _____ (conocer) a tres famosos pintores italianos: Miguel Ángel, Correggio y Tiziano. Éste _____ (ser) su maestro (*teacher*) por muchos años pero también los otros dos _____ (tener) gran influencia en su obra (*work*) futura. Pero parece que el Greco no _____ (querer) quedarse en Italia. Unos años después _____ (viajar) a España y a los treinta y seis años _____ (decidir) ir a vivir a la ciudad de Toledo. Allí _____ (pasar) el resto de su vida. ¿Por qué no _____ (volver) a Grecia? Probablemente porque en España, y especialmente en Toledo, _____ (poder) encontrar ese gran misticismo y ese espíritu (*spirit*) religioso que están presentes en todas sus obras. El Greco _____ (morir) en Toledo en 1614.

C. Give the Spanish equivalent of the following sentences.

1. I knew the Johnsons when they were living in Mexico.
2. I met them in Spain.
3. Enrique found it out last week.
4. Jaime never wanted to go to the movies alone.
5. She could take her children there but she didn't want to (she refused to).
6. Amalia couldn't come to class today because she had an accident.
7. Ramona always knew all the answers (*respuestas*).
8. Marisa couldn't dance well because she never used to practice.

UN IMPORTANTE CENTRO CULTURAL

En un autobús de turismo que entra en la ciudad de Toledo

Guía: . . . en la época del rey Alfonso X,[1], Toledo era un importante centro cultural. Aquí, el rey estableció la famosa Escuela de Traductores donde trabajaban juntos los maestros árabes, cristianos y judíos y . . .

Sr. Blanco: ¡Cómo habla este guía!

Sofía: Pero dice cosas que yo no sabía. Es interesante.

Sra. Vega: Para usted, quizás. Yo venía con la idea de comprar joyas.[2]

Sofía: Quizás me interesa porque soy judía y . . .

David: ¡Ah!, tú eres judía también. Yo me llamo David Blum. Soy argentino.

Sofía: Mucho gusto. Sofía Marcus. Conocí a un Blum en Bogotá cuando era niña y . . .

Guía: . . . iban y venían los sabios de Europa por estas calles. Bueno. Creo que mientras hablaba, alguien hizo una pregunta ¿fue usted, señor Blanco?

Sr. Blanco: Sí. ¿Cuántos años tenía el Greco[3] cuando pintó la «Vista de Toledo»?

Guía: Bueno . . . el Greco tenía . . . Pues lo sabía, pero ahora . . . en fin, ustedes tienen dos horas para visitar la ciudad. Salimos a las once en punto.

David: ¿Tú también pensabas ir a las joyerías, Sofía?

Sofía: No, quiero visitar la Sinagoga del Tránsito[4] y el Museo Sefardí que está dentro de ella.

David: No está lejos, creo. ¿Puedo ir contigo? Yo viajo solo porque soy soltero ¿y tú?

Dos horas más tarde

Sra. Vega: Todos los anillos eran lindísimos. Me pedían 200 pesetas por éste, pero yo les ofrecí 100 y aceptaron.

Sr. Blanco: ¿Y por qué no compró más joyas? ¿No le gustaban?

Sra. Vega: Costaban demasiado.

Guía: ¡Hora de salir! ¿Estamos todos?

Sra. Vega:	Creo que faltan los dos jóvenes, Sofía y David. Los vi en la plaza. Iban del brazo y parecían muy felices.
Sr. Blanco:	¡Qué escándalo! Esta generación es terrible. Nunca pude entender eso. Ese joven la conoció esta mañana y ahora seguramente se besan y se abrazan en público. ¿No podían esperar?
Sra. Vega:	¿Y no hacíamos lo mismo nosotros, cuando éramos jóvenes?
Sr. Blanco:	Posiblemente lo hacía usted, señora. Pero yo . . . nunca fui tan joven.
Sra. Vega:	Ya lo creo.

guía *guide*   **me interesa** *it interests me*   **hizo una pregunta** *asked a question*   **hora de salir** *time to go*   **faltan** *are missing*   **escándalo** *scandal*   **seguramente** *surely*   **lo mismo** *the same*

Preguntas

1. ¿Dónde estableció el rey Alfonso X la Escuela de Traductores?   2. ¿Quiénes trabajaban en esa escuela?   3. ¿Con qué idea venía la señora Vega?   4. ¿Qué pregunta le hizo el señor Blanco al guía?   5. ¿Sabía contestarla el guía?   6. ¿Dónde quería ir Sofía?   7. ¿Iban del brazo o de la mano Sofía y David?   8. ¿Cuál fue la reacción del señor Blanco? ¿Qué opina usted de su reacción?

NOTAS CULTURALES

1. Alfonso X of Castile was known as **El Sabio** (*the wise man*) because he devoted most of his energies to scholarly projects such as poetry, law codes, and the writing of a history of the world. Many ancient manuscripts (including those of Aristotle, Euclid, Ptolemy, Hippocrates, and Averroës) would have been lost to the Western world were it not for the School of Translators, greatly encouraged by Alfonso X, which employed Arab, Jewish, and Christian scholars to translate ancient texts into Latin.

2. The jewelry and metal work of Toledo have been distinctive and famous for centuries. During the Middle Ages, Toledo was also famous for the making of swords, which are still made for decorative use.

3. Domenico Theotocopoulos (1541–1614), known as El Greco (*the Greek*), is considered one of the world's great painters. For more information on his life, see Ejercicio B., page 205.

4. The synagogue called **El Tránsito,** located in the Jewish Quarter **(la Judería)** of Toledo, is considered one of the most beautiful in the world. The building is a fine example of the **mudéjar** style of architecture, the style perfected by Arab craftsmen living under Christian rule. Attached to the synagogue is a small museum on the history of the Sephardic Jews **(los sefardíes),** the Jews who lived in Spain and Portugal before they were expelled from Spain at the end of the fifteenth century, and their descendants.

ACTIVIDADES

Melodrama de amor

Read the following picture story. Then change it to the past by filling in each blank with the correct preterite or imperfect of the verb. (You may wish to review first the differences between these two tenses.)

Pepe y Pepita se *conocen* (   ) en una fiesta. Ella *es* (   ) bonita y simpática. Por eso, Pepe se *enamora* (   ) de ella.

Un día, Pepe le *dice* (   ) a Pepita «Yo te amo». Ella *responde* (   ) «Yo también te amo». Entonces se *besan*: (   ) ¡el primer beso!

Una noche, Pepita *habla* (   ) con Pepón en un café cuando *entra* (   ) Pepe. Furioso, Pepe *rompe* (   ) con ella.

Veinte años después: Una tarde, Pepita *sabe* (   ) por una amiga que Pepe *vive* (   ) en la ciudad. Ella *va* (   ) a verlo. ¡Sorpresa! ¡Se *aman* (   ) todavía! (*still*) Se *casan* (   ) en seguida. ¡Qué felicidad!

Entrevista

Ask a classmate the following questions. Then report the information to the class.

1. ¿Qué hacías cuando eras niño(-a)? ¿jugabas al fútbol? ¿al tenis?
2. ¿Te gustaba ir a la escuela o no? ¿por qué?

3. ¿Salías por la noche cuando tenías doce años? ¿Ibas al cine solo(-a)?
4. ¿Conocías otras ciudades cuando tenías ocho años? ¿Qué ciudades conocías?
5. ¿Cuándo conociste a tu primer(-a) novio(-a)? ¿Cómo era él/ella?
6. ¿Podías verlo(-a) todos los días? ¿Era celoso(-a)? ¿Eras tú celoso(-a)?

Situación

Durante la excursión

Two older travelers, Mr. Blanco and Mrs. Vega, are sitting in the plaza of a Spanish city, waiting for the tour bus. Mr. Blanco says he saw a boy and a girl from the tour in the museum. They were going along arm in arm and seemed very happy. Mrs. Vega reacts strongly saying, "What a scandal! This generation is awful." When she was young, the world was different, people were better, etc. Mr. Blanco says that he thinks that they did the same things when they were young. But he agrees (*está de acuerdo*) that the world was different. They both talk about where they met their first sweetheart. The guide interrupts to say it's time to go. He asks if they saw the boy and the girl from the tour (*de la excursión*).

VOCABULARIO ACTIVO

Verbos útiles

abrazar   *to embrace, hug*
adorar   *to adore, love*
amar   *to love*
casarse   *to get married*
divorciarse   *to get a divorce*
enamorarse de   *to fall in love with*
engañar   *to deceive*
establecer (zc)   *to establish*
faltar   *to lack, to need*
guardar   *to keep*
ignorar   *to not know, be unaware of*
llevarse (bien)   *to get along (well)*
obtener   *to obtain, get*
ofrecer (zc)   *to offer*
organizarse   *to organize oneself*
parar   *to stop*
romper   *to break;* **romper con**   *break up with*
tener celos   *to be jealous*

Los novios

el anillo   *ring*
la boda   *wedding*
cariñoso(a)   *loving, affectionate*
ir del brazo   *to walk arm in arm;* **ir de la mano**   *to go hand in hand*
soltero(a)   *single, unmarried*

Otras palabras útiles

cristiano(a)   *Christian*
demasiado   *adv. too much*
dentro de   *in, inside of*
en serio   *seriously*
la época   *epoch, era*
la joya   *jewel*
la joyería   *jewelry store*
judío(a)   *Jewish*
el maestro (la maestra)   *teacher, master*
mientras   *while*
el periódico   *newspaper*
la sorpresa   *surprise*
el turismo   *tourism*

SEGUNDO REPASO

I. VERBS WITH IRREGULARITIES IN THE PRESENT TENSE

A. Review the following verbs with irregularities in the present tense.

1. Stem-changing verbs:
   a. **o** to **ue (volver): vuelvo, vuelves, vuelve, volvemos, volvéis, vuelven**
   b. **u** to **ue (jugar): juego, juegas, juega, jugamos, jugáis, juegan**
   c. **e** to **ie (pensar): pienso, piensas, piensa, pensamos, pensáis, piensan**
   d. **e** to **i (pedir): pido, pides, pide, pedimos, pedís, piden**

2. Verbs with an irregularity in the first-person singular: **conocer (conozco), dar (doy), poner (pongo), saber (sé), salir (salgo), traer (traigo), ver (veo).**

3. Irregular verbs:
   a. **decir: digo, dices, dice, decimos, decís, dicen**
   b. **oír: oigo, oyes, oye, oímos, oís, oyen**
   c. **venir: vengo, vienes, viene, venimos, venís, vienen**

B. Complete the following sentences with the present tense of the verb in parentheses.

1. Yo nunca (recordar) _____ su número de teléfono.
2. Raúl y Jacinto no (poder) _____ trabajar aquí.
3. ¿Qué (servir) _____ tú esta noche? ¿Vino o cerveza?
4. Pues, yo te (decir) _____ la verdad. Todo el mundo (decir) _____ que Enrique tiene mucho dinero.
5. ¿El postre? Yo se lo (traer) _____ inmediatamente, señora.
6. Desde aquí nosotros (ver) _____ la torre. ¿Qué (hacer) _____? ¿Subimos?
7. Yo (poner) _____ el pan aquí, y tú (poder) _____ poner el queso allí.
8. Yo (venir) _____ del concierto; ¿y ustedes de dónde (venir) _____?
9. Yo (salir) _____ ahora para ir al partido de fútbol. (saber) _____ ustedes a qué hora empieza?
10. Yo (conocer) _____ a varios jugadores de jai alai, y mi hermana Antonia (conocer) _____ a Pardo, el mejor jugador de España.
11. ¿Me preguntas qué (hacer) _____ yo los fines de semana? Pues, mi novia y yo (hacer) _____ deportes, vamos al cine o miramos televisión juntos.
12. Yo (saber) _____ que a mis hermanos les gusta el chocolate, pero mamá nunca se lo (dar) _____.

13. ¿Qué (pedir) _____ usted? ¿Café negro o café con leche?
14. Ernesto no (saber) _____ si Teresa (seguir) _____ tres o cuatro cursos este semestre.

II. SUBJECT AND OBJECT PRONOUNS IN SPANISH

A. Review the following chart of subject, indirect object, and direct object pronouns in Spanish.

Subject Pronouns	Object Pronouns	
	Indirect	*Direct*
yo	me	me
tú	te	te
él, ella, usted	le (se)	lo la
nosotros(-as)	nos	nos
vosotros(-as)	os	os
ellos, ellas, ustedes	les (se)	los las

1. Subject pronouns generally tell who carries out the action expressed by a verb: **Ustedes van a México, ¿no?**
2. Indirect object pronouns generally answer the question *To whom (what)?* or *For whom (what)?*: **Adela me escribe y me dice que hay mucha contaminación del aire en Madrid.**
3. Direct object pronouns tell who or what receives the action expressed by a verb: **Juan critica mucho el gobierno. Juan lo critica mucho.**
4. The indirect object pronoun **se** replaces **le** or **les** before the direct objects **lo, la, los,** or **las**: **¿Quieren tres cafés? Ahorita se los sirvo.**

B. Answer the following questions in the affirmative, replacing the words in italics with the appropriate direct or indirect object pronoun.

Modelo: *¿Me* puedes preparar *el almuerzo?* **Sí, te lo puedo preparar.**

1. ¿Puede decir*nos el nombre del restaurante?*
2. *¿Me* puede usted esperar *unos minutos?*
3. *¿Te* puedo visitar mañana?
4. ¿Quiere dar*me* usted *esos pasaportes?*
5. *¿Le* vas a dar *tu dirección (a Ramón)?*

6. ¿*Me* necesitas ahora?
7. ¿*Les* habla Eduardo todos los días *(a ustedes)*?
8. ¿*Te* gustan las frutas?
9. ¿*Le* haces *el desayuno (a Pablo)*?
10. ¿Buscas *a tu novia* para confesar*le la verdad*?
11. ¿*Nos* van a pagar *cien pesos* ustedes si ese equipo gana hoy?
12. ¿*Te* van a traer *las maletas* aquí?

III. REFLEXIVE VERBS

A. The reflexive pronouns in Spanish are **me, te, se, nos, os,** and **se.** These pronouns are used with certain verbs to show that the subject of the sentence receives the action indicated by the verb **(lavarse, divertirse).** Reflexive pronouns precede a conjugated verb form **(¿Nos sentamos aquí?)** or follow and are attached to an infinitive **(Voy a quedarme en casa).** Some reflexive verbs have reflexive equivalents in English **(lavarse** *to wash oneself),* but there are many that do not **(quitarse** *to take off (clothing)).*

B. Restate, changing the pronouns and verbs from the plural to the singular.

   Modelo: ¿Nos sentamos aquí?   **¿Me siento aquí?**

   1. Siempre nos divertimos con ellas.
   2. Ellos se van de aquí a las seis.
   3. ¿Os quitáis el sombrero?
   4. Nos levantamos temprano todos los días.
   5. Ustedes se casan el próximo sábado, ¿no?
   6. Siempre nos ponemos el abrigo cuando hace frío.
   7. ¿Os quedáis en Madrid?
   8. ¿Por qué no se ponen ustedes los zapatos? ¡Es hora de ir a clase!

IV. FORMATION OF THE PRETERITE AND IMPERFECT TENSES

A. Review the following verbs in the preterite and imperfect tenses.

   1. The preterite tense
      a. Regular **-ar** verbs **(pensar): pensé, pensaste, pensó, pensamos, pensasteis, pensaron.** (Note that the changes **e → ie** and **o → ue** affect the present tense only: **pienso, piensas** . . . .)
      b. Regular **-er** and **-ir** verbs **(volver): volví, volviste, volvió, volvimos, volvisteis, volvieron.** (But **vuelvo, vuelves** . . . .)

c. Vowel change **e → i** and **o → u** in the third-persons singular and plural of **-ir** stem-changing verbs: **pedir, divertirse, seguir, servir, preferir, dormir, morir (me divertí, te divertiste, se divirtió . . . se divirtieron; dormí, dormiste, durmió . . . durmieron)**

d. Irregular verbs:

1. Verbs with **u** stems, first person: **pude (poder), puse (poner), supe (saber), estuve (estar), tuve (tener)**
2. Verbs with **i** stems, first person: **quise (querer), vine (venir), hice (hacer)**
3. Verbs with **j** stems: **dije (decir), traje (traer)**
4. The verbs **ir** and **ser: fui, fuiste, fue, fuimos, fuisteis, fueron.** (The context indicates the meaning of these verbs.)
5. The verb **dar: di, diste, dio, dimos, disteis, dieron**

2. The imperfect tense

a. Regular **-ar** verbs **(entrar): entraba, entrabas, entraba, entrábamos, entrabais, entraban**

b. Regular **-er** and **-ir** verbs **(hacer): hacía, hacías, hacía, hacíamos, hacíais, hacían**

c. Three irregular verbs:
ir: iba, ibas, iba, íbamos, ibais, iban
ser: era, eras, era, éramos, erais, eran
ver: veía, veías, veía, veíamos, veíais, veían

B. Change the verbs in the following sentences from the present to the preterite.

Modelo: Raúl va al centro. **Raúl fue al centro.**

1. Tienen que aprender el inglés.
2. ¿Qué pides?
3. Ya los veo.
4. Se lo damos gratis.
5. ¿Quién pierde? ¿Quién gana?
6. No tienes tiempo para ver el partido.
7. Tío Felipe es arquitecto y jugador profesional de fútbol.
8. Los árabes traen a España una rica cultura.
9. Salgo temprano.
10. Fernando se va a casa a acostarse.
11. Se divierten mucho.
12. No nos quiere ver.
13. Conocen a María.
14. Sabe la verdad.
15. Me levanto a las ocho.

Now change the verbs in the following sentences of the preceding exercise to the imperfect: 1, 2, 5, 6, 7, 9, 10, 11, 12, 13, 14, and 15.

Modelo: Raúl va al centro. **Raúl iba al centro.**

V. USE OF THE PRETERITE AND THE IMPERFECT TENSES

A.   The preterite tense emphasizes the completion of an action and is used to pinpoint actions and events at some point in the past: **Entré en la cafetería. Primero comí, después pagué, por fin salí.** The imperfect emphasizes the duration or repetition of a past action or event: **Los surrealistas creían que sus ideas eran nuevas.**

B.   Complete the following paragraph using the imperfect or preterite tense, as appropriate. State the reasons for your choices.

Ayer (llamar) _____ a Pedro a las once y (pasar) _____ por su oficina a las once y media. (querer) _____ invitarlo a almorzar pero él no (estar) _____ allí. Yo (tener) _____ mucha hambre y por eso (decidir) _____ comer sola. (pedir) _____ una hamburguesa, una ensalada grande y una taza de café. Cuando (terminar) _____ mi almuerzo, (volver) _____ a la oficina de Pedro. Él me (decir) _____ que no (ir) _____ a tener tiempo para nuestro partido de tenis diario *(daily)*. (decidir) _____ ir de compras pero no (comprar) _____ nada porque los zapatos que me (gustar) _____ (costar) _____ demasiado. (ser) _____ las ocho cuando yo (llegar) _____ a casa. (mirar) _____ televisión por unas horas y después (acostarse) _____ .

VI. QUESTIONS FOR CONVERSATION

1. ¿Conoce usted a muchas personas interesantes? ¿Dónde y cuándo las conoció?   **2.** ¿Qué consejos les pide a sus padres? ¿a sus amigos?   **3.** ¿Qué comidas le gustan a usted? ¿Cuáles no le gustan?   **4.** ¿Qué deportes le gustan a usted? ¿Qué deportes no le gustan? ¿Por qué? ¿Practica usted algún deporte? ¿Cuál(es)?   **5.** ¿Es el español una lengua tan difícil como el inglés? ¿Cree usted que hay lenguas más difíciles que otras? ¿por ejemplo?

VII. SUPPLEMENTARY TRANSLATION EXERCISE

1. Of all your friends, I'm the most intelligent and least boring, right?   **2.** Don't you want any fruit either?   **3.** Someone called but no one answered.   **4.** We understand each other well.   **5.** I know Elvira, but I don't know where she lives.   **6.** I asked my father for the car, and he asked why I wanted it.   **7.** Where are Manuel and Silvia? It's already five o'clock.

EL CUERPO

—¿Y las piernas? ¿Y los pies?
—¿Y los brazos? ¿Y las manos?

—Están en otro museo.

OBJECTIVES

LANGUAGE: In this chapter we introduce, discuss, and practice:

1. commands in the **usted** or **ustedes** form
2. how to add object pronouns to commands
3. adjectives used as nouns

You will also learn vocabulary for parts of the body.

CULTURE: The dialogue at the end of the chapter takes place in a doctor's office in Panama City. You will learn something about the Central American state situated on the S-shaped Isthmus of Panama, which joins North and South America.

EXPLICACIÓN

I. FORMAL USTED AND USTEDES COMMANDS

En la sección de cosméticos.

(1) **Experta:** *Compren,* señoras, esta crema para la piel. *Pierdan* diez años en una semana.

(2) **Señora I:** ¡Qué milagro! Por favor, señorita, *explique* cómo usarla.

(3) **Experta:** Es muy fácil. *Usen* la crema todas las noches. *Tengan* cuidado, no *apliquen* crema sobre los ojos. *Extiendan* la crema en la cara y sobre todo en la frente.

(4) **Señora II:** Y *diga* usted, por favor, ¿también en el cuello?

(5) **Experta:** No, no *toquen* el cuello con la crema, ni tampoco las orejas. Pero *cubran* bien la nariz.

(6) **Señora I:** Y . . . *sea* sincera ¿vamos a parecer jóvenes en una semana?

(7) **Experta:** ¡Por supuesto! En una semana, o en dos, o en tres. . . .

1. ¿Dónde están las dos señoras? 2. ¿Para qué es la crema? 3. ¿Cuándo deben usar la crema? 4. ¿Deben usar la crema sobre los ojos y en el cuello? 5. ¿Deben cubrir las orejas y la nariz con la crema? 6. ¿Dice la experta que las señoras van a parecer jóvenes en una semana? 7. ¿Cree usted que las personas que trabajan en tiendas pueden ser sinceras? ¿Por qué?

A. To form the singular formal (**usted**) command of regular verbs, drop the **-o** ending from the first person singular (**yo**) form of present tense and add **-e** for **-ar** verbs and **-a** for **-er** and **-ir** verbs.

In the cosmetics department.

(1) Buy, ladies, this skin cream. Lose ten years in one week. (2) What a miracle! Please, Miss, explain how to use it. (3) It's very easy. Use the cream every night. Be careful, don't apply cream over your eyes. Spread the cream on your face and especially on your forehead. (4) And tell (us) please, also on the neck? (5) No, don't touch the neck with the cream nor your ears either. But cover the nose well. (6) And . . . be honest. Are we going to look young in one week? (7) Of course! In one week, or in two, or in three . . .

(Yo) compro esta crema. Compre (usted) esta crema.	*I am buying this cream. Buy this cream.*
(Yo) manejo con cuidado. Maneje (usted) con cuidado.	*I drive carefully. Drive carefully.*
(Yo) leo la explicación. Lea (usted) la explicación.	*I am reading the explanation. Read the explanation.*

B. The **ustedes** command is formed by adding an **-n** to the singular **usted** command form. This form is used in the same situation in which one would use the **ustedes** form of address.

Compren (ustedes) esta crema.	*Buy this cream.*
Manejen (ustedes) con cuidado.	*Drive carefully.*
Lean (ustedes) la explicación.	*Read the explanation.*

C. The negative command is formed by adding **no** before the verb.

No hable con la boca llena.	*Don't talk with your mouth full.*
No extiendan los brazos así.	*Don't stretch out your arms like that.*
¡No miren la nariz del señor!	*Don't look at the man's nose!*

D. If a verb has an irregularity or a stem change in the first person singular, present tense, this irregularity or stem change is carried over into the command forms.

No ponga los pies en la mesa.	*Don't put your feet on the table.*
No salga todavía.	*Don't leave yet.*
No pierdan el dinero.	*Don't lose the money.*
¡Haga una fiesta!	*Have a party!*
Recuerden el refrán: al mal tiempo, buena cara.	*Remember the proverb: grin and bear it (in bad times, show a good face).*

E. A number of verbs have a spelling change in the **usted** and **ustedes** command forms to preserve the sound of the infinitive ending.

c to **qu**   buscar   yo busco→   busque(n)

g to **gu**   llegar   yo llego→   llegue(n)

z to **c**   empezar   yo empiezo→ empiece(n)

F. Some irregular formal **usted** and **ustedes** commands are:

ir	**vaya(n)**	estar	**esté(n)**
ser	**sea(n)**	dar	**dé, den**
saber	**sepa(n)**		

Vayan a hablar con la enfermera.	*Go to talk with the nurse.*
Sean simpáticos con esos extranjeros.	*Be nice to those foreigners.*

Sepan la lección para mañana.   *Know the lesson for tomorrow.*
No esté triste.   *Don't be sad.*
Dése cuenta, doctor, que no tengo   *(You must) realize, doctor, I don't have*
    tiempo para descansar.   *time to rest.*

G. Although the pronouns **usted** and **ustedes** are generally omitted, they may be used to soften a command.

Entre tanto, observe usted esto, por   *Meanwhile, observe this, please.*
    favor.

Levanten ustedes las manos, por   *Raise your hands, please, if you have*
    favor, si tienen preguntas.   *questions.*

Ejercicios

A. Create new sentences, substituting the verbs in the lists for those in italics.

1. (*observar*) Observe usted esos ojos.
   a. cerrar   **b.** abrir   **c.** cuidar   **d.** cubrir   **e.** usar
2. No (*perder*) pierdan ustedes la crema, por favor.
   a. olvidar   **b.** traer   **c.** comprar   **d.** tocar   **e.** pedir

B. Make formal **usted** or **ustedes** commands from the following statements.

Modelo: a. Usted levanta la mano.   **Levante la mano.**

1. Usted llega temprano.
2. Usted extiende los brazos.
3. Usted no sale ahora.
4. Ustedes dan consejos a Susana.
5. Ustedes no compran esa crema.
6. Ustedes no cierran los ojos.

Modelo: b. La señora tiene mucho cuidado.   **Señora, tenga mucho cuidado.**

1. El señor viene a las tres.
2. La señora no pide nada.
3. El señor descansa un poco.
4. Los niños abren la boca.
5. Las chicas van a clase.
6. Los señores vuelven pronto.
7. La señorita cuida su piel.
8. El doctor observa la nariz del bebé.

C. It is the first day of school for Spanish 1 and the students are asking their teacher many questions. Answer their questions with an affirmative **usted** or **ustedes** command, as the teacher would.

Modelos: ¿Debo hablar español ahora? **Sí, hable español ahora.**

¿Debemos practicar el diálogo? **Sí, practiquen el diálogo.**

1. ¿Debo levantar la mano?
2. ¿Debo hacer los ejercicios?
3. ¿Debo buscar eso en el diccionario?
4. ¿Debemos empezar la lección trece?
5. ¿Debemos ir al laboratorio hoy?
6. ¿Debemos comprar el cuaderno de ejercicios?

D. Answer the students' questions from *Ejercicio C* with a negative **usted** or **ustedes** command, as appropriate.

Modelos: ¿Debo hablar español ahora? **No, no hable español ahora.**

¿Debemos practicar el diálogo? **No, no practiquen el diálogo.**

E. Give the Spanish equivalent of the following sentences.

1. Don't open the window, sir.
2. Follow Florida Street, ma'am.
3. Eat, children.
4. Wait a minute, gentlemen.
5. Don't go tomorrow, miss; go Tuesday.

Preguntas

1. ¿Cómo voy de aquí a la biblioteca? ¿de aquí a la cafetería? ¿de aquí a la oficina del director? (Use **usted** commands in all your answers.) **2.** ¿Qué debo hacer para perder peso? ¿para aumentar de peso? ¿para ganar más dinero?

II. OBJECT PRONOUNS WITH COMMANDS

(1)	**Hombre I:**	¿La cabeza? *¡Córtesela*, hombre!
(2)	**Hombre II:**	Bueno, pero ¿qué hago con los brazos? ¿Los pongo sobre la mesa?
(3)	**Hombre I:**	No, no los ponga allí. *Déjelos* en el suelo. Y *hágame* el favor de buscar las piernas debajo de la mesa.
(4)	**Hombre II:**	Aquí están, pero no encuentro los pies.
(5)	**Hombre I:**	No importa. *Levántese* del suelo que ya viene el jefe.
(6)	**Jefe:**	Bueno, ahora que ya deshicieron el maniquí, *guárdenlo* en el depósito. Gracias por la ayuda.

1. ¿Qué debe hacer el hombre II con la cabeza? ¿con los brazos? 2. ¿Qué tiene que buscar debajo de la mesa? 3. ¿Qué no encuentra el hombre II? 4. ¿Por qué se levanta del suelo? 5. ¿Qué deshicieron los hombres? ¿Fue un cadáver?

A. Reflexive and object pronouns are attached to affirmative commands. A written accent is required over the stressed vowel of the command form in order to maintain the proper stress pattern when pronouns are added. Reflexive or indirect object pronouns precede direct object pronouns.

Mueva* el periódico.	*Move the newspaper.*
Muévalo.	*Move it.*
Cierren los ojos.	*Close your eyes.*
Ciérrenlos.	*Close them.*
Déle una sorpresa a sus hijos.	*Give your children a surprise.*
Désela.	*Give it to them.*
Compre usted este champú para el pelo.	*Buy this shampoo for your hair.*
Cómprelo usted.	*Buy it.*
Lávense las manos y la cara.	*Wash your hands and face.*
Lávenselas.	*Wash them.*

(1) The head? Cut it off, man! (2) All right, but what do I do with the arms? Shall I put them on the table? (3) No, don't put them there. Leave them on the floor. And please look for the legs under the table. (4) Here they are, but I can't find the feet. (5) It doesn't matter. Get up from the floor because here comes the boss. (6) Well, now that you took the manikin apart, put it away in the warehouse. Thanks for your help.

* **Mover** is an **o** to **ue** stem-changing verb.

B. Object pronouns precede negative commands. Again, reflexive or indirect object pronouns precede direct object pronouns.

No le pida el auto a su tío al principio. — *Don't ask your uncle for the car at first.*

No se lo pida a su tío al principio. — *Don't ask your uncle for it at first.*

No se quite el suéter. — *Don't take off your sweater.*

No se lo quite. — *Don't take it off.*

Ejercicios

A. Create new sentences, substituting the words in the lists for those in italics.

1. *(las cartas)* Déje*las* aquí.
   a. el postre **b.** la cerveza **c.** las maletas **d.** los zapatos **e.** la sopa

2. *(los brazos)* No *los* muevan, niños.
   a. las manos **b.** el cuello **c.** los pies **d.** las piernas **e.** la cabeza

B. Replace the nouns with object pronouns.

Modelo: a. Cierre los ojos, señora. **Ciérrelos, señora.**

1. Compre esta crema para la piel, señorita.
2. Córtense el pelo, muchachos.
3. Abran la boca, niños.
4. Deshaga ese trabajo, joven.
5. Lávense las manos, muchachas.
6. Cúbrale los pies al niño, señora.

Modelo: b. No se quite la camisa, señor. **No se la quite, señor.**

1. No llame a la enfermera, señor.
2. No abran los ojos, muchachos.
3. No se cubran las orejas, niños.
4. No tomen ese vino, señores.
5. No se toquen la cara, señoritas.
6. No mueva los brazos, señora.

C. Make affirmative **usted** or **ustedes** commands from the following sentences.

Modelos: La señora se sienta. **Señora, siéntese.**
Los niños se lavan la cabeza. **Niños, lávense la cabeza.**

1. La señorita se aplica la crema.
2. Los niños se lavan las manos.
3. El señor se queda aquí.
4. Las señoras se cuidan la piel.
5. Los muchachos se levantan temprano.
6. La señora se va.

7. Los niños se acuestan ahora.
8. El profesor se olvida de los exámenes.

D.   Make the commands in *Ejercicio C* negative.

E.   Give the Spanish equivalent of the following sentences.

1. Sit down, Mrs. Alvarado.
2. Don't close your mouth, Mr. Gómez.
3. Take care of your eyes, young ladies.
4. Don't take off your hat, sir.
5. Don't stay here, boys.
6. Give it (the money) to the foreigners, Miss Ramírez.

III. ADJECTIVES USED AS NOUNS

(1) **Beto:** ¿Tú prefieres a los hombres rubios o a los *morenos?*
(2) **Elba:** Prefiero a los *morenos,* pero los *rubios* también me gustan.
(3) **Beto:** Y . . . ¿de qué nacionalidad los prefieres?
(4) **Elba:** Bueno . . . los *mexicanos* tienen ojos hermosos, los *colombianos* cuerpos hermosos y los *españoles* pelo hermoso.
(5) **Beto:** Veo que los prefieres a todos. Y yo ¿te gusto?
(6) **Elba:** ¡Qué va! Tú eres mi marido.

1. ¿A quiénes prefiere Elba: a los rubios o a los morenos?   2. ¿Qué dice ella de los mexicanos? ¿de los colombianos? ¿y de los españoles?   3. ¿Le gusta (a ella) Beto?

A.   Many adjectives can be used as nouns. When used in this way adjectives are generally preceded by a definite article or a demonstrative adjective. They must agree in gender and number with the nouns they represent.

la mano derecha   → la derecha
el joven inglés   → el inglés
estos zapatos pequeños   → estos pequeños

(1) Do you prefer blond men or dark-haired (ones)? (2) I prefer dark-haired (ones), but I also like blonds. (3) And what nationality do you prefer? (4) Well . . . Mexicans have beautiful eyes, Colombians (have) beautiful bodies and Spaniards (have) beautiful hair. (5) I see that you prefer all of them. And do you like me (Do I appeal to you)? (6) Come on! You're my husband.

B. As shown above, adjectives of nationality and descriptive adjectives (those that state color, size, height and so forth) are commonly used as nouns. Equivalent English expressions usually require a noun or the word *one* or *ones*.

La francesa baja que discute mucho es mi vecina.	*The short French woman who argues a lot is my neighbor.*
No me gusta el vino tinto; prefiero el blanco.	*I don't like red wine; I prefer white wine.*
Me gustan los ojos castaños, pero me gustan más los verdes.	*I like brown (chestnut-colored) eyes, but I like green ones better.*

Ejercicios

A. Create new sentences, substituting the words in the lists for those in italics.

1. *La ropa* española me gusta más que la francesa.
   a. la música **b.** el cine **c.** los muchachos **d.** las sopas **e.** los bailes

2. *Los ojos* azules son más bonitos que los verdes.
   a. el vestido **b.** las blusas **c.** la bicicleta **d.** el color **e.** los pantalones

B. It's Anita's birthday, and her mother takes her shopping and then to a restaurant. Answer Anita's mother's questions as Anita would, following the example.

Modelo: ¿Te gustan más *los zapatos rojos* o los zapatos negros? Me gustan más *los rojos.*

1. ¿Quieres la muñeca (*doll*) rubia o *la muñeca morena?*
2. ¿Prefieres *el vestido verde* o el vestido amarillo?
3. ¿Vas a comprar los pantalones cortos o *los pantalones largos?*
4. ¿Deseas comer en *el barrio italiano* o en el barrio cubano?
5. ¿Prefieres ir al restaurante caro o *al restaurante barato?*
6. ¿Prefieres *la sopa de tomates* o la sopa de pollo?
7. ¿Te gustan más *las tortas de chocolate* o las tortas blancas?
8. ¿Quieres una bicicleta pequeña o *una bicicleta grande?*

Preguntas

1. ¿Qué tipo de música prefiere usted? ¿la clásica o la folklórica? **2.** ¿A quiénes prefiere usted? ¿a los (las) rubios(as) o a los (las) morenos(as)? **3.** ¿Prefiere usted el vino blanco ó el tinto? ¿el español o el chileno? **4.** ¿Cree usted que los ojos azules son más atractivos que los castaños? **5.** ¿Piensa usted que las mujeres altas son más elegantes que las bajas? ¿y los hombres? **6.** ¿Qué autos le gustan más a usted? ¿los americanos o los japoneses? ¿Cuáles son mejores? ¿más económicos? **7.** ¿Con cuál mano agarra (*hold*) usted el tenedor? ¿con la izquierda o con la derecha? ¿y el cuchillo?

UNA SORPRESA

En el consultorio de una doctora, en la ciudad de Panamá.

Enfermera:	Buenas tardes, señora Seara. Hace buen tiempo, ¿verdad?
Sra. Seara:	No me hable del tiempo. El calor es terrible.
Enfermera:	¿A usted también le molesta el calor, señor Seara?
Sr. Seara:	¿A mí? Bueno, el calor lo tolero, pero no tolero el tráfico. ¡Y la gente en el barrio del Marañón![1] No mueven los pies. Me dan ganas de gritarles: «¡Caminen de prisa!»
Enfermera:	Sí, es difícil manejar a estas horas. Bueno, siéntense y descansen.
Sra. Seara:	Gracias. Y, por favor, dígale a la doctora que llegamos.
Enfermera:	No se preocupe, señora. Enseguida los va a atender. Entre tanto, llenen este formulario. No olviden llenar la sección sobre alergias. Y dénmelo después.

Con la doctora

Sra. Seara:	. . . y siento el cuerpo [2] hinchado. Mire mis manos ¡están horribles! Y el vientre ¡tóquelo! ¡parece de piedra!
Doctora:	Sí, voy a examinarla. Abra la boca y diga «aaaaaaaaa». A ver . . .
Sr. Seara:	No sabemos qué le pasa, doctora. La francesa que vive frente a casa dice que debe ser algo en el cerebro.
Sra. Seara:	¡No lo escuche, doctora! Nuestra vecina no es francesa, es inglesa. Él siempre escucha a los extranjeros. A mí no me escucha ¡Y me muero de dolores!
Sr. Seara:	Bueno . . . sí, te escucho, ya ves que me preocupo.

Doctora:	Por favor, terminen de discutir que no puedo trabajar así. Dígame, señora ¿son nuevos estos dolores?
Sra. Seara:	No, pero al principio no les di importancia. Primero eran dolores en los brazos y en la espalda. Después, palpitaciones en el corazón y calores en la cara, y . . .
Doctora:	Espere un momento. ¿Cuándo empezó a estar mal?
Sra. Seara:	A ver . . . en junio; sí, en junio, después que fuimos al restaurante Jade. A mi marido le encanta la comida china, pero a mí no. Prefiero la italiana.
Sr. Seara:	Debes recordar que fuimos al Jade porque tú querías comprar unas molas⁽³⁾ en la tienda que está al lado. ¿Te acuerdas?
Sra. Seara:	No me acuerdo. Pero imagínese, doctora, después de la comida, la indigestión. Póngase en mi lugar, una indigestión con comida que no me gusta ¡dése cuenta!
Doctora:	Señora Seara, creo que su indigestión, dentro de seis meses, se va a llamar Dorita o Pablito. Compre vitaminas para el embarazo y vuelva a verme el mes próximo.

consultorio *doctor's office*	**atender** *take care of*	**hinchado** *swollen*
palpitaciones *palpitations*	**embarazo** *pregnancy*	

Preguntas

1. ¿Por qué dice la señora Seara «No me hable del tiempo»? **2.** ¿Qué no tolera el señor Seara? **3.** ¿Qué les da la enfermera para llenar? **4.** ¿De qué problemas físicos habla la señora Seara cuando está con la doctora? **5.** ¿Cuál fue la opinión de la francesa (o inglesa) que vive frente a su casa? **6.** ¿Cuándo empezaron los dolores de la señora Seara? ¿Qué le dolía? **7.** ¿Qué clase de comida le encanta al señor Seara? ¿Y a su esposa? **8.** Según la doctora, ¿tiene realmente una indigestión la señora Seara o algún otro problema? Explique.

NOTAS CULTURALES

1. El Marañón is a district within Panama City, close to the commercial area. It was built around 1906 to house the labor force engaged in constructing the Panama Canal. After completion of the canal in 1914, the houses—mostly two-storied, wooden townhouses—were rented to other people. The district has been neglected for many years and now the houses are completely run-down, especially due to the constant humidity and heat. At present, the government is trying to develop a new commercial area in **Marañón.**

2. Notice that it is common in Spanish to use the definite article rather than the possessive adjective with parts of the body and articles of clothing, when it is obvious to whom they belong; e.g. **tengo el cuerpo hinchado.** This will be discussed in the grammar section of chapter 18.

3. Molas are rectangular needlework panels, intricately designed by the Cuna Indian women of the San Blas Islands, near the eastern coast of Panama. They consist of several layers of cloth with slots cut in the top layer to show the colors of the under layers. The designs are traditionally abstract, continuous-line compositions, often based on the patterns of Brain Coral. These brightly-colored **molas** are used to decorate blouses, dresses, cushions, purses, table-cloths or other items and are now in great demand by tourists.

ACTIVIDADES

Dibuje, por favor

Study the labelled picture for several minutes. Then close the book. Your teacher will draw a head on the blackboard and then hand the chalk to someone else, saying: «Dibuje el (la, los, las) . . . , por favor.» The person chosen will then draw what is asked for and hand the chalk to someone else, with a similar command, and so on until all the items on the list have been drawn.

el cuello	la pierna derecha
los ojos	los dos pies
el brazo izquierdo	la nariz
el brazo derecho	la boca
la mano izquierda	las orejas
la mano derecha	el corazón
la pierna izquierda	el pelo

El Cuerpo Humano

Give each of the following commands in the *usted* form, substituting the correct word for the drawing. Then use the appropriate direct object pronoun (*lo, la, los, las.*)

Modelo: bajar la = baje la cabeza (*lower your head*); bájela (*lower it*)

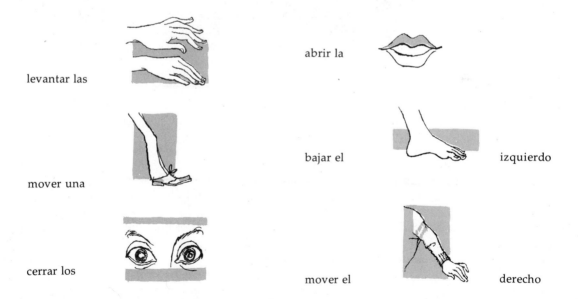

levantar las

abrir la

mover una

bajar el   izquierdo

cerrar los

mover el   derecho

Now, with your book closed, listen to the commands the teacher gives to you or to the whole class and do what he/she says. Afterwards, your teacher may call on you to give commands to someone else.

Entrevista

Ask a classmate the following questions. Then report the information to the class.

1. ¿Qué mano usas para escribir: la derecha o la izquierda?
2. ¿Prefieres el pelo corto o el largo? ¿Por qué?
3. ¿Qué te atrae más en la gente: la belleza de la cara, la inteligencia, la personalidad o alguna otra cosa?
4. Según tu opinión ¿qué actor o actriz es popular a causa de la belleza de su cara?
5. ¿Crees en el alma (soul)? ¿En qué parte del cuerpo crees que está?

Situación

Lugar: en la farmacia.
Personajes: el boticario (the pharmacist) y **Alejandra,** una turista que tiene dolores (pains) y necesita comprar medicinas.

El boticario:	*¿En qué puedo ayudarla, señorita?*
Alejandra:	explica que tiene dolor de cabeza y dolores en los brazos, en los pies, etc. . . . en todo el cuerpo. Dice que es horrible.
El boticario:	le da varias órdenes: «Abra la boca», «Ciérrela», «Levante el brazo», etc. . . .
Alejandra:	le pregunta qué debe tomar.
El boticario:	dice que debe comprar aspirinas y tomar dos. Le da varios consejos: acostarse temprano, descansar mucho, comer poco, etc....
Alejandra:	pregunta cuánto cuestan las aspirinas. Paga al boticario. Le da las gracias y sale.

VOCABULARIO ACTIVO

Verbos útiles

aplicar   *to apply*
caminar   *to walk*
cortar   *to cut, cut off*
cubrir   *to cover*
darse cuenta de   *to realize*
descansar   *to rest*
deshacer   *to take apart, undo*
discutir   *to discuss, argue*
extender (ie)   *to spread, extend*
guardar   *to keep*
llenar   *to fill, fill out*
manejar   *to drive*
mover (ue)   *to move*
observar   *to observe*
tocar   *to touch*

El cuerpo humano

la boca   *mouth*
el brazo   *arm*
la cabeza   *head*
la cara   *face*
el cerebro   *brain*
el cuello   *neck*
el cuerpo   *body*
la espalda   *back*
la frente   *forehead*
la mano   *hand*
la nariz   *nose*
la oreja   *ear*
el pelo   *hair*

el pie   *foot*
la piel   *skin*
la pierna   *leg*
el vientre   *stomach, abdomen*

Adjetivos

bajo(a)   *short, low*
castaño(a)   *chestnut-colored*
hermoso(a)   *beautiful, handsome*
moreno(a)   *dark (in hair color or complexion), brunette*

Sustantivos

la crema   *cream*
el enfermero (la enfermera)   *nurse*
el extranjero (la extranjera)   *foreigner*
la nacionalidad   *nationality*
la piedra   *stone, rock*
la prisa   *hurry;* **de prisa**   *in a hurry*
la sorpresa   *surprise*
el suelo   *floor, ground*
el suéter   *sweater*
el tinto   *red wine*
el vecino (la vecina)   *neighbor*

Otras palabras

al principio   *in the beginning, at first*
entre tanto   *in the meantime*

La España del pasado

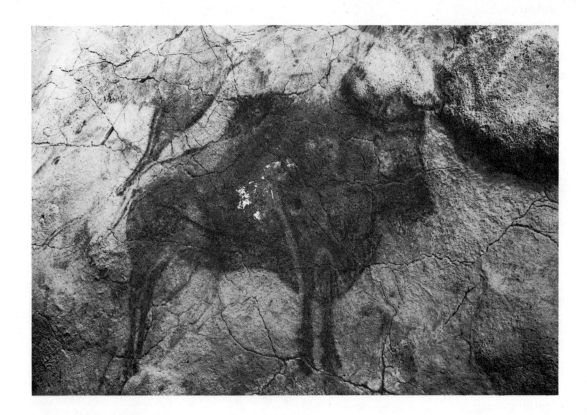

En las Cuevas de Altamira, al norte de España, podemos ver algunas de las pinturas más antiguas del mundo. Son *dibujos* de animales que tienen 20.000 o 30.000 años. En tiempos prehistóricos *se desarrollaba* allí una cultura de origen europeo, *mientras que* en el sur de la península *floreció* una cultura africana que dejó testimonios muy diferentes: figuras estilizadas de hombres y mujeres.

drawings
was developing
while
flourished

Los primeros habitantes históricamente conocidos de España fueron los *iberos*. Estos *se mezclaron* después con los *celtas, invasores del norte*. *Alrededor del* siglo XI *a.C.* llegaron los *fenicios* y griegos, y establecieron centros comerciales en las costas. Luego vinieron los *cartagineses* del norte de África. Explotaron las numerosas minas y convirtieron el país en una base militar para atacar a los romanos, sus enemigos mortales. La guerra entre ellos fue larga y terrible, pero terminó en 218 a.C. con el triunfo de los romanos.

Iberians / were mixed / Celts / invaders /Around / antes de Jesucristo (B.C.) /Phoenicians / Carthaginians

Los romanos eran ingenieros *formidables* y construyeron puentes, edificios, *caminos* y acueductos por todo el país. Algunas de estas construcciones sirven todavía, como el famoso acueducto de Segovia, que vemos en la foto. Pero ninguna de estas construcciones puede compararse con el *legado* cultural de Roma. Esta influencia está presente en la lengua, *ya que* el latín vulgar fue la base del español moderno; en el sistema de leyes; en las ideas estéticas; y también en la religión católica, proclamada como religión oficial por Teodosio, un *emperador* romano que nació en España.

Por otra parte, también fueron importantes las contribuciones que España hizo a Roma. Además de sus *recursos* naturales, le dio tres emperadores y algunos de sus mejores escritores: el poeta Lucano, el satírico Marcial y el filósofo Séneca.

Con el tiempo, el Imperio Romano empezó a *decaer*. En el siglo V, algunas tribus de origen germánico penetraron sus fronteras. Los *visigodos* y otras tribus ocuparon España, pero su cultura tuvo poca influencia en el *modo de ser* del pueblo.

En el año 711 los musulmanes invadieron la península ibérica. En siete años conquistaron la península y sólo *fueron derrotados* cuando llegaron a los *Pirineos*. Los musulmanes establecieron en España una cultura que durante mucho tiempo fue la más espléndida del mundo

superb
roads

legacy
since

emperor

resources

decay

Visigoths
lifestyle

were defeated
Pyrenees

occidental. Construyeron verdaderas maravillas, tales como la *Mez-*   mosque
quita de Córdoba, que vemos en esta foto. En el siglo X, los sabios
de toda Europa viajaban a Córdoba, Granada y otros centros para
aprender de los musulmanos nuevos conocimientos de ciencias,
matemáticas, medicina, agricultura y poesía.

    Poco después de la *llegada* de los musulmanes, grupos de cris-   arrival
tianos *rebeldes* se refugiaron en las montañas del norte de España.   rebels
Desde allí empezaron la guerra de la *Reconquista,* que *duró* casi ocho   reconquest / lasted
siglos. El momento crítico llegó en la Castilla del siglo XI, cuando los
cristianos *alcanzaron* la superioridad militar. La figura principal de   reached
esta época fue El Cid, héroe nacional de España, cuyas aventuras
forman la base de un gran poema épico. Este *dibujo* del Cid es de un   drawing
libro antiguo. El Cid nunca perdió una batalla y ganó el respeto de
los musulmanes por su gran talento diplomático.

Poco a poco los reinos cristianos del norte se unían y ganaban terreno, mientras que el poder musulmán se desintegraba por disensiones internas. *A fines* del siglo XV, la España cristiana se unificó gracias al matrimonio de Fernando de Aragón e Isabel de Castilla, conocidos como los Reyes Católicos. Ésta es su tumba en la Catedral de Granada. En 1492, Granada, el último reino musulmán, *cayó bajo* las fuerzas armadas de los Reyes Católicos, y el mismo año Cristóbal Colón descubrió un Nuevo Mundo en nombre de España. Para los españoles se cerró la larga época de la Reconquista, pero también empezó otra de nuevas conquistas. Ahora los españoles podían utilizar la disciplina militar y psicológica adquirida durante los 700 años de la Reconquista en la colonización del Nuevo Mundo. En los siglos XVI y XVII, el imperio español era más vasto que el antiguo imperio romano y España la nación más poderosa del mundo.

at the end

fell under

Preguntas

1. ¿Dónde podemos ver algunas de las pinturas más antiguas del mundo? ¿Cómo son?
2. ¿Cómo se llamaron los primeros habitantes de España? ¿Qué otros grupos llegaron después?   **3.** ¿Qué ejemplos puede usted dar de la influencia de Roma sobre la cultura española?   **4.** ¿Cuáles fueron algunas de las contribuciones que España hizo a Roma?
5. ¿Quiénes invadieron la península ibérica en el año 711?   **6.** En el siglo X ¿para qué viajaban a Córdoba los sabios de toda Europa?   **7.** ¿Dónde se refugiaron los cristianos rebeldes que empezaron la Reconquista?   **8.** ¿Quién fue el Cid?   **9.** ¿Cuándo y cómo se unificó la España cristiana?   **10.** ¿Por qué podemos decir que el año 1492 fue doblemente importante para España?

VIAJES Y PASEOS

OBJECTIVES

LANGUAGE: In this chapter we introduce, discuss, and practice:

1. commands in the **tú** or **vosotros** form
2. other uses of **se:** the impersonal **se** and a construction with **se** that is used instead of the passive voice (the **se** for passive)
3. **hace** + time expressions

4. long forms of possessive adjectives and possessive pronouns

You will also learn vocabulary related to travel and transportation.

CULTURE: The dialogue at the end of the chapter takes place in Mexico City in an office near the **Zócalo,** or main square. You will learn something about the history and past cultures of Mexico.

EXPLICACIÓN

I. TÚ AND **VOSOTROS** COMMANDS

Cerca del puerto de Cádiz.

(1) **Fermín:** *Dime,* Tito ¿qué hago para llegar al puerto?

(2) **Tito:** *Hazlo* de la siguiente forma: *toma* el autobús aquí en la parada, y *baja* en la estación de autobuses; allí, *dobla* a la derecha. Después *ve* hasta el hotel El Viajero pero ¡cuidado! no *dobles* a la izquierda. *Sigue* derecho hasta el edificio de la aduana.

(3) **Fermín:** ¿Crees que llego a tiempo para reservar los pasajes?

(4) **Tito:** No te *preocupes,* los niños te acompañan. *(Llama a los niños)* ¡Tatín! ¡Beba! *Acompañad* al tío Fermín adonde están los barcos ¿eh? Y *estad* atentos, no os *perdáis.*

(5) **Tatín:** ¡Beba! Vamos a la juguetería con el tío Fermín ¡*Date* prisa!

1. ¿Adónde quiere ir Fermín? 2. Según las instrucciones de Tito ¿dónde debe doblar Fermín? 3. ¿Para qué quiere Fermín llegar al puerto? 4. ¿Quiénes lo van a acompañar? 5. ¿Adónde cree Tatín que van a ir? 6. En general, ¿prefiere usted viajar en autobús, en barco o en avión? ¿Por qué?

A. Informal singular **(tú)** affirmative commands for regular verbs are the same as the third-person singular, present-tense form. The pronoun **tú** is not used, except very rarely, for emphasis.

Gloria toma el tren.	*Gloria is taking the train.*
Toma (tú) el tren.	*Take the train.*

Near the port of Cádiz.
(1) Tell me, Tito, what do I do to get to (to arrive at) the harbor? (2) You do it in the following way: take the bus here at the bus stop and get off at the bus station; there turn to the right. Afterwards go until the hotel El Viajero but, careful! Don't turn to the left. Continue straight until the customs building. (3) Do you think I'll arrive in time to reserve the tickets? (4) Don't worry, the children will accompany you. (He calls the children) Tatín! Beba! Accompany Uncle Fermín to where the boats are, okay? And be alert. Don't get lost. (5) Beba! We're going to the toy store with Uncle Fermín. Hurry up!

Juan lee el mapa.	Juan is reading the map.
Lee el mapa.	Read the map.
Julia sube al autobús.	Julia gets on the bus.
Sube al autobús.	Get on the bus.

B. Some irregular affirmative **tú** commands are:

di	(decir)	**sal**	(salir)
haz	(hacer)	**sé**	(ser)
ve	(ir)	**ten**	(tener)
pon	(poner)	**ven**	(venir)

Irene, di gracias.	Irene, say thank you.
Ve a la aduana, Jorge.	Go to the customs office, Jorge.
Haz la maleta.	Pack (make) your suitcase.
Sé puntual, Paco.	Be punctual, Paco.
Ven acá, María.	Come here, María.
¡Ten cuidado, José!	Be careful, José!
Sal ahora.	Leave now.
Pon el equipaje aquí.	Put the luggage here.

C. Negative **tú** commands are formed by adding an **-s** to the formal **usted** forms.

No doble (usted) aquí.⎫ No dobles (tú) aquí. ⎭	Don't turn here.
No saque (usted) malas notas.⎫ No saques (tú) malas notas. ⎭	Don't get bad grades.
No deje (usted) las maletas aquí.⎫ No dejes (tú) las maletas aquí. ⎭	Don't leave the suitcases here.
No ocupe (usted) esa silla, por favor.⎫ No ocupes (tú) esa silla, por favor. ⎭	Please don't occupy that chair.

D. Affirmative plural **(vosotros)** commands are formed by dropping the **-r** of the infinitive ending and adding **-d:**

Hablad.	Speak.
Comed.	Eat.
Escribid.	Write.

The final **-d** is dropped before the reflexive **os** is added:

Levantaos.	Get up.
Vestíos.*	Get dressed.

---

* An accent is required over the final **-i** of **-ir** verbs.

E. Negative **vosotros** commands are formed by dropping the **-o** from the first-person singular **(yo)** form of the present tense and adding **-éis** to **-ar** verbs and **-áis** to **-er** or **-ir** verbs.

No habléis.	*Don't speak.*
No comáis.	*Don't eat.*
No escribáis.	*Don't write.*
No os levantéis.	*Don't get up.*

F. Reflexive and object pronouns are added to informal commands in the same way they are added to formal commands; they precede negative commands and follow and are attached to affirmative commands.

Preséntaselos a papá.	*Introduce them to Dad.*
No se los presentes a papá.	*Don't introduce them to Dad.*
Dímelo.	*Tell it to me.*
No me lo digas.	*Don't tell me.*
Oponte a eso.	*Oppose it.*
No te opongas a eso.	*Don't oppose it.*
Dejadlos.	*Leave them.*
No los dejéis.	*Don't leave them.*

Ejercicios

A. Create new sentences, substituting the verbs in the lists for those in italics.

1. (*venir*) Ven (tú) más temprano hoy.
   a. comer **b.** salir **c.** llegar **d.** dormir **e.** llamar
2. No (*hacer*) hagas (tú) eso aquí.
   a. poner **b.** comprar **c.** escribir **d.** decir **e.** buscar
3. No (*perder*) perdáis (vosotros) los pasajes.
   a. llevar **b.** comprar **c.** olvidar **d.** reservar **e.** pedir

B. Eliana has invited Lelia to come to her house at around 8 p.m. With the infinitive phrases provided, form affirmative **tú** commands to give Lelia directions on how to get to her friend's house, as Eliana would.

Modelo: Salir antes de las siete. **Sal antes de las siete.**

1. Tomar la calle Colonia.
2. Caminar tres cuadras hacia el centro.
3. Doblar a la izquierda.
4. Ir a la estación de autobuses.
5. Subir al autobús número 85.
6. Sentarse cerca de la puerta de salida (*exit*).
7. Leer los nombres de las calles.
8. Bajarse en Colón, después de pasar cinco paradas.

9. Seguir por Colón hasta el número 121 que es donde vivo.
10. ¡Ser puntual!

C. Vacation time is here again, but poor Rubén is very confused and doesn't know what to do! His father tells him to do one thing but his mother advises him to do just the opposite! Play the role of his mother, following the example.

Modelo: ¡Quédate en casa con nosotros! **¡No te quedes en casa con nosotros!**

1. ¡Busca trabajo en el hotel!
2. ¡Ve a visitar a tus abuelos!
3. ¡Escribe cartas a tus tíos!
4. ¡Córtate el pelo hoy!
5. ¡Levántate más temprano!
6. ¡Haz viajes cortos!
7. ¡Practica piano los fines de semana!
8. ¡Estudia español durante tus vacaciones!
9. ¡Juega al fútbol con tus amigos!
10. ¡Sigue los consejos de tu padre!

D. Eduardito and Martita are visiting their grandmother in Madrid. Using **vosotros** commands, answer the children's questions as their grandmother would.

Modelos: ¿Podemos acostarnos tarde hoy? **Sí, acostaos tarde hoy.**
¿Podemos ir al cine solos? **No, no vayáis al cine solos.**

1. ¿Podemos mirar televisión ahora? No, _____
2. ¿Podemos comer algunos dulces? Sí, _____
3. ¿Podemos escribir en la pared? No, _____
4. ¿Podemos levantarnos a las siete? Sí, _____
5. ¿Podemos pedir una coca-cola? No, _____
6. ¿Podemos volver en diciembre? Sí, _____

Preguntas

(Ask these questions of a fellow student.)

1. ¿Cómo puedo ir de aquí al correo? ¿a la librería universitaria? ¿a la oficina del (de la) profesor(a)? (Use **tú** commands in all your answers.)   **2.** ¿Qué debo hacer para sacar buenas notas? ¿para hablar bien el español? ¿para tener muchos amigos?

II. OTHER USES OF SE

(1)	**Janet:**	¿A qué hora *se abren* los negocios en este país?
(2)	**Patricia:**	A las nueve de la mañana, y *se cierran* a las siete de la tarde.
(3)	**Janet:**	*¿Se puede* cambiar dinero aquí?
(4)	**Patricia:**	Sí, hay una agencia frente a la estación del ferrocarril donde *se cambian* diferentes monedas. Pero a esta hora no *se hace* nada.
(5)	**Janet:**	¿Por qué? Son sólo las dos de la tarde.
(6)	**Patricia:**	Casi todo *se cierra* entre el mediodía y las tres.
(7)	**Janet:**	Veo que aquí *se respeta* la siesta hispana.
(8)	**Patricia:**	Y si no ¿cómo *se puede* estar despierto para salir a la noche?

1. ¿A qué hora se abren los negocios en el país de Patricia?   **2.** ¿A qué hora se cierran?   **3.** ¿Qué quiere cambiar Janet?   **4.** ¿Por qué no puede hacerlo ahora?   **5.** ¿Por qué es buena la siesta hispana, según Patricia?

A. The pronoun **se** followed by a verb in the third-person singular is a construction frequently used when it is not important to express or identify the agent or doer of an action. This use of **se** is often translated in English with *one, people, we, you,* or a passive construction. It is known as the impersonal **se.**

Se sabe que llevar cheques de viajero es mejor que llevar dinero.	*It is known that it is better to carry travellers' checks than to carry money.*
¿Es cierto que aquí se duerme siesta siempre?	*Is it true they (people) always take naps here?*

---

(1) What time do businesses open in this country? (2) At nine in the morning and they close at seven at night. (3) Can one exchange money here? (4) Yes, there is an agency across from the railroad station where different currencies are exchanged. But at this hour, you can't do anything. (5) Why? It's only two in the afternoon. (6) Almost everything is closed between noon and three o'clock. (7) I see that here people honor the hispanic *siesta.* (8) And if not, how can we be awake to go out at night?

Se cree que el poder de los antiguos sacerdotes aztecas era muy grande.	*It is believed (people believe) that the power of the ancient Aztec priests was very great.*
Antes de tomar una copa, se dice «¡Salud!»	*Before having a drink, one says "Cheers!"*

B. **Se** plus a verb in the third-person singular or plural is another common construction in Spanish, called the **se** for passive, since it is used instead of the passive when the agent is not expressed. The verb is in the singular or plural to agree with the subject.

Se necesita secretario(-a) bilingüe.	*Bilingual secretary (is) needed.*
Se necesitan camareros experimentados.	*Experienced waiters (are) needed.*
¿Se vende este auto?	*Is this car for sale?*
¿Se venden boletos de ida y vuelta allí?	*Are round-trip tickets sold there?*

C. The **se** and third-person verb construction is also commonly used with an indirect object pronoun to make unexpected actions impersonal. Instead of saying **Perdí el dinero** (*I lost the money*) one can say **Se me perdió el dinero** (*The money [in my possession] was lost*). The indirect object pronoun is placed after **se** and before the verb, which must agree in number with the subject.

Se me olvidó la dirección.	*I forgot the address.*
A Juan se le perdió la guía.	*Juan lost the guidebook.*
¿Se te olvidó informarte de la hora de partida?	*You forgot to find out the departure time?*

This construction puts a certain polite distance between an event and the person responsible for it or implies that something happened accidentally.

Ejercicios

A. Create new sentences by substituting the words in the lists for those in italics.

1. En la *librería* se venden *libros*.
    a. zapatería / zapatos **b.** cervecería / cerveza **c.** panadería / pan **d.** carnicería / carne **e.** frutería / frutas

2. Se necesita *secretario* experimentado.
    a. doctores **b.** telefonista **c.** profesores **d.** agentes **e.** dentista

B. Susan Johnson, who is spending a few months in Montevideo, Uruguay, as an exchange student, has many questions for Gloria, her Uruguayan "sister". Using an expression with **se,** answer Susan's questions in the affirmative or negative, as Gloria would.

Modelos: ¿Estudian aquí lenguas en la escuela secundaria? (sí) **Sí, aquí se estudian lenguas en la escuela secundaria.**

¿Juegan aquí mucho al béisbol? (no) **No, aquí no se juega mucho al béisbol.**

1. ¿Van aquí mucho a la playa en el verano? (sí)
2. ¿Pagan aquí para asistir a la universidad? (no)
3. ¿Ven aquí películas norteamericanas? (sí)
4. ¿Practican aquí tantos deportes como en los Estados Unidos? (no)
5. ¿Juegan aquí mucho al fútbol? (sí)
6. ¿Siguen aquí el sistema de semestres? (no)
7. ¿Cierran aquí los negocios en general entre el mediodía y las tres? (sí)
8. ¿Traen aquí muchos autos de los Estados Unidos? (no)

C. Give the Spanish equivalent of the following sentences.

1. Spanish is spoken here.
2. You can't exchange money in that agency.
3. They don't make cars in Uruguay.
4. Wine is not served there.
5. Spanish teachers needed.
6. They say he is very jealous.
7. I forgot the passports.
8. They lost your address.

Preguntas

1. ¿Sabe usted cómo se dice *"Cheers!"* en español? ¿en alemán? ¿en francés? **2.** ¿Qué se necesita para viajar a otro país? ¿a otro estado? **3.** Se dice que en el futuro vamos a poder vivir en la luna (*moon*). ¿Cree usted que eso va a ser posible? ¿Por qué? **4.** ¿A qué hora se abren los negocios aquí? ¿Y a qué hora se cierran? **5.** ¿Se juega mucho al béisbol en América del Sur? ¿Y en los Estados Unidos? ¿Se pratican aquí más o menos deportes que allí?

III. HACE + TIME EXPRESSIONS

En la pensión de doña Telma.

(1) **Doña Telma:** Bienvenido, Ruperto. Mire qué casualidad . . . *hace unos días* me acordé de usted.

(2) **Ruperto:** ¡Qué amable, doña Telma! *Hace mucho* que no oigo un cumplido tan gentil. ¿Y por qué se acordó usted de mí?

(3) **Doña Telma:** Bueno . . . ¿cómo no acordarme del primer huésped . . . ?

(4) **Ruperto:** Pero, doña Telma, *hacía tres años* que usted

tenía esta pensión cuando yo llegué. ¿Fui yo el
primer huésped?

(5) **Doña Telma:** Sí, fue usted el primer huésped que se marchó
sin pagar la cuenta.

---

1. ¿De quién se acordó doña Telma hace unos días? **2.** ¿Quién dice que doña Telma es amable? **3.** ¿Fue realmente Ruperto el primer huésped de la pensión?

A. **Hacer** with Expressions of Time to Indicate Duration

1. To express the duration of an action that began in the past and continues into the present use:

hace + period of time + **que** + clause in the present

Hace tres años que vivo aquí.	*I have lived (have been living) here for three years (and still do).*
Hace cuatro meses que trabajo en la aduana.	*I've been working in the custom's office for four months (and still do).*

2. To express the duration of an action that began in the past and continued until some later time in the past, use:

hacía + period of time + **que** + clause in the imperfect

Hacía tres años que vivía aquí cuando me mudé.	*I had lived (had been living) here for three years when I moved.*
Hacía cuatro meses que trabajaba en la aduana.	*I had been working in the custom's office for four months.*

3. The **hacía** construction usually implies that the action or event in progress was interrupted by something else. It does not give the idea of a completed action or event. Compare the following examples.

Hacía tres años que vivía aquí cuando me trasladaron.	*I had lived (had been living) here for three years when they transferred me.*
Viví aquí durante tres años: desde 1969 hasta 1972.	*I lived here for three years: from 1969 to 1972.*

At doña Telma's boarding house.
(1) Welcome, Ruperto. Look what a coincidence . . . I thought of you a few days ago. (2) How kind, doña Telma! I haven't heard such a nice compliment in a long time! And why did you think of me? (3) Well . . . how could I not think of the first guest. . .? (4) But, doña Telma, you had had the boarding house for three years when I arrived. Was I the first guest? (5) Yes, you were the first guest who left without paying the bill.

4. The present or imperfect clause can also be placed at the beginning of the construction, and in this case **que** is omitted.

clause in the present + **hace** + period of time
clause in the imperfect + **hacía** + period of time

Vivo aquí hace tres años.   *I have been living here for three years.*
Vivía aquí hacía tres años.   *I had been living here for three years.*

The word **desde** frequently precedes **hace** or **hacía** in this construction.

Vivo aquí desde hace tres años.   *I have been living here for three years.*
Vivía aquí desde hacía tres años.   *I had been living here for three years.*

B. **Hacer** with Expressions of Time to Indicate *Ago*

1. To express the amount of time that has gone by since a past action occurred, use the following construction (note that **que** is frequently omitted.):

hace + period of time + **(que)** + clause in the preterite

Hace dos meses (que) me pasó algo extraño.   *Something strange happened to me two months ago.*
Hace una semana (que) ella consultó al médico.   *She consulted the doctor a week ago.*

2. The clause in the preterite can also be placed at the beginning of the construction, and in this case **que** is always omitted.

clause in the preterite + **hace** + period of time

Me pasó algo extraño hace dos meses.   *Something strange happened to me two months ago.*
Ella consultó al médico hace una semana.   *She consulted the doctor a week ago.*

Ejercicios

A. Answer the following questions according to the examples.

Modelo: 1. ¿Cuándo llamó Eugenio?   **Hace una semana que llamó.**

a. ¿Cuándo viajó Amparo?
b. ¿Cuándo escribió Rogelio?
c. ¿Cuándo vino tu hermana?
d. ¿Cuándo consultaste al dentista?

Modelo: 2. ¿Escuchas ese programa todos los días?   **No, hace tres días que no lo escucho.**

a. ¿Tocas la guitarra todos los días?
b. ¿Ves a esas muchachas todos los días?

c. ¿Lees el periódico todos los días?

d. ¿Comes chocolates todos los días?

Modelo: 3. Anoche dormiste bien, ¿verdad?   **Sí, pero hacía un mes que no dormía bien.**

a. Anoche bailaste con Pedro, ¿verdad?

b. Anoche fuiste al cine, ¿verdad?

c. Anoche comiste flan, ¿verdad?

d. Anoche miraste televisión, ¿verdad?

B.   Mrs. Sánchez is asking her daughter Rosita if she took care of the things she had to before their trip to Europe. Answer Mrs. Sánchez' questions in the negative, using **hace** + a time expression, as Rosita would.

Modelo: ¿Compraste los pasajes la semana pasada? (tres días)   **No, compré los pasajes hace tres días.**

1. ¿Hablaste con Amalia anoche? (una hora)
2. ¿Fuiste al doctor el lunes pasado? (dos semanas)
3. ¿Pusiste los regalos en las maletas ayer? (unos minutos)
4. ¿Encontraste tu pasaporte el mes pasado? (seis meses)
5. ¿Reservaste cuarto en el hotel la semana pasada? (un mes)
6. ¿Pediste un taxi esta mañana? (exactamente quince segundos)

C.   Felipe Torres is being interviewed for a job as a bilingual secretary for a big company in New York City. Here are some of the questions he is being asked. Answer them in the affirmative, using **hace** + a time expression, as he would.

Modelo: Usted busca trabajo como secretario bilingüe, ¿no? (diez días)   **Sí, hace diez días que busco trabajo como secretario bilingüe.**

1. Usted desea cambiar de empleo, ¿no? (unas seis semanas)
2. Su familia vive en Nueva York, ¿no? (cinco años)
3. Uno de sus amigos trabaja aquí, ¿no? (cuatro meses)
4. Usted enseña español en una universidad, ¿no? (mucho tiempo)
5. Usted y su esposa ocupan un apartamento cerca de aquí, ¿no? (cuatro años)
6. Su hija y mi hijo se ven todos los días, ¿no? (varios meses)
7. Nuestros hijos piensan casarse, ¿no? (unas tres semanas)
8. Usted quiere trabajar en esta compañía, ¿no es cierto? (varios días)

¡Pues hace varios años que necesito una persona como usted! ¡Desde hoy forma parte de nuestra compañía!

D.   Give the Spanish equivalent of the following sentences.

1. We were transferred three weeks ago.
2. Sergio has been working here for ten years.
3. They had been living in Buenos Aires for about eight months.
4. My brother has not come here for years.

5. You (**tú**) had been in Madrid for five days when you met Pablo, right?
6. When the other guests arrived, I had been visiting there for a week.

Preguntas

1. ¿Cuánto tiempo hace que usted estudia español? ¿que asiste a esta universidad?
2. ¿Cuántas semanas hace que comenzó este semestre? **3.** ¿Viajó alguna vez a un país hispano? ¿A qué país? ¿Cuántos años hace que viajó? **4.** ¿Qué comió anoche? ¿Cuánto tiempo hacía que no comía eso? **5.** ¿Qué programa(s) de televisión miró el fin de semana pasado? ¿Cuántos días hacía que no miraba ese (esos) programa(s)?

IV. LONG FORMS OF POSSESSIVE ADJECTIVES

(1) **Oscar:** Esta llave es *mía* ¿no?
(2) **Raúl:** Sí, es *tuya*. Y dime ¿es éste el pasaporte de Enrique?
(3) **Oscar:** Claro, es el *suyo*. Pero . . . no veo mi maleta.
(4) **Empleada:** ¿La maleta azul era la *de usted*? ¡Yo creía que era *de esos turistas* venezolanos!
(5) **Oscar:** No, señorita, la *mía* era la única azul. Las *de ellos* eran todas negras.
(6) **Empleada:** ¡Dios mío! Vino un hombre con barba, dijo que era amigo *de ellos* ¡y se la llevó!

1. ¿Es de Oscar la llave? **2.** ¿De quién es el pasaporte? **3.** ¿De qué color era la maleta de Oscar? **4.** ¿De quiénes eran las maletas negras? **5.** ¿Quién se llevó la maleta azul?

(1) This key is mine, isn't it? (2) Yes, it's yours. And tell me, is this passport Enrique's? (3) Sure, it's his. But. . . I don't see my suitcase. (4) The blue suitcase was yours? I thought that it (belonged to) was those Venezuelan tourists'! (5) No, miss, mine was the only blue one. All of theirs were black. (6) Good heavens! A man with a beard came, said he was a friend of theirs, and took it away!

A. There are other forms of possessive adjectives than those presented in Chapter 5. These longer forms follow rather than precede the nouns they modify and agree with them in gender and number.

LONG FORMS OF POSSESSIVE ADJECTIVES

Singular	Plural	
mío, mía	míos, mías	*my, of mine*
tuyo, tuya	tuyos, tuyas	*your, of yours*
suyo, suya	suyos, suyas	*his, of his; her, of hers; your, of yours*
nuestro(-a)	nuestros(-as)	*our, of ours*
vuestro(-a)	vuestros(-as)	*your, of yours*
suyo(-a)	suyos(-as)	*their, of theirs; your, of yours*

Esa amiga tuya es fascinante.   *That friend of yours is fascinating.*

Durante el mes de julio, voy de vacaciones con unos primos míos.   *During the month of July, I'm going on vacation with some cousins of mine.*

Éste es el mapa suyo, ¿verdad?   *This is your map, right?*

B. Possessive pronouns have the same forms as the long forms of the possessive adjectives. They are usually preceded by the definite article. The article and the pronoun agree in gender and number with the noun referred to, which is omitted.

Voy a vender el (auto) mío porque no funciona bien.   *I'm going to sell mine (my car) because it doesn't run well.*

¿Dónde están las (maletas) tuyas? — En medio del cuarto.   *Where are yours (your suitcases)? —In the middle of the room.*

Su casa está a la derecha. La nuestra está a la izquierda.   *Their house is on the right. Ours is on the left.*

Mi hijo no salió con el suyo, Sr. López, ¿no es cierto?   *My son didn't leave with yours, Mr. López, isn't that right?*

C. After the verb **ser** the definite article is usually omitted.

La roja es nuestra.   *The red one is ours.*

Esas guías no son tuyas.   *Those guidebooks aren't yours.*

¿Son míos estos pasajes?   *Are these tickets mine?*

D. Since **suyo(-a)** and **suyos(-as)** have several meanings, depending on the possessor, these pronouns may be replaced by a prepositional phrase with **de**.

de +
él
ella
usted
ellos
ellas
ustedes

—El traje mío es viejo.   —*My suit is old.*
—¿El suyo es nuevo? (¿El de usted es   —*Yours is new?*
nuevo?)
—¿Y las llaves?   —*And the keys?*
—Las suyas no están aquí. (Las de   —*Hers aren't here.*
ella no están aquí.)

Ejercicios

A. Create new sentences, substituting the words in the lists for those in italics.

1. Hace dos meses que un *primo* mío está en Chile.
   a. amigas **b.** hija **c.** tíos **d.** profesores **e.** hermano
2. Es la *maleta* suya.
   a. pasaporte **b.** libros **c.** cámara **d.** camisas **e.** pasaje

B. Restate, using first the long form of the possessive adjective and then changing the sentence to use the corresponding possessive pronoun.

Modelo: Mi casa es pequeña. **La casa mía es pequeña. La mía es pequeña.**

1. Tu amigo está allí.
2. Él vendió sus libros.
3. Nuestras hijas son rubias.
4. Dejé mi maleta en el hotel.
5. Pepe perdió su pasaporte anoche.

C. Mrs. Ruiz is helping a friend unpack after a trip. Answer her questions in the affirmative, following the model.

Modelo: ¿Son de Luis estas corbatas? **Sí, son suyas.**

1. ¿Es tuya esta falda?
2. ¿Son de Irene estas sandalias?
3. ¿Es de Luisito esta camisa?
4. ¿Son de los niños estos zapatos?
5. ¿Es tuyo este vestido?
6. ¿Es de Luis este sombrero?
7. ¿Son de ustedes estos pasaportes?

D. Give the Spanish equivalent of the following phrases.

1. my trip and yours (**tú** form)
2. your (**usted** form) beard and mine
3. our address and his
4. her key and mine
5. their boarding house and hers
6. your (**ustedes** form) guests and ours
7. my maps and theirs
8. your (**tú** form) ticket and his

EN LA ANTIGUA CAPITAL AZTECA

En una oficina del Zócalo[(1)], México, D.F. Dos agentes de la compañía Turismo Mundial le dan la bienvenida a Amalia Mercado, una agente española en viaje de negocios.

Héctor: ¡Bienvenida, Amalia! ¿Cómo estás?

Amalia: Bien, gracias. Hace mucho que no nos vemos ¿eh?

Héctor: Es cierto, hace unos tres años ¿no? ¡Cómo pasa el tiempo! Ven, que te presento a Alonso Rodríguez. Él es el encargado de las excursiones al Caribe en barco y en avión, y de la reserva de pasajes.

Amalia: ¡Pero si ya nos conocemos! ¿Recuerdas, Alonso? Fue en Málaga.

Alonso: ¡Claro! Y me acuerdo de aquel auto tuyo que no funcionaba bien.

Amalia: Ya no lo tengo. Pero no sabía que ahora vivías en México.

Alonso: Estoy aquí desde marzo. La compañía quiso trasladarme y no pude oponerme.

Amalia: ¿Hacía mucho tiempo que vivías en Málaga?

Alonso: Cinco años. Se vivía bien allá. No quería mudarme, pero . . .

Héctor: Bueno, aquí también se vive bien. Y . . . ¿es tu primer viaje a México, Amalia?

Amalia: Sí. Vine por una invitación de la Compañía Mexicana de Aviación. Un viaje de ida y vuelta en primera clase. Mirad qué buena suerte.[(2)] Y todo esto me parece extraño y fascinante.

Héctor: Es cierto. La ciudad está construida sobre las ruinas de la antigua capital azteca, que estaba en medio de un lago.[(3)] Por eso, algunas partes de la ciudad se hunden y otras se elevan un poco cada año.

Alonso: Aquí cerca, en el sitio que ocupa ahora la catedral, se dice que los aztecas tenían su gran templo.

Amalia: ¡Eso sí que es interesante! Y dime, Héctor, ¿te vas a quedar aquí para siempre?

Héctor: ¿Quién sabe? Hace tres meses, la compañía iba a trasladarme. Pero mi esposa no quiso mudarse. Y no pude convencerla.

Amalia: Ten cuidado. No te olvides que puedes perder el ascenso.

Alonso: Estos jefes nuestros son como los antiguos sacerdotes aztecas, y nosotros somos los sacrificados.[4] Ellos tienen todo el poder.

Amalia: ¡Caramba! Tú estás muy pesimista hoy. Pero ¿se trabaja mucho acá?

Héctor: Bueno, se trabaja las horas necesarias.

Alonso: ¿Qué les parece si vamos a tomar una copa al bar de la Torre Latinoamericana[5]? Se tiene una hermosa vista de la ciudad desde allí.

Amalia: Me parece bien, pero esperadme un momento, que debo llamar por teléfono. ¡Ay, se me perdió el número! ¡No, no! Aquí está. Vuelvo en cinco minutos. No me abandonéis.

Héctor: ¡Qué mujer! Siempre se te pierden las cosas y se te olvidan los números de teléfono. No te preocupes, que aquí te esperamos.

---

encargado *man in charge*   **construida** *built*   **se hunden** *sink*   **se elevan** *rise*
ascenso *promotion*

Preguntas

1. ¿Dónde están los tres agentes?   **2.** ¿Cuánto tiempo hace que no se ven Amalia y Héctor?   **3.** ¿De qué se acuerda Alonso?   **4.** ¿Cuánto tiempo hacía que Alonso vivía en Málaga antes de mudarse?   **5.** Según se dice ¿dónde tenían los aztecas su gran templo? **6.** ¿Por qué a veces cree Alonso que los jefes suyos son como los antiguos sacerdotes aztecas?   **7.** ¿Para qué piensan ir a la Torre Latinoamericana?   **8.** ¿Qué se le perdió a Amalia? ¿Qué cosas se le pierden a usted generalmente? ¿qué cosas se le olvidan?

NOTAS CULTURALES

1. El Zócalo (officially called **Plaza de la Constitución**) is one of the biggest squares in the world and the center of Mexico City (**México, Distrito Federal**). One side is occupied by the cathedral, one of the largest in America, built on the site of a former Aztec temple, the **Teocali** or **Gran Templo de Moctezuma.** Another side is occupied by the **Palacio Nacional,** which contains the offices of the president and other government officials. It was built over the site of Moctezuma's palace.

2. Since Amalia is from Spain, she uses the **vosotros** command forms when she speaks to friends; these forms are not used by people from other parts of the Hispanic world.

3. The subsoil of Mexico City, for the reasons alluded to in the dialogue, is like a giant sponge: about 85 percent of it is water, much of which is extracted from time to time for use in the growing city. For this reason, there are many differences in levels in some older public buildings. Many have been thrust upwards and must be entered by stairways added later to the original structure. Others have sunk and must now be reached by descending a stairway.

4. The Aztec Indians, who had conquered most of the other Indians of Mexico by the time the Spanish arrived, practiced a religion in which human sacrifices were performed regularly. They believed that the sun needed to be fed human blood to maintain its energy. The usual procedure was to tear open the victim's chest with an ornate knife and rip out the still-beating heart as an offering to the sun.

5. The **Torre Latinoamericana** is a 44-story skyscraper. It literally floats on its foundation, which consists of piers sunk deep into the clay beneath Mexico City. An observatory on top affords a panoramic view of the city and is popular with tourists.

ACTIVIDADES

¿Qué hace el turista experimentado?

Eduardo has not travelled very much and asks his friend Ana, an experienced traveller, what are the most important rules for travelling. Formulate six rules (in the *tú* command form, negative and affirmative) that Ana might give to Eduardo.

Modelo: No *dejes* las cosas para el último momento. *Compra* los boletos temprano.

A. No deja las cosas para el último momento. Compra los boletos (de barco, tren o avión) con tiempo.

D. Lee varios libros y guías sobre el país donde va a viajar. También consulta mapas de las diferentes ciudades y regiones.

B. Hace la maleta varios días antes de la partida. Nunca lleva mucho equipaje; prefiere llevar una sola maleta.

E. Nunca se olvida de las tres cosas más importantes: los boletos, el dinero (o cheques de viajero) y el pasaporte.

C. Llega temprano al aeropuerto, al puerto o a la estación de trenes. No llega tarde nunca.

F. Siempre se informa sobre los precios antes de quedarse en un hotel.

Un viaje imaginario

One student should begin by saying the following phrase:

«*Mañana me voy de viaje. Pongo en la maleta . . . mi pasaporte*»
The next student should repeat the phrase and add another object, for example:
«*Mañana me voy de viaje. Pongo en la maleta mi pasaporte y dinero.*»
The game continues until someone can't remember all the objects or makes a mistake.
Then someone begins again.

Entrevista

Ask a classmate the following questions. Then report the information to the class.

1. ¿Cuánto tiempo hace que no sales de viaje?
2. ¿Crees que se viajaba mejor hace diez años, o que es más fácil viajar ahora?
3. ¿Prefieres viajar en avión, en tren o en barco? ¿Por qué?
4. ¿Qué lugares quieres conocer? ¿Por qué?
5. ¿Crees que se necesita mucho dinero para viajar o tienes el secreto para viajar bien y barato? Si es así ¡dímelo!
6. ¿Qué tipo de ropa llevas en tu maleta cuando sales de vacaciones?

Situación

Lugar: en la estación de trenes
Personajes: el **empleado** que vende los boletos; **Turista I** y **Turista II**

El empleado:	«*Buenos días ¿qué desea?*»
Turista I:	«*Buenos días*»; pide dos boletos para el tren expreso que va a Málaga.
El empleado:	dice que el tren salió hace veinte minutos.
Turista I:	dice que qué mala suerte; pregunta cuándo va a salir el próximo tren para Málaga.
El empleado:	dice que el próximo tren sale mañana a las diez.
Turista II:	interrumpe (*interrupts*) para decir que se puede ir a Málaga en autobús.
Turista I:	dice que es una buena idea; pregunta dónde está la estación de los autobuses.
Turista II:	explica que la parada del autobús está cerca, en la calle Flores, dos cuadras a la derecha, etc. . . . .
Turista I:	da las gracias; dice que va enseguida.

VOCABULARIO ACTIVO

Verbos útiles

acompañar *to accompany*
acordarse (ue) de *to remember*
cambiar *to change, to exchange*
consultar *to consult*
convencer *to convince*
dejar *to leave, leave behind; to allow or permit*
doblar *to turn*
funcionar *to work, function*
informarse *to inform oneself, find out*
marcharse *to leave, go away*
mudarse *to move, change residence*
ocupar *to occupy*
olvidar *to forget*
oponerse *to oppose, be against*
presentar *to introduce, present*
respetar *to respect*
sacar *to take out;* **sacar una nota** *to get a grade*
subir *to go up;* **subir a** *to get on*
trasladar *to transfer*

Los viajes

la aduana *customs, customs office*
el barco *ship, boat*
la bienvenida *welcome;* **dar la bienvenida** *to welcome*
el boleto *ticket*
el cheque de viajero *traveler's check*
la dirección *address*
el equipaje *luggage*
la estación *station*
el ferrocarril *railroad*
la guía *guidebook (also, woman guide)*
el huésped *guest*
el mapa *map*
la moneda *coin, currency*
la parada *stop*
la partida *departure*
el pasaje *ticket*

la pensión *boarding house, hotel that offers meals*
el puerto *port, harbor*
el tren *train*

Sustantivos

la barba *beard*
la compañía *company*
la copa *drink;* **tomar una copa** *to have a drink*
el cumplido *compliment*
la llave *key*
el negocio *business;* **viaje de negocios** *business trip*
el poder *power*
la ruina *ruin*
el sacerdote *priest*
el secretario (la secretaria) *secretary*
el templo *temple*

Adjetivos

antiguo(a) *ancient; former*
atento(a) *alert*
cierto(a) *certain, sure*
despierto(a) *awake, alert*
experimentado(a) *experienced*
extraño(a) *strange*
fascinante *fascinating*
gentil *nice*
necesario(a) *necessary*
pesimista *pessimistic*
puntual *punctual*
único(a) *only; unique*

Otras palabras

a mediodía *at noon*
de ida y vuelta *roundtrip*
durante *during*
en medio de *in the middle of*
¡Qué casualidad! *What a coincidence!*

CAPÍTULO 14

ARTE Y LITERATURA

UN DETALLE DE LAS MENINAS, DE VELÁZQUEZ

OBJECTIVES

LANGUAGE: In this chapter we introduce, discuss, and practice:
1. past participles (like *said, made, written,* or *painted*) and their use as adjectives
2. the present and past perfect tenses, two compound past tenses
3. a contrast of the four past tenses you have studied: the preterite, imperfect, present perfect, and past perfect

You will also learn vocabulary related to art and literature.

CULTURE: The dialogue at the end of the chapter takes place in the famous **Museo del Prado** in Madrid, where a professor of art and some students are looking at several of the paintings on display there. You will learn something about some of the many renowned Spanish artists and their works.

EXPLICACIÓN

I. THE PAST PARTICIPLE USED AS AN ADJECTIVE

En el Museo del Prado.

(1) **Lucía:** ¡Estos cuadros de Goya son muy hermosos! Parecen *inspirados* por la naturaleza misma . . .

(2) **Arturo:** Sin embargo, éstos de aquí tienen otro estilo . . . Representan actos brutales, cuerpos *rotos*, monstruos . . .

(3) **Lucía:** Sí, son obras *pintadas* después de la guerra napoleónica. A Goya le impresionó mucho tanto sufrimiento y muerte. Estaba *obsesionado*. Pintaba personas y cosas *destruidas* . . .

(4) **Arturo:** Es verdad, pero sólo un genio como Goya podía crear algo tan trágico y bello como *El tres de mayo.*

1. ¿Cómo son los cuadros de Goya que mira Lucía?   **2.** ¿Por qué dice Arturo que los cuadros de Goya que él mira tienen otro estilo?   **3.** ¿Cómo explica este cambio Lucía? **4.** ¿Por qué cree Arturo que Goya es un genio?   **5.** ¿Qué cuadros de Goya conoce usted? ¿Le gustan?

A. To form the past participle of regular **-ar** verbs, add **-ado** to the stem of the infinitive.

habl**ado**   *spoken*

B. To form the past participle of regular **-er** or **-ir** verbs, add **-ido** to the stem of the infinitive.

com**ido**   *eaten*
viv**ido**   *lived*

At the Prado museum
(1) These pictures of Goya are very beautiful! They seem inspired by nature itself . . . (2) Nevertheless, these over here have another style . . . They depict brutal acts, broken bodies, monsters . . . (3) Yes, they are works painted after the Napoleonic war. So much suffering and death impressed Goya a great deal. He was obsessed. He painted people and things destroyed . . . (4) It's true, but only a genius like Goya could create something so tragic and beautiful as *The Third of May.*

If the stem of an **-er** or **-ir** verb ends in **-a, -e,** or **-o,** the **-ido** ending takes an accent.

traído	*brought*
creído	*believed*
oído	*heard*

The past participle of **ser** is **sido,** and of **ir, ido.**

C.   The past participle is often used as an adjective and agrees in gender and number with the noun it modifies. It is often used with **estar,** frequently to show the result of an action.

La novela está inspirada en la vida de Goya.	*The novel is inspired on Goya's life.*
El cuadro pintado en México es de la señora Ordóñez.	*The picture painted in Mexico is Mrs. Ordóñez'.*
Después de escribir toda la noche, el autor estaba cansado.	*After writing all night, the author was tired.*

D.   Some irregular past participles are:

abierto *open, opened* (abrir)	muerto *died, dead* (morir)
cubierto *covered* (cubrir)	puesto *put* (poner)
descrito *described* (describir)	resuelto *solved* (resolver)
dicho *said* (decir)	roto *broken* (romper)
escrito *written* (escribir)	visto *seen* (ver)
hecho *made, done* (hacer)	vuelto *returned* (volver)
¿Lees una revista escrita en español?	*Do you read a magazine written in Spanish?*
Julia tiene el bolso abierto.	*Julia has her purse open.*

Ejercicios

A.   Create new sentences, substituting the words in the lists for those in italics.

1.   ¿Tienes *algo* hecho en México?
   a. una guitarra   **b.** un poncho   **c.** dos maletas   **d.** unos zapatos   **e.** un bolso

2.   ¿Leen *una novela* escrita en español?
   a. un poema   **b.** libros   **c.** una obra   **d.** revistas   **e.** diálogos

B.   Mrs. Ibáñez is asking Ricardo if he has already done the following things. Answer her questions in the affirmative, following the model, as Ricardo would.

Modelo: ¿Abriste las puertas?   **Sí, las puertas ya están abiertas.**

1.   ¿Lavaste el auto?
2.   ¿Pusiste la mesa?
3.   ¿Escribiste las cartas?
4.   ¿Resolviste el problema?
5.   ¿Hiciste los ejercicios?
6.   ¿Pagaste la cuenta?

C. *Mini-misterio.* There has been a murder at the home of Mr. and Mrs. Solís. After surveying the scene of the crime, Detective Jolmez is able to solve the case. In the paragraph that follows, fill in the blanks with the correct past participles of the verbs provided, and then try to guess who is the murderer...

Modelo: Jolmez ve muchas cosas _____**rotas**_____(romper) y una silla en el suelo.

A la derecha de la silla ve a un hombre _____ (morir). Parece que los señores Solís se preparaban para cenar. La mesa ya estaba _____ (poner) y allí se veían platos y vasos muy caros, probablemente _____ (comprar) en Francia. Jolmez se da cuenta de que los Solís son gente rica. Tienen un cuadro _____ (pintar) por Goya, varios objetos artísticos _____ (traer) de Europa y el Oriente, y una colección de libros _____ (escribir) en el siglo XVI. Pero en medio de todo esto también hay una persona _____ (morir). Jolmez observa que es el señor Solís y que tiene las dos manos fuertemente _____ (cerrar). En la mano derecha tiene un papel. Es una carta _____ (escribir) por una mujer _____ (llamar) Carolina. Dice la carta: «(Querer) _____ amor mío: Tu esposa lo sabe todo. ¡Cuídate, por favor! Te besa, Carolina.» Jolmez descubre después que en la mano izquierda el señor Solís tiene _____ (guardar) un botón *(button)* verde. Observa también que tiene la camisa _____ (cubrir) de sangre. Jolmez va después al baño *(bathroom)* y allí encuentra a la señora Solís, _____ (vestir) de verde y _____ (sentar) en el suelo. Parece _____ (dormir) pero está realmente _____ (morir). Jolmez observa la escena por unos minutos y dice: «El misterio está _____ (resolver).»...¿Qué ve Jolmez en el baño? Muy poco: un bolso _____ (abrir), una botellita *(little bottle)* vacía *(empty)* de píldoras *(pills)* de dormir y un cuchillo _____ (cubrir) de sangre. ¿Quién mató a los señores Solís? ¿Por qué? (La solución está incluida en el Ejercicio D. de la página 260.)

Preguntas

1. ¿Está usted inspirado(a) en este momento? ¿cansado(a)? ¿preocupado(a)? ¿Por qué? **2.** ¿Está usted sentado(a) cerca de la ventana? ¿de la puerta? **3.** ¿Tiene usted el libro de español abierto o cerrado ahora? **4.** ¿Vio usted alguna vez un cuadro pintado por Picasso? ¿por Velázquez? ¿por el Greco? ¿por algún otro pintor español conocido? ¿Qué cuadro(s)? **5.** ¿Leyó alguna novela escrita por Hemingway? ¿Faulkner? ¿Jules Verne? ¿García Márquez? ¿Qué novela(s)?

II. THE PRESENT AND PAST PERFECT TENSES

(1) **Primer Señor:** Perdone, señor. *¿Ha visto* usted a algún policía por esta calle?

(2) **Segundo Señor:** Por aquí, no, pero *he encontrado* a unos policías frente al Teatro de Comedias.

(3) **Primer Señor:** ¿No *ha visto* a nadie por aquí?

(4) **Segundo Señor:** No, antes de encontrarme con usted, no
había visto a nadie.

(5) **Primer Señor:** Entonces, ¡arriba las manos!

---

1. ¿Ha visto el señor a algún policía por la calle?   **2.** ¿Y frente al Teatro de Comedias?
3. ¿Se ha encontrado con alguien?   **4.** ¿Qué le dice el otro hombre después de todas las preguntas?

A. The present perfect tense is formed with the present tense of the auxiliary verb **haber** plus a past participle.

haber

he	hemos
has	habéis + past participle
ha	han

It is used to report an action or event that has recently taken place or been completed and still has a bearing upon the present. It is generally used without reference to any specific time in the past, since it implies a reference to the present day, week, month, etc.

La obra de ese pintor ha sido muy admirada recientemente.	*That painter's work has been much admired recently.*
Ellos han hablado conmigo hoy.	*They have spoken with me today.*
¿Ya has firmado la carta, querido?	*Have you already signed the letter, dear?*
A pesar de que Julio escribe poesía constantemente, no ha escrito un solo poema bueno.	*In spite of the fact that Julio writes poetry constantly, he hasn't written a single good poem.*
¿Has visto el retrato?	*Have you seen the portrait?*

The past participle always ends in **-o** when used to form a perfect tense; it does not agree with the subject in gender or number.

B. The past perfect tense is formed with the imperfect of **haber** plus a past participle.

haber

había	habíamos
habías	habíais + past participle
había	habían

(1) Excuse me, sir. Have you seen a policeman on this street? (2) Not around here, but I came across a few policemen in front of the Comedy Theater. (3) You haven't seen anyone around here? (4) No, before meeting you, I hadn't seen anyone. (5) Then, hands up!

It is used to indicate that an action or event had taken place at some time in the past prior to another past event, stated or implied. If the other past event is stated, it is usually in the preterite or imperfect.

Leí que un escritor peruano había ganado el premio.

I read that a Peruvian writer had won the prize.

Ya habían vendido la pintura cuando yo llegué.

They had already sold the painting when I arrived.

C. The auxiliary form of **haber** and the past participle are seldom separated by another word. Negative words and pronouns normally precede the auxiliary verb.

No he recibido el recado.

I haven't received the message.

¿Ya me has enviado el cuento?

Have you already sent me the story?

No, no te lo he enviado todavía.

No, I haven't sent it to you yet.

Ejercicios

A. Create new sentences, substituting the words in the lists for those in italics.

1. *Javier* ha visitado ese museo muchas veces.
   a. nosotros **b.** yo **c.** Luis y Estela **d.** tú **e.** ustedes

2. *Ustedes* nunca habían venido aquí antes, ¿verdad?
   a. Fernando **b.** tú **c.** usted **d.** nosotros **e.** su amiga

3. *Nosotros* dijimos que ya habíamos visto ese cuadro.
   a. usted **b.** yo **c.** Celia **d.** los González **e.** tú

B. Mrs. Díaz is telling her husband how very happy she is because of the many good things that have happened to them recently. Fill in the blanks with the present perfect form of the verbs in parentheses and you'll see why she is so happy.

1. (sacar) Los niños _____ muy buenas notas en la escuela.
2. (ganar) Tú _____ más dinero que nunca.
3. (escribir) Yo _____ la novela más leída del año.
4. (pintar) Nuestra hija _____ sus mejores cuadros.
5. (hacer) Tú y yo _____ muchos viajes.
6. (casarse) Pedro _____ con una muchacha muy buena.
7. (resolver) Carlos y Marisa _____ sus problemas sentimentales.
8. (pedir) ¡Y nadie nos _____ dinero!

C. Complete the sentences with the past perfect form of the verbs in parentheses.

1. (cenar) Ellos ya _____ cuando llegué.
2. (llamar) Roberto me dijo que tú _____.
3. (romper) Carlitos confesó que fue él quien _____ esa puerta.
4. (vender) No sabía que tus padres _____ su casa.
5. (ser) Tina me contó que tú y ella _____ novios antes.

6. (desayunar) Tú ya _____ cuando Rita te llamó, ¿no?
7. (acostarse) ¿Creías que yo _____ tan temprano?
8. (traer) Susana me contó que usted _____ un postre delicioso.

D. Give the Spanish equivalent of the following sentences.
1. We have seen that painting many times.
2. Fernando had said that you were coming.
3. She had already talked to you when she called me.
4. They have been very busy lately.
5. Did you realize that Mrs. Solís had killed her husband before committing suicide because she was jealous of Carolina?

Preguntas

1. ¿Qué ha hecho usted esta mañana? ¿algo interesante?   2. ¿Ha ido al cine recientemente? ¿Qué película(s) ha visto? ¿Le ha(n) gustado?   3. ¿Ha visitado algún museo en los últimos dos meses? ¿Cuál? ¿Había estado en ese mismo museo antes? ¿Cuándo?   4. ¿Ha visto algún cuadro pintado por Goya? ¿por algún otro pintor español?   5. ¿Ha ido a Europa este verano? ¿Había estado allí antes? ¿Cuándo?   6. ¿Ha perdido algo importante recientemente? ¿Qué ha perdido?   7. ¿Ha sacado una buena nota en su último examen de español? ¿Había sacado mejor o peor nota antes?

III. CONTRAST OF PAST INDICATIVE TENSES

(1) **Pedro:** ¡Hola, Elba! ¿No me *dijiste* que *habías enviado* un cuento al concurso?

(2) **Elba:** Sí, pero ¡qué rabia! Creo que los jurados no *han sido* honestos. No me *dieron* el premio a pesar de que *era* un cuento sensacional. Lo *escribió* un escritor muy famoso.

(3) **Pedro:** Pero, ¿cómo? Yo *suponía* que *era* tuyo.

(4) **Elba:** Bueno . . . no del todo. Yo *cambié* el nombre de los personajes, *firmé* como autora y lo *envié*. ¡Qué ofensa para Ernest Hemingway!

1. ¿Quién envió el cuento al concurso?   2. ¿Qué cree ella de los jurados?   3. ¿Quién es el autor verdadero del cuento?

(1) Hi, Elba! Didn't you tell me that you had sent a story to the contest? (2) Yes, but boy am I angry! (What anger) I think that the judges (members of the jury) have not been honest! They didn't give me the prize in spite of (the fact) that it was a sensational story. A very famous author wrote it. (3) But, what? I supposed that it was yours. (4) Well . . . not exactly. I changed the name of the characters, signed as the author and sent it. What an offense to Ernest Hemingway!

Spanish has four widely used tenses in the indicative mood that deal with past actions or events. Two of them—the preterite and the imperfect—are simple tenses, and two—the present perfect and the past perfect—are compound tenses. Although all four tenses describe past events, as we have seen in this and previous chapters, they differ in interpretation and emphasis.

A. The preterite deals with completed past events that are independent of the present. This tense emphasizes the completion of an action in the past.

Ayer a las cuatro hablé con José Luis.	*Yesterday at four o'clock I spoke with José Luis.*
¿Qué hiciste la semana pasada?	*What did you do last week?*
Ayer me ocurrió algo interesante.	*Something interesting happened to me yesterday.*

B. The imperfect emphasizes the duration or repetition of a past action or event.

Hablaba con José Luis cuando ocurrió el accidente.	*I was talking to José Luis when the accident occurred.*
¿Qué hacías los fines de semana cuando estabas en Guatemala?	*What did you use to do on weekends when you were in Guatemala?*
Siempre me ocurrían cosas interesantes.	*Interesting things always used to happen to me.*

C. The present perfect, like the preterite, deals with completed past events. However, unlike the preterite, this tense emphasizes a present perspective or result.

He hablado con José Luis recientemente.	*I spoke with José Luis recently.*
¿Qué has hecho esta semana?	*What have you done this week?*
Hoy no me ha ocurrido nada interesante.	*Nothing interesting has happened to me today.*

D. The past perfect deals with a past event prior to another past event (stated or implied).

Lo sabía porque había hablado con José Luis.

I knew it because I had spoken with José Luis.

¿Qué habías hecho antes de casarte?

What had you done before you got married?

Nunca me había ocurrido nada interesante antes de conocerte.

Nothing interesting had ever happened to me before I met you.

Ejercicios

A. Choose the correct Spanish equivalent of the sentences or phrases in italics.

1. *He used to come at eight o'clock.*
   a. Vino a las ocho. **b.** Venía a las ocho. **c.** Había venido a las ocho.

2. *They have already seen that painting.*
   a. Ya han visto ese cuadro. **b.** Ya vieron a ese pintor. **c.** Ya habían visto ese cuadro.

3. We were eating *when he came in.*
   a. cuando entraba **b.** cuando ha entrado **c.** cuando entró

4. *What have you done!*
   a. ¡Qué había hecho! **b.** ¡Qué hice! **c.** ¡Qué has hecho!

5. I knew how to do it because *I had done it* before.
   a. lo hice **b.** lo había hecho **c.** lo he hecho

6. We did our homework while *we waited for you.*
   a. te hemos esperado **b.** te esperábamos **c.** te habíamos esperado

B. Complete the paragraph with the appropriate past tense form of the verbs in parentheses.

Ayer, mientras yo (esperar) _____ el autobús, (ver) _____ a Juan, un amigo mío muy querido. Recuerdo que en 1970, cuando él y yo (conocerse) _____, los dos (querer) _____ ser pintores famosos. Él (admirar) _____ profundamente a Goya y (tener) _____ un cuadro suyo que (heredar) (*inherit*) _____ de una tía rica. No (ver) _____ a Juan desde 1975 y noté (*I noticed*) que en estos últimos años mi amigo (cambiar) _____ mucho. Tenía la intuición de que ahora (ser) _____ muy rico. Cuando lo (ver) _____, (llevar) _____ un traje elegante y zapatos muy caros. Yo le (decir) _____ que (estar) _____ muy contento de verlo y le (preguntar) _____ si (seguir) _____ obsesionado por las obras de Goya. Me (decir) _____ que ya no, que ahora (dedicarse) _____ a viajar y a visitar casinos por todo el mundo. Juan me (contar) _____ que en 1976 (conocer) _____ a una mujer admirable, (enamorarse) _____ de ella y en menos de un mes (decidir) _____ casarse. La mujer (tener) _____ mucho dinero porque (ser) _____ la única hija de un millonario italiano. Me contó mi amigo que él y su esposa (vivir) _____ muy felices hasta hace unos diez días, cuando el doctor de la familia (descubrir) _____ que su esposa (tener) _____ cáncer. La tragedia de mi amigo me (dejar) _____ muy triste pero (inspirar) _____ este cuadro que (empezar) _____ hace unas horas y cuyo título (*title*) va a ser «Los dólares todavía no (poder) _____ curar todos los dolores del mundo».

Preguntas

1. ¿Ha pintado usted algo alguna vez? ¿un cuadro? ¿una casa? ¿una mesa? ¿Qué ha pintado? **2.** ¿Ha perdido dinero recientemente? ¿Dónde? **3.** ¿Cuál era su programa de televisión favorito cuando usted era niño(a)? **4.** ¿Qué quería ser usted cuando tenía seis o siete años? ¿Qué quiere ser ahora? **5.** ¿Visitó usted algún país de habla española el verano pasado? ¿Qué país? ¿Había ido allí usted antes? ¿Cuándo?

EN EL PRADO

Una profesora de arte y unos estudiantes visitan el Museo del Prado,[1] *en Madrid.*

Profesora: Podemos descansar aquí. Hemos visto las obras de Velázquez, el Greco y Goya. ¿Cuál de los tres pintores les ha gustado más?

Ana: A mí me ha gustado el Greco por su estilo único y original.

Jorge: ¿Esas figuras largas y deformadas?[2] Nunca he visto cosa igual.

Ana: Son las visiones de un místico.

Jorge: ¡O quizás de un loco!

Pablo: Me han impresionado más los retratos de Velázquez. Son tan realistas que las personas que pinta parecen estar vivas, ¿no?

Ana: Tengo una pregunta sobre *Las Meninas*. ¿Por qué lo han puesto en una sala aparte?[3]

Profesora: Porque es uno de los cuadros más famosos del museo. En la historia del arte significa un problema resuelto: la representación perfecta del espacio en sus tres dimensiones por medio de la manipulación de distintas intensidades de luz.

Ana: Mientras lo miraba, me di cuenta de que el cuadro juega con los conceptos de ilusión y realidad.

Jorge: Francamente me parece que Goya tiene más valor universal. Sus obras son una sátira de la humanidad.

Ana: Estoy de acuerdo. El realismo de Velázquez era importante para los hombres del siglo XVII porque todavía no habían inventado la fotografía. Hoy día interesa más la expresividad de Goya.

Pablo: Son obras demasiado deprimentes para mí. No me gusta ver escenas brutales, cuerpos fracturados ni monstruos.[4]

Ana: Sin embargo, sus obras han tenido una gran influencia en el arte del siglo XX.

Jorge: ¿Podemos continuar esta discusión en la cafetería? Estoy a punto de morder una naturaleza muerta.[5]

deformadas	*deformed*	**sala**	*room*	**distintas**	*different*	**humanidad** *humanity*
expresividad	*expressiveness*	**a punto de morder**	*about to bite*		

deformadas *deformed* **sala** *room* **distintas** *different* **humanidad** *humanity*
expresividad *expressiveness* **a punto de morder** *about to bite*

Preguntas

1. ¿Dónde están la profesora y sus estudiantes? 2. ¿De qué pintores hablan? 3. ¿Cómo son las figuras que pintó el Greco? 4. ¿Quién pintó *Las Meninas?* 5. ¿Por qué han puesto esta obra en una sala aparte? 6. ¿Con qué conceptos juega el cuadro? 7. Según Jorge ¿por qué tienen más valor universal las obras de Goya? 8. ¿Por qué era importante el estilo de Velázquez para los hombres del siglo XVII? 9. ¿Cuál de los tres pintores le gusta más a usted? Hay ejemplos de sus cuadros en este capítulo (página 254) y en *La pintura* (páginas 269, 270, 271).

NOTAS CULTURALES

1. **The Prado Museum** of Madrid, founded in the early nineteenth century, is one of the great art museums of the world, particularly noted for its fine collections of Spanish and Flemish paintings.

2. El Greco, discussed in the dialogue of Chapter 11, is usually considered a Spanish painter since his greatest works were done after his arrival in Spain and reflect the fervent mysticism sometimes associated with that country. The figures in his paintings appear elongated, and for many years this was thought to be due to a visual problem of the artist. Modern critics, however, have classified el Greco as one of the world's great painters who distorted outward form in order to express the inward spirit.

3. Las Meninas *(The Maids of Honor),* shown at the beginning of this chapter, is one of the most important paintings of Diego Velázquez. The effect of three dimensionality is not achieved by the traditional method of geometric perspective, but by the contrasting of light and shadow, a technique which was to have a great impact on later artists.

The painting seems to be totally unposed. The princess Margarita, two maids of honor, two dwarfs (used for entertainment in the court), and a dog seem to have entered the painter's studio and appear in the foreground. To the left behind them is Velázquez himself busily painting on his canvas. To the right are two ladies of the court. On the far back wall hangs a mirror in which appear the reflections of the king and queen, who would therefore seem to be standing in the place where we, the observers, now are. Finally, farther back still, a court official stands in an open doorway. By looking at the picture we are seeing, as though we looked through the eyes of the king and queen, an impromptu view of the daily reality of the court. Is the painting the artist is shown doing of the royal couple, of us, or is it the very painting we now see, assuming he is gazing into a mirror directly in front of him? The observer is invited to ponder on a theme suggested by the painting: where is the line between illusion and reality?

4. Francisco de Goya (1746–1828) is a Spanish painter who produced an enormous variety of paintings, drawings, and engravings. His later works portray in grotesque detail the horrors of war (which he viewed close at hand), the cruelty and vices of society, and terrifying images drawn from witchcraft, superstition, dreams, and myths.

5. Naturaleza muerta is the Spanish term for *still life*, a painting which portrays small inanimate objects (such as bottles, flowers, books, and—very often— food) painted in a very realistic manner.

ACTIVIDADES

Palabra secreta

How many Spanish words related to the fine arts can you find in the rectangle? If you find all nine of the words you will be left with five extra letters which spell out the *secret word* which refers to something which has proven to be essential to many great artists and writers through the ages. The words go left to right, up and down, sideways, backwards or diagonally. Individual letters may be used more than once. English equivalents are given below and the first word is done for you.

1. portrait
2. style
3. picture
4. story
5. a 19th Spanish painter
   whose name beings with G.
6. novel
7. poetry
8. opera
9. art

R	E	S	T	I	L	O
E	C	U	A	D	R	O
T	U	A	A	P	☺	A
R	E	L	R	I	L	I
A	N	☺	A	E	Z	S
T	T	Y	V	☺	P	E
O	O	O	☺	☺	☺	O
G	N	A	R	T	E	P

Entrevista

Ask a classmate the following questions. Then report the information to the class.

1. ¿Qué obras de arte abstracto has visto? ¿Dónde? ¿Te han gustado?
2. ¿Crees que los grandes artistas han sido felices? ¿Por qué?
3. ¿Consideras que aun hoy, cuando tenemos la fotografía, es importante el realismo en el arte? ¿Por qué?

4. Muchos dicen que el cine es al arte de nuestro tiempo. ¿Qué película te ha parecido realmente artística?
5. ¿Qué habilidades (*abilities*) artísticas tienes? ¿Has hecho alguna vez una escultura (*sculpture*), una pieza de alfarería (*pottery*), un tejido (*weaving*) o has pintado?
6. ¿Cómo se llama tu autor(-a) favorito(-a)? ¿Qué libros has leído escritos por él o ella?

Situación

Lugar: en el mercado
Personajes: una **india** que vende cuadros y estatuas (*statues*); **Ana** y **Francisco,** dos turistas.

Francisco:	*«Mira, Ana, qué lindos cuadros.»*
Ana:	responde que sí, que son muy bonitos, que le gustan los colores, las figuras, etc. . . Le pregunta a la india quién los ha pintado.
La india:	dice que su hermano los pintó hace dos semanas. Dice que también tiene estatuas muy bellas.
Francisco:	declara que le gustan más las estatuas, que nunca ha visto estatuas más lindas. Le pregunta a la india cuánto cuestan.
La india:	responde que las estatuas cuestan un dólar cada una.
Ana:	*«Qué lástima».* Dice que ella había pensado comprar cuatro por dos dólares.
La india:	dice que por dos dólares le puede dar dos estatuas y un cuadro.
Ana:	dice que está de acuerdo; dice que va a llevar la estatua de la mujer.
Francisco:	elige otras estatuas.
Ana:	da las gracias y se va.

VOCABULARIO ACTIVO

Verbos útiles

admirar to admire
crear to create
describir to describe
destruir to destroy
enviar to send
firmar to sign
impresionar to impress
inspirar to inspire
ocurrir to occur
pintar to paint
representar to represent
significar to mean, signify
suponer to suppose

El arte y la literatura

el acto act
el autor (la autora) author
el concurso contest
el cuadro painting
el cuento story, short story
la escena scene
el escritor (la escritora) writer
el estilo style
el, la genia(o) genius
la ilusión illusion
la influencia influence
la novela novel
la obra work
el personaje character (as in a literary work)
la pintura painting
la poesía poetry
el premio prize
la realidad reality
el retrato portrait
la revista magazine
la sátira satire

Adjetivos

abierto(a) open
bello(a) beautiful
cansado(a) tired
cubierto(a) covered
deprimente depressing
descrito(a) described
destruido(a) destroyed
dicho(a) said, told
escrito(a) written
hecho(a) made, done
honesto(a) honest
inspirado(a) inspired
largo(a) long
loco(a) crazy
místico(a) mystical
muerto(a) dead
obsesionado(a) obsessed
pintado(a) painted
puesto(a) put
querido(a) dear
realista realistic
resuelto(a) solved
roto(a) broken
sensacional sensational
trágico(a) tragic
visto(a) seen
vivo(a) alive, bright, vivid
vuelto(a) returned

Otras palabras útiles

a pesar de in spite of
la guerra war
el, la jurado juror
la luz light
el monstruo monster
la muerte death
la naturaleza nature
por medio de through, by means of
¡Qué rabia! What anger! How angry I am!
el recado message
sin embargo however
el sufrimiento suffering

La Pintura

Entre los muchos pintores excelentes de España, hay tres que con frecuencia son considerados como «los más españoles» porque *encarnan* cualidades esenciales de la cultura española. Irónicamente, uno de ellos es *griego:* Doménico Theotocópoulos, más conocido como el Greco. Vivió en España la mayor parte de su vida y murió allí en 1614. El Greco representa la profunda religiosidad española. Su arte es expresionista. No trata de reproducir la realidad externa *sino* de *captar* el *alma* interior y expresar su exaltación o dolor espiritual. Por eso, muchas veces pinta figuras *alargadas* con *gestos* dramáticos. Usa colores vibrantes y *escoge* escenas de movimiento y agitación. Muchos lo han considerado un pintor místico. *La Resurrección* representa una escena del Nuevo Testamento, la del triunfo de Cristo sobre la muerte.

embody
Greek

but rather / to capture / soul / elongated / gestures
chooses

Otro pintor, quizás « el más español » de todos, es Diego de Silva y Velázquez. También vivió en el siglo XVII, pero su estilo es muy diferente al de el Greco. Velázquez representa el realismo y la *sobriedad*. Por la manipulación de la luz y la *sombra*, sus cuadros dan la ilusión de un espacio real y palpable. Su principal interés son las personas, y muchas de sus pinturas son retratos que revelan gran penetración sicológica.

*La **rendición** de Breda* representa la terminación de una *guerra*, el momento en que el capitán *holandés entrega* las llaves de la ciudad de Breda al victorioso capitán español. La *bondad* del *vencedor* se revela en la expresión de su *rostro* y en su gesto de compasión. También se pueden observar otras reacciones en las expresiones y gestos de varios soldados: *piedad, inquietud,* disgusto o *aburrimiento.* El grupo de *lanzas al fondo,* da al cuadro un sentido de equilibrio y serenidad, otra de las características de Velázquez.

moderation
shadow

surrender / war
Dutch / gives
goodness / victor
face

pity / restlessness /
  boredom
lances in the background

El tercer pintor considerado como típicamente español es Francisco de Goya (1746–1828). Representa la pasión y la intensidad del carácter español. Vivió en tiempos de gran decadencia. En este cuadro oficial de la *corte,* Goya muestra al rey y su familia con un realismo brutal: al rey, *gordo* y estúpido; a la reina, cruel y depravada; y al *príncipe* con la cara del *amante* de la reina. Y, *cosa increíble,* ¡los reyes estaban muy contentos porque sólo vieron en el cuadro la elegancia de su ropa!

royal court
fat
prince / lover / the
  unbelievable thing

El tres de mayo, otro cuadro de Goya, representa la *ejecución* de   execution
unos campesinos en 1808, durante la rebelión española contra Na-
poleón. Es una escena real que Goya vio. También es una protesta
universal contra la guerra. Hay un fuerte contraste entre la masa
indiferenciada de los soldados que actúan como una *máquina* y las   machine
víctimas, que revelan características humanas individuales y particu-
lares. Una de ellas, con los brazos *en cruz* como Cristo, parece re-   in the form of a cross
presentar el espíritu de la *lucha.*   struggle

También en el siglo XX España ha producido grandes pintores como Joan Miró, Salvador Dalí, Juan Gris y otros. Pero el más famoso es Pablo Picasso. *Aunque* vivió la mayor parte de su vida en Francia, although muchos de sus cuadros revelan un espíritu español. Sin embargo, su arte ha sido, casi siempre, independiente y universal. Entre sus obras más notables están los cuadros cubistas como *Los tres músicos*. Picasso y los otros pintores cubistas trataron de captar el movimiento del objeto o de la persona que pintaban, *mostrando* varios ángulos showing diferentes *al mismo tiempo*. Así querían presentarnos una realidad at the same time más completa *que la del* cuadro tradicional. Pero Picasso *no se limitó* than that of / did not al cubismo; *produjo* una obra muy variada y original, de gran in- limit himself
he produced fluencia.

Pablo Picasso. *Three Musicians*, 1921, (summer). Collection, The Museum of Modern Art, New York. Mrs. Simon Guggenheim Fund.

España no es la única que ha dado al mundo pintores conocidos. En los tiempos modernos, varios países hispanoamericanos han producido pintores de interés. Entre los más importantes están los pintores que *integran* la escuela mexicana de la Revolución, espe- compose, make up cialmente Diego Rivera, José Clemente Orozco y David Alfaro Si- queiros. Sus murales y pinturas representan temas históricos: las civilizaciones precolombinas, la conquista, la vida colonial y los tiempos modernos de México. El tema más repetido es el de la revo- lución, con alusión especial a la Revolución Mexicana de 1910. La perspectiva es predominantemente marxista. Este mural de Diego Rivera es una representación de Emiliano Zapata, revolucionario mexicano y promotor de la reforma agraria.

Diego Rivera. *Zapata*. Lithograph, 1932. © Sotheby Parke-Bernet. Agent: Editorial Photocolor Archives.

1. ¿Cuál de los tres pintores considerados «los más españoles» era griego?   **2.** ¿Por qué cree usted que muchos lo han llamado un pintor místico?   **3.** ¿Qué representa el estilo de Velázquez?   **4.** Describa el cuadro *La rendición de Breda*.   **5.** ¿Qué muestra Goya en el cuadro oficial de la corte?   **6.** ¿Qué ve usted en *El tres de mayo?*   **7.** ¿Cuál es el más famoso de los pintores españoles de este siglo? ¿Qué trataba de hacer durante su período cubista?   **8.** ¿Cuáles son los pintores más importantes de la escuela mexicana de la revolución?   **9.** ¿Cuáles son los temas de sus cuadros y murales?   **10.** De los cuadros reproducidos aquí ¿cuál le gusta más? ¿por qué?

FIESTAS Y FERIADOS

Mañana empieza Janucá

¡Feliz Navidad!

¡Feliz cumpleaños!

OBJECTIVES

LANGUAGE: In this chapter we introduce, discuss, and practice:
1. the present subjunctive of regular verbs
2. the present subjunctive of irregular, orthographic, and stem-changing verbs
3. some additional command forms, the first-person plural (corresponding to *let's . . .* in English) and third-person forms

You will also learn vocabulary related to holidays and celebrations.

CULTURE: The dialogue at the end of the chapter takes place in Querétaro, Mexico, where a family and friends are celebrating the **Posadas,** a Christmas tradition in Mexico. You will learn something about Mexican holidays and particularly about the elaborate Christmas-time festivities.

EXPLICACIÓN

I. THE PRESENT SUBJUNCTIVE OF REGULAR VERBS

(1)	**Pedrito:**	Papá, quiero organizar una protesta pública con los otros niños del barrio para el día de mi santo.*
(2)	**El padre:**	Pero ¿por qué?
(3)	**Pedrito:**	Porque todos ustedes—tíos, abuelos, padres— siempre nos mandan que *estudiemos*, que *comamos*, que *abramos* la puerta, que nos *lavemos* las manos, que . . .
(4)	**El padre:**	¿Por qué dices todo eso, Pedrito?
(5)	**Pedrito:**	Porque estoy cansado de escuchar, «Pedrito, te pido que le *envíes* una tarjeta a tu abuela», . . . «Pedrito, te prohíbo que *mires* la televisión ahora», «Pedrito, te mando que *asistas* a la Misa de Noche- buena . . .»
(6)	**El padre:**	Pero, es que quiero que *aprendas*, hijo.
(7)	**Pedrito:**	¡Aprendo que no hay justicia en este mundo!

1. ¿Qué quiere organizar Pedrito? ¿Con quién?   **2.** ¿Qué hacen los tíos, abuelos y papás, según Pedrito?   **3.** ¿De qué está cansado Pedrito?   **4.** Según el padre, ¿por qué hay que hacer todo eso?   **5.** ¿Qué aprende Pedrito?   **6.** ¿Está usted cansado de recibir órdenes? ¿Quién se las da?

So far in this text, the tenses presented have been in the indicative mood, except commands, which are in the imperative mood. In this chapter, the *subjunctive* mood is introduced. While the indicative mood is used to state

---

(1) Dad, I want to organize a public protest with the other children in the neighborhood on my Saint's Day. (2) But why? (3) Because all of you—aunts and uncles, grandparents, parents—are always ordering us to study, to eat, to open the door, to wash our hands, to . . . (4) Why are you saying (all) this, Pedrito? (5) Because I am tired of hearing, "Pedrito, I'm asking you to send a card to your grandmother," "Pedrito, I forbid you to watch television now," "Pedrito, I order you to attend Mass on Christmas Eve . . . ." (6) But I want you to learn, son. (7) I'm learning that there's no justice in this world!

---

* Day of the saint after whom a person is named. In Spain and in some Latin American countries, this day is celebrated more than one's birthday.

facts or ask direct questions and the imperative mood is used to give commands, the subjunctive is used:

1. for *indirect* commands or requests

My boss requests that I *be* at work at eight o'clock sharp.
Mary's mother asks that she *celebrate* Christmas with the family.

2. for situations expressing doubt, probability, or something hypothetical or contrary to fact

If I *were* rich, I would go to Sevilla for the Easter celebrations.
Be that as it *may* . . .

3. for statements of emotion, hope, wishing or wanting

May you *succeed* at everything you do.
Sally wishes that Tom *were* going to the party.

4. for statements of necessity

It is necessary that he *do* the honors and make a toast to the host.

5. for statements of approval or disapproval, permission, or prohibiting

Father forbids that he even *think* about going to Mexico for Christmas.
It's better that we *stay* home.

The subjunctive is used in Spanish far more than it is in English, and the discussion of the uses of the subjunctive in Spanish will be continued in Chapters 16 and 17. In this chapter we will concentrate on the formation of the present subjunctive. We will limit its use to indirect requests or commands with four verbs: **mandar** (*to order*), **pedir** (*to ask, request*), **querer** (*to wish, want*) and **prohibir** (*to prohibit, forbid*). First let's see how the subjunctive of regular verbs is formed.

A. To form the present subjunctive of regular **-ar** verbs, drop the ending **-o** from the first-person singular **(yo)** form of the present indicative and add the endings **-e, -es, -e, -emos, -éis, -en.** For **-er** and **-ir** verbs, add the endings **-a, -as, -a, -amos, -áis, -an.**

hablar		comer		vivir	
hable	hablemos	coma	comamos	viva	vivamos
hables	habléis	comas	comáis	vivas	viváis
hable	hablen	coma	coman	viva	vivan

Mis padres quieren que celebremos las Navidades en casa de mis tíos.	My parents want us to celebrate Christmas at my aunt and uncle's.
Le pido que me presente a los invitados.	I'm asking him to introduce the guests to me.
Nos mandan que organicemos la próxima fiesta.	They're asking (ordering) us to organize the next party.
Nos prohíben que fumemos aquí.	They forbid us to smoke here.

Quiero que le compres un regalo de cumpleaños a tu hermana. *I want you to buy a birthday present for your sister.*

¿Quiere el profesor que terminemos la lectura la próxima semana? *Does the instructor want us to finish the reading next week?*

B. You may have noticed that the **usted** and **ustedes** forms of the present subjunctive are the same as the **usted** and **ustedes** command forms and that the **tú** form is like the negative **tú** command form. Compare the following sentences.

Lean el periódico. *Read the newspaper.*
Quiero que ustedes lean el periódico. *I want you to read the newspaper.*
Llame a mi nuera, por favor. *Call my daughter-in-law, please.*
Quiero que usted llame a mi nuera. *I want you to call my daughter-in-law.*
No vayas al desfile. *Don't go to the parade.*
Prohíben que vayas al desfile. *They forbid you to go to the parade.*

In an indirect command or request, there is an implied command, as you can see. Notice one other important thing about these sentences: where the Spanish sentence uses the subjunctive, the English sentence uses the infinitive. That is, instead of saying, "I want that you read the newspaper" or "They forbid that you go to the parade," we often use an infinitive construction in English. In Spanish you must use the subjunctive and the **que,** unless there is no change in subject:

Quiero celebrar el Día de la Raza con tío Jorge. *I want to celebrate Columbus Day with Uncle Jorge.*

Quiero que mis hijos celebren el Día de la Raza con tío Jorge. *I want my children to celebrate Colombus Day with Uncle Jorge.*

Quieren acostarse a media noche. *They want to go to bed at midnight.*

Quieren que nosotros nos acostemos a medianoche. *They want us to go to bed at midnight.*

Ejercicios

A. Create new sentences, substituting the words in the lists for those in italics.

1. Don Antonio quiere que *su hijo* estudie español.
   a. ellos **b.** yo **c.** tú **d.** ustedes **e.** Ernesto y yo

2. El doctor no quiere que *tú* comas mucho.
   a. usted **b.** ellas **c.** yo **d.** nosotros **e.** Guillermo

3. Papá prohíbe que *yo* escriba eso.
   a. tú **b.** ustedes **c.** nosotros **d.** ellas **e.** José

4. Ellas piden que *nosotros* pasemos Navidad aquí.
   a. tú y Sonia **b.** yo **c.** tú **d.** usted **e.** Gerardo

B.   Restate, adding the request as in the example.

Modelo: Hablo con los niños. Me pide que . . .   **Me pide que hable con los niños.**

1. Pedrito nos invita a su cumpleaños. Quiero que . . .
2. Tus hijos van al desfile. No quieres que . . .
3. Vivimos cerca de la universidad. Nos piden que . . .
4. Leo el periódico. ¿Prohíbes que . . .?
5. Beben vino con la comida. No quiero que . . .
6. Escribo una carta a mi nuera. ¿Quiere que . . .?
7. Estudian el capítulo quince. Manda que . . .
8. Comes sólo frutas y pescado. ¿Te pide que . . .?
9. Recibimos a los estudiantes. Mandan que . . .
10. Teresa y Jorge hablan por teléfono. Prohíben que . . .

C.   Estela missed class today and Rita, a classmate, is telling her what their Spanish teacher wants them to do for tomorrow. Form sentences with the following elements, as Rita would.

Modelo: pedir/todos/leer la lectura sobre «Las Fiestas»
         Pide que todos leamos la lectura sobre «Las Fiestas».

1. prohibir/nosotros/usar diccionario durante el examen
2. mandar/todos/estudiar la próxima lección
3. querer/tú/escribir una composición extra
4. no querer/nadie/hablar inglés en clase
5. pedir/Juan y Elba/preparar preguntas sobre la lectura
6. querer/yo/describir mi viaje a México
7. prohibir/Ramón/fumar en clase
8. pedir/nosotros/aprender bien el vocabulario

D.   Give the Spanish equivalent of the following sentences.

1. I want you (*tú*) to send a birthday card to your grandmother.
2. She is asking us to read the book.
3. The teacher is ordering Rodrigo to study more.
4. We want you (*ustedes*) to call us tomorrow.
5. They always prohibit us from writing in the books.
6. Elena, I am asking you to drink your milk!
7. My parents forbid me from staying at my girlfriend's (boyfriend's) house.
8. He wants you (*ustedes*) to attend his birthday party.

Preguntas _____

1. ¿Quiere usted que sus padres le escuchen más? ¿que lo llamen por teléfono todos los días? ¿que le manden más dinero?   **2.** ¿Quieren sus padres que usted les escriba más? ¿que usted los visite todas las semanas?   **3.** ¿Les pide usted a sus amigos que lo (la) lleven al cine? ¿que lo (la) inviten a cenar?   **4.** ¿Le prohíbe usted a su novio(a) que fume? ¿que tome bebidas alcohólicas? ¿que baile con otras personas?

II. PRESENT SUBJUNCTIVE OF IRREGULAR, ORTHOGRAPHIC, AND STEM-CHANGING VERBS

(1) **Alicia:** Mamá, quiero que *conozcas* a John. Llegó hace unas horas de California.

(2) **Madre:** Mucho gusto, John. ¿Qué tal el viaje?

(3) **John:** Fue un poco largo, pero interesante.

(4) **Alicia:** ¿Quieres que *salgamos* para ver la ciudad?

(5) **John:** ¡Cómo no!, porque tengo que volver el viernes.

(6) **Madre:** ¡Qué lástima! El sábado empiezan las Posadas.*

(7) **John:** Es que . . . mis padres quieren que *vuelva.*

(8) **Madre:** ¿Por qué no les *pides* que te *permitan* quedarte unos días más?

(9) **Alicia:** ¡Sí, John! Quiero que los *llames* y les *digas* que estás invitado a pasar las Navidades con nosotros.

1. ¿A quién quiere Alicia que su madre conozca?   **2.** ¿De dónde es él?   **3.** ¿Qué quiere Alicia que John y ella hagan?   **4.** ¿Cuándo debe volver John? ¿Por qué?   **5.** ¿Cuándo empiezan las Posadas?   **6.** ¿Qué quiere Alicia que haga su amigo?

(1) Mom, I want you to meet John. He arrived from California a few hours ago. (2) Glad to meet you, John. How was the trip? (3) It was a bit long, but interesting. (4) Do you want us to go out to see the city? (5) Of course! Because I have to return Friday. (6) What a shame! The **Posadas** start on Saturday. (7) It's just that my parents want me to return. (8) Why don't you ask them to allow you to stay a few days longer? (9) Yes, John! I want you to call them and tell them that you are invited to spend Christmas with us.

*See **Nota Cultural 1** of this chapter.

A. Verbs that have an irregularity in the first person singular of the present indicative carry this irregularity over into the subjunctive. The endings are regular.

decir		conocer		tener	
diga	digamos	conozca	conozcamos	tenga	tengamos
digas	digáis	conozcas	conozcáis	tengas	tengáis
diga	digan	conozca	conozcan	tenga	tengan

Other verbs that follow this pattern are:

construir	construy-	salir	salg-
destruir	destruy-	traer	traig-
hacer	hag-	valer	valg-
oír	oig-	venir	veng-
poner	pong-	ver	ve-

B. The following verbs are irregular:

dar		estar		haber	
dé	demos	esté	estemos	haya	hayamos
des	deis	estés	estéis	hayas	hayáis
dé	den	esté	estén	haya	hayan

ir		saber		ser	
vaya	vayamos	sepa	sepamos	sea	seamos
vayas	vayáis	sepas	sepáis	seas	seáis
vaya	vayan	sepa	sepan	sea	sean

C. Most stem-changing -ar and -er verbs retain the same pattern of stem change in the present subjunctive that they have in the indicative.

encontrar		poder	
encuentre	encontremos	pueda	podamos
encuentres	encontréis	puedas	podáis
encuentre	encuentren	pueda	puedan

entender		pensar	
entienda	entendamos	piense	pensemos
entiendas	entendáis	pienses	penséis
entienda	entiendan	piense	piensen

D. Stem-changing **-ir** verbs that have a change in stem of **e** to **ie**, **e** to **i**, or **o** to **ue** in the present indicative follow the same pattern in the subjunctive with one additional change: in the **nosotros** and **vosotros** forms the **e** of the stem is changed to **i**; the **o** is changed to **u**.

sentir		**morir**		**dormir**	
sienta	sintamos	muera	muramos	duerma	durmamos
sientas	sintáis	mueras	muráis	duermas	durmáis
sienta	sientan	muera	mueran	duerma	duerman

pedir		**vestirse**	
pida	pidamos	me vista	nos vistamos
pidas	pidáis	te vistas	os vistáis
pida	pidan	se vista	se vistan

Ejercicios

A. Create new sentences, substituting the words in the lists for those in italics.

1. Quiero que *tú* conozcas a Juan.
   a. mis padres   **b.** ella   **c.** ustedes   **d.** esta señora   **e.** tu amigo

2. ¿Quieres que *nosotros* salgamos para ver la ciudad?
   a. los niños   **b.** yo   **c.** tus primos   **d.** Isabel   **e.** tú y yo

3. Mandan que *ustedes* les den dinero.
   a. yo   **b.** nosotros   **c.** el gobierno   **d.** tú   **e.** los González

4. Pido que *Marisa* vaya con nosotros.
   a. el guía   **b.** ustedes   **c.** tú   **d.** Ana y Tomás   **e.** usted

5. Queremos que *el doctor* nos entienda.
   a. usted y su esposo   **b.** tú   **c.** nuestra hija   **d.** usted   **e.** todos

6. ¿Mandan que *nosotros* sirvamos la cena?
   a. las chicas   **b.** el mozo   **c.** ustedes   **d.** yo   **e.** tú

B. Mrs. Gil is going to a birthday party. Following the examples, answer the questions that her children and the babysitter ask her before she leaves.

Modelos: ¿Debo dormirme temprano? Sí, quiero que (tú) . . .   **Sí, quiero que (tú) te duermas temprano.**
¿Debemos hacer eso? No, prohíbo que (ustedes) . . .   **No, prohíbo que (ustedes) hagan eso.**

1. ¿Debemos decir la verdad? Sí, les pido que (ustedes) . . .
2. ¿Debe ir a la fiesta Susana? No, no quiero que (ella) . . .
3. ¿Debo estar aquí hasta medianoche? Sí, quiero que (usted) . . .
4. ¿Deben saber eso ellos? No, prohíbo que (ellos) . . .

5. ¿Debo permitirles salir? No, le pido que (usted) no . . .
6. ¿Debemos ver ese programa? No, prohíbo que (ustedes) . . .
7. ¿Debo acostarme en el sofá? No, te pido que (tú) . . .
8. ¿Deben ponerse pijamas los niños? Sí, mando que (ellos) . . .

C. Fill in the blanks with the appropriate forms of the verbs in parentheses.
1. Quieren que nosotros (ir) ——————— a su casa.
2. Te pido que (traer) ——————— a tu novio a mi fiesta de cumpleaños.
3. Los médicos me prohíben que (pensar) ——————— en los problemas de todo el mundo.
4. Mamá nos manda que (hacer) ——————— la cena.
5. Queremos que tú (seguir) ——————— un curso con la señora Rodríguez.
6. ¡No pueden prohibirme que (volver) ——————— tarde!
7. ¿Te pide ella que le (dar) ——————— chocolates para el día de su santo?
8. El policía manda que usted le (mostrar) ——————— algún documento de identidad.

D. Give the Spanish equivalent of the following sentences.
1. I want you to be good, Miguelito.
2. Carla, ask your mother to give you ten dollars.
3. Do you (*usted*) want us to bring something to the party?
4. Her mother prohibits her from going out at night.
5. Are you (*ustedes*) asking me to do you a favor?
6. The doctor asks him to get dressed.
7. The policeman orders her to tell the truth.
8. They are asking us to be here before Christmas.

Preguntas ——————————————————————————————————

1. ¿Cree usted que se debe prohibir que haya huelgas (*strikes*) de estudiantes durante el año académico? ¿de profesores? ¿Por qué? 2. En general, ¿quieren los profesores que los estudiantes vengan a clase regularmente? ¿que sepan la lección? ¿que duerman durante la clase? 3. ¿Deben los profesores prohibir que los estudiantes traigan televisores o radios a clase? 4. ¿Qué quiere su profesor(a) que usted haga para mañana?

III. FIRST-PERSON PLURAL (NOSOTROS) AND THIRD-PERSON COMMANDS

————————————————————————————————————

(1)   **Padre:**   ¿Qué quieren que les traigan los Reyes Magos,*
niños?
(2) **Juanito:** Um . . . *pensemos* . . .

———————————

* In Spain, Argentina, Mexico and certain other parts of the Hispanic world, children receive presents on January 6th, the Feast of the Epiphany or Coming of the Magi, rather than on Christmas.

(3) **Pepito:** No, mejor *escribámosles* una carta.
(4) **Padre:** Bueno, pero no debe ser una carta muy larga, ¿eh?
(5) **Juanito:** No te preocupes por los regalos, papá. ¡Que se *preocupen* los Reyes!

---

1. ¿Qué les pregunta el padre a sus dos hijos? **2.** ¿Quién quiere que escriban una carta? **3.** ¿Quiere el padre que la carta sea larga o corta? **4.** Según Juanito ¿quiénes deben preocuparse por los regalos?

A. As you have seen the **usted** and **ustedes** command forms are the same as the **usted** and **ustedes** forms of the present subjunctive, and the negative **tú** command forms are the same as the **tú** form of the present subjunctive. Similarly, the **nosotros** form of the present subjunctive is equivalent to the first-person plural command form; it corresponds to *Let's . . .* or *Let's not . . .* in English.

Hablemos con tu yerno. (No hablemos con tu yerno.)	*Let's speak with your son-in-law. (Let's not speak with your son-in-law.)*
Comamos pavo. (No comamos pavo.)	*Let's eat turkey. (Let's not eat turkey.)*
Escribamos tarjetas de Navidad. (No escribamos tarjetas de Navidad.)	*Let's write Christmas cards. (Let's not write Christmas cards.)*

One exception is the affirmative **Vamos** (*Let's go*). *Let's not go* is **No vayamos. Vamos a** + infinitive can also be used for the **nosotros** command form:

Vamos a rezar por la paz.⎫ Recemos por la paz.　⎭	*Let's pray for peace.*
Vamos a saludar a mi padrino.⎫ Saludemos a mi padrino.　　⎭	*Let's say hello to my godfather.*

Pronouns are added to the **nosotros** command forms just as they are added to other command forms. When **nos** is added to an affirmative command the final **-s** of the verb is dropped.

Levantémonos. (No nos levantemos.)	*Let's stand up. (Let's not stand up.)*
Vámonos. (No nos vayamos.)	*Let's go. (Let's not go.)*
Celebrémoslo con nuestros nietos. (No lo celebremos con nuestros nietos.)	*Let's celebrate it with our grandchildren. (Let's not celebrate it with our grandchildren.)*

(1) What do you want the Wise Men to bring you, children? (2) Hummm . . . Let's think . . . (3) No, (better) let's write them a letter. (4) All right, but it shouldn't be a very long letter. (5) Don't you worry about the gifts, Dad. Let the Kings worry!

B. Indirect commands are commands introduced by **que** that are given to someone else (indirectly). The verb is in the subjunctive; it usually follows **que** and precedes the subject.

Que les vaya bien.*   *May all go well with you.*

Que tu madrina vea el nacimiento.   *Let (have) your godmother look at the nativity scene.*

¡Que terminen de poner los adornos en el árbol de Navidad!   *Let them finish putting the decorations on the Christmas tree!*

Ejercicios

A. Create new sentences, substituting the verbs in the lists for those in italics.

1. (*comer*) Comamos (nosotros) un poco más temprano hoy.
   a. irse   **b.** dormir   **c.** levantarse   **d.** salir   **e.** acostarse

2. ¡Que no lo (*hacer*) haga (él)!
   a. decir   **b.** construir   **c.** pedir   **d.** buscar   **e.** mirar

3. ¡Que (*descansar*) descansen (ustedes) mucho!
   a. dormir   **b.** bailar   **c.** salir   **d.** estudiar   **e.** divertirse

B. Answer the questions in the affirmative, following the example.

Modelo: ¿Escribimos a los Reyes Magos?   **Sí, escribámosles.**

1. ¿Saludamos a Ernesto?
2. ¿Nos vamos ahora?
3. ¿Salimos con ellos?
4. ¿Ponemos los adornos en el árbol?
5. ¿Visitamos a abuelo el día de su santo?
6. ¿Pedimos dos cervezas?

C. It's Saturday afternoon and Juan and María don't have any plans, yet they don't seem to agree on how to spend the rest of the day. . . Answer Juan's suggestions in the negative, as María would. Use **nosotros** command forms and object pronouns whenever possible, following the examples.

Modelo: ¿Vamos a visitar a Teresa?   **No, no vayamos a visitarla.**

1. ¿Hacemos la sopa?
2. ¿Escribimos la carta a tus padrinos?
3. ¿Preparamos un pavo para la cena?
4. ¿Nos sentamos en la sala?
5. ¿Vamos a poner el nacimiento?
6. ¿Pedimos una pizza grande?

---

* These forms are similar to the indirect commands with **querer** or other verbs discussed earlier in the chapter; understood is **Quiero que les vaya bien.**

Preguntas

1. ¿Qué quiere usted que hagamos hoy? ¿Quiere que leamos el diálogo o que conversemos por unos minutos? **2.** ¿Quiere usted que tengamos una fiesta aquí en la clase la próxima semana? ¿antes de terminar el semestre? ¿el día de su santo? **3.** ¿Qué quiere usted que hagamos mañana? ¿que hagamos muchos ejercicios? ¿que hablemos de algunas fiestas hispanas típicas? ¿que escuchemos algunas canciones en español?

LAS POSADAS

Don Antonio, un español de 75 años, está en el pueblo de Querétaro, México, de visita en casa de su hija, su yerno mexicano y sus dos nietos. Es época de Navidad. Varias familias se han reunido en la casa de unos vecinos para celebrar las Posadas.[1]

La vecina:	Entren, por favor. Están en su casa.[2]
La hija:	¡Qué bonitos están los adornos y el Nacimiento![3]
La vecina:	Gracias. Siéntese aquí usted, Don Antonio, quiero que vea bien las Posadas.
Don Antonio:	Muchas gracias, señora. Y como no sé mucho de esto les pido que me expliquen el origen de la celebración.
La hija:	Es muy típica de México. Que yo sepa, viene de la época de los aztecas.
La vecina:	¡Escuchen! Ya han empezado las canciones.

Dos hombres empiezan a cantar; uno hace el papel de San José y el otro hace el papel del dueño de casa.

San José:	En nombre del cielo, danos posada. Ábrele la puerta a mi esposa amada.
El dueño:	Aquí no hay mesón. Sigan adelante. Ya no me hables más, ¡ladrón o tunante![4]

Una hora después. Las canciones han terminado.

El vecino:	Bueno, que pasen todos al comedor. La comida está en la mesa.
La vecina:	Sí, entremos y comamos. ¡A ver . . . !, que traigan la piñata![5]
La hija:	Me pregunto quién va a ser el padrino el año que viene.[6]
La nieta:	Abuelo, ¡te pido que te despiertes! No duermas más.
Don Antonio:	¿Cómo? ¡Qué pasa! Oh, yo no dormía, preciosa. Rezaba con los ojos cerrados.

La nieta: ¡Mira qué grande que es la piñata, abuelo! ¿Tienen piñatas en España?
Don Antonio: No, mi tesoro. No es nuestra costumbre.
El nieto: ¡Pobres niños españoles!

que yo sepa   *as far as I know*

Preguntas

1. ¿Para qué se han reunido varias familias mexicanas? 2. ¿Qué pide Don Antonio que le expliquen? ¿Por qué no sabe mucho de esto? 3. ¿Cuáles son los papeles que hacen los dos hombres que cantan? 4. Después de las canciones ¿adónde quiere el vecino que pasen todos? ¿Por qué? 5. ¿Qué manda la vecina que traigan? 6. ¿Qué le pide la nieta a su abuelo? 7. ¿Admite Don Antonio que él dormía? 8. ¿Ha visto usted una piñata alguna vez? ¿Ha estado usted en México o en algún otro país hispano durante una celebración?

NOTAS CULTURALES

1. The **Posadas** (literally *the inns*) are Christmas celebrations in Mexico commemorating the search of Joseph and Mary for lodging during their journey to Bethlehem. The festivities are held on nine consecutive nights, beginning on December 16 and ending on Christmas Eve. Nine families usually participate, with each family sponsoring one evening. The celebration begins around eight o'clock with prayers and songs; then the company divides into two groups, one group acting as Joseph and Mary seeking lodging on the journey to Bethlehem, the other acting as the innkeepers. The groups converse in song. At the end of each evening the identity of those seeking shelter is revealed, they are admitted to the "inn," and there is much celebrating. For the first eight nights there are fruits, nuts, candies, and punch; on Christmas Eve the host family for that year provides a large dinner after midnight mass. The origin of the custom is said to be in an Aztec ceremony which a Spanish priest, Diego de Soria, adapted to Christian purposes.

2. This is the traditional greeting by which a host in the Hispanic world welcomes a guest into his home. It means *You are in your own house.*

3. In the house of the host family is a **nacimiento,** or nativity scene, with the manger, the landscape of Bethlehem with traditional pine boughs, the star of the East, the animals, and, of course, statues of Mary and Joseph. Every **nacimiento** has nine levels or steps. Each night of the **Posadas** the statues are moved up one level. Thus, the holy family symbolically arrives at the manger at the same time the community celebrates Christmas Eve.

4. *In the name of Heaven,
give us shelter.
Open the door
to my beloved wife.*

*There is no inn here.
Continue (on your search).
Speak to me no further,
thief or rogue.*

5. A **piñata** for the children is part of every night of the **Posadas**. The **piñata** is a brightly colored figure made of tissue paper, usually in the shape of an animal or toy, which covers a clay or cardboard container full of fruits, candies, and coins. The children take turns at being blindfolded and trying to break the **piñata** with a bat. When it is finally broken, the contents spill out and all the children leap upon them happily. **Piñatas** are also used for children's birthday parties in many countries.

6. On Christmas Eve, the figurine of the child Jesus is rocked to sleep, and godparents **(padrinos)** are chosen from among the guests. They will be the host family of the next year's **Posadas**.

ACTIVIDADES

Los días feriados

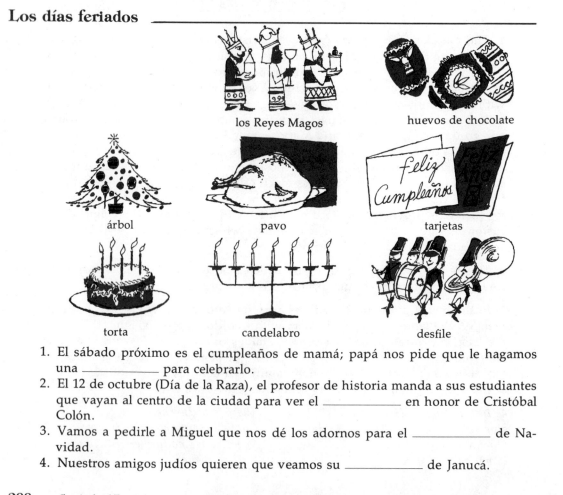

los Reyes Magos

huevos de chocolate

árbol

pavo

tarjetas

torta

candelabro

desfile

1. El sábado próximo es el cumpleaños de mamá; papá nos pide que le hagamos una _____ para celebrarlo.
2. El 12 de octubre (Día de la Raza), el profesor de historia manda a sus estudiantes que vayan al centro de la ciudad para ver el _____ en honor de Cristóbal Colón.
3. Vamos a pedirle a Miguel que nos dé los adornos para el _____ de Navidad.
4. Nuestros amigos judíos quieren que veamos su _____ de Janucá.

5. Yo quiero comer jamón para Navidad, pero mamá quiere que comamos _____.
6. Andresito va a pedirles a _____ que le traigan muchos regalos.
7. Comprémosles _____ a los niños para Pascuas (*Easter*).
8. Mi madre me pide que no me olvide de enviarles _____ de Navidad y de cumpleaños a mis padrinos.

Las fechas de cumpleaños.
¿Cuáles son los meses más populares? _____

¿Sabe usted en qué meses hay más cumpleaños? Pues . . . depende del país. En Argentina, por ejemplo, los dos meses más comunes son septiembre y octubre. Allí la gente llama a los bebés que llegan en esos meses «hijos de las vacaciones» porque su fecha de concepción probablemente coincide con los dos meses de más calor, cuando la mayoría de la gente sale de vacaciones. En los Estados Unidos, los dos meses más comunes para los nacimientos son julio y agosto.
¿Puede usted pensar en alguna explicación de este fenómeno?
Esta clase de español ¿es típica de la población norteamericana en este aspecto?

Entrevista _____

Ask a classmate the following questions. Then report the information to the class.
1. ¿Quiere tu familia que estés con ellos para Navidad? ¿Quieres tú estar con ellos?
2. ¿Qué te gusta hacer para celebrar tu cumpleaños? ¿dar una fiesta en tu casa? ¿salir a comer con tus amigos?
3. La víspera (*eve*) del Año Nuevo ¿quieres que tus amigos vayan a tu casa o prefieres ir a otra parte?
4. ¿Qué día de fiesta es más importante para ti: Navidad, Año Nuevo o algún otro día? ¿Por qué?
5. ¿Te gusta dar y recibir regalos para Navidad o crees que esa costumbre es simplemente un buen negocio para los comerciantes?
6. En una fiesta en tu casa ¿prohíbes a tus amigos que fumen o no? ¿Por qué?

Situación _____

Lugar: en casa de Graciela, el día de Navidad.
Personajes: Graciela, Consuelo (una invitada) y **Manolo** (un invitado)

Graciela:	*«Hola, Consuelo, feliz Navidad. Me alegro de verte. ¿Cómo estás?»*
Consuelo:	dice que está bien y que le encantan los adornos de la casa, etc. . .
Graciela:	le da las gracias y le dice que quiere que ella conozca a su vecino Manolo. Llama a Manolo.

Manolo:	saluda a Graciela y le dice que la fiesta es muy agradable y que la comida es deliciosa . . . etc.
Graciela:	presenta a Manolo y Consuelo.
Consuelo y Manolo:	*«Mucho gusto».*
Manolo:	pregunta a Consuelo si quiere que le traiga una copa (*glass*) de champaña.
Consuelo:	dice que sí, que adora el champaña y que entonces van a poder brindar (*toast*) por una feliz Navidad para todos.

VOCABULARIO ACTIVO

Verbos útiles

celebrar   *to celebrate*
fumar   *to smoke*
mandar   *to order, command*
permitir   *to permit, allow*
rezar   *to pray*
reunirse   *to meet, get together*
saludar   *to greet*
terminar   *to end, finish*

Las fiestas

el adorno   *decoration*
el árbol de Navidad   *Christmas tree*
la celebración   *celebration*
el comedor   *dining room*
la costumbre   *custom*
el cumpleaños   *birthday*
el desfile   *parade*
la época   *era, epoch*
el invitado (la invitada)   *guest*
Janucá   *Chanukah*
la madrina   *godmother*
la misa   *mass*
el nacimiento   *nativity scene; birth*
la Navidad   *Christmas*
la Nochebuena   *Christmas Eve*

el padrino   *godfather;* **los padrinos**   *godparents*
el papel   *role;* **hacer un papel**   *to play a role*
el pavo   *turkey*
los Reyes Magos   *Three Kings (Three Wise Men)*
el santo (patrón)   *patron saint*
la tarjeta   *card*

Otras palabras útiles

despacio   *slowly*
el dueño (la dueña)   *owner*
la justicia   *justice*
la lectura   *reading*
medianoche   *midnight*
el nieto (la nieta)   *grandson (granddaughter)*
la protesta   *protest*
próximo(a)   *next*
público(a)   *public*
el pueblo   *town*
el tesoro   *treasure*
varios(as)   *several*
el yerno (la nuera)   *son-in-law (daughter-in-law)*

LA SALUD

—¿Sólo una aspirina?

MEDICINAS

PENICILINA

LAXANTES

DIGESTIVOS

ANTIBIÓTICOS

OBJECTIVES

LANGUAGE: In this chapter we introduce, discuss, and practice:
1. the subjunctive in noun clauses
2. the subjunctive with impersonal expressions, like *It's important that . . .* or *It's good that . . .*
3. endings that can be added to a word to form diminutives, words that imply smallness of size, endearment, or sometimes contempt

You will also learn vocabulary related to health or illness.

CULTURE: The dialogue at the end of this chapter takes place in Colombia, off the coast of the Caribbean. You will learn something about that region and especially about some of the country people and their way of life and customs. Close family ties and a spirit of cooperation prevail there through bad times as well as good.

EXPLICACIÓN

I. THE SUBJUNCTIVE IN NOUN CLAUSES

(1)	**La doctora:**	Primero quiero *que la enfermera le tome la temperatura.*
(2)	**La enferma:**	Ya lo hizo, doctora, y no tengo fiebre. Pero me siento muy mal.
(3)	**La doctora:**	No me sorprende *que se sienta mal.* Quiero *que usted vaya al hospital inmediatamente.*
(4)	**La enferma:**	Pero, doctora, ¿qué es lo que tengo?
(5)	**La doctora:**	Por ahora sólo sé que su aspecto físico es horrible. Mírese en ese espejo. Está usted muy pálida, tiene los ojos nublados, los labios . . .
(6)	**La enferma:**	¡Basta ya! ¡Tampoco usted es una Venus!

1. ¿Qué quiere la doctora que haga la enfermera? **2.** ¿Cómo se siente la enferma? **3.** ¿Qué quiere la doctora que haga la enferma? **4.** ¿Sabe la doctora qué tiene la enferma? **5.** ¿Qué hace usted cuando se siente muy mal?

A. Many sentences are composed of two or more clauses, or groups of words containing a subject and a verb. For instance, in the sentence *We wish that he were coming, We wish* is a main clause and *that he were coming* is a dependent clause. A dependent clause contains a subject and a verb, but it cannot stand alone as a sentence; it is dependent upon the verb in the main clause. When a dependent clause functions as the subject or object of the verb of the main clause, it is called a noun clause. In Spanish, noun clauses are always introduced by **que,** but in English *that* is often omitted or an infinitive is used in place of the noun clause.

Espero que Juan se sienta mejor.	*I hope (that) Juan feels better.*
Quiero que tome dos aspirinas.	*I want you to take two aspirins.*

(1) First, I'd like the nurse to take your temperature. (2) She already took it, doctor, and I don't have a fever. But I feel terrible. (3) I'm not surprised that you feel badly. I want you to go to the hospital immediately. (4) But doctor, what do I have? (5) Right now I only know that your physical appearance is horrible. Look at yourself in that mirror. You are very pale, your eyes are blurry, your lips . . . (6) That's enough! You're no Venus yourself!

B. The verb in the noun clause must be in the subjunctive when the subject is different from that in the main clause and the main clause expresses one of the following.

1. an order, request, or plea

Insiste en que su hijo estudie medicina.	*He insists that his son study medicine.*
Les pido (a ellos) que me traigan cigarrillos.	*I am asking them to bring me cigarettes.*
¡Te digo que tomes la sopa!	*I'm telling you to eat the soup!*
El doctor prohíbe que se levante de la cama.	*The doctor forbids him to get out of bed.*

2. will, desire, or preference

No quiero que usted pierda tiempo.	*I don't want you to waste time.*
Desean que tú arregles la radio.	*They want you to fix the radio set.*
Elena prefiere que su esposo fume cigarros.	*Elena prefers that her husband smoke cigars.*

3. expectations, emotions, and feelings

Tengo miedo de que se enfermen.	*I am afraid that they will get sick.*
Ojalá que los jóvenes lleguen pronto.	*I hope that the young people arrive soon.*
Me alegro de que no tengas deudas.	*I'm glad you don't have any debts.*
No me sorprende que Ernesto esté enfermo, porque no come bien.	*I'm not surprised that Ernesto is sick because he doesn't eat well.*
Siento que Juan tenga dolor de oídos.	*I'm sorry Juan has an earache.*

4. approval, permission, or advice

Me gusta que Ana diga eso.	*I'm pleased (it pleases me) that Ana says that.*
El profesor permite que llegue tarde hoy.	*The teacher is permitting me to arrive late today.*

5. necessity

Necesitan que alguien los lleve al doctor.	*They need someone to take them to the doctor.*

6. doubt or uncertainty

Dudo que encuentren la cura para esa enfermedad.	*I doubt they will find the cure for that disease.*
No estoy seguro que José sepa hacerlo.	*I'm not sure that José knows how to do it.*

C. The verbs **creer** and **pensar** require the subjunctive in interrogative or negative sentences when surprise or doubt is implied. The indicative is used in affirmative sentences or when there is no uncertainty in the speaker's mind.

¿Crees que Alicia esté embarazada? *Do you think that Alicia is pregnant? (doubt implied)*

¿Crees que Alicia está embarazada? *Do you think Alicia is pregnant? (simple question)*

No creo que Alicia esté embarazada. *I don't believe that Alicia is pregnant.*

¿Piensas que Ramón esté contento? *Do you think Ramón is happy? (doubt implied)*

No pienso que Ramón esté contento. *I don't think that Ramón is happy.*

Pienso que Ramón está contento. *I think that Ramón is happy.*

Ejercicios

A. Create new sentences, substituting the expressions in the lists for those in italics.

1. *Me alegro de que ustedes* estén bien.
   a. Dudo que nosotros **b.** No creo que ellos **c.** Ojalá que mamá **d.** Espero que tú **e.** Deseo que Pablo

2. *No creo que tú* me lo traigas.
   a. Mando que Anita **b.** Prefiero que tú y Lelia **c.** Pido que usted **d.** Necesito que ellos **e.** Quiero que los Rodríguez

3. *¿Quieren que yo* llame al doctor?
   a. Insisten en que los muchachos **b.** Esperan que Alicia **c.** Dudan que Ernesto y yo **d.** Prefieren que tú **e.** Tienen miedo de que ustedes

4. *Esperamos que papá* nos dé las medicinas.
   a. Ojalá que tus amigos **b.** Necesitamos que tú **c.** Queremos que el gobierno **d.** Nos alegramos de que ustedes **e.** Dudamos que alguien

B. Complete the sentences with the correct form of the verb in parentheses.

1. (llegar) ¡Ojalá que la enfermera _____ pronto!
2. (conocer) Queremos que tú _____ a Jesús.
3. (dar) Le pido que no le _____ aspirinas al niño.
4. (volver) ¿Dudas que el doctor _____ mañana?
5. (saber) Esperamos que ellas _____ hacerlo.
6. (venir) No creo que él _____ porque tiene dolor de oídos.
7. (tener) ¿Te sorprende que yo _____ dolor de cabeza?
8. (ser) ¿No creen que ella _____ mi hermana?
9. (estar) Sentimos que usted _____ enferma.
10. (trabajar) ¿No le gusta que su esposa _____ en el hospital?

C. Give the Spanish equivalent of the following sentences.

1. I hope (that) he helps the family.
2. I want him to help the family.

3. She believes you are at the hospital.
4. She doubts that you are at the hospital.
5. They don't believe you are at the hospital.
6. Do you (*tú*) think he has a fever?
7. I think he has a fever.
8. We don't think that he has a fever.

Preguntas

1. ¿Cree usted que los doctores generalmente les dicen la verdad a sus pacientes? ¿mentiras? ¿un poco de verdad y otro poco de mentiras? ¿Por qué? **2.** ¿Piensa usted que los países más ricos tienen que ayudar a los más pobres? ¿Sí o no? ¿Por qué? **3.** ¿Qué tipo de ayuda prefiere usted que se dé a los países pobres? ¿económica (dinero, comida)? ¿cultural (construcción de escuelas, universidades, bibliotecas)? ¿médica? ¿humana (doctores, técnicos, ingenieros, etc.)? ¿Por qué?

II. THE SUBJUNCTIVE WITH IMPERSONAL EXPRESSIONS

(1) **Señor Álvarez:** Si piensa casarse con mi hija *es importante que me diga* qué hace y cuánto gana.

(2) **El novio:** Pues mire, señor Álvarez, *es preferible que ella sea* feliz y no rica. Yo gano ochenta pesos al mes; soy enfermero.

(3) **Señor Álvarez:** Entonces *no es possible que yo permita* que se case con mi hija. *Es mejor que usted cambie* o de empleo o de novia.

1. ¿Qué quiere saber el señor Álvarez? **2.** ¿Cuánto gana el novio? **3.** ¿Va a permitir el señor Álvarez que se casen? ¿Por qué?

A. The subjunctive is used after many impersonal expressions that express doubt, emotion, expectation, or personal judgment. Some of the more commonly used impersonal expressions that require the subjunctive in affirmative, negative, or interrogative sentences are:

Es bueno.	*It's good.*	Es impossible.	*It's impossible.*
Es malo.	*It's bad.*	Es posible.	*It's possible.*
Es mejor.	*It's better.*	Es importante.	*It's important.*

---

(1) If you intend to marry my daughter it's important that you tell me what you do and how much you earn. (2) Well (look), Mr. Álvarez, it's preferable for her to be happy not rich. I earn 80 pesos a month, I'm a male nurse. (3) Then it's not possible for me to permit you to marry my daughter. It's better that you change your job or your girlfriend.

Es una lástima.	*It's a pity.*	Es necesario.	*It's necessary.*
Es difícil.	*It's difficult.*	Es terrible.	*It's terrible.*
Es probable.	*It's probable.*	Es ridículo.	*It's ridiculous.*

¿Es bueno que ellos hagan ejercicios?   *Is it good that they exercise?*

Es mejor que me vaya porque tengo mareos.   *It's better for me to leave because I feel dizzy.*

Es importante que tomes vitaminas.   *It's important that you take vitamins.*

No es posible que sea tan valiente.   *It's not possible that he's so brave.*

B. The following expressions require the subjunctive when used in the negative or interrogative if doubt is strongly implied.

Es verdad.	*It's true.*	Es (está) claro.	*It's clear.*
Es cierto.	*It's certain.*	Es seguro.	*It's certain.*
Es evidente.	*It's evident.*	Es obvio.	*It's obvious.*

No es verdad que él tenga un resfrío.   *It's not true that he has a cold.*

¿Es verdad que él tenga un resfrío?   *Is it true that he has a cold? (doubt implied)*

¿Es verdad que él tiene un resfrío?   *Is it true that he has a cold? (simple question)*

Es verdad que él tiene un resfrío.   *It's true that he has a cold.*

No es cierto que esa enfermedad sea incurable.   *It's not true that that disease is incurable.*

Es cierto que esa enfermedad es incurable.   *It's true that that disease is incurable.*

C. The expressions **tal vez** and **quizás,** which both mean *perhaps,* normally require the subjunctive. They are followed by the indicative if the speaker or writer wants to express belief or conviction.

Quizás fume demasiado.   *Perhaps he smokes too much (speaker not sure).*

Quizás fuma demasiado.   *Perhaps he smokes too much (he probably does)*

Tal vez Enrique lo sepa.   *Maybe Enrique knows about it.*

Tal vez Enrique lo sabe.   *Maybe Enrique knows about it (he probably does).*

Ejercicios _____

A. Create new sentences, substituting the words in the lists for those in italics. Use the subjunctive or indicative, as required by the impersonal expression.

1. *Es una lástima* que Jesusito esté enfermo.
   a. Es verdad   **b.** Es probable   **c.** No es cierto   **d.** Es evidente   **e.** Es posible

2. *Es mejor* que ellos se levanten a las cinco de la mañana.
   a. Es ridículo   **b.** Es difícil   **c.** Es cierto   **d.** Es imposible   **e.** Es verdad

B. Create new sentences, replacing the words in italics with **que** + a clause. Use the word or words in parentheses as subjects.

Modelo: Es bueno *ser bilingüe.* (Tomás)   **Es bueno que Tomás sea bilingüe.**

1. Es una lástima *no llegar temprano.* (Eduardo y Carolina)
2. Es importante *no trabajar demasiado.* (tú)
3. Es posible *tener fiebre.* (la hija del doctor)
4. Es mejor *no hacerlo.* (nosotros)
5. Es ridículo *decir esas cosas.* (usted)
6. Es necesario *ver al doctor regularmente.* (yo)

C. Mrs. Ramos is pregnant with her first baby and goes to see the family doctor. Form sentences with the following elements, starting them with **Es necesario que,** as the doctor would.

Modelo: usted/tomar mucha leche   **Es necesario que usted tome mucha leche.**

1. su marido/ayudar más en la casa
2. usted/dormir ocho horas por día
3. usted y su marido/querer tener este bebé
4. usted/comer bien y tomar vitaminas
5. ustedes/buscar un buen hospital.
6. usted/no fumar
7. su marido/aprender a cambiar pañales (*diapers*)
8. usted/no tomar bebidas alcohólicas
9. usted/no cansarse mucho
10. usted/volver aquí la próxima semana

D. Write three sentences using **quizás** or **tal vez.**

Preguntas

1. ¿Es importante o no que uno vea al doctor regularmente? ¿Por qué? **2.** ¿Es posible que en el futuro exista la posibilidad de vivir eternamente? ¿Le gusta o no la idea de no morir? ¿Por qué sí o por qué no? **3.** ¿Es probable que podamos llegar a Venus en esta década (*decade*)? ¿que podamos hablar con habitantes de otros planetas? ¿que se encuentre una cura para el cáncer? **4.** ¿Es posible que no tengamos guerras en el futuro? ¿problemas económicos? ¿enfermedades? **5.** ¿Es mejor que una familia no tenga hijos? ¿tenga solamente un hijo? ¿tenga dos o más hijos? ¿Por qué?

III. DIMINUTIVES

(1)	**Sr. González:**	¿No te sientes bien, *hijita*?
(2)	**Isabelita:**	Sabes *papito* . . . tengo un *dolorcito* de garganta. Creo que no debo ir a la escuela. Y tengo un *poquito* de tos también.
(3)	**Sr. González:**	¡Qué lástima! Yo pensaba llevarte al cine después de la escuela a ver «Los tres *chanchitos*».
(4)	**Isabelita:**	Pues . . . en ese caso, tomo una *pildorita* y me pongo *buenita* ¿eh?

1. ¿Por qué cree Isabelita que no debe ir a la escuela? **2.** ¿Adónde pensaba llevarla su papá? **3.** En ese caso, ¿qué va a hacer la niña?

A. In Spanish, certain endings may be added to a word to form diminutives. Learn to recognize these common endings:

1. **-ito, -ita, -(e)cito, -(e)cita**

   These endings are added to a word ending in a consonant to indicate smallness of size or fondness. If the word ends in a vowel, the final vowel is dropped.

casita	*(small) house*	pobrecito	*poor (little) thing*
hermanitos	*little brothers*	Miguelito	*little Michael*
cosita	*small or insignificant*	mujercita	*little woman*
	thing	momentito	*moment*
hombrecito	*little man*	rubiecito	*little blond boy*

(1) Don't you feel well, little daughter? (2) You know, Daddy . . . I have a little sore throat. I think I shouldn't go to school. I have a slight cough too. (3) What a shame! I was thinking of taking you to the movies after school to see *The Three Little Pigs*. (4) Well . . . in that case I'll take a little pill and be just fine, eh?

2. **-illo, -illa, -(e)cillo, -(e)cilla**

These endings can also indicate smallness of size or fondness, but they sometimes indicate contempt or sarcasm.

panecillo	*small loaf of bread*	platillo	*small dish*
autorcillo	*insignificant author*	chiquilla	*little girl*
reyecillo	*petty king*		

B. Note that some words require a spelling change before a suffix is added in order to preserve the sound of the consonant when the final vowel is dropped.

amiguito	*little friend*	chiquito	*little one*
poquito	*little bit*	cerquita	*very near*

Ejercicios

A. Restate the following sentences, using a diminutive form of the word in italics.

Modelo: Dame un *poco* de agua, por favor. **Dame un poquito de agua, por favor.**

1. ¿Quién es este *chico?*
2. ¿Qué tiene mi *hijo,* doctor?
3. Creo que las aspirinas están en la *mesa.*
4. Espéreme un *momento,* por favor.
5. Viven *cerca* del hospital.
6. Tengo un *dolor* aquí, mamá. ¿Qué puede ser?
7. ¿No se sienten bien tus *amigas?*
8. ¿Tiene mucha fiebre su *hermana?*

Preguntas

Choose the appropriate response.

1. ¿Conoces a la chiquilla rubia?
   a. ¿Esa mujer? Sí, la conozco.   **b.** ¡Claro!, es mi hermanita.   **c.** Lo conocí en la calle.

2. ¿Dónde está tu papito?
   a. Está con mi mamita.   **b.** Está sobre la mesita.   **c.** Ella no está aquí.

3. Me gustan mucho estos panecillos.
   a. Los hice hace veinte años.   **b.** Son para tomar la temperatura, Luis.   **c.** Son realmente muy fáciles de hacer, Susana.

UN RANCHO EN LA COSTA DEL CARIBE

Un rancho en la costa del Caribe.

Antonia: ¡Jesús![1] ¡Jesusito, ven acá! Necesito que me traigas leña. Me duele mucho la espalda. ¿Qué hacías?
Jesusito: Miraba los gallos.[2] ¡Qué valiente parece el chiquito!
Antonia: ¡Otra vez! Es tonto que pierdas el tiempo así. Sabes que ya eres un hombrecito. Es importante que empieces a ayudar a la familia. Tu padre no está bien.
Jesusito: Sí, mamá. Voy por la leña y después iré a pescar. ¿Está enfermo papá?
Antonia: No, sólo es un poco de fatiga. Ojalá que regreses con un buen pescado.
Jesusito: Sí, mamá. Y ojalá que papá no se enferme.
Antonia: ¿Y tu hermanita? Espero que no esté cerca del río.
Jesusito: No, mamá. Está con papá en el arrozal.[3]

El niño sale, pero regresa en seguida.

Jesusito: Mamá, por el río llega gente en canoa.

Antonia: ¿Estás seguro? ¿Quiénes pueden ser? ¡Ah, sí!, son Félix y Marta. ¡Bienvenidos!

Félix: Buenos días, comadre[4] Antonia.

Antonia: Muy buenos días, compadres. Pasen adelante.

Félix: ¿Y el compadre Ezequiel?

Antonia: Está en el arrozal. Jesús, ve por tu papá.

Jesusito: Sí, mamá. Ya le digo a papá que venga.

Antonia: En un momentito les hago un rico tinto.[5]

Félix: Bueno, si usted insiste.

Antonia: Claro, y también insisto en que almuercen con nosotros.

Félix: En estos momentos, es mejor que nos haga una burundanga.[6]

Antonia: Pero, ¿por qué? ¿se siente mal? La veo pálida.

Marta: Es que tenemos muchos problemas. El señor Álvarez nos ha quitado el rancho y la tierra porque no podíamos pagar las deudas.

Félix: La señora Álvarez quiere que trabajemos para ella en su casa. Pero, ¡qué va! No queremos ser sirvientes.

Antonia: Claro. Es mejor ser pobres pero libres. ¿Por qué no vienen a vivir con nosotros?

Marta: Gracias, comadre. Pero no creo que aquí haya suficiente tierra para dos familias. Además, como usted puede ver, estoy embarazada.

Antonia: No lo sabía. ¡Felicitaciones! ¡Qué contenta estoy! Con mayor razón, Ezequiel no va a permitir que se vayan. Es verdad que no tenemos mucha tierra, pero con más manos para el trabajo, va a rendir más.

Félix: Se lo agradecemos de todo corazón, comadre. Vamos a ver qué pasa.

Antonia: ¡No se preocupen! Todo se va a arreglar.

Caribe *Caribbean*   **rendir** *produce*

1. ¿Qué quiere Antonia que Jesús le traiga?   2. ¿Qué hacía Jesús?   3. ¿Qué va a hacer Jesús después de ir por leña?   4. ¿Con quién está la hermanita de Jesús?   5. ¿Quiénes llegan en canoa?   6. ¿Qué le va a decir Jesús a su papá?   7. ¿En qué insiste Antonia? 8. ¿Cuáles son los problemas de Félix y Marta?   9. ¿Qué quiere la señora Álvarez que Félix y Marta hagan?   10. «Es mejor ser pobre pero libre». ¿Está usted de acuerdo? ¿O es necesario tener dinero para ser verdaderamente libre?

NOTAS CULTURALES

1. Jesús is a common proper name in the Hispanic world, and it is used for both males and females, often in compound names like **María de Jesús** or **Roberto de Jesús.**

2. Many country people in the Hispanic world breed roosters for cockfighting, **la pelea de gallos,** a favorite sport in Mexico and the Caribbean. In some places it is considered cruel and is now banned by law.

3. Rice is cultivated in many of the marshy areas of Colombia. An **arrozal** is a rice field. Similarly, a corn field is called a **maizal,** a coffee field a **cafetal,** and so forth.

4. The words **comadre** and **compadre** are used in many areas of the Hispanic world to mean *good friend,* particularly among families joined together by the system of **compadrazgo.** This often means that the husband and wife of each of the families are godparents to the children of the other family and so are bound to help them in times of trouble.

5. The word **tinto** is used in Colombia and certain other places to mean *black coffee.* It normally refers to *red wine* (**vino tinto**) and is used to distinguish it from *white wine* (**vino blanco**) in all parts of the Hispanic world.

6. A **burundanga** is a drink made from herbs; it is supposed to cause certain spiritual changes in the person who drinks it. The word is of African origin, as are many of the words used in the Caribbean and the coastal areas of Colombia, since many of the people there are of African ancestry, often mixed with Indian and Caucasian.

ACTIVIDADES

¿Qué tengo, Doctor?
Síntomas
Me duele:

| la cabeza | la espalda | la garganta | el estómago |

Me duelen:

| los pies | los huesos | los ojos | los oídos |

Tengo:

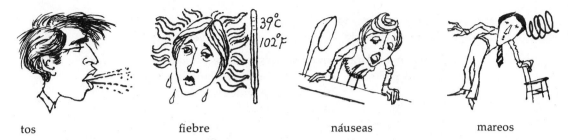

tos   fiebre   náuseas   mareos

A "volunteer" should act the part of a patient who comes to a doctor's office and describes his/her symptoms. The class should then decide on the appropriate diagnosis and remedy, consulting the *Vocabulario Activo* and the *Vocabulario Auxiliar* when necessary. The activity should be repeated several times.

Vocabulario Auxiliar

la alergia	el problema
el antibiótico	ortopédico
la artritis	la radiografía (*X-ray*)
la gripe (*flu*)	
la indigestión	tomar líquidos
la operación	las úlceras

Conversación con un hipocondríaco

One student should play the role of a hypocondriac and make statements about his/her medical problems based on the vocabulary given on page 305. Other students should respond to each statement with sentences using impersonal expressions (given on pages 295–296) and the subjunctive.

Modelos: —Me duelen los huesos.
—Es una lástima que te duelan los huesos.
—Necesito una operación.
—Es ridículo que usted necesite una operación.

Entrevista

Ask a classmate the following questions. Then report the information to the class.

1. Cuando te duele la cabeza ¿qué haces?
2. ¿Cuántas veces tuviste un resfrío el invierno pasado?
3. Si tienes fiebre y náuseas, ¿te acuestas? ¿consultas con un médico? ¿no haces nada?
4. Según tu opinión, ¿es probable que la medicina descubra una cura para el cáncer? ¿Cuándo?
5. ¿Es necesario que nuestros hospitales cambien la manera de recibir a los enfermos que no tienen dinero? ¿Cómo?

Situación

Lugar: en la oficina del doctor Fernández.
Personajes: La **recepcionista**, el **paciente**, el **doctor Fernández.**

La recepcionista:	*«Buenos días. ¿Viene usted a ver al doctor?»*
El paciente:	dice que sí, que se siente muy mal y que necesita que el doctor lo vea inmediatamente.
La recepcionista:	le pide que describa sus síntomas.
El paciente:	le describe los síntomas que tiene. . . .
La recepcionista:	dice que es una lástima que el doctor Fernández no esté, que tuvo que salir por una emergencia. Le pregunta si quiere dejar un recado.

*En ese momento regresa el doctor Fernández con unos palos (clubs) de golf
bajo el brazo.*

Dr. Fernández:	saluda a la recepcionista y le pregunta *«¿Qué hay de nuevo?»*
La recepcionista:	dice que está el paciente allí.
Dr. Fernández:	dice que puede ver al paciente.

El Dr. Fernández y el paciente entran al consultorio (examining room).

VOCABULARIO ACTIVO

Verbos útiles

agradecer (zc) *to thank*
alegrarse de *to be glad*
arreglar *to fix, arrange;* **arreglarse** *to be okay, turn out all right*
dudar *to doubt*
enfermarse *to get sick*
insistir *to insist*
quitar *to take away*
sentir *to feel or sense;* **sentirse +**
    adj. *to feel a certain way;* **sentir**
    que . . . *to be sorry that . . .*
sorprender *to surprise*
tener miedo (de) *to be afraid*

La salud

el aspecto (físico) *(physical) appearance*
la aspirina *aspirin*
la cama *bed*
el cigarro *cigar;* **el cigarrillo** *cigarette*
la cura *cure*
la enfermedad *illness*
la fatiga *fatigue*
la garganta *throat*
el hospital *hospital*
el labio *lip*
la medicina *medicine*
el oído *hearing, ear*
la píldora *pill*
el resfrío *cold*
el síntoma *symptom*
tener mareos *to be dizzy*
tener tos *to have a cough*
la tos *cough*
la vitamina *vitamin*

Adjetivos

claro(a) *clear, obvious*
evidente *evident, obvious*
libre *free*
médico(a) *medical*
obvio(a) *obvious*
pálido(a) *pale*
preferible *preferable*
seguro(a) *sure, certain*
tonto(a) *silly, foolish*
valiente *brave*

Otras palabras útiles

la canoa *canoe*
la comadre *close family friend, often godmother of one's child;* **el compadre** *close friend, often godfather of one's child*
demasiado *too much*
la deuda *debt*
el espejo *mirror*
el gallo *cock, rooster*
la leña *firewood*
Ojalá que . . . *I hope (it is to be hoped) that . . .*
pasar adelante *to come in, go on in*
perder (el) tiempo *to waste time*
el rancho *ranch; in Venezuela and Colombia a small, poor dwelling*
el, la sirviente *servant*
tal vez *perhaps*
la tierra *land, earth*

Las Fiestas

A los hispanos les gustan las fiestas y los *espectáculos*. En cada
comunidad se celebran, anualmente, varias fiestas. En el pueblo de
Guatemala que se ve en la foto los indios, vestidos de conquistadores
españoles o de jefes *indígenas*, participan en una representación de
la conquista. La fiesta es una ocasión muy especial para los habitantes de las regiones pobres y remotas. Durante un tiempo pueden
olvidar su vida *cotidiana* de trabajo y miseria y ser parte de las ricas
tradiciones del pasado.

En España y en ciertos países de Hispanoamérica, una parte importante de muchas fiestas es la *corrida de toros*. Generalmente los
extranjeros la consideran como un deporte, pero para el hispano es
un espectáculo o un rito que tiene *valor* técnico, estético y espiritual.
Simboliza el drama *íntimo* y personal de *todo ser humano al enfrentarse con* la muerte.

La corrida empieza con el desfile de los toreros. Hay tres clases de
toreros: los picadores, los banderilleros y los matadores, y cada uno
tiene un papel distinto. Cuando el toro entra en la plaza la *lucha*
comienza. Durante la corrida los toreros *tratan de descubrir* los *puntos
fuertes y débiles* del toro *por medio de* una serie de movimientos tra-

shows, pageants

native

daily

bullfight
foreigners
value
*intimate / every
human being upon
confronting*

fight
*try to discover / strong
and weak points /
through*

dicionales y exactos. Pero el toro también aprende a defenderse. Así, cuando la corrida es buena, es prácticamente un duelo, tanto intelectual como físico, entre el hombre y el animal. Cuando llega el momento más importante, llamado por los aficionados «el momento de la verdad», el torero se enfrenta con el toro. Si el torero es excelente, lo mata inmediatamente con un solo *golpe* de la *espada*. blow / sword

La mayoría de la gente hispana es católica y, *por lo tanto*, las fiestas therefore católicas se celebran con mucho entusiasmo. Cada pueblo o ciudad tiene su santo patrón, y cada año se organiza una fiesta para *honrar* honor su día. También cada persona tiene, generalmente, una fecha en que celebra el día del santo cuyo nombre lleva. Por ejemplo, el santo de José es el 19 de marzo, día de San José. Es común celebrar ese día con un almuerzo o una cena especial.

Una de las festividades religiosas más conocidas es la celebración de la *Semana Santa* en Sevilla. La semana *anterior al domingo de Pascua* toda la ciudad se transforma. *Se adornan* las casas con *mantos* violetas, estatuas y flores. Los niños se visten de ángeles o de Jesús,

Holy Week / before
Easter Sunday
they decorate / cloths

y muchos adultos se ponen la ropa violeta del penitente. Hay procesiones lentas y silenciosas de enormes «pasos» (plataformas decoradas con estatuas que representan escenas religiosas) que a veces *pesan* más de 3.000 kilos. Estos «pasos» no están *montados en* automóviles: son *cargados por* los hombres de Sevilla, vestidos de penitentes. Luego, el tono pasa de la tristeza a la alegría cuando, una semana después de la Pascua, se celebra una gran *feria* con bailes, carreras de caballos, corridas de toros, música y *fuegos artificiales*.

En las fiestas religiosas de los pueblos pequeños y remotos de la América Hispana se encuentra, muchas veces, una *mezcla* curiosa de cristianismo y paganismo. En algunas partes del Perú y de Bolivia, la gente honra simultáneamente a la Virgen María y a la Pachamama, o Madre-Tierra de la religión indígena. Los indios bolivianos de la foto son del pueblo de Oruro, famoso por su «fiesta de la diablada». *Llevan máscaras* que representan al mismo tiempo a los antiguos *demonios* de los Andes y a los *diablos* cristianos. La diablada es un baile que simboliza la eterna lucha entre *el bien y el mal. Al final,* hombres vestidos de ángeles matan a los diablos, y la ceremonia termina con un servicio religioso.

(marginal glosses:)
weigh / mounted on / carried by

fair
fireworks

mixture

they wear / masks
demons / devils
good and evil / at the end

Preguntas

1. ¿Por qué es la fiesta una ocasión muy especial para los habitantes de las regiones pobres y remotas? **2.** ¿Es un deporte la corrida de toros? ¿Qué simboliza? **3.** ¿Qué es «el momento de la verdad»? **4.** ¿Qué significa «el día del santo» para una persona hispana? **5.** ¿Dónde se celebra una Semana Santa famosa? ¿Qué hacen allí? **6.** ¿Qué pasa una semana después de Pascuas? **7.** ¿Cuál es la mezcla frecuente en las fiestas de ciertos países hispanos? ¿Qué ejemplo de esto puede dar usted? **8.** ¿En qué fechas celebramos fiestas en nuestra sociedad? ¿Cuál es su fiesta (día feriado) preferida?

SENTIMIENTOS Y EMOCIONES

¡Qué risa!

¡Qué susto!

¡Qué rabia!

OBJECTIVES

LANGUAGE: In this chapter we introduce discuss, and practice:
1. the subjunctive in adjective clauses
2. the subjunctive in adverbial clauses
3. various uses of the infinitive in Spanish

You will also learn vocabulary related to feelings and expressions of emotion.

CULTURE: The dialogue at the end of the chapter takes place in Asunción, Paraguay, in a beauty parlor, where two women are discussing men, their women friends, and the **altibajos** (*ups and downs*) of life in general.

EXPLICACIÓN

I. SUBJUNCTIVE IN ADJECTIVE CLAUSES

(1) **Señor Méndez:** ¿Es usted la persona que quiere trabajar aquí?

(2) **Señor Gómez:** Sí, señor, yo soy profesor y busco un empleo *que me guste*. Puedo enseñar historia, literatura . . . cualquier curso *que usted mande*.

(3) **Señor Méndez:** ¡Qué bien! Me alegro de conocer a alguien que sabe tanto . . . Dígame, ¿sabe usted quién mató a Julio César?

(4) **Señor Gómez:** Pero señor, pregúntele eso a alguien *que sea detective*.

(5) **Señor Méndez:** ¡Bruto!

(6) **Señor Gómez:** Por favor, señor, sin ofender . . .

1. ¿Quién busca un empleo que le guste? 2. ¿Qué es el Sr. Gómez? 3. ¿Qué puede enseñar él? 4. Aparentemente, ¿sabe él quién mató a Julio César? 5. ¿A quién hay que preguntarle quién lo mató, según el Sr. Gómez? 6. ¿Trabaja usted además de estudiar? ¿Está contento(-a) con su trabajo?

A. An adjective clause is a dependent clause that modifies a noun or pronoun. In the sentence **Salgo con una chica que es inteligente y simpática,** the adjective clause is **que es inteligente y simpática,** and the noun it modifies is **chica.** In Spanish, adjective clauses are introduced by **que.**

B. If the noun or pronoun (including **alguien, alguno,** and **algo**) that the adjective clause modifies is known, definite or existent, the verb in the adjective clause should be in the indicative. But if the noun or pronoun is unknown, indefinite

---

(1) Are you the person who wants to work here? (2) Yes, sir, I am a teacher, and I'm looking for a job that I like. I can teach history, literature . . . any course you like (order). (3) Great! (How good). I'm glad to meet someone who knows so much . . . Tell me, do you know who killed Julius Caesar? (4) But sir, ask that of someone who is a detective. (5) Brutus! (also, Brute! Ignoramus!) (6) Please, sir, without being insulting (there's no need to be insulting).

or non-existent, then the verb in the adjective clause should be in the subjunctive. Compare the following examples:

Busco una peluquería que me guste.	*I'm looking for a hairdresser's I like.*
Voy a una peluquería que me gusta.	*I go to a hairdresser's that I like.*
¿Hay alguien allí que comprenda francés?	*Is there anyone there who understands French?*
Sí, hay alguien allí que comprende francés.	*Yes, there is someone there who understands French.*
Busco un hombre que me trate con toda igualdad.	*I'm looking for a man who would treat me with complete equality.*
Busco a un hombre que trabaja aquí los lunes.*	*I'm looking for a man who works here on Mondays.*
Necesito a alguien que me quiera ayudar.	*I need someone who wants to help me.*
Encontré a alguien que me quiere ayudar.	*I found someone who wants to help me.*

Ejercicios

A. Create new sentences, substituting the words in the lists for those in italics.

1. Necesitamos *una persona* que sepa inglés.
   a. enfermeros **b.** un profesor **c.** jóvenes **d.** gente **e.** una secretaria

2. Espero que encuentres *algo* que te guste.
   a. un auto **b.** zapatos **c.** una casa **d.** un empleo **e.** blusas

B. Create new sentences by substituting the words in parentheses for the italicized words, and by changing the verbs to the present subjunctive.

Modelo: Quiero asistir a *la clase* que empieza a las diez. (una clase)
   Quiero asistir a una clase que empiece a las diez.

1. Queremos visitar *el museo* que tiene obras de Goya. (un museo)
2. Necesito encontrar *a la persona* que habla portugués. (una persona)
3. Busco *a las chicas* que quieren trabajar aquí. (unas chicas)
4. Aquí *hay alguien* que sabe hablar español, ¿verdad? (no hay nadie)
5. Vamos a *la cafetería* donde sirven café colombiano. (una cafetería)
6. Queremos comprar *los zapatos* que te gustan. (unos zapatos)
7. Aquí *hay algo* que te puede ofender. (no hay nada)
8. Voy a pasar la noche en *el hotel* que está cerca del parque. (un hotel)

* The personal **a** is used before a direct object that is a person when the speaker or writer has someone definite in mind, but not when the person is indefinite or unspecified. The personal **a** is nearly always used before the pronouns **alguien, nadie, alguno,** and **ninguno,** when referring to a person.

C. Mr. Riquelme and his family are thinking about moving to a different neighborhood. To know why they want to move, complete Mr. Riquelme's comments using the present indicative or subjunctive of the verbs indicated, as appropriate.

Modelo: (gustar) a. Vivimos en un barrio que no nos <u>gusta</u>.
b. Buscamos un barrio que nos <u>guste</u>.

1. (enseñar) Mi hija asiste a un liceo (*high school*) donde no se _____ música.
2. Ella quiere asistir a un liceo donde se _____ música.
3. (ser) Tenemos una casa que _____ muy pequeña.
4. Necesitamos una casa que _____ más grande.
5. (gustar) Aquí no hay restaurantes que nos _____.
6. Sólo hay restaurantes que no nos _____.
7. (estar) Los niños quieren ir a una escuela que _____ cerca de casa.
8. Ahora ellos van a una escuela que _____ muy lejos.

D. Give the Spanish equivalent of the following sentences.

1. I'm looking for a man who knows French.
   I'm looking for the man who knows French.
2. Let's go to the restaurant that she likes.
   Let's go to a restaurant that she likes.
3. There's someone here who knows me.
   There's no one here who knows me.
4. We need a Spanish teacher who can teach literature.
   We need the Spanish teacher who can teach literature.

Preguntas

1. ¿Tiene usted amigos que vivan cerca de su casa? ¿en el campo? ¿en México? **2.** ¿Es usted amigo(a) de alguien que sea muy importante? ¿que tenga mucho dinero? ¿que haga muchos deportes? **3.** ¿Conoce usted a alguien que tenga más de cien años? ¿que escriba poemas o cuentos? ¿que viaje mucho? **4.** ¿Dan aquí alguna película que le guste? ¿que esté en español? **5.** ¿Hay alguien en esta clase que sepa hablar árabe? ¿japonés? ¿Hay alguien que pueda tocar la guitarra? ¿cantar?

II. SUBJUNCTIVE IN ADVERBIAL CLAUSES

(1) **Doña Ramona:** Noto que estás un poco deprimida, Jane . . . ¿Quieres que te enseñe algunas palabras en guaraní* *antes de que vuelvas a tu país?*

(2) **Jane:** ¡Sí, doña Ramona! Las despedidas siempre me causan tristeza. Pero puede empezar a enseñarme guaraní *cuando desee.* Por ejemplo, ¿cómo se dice «yo te quiero»?

* See **Nota cultural 3** of this chapter.

Quiero decírselo a Teddy *cuando lo vuelva a ver.*

(3) **Doña Ramona:** Pues eso se dice «che ro jaijú». Sé que él se va a sentir muy feliz *tan pronto como le digas qué significa.*

---

1. ¿Quién parece estar un poco deprimida?   **2.** ¿Qué quiere aprender Jane antes de volver a su país?   **3.** ¿Qué le causa tristeza a Jane?   **4.** ¿Qué quiere decirle Jane a Teddy cuando lo vuelva a ver?   **5.** ¿Cómo se dice «yo te quiero» en guaraní?

A. An adverbial clause is a dependent clause that modifies a verb and, like an adverb, expresses time, manner, place, or purpose. Adverbial clauses are introduced by a conjunction. The adverbial clauses are shown below in bold.

Un momento, señora; voy a atenderla **tan pronto como pueda.**	*Just a moment, ma'am; I'll wait on you as soon as I can.*
Te voy a contar lo que pasó **con tal que no te rías.**	*I'll tell you what happened, provided that you don't laugh.*

B. The following conjunctions always require the subjunctive, since they indicate that an action or event is indefinite or uncertain (it may not necessarily take place):

antes (de) que† *before*	en caso (de) que† *in case*
a menos que *unless*	para que *so that*

No voy a ir a menos que me sienta mejor.	*I'm not going unless I feel better.*
Sea cortés, para que no se ofendan.	*Be polite, so that they are not offended.*
¿Por qué no salen ahora, chicos, antes que papá se ponga ansioso?	*Why don't you go out now, children, before papa gets upset (anxious)?*
No quiero gastar este dinero en caso que lo necesite más tarde.	*I don't want to spend this money in case I need it later.*

(1) I notice you are a little depressed, Jane . . . Do you want me to teach you some words in guaraní before you go back to your country? (2) Yes, doña Ramona! Farewells always make me sad (lit.: . . . cause me sadness). But you can start teaching me guaraní whenever you want. For example, how does one say "I love you"? I want to say it to Teddy when I see him again. (3) Well, you say «che ro jaijú». I know he will feel very happy as soon as you tell him what it means.

† The **de** may be omitted.

C. **Aunque** is followed by the subjunctive to indicate conjecture or uncertainty, but by the indicative to indicate fact or certainty.

Aunque María sea supersticiosa, no tiene miedo de los gatos negros.	*Although María may be superstitious, she's not afraid of black cats.*
Aunque María es supersticiosa, no tiene miedo de los gatos negros.	*Although María is superstitious, she's not afraid of black cats.*
Jorge no va a mentir aunque tenga vergüenza de confesar la verdad.	*Jorge is not going to lie, even though he may be ashamed to confess the truth.*
Jorge no va a mentir aunque tiene vergüenza de confesar la verdad.	*Jorge is not going to lie, even though he is ashamed to confess the truth.*

D. The conjunctions of time listed below can take either the subjunctive or indicative.

cuando *when*	luego que *as soon as*
después (de) que *after*	mientras (que) *while*
en cuanto *as soon as*	tan pronto como *as soon as*
hasta que *until*	

A Elena le va a dar mucha rabia en cuanto lo descubra.	*Elena is going to get very angry as soon as she finds out.*
A Elena le dio mucha rabia en cuanto lo descubrió.	*Elena got very angry as soon as she found out.*
Cuando le cuente el chiste, va a morirse de risa.	*When I tell her the joke, she's going to die of laughter.*
Cuando le conté el chiste, se murió de risa.	*When I told her the joke, she was dying of laughter.*
No le digamos eso al jefe hasta que se calme.	*Let's not tell the boss that until he calms down.*
No le dijimos eso al jefe hasta que se calmó.	*We didn't tell the boss that until he calmed down.*

The indicative is used if the adverbial clause expresses a fact or a definite event: for instance, a customary or completed action. However, if the adverbial clause expresses an action that may not necessarily take place or that will probably take place but at an indefinite time in the future, the subjunctive is used.

E. Some of the conjunctions just discussed are prepositions combined with **que** (**para que, sin que, antes de que, hasta que, después de que**). These prepositions are often followed by infinitives if there is no change in subject.

Después de enojarse, Juan se puso muy triste.	*After getting angry, Juan became very sad.*
Después de que ella se enojó, Juan se puso muy triste.	*After she got angry, Juan became very sad.*

Ejercicios

A. Create new sentences, substituting the words in the lists for those in italics.

1. Voy a estar aquí hasta que *ellos* vuelvan.
   a. tú **b.** usted **c.** doña Ramona **d.** ustedes **e.** mi hermana
2. Lo hacen para que *usted* no se enoje.
   a. yo **b.** sus padres **c.** tú **d.** ustedes **e.** nosotros
3. Vamos a estar tristes cuando *tú* te vayas.
   a. ella **b.** usted **c.** nuestros hijos **d.** Rubén **e.** ustedes

B. Complete the following sentences with the correct subjunctive form of the verb in parentheses.

1. (estar) Voy a pasar la noche aquí para que tú no _____ sola.
2. (llegar) Quieren irse antes de que _____ Alberto y Antonia.
3. (levantarse) Pensamos llegar a las siete a menos que (nosotros) _____ tarde.
4. (volver) ¿Por qué no vamos al cine antes de que _____ papá?
5. (llover) Ellos van a clase a menos que _____ mucho.
6. (saber) ¿Piensan hacerlo sin que ella lo _____?
7. (entender) El profesor habla despacio para que nosotros lo _____.
8. (ofenderse) ¿Realmente no puedes hacer nada sin que ellos _____?

C. Combining one element from each of the three columns, create ten original—but logical—sentences, using the indicative or subjunctive form of the verbs given in column III, as appropriate.

Modelos: a. **Debes comer tan pronto como tengas hambre.**
   b. **Fuimos al cine aunque llovía.**

I	II	III
Debes comer	mientras	ver a Luis
Fuimos al cine	aunque	tener hambre
Pensamos asistir a clase	cuando	ellos acostarse
Sara empezó a estudiar	después de que	llover
Van a sentirse felices	tan pronto como	estar deprimidos
Ustedes cantaban	hasta que	llegar su tía

D. Give the Spanish equivalent of the following sentences.

1. Call me before you leave.
2. She went to his birthday party, although she didn't feel well.
3. I usually play the piano whenever I am a little depressed.
4. They waited for us until we arrived.
5. He is going to use the car without his father knowing about it.
6. You (*tú*) can't sleep unless you are very tired, right?

Preguntas

1. ¿Adónde piensa ir usted cuando termine esta clase? ¿cuando lleguen las vacaciones? ¿cuando complete sus estudios universitarios? **2.** ¿Qué quiere hacer usted en cuanto sepa hablar bien el español? ¿antes de que termine esta década (*decade*)? ¿cuando cumpla noventa años? **3.** ¿Asiste usted a clase aunque llueva? ¿aunque esté muy cansado? **4.** ¿No puede estudiar usted a menos que tome café? ¿a menos que esté solo? **5.** ¿Qué cree usted que debe hacer un estudiante para que le sea más fácil aprender español? ¿para que le sea más interesante?

III. THE INFINITIVE

De Barcelona a Valencia.

(1)	**La pasajera:**	Señor, ¿es posible *ir* a Valencia en tren?
(2)	**El agente:**	Sí, señorita. Puede *tomar* el Talgo* si desea *viajar* de día o el Expreso si no teme *viajar* de noche. ¿Cuándo quiere *partir*?
(3)	**La pasajera:**	Ahora mismo. Tengo esperanza de *estar* allí mañana antes de las seis. ¡Estoy ansiosa por *conocer* a mis futuros suegros!
(4)	**El agente:**	Pues vamos a *ver* . . . Son las doce menos cinco. ¡Hoy es su día de suerte, señorita! A medianoche—dentro de cinco minutos—va a *salir* un Expreso para Valencia.
(5)	**La pasajera:**	¡Qué alegría! ¿Y a qué hora llega?
(6)	**El agente:**	A las seis menos diez. Éste lleva un coche-cama, en caso de que quiera *dormir* unas horas.
(7)	**La pasajera:**	¡Buena idea! Deme un pasaje de ida y vuelta. ¡Pero apúrese, por favor! ¡No quiero *perderlo*!

* In Spain, the **Talgo** is a very fast, modern train.

1. ¿Se puede viajar de Barcelona a Valencia en tren? **2.** ¿Se debe tomar el Talgo si se quiere viajar de noche? ¿el Expreso? **3.** ¿A qué hora quiere estar la señorita en Valencia? ¿Por qué? **4.** ¿Perdió ella el Expreso de las seis y cinco? **5.** ¿A qué hora llega ese Expreso a Valencia? ¿Lleva o no un coche-cama? **6.** ¿Qué clase de pasaje quiere ella? ¿sólo de ida o de ida y vuelta?

A. In Spanish the infinitive can be used:

1. As a noun. In Spanish the infinitive form is often used as the subject or object of a verb in much the same way that the *-ing* form of the English verb is used. It can be used with or without the definite article.

   Creen que (el) esquiar es peligroso.   *They believe that skiing is dangerous.*

2. As a verb complement. In Spanish most verbs may be followed by an infinitive. Certain verbs require the preposition **a,** or the prepositions **de** or **que** in idiomatic expressions like **tener que.**

¿Te gusta hacer deportes?	*Do you like to play sports?*
¿Puedes estudiar y mirar televisión a la vez?	*Can you study and watch television at the same time?*
Fuimos a ver «La venganza del Zorro».	*We went to see "The revenge of Zorro."*
Espero poder estudiar esta noche.	*I hope to be able to study tonight.*
Necesito saber la verdad.	*I need to know the truth.*
¿Te ayudo a hacer la torta?	*Can I help you make the cake?*
Tenemos que comprar el pasaje.	*We have to buy the ticket.*

3. As the object of a preposition.

Antes de comprender el problema, Marta lo pensó bien.	*Before understanding the problem, Marta thought about it carefully.*
Después de llorar casi una hora, Ana se calmó.	*After crying almost an hour, Ana calmed down.*
En vez de trabajar, él va a la playa todos los días.	*Instead of working, he goes to the beach every day.*

From Barcelona to Valencia.
(1) Sir, is it possible to go to Valencia by train? (2) Yes, miss, you can take the Talgo if you want to travel by day or the Express if you are not afraid of traveling at night. When do you want to leave? (3) Right now. I'm hoping to be there tomorrow before six. I'm anxious to meet my future in-laws! (4) Well, we'll see . . . It's now five to twelve. Today is your lucky day, miss! At midnight—in five minutes—an Express is going to leave for Valencia. (5) How wonderful! And at what time does it arrive? (6) At ten to six. This one has a Pullman (sleeping-car), in case you want to sleep a few hours. (7) Good idea! Give me a round-trip ticket. But hurry, please! I don't want to miss it!

4. With **al. Al** plus infinitive expresses the idea of *on* or *upon* plus the *-ing* form of the verb.

Al hablar con Mamá de lo que sucedió, nos dimos cuenta que estaba enojada.	*When we talked with Mom about what happened, we realized she was angry.*
Al recibir la noticia, Pedro se la contó a todo el mundo.	*When he received the news (upon receiving the news), Pedro told it to everyone.*

5. With a conjugated form of **hacer** or **mandar** to mean *to have something done.*

Isabel se hizo teñir el pelo.	*Isabel had her hair dyed.*
A la señora le mandaron esperar.	*They had the lady wait.*

6. With verbs like **prohibir** and **permitir** instead of a subjunctive form. In these cases, indirect objects are necessary. Compare:

¿Me permite acompañarla?	
¿Permite que la acompañe?	*Will you allow me to go with you?*
Nos prohíben fumar.	
Prohíben que fumemos.	*They forbid us to smoke.*

Ejercicios

A. Answer the following questions in the negative, using the verb in parentheses as in the examples.

Modelo: ¿Gasta mucho Susana? (querer) **No, ella no quiere gastar mucho.**
¿Lo hace Ernesto? (poder)   **No, él no puede hacerlo.**

1. ¿Va allí María? (pensar)
2. ¿Lo sabe tu hermano? (ir a)
3. ¿Duerme Pepito? (tener ganas de)
4. ¿Se queda aquí Roberto? (poder)
5. ¿Toma ella el Talgo? (querer)
6. ¿Lo paga su esposo? (ir a)

B. Answer the questions in the affirmative, according to the examples. Use object pronouns whenever possible.

Modelo: ¿Vas a ver a tu prima? (mañana) **Sí, voy a verla mañana.**
¿Piensan viajar a Valencia? (esta tarde)   **Sí, pensamos viajar a Valencia esta tarde.**

1. ¿Quieres hablar con él? (hoy)
2. ¿Pueden buscar a las chicas? (a las seis)
3. ¿Vas a comprar esos libros? (la semana próxima)
4. ¿Están ansiosos por conocer a Ricardo? (antes de la fiesta)

5. ¿Tienes ganas de llamar a Susana? (esta noche)
6. ¿Piensan ir allí ustedes? (después de la clase)

C. Give the Spanish equivalent of the following sentences.

1. I have to hurry.
2. We left before eating.
3. Susana is anxious to meet her future in-laws.
4. Was he angry? He went away without saying anything.
5. Seeing is believing.
6. Upon receiving her letter, we all felt very happy.
7. I saw you (*tú* form) upon opening the door.
8. Why doesn't she laugh instead of crying?

Preguntas

1. ¿Qué hizo usted anoche al llegar a su casa? ¿esta mañana al levantarse?   2. ¿Se sintió usted triste o feliz al terminar sus estudios secundarios? ¿al recibir la nota de su primer examen de español?   3. ¿Prefiere usted viajar de día o de noche? ¿Tiene usted miedo de viajar en avión? ¿en auto? ¿Por qué?   4. ¿Qué debe decir uno al encontrarse con un amigo? ¿al recibir un regalo? ¿al entrar a clase? ¿al salir?

EL HOMBRE Y LA MUJER

Dos mujeres se encuentran en una peluquería de Asunción, Paraguay.[1]

Gloria: ¡Hola, Elena! Me alegro de verla. ¿Cómo está?

Elena: Muy bien, Gloria. ¿Qué hace aquí?

Gloria: Vengo todos los meses para que me tiñan el pelo. Hay una muchacha aquí que me lo hace muy bien, sin que nadie pueda notarlo.

Elena: ¿Para qué gasta el dinero así?

Gloria: Para que mi marido no descubra que no soy rubia natural. Me da vergüenza decírselo.

Elena: Pero en cuanto su marido sepa la verdad, se va a sentir desilusionado.

Gloria: No importa. Por ahora no lo sabe y está contento.

Entra María, la peluquera.

María: Buenas tardes, señora Martínez. Tan pronto como termine con la señora Ospina, la atiendo.

Gloria: Gracias, María. No tengo prisa.

María: ¿Y usted, señorita? ¿En qué puedo servirla?

Elena: Tengo que dar una conferencia esta noche y necesito un peinado que sea elegante y sencillo a la vez.

María: No hay problema, con tal que usted pueda esperar veinte minutos. Alicia la va a atender.

Elena: Cómo no. Francamente, Gloria, me parece triste que una mujer le tenga que mentir a su esposo.

Gloria: Pues ellos nos mienten a nosotras. Hace algunos días Olga me llamó por teléfono para contarme que su esposo tiene una amante. ¡Lloraba tanto la pobre!

Elena: ¡Qué barbaridad! ¿Y qué va a hacer?

Gloria: Nada. ¿Qué puede hacer? Pero sufre.

Elena: Puede buscarse un amante ella también.

Gloria: ¿Para qué? La venganza es estúpida. ¿Va a ser más feliz?

Elena: Entonces puede divorciarse.

Gloria: Tampoco. A pesar de que su esposo la engaña, Olga todavía lo quiere. Cuando usted se case, Elena, va a pensar de otra manera.

Elena: Es difícil que me case aquí.[2]

Gloria: ¿No conoce a algún hombre que sea simpático?

Elena: Hombres hay muchos, pero no hay ninguno que me guste. Casi todos son extranjeros y no hablan ni español ni guaraní.[3] Además, busco un hombre que me trate de igual a igual.

Gloria: Espero que no muera soltera.

Elena: Soltera, puede ser que muera, pero por lo menos, voy a morir contenta.

Preguntas

1. ¿Dónde se encuentran Gloria y Elena?   2. ¿Por qué viene Gloria a este lugar todos los meses?   3. ¿Cómo se va a sentir el marido de Gloria cuando sepa la verdad?   4. ¿Qué le parece triste a Elena? ¿Le parece triste a usted? ¿Por qué?   5. ¿Qué le contó a Gloria su amiga Olga cuando la llamó por teléfono?   6. ¿Qué va a hacer Olga? ¿Por qué no va a divorciarse? ¿Qué cree usted que ella debe hacer?   7. ¿Qué busca Elena?   8. ¿Es mejor que muera soltera o que cambie sus ideales?

NOTAS CULTURALES

1. Asunción, one of the oldest cities of South America (founded in 1537), is the capital city and port of Paraguay, on the eastern bank of the Paraguay River. It is the center of trade and government of the nation. With a population of about 500,000, Asunción still conserves a picturesque charm with pastel-colored buildings and numerous orange trees.

2. In Paraguay the ratio of men to women is rather low because many men emigrate to nearby Brazil and Argentina where there is a higher standard of living and more opportunities for work. The tradition of male scarcity dates from the War of the Triple Alliance (1865–1870), when President Solano López waged a war against Argentina, Brazil, and Uruguay that killed half of Paraguay's population. Only 13 percent of the survivors were male, mostly old men and very young boys. It took many years for the sex ratio of young people at a marriageable age to return to an approximately even balance. It is said that some of the priests in those times went so far as to advocate polygamy.

3. Paraguay is the only Latin American country that has officially adopted an Indian language. **Guaraní** is the language of the Indians who inhabited Paraguay before the Spanish conquest. Almost all Paraguayans are mestizo and bilingual, and street signs, newspapers, and books appear in both languages. Spanish is the official language, but **Guaraní** is favored for social discourse in all levels of society.

ACTIVIDADES

Ana, Alberto y las emociones

¿Qué hace Ana?

se alegra

se ríe

se enoja

llora

¿Qué le da a Ana?

le da vergüenza

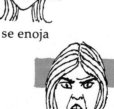

le da rabia

¿Cómo está Alberto?

está contento (feliz)   está deprimido   está asustado (tiene miedo)   está enojado

Using the above illustrations as a guide, complete the following sentences.
A. *¿Qué hace usted?*
   1. Al ver una película trágica, yo . . .
   2. Al escuchar un chiste, yo . . .
   3. Al recibir la visita de un buen amigo, yo . . .
   4. Al perder la única llave de la casa que tenemos, yo . . .
B. *¿Qué le da a usted?*
   1. Al descubrir que no tiene dinero para pagar la cuenta del hotel, . . .
   2. Al saber que su novio(-a) sale con otro(-a), . . .
C. *¿Cómo va a estar usted?*
   1. Cuando suban el precio de la gasolina, voy . . .
   2. Cuando lleguen visitantes de otros planetas, voy . . .
   3. Cuando terminen las vacaciones, voy . . .
   4. Cuando tenga dinero para ir de viaje, voy . . .

Un anuncio

Write a newspaper classified ad beginning with *Se necesita(n)* and combining elements from the following columns:

Modelo: Se necesita un detective que nunca esté asustado.

un(-a) profesor(-a) de secundaria   que se ría mucho
un(-a) agente de viaje   que no se enoje fácilmente
un(-a) compañero(-a) de cuarto   que no esté deprimido(-a)
un(-a) detective   que siempre esté contento(-a)
un(-a) novio(-a)   que nunca esté asustado(-a)
                                        que no le dé vergüenza mentir

Entrevista

Ask a classmate the following questions. Then report the information to the class.
1. ¿Qué prefieres: una persona que sea inteligente o una que sea honesta? ¿Por qué?
2. ¿Durante cuánto tiempo deben conocerse un hombre y una mujer antes de pensar en casarse?
3. ¿Crees que una mujer debe divorciarse cuando sabe que su marido no le es fiel? ¿Y un hombre?

4. ¿Crees que el pelearse (*to fight*) de vez en cuando es bueno o malo para un matrimonio?
5. Cuando salgas de la universidad ¿vas a buscar trabajo en esta ciudad o quieres ir a otra?
6. ¿Vas a buscar trabajo en cuanto termines de estudiar o vas a esperar?

VOCABULARIO ACTIVO

Verbos útiles

apurarse   *to hurry*
atender (ie)   *to wait on*
calmarse   *to calm down*
causar   *to cause*
enojarse   *to become angry, get mad*
gastar   *to spend*
llorar   *to cry*
mentir (ie)   *to lie*
notar   *to notice*
ofender   *to offend;* **ofenderse**   *to take offense*
partir   *to leave*
reírse (i)   *to laugh*
suceder   *to happen*
sufrir   *to suffer*
teñir (i)   *to dye*
tratar (de)   *to try (to); to treat, deal (with)*

Las emociones

la alegría   *happiness*
ansioso(a)   *anxious, nervous*
asustado(a)   *frightened, startled*
deprimido(a)   *depressed*
desilusionado(a)   *disappointed, disillusioned*
enojado(a)   *angry*
la esperanza   *hope*
estúpido(a)   *stupid, ridiculous*
la rabia   *anger, rage*
la risa   *laughter*
supersticioso(a)   *superstitious*
el susto   *fright*
la tristeza   *sadness*
la venganza   *revenge*
la vergüenza   *shame;* **darle vergüenza a alguien**   *to make someone ashamed*

Conjunciones

a menos que   *unless*
antes (de) que   *before*
aunque   *although*
con tal (de) que   *provided that*
en caso (de) que   *in case*
en cuanto   *as soon as*
hasta que   *until*
luego que   *as soon as*
mientras que   *while*
para que   *so that*
sin que   *without*
tan pronto como   *as soon as*

Otras palabras útiles

a la vez   *at once, at the same time*
el, la amante   *lover*
el coche-cama   *Pullman car, sleeper*
la conferencia   *lecture*
cortés   *polite*
dentro de   *within*
la despedida   *farewell, leave-taking*
en vez de   *instead of*
igual   *equal*
la igualdad   *equality*
hacer + inf.   *to have something done*
mandar + inf.   *to order something done*
la noticia   *news item;* **las noticias**   *news*
el peinado   *hairdo*
peligroso(a)   *dangerous*
la peluquería   *hairdresser's*
el peluquero (la peluquera)   *barber (hairdresser)*
sencillo(a)   *simple*
el suegro (la suegra)   *father-in-law (mother-in-law)*
el (tren) expreso   *fast train*

TERCER REPASO

I. COMMAND FORMS

A. 1. Review the following table of command forms.

PERSON	INFINITIVE	AFFIRMATIVE	NEGATIVE
tú	cantar	canta	no cantes
	comer	come	no comas
	pedir	pide	no pidas
vosotros	cantar	cantad	no cantéis
	comer	comed	no comáis
	pedir	pedid	no pidáis
usted	cantar	cante	no cante
	comer	coma	no coma
	pedir	pida	no pida
ustedes	cantar	canten	no canten
	comer	coman	no coman
	pedir	pidan	no pidan

2. Some irregular **usted** and **ustedes** commands are:

   ir: vaya(n)   **estar: esté(n)**
   ser: sea(n)   **dar: dé, den**
   saber: sepa(n)

3. Some irregular affirmative **tú** commands are:

   decir: di   **salir: sal**
   hacer: haz   **ser: sé**
   ir: ve   **tener: ten**
   poner: pon   **venir: ven**

4. Reflexive and object pronouns are attached to affirmative commands: **Lávate las manos; lávatelas en seguida.** With negative commands, these same pronouns precede the verb: **No te laves las manos; no te las laves.**

B. Convert the following statements into commands.

Modelos: Usted no se pone el abrigo. **No se ponga el abrigo.**
Ustedes levantan la mano derecha. **Levanten la mano derecha.**
Tú me lo dices. **Dímelo.**

1. Ustedes se lavan la cara.
2. Usted no nos lo explica.
3. Tú no te vas ahora, Rosa.
4. Usted me las sirve inmediatamente.
5. Tú le dices algo en español.
6. Usted me trae una cerveza fría.
7. Tú tienes mucho cuidado, Patricia.
8. Ustedes no se ponen nerviosos.
9. Usted me da una crema para la piel.
10. Tú vienes al centro conmigo.
11. Ustedes no van a ese partido de fútbol.
12. Tú no eres pesimista.
13. Usted me invita a su fiesta de cumpleaños.
14. Vosotros habláis con la secretaria.
15. Vosotros no escribís la carta.

II. THE REFLEXIVE; THE PRONOUN SE

A. Review these uses of the reflexive and the pronoun **se.**

1. The reflexive
The reflexive pronouns **me, te, se, nos, os,** and **se** are used to indicate that an action reflects back to the subject, that the subject receives the action of the verb: **Me desperté a las nueve. Se puso los zapatos.**

2. The pronoun **se**
a. The impersonal **se** is used in third-person constructions when it is not necessary to identify the agent of an action: **Se come bien en España. Se dice que él es muy honesto.** The verb is in the singular.

b. **Se** for passive
In this construction, the verb is in either the third-person singular or plural, to agree with the subject: **Aquí se venden frutas. Allí se vende carne.** Direct or indirect objects can be used with this construction: **Se me perdió el pasaporte. Se le olvidaron las llaves.** This often implies an accidental or unplanned occurrence.

B. Complete the following groups of sentences with one of the verbs listed in parentheses in its correct form. Use the present or preterite tense according to the context.

(Active subject: **sentirse, llamarse, sentarse, darse cuenta de**)

1. El artista que pintó la «Vista de Toledo» _____ El Greco.
2. Elsita no está en clase porque _____ mal.
3. Podemos _____ en aquella mesa, ¿de acuerdo?
4. Cuando lo vi, _____ que el cuadro era una obra maestra.

(Passive subject: **verse, decirse, necesitarse, poderse**)

5. En este hospital _____ más doctores bilingües.
6. ¡Hola, buenos días! ¿ _____ entrar?
7. Esta mañana no _____ el sol; está muy nublado.
8. Cuando una persona duerme profundamente _____ que duerme como una piedra.

(Unplanned occurrences: **olvidársele, perdérsele**)

9. A mí _____ que hoy es el día de tu santo.
10. Adolfo, ¿dijiste que _____ todos tus documentos y tu pasaje de vuelta también?

III. THE PERFECT TENSES; CONTRAST OF PRETERITE, IMPERFECT, AND PERFECT TENSES

A. The perfect tenses

1. Regular past participles: **hablado, comido, vivido**
2. Irregularly formed past participles: **abierto, cubierto, dicho, escrito, hecho, ido, muerto, puesto, resuelto, roto, visto, vuelto**
3. The present perfect (**dar**): **he dado, has dado, ha dado, hemos dado, habéis dado, han dado**
4. The past perfect (**tener**): **había tenido, habías tenido, había tenido, habíamos tenido, habíais tenido, habían tenido**

B. Change the following sentences to the present perfect.

Modelo: Pedro va al doctor. **Pedro ha ido al doctor.**

1. Alberto está en ese hospital.
2. Los niños se acuestan tarde.
3. Tú tienes mucha fiebre.
4. Usted nos da buenos consejos.
5. Yo me pongo el vestido nuevo.
6. Nosotros vemos un programa interesante.
7. Tú y Marisa escriben una composición muy buena.
8. Ese candidato dice muchas mentiras.

C. Change the sentences in exercise B above to the past perfect.

Modelo: Pedro va al doctor. **Pedro había ido al doctor.**

D. Change the verbs in the following sentences to the tense indicated in parentheses.

(Imperfect)
1. María está enferma.
2. Son las seis de la tarde.
3. Ellos viven cerca del aeropuerto.

(Preterite)
4. Ustedes saben que Juanita se casa, ¿no?
5. Nosotros nos ponemos nerviosos cuando vemos al doctor.
6. Ana dice que Alejandro viene a las ocho.

E. Choose the correct Spanish equivalent of the sentence or phrases in italics.

1. *He used to come at eight o'clock.*
   a. Vino a las ocho.   **b.** Venía a las ocho.   **c.** Había venido a las ocho.
2. *They haven't yet bought the ticket.*
   a. No han comprado el pasaje todavía.   **b.** No habían comprado el pasaje todavía.   **c.** Ya no compraron el pasaje.
3. We were dining *when he came in.*
   a. cuando entraba   **b.** cuando ha entrado   **c.** cuando entró
4. *She was leaving.*
   a. Salió   **b.** Ha salido.   **c.** Salía.
5. *He began to study* at seven o'clock and finished at ten.
   a. Empezó a estudiar   **b.** Empezaba a estudiar   **c.** Había empezado a estudiar
6. *What have you done!*
   a. ¡Qué había hecho!   **b.** ¡Qué hice!   **c.** ¡Qué has hecho!
7. I believed her because *she had spoken* to my mother about it.
   a. le habló   **b.** le había hablado   **c.** le ha hablado
8. He played the guitar while *he waited for dinner.*
   a. ha esperado la comida   **b.** esperaba la comida   **c.** esperó la comida

IV. THE PRESENT SUBJUNCTIVE

A. Formation of the present subjunctive.

1. Regular **-ar** verbs **(visitar): visite, visites, visite, visitemos, visitéis, visiten**
2. Regular **-er** and **-ir** verbs **(comer): coma, comas, coma, comamos, comáis, coman**

3. Verbs with an irregularity in the first-person singular of the present indicative (hacer): haga, hagas, haga, hagamos, hagáis, hagan
4. Stem-changing -ir verbs (pedir): pida, pidas, pida, pidamos, pidáis, pidan
5. Stem-changing -ar and -er verbs (volver): vuelva, vuelvas, vuelva, volvamos, volváis, vuelvan
6. Irregular verbs:
    a. dar: dé, des, dé, demos, deis, den
    b. estar: esté, estés, esté, estemos, estéis, estén
    c. ir: vaya, vayas, vaya, vayamos, vayáis, vayan
    d. haber: haya, hayas, haya, hayamos, hayáis, hayan
    e. ser: sea, seas, sea, seamos, seáis, sean
    f. saber: sepa, sepas, sepa, sepamos, sepáis, sepan

B. Complete the following sentences with the present subjunctive of the verbs in parentheses.

1. Mamá tiene miedo que nosotros no _____ (estar) allí a las doce.
2. Ojalá que él _____ (tener) la dirección.
3. Le prohíbo que _____ (mentir).
4. Te pido que _____ (traer) a tu hermana a mi fiesta.
5. Preferimos que él no _____ (venir).
6. Quiero que tú _____ (conocer) a Anita.
7. Me gusta que ellos _____ (ganar) el partido.
8. El médico no permite que yo _____ (fumar).
9. Necesitan que el señor Villa les _____ (hacer) un favor.
10. Dudo que José _____ (comer) bien.
11. No estamos seguros que _____ (ser) ellos.
12. ¿Cree usted que nosotros _____ (tener) razón?
13. Tal vez Eduardo _____ (ir) en auto a Toledo, pero lo dudo.
14. Es necesario que nosotros _____ (acostarse) temprano.
15. Es mejor que yo _____ (irse).
16. No es seguro que Elena _____ (salir) mañana.
17. ¿Es cierto que Felipe _____ (tener) mucho dinero en Suiza (Switzerland)?
18. Busco una bicicleta que _____ (funcionar) bien y que _____ (ser) barata.
19. El señor Juárez invita a los Hernández sin que su esposa lo _____ (saber).
20. Vamos a cenar a las nueve a menos que ellos _____ (llegar) tarde.

C. The subjunctive is used:

1. with verbs of expectations and feelings: alegrarse, temer, sentir, etc.
2. with verbs expressing an order, request, or plea: mandar, pedir.
3. with verbs expressing will, desire, or preference: preferir, querer, desear.
4. with verbs of approval or permission: permitir, prohibir.
5. with verbs of necessity: necesitar.
6. with verbs expressing doubt or uncertainty: dudar, no estar seguro(-a) de.
7. with creer, pensar, and tal vez or quizás in the negative or interrogative, when doubt is implied.

8. with certain impersonal expressions: **es bueno que, es necesario que.**
9. with **es verdad (cierto, seguro, claro)** in the negative or interrogative, when doubt is implied.
10. with descriptions of the unknown or indefinite.
11. with certain adverbial conjunctions: **a menos que, sin que, antes de que, para que, con tal de que, en caso de que**.

D. Cross out the words that a Spanish speaker would not be likely to say.

Modelo: ~~Es mejor~~/Es cierto que yo estoy muy contento.

1. *Nos alegramos mucho/No sabemos* que se casen.
2. *Sabe/Tiene miedo* que su equipo pierda el partido.
3. *Me sorprende/Creo* que ellos viajan mañana.
4. *Dudo/Sé* que Susana vaya a esa conferencia.
5. *Es cierto/No es cierto* que él tenga dolor de cabeza.
6. *No hay nadie/Hay alguien* allí que pueda hacerlo.
7. *Sabe/Espera* que ellos llegan temprano.
8. El médico *cree/no cree* que Silvia esté enferma.

V. QUESTIONS FOR CONVERSATION

1. A ti, ¿qué te gusta hacer los sábados? ¿Te gusta quedarte en casa o prefieres salir? ¿por qué?   **2.** ¿Vas mucho al cine? ¿Cuánto tiempo hace que no vas? ¿Cuál fue la última película que viste?   **3.** ¿Cuánto tiempo hace que asistes a esta universidad? ¿que estudias español?   **4.** ¿Leíste alguna vez algún cuento escrito en español? ¿qué cuento? ¿algún cuento español traducido al inglés? ¿qué cuento? ¿Te gustó?   **5.** ¿Has viajado recientemente? ¿Adónde has ido?   **6.** ¿Qué quieres hacer este fin de semana? ¿Qué quieres que hagamos aquí mañana? ¿el último día de clase?

VI. SUPPLEMENTARY TRANSLATION EXERCISE

1. I've known Marta for four years. I met her in Mexico.
2. Don't stay here during the summer. Go visit your friends in Guatemala.
3. Yesterday I went to see my doctor. Can you believe that I hadn't seen her for two years?
4. Why didn't you (*tú*) tell me that you had been here before Christmas?
5. This city has always been an important cultural center.
6. The accident has affected me very much, physically as well as economically.
7. Who said that Hector got married two days ago?
8. I hope (that) you and Susana will be able to come to our party tonight.

PROFESIONES Y OFICIOS

OBJECTIVES

LANGUAGE: In this chapter we introduce, discuss, and practice:

1. the present participle (corresponding to -ing words in English) and the progressive tenses (*we are going, he was waiting* are examples in English)
2. the neuter article **lo, lo que (cual)** and **el que (cual)**
3. uses of the definite article in Spanish where it would not be used in English
4. omission of the indefinite article in Spanish where it would be used in English

You will also learn vocabulary related to professions, careers, and jobs.

CULTURE: The dialogue takes place in Machu Picchu, Peru, an Inca city that was abandoned long ago and is now a very beautiful attraction for tourists and for anyone interested in Latin American history. You will learn something about this area in the Andes mountains and about its people.

EXPLICACIÓN

I. THE PRESENT PARTICIPLE AND THE PROGRESSIVE TENSES

(1)	**Secretario:**	El ingeniero lo *está esperando* abajo, señor Ramos . . . ¡Perdóneme! ¿*Estaba durmiendo*?
(2)	**Jefe:**	No, *estaba descansando* porque me *están doliendo* mucho los músculos.
(3)	**Secretario:**	¿Pero por qué? ¿Está enfermo, señor?
(4)	**Jefe:**	No, creo que no. Hace unos minutos *estaba leyendo* el periódico, sentado en una de esas sillas modernas que compraron ayer.
(5)	**Secretario:**	Así que *estaba probando* los muebles nuevos . . . Pero señor Ramos, eso no es una silla . . . ¡Es un canasto de basura!

1. ¿A quién está esperando el ingeniero? ¿Dónde lo está esperando? **2.** ¿Estaba durmiendo el señor Ramos? ¿Qué estaba haciendo? ¿por qué? **3.** ¿Qué estaba leyendo él hace unos minutos? **4.** ¿En qué creía el señor Ramos que estaba sentado? ¿En qué estaba sentado realmente? **5.** ¿En qué está sentado(a) usted? ¿Qué está haciendo? ¿Qué estaba haciendo hace unos minutos?

A. To form the present participle of most Spanish verbs, **-ando** is added to the stem of the infinitive of **-ar** verbs and **-iendo** to the stem of the infinitive of **-er** and **-ir** verbs.

hablando	*speaking*
comiendo	*eating*
viviendo	*living*
Hablando de arqueología, ¿sabes cómo los incas construían muros de piedra?	*Speaking of archeology, do you know how the Incas built stone walls?*

(1) The engineer is waiting for you downstairs, Mr. Ramos. . . Forgive me! Were you sleeping? (2) No, I was resting because my muscles are aching a lot. (3) But why? Are you sick, sir? (4) No, I don't think so. A few minutes ago I was reading the newspaper, seated on one of those modern chairs that you bought yesterday. (5) So you were trying the new furniture. . . But Mr. Ramos, that's not a chair. . . It's a wastebasket!

B. A form of **estar** in the present tense can be combined with a present participle to form the present progressive tense. This tense is used to emphasize that an action is in progress—taking place—at a particular moment in time. It is only used to stress that an action is occurring at a specific point in time; otherwise the present tense is used.

El arqueólogo está hablando de las ruinas mayas.
The archeologist is talking about the Mayan ruins (at this very moment).

La dentista está trabajando; no puede venir al teléfono.
The dentist is working; she can't come to the telephone.

Me están doliendo los músculos.
My muscles are aching (right now).

C. A form of **estar** in the imperfect tense can be combined with a present participle to form the past progressive tense, a tense that indicates that an action was in progress at a given moment in the past.

El arqueólogo estaba hablando de las ruinas mayas (cuando se le ocurrió la teoría).
The archeologist was talking about the Mayan ruins (when the theory occurred to him).

Ella estaba trabajando (ayer a las dos).
She was working (yesterday at two o'clock).

Jorge estaba haciendo un problema de geometría (cuando llegué).
Jorge was doing a geometry problem (when I arrived).

D. Present participles of verbs with a stem ending in a vowel take the ending **-yendo** rather than **-iendo,** since in Spanish an unaccented **i** between two vowels becomes a **y.**

creyendo (creer) oyendo (oír)
leyendo (leer) trayendo (traer)

E. Stem-changing **-ir** verbs show a change in the stem of the present participle from **e** to **i** or **o** to **u** (as they do in the third-persons singular and plural of the preterite).

diciendo (decir) durmiendo (dormir)
pidiendo (pedir) muriendo (morir)
prefiriendo (preferir)
siguiendo (seguir)
sirviendo (servir)

F. **Seguir** (instead of **estar**) is often used to form a progressive tense to imply that an action is continuing (not yet finished).

Los científicos—un biólogo, un químico, y un médico—seguían hablando de manera muy animada.
The scientists—a biologist, a chemist, and a doctor—kept on talking in an animated manner.

| Todo el mundo está muy ocupado: el ingeniero sigue hablando con el jefe y la mecanógrafa sigue escribiendo a máquina. | *Everyone is very busy; the engineer is still talking to the boss and the typist keeps on typing.* |

Ejercicios

A. Create new sentences, substituting the words in the lists for those in italics.

1. *Marta* está esperando al jefe.
   a. tú **b.** Teresa y José **c.** yo **d.** nosotros **e.** el ingeniero Ruíz
2. En este momento *yo* estoy leyendo el periódico.
   a. nosotros **b.** el biólogo. **c.** tú **d.** la profesora **e.** ustedes
3. *El secretario* estaba escribiendo a máquina.
   a. yo **b.** tú y Pablo **c.** nosotros **d.** los científicos **e.** tú
4. *Tú* seguías durmiendo cuando se fue el doctor.
   a. Manuel **b.** ustedes **c.** Silvia y yo **d.** usted **e.** yo

B. Restate, changing the verbs from the present progressive to the past progressive.

1. La mecanógrafa está trabajando.
2. ¿Qué estás haciendo?
3. Ellos están descansando.
4. Los muchachos siguen estudiando geometría.
5. Estoy jugando al tenis.

C. Luis is writing Felipe, an old roommate of his, and telling him about himself and his family. Restate Luis' sentences, changing the verbs from the present to the present progressive, as in the example.

Modelo: Inés y yo vivimos cerca de la universidad. **Inés y yo estamos viviendo cerca de la universidad.**

1. Ahora yo trabajo con un grupo de ingenieros.
2. También asisto a una clase de programación (*programming*) por la noche.
3. Inés estudia lenguas.

4. En su clase de español ya leen cuentos y novelas cortas.
5. En estos días, papá y mamá viajan mucho.
6. Y tú, ¿todavía piensas visitar el Perú este verano?
7. En este momento Inés duerme . . .
8. Y a mí me duele la mano de tanto escribir.

D. Teresa is telling a friend that practically nobody she knows was home during the last big earthquake in Lima (Perú). Restate what she says, changing the verbs from the imperfect to the past progressive, as in the example.

Modelo: Mi marido viajaba a la Argentina. **Mi marido estaba viajando a la Argentina.**

1. Yo enseñaba arqueología en la universidad.
2. Uno de mis estudiantes dormía en clase.
3. Mis vecinos visitaban a unos amigos en Arequipa.
4. María y Juan trabajaban en la oficina.
5. Tus hermanos jugaban fútbol en el parque.
6. Papá y mamá salían del consultorio (office) del dentista.

E. Complete the following sentences with the correct present participle of the verb in parentheses.

1. (mirar) ¿Qué está _____ ese pintor?
2. (esperar) Estamos _____ a la doctora.
3. (pedir) Enrique le estaba _____ consejos a su profesor.
4. (hacer) ¿Qué estaban _____ ustedes cuando llegó el jefe?
5. (explicar) El ingeniero nos estaba _____ el problema.
6. (doler) ¿Todavía te siguen _____ los brazos?
7. (leer) Estaba _____ un artículo de un químico famoso cuando me llamaste.
8. (seguir) ¿Por qué les estaba _____ el policía?

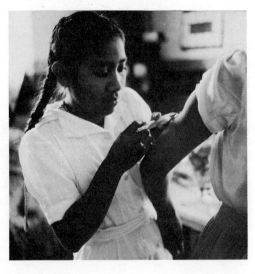

Preguntas

1. ¿Qué está haciendo usted en este momento? ¿Está descansando? ¿contestando preguntas en español? **2.** ¿Le está doliendo la cabeza ahora? ¿el estómago? **3.** ¿En qué (quién) estaba pensando usted hoy cuando entró a clase? ¿anoche cuando se acostó? **4.** ¿Qué estaba haciendo usted ayer por la tarde? ¿por la noche?

II. THE NEUTER ARTICLE LO; LO QUE (CUAL) AND EL QUE (CUAL)

En una exposición de arte abstracto.

(1) **Angelina:** ¿Te gusta el arte abstracto, Eva?

(2) **Eva:** Más o menos. *Lo que* no me gusta del arte abstracto es . . . *lo abstracto.* Me gusta más el realismo. Pero recuerda que yo soy dentista. No soy pintora como tú.

(3) **Angelina:** Pero Eva, ¡*lo que* a ti no te gusta es justamente *lo bueno* del arte abstracto! Todas estas obras tienen un significado diferente para cada persona.

(4) **Eva:** ¿Y crees que eso es importante, Angelina?

(5) **Angelina:** ¡Claro que *lo* es! Gracias a eso el arte abstracto es un arte activo, porque cada persona que lo mira está creando una obra diferente.

1. ¿Le gusta el arte abstracto a Eva? **2.** ¿Prefiere ella el arte realista? **3.** ¿Es Eva dentista o pintora? ¿y Angelina? **4.** Según Angelina, ¿qué es lo bueno del arte abstracto? **5.** ¿Por qué cree ella que el arte abstracto es activo?

A. The neuter article **lo** can be used with the masculine, singular form of an adjective to express an abstract quality or idea.

Lo bueno de ser escultor es la libertad de expresión.	*The good thing about being a sculptor is the freedom of expression.*
¿Qué es lo mejor de tu carrera? ¿y lo peor?	*What's the best thing about your career? And the worst thing?*

At an abstract art exposition.
(1) Do you like abstract art, Eva? (2) More or less. What I don't like about abstract art is . . . the abstractness. I like realism better. But remember that I am a dentist. I am not a painter like you. (3) But Eva, what you don't like is precisely what's good about abstract art! All these works have a different meaning for each person. (4) And do you believe that is important, Angelina? (5) Of course it is! Thanks to that abstract art is an active art, because each person who looks at it is creating a different work.

However, if the reference is to a specific person or thing the gender of which is known, **el** or **la** must be used.

El más chistoso de la clase es Juan.　*The funniest one in the class is Juan.*
Esta artista es la más ambiciosa del　*This artist is the most ambitious in the*
　grupo.　*group.*

B.　**Lo** can replace an adjective or refer to a whole idea previously stated.

¿Eres estudioso? —Sí, lo soy.　*Are you studious? —Yes, I am.*
¿Es Luis comerciante? —No, no lo es.　*Is Luis a businessman? —No, he's not.*
　Es arquitecto.　*He's an architect.*

C.　**Lo que** or **lo cual** can be used to express something imprecise or to sum up a preceding idea.

Lo que quiero es que seas más　*What I want is for you to be more*
　generoso.　*generous.*
El mecánico pudo arreglar el auto, lo　*The mechanic was able to fix the car,*
　cual nos alegró mucho.　*which pleased us very much.*

D.　However, if the reference is to a specific thing or person, **el que (cual), la que (cual), los que (cuales),** or **las que (cuales)** must be used.

Esa muchacha de la cual me hablabas,　*That girl you were telling me about is*
　es muy egoísta, ¿verdad?　*very selfish, isn't she?*
El reloj de mi marido, por el que (el　*My husband's watch, the one he paid so*
　cual) pagó tanto dinero, no anda　*much money for, doesn't run well.*
　bien.
Conozco a un periodista francés con　*I know a French journalist with whom I*
　el que (con el cual) salgo de vez en　*go out once in a while.*
　cuando.
Aquellos son los carpinteros con los　*Those are the carpenters with whom we*
　cuales (con los que) tuvimos la　*had the argument.*
　disputa.

In the preceding two examples **quien** or **quienes** could also be used since the references are to people.

Ejercicios

A.　Create new sentences, substituting the words in the lists for those in italics. Make all other necessary changes.

1. Aquel *cuadro,* el que compramos ayer, es para Sonia.
   a. zapatos　**b.** pintura　**c.** abrigo　**d.** blusas　**e.** crema
2. ¿Son colombianas las *chicas* con las cuales estabas hablando?
   a. profesores　**b.** pintora　**c.** secretarios　**d.** ingenieros　**e.** doctoras

B. Answer affirmatively or negatively, as the case may be.

Modelo: ¿Es mejor decir la verdad? **Sí, lo es.**
No, no lo es.

1. ¿Es bueno mentir?
2. ¿Es útil hablar dos lenguas?
3. ¿Son estudiosos sus amigos? ¿ambiciosos? ¿egoístas? ¿generosos?
4. ¿Está usted cansado(a) hoy? ¿nervioso(a)? ¿contento(a)? ¿triste?
5. ¿Sabe usted lo que quiere ser en el futuro? ¿lo que quiere hacer?

Preguntas

1. ¿Qué es lo más interesante de la vida universitaria? ¿lo más aburrido? ¿lo más divertido? **2.** ¿Qué profesores le gustan más a usted—los que divierten mucho a sus estudiantes o los que los hacen trabajar? ¿Por qué? **3.** ¿Quién aprende más—el que lee mucho pero viaja poco o el que lee poco pero viaja mucho? ¿Por qué? **4.** ¿Cuál carrera es la que a usted le gusta más? ¿Por qué? ¿Cuál es la que le gusta menos? ¿Por qué **5.** ¿Qué es lo interesante de la vida de un doctor? ¿de un ingeniero? ¿de un arquitecto? ¿de un arqueólogo?

III. OTHER USES OF THE DEFINITE ARTICLE

En la panadería.

(1) **El panadero:** Señora, tiene *la* cartera abierta. Ciérrela.
(2) **La señora:** Gracias. Me podían haber robado *el* dinero. Dígame, ¿a cuánto está *el* pan esta semana?
(3) **El panadero:** A quince pesos *el* kilo.
(4) **La señora:** ¡Qué barbaridad! *El* pan está por las nubes estos días. Y *los* bizcochos, ¿a cuánto están?
(5) **El panadero:** A veintiocho, señora. Es que *el* azúcar está carísimo.
(6) **La señora:** Lo sé. Me gustan *las* cosas dulces, pero a esos precios . . . Bueno, al menos parece que *la* inflación sirve para no aumentar de peso.

1. ¿Quién debe tener cuidado? ¿Por qué? **2.** ¿A cuánto está el pan? ¿Cree la señora que el pan está caro o barato? **3.** ¿Por qué están caros los bizcochos? **4.** Según la señora, ¿qué es lo bueno de la inflación?

At the bakery.
(1) Ma'am, your purse is open. Close it. (2) Thanks. They could have stolen my money. Tell me, how much is bread this week? (3) Fifteen pesos a kilo (2.2 pounds). (4) How awful! Bread is sky-high these days. And biscuits, how much are they? (5) Twenty-eight, ma'am. Sugar is very expensive. (6) I know. I like sweets, but at those prices . . . Well, at least it seems inflation is good for not gaining weight.

Several uses of the definite article have already been presented, such as the article with titles (Chapter 1) and the article with dates and days of the week (Chapter 4). Other uses of the definite article are:

A. With parts of the body, personal effects, and articles of clothing, when it is clear who the possessor is. The possessive adjective is not used in these instances.

El médico se lava las manos.	*The doctor washes his hands.*
El farmacéutico se puso el abrigo.	*The pharmacist put on his coat.*
Dame la mano.	*Give me your hand.*

B. Before a noun used in a general sense as representative of its class or type. The noun can be singular or plural, concrete or abstract.

Me gusta el arte moderno.	*I like modern art.*
Así es el amor.	*That's love.*
¿Te importan el dinero y la fama?	*Are money and fame important to you?*

C. With names of languages or fields of study, except after the preposition **en** and after **hablar, escribir, enseñar, estudiar, aprender,** and **leer,** when it is usually omitted.

Aprendo alemán. —El alemán es una lengua muy útil.	*I'm learning German. —German is a very useful language.*
Me gustan las ciencias: la biología, la química . . .	*I like sciences—biology, chemistry . . .*
¿Lees francés? —Sí, pero con dificultad.	*Do you read French? —Yes, but with difficulty.*
¿Cómo se dice «buen viaje» en francés? —«Bon voyage.»	*How do you say "Have a good trip" in French? —"Bon voyage."*

D. For rates and prices.

Aquí se venden huevos a setenta centavos la docena.	*Eggs are sold here for seventy cents a dozen.*
Compré un vino excelente a cuarenta pesos el litro.	*I bought an excellent wine for forty pesos a liter.*

E. Before each noun in a series.

El paraguas, el periódico y la cartera son míos.	*The umbrella, newspaper, and wallet are mine.*
El fútbol, el jai alai y el boxeo son tres deportes populares en el mundo hispano.	*Soccer, jai alai, and boxing are three popular sports in the Hispanic world.*

F. With the preposition **a** + a time expression to mean *per*.

El abogado va de vacaciones dos
veces al año.

*The lawyer goes on vacation twice a
year.*

El arqueólogo va a Bogotá tres veces al
mes.

*The archeologist goes to Bogota three
times per (a) month.*

Ejercicios

A. Complete the following paragraph with the appropriate definite articles, if needed.

Un día en la vida de Miguel y Cristina Sáenz

Miguel Sáenz estudia para farmacéutico. Ayer se despertó a _____ siete de _____ mañana. Abrió _____ ojos y con gran esfuerzo (*effort*) puso _____ pies en _____ suelo. Estaba cansado. Se lavó _____ cara y _____ manos. Como le dolía _____ cabeza, tomó una aspirina. Empezó a vestirse. Se puso _____ camisa, _____ pantalones, _____ calcetines y _____ zapatos. En _____ cocina, su mamá lo esperaba con _____ desayuno. Allí su hermana Cristina, una profesora de lenguas, leía las obras completas de Pirandello en _____ italiano. A Cristina le encantan _____ lenguas. Además de hablar _____ inglés, habla _____ italiano, _____ francés, _____ portugués y _____ español perfectamente. Anoche fue a ver *Seis personajes en busca de autor*, probablemente _____ obra más famosa de Pirandello. A _____ seis de _____ tarde, Cristina se lavó _____ pelo y se bañó. Después de bañarse, se puso _____ ropa, se pintó _____ ojos y _____ labios, le dio un beso a _____ señora Sáenz y salió de su casa con _____ bolso en _____ mano. En _____ teatro la esperaba _____ doctor Rossi, un médico italiano amigo suyo. La obra fue totalmente en _____ italiano, pero Cristina no tuvo ningún problema porque _____ italiano es una de las varias lenguas que ella habla y entiende muy bien.

B. Give the Spanish equivalent of the following sentences.

1. Two very important languages are Spanish and French.
2. In the United States many people speak Spanish.
3. She put on her shoes.
4. Give me your hand.
5. Children need milk.
6. My arm hurts very much.

Preguntas

1. Cuando usted se despierta por la mañana, ¿abre los ojos fácilmente o con mucha dificultad? **2.** ¿Le duele a usted a veces la cabeza? ¿el estómago? ¿la garganta? ¿Qué toma o qué hace usted entonces? **3.** ¿Qué ropa se pone usted cuando hace frío? ¿cuando hace calor? ¿cuando llueve? **4.** ¿Le interesa a usted el arte? ¿la política? ¿la literatura? ¿la ecología?

IV. OMISSION OF THE INDEFINITE ARTICLE

(1)	**Señorita Rojas:**	¿Sabías que mi doctora tuvo otro hijo?
(2)	**Señora de Pérez:**	¡No, no lo sabía! ¿Y cómo se llama el bebé?
(3)	**Señorita Rojas:**	OKSNEDZSKI, como su abuelo.
(4)	**Señora de Pérez:**	¿Es escandinavo su abuelo?
(5)	**Señorita Rojas:**	No, es oculista.

1. ¿Qué tuvo la doctora de la señorita Rojas? **2.** ¿Lo sabía la señora de Pérez? **3.** ¿Qué es el abuelo del nuevo bebé? **4.** ¿Es él francés? ¿escandinavo? ¿Por qué tiene ese nombre?

A. The indefinite article is omitted before an unmodified noun that indicates profession, occupation, religion, nationality, or political affiliation, following the verb **ser**. However, the indefinite article is used if the noun is modified. Compare the following examples.

¿Qué oficio tiene Juan? —Es cocinero.	*What job does Juan have? —He's a cook.*
El primo de Ana es panadero.	*Ana's cousin is a baker.*
¿Eres católica? —No, soy protestante.	*Are you a Catholic? —No, I'm a Protestant.*
El señor Cruz es colombiano.	*Mr. Cruz is a Colombian.*
Gloria es socialista.	*Gloria is a socialist.*
Armando es un demócrata fanático.	*Armando is a fanatical Democrat.*
¿Eres una católica devota?	*Are you a devout Catholic?*
Miguel Ángel fue un gran artista.	*Michelangelo was a great artist.*

(1) Did you know that my doctor had another baby? (2) No, I didn't know (about) it! And what's the baby's name? (3) OKSNEDZSKI, after his grandfather. (4) Is his grandfather a Scandinavian? (5) No, he's an optometrist.

B. The indefinite article is not used before words such as **medio, otro** and **cierto.** The latter agree in gender and number with the nouns they modify.

Quiero media docena de huevos.	*I want a half-dozen eggs.*
Encarnita compró otro reloj.	*Encarnita bought another watch.*
Cierto filósofo dijo eso.	*A certain philosopher said that.*

Ejercicios

A. Create new sentences, substituting the words in the lists for those in italics. Make all other necessary changes.

1. (*esa señora/argentino*) → Esa señora es argentina.
   a. mis amigos/protestante **b.** Juan y José/pintor **c.** Ana/doctor **d.** nosotros/católico **e.** los Pérez/cubano
2. (*Luis/buen oculista*) → Luis es un buen oculista.
   a. Marisa/buen escultor **b.** tu hermano/buen político **c.** Julio/buen artista **d.** Elena/buen profesor **e.** esa muchacha/buen mecanógrafo

B. Give the Spanish equivalent of the following sentences.

1. Mrs. García is a teacher.
2. Mr. Cárdenas is a Protestant.
3. Isabel is a fanatical socialist.
4. The Montoyas are Argentinean.
5. I want a half-dozen oranges, please.

Preguntas

1. ¿Qué profesión u oficio tiene su padre? ¿su madre? ¿su mejor amigo(a)? 2. ¿Qué quiere ser usted? ¿doctor? ¿profesor? ¿ingeniero? ¿pintor? ¿escultor? ¿oculista? ¿panadero? ¿Por qué? 3. ¿Puede nombrar (*name*) usted a un socialista o comunista famoso? ¿a un católico devoto? ¿a un pintor español? 4. ¿Conoce usted personalmente a algún político importante? ¿a algún escritor contemporáneo? ¿a algún pintor o escultor conocido?

LA MISTERIOSA CIUDAD DE LOS INCAS

Eva y su novio Juan están visitando las ruinas de Machu Picchu, en el Perú.[1] *Ella está buscando inspiración para unas pinturas.*

Juan: ¿Qué haces, mi amor?
Eva: Estoy admirando estos muros imponentes.[2] Parecen más bellos ahora, sin los turistas.
Juan: ¿Por qué no me despertaste?
Eva: Salí a las cinco y seguías durmiendo como una piedra. Hace dos horas que espero el amanecer, pero creo que hoy no vamos a poder ver el sol por la niebla.
Juan: ¡Qué lástima!

Eva: ¡Al contrario! Creo que las ruinas me gustan más en medio de la niebla. Les da cierto aire misterioso.

Juan: Fíjate en aquella piedra. Parece obra de un escultor moderno. Creo que es la que usaba el Inca para atrapar el sol.[3]

Eva: Sí, lo es. Conozco la leyenda. Me la contó el camarero del hotel.

Juan: Mira. Allí está el muchacho indio que vimos anoche.

Tano: Muy buenos días, señores.

Eva: Buenos días. No sabía que hablaba castellano.[4]

Tano: En casa hablamos quechua,[5] señora, pero en la escuela nos enseñan castellano. ¿Usted es arqueóloga?

Eva: No. Yo soy pintora, y él es biólogo. Usted trabaja en el hotel, ¿verdad?

Tano: Sí, soy ayudante del cocinero. ¿Les gusta la comida peruana?

Eva: Sí, lo que comimos anoche estuvo excelente.

Tano: Usted es muy amable. Perdone, pero ahora tengo que regresar, porque el panadero me espera para que saque el pan del horno.

Eva: Hasta luego entonces.

Juan: Nosotros también debemos volver, Eva. Dame la mano.

Eva: Ponte el abrigo primero. ¿No te estás muriendo de frío?

Juan: No, antes de venir tomé un té de coca[6] para calentarme y para no sentir tanto la altura.

Eva: Sí, es difícil acostumbrarse a esta altura. Me estoy imaginando que estamos en el cielo.

Juan: No te lo estás imaginando. Esta niebla en realidad no es niebla. ¡Es una nube baja!

imponentes *imposing*   **ayudante** *helper*

Preguntas

1. ¿Qué están haciendo Eva y Juan? **2.** ¿Qué está haciendo Eva? **3.** ¿Por qué no despertó a Juan? **4.** ¿Por qué le gustan a Eva las ruinas en medio de la niebla? **5.** ¿Qué idiomas habla Tano? ¿Por qué? **6.** ¿Cuáles son las profesiones de Eva, de Juan y de Tano? **7.** ¿Qué quiere Eva que se ponga Juan? ¿Por qué no necesita hacerlo él? **8.** ¿Por qué dice Juan que Eva no se está imaginando que está en el cielo? ¿Ha estado usted en algunas montañas altas? ¿Dónde?

NOTAS CULTURALES

1. Machu Picchu is the ancient fortress city of the Incas, located high in the Andes mountains not far from Cuzco, Peru, which was the capital of the Inca empire when the Spanish arrived. Machu Picchu cannot be seen from the valley below and remained unknown to the outside world until 1911, when it was discovered by the noted American explorer Hiram Bingham. Temples, stairways, walls, and houses still stand, offering a unique glimpse into the life of the ancient Incas.

2. The Incas were master stonecutters. They built massive walls from huge polygonal blocks so precisely shaped and chiseled that no mortar was necessary. Stones with as many as twelve sides fit so perfectly together that a razor blade cannot be inserted between them. Many of these walls are still in use today.

3. According to legend, this beautifully sculptured stone was an important part of a ceremony performed once a year by the Inca emperor (who was the only one called **Inca** in those days). The priests would tell the Inca which day was to be the shortest of the year, and on that day he would go forth at sunset and ceremonially "tie" the sun to the earth, using this stone, called "the hitching post of the sun." This was supposed to prevent the sun from continuing to slip away from the earth gradually, day by day. The proof came, of course, when the days that followed turned out to be longer, thus corroborating the general belief that the Inca was a direct descendant of the sun and had a special power over it.

4. In many parts of Latin America, the Spanish language is frequently referred to as **(el) castellano.** However, the term **(el) español** is also used and understood.

5. Quechua, the language spoken by the Incas, was imposed upon all new members of the Inca empire after conquest. Quechua and Aymara are the most common Indian languages in Peru, and many Peruvians learn Spanish only as a second language.

6. Coca-leaf tea is made from the leaf of the coca plant, from which cocaine is extracted. The tea is strictly for medicinal purposes and does not have the effects of cocaine. It is sometimes served to tourists to prevent altitude sickness. The leaves of the coca plant, however, in combination with some other ingredients, are chewed as a narcotic by many Indians of the Peruvian and Bolivian sierra.

ACTIVIDADES

¿Qué está haciendo?

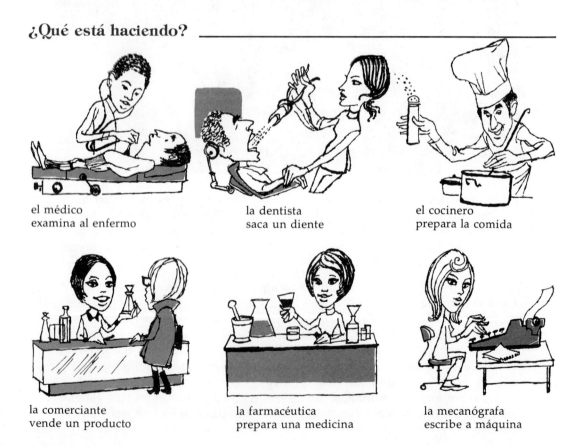

el médico
examina al enfermo

la dentista
saca un diente

el cocinero
prepara la comida

la comerciante
vende un producto

la farmacéutica
prepara una medicina

la mecanógrafa
escribe a máquina

el mecánico
arregla el auto

A student will begin by a question concerning one of the professions shown, using the present participle. The student who answers, should then phrase a similar question, etc.

Modelo: —¿Qué *está haciendo* la farmacéutica?
—La farmacéutica *está preparando* una medicina.

Lo bueno y lo malo

Choose three professions and write two original sentences for each about what you consider to be the good aspects (lo bueno) *and the bad aspects* (lo malo).

Modelo: Cocinero(-a):   Lo bueno es que puedes ser creativo(-a).
Lo malo es que puedes comer mucho y no recibes un salario grande.

Entrevista

Ask a classmate the following questions. Then report the information to the class.

1. ¿Qué querías ser cuando eras niño? ¿Sigues pensando que ésa es una buena profesión?
2. ¿Para qué estás estudiando ahora?
3. ¿Te faltan muchos años para terminar tus estudios?
4. ¿Ya estás buscando trabajo? ¿Dónde?
5. ¿Qué te parece lo más importante en la elección de una profesión?
6. ¿Por qué estás estudiando español? ¿Qué es lo que más te interesa del estudio del español?

Situación

Choose one of the professions mentioned in this chapter. If called upon, you should act it out in front of the class, then call on students and ask them: *¿Qué estoy haciendo? ¿Qué soy yo?*. A correct answer might be: *Usted está haciendo pan. Usted es panadero.*

VOCABULARIO ACTIVO

Verbos útiles

andar *to walk;* **El reloj anda bien.** *The watch runs well.*
atrapar *to catch*
calentar *to heat, warm*
escribir a máquina *to type*
robar *to steal*

Las profesiones y los oficios

el abogado *lawyer*
el, la arqueólogo *archeologist*
el, la arquitecto *architect*
el, la artista *artist; actor (actress)*
el, la biólogo *biologist*
el, la carpintero *carpenter*
el, la científico *scientist*
el cocinero (la cocinera) *cook, chef*
el, la comerciante *businessman or businesswoman*
el, la dentista *dentist*
el, la escultora *sculptor*
el, la farmacéutico *druggist, pharmacist*
el, la filósofo *philosopher*
el, la ingeniero *engineer*
el ladrón *thief*
el, la mecánico *mechanic*
el mecanógrafo (la mecanógrafa) *typist*
el, la médico *doctor*
el, la oculista *optometrist*
el oficio *job, occupation*
el panadero/, la panadera *baker*
el, la periodista *journalist*
el pintor (la pintora) *painter*
el, la químico *chemist*

Sustantivos

la altura *altitude*
el amanecer *dawn*
la arqueología *archeology*
el bizcocho *cookie, biscuit*
el canasto de basura *wastebasket*
la carrera *career*
la cartera *wallet*
el castellano *Spanish language (Castilian)*
el cielo *sky, heaven*
la dificultad *difficulty*
la disputa *dispute*
la docena *dozen*
la expresión *expression*
la geometría *geometry*
el horno *oven*
la leyenda *legend*
la libertad *freedom, liberty*
el mueble *item of furniture*
el muro *wall*
el músculo *muscle*
la niebla *fog*
la nube *cloud*
la panadería *bakery*
el realismo *realism*
el significado *meaning*
la teoría *theory*

Adjetivos

abstracto(a) *abstract*
activo(a) *active*
ambicioso(a) *ambitious*
animado(a) *lively, animated*
católico(a) *Catholic*
cierto(a) *certain, a certain*
chistoso(a) *funny*
egoísta *selfish*
estudioso(a) *studious*
generoso(a) *generous*
inca *Inca (indigenous culture of the Andes)*
maya *Mayan (indigenous culture of Central America)*
misterioso(a) *mysterious*
protestante *Protestant*
socialista *socialist*
útil *useful*

Otras palabras útiles

al contrario. *on the contrary.*
de vez en cuando *from time to time*
infinitamente *infinitely*
por las nubes *sky-high*

Hispanoamérica: Antes y Después de la Conquista

Mucho antes de la *llegada* de los españoles al Nuevo Mundo, ya existían varias importantes civilizaciones *indígenas*. Una de las más avanzadas fue la de los mayas, que *se desarrolló* en México y Centroamérica. La civilización maya se distinguió en los *campos* de las matemáticas, la astronomía, el arte y la escritura pictográfica.

arrival
native
developed
fields

Otra civilización bastante avanzada fue la tolteca. Los toltecas construyeron pirámides como la que se ve en la fotografía. Ésta es la Pirámide del Sol y está en Teotihuacán, antiguo centro tolteca cerca de la ciudad de México.

Cuando los españoles llegaron a México, hace casi 500 años, la civilización dominante era la azteca y su capital era la ciudad de Tenochtitlán. Los aztecas controlaban un vasto imperio. Eran un *pueblo guerrero* y practicaban un culto muy *sanguinario*. Como creían que el Sol necesitaba beber sangre humana, los sacrificios humanos eran parte esencial de sus ritos religiosos. Sus víctimas eran, normalmente, *miembros* de tribus subordinadas.

warlike people /
bloody

members

En 1519 el conquistador español Hernán Cortés llegó a México con unos 400 soldados, y consiguió la alianza de las tribus que odiaban a sus opresores, los aztecas. Con la ayuda de estas tribus, Cortés capturó al emperador Moctezuma y, en tres años, conquistó todo el imperio azteca. Otros factores que ayudaron a Cortés fueron la vulnerabilidad de los indios a las enfermedades introducidas por los españoles, la superioridad de las *armas* españolas, sus *caballos* que

arms, weapons /
horses

atemorizaron a los indios y la curiosa leyenda de Quetzalcóatl, un hombre-dios, blanco y con barba, que *según las profecías* debía volver a gobernar al pueblo. Por eso, Moctezuma recibió a Cortés con *amabilidad* y regalos, creyendo que era el dios.

terrified
according to the
prophecies
kindness

En Sudamérica había otra gran civilización indígena: la de los incas, que *comprendía* mucho de lo que es hoy Ecuador, Perú, Bolivia y Chile. Para los incas, la organización social era muy importante. La sociedad incaica tenía una estructura social piramidal. *En lo más alto* estaba el Inca, o jefe supremo, y sus nobles. Esta clase privilegiada llevaba una vida *lujosa. En cambio*, la gente común trabajaba en tierras colectivas y tenía sólo lo necesario para vivir. Los viejos y enfermos recibían ayuda del estado, pero todos trabajaban y vivían

comprised

on the top

luxurious / on the
other hand

donde su jefe les decía. Había poco crimen, *ya que* el *castigo* era inmediato y severo.

since / punishment

La astronomía y las matemáticas no estaban tan desarrolladas como entre los mayas y aztecas, pero los incas estaban más avanzados en medicina y en ingeniería. Construyeron excelentes caminos, puentes, acueductos y *fortalezas* que aún hoy se conservan, como se puede ver en esta foto.

fortresses

Ésta es la estatua del conquistador Francisco Pizarro, en Lima. Pizarro llegó al Perú en el año 1531 con menos de 200 soldados. Con este pequeño *ejército* conquistó en pocos meses a los incas, un imperio de seis o siete millones de personas. Pizarro siguió el ejemplo de Cortés y así, *aparentando amistad,* pudo capturar al emperador Atahualpa. Los indios del Perú estaban acostumbrados a *obedecer*, *de modo que* con la captura de su jefe supremo, el poder pasó fácilmente a manos de los españoles. El caso de esta conquista es un

army

pretending friendship
to obey
so that

ejemplo de las oportunidades que ofrecía el Nuevo Mundo. Pizarro pertenecía a la clase más pobre de España, pero en el Perú llegó a ser rico y poderoso.

Durante los tres siglos coloniales la sociedad hispanoamericana era básicamente feudal. Estaba formada por cuatro grupos: los indios, los mestizos, los criollos o blancos nacidos en América, y los peninsulares o españoles. Los indios trabajaban en las minas o en las haciendas de los criollos. El número de mestizos *crecía* día a día y   was growing
formaba un puente entre los grupos de indios y criollos. Los peninsulares estaban *por encima de* todos, ya que el gobierno español   above
les daba a ellos todos los *puestos* políticos. Los criollos, que estaban   positions
resentidos por esta discriminación, *prestaron atención* a las ideas re-   paid attention
volucionarias que circulaban en el siglo XVIII.

La revolución hispanoamericana empezó a principios del siglo XIX. En México, un *humilde* sacerdote, el Padre Miguel Hidalgo,   humble

encabezó una rebelión de los indios bajo la *bandera* de la Virgen de   headed, led / flag
Guadalupe. Poco después, en la Argentina, el General José de San Martín, un criollo, *tomó el mando* de las fuerzas revolucionarias que   took command
liberaron a la Argentina y Chile, mientras que otro jefe criollo, Simón Bolívar, ganó la liberación del norte de Sudamérica. Ya en 1825 toda Hispanoamérica era independiente. Arriba se puede ver un retrato del padre Hidalgo, y en la página siguiente hay retratos de San Martín y Bolívar.

Aunque Bolívar soñaba con la unión de toda la América Española en un solo país poderoso, las naciones se formaron separadamente, y este deseo no se realizó. Como los criollos, excluidos de la política por tres siglos, no tenían experiencia en el gobierno, muchas naciones pasaron a manos de dictadores, a pesar de sus constituciones democráticas. La independencia fue sólo el primer paso hacia el camino de la libertad.

José de San Martín

Simón Bolívar

Preguntas

1. ¿Dónde se desarrolló la civilización maya? ¿En qué campos se distinguió? 2. ¿Quiénes construyeron la Pirámide del Sol que está en Teotihuacán, cerca de la ciudad de México? 3. ¿Cómo eran los aztecas cuando llegaron los españoles a México? 4. ¿Cuáles fueron los factores que ayudaron a Cortés en la conquista del imperio azteca? 5. ¿Cómo era la organización social de los incas? 6. ¿En qué campos estaban avanzados los incas? ¿Qué construyeron? 7. ¿Cómo pudo Pizarro conquistar el gran imperio de los incas en pocos meses? ¿Tenía un ejército muy grande? 8. ¿Cuáles eran los cuatro grupos que formaban la sociedad colonial hispanoamericana? 9. ¿Cómo se llaman los tres grandes héroes de las revoluciones hispanoamericanas? 10. ¿Con qué soñaba Bolívar? ¿Qué les pasó después a muchas de las naciones, a pesar de sus constituciones democráticas?

EN CASA

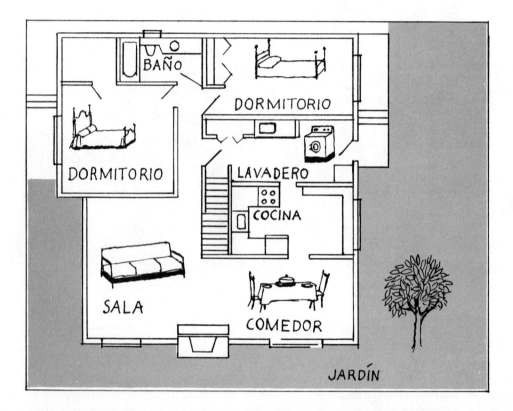

OBJECTIVES

LANGUAGE: In this chapter we introduce, discuss, and practice:
1. the future tense
2. the conditional tense
3. cardinal numbers 100 and above

You will also learn words for rooms of the house, furniture, and other vocabulary related to the home.

CULTURE: The dialogue takes place on a train from the coastal city of Guayaquil over the Andes mountains to Quito, the capital of Ecuador.

EXPLICACIÓN

I. THE FUTURE TENSE

(1)	**Sra. Duarte:**	Miguelito, te *diré* un secreto si prometes subir a tu dormitorio y acostarte pronto.
(2)	**Miguelito:**	*Subiré* a mi dormitorio y *me acostaré* ahora mismo, mamá. Pero primero dime el secreto.
(3)	**Sra. Duarte:**	Tu papá y yo te vamos a dar un regalo muy lindo. Está aquí mismo en la cocina con nosotros . . .
(4)	**Miguelito:**	¿En serio? ¿Y cuándo *podré* verlo?
(5)	**Sra. Duarte:**	*Tendrás* que esperar unos cinco meses.
(6)	**Miguelito:**	¡Cinco meses! Entonces, ¿no lo *veré* mañana?
(7)	**Sra. Duarte:**	No, pero te *contaré* lo que es. ¡Tu papá y yo te *daremos* un hermanito o una hermanita!
(8)	**Miguelito:**	¿Un hermano? . . . ¿una hermana? ¿Y por qué no mejor una bicicleta? . . .

1. ¿Qué le dirá la mamá a Miguelito?   **2.** ¿Qué promete Miguelito?   **3.** ¿Quiénes le van a dar un regalo a él?   **4.** ¿Cuándo podrá ver él el regalo?   **5.** ¿Le gusta mucho a Miguelito el regalo que le promete su madre?   **6.** ¿Qué prefiere él?   **7.** ¿Tiene usted algún secreto ahora? ¿Nos lo podrá contar antes de que terminen las clases?

A. To form the future tense, add to the complete infinitive the endings **-é, -ás, -á, -emos, -éis, -án.** The endings are the same for **-ar, -er,** and **-ir** verbs. Except for the first-person plural, all forms have written accents.

hablar		comer		vivir	
hablar**é**	hablar**emos**	comer**é**	comer**emos**	vivir**é**	vivir**emos**
hablar**ás**	hablar**éis**	comer**ás**	comer**éis**	vivir**ás**	vivir**éis**
hablar**á**	hablar**án**	comer**á**	comer**án**	vivir**á**	vivir**án**

(1) Miguelito, I'll tell you a secret if you promise to go up to your room and go to bed soon. (2) I'll go up to my room and I'll go to bed right away, Mom. But first tell me the secret. (3) Your father and I are going to give you a very nice present. It's right here in the kitchen with us . . . (4) Really? And when will I be able to see it? (5) You'll have to wait about five months. (6) Five months! Then I won't see it tomorrow? (7) No, but I'll tell you what it is. Your father and I are going to give you a little brother or sister! (8) A brother? . . . a sister? And why not a bicycle instead?

Te acompañaré a comprar los muebles.	*I'll go with you to buy the furniture.*
¿Crees que el vendedor los convencerá de que compren esa propiedad?	*Do you think the salesman will convince them to buy that property?*
El miércoles próximo iremos a ese lugar.	*Next Wednesday we will go to that place.*

B. Some verbs are irregular in the future. However, the irregularity is only in the stem; the endings are the same as for regular verbs.

dir-	(decir)	sabr-	(saber)
habr-	(haber)	saldr-	(salir)
har-	(hacer)	tendr-	(tener)
podr-	(poder)	valdr-	(valer)
pondr-	(poner)	vendr-	(venir)
querr-	(querer)		

Jaime no podrá ir a visitar a sus parientes.	*Jaime will not be able to go visit his relatives.*
¡Limpia la cocina! —Lo haré mañana.	*Clean the kitchen!—I'll do it tomorrow.*
Tendrán que esperar un rato.	*They'll have to wait a while.*
Querrán un cuarto con dos camas, televisor, baño y una buena vista.	*They'll want a room with two beds, a television, a bath, and a good view.*

C. The future tense can also be used to express probability or doubt in the present.

¿Qué hora será?	*What time can it be? (I wonder what time it is.)*
Serán las ocho.	*It must be eight o'clock. (It is probably eight o'clock.)*
¿Dónde estará Tomás?	*Where can Tomás be? (Where might Tomás be?)*
Tomás estará en su dormitorio.	*Tomás is probably (must be) in his room.*

Ejercicios

A. Create new sentences, substituting the words in the lists for those in italics.

1. *Ernesto* hablará con el vendedor mañana.
   a. nosotros **b.** sus padres **c.** tú **d.** usted **e.** yo

2. El año que viene *mis tíos* irán a Europa.
   a. Ana y yo **b.** él **c.** los Zelaya **d.** yo **e.** Raquel

3. *Yo* no lo haré hasta las vacaciones.
   a. ellas **b.** tú **c.** ustedes **d.** la pintora **e.** usted y yo

4. *Los Rojas* tendrán que comprar una casa más grande.
   a. tú **b.** Elena y Miguel **c.** nosotros **d.** yo **e.** José Luis

B. Restate, changing the verbs to the future.

1. El autobús viene a las cuatro.
2. No vuelven esta noche.
3. Desayunamos a las siete y media.
4. ¿A qué hora salen ustedes de aquí?
5. ¿Está el gato en la cocina?
6. El tío de Carmela nos vende su auto.
7. Nadie te quiere ayudar.
8. Nunca puedo ir al cine.
9. Miguelito sube a su dormitorio a las ocho.
10. ¿Cuándo vas a ver la propiedad?

C. Complete the following paragraph with the appropriate future forms of the verbs in parentheses.

El próximo verano mi familia y yo (ir) _____ a México. Primero (visitar) _____ la ciudad de Monterrey, donde papá (ver) _____ a un amigo suyo. Después, mamá y él (ir) _____ a Guanajuato. Allí tenemos varios parientes y mis padres (sentirse) _____ muy felices de verlos. Sé que todos (querer) _____ tenerlos en su casa, pero estoy seguro de que papá y mamá (preferir) _____ estar solos en algún hotel. Lo único que ellos (necesitar) _____ es un dormitorio cómodo con una cama grande. Durante ese tiempo, mi hermano y yo (viajar) _____ y (conocer) _____ muchos lugares interesantes. (Hacer) _____ una visita a Guadalajara, donde mi hermano (poder) _____ ver algunos cuadros de Orozco, el famoso pintor mexicano, y yo (divertirse) _____ escuchando música en la Plaza de los Mariachis. Finalmente, los cuatro (encontrarse) _____ en la ciudad de México. Mis padres (venir) _____ allí en auto desde Guanajuato y nosotros en avión desde Guadalajara.

D. Give the Spanish equivalent of the following sentences.

1. You (tú) will find what you need in the kitchen.
2. Hernando will buy all the furniture that we'll need.
3. We'll meet her family next week.
4. Next time they'll bring more money.
5. It must be two o'clock.
6. I wonder where Alicia is.

Preguntas

1. ¿Qué hará usted el próximo domingo? ¿Se quedará en su casa o irá a alguna parte? ¿Adónde? 2. ¿A qué hora se acostará usted esta noche? ¿A qué hora se levantará mañana? 3. ¿Va a viajar usted el próximo verano? ¿Adónde irá? Si no va a viajar a ninguna parte, ¿qué hará? 4. ¿Qué hora será ahora? 5. ¿Dónde estará su mamá en este momento? ¿su papá? ¿su novio(a)?

II. THE CONDITIONAL TENSE

(1) **Marisa:** ¿Recuerdas la promesa que me hiciste la semana pasada mientras pintábamos las paredes de la sala?

(2) **Pablo:** ¿La semana pasada? ¡Ah!, te dije que *iríamos* al cine, ¿no?

(3) **Marisa:** No, dijiste que *harías* algo que me *gustaría* muchísimo . . .

(4) **Pablo:** ¿Qué te *prometería* yo? . . . ¡No lo recuerdo! Tal vez te dije que *limpiaría* las alfombras . . .

(5) **Marisa:** ¡No! ¡Me prometiste que no *fumarías* más!

(6) **Pablo:** ¡Y no fumo más, Marisa! Fumo exactamente igual que siempre, querida . . .

1. ¿Recuerda Pablo lo que dijo que haría? 2. ¿Le prometió él a Marisa que irían al cine? ¿que limpiaría la sala? 3. ¿Cuál fue la promesa de Pablo? 4. Según Marisa, ¿cuándo prometió Pablo que no fumaría más? 5. Según Pablo, ¿cumplió él su promesa? ¿Por qué?

(1) Remember the promise you made me last week while we were painting the living room walls? (2) Last week? Oh, I told you we would go to the movies, right? (3) No, you said you'd do something that I would like very much . . . (4) I wonder what I promised you . . . I don't remember it! Maybe I told you that I would clean the carpets . . . (5) No! You promised me you wouldn't smoke any more! (6) And I am not smoking any more, Marisa! I am smoking exactly the same as always, dear . . .

A. To form the conditional tense, add to the complete infinitive the endings **-ía,**
-ías, -ía, -íamos, -íais, -ían. The endings are the same for **-ar, -er,** and **-ir** verbs.

hablar		comer		vivir	
hablaría	hablaríamos	comería	comeríamos	viviría	viviríamos
hablarías	hablaríais	comerías	comeríais	vivirías	viviríais
hablaría	hablarían	comería	comerían	viviría	vivirían

The conditional usually conveys the meaning *would* in English.

Él no compraría una casa sin seis
  habitaciones, dos baños, comedor y
  un lavadero.

He wouldn't buy a house without six
* rooms, two bathrooms, dining room,*
* and a laundry.*

Ellos no vivirían en un apartamento
  tan pequeño.

They would not live in such a small
* apartment.*

However, remember that the imperfect in Spanish can also be translated as
would referring to a repeated event in the past:

Durante el verano, comíamos en el
  patio todos los días.

During the summer we would eat on the
* patio every day.*

B. The conditional often refers to a projected or possible action in the future in
relation to a past moment.

Prometieron que traerían el sofá y los
  sillones antes de las dos.

They promised they would bring the sofa
* and the armchairs before two o'clock.*

No sabíamos si José llegaría hoy o
  mañana.

We didn't know if José would arrive
* today or tomorrow.*

Dijo que alquilaría la casa que da al
  parque.

He said he would rent the house that
* faces the park.*

C. The verbs that have irregular stems in the future also have the same irregular
stems in the conditional. The endings are the same as for verbs with regular
stems.

dir-	(decir)	sabr-	(saber)
habr-	(haber)	saldr-	(salir)
har-	(hacer)	tendr-	(tener)
podr-	(poder)	valdr-	(valer)
pondr-	(poner)	vendr-	(venir)
querr-	(querer)		

Lucía no diría eso.

Lucía wouldn't say that.

Pedro prometió que pondría los
  juguetes en el armario.

Pedro promised he would put the toys in
* the cupboard.*

Creo que ellos podrían ayudarte a
  arreglar el techo.

I think they could (would be able to)
* help you fix the roof.*

D. The conditional may be used to express probability in the past.

¿Qué hora sería cuando ellos llegaron?   *What time was it (probably) when they arrived?*

Serían las nueve.   *It must have been (was probably) nine o'clock.*

¿Qué edad tendría Pepito cuando fueron a España?   *Approximately how old was Pepito when they went to Spain?*

Tendría once o doce años.   *He was around eleven or twelve years old (he must have been eleven or twelve years old).*

E. The conditional may also be used to indicate an attitude of politeness or deference.

Usted debería tomar un taxi.   *You should take a taxi.*

¿Me podría usted decir cómo llegar al Hotel Continental?   *Can you tell me how to get to the Hotel Continental?*

Ejercicios

A. Create new sentences, substituting the words in the lists for those in italics.

1. *Ustedes* no venderían esta casa por tan poco.
   a. El arquitecto **b.** Tú **c.** Los García **d.** Yo **e.** Dina y yo

2. Le dije que *él* vendría al parque a las cinco.
   a. los jóvenes **b.** usted **c.** yo **d.** tú **e.** nosotros

3. ¿Qué haría *usted* sin mí?
   a. el jefe **b.** los estudiantes **c.** tú **d.** la doctora **e.** ustedes

4. *Yo* tendría un año cuando empecé a hablar.
   a. Mi papá **b.** Ellos **c.** Nosotros **d.** Juanita **e.** Tú

B. Restate, changing the verbs to the plural and making any other necessary changes.

1. Yo no limpiaría las alfombras antes de pintar.
2. ¿No haría usted ese viaje?
3. Él tendría mucha sed.
4. Tú estarías en el jardín.
5. Ella podría llevar los sillones a la sala.

C. Mr. Benítez is telling his wife Leonor how he would spend his money and how their life would change if he suddenly became a millionaire. With the elements given, form sentences in the conditional, as Mr. Benítez would.

Modelo: yo / dar algún dinero a los pobres. **Yo daría algún dinero a los pobres.**

1. tú y yo / viajar por todo el mundo
2. nuestros hijos / asistir a una buena universidad

3. yo / comprarte un Mercedes
4. nosotros / vivir en una casa muy grande
5. nuestra casa / tener ocho dormitorios y cuatro baños
6. tú / no trabajar en la oficina
7. Anita / poder tener muchos juguetes lindos
8. Pedrito / ir a un campamento (*camp*) de verano todos los años
9. yo / hacer muchas cosas que ahora no puedo hacer
10. todos / ser muy felices

Preguntas

1. ¿Podría decirme cuál es la ciudad más grande del mundo? ¿Sería usted feliz viviendo allí? ¿Por qué? **2.** ¿Le gustaría ser rico? ¿Cree usted que sería más feliz siendo rico? **3.** ¿Qué hora sería cuando usted llegó a la universidad? ¿a clase? **4.** ¿Sabía usted que hoy estudiaríamos el condicional? ¿Creía que tendríamos un examen? ¿Pensaba que no haríamos estos ejercicios? **5** ¿Podría usted decirnos cómo sería su casa ideal? ¿Tendría muchos dormitorios? ¿baños? ¿Tendría sala? ¿cocina? ¿patio? ¿jardín? ¿garage? ¿Para cuántos autos? ¿Qué más tendría?

III. CARDINAL NUMBERS 100 AND ABOVE

En un hotel del centro

(1) **Enrique:** Buenas tardes.
(2) **El gerente:** Buenas tardes, señor.
(3) **Enrique:** ¿Cuánto cuesta una habitación con televisor y dos camas?
(4) **El gerente:** *Ochocientos* pesos por noche.
(5) **Enrique:** ¿Y sin televisor?
(6) **El gerente:** *Quinientos* pesos.
(7) **Enrique:** ¿Y con sólo una cama?
(8) **El gerente:** *Doscientos cincuenta* pesos. Y si usted duerme en el parque, no le costará absolutamente nada.

1. ¿Dónde está Enrique? **2.** ¿Cuánto cuesta una habitación con televisor y dos camas? ¿sin televisor? ¿con sólo una cama? **3.** Según el gerente, ¿dónde debe dormir Enrique para no pagar nada?

At a downtown hotel.
(1) Good afternoon. (2) Good afternoon, sir. (3) How much is a room with a T.V. set and two beds? (4) Eight-hundred pesos per night. (5) And without a T.V. set? (6) Five-hundred pesos. (7) And with only one bed? (8) Two-hundred and fifty pesos. And if you sleep in the park, it will cost you absolutely nothing.

100 cien(to)	600 seiscientos
101 ciento uno	700 setecientos
200 doscientos	800 ochocientos
300 trescientos	900 novecientos
400 cuatrocientos	1.000 mil
500 quinientos	1.000.000 un millón (de)

A. Before all nouns and before the number **mil** (*one thousand*), **cien** is used to mean *one hundred*.

cien años   *100 years*   cien mil dólares   *100,000 dollars*
cien millas   *100 miles*   cien mil promesas   *100,000 promises*

B. **Ciento** is used in all other cases. **Ciento** does not have a feminine form. However, the numbers 200–900 do agree with a noun in gender. For instance, **doscientos** becomes **doscientas** before a feminine noun.

ciento una noches   *101 nights*
ciento un días   *101 days*
ciento cincuenta muchachas   *150 girls*
ciento noventa muchachos   *190 boys*
doscientos parientes   *200 relatives*
cuatrocientos diez libros   *410 books*
quinientas cuatro lámparas   *504 lamps*

C. **Un millón** (*one million*) is followed by **de** before a noun. The plural is **millones.**

La población actual de Trinidad es de un   *The current population of Trinidad is a*
   poco más de un millón de personas.   *little more than one million people.*
Actualmente ella tiene tres millones   *At the present time, she has three*
   de dólares.   *million dollars.*

D. To express numbers above 1,000, **mil** is always used.

mil novecientos ochenta y ocho   *1988*
mil sesenta y seis   *1066*
dos mil uno   *2001*
dos mil treinta y tres   *2033*

In expressing dates, the day, month, and year are connected by **de.**

el trece de enero de mil ochocientos   *January 13, 1863*
   sesenta y tres
el ocho de diciembre de mil   *December 8, 1941*
   novecientos cuarenta y uno
el 28 de febrero de 1938   *February 28, 1938*
el 4 de julio de 1990   *July 4, 1990*

E. The verb **nacer** means *to be born.*

¿En qué año nació Pablo Picasso?   *In what year was Pablo Picasso born?*
—En 1879.   *—In 1879.*

Ejercicios

A. Read the following in Spanish:

Modelos: 250 + 150 = 400   **doscientos cincuenta más ciento cincuenta son cuatro-cientos**
          300 − 100 = 200   **trescientos menos cien son doscientos**

1. 50 + 50 = 100
2. 320 + 210 = 530
3. 960 − 605 = 355
4. 1.000 − 875 = 125
5. 9.000 − 7.000 = 2.000
6. 425 + 201 = 626
7. 100.000 + 50.000 = 150.000
8. 1.000.000 − 7.500 = 992.500

B. *Algunas fechas históricas importantes.* Read the following sentences aloud; then copy them, spelling out the numbers.

1. En el año 711 los moros invadieron la península ibérica.
2. Cristóbal Colón descubrió América en 1492.
3. Hernán Cortés nació en 1485 y murió en 1547.
4. Francisco Pizarro llegó al Perú en 1531.
5. Miguel de Cervantes, autor del *Quijote,* nació en 1547 y murió en 1616.
6. La mayoría de los países latinoamericanos se hicieron independientes entre 1810 y 1825.
7. Entre 1936 y 1939 España sufrió una guerra civil conocida hoy como la *Guerra Civil Española.*
8. Después de la *Guerra Civil Española,* el dictador Francisco Franco gobernó España hasta su muerte en 1975.

C. Write out each of the following phrases.

1. 750 ventanas
2. 318 sofás
3. 451 dormitorios
4. 1.001 noches
5. 846 televisores
6. 179 hoteles
7. 521 camas
8. 1.000.000 casas
9. 230 habitaciones
10. 999 millas

Preguntas

1. ¿En qué año nació usted? ¿su padre? ¿su madre?   **2.** ¿Recuerda usted la fecha de la Revolución Francesa? ¿de la Revolución Americana?   **3.** ¿Ha comprado usted algo muy caro recientemente? ¿Cuánto le ha costado?   **4.** ¿Cuánto cuesta, más o menos, una casa de dos dormitorios? ¿de cinco dormitorios? ¿Cuánto cuesta un Toyota? ¿un Mercedes? **5.** ¿Sabe usted cuánto cuesta aproximadamente un pasaje de ida y vuelta a México? ¿a España? ¿a la Argentina?   **6.** ¿Sabe usted cuál es la población actual de los Estados Unidos? ¿Cuántas personas de origen hispano viven actualmente aquí?

LA CIUDAD DE LA ETERNA PRIMAVERA

Una familia viaja en tren por las altas montañas del Ecuador.

Miguel:	¿Podrías contarme un cuento, abuela?
Abuela:	Bueno. Cuando yo era niña vivía en Quito,[1] en una casa muy grande de doce habitaciones. Tenía hermosos pisos de mosaicos y un jardín maravilloso porque allí, como tú sabes, siempre es primavera. Y detrás del armario que estaba en mi dormitorio, había una puerta secreta que daba a una escalera. Un día, mis hermanos y yo la subimos y nos encontramos en el techo.
Miguel:	¿Qué edad tenías entonces, abuela?
Abuela:	¿Qué edad tendría yo? A ver . . . Tendría unos siete años, como tú. Nunca me olvidaré de la vista desde allí: toda la ciudad y los veinte volcanes que la rodean. El Pichincha es uno de los más conocidos. Deberíamos ir a los Mercados de San Roque[2] que están por allí.
Miguel:	Anoche me dijiste que me comprarías un juguete. ¿Recuerdas, abuelita?
Abuela:	Por supuesto. Y también te compraré un santo de madera.

Mamá: A mí me gustaría ver las famosas esculturas de Capiscara.[3]

Papá: Iremos a verlas. Y también querremos visitar esa iglesia colonial que tiene el altar y las paredes totalmente cubiertos de oro. ¿Cómo se llama?

Abuela: Es la Iglesia de la Compañía.[4] Es una maravilla.

Una turista norteamericana interrumpe la conversación

Turista: Perdonen. ¿Saben ustedes por qué el tren marcha ahora más despacio que antes? ¿Habrá algún problema?

Papá: No se preocupe, señora. Es que pronto llegaremos a una sección muy empinada, la Nariz del Diablo[5] y el tren tendrá que subirla poco a poco.

Turista: ¡Ah, qué alivio! Querría hacerles otra pregunta también. ¿Saben algo sobre la ciudad de Riobamba? Unos amigos nos dijeron que podríamos pasar la noche allí.

Mamá: (*leyendo de una guía de turismo*) Aquí dice que Riobamba se encuentra a 138 millas de Quito, a una altura de 9.028 pies sobre el nivel del mar . . .

Abuela: Es una ciudad preciosa, con edificios coloniales. Yo diría que ustedes lo pasarían muy bien allí.

Mamá: ¿De dónde será esa señora?

Abuela: No sé, pero hace un rato hablaba en inglés con otros extranjeros.

Papá: Entonces será inglesa o norteamericana.

El tren se para.

Mamá: ¡Jesús! ¿Qué pasa?

Abuela: Estaremos llegando a la Nariz del Diablo.

Miguel: No tengas miedo, mamá. Si estás nerviosa, la abuela te puede contar un cuento.

mosaicos *tiles*   **santo de madera** *wooden statue of a saint*   **empinada** *steep*

Preguntas

1. ¿Dónde vivía la abuela cuando era niña? 2. ¿Qué había detrás del armario que estaba en su dormitorio? 3. ¿Qué edad tendría cuando subió al techo? 4. ¿Cuántos volcanes rodean a Quito? 5. ¿Qué le comprará la abuela a Miguel en el mercado? 6. ¿Por qué va más despacio el tren en ese momento? 7. ¿Qué le dijeron unos amigos a la turista? 8. ¿Qué información sobre Riobamba encuentra Mamá en su guía? 9. ¿Qué diría la abuela? 10. Según Papá ¿de dónde será la turista?

NOTAS CULTURALES

1. Quito, the capital city of Ecuador (elevation: 9,500 feet), has been aptly called "a great outdoor museum" because of its numerous buildings in the ornate Spanish colonial style. The city was founded in 1534 on the site of the capital of the pre-Inca kingdom of the Scyris, which had fallen to the Incas shortly before the arrival of the Spaniards. Because it is so close to the equator (**ecuador** in Spanish), there is little seasonal variation of temperature.

2. San Roque, a picturesque suburb with narrow streets, is located on the side of the volcano **el Pichincha.** It has frequently been a hideout for revolutionaries. It is now known for many small bazaars where excellent wood carvings and other items can be purchased at low prices.

3. Caspicara is the popular name for Manuel Chili, an eighteenth-century Ecuadorean sculptor who produced religious statues of startling realism. Most of the figures were first carved out of wood, then covered with silver or gold, then painted. The precious metal beneath gave a rich shine to the colors. To endow many of the larger statues with a more life-like appearance, actual human hair, fingernails, and eyelashes were affixed to them.

4. La Iglesia de la Compañía, *the Church of the Company* (the company of Jesus, that is, the Jesuits), is an excellent example of colonial baroque architecture. Built by the Jesuits in the seventeenth century, the church contains a dazzlingly rich interior of gold, red, and white stucco.

5. La Nariz del Diablo (*The Devil's Nose*) is a particularly steep section of the railroad between the coastal city of Guayaquil and Quito. At this point the track ascends one thousand feet through a series of zigzags. The entire trip of 288 miles takes twelve to eighteen hours.

ACTIVIDADES

La Casa y Sus Muebles

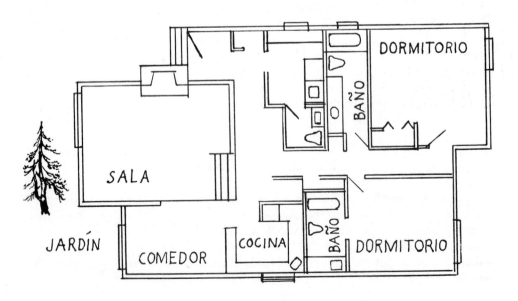

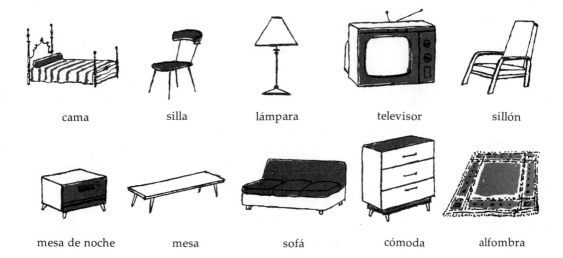

cama   silla   lámpara   televisor   sillón

mesa de noche   mesa   sofá   cómoda   alfombra

If you had just bought the house and furniture above . . .

1. ¿En qué habitación pondría usted el televisor? ¿Por qué?
2. ¿Qué muebles pondría usted en el comedor?
3. ¿Qué muebles pondría usted en los dormitorios?
4. ¿Qué muebles no usaría nunca en la sala?
5. ¿En cuál de los dormitoriós dormiría usted?
6. ¿Cuál de las habitaciones sería su favorita?

¿Dice La Verdad El Vendedor De Propiedades?

Imagine that a Real Estate Agent is trying to sell the house on page 312 to a couple who have three teen-age boys and four-year old twin girls. Tell which parts of his sales pitch seem true and which strike you as lies (*mentiras*) and explain why.

Vendedor:—Señores Smith, pronto entrarán en la casa de sus sueños y verán que esta casa es perfecta para todas sus necesidades. No importa que sólo tenga dos dormitorios. Es mucho mejor para mantener la unidad de la familia. Además, dos baños son un número suficiente para una familia como ustedes. Estoy seguro que no necesitarán más espacio porque la sala es grande. La cocina es pequeña pero esto no es malo sino bueno porque el piso que tendrán que limpiar será más pequeño. Créanme, señores: esta casa es un regalo porque el precio es muy razonable. Cuesta solamente 200.000 dólares.

Entrevista

Ask a classmate the following questions. Then report the information to the class.

1. Cuando puedas ¿comprarás una casa con jardín o prefieres alquilar un apartamento que quede cerca del centro?
2. ¿Preferirías poner en tu sala muebles tradicionales o modernos?
3. Dime cómo será tu «casa ideal».
4. ¿En qué país te gustaría más vivir? ¿Por qué?
5. ¿Cuántos años tendrás en el año 2000? ¿Te gustaría vivir hasta el año 2050?

Situación

Los muebles y la personalidad

Se dice que los muebles revelan la personalidad de la gente que los compra. Abajo hay algunas fotos de diferentes muebles. ¿Qué piensa usted de sus dueños? Usando el futuro de probabilidad, diga dos cosas sobre el dueño de cada mueble.

Modelo: La dueña será una persona vieja, probablemente una maestra.

  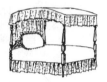 

VOCABULARIO ACTIVO

Verbos útiles

alquilar   *to rent*
dar a   *to face, be facing*
interrumpir   *to interrupt*
limpiar   *to clean*
nacer(zc)   *to be born*
parar(se)   *to stop*
perdonar   *to forgive*
prometer   *to promise*
rodear   *to surround*

La casa

la alfombra   *rug, carpet*
el armario   *armoire, cupboard*
el baño   *bathroom*
la cocina   *kitchen*
la cómoda   *chest of drawers*
el dormitorio   *bedroom*
la escalera   *stairway*
la habitación   *room*
la lámpara   *lamp*
el lavadero   *laundry room*
la pared   *wall*
el patio   *patio*
la sala   *living room*
el sillón   *armchair*
el sofá   *sofa*

el techo   *roof*
el televisor   *television set*

Otras palabras útiles

actual   *current;* **actualmente**   *currently, at present*
ahora mismo   *right away*
cómodo   *comfortable*
la edad   *age;* **¿Qué edad tienes?**   *How old are you?*
la escultura   *sculpture*
el juguete   *toy*
el lugar   *place, spot*
la milla   *mile*
el nivel   *level;* **el nivel del mar**   *sea level*
el, la pariente   *relative*
el parque   *park*
poco a poco   *little by little*
la promesa   *promise*
la propiedad   *property, real estate*
¡Qué alivio!   *What a relief!*
el rato   *short time;* **hace un rato**   *a while ago*
el vendedor (la vendedora)   *salesman (saleswoman)*
el volcán   *volcano*

CAPÍTULO 20

¿QUÉ HAY DE NUEVO?

¡ Últimas noticias !
¡ Llegó Cristóbal Colón a América !

NOVEDADES

OBJECTIVES

LANGUAGE: In this chapter we introduce, discuss, and practice:
1. the uses of **por** and **para**
2. the change of the conjunctions **y** to **e** and **o** to **u**
3. the verb **acabar** (*to finish*), **acabar** + an infinitive (*to have just*) and other idioms with **acabar**
4. verbs that end in **-ucir**

You will also learn vocabulary related to news and the media.

CULTURE: The dialogue takes place in a shop in San Jose, Costa Rica, where the owner is talking about the news of the day with some customers. You will learn something about this Central American country with a high per capita income and a long tradition of democracy.

EXPLICACIÓN

I. POR AND PARA

(1) **Manuel:** *¿Por* qué no prendes la radio *para* escuchar el noticiero?

(2) **Marisa:** Porque tengo que salir inmediatamente *para* llegar al aeropuerto *para* las siete.

(3) **Manuel:** ¿Al aeropuerto? *¿Para* qué quieres ir allí?

(4) **Marisa:** *Para* conocer al diplomático inglés que llega hoy. Quiero hacerle una entrevista *para* publicarla en nuestro periódico universitario. Dicen que *para* un inglés, habla español muy bien.

(5) **Manuel:** Eso dicen . . . ¿Pero no sabías que cambiaron la hora de su llegada? Y ahora no se sabe si llega *por* avión o *por* tren.

(6) **Marisa:** Probablemente eso es lo que te estaba diciendo Carlos *por* teléfono cuando yo llegué, ¿no?

(7) **Manuel:** Exacto. Pero también me contó que el canal seis iba a filmar su llegada y su discurso en la casa presidencial *para* transmitirlos esta noche a las once. ¿Quieres ver ese programa?

(8) **Marisa:** ¡Claro que sí! Pero mientras tanto, ¿qué te parece si salimos a comer algo *para* calmar los ruidos que están transmitiendo nuestros estómagos? . . .

(1) Why don't you turn on the radio to listen to the news broadcast? (2) Because I have to leave immediately to get to the airport by seven. (3) To the airport? What do you want to go there for? (4) To meet the English diplomat who arrives today. I want to have an interview with him to publish it in our university newspaper. They say that for an Englishman, he speaks Spanish very well. (5) That's what they say. . . But didn't you know that they have changed the time of his arrival? And now they don't know whether he's arriving by plane or by train. (6) That's probably what Carlos was telling you on the phone when I arrived, right? (7) Right. But he also told me that channel six was going to film his arrival and his speech at the presidential home to transmit them tonight at eleven. Do you want to see that program? (8) Of course! But meanwhile . . . what do you think about going out to eat something to calm down the noises that our stomachs are transmitting?. . .

1. ¿Por qué Marisa no prende la radio?   **2.** ¿Adónde quiere ir ella? ¿Para qué quiere ir allí?   **3.** ¿Para qué quiere hacerle ella una entrevista al diplomático inglés?   **4.** ¿Habla español él? ¿Lo habla bien o mal?   **5.** ¿Se sabe si él llega por avión o por tren?   **6.** ¿Qué le contó Carlos a Manuel por teléfono?   **7.** ¿Qué quiere hacer Marisa antes de las once? ¿Para qué?   **8.** ¿Habla usted mucho por teléfono con sus amigos? ¿Con quién(es) habla por teléfono?

Por and para each have a wide variety of uses in Spanish. While both prepositions are often translated by *for* in English, there is a great difference in usage between them.

A.   **Por** is generally used to express:

  1. Cause or motive *(because of, on account of, for the sake of).*

Los precios suben por la inflación y la inflación ocurre porque los precios suben. —¡Qué círculo vicioso!	*Prices go up because of inflation, and inflation happens because prices go up. —What a vicious cycle!*
Las noticias son siempre malas: asesinatos, huelgas, secuestros . . . Por eso no las escucho.	*The news is always bad: murders, strikes, kidnappings . . . That's why I don't listen to it.*
Lo hizo por amor.	*He (she) did it for (for the sake of) love.*
¿Por qué apareció José en ese programa de televisión?	*Why did José appear in that television program?*

  2. Duration, length of time.

El periodista irá a Lima por dos semanas.	*The journalist will go to Lima for two weeks.*
Me enteré que por la tarde habrá una demostración en la universidad.	*I found out that in the afternoon there will be a demonstration at the university.*

  3. Exchange *(in exchange for).*

Inés consiguió una docena de huevos por diez pesos.	*Inés got a dozen eggs for (in exchange for) ten pesos.*
Cambiamos nuestro televisor viejo por uno nuevo.	*We exchanged our old television set for a new one.*
Pagué cien pesetas por las tazas.	*I paid a hundred pesetas for the cups.*

  4. *In place of (as a substitute for, on behalf of).*

El secretario dio el discurso por el presidente.	*The secretary gave the talk for (on behalf of) the president.*
Juan está trabajando por Jaime en la farmacia.	*Juan is working for (instead of, as a substitute for) Jaime at the pharmacy.*

5. The equivalent of *through, around, by,* or *along.*

José caminó por la avenida principal. | José walked along the main avenue.

Pasaron por la casa a las ocho. | They came by the house at eight o'clock.

Tomás no podía ver mucho por la ventana. | Tomás couldn't see much through the window.

Se comunicaron por teléfono. | They communicated by telephone (on the telephone).

Transmitieron las noticias por radio. | They transmitted the news by radio.

6. The object of an errand.

Pepito fue a la panadería por pan. | Pepito went to the bakery for bread.

Vendré por ti a las siete. | I'll come for you at seven o'clock.

El reportero vino por una copia del discurso. | The reporter came for a copy of the speech.

7. Number, measure or frequency *(per).*

Venden los huevos por docena. | They sell eggs by the dozen.

Van a ochenta kilómetros por hora. | They are going eighty kilometers per hour.

El canal 9 pasa cuatro telenovelas por día. | Channel 9 shows four soap operas a day.

B. **Para** is generally used to express:

1. Intended recipient *(for someone or something)*

Esto no es para ti sino para Jorge. | This is not for you but for Jorge.

Trabajo para el Canal 2. | I work for Channel 2.

Hizo el reportaje para una estación de radio. | He made the report for a radio station.

2. Direction *(toward)*

Salieron para España ayer. | They left for Spain yesterday.

3. Purpose *(in order to)*

Miramos las noticias para informarnos. | We watch the news to inform ourselves.

Fuimos a Acapulco para entrevistarla. | We went to Acapulco to interview her.

4. Lack of correspondence in an expressed or implied comparison.

Pedrito es muy inteligente para su edad. | Pedrito is very intelligent for his age.

¡Él es muy viejo para ti! | He is very old for you (in comparison)!

5. A specific event or point in time.

Tienen que terminar de filmar la documental para el jueves.	*They have to finish filming the documentary by Thursday.*
Iré a visitarte para Navidad.	*I will visit you for Christmas.*

6. The use for which something is intended.

Esta taza es para café.	*This cup is for coffee.*
Esas cámaras son para la conferencia de prensa.	*Those cameras are for the press conference.*

Ejercicios

A. A journalist is interviewing Mr. Ramos, the Bolivian president's private secretary, at a press conference in Costa Rica. Answer the journalist's questions using **por** with the words in parentheses, as Mr. Ramos would.

Modelo: ¿Por quién vino usted aquí? (el presidente boliviano) **Vine aquí por el presidente boliviano.**

1. ¿Por qué no pudo venir él? (problemas familiares)
2. ¿Cómo llegó usted aquí? (avión)
3. ¿Por cuánto tiempo va a quedarse con nosotros? (una semana)
4. ¿Por qué países piensa pasar antes de volver a Bolivia? (Venezuela y Colombia)
5. ¿Por qué está usted en Costa Rica? (la conferencia de prensa)
6. ¿Por qué canal la van a transmitir? (el canal doce)
7. ¿A qué hora van a transmitir su discurso mañana? (radio a las dos de la tarde)
8. ¿Cómo van a saber los bolivianos los detalles de la conferencia (la prensa, la televisión y la radio)

B. Answer Leonor's questions to her father using **para** with the words in parentheses, as he would. Use pronouns whenever possible.

Modelo: ¿Para qué escuchas todos los noticieros? (informarme de todas las noticias) **Los escucho para informarme de todas las noticias.**

1. ¿Para cuándo tienes que terminar ese artículo? (el lunes)
2. ¿Para qué vas a la casa presidencial? (hacerle un reportaje a un diplomático francés)
3. ¿Para qué periódico te gustaría trabajar? («Noticias de último momento»)
4. ¿Para qué hora dijo abuelita que vendría? (las dos)
5. ¿Para qué viene ella tan temprano? (ver su telenovela favorita)
6. ¿Para dónde tiene que viajar Luis? (Costa Rica)
7. ¿Para qué tiene que estar allí él? (filmar una película documental)
8. ¿Para dónde tienes que ir ahora? (mi trabajo)

C. Give the Spanish equivalent of the following sentences.

1. They did it for love.
2. She got that radio for eighty pesos.
3. Does Mario plan to go to Costa Rica by plane or by bus?
4. This program is not for children; it has too many murders.
5. I'll be home by Christmas.
6. He is very tall for his age.
7. Why aren't we going to the press conference?
8. The president's wife is here for (on behalf of) her husband.
9. Who is the newspaper for?
10. My interview with the English diplomat is going to be transmitted by television.

D. Complete the following sentences with **por** or **para.**

1. Me dio cinco pesos _____ comprar el periódico.
2. Es periodista. _____ eso estuvo en la conferencia de prensa.
3. Ella prendió la radio _____ escuchar el noticiero.
4. Estos dos libros son _____ Jorge.
5. Mamá fue a la panadería _____ pan.
6. Piensan continuar la investigación del secuestro _____ tres semanas más.
7. Vinieron _____ contarnos que había empezado la huelga.
8. Pasamos _____ su casa a las nueve _____ hacerle una entrevista.
9. ¿Cuánto pagó usted _____ la radio que compró _____ Eduardito?
10. _____ llegar a la estación de radio, tienes que pasar _____ el parque y luego caminar tres cuadras _____ la calle Corrientes.

E. Complete the following paragraph with **por** or **para,** as appropriate.

A Ernesto y a Gerardo les gusta hacer planes _____ el futuro. Ernesto sólo tiene siete años pero es muy inteligente _____ su edad. Gerardo es dos años menor y _____ eso todavía no va a la escuela. En este momento los dos niños se están preparando _____ ir a dormir. Sólo les queda media hora _____ hablar porque _____ las nueve tienen que estar en la cama y en silencio. «¿Qué vas a ser cuando seas grande?», le pregunta Gerardo a su hermano. «Voy a ser periodista como papá, _____ entrevistar a personas famosas. Estoy seguro que voy a trabajar _____ un periódico importante como *La nación*.» «Yo prefiero ser reportero, como mamá—dice Gerardo— _____ que mis amigos me vean _____ televisión tres veces _____ semana, como la ven a ella.» Cuando la mamá viene _____ darles las buenas noches, uno de sus hijos le pregunta: «¿Qué es mejor ser _____ viajar por todo el mundo y _____ ganar mucho dinero? ¿periodista o reportero?» Ella piensa _____ unos segundos y luego les responde que _____ ser rico es mejor ser doctor o abogado. «Pero ahora es hora de dormir», les dice, y se acerca _____ darles un beso a cada uno.

Preguntas

1. ¿Viene usted a alguna clase por la mañana? ¿por la tarde? ¿por la noche? **2.** ¿Cuántas veces por semana va usted al laboratorio de lenguas? ¿a la biblioteca? **3.** ¿Estudia usted para periodista? ¿reportero? ¿Para qué estudia usted? **4.** ¿Ha escrito algún artículo para el periódico de su universidad? ¿para el periódico de su escuela secundaria? **5.** ¿Cómo se entera usted de las noticias? ¿por radio? ¿por televisión? ¿por los periódicos? **6.** ¿Para cuándo piensa usted terminar sus estudios? **7.** ¿Ha viajado mucho por avión? ¿por tren? ¿Adónde ha viajado? ¿Por qué países le gustaría viajar en el futuro?

II. THE CHANGE OF THE CONJUNCTIONS **Y** TO **E** AND **O** TO **U**

(1) **Un señor:** ¿Está en casa el señor o la señora González?

(2) **Una niña:** ¿Qué señor y qué señora González? ¿Mis padres o mis tíos Juana **e** Ignacio?

(3) **Un señor:** Unos *u* otros, no me importa.

(4) **Una niña:** Bueno, mamá y papá salieron, y mis tíos están pero hoy no reciben.

(5) **Un señor:** Pues en este caso no deben recibir, sino dar. Vengo por el alquiler.

1. ¿Quiénes están en casa? ¿los padres o los tíos de la niña? **2.** ¿Cómo se llaman sus tíos? **3.** ¿Reciben ellos hoy? **4.** ¿Qué quiere el señor?

(1) Is Mr. or Mrs. González home? (2) Which Mr. and Mrs. González? My parents or my aunt and uncle, Juana and Ignacio? (3) Either one, it doesn't matter to me. (4) Well, Mom and Dad went out, and my aunt and uncle are in, but they're not receiving visitors today. (5) Well, in this case they don't have to receive, but give. I've come for the rent.

A. When the word following the conjunction **y** (*and*) begins with an **i** or **hi**, the **y** is changed to **e**. It does not change if followed by a word beginning with **hie.**

noticias e información	*news and information*
trabajador e inteligente	*hard-working and intelligent*
verano e invierno	*summer and winter*
madera y hierro.	*wood and iron*

B. When the word following the conjunction **o** (*or*) begins with an **o** or **ho**, the **o** is changed to **u**.

diez u once	*ten or eleven*
primavera u otoño	*spring or fall*
plata u oro	*silver or gold*
ayer u hoy	*yesterday or today*

Ejercicios

A. Create new sentences, substituting the words in the lists for those in italics.

1. Carlos e *Inés* han visto el programa.
   a. Roberto **b.** Isabel **c.** Hilda **d.** Ignacio **e.** Teresa

2. Sé que Anita u *Olga* conoce a ese periodista.
   a. Ofelia **b.** Silvia **c.** Óscar **d.** Héctor **e.** Homero

B. Give the Spanish equivalent of the following phrases.

1. reporters and journalists
2. French and Italian
3. mathematics and history
4. father and son
5. radio and television
6. to teach and to inform
7. to live or to die
8. seven or eight
9. woman or man
10. one or another
11. film or book
12. minutes or hours

Preguntas

1. ¿Habla usted español e inglés? ¿francés e italiano? **2.** ¿Ha visitado usted Dinamarca (*Denmark*) u Holanda? ¿España o Portugal? ¿Cuándo? **3.** ¿Era Rembrandt inglés u holandés? ¿Y Van Gogh? **4.** ¿Cree usted que actualmente hay en este país más problemas de desempleo e inflación que en el pasado? ¿de pobreza e ignorancia? ¿Afectan estos problemas más a América Latina que a los Estados Unidos?

III. IDIOMS WITH ACABAR

(1) **César:** *Acabo de escuchar* una noticia muy deprimente, Tulio. Sabes que después de ver la película «Y todo *se acabó*», dos locos que *acababan de verla* mataron a seis personas en la calle.

(2) **Tulio:** ¡Eso es horrible! Pero la culpa la tiene esa película. Tú sabes que *acaba muy mal*, ¿no?

(3) **César:** Sí, lo sé. Lo que más me deprime es que todo eso pasó hace unos veinte minutos. Lo *acaban de transmitir* por radio.

(4) **Tulio:** Todavía no entiendo por qué eso te deprime tanto . . . Hay noticias de ese tipo todos los días . . .

(5) **César:** Es que Elena y yo *acabamos de pasar* por ese cine . . .

(6) **Tulio:** ¡Pero eso en vez de deprimirte tiene que alegrarte! ¡Ustedes todavía están vivos!

(7) **César:** Tienes razón. Vamos a celebrar nuestra suerte *acabando* la botella de whisky que abrimos ayer.

(1) I've just heard a very depressing piece of news, Tulio. You know that after watching the movie "And everything ended", two crazy people who had just seen it killed six people in the street. (2) That's horrible! But the fault lies with the movie. You know that it has a very unhappy ending, right? (3) Yes, I know it. What depresses me the most is that all this happened some twenty minutes ago. They've just transmitted it by radio. (4) I still don't understand why that depresses you so much. . . There is news of that kind every day. . . (5) It's that Elena and I just passed by that movie theater. . . (6) But that has to make you happy instead of depressing you! You are still alive! (7) You are right. Let's celebrate our (good) luck by finishing up the bottle of whisky that we opened yesterday.

1. ¿Qué acaba de escuchar César? **2.** ¿Qué pasó después de terminar la película «Y todo se acabó»? **3.** ¿Por qué cree Tulio que la película tiene la culpa del crimen? **4.** ¿Cuándo pasó todo eso? ¿Lo transmitieron por televisión? **5.** ¿Por qué esta noticia le deprime de manera especial a César? **6.** ¿Cómo van a celebrar el hecho de que aún están vivos él y Elena?

A. **Acabar** means *to end, finish, run out.*

Se nos acabó el tiempo y no pudimos terminar la entrevista.	*We ran out of time and couldn't finish the interview.*

B. **Acabar de** + infinitive in the present tense means *to have just.* In the imperfect, it means *had just.*

Luis acaba de aceptar un trabajo como periodista.	*Luis has just accepted a job as a journalist.*
Acabo de pagar mis impuestos.	*I've just paid my taxes.*
Acabábamos de llegar cuando el reportero entró.	*We had just arrived when the reporter came in.*
Acababan de terminar una película documental sobre los acontecimientos en Nicaragua.	*They had just finished a documentary about the events in Nicaragua.*

C. **Acabar bien (mal)** means *to have a happy (unhappy) ending.*

La película acabó bien.	*The film had a happy ending.*

D. **Acabar por** + infinitive means *to end up (by).*

Acabamos por cambiar el canal.	*We ended up changing the channel.*

Ejercicios

A. Create new sentences, substituting the words in the lists for those in italics.

  1. *Nosotros* acabamos de escuchar las noticias.
     a. yo **b.** Elena y Luis **c.** tú **d.** papá **e.** ustedes
  2. *El presidente* acabó por aceptar la entrevista.
     a. usted **b.** los diplomáticos ingleses **c.** tú **d.** Bernardo y yo **e.** yo

B. Rogelio's father has just arrived home from work and is asking his son a few questions. Answer them affirmatively, as Rogelio would. Use direct object pronouns.

  Modelo: ¿Ya prendieron la radio? (Anita y Pepito) **Sí, Anita y Pepito acaban de prenderla.**

  1. ¿Ya escucharon las noticias? (mamá y yo)
  2. ¿Ya aceptaron el nuevo plan económico? (el presidente)

3. ¿Ya transmitieron la conferencia de prensa? (el canal seis y el canal doce)
4. ¿Ya vieron el programa de las seis? (mamá y Anita)
5. ¿Ya aumentaron los impuestos? (el gobierno)
6. ¿Ya llamaron a la profesora de Anita? (yo)
7. ¿Ya estudiaron sus lecciones? (Pepito y yo)
8. ¿Ya pusieron la mesa (Pepito)

C. Give the Spanish equivalent of the following sentences.

1. The course ended last week.
2. He ended up watching a soap opera.
3. Those reporters had just attended the press conference.
4. I have just heard some very depressing news.
5. They had just talked to the president.
6. The movie we have just seen has a happy ending.
7. The newscast ended at eight.
8. Mary has just read an article about the events in El Salvador.

IV. VERBS ENDING IN -UCIR

(1) **Roberto:** ¿Qué haces, Cecilia? ¿*Traduces* algo?
(2) **Cecilia:** Sí, *traduzco* un artículo de una revista norteamericana sobre las razones más comunes de los accidentes de tránsito. Deberías leerlo; tú *conduces* bastante mal.
(3) **Roberto:** No *conduzco* mal; por lo contrario, *conduzco* muy bien.
(4) **Cecilia:** Entonces, por qué esta mañana señalaste que ibas a doblar a la izquierda y luego doblaste a la derecha?
(5) **Roberto:** Eso no fue porque sea mal conductor—es sólo que nunca aprendí a distinguir entre la izquierda y la derecha.

1. ¿Qué hace Cecilia? **2.** ¿Sobre qué es el artículo que traduce? **3.** Según Roberto, ¿conduce él mal o bien? **4.** ¿Qué hizo Roberto esta mañana? **5.** ¿Por qué lo hizo? ¿Fue porque conduce mal?

(1) What are you doing, Cecilia? Are you translating something? (2) Yes, I'm translating an article from an American magazine about the most common causes of traffic accidents. You should read it; you drive pretty badly. (3) I don't drive badly; on the contrary, I drive very well. (4) Then, how come this morning you signaled you were going to turn left and then you turned right? (5) That wasn't because I'm a bad driver—it's only that I never learned to tell left from right.

A. Verbs that end in **-ucir** have the ending **-zco** in the first-person singular of the present tense. The other present-tense forms are regular.

traducir		**conducir**	
(to translate)		*(to drive, lead, conduct)*	
traduzco	traducimos	conduzco	conducimos
traduces	traducís	conduces	conducís
traduce	traducen	conduce	conducen

Si quieres, te traduzco el reportaje.   *If you want, I'll translate the report for you.*

No tomo sangría porque esta noche conduzco.   *I'm not drinking sangría because tonight I'm driving.*

B. These verbs are also irregular in the preterite.

traducir		**conducir**	
traduje	tradujimos	conduje	condujimos
tradujiste	tradujisteis	condujiste	condujisteis
tradujo	tradujeron	condujo	condujeron

¿Tradujeron esta telenovela al inglés?   *Did they translate this soap opera into English?*

Condujimos a Juárez para filmar una película documental sobre los inmigrantes ilegales.   *We drove to Juarez to film a documentary about illegal immigrants.*

Ejercicios

A. Create new sentences, substituting the words in the lists for those in italics.

1. *José* conduce un coche nuevo.
   a. Eduardo **b.** Irma y yo **c.** ustedes **d.** yo **e.** tú

2. *Nosotros* le traducimos las noticias a papá.
   a. Paco **b.** yo **c.** tú **d.** mi novio **e.** Cristina y Luis

3. *El periodista* lo condujo allí pero *tú* tradujiste su discurso.
   a. yo/Marisa **b.** nosotros/Ana e Isabel **c.** tú/yo **d.** la reportera/Óscar y yo
   e. los muchachos/ustedes

B. Restate, changing the verbs to the singular.

1. Conducen muy bien.
2. Conducimos un auto usado.
3. ¿Traducen ustedes la entrevista con Esteban?
4. Te traducimos el discurso del general Díaz.
5. ¿Adónde la conducen ellos?

C.   Change the verbs in Exercise B to the preterite.

Preguntas

1. ¿Sabe conducir usted? ¿Qué tipo de coche conduce?   **2.** ¿Conducía usted el mismo coche el año pasado?   **3.** ¿Diría usted que los jóvenes conducen mejor que las personas de más edad? ¿Por qué sí o por qué no?   **4.** Cuando usted habla español, ¿traduce literalmente del inglés? ¿Quiere su profesor que traduzca literalmente o que trate de pensar en español? ¿Por qué?

PRIMERO, LAS MALAS NOTICIAS

En un comercio que está en la Avenida Central de San José[1] *de Costa Rica, Carola y el dueño conversan.*

Carola: Acabo de escuchar el noticiero de las nueve. No sé para qué lo escucho. Es deprimente.

Dueño: ¿Te preocupas por las malas noticias?

Carola: ¡Claro! Y todas son malas. Por una u otra razón, parece que todo anda mal en el mundo. O, tal vez, eso lo hacen los periodistas para llamar la atención.

Dueño: ¿Tú prefieres las historias que acaban bien? En ese caso, es mejor que no escuches la radio, ni mires la televisión, ni leas los periódicos. O puedes leer los chistes y mirar las telenovelas.

Carola: No exageres. Es necesario enterarse de lo que ocurre. ¿Qué me dices del nuevo plan económico?

Dueño: Para nosotros, los comerciantes, no será bueno. Por lo que leí, el gobierno va a aumentar los impuestos a las ventas. Entonces, naturalmente, yo tendré que aumentar los precios.

Carola: Y los trabajadores perderemos, como siempre, porque eso aumentará la inflación.

Dueño: Bueno, lo implementarán para marzo. Por seis meses tendremos todavía el plan viejo. En realidad, no entiendo a estas autoridades económicas. ¿No pueden conducir el país como yo conduzco mi negocio?

Entra Estela

Estela: ¡Hola, hola! Buen día. Tengo mucha prisa. Voy por carne al mercado central, pero quería decirles que miren un programa que dan por televisión esta noche. Transmiten desde el Teatro Nacional.[2] Es una adaptación de «Requiem para una monja» de William Faulkner. La misma que yo ahora traduzco para mi clase de inglés. Me voy. ¡Hasta luego!

Carola: ¡Qué muchacha! Siempre pasa por aquí como un ciclón. Y conoce todas las novedades.

Dueño: Es por eso que me gusta. Va de acá para allá y se entera de todo. Además, estudia filosofía e inglés, y tres veces por semana sigue un curso de teatro.

Carola: ¿Sabías que su padre es uno de los candidatos a la Asamblea Legislativa por la provincia de Limón? [3]

Dueño: Sí, leí un discurso suyo en el periódico, pero, para mí, la política es una cuestión para especialistas.

Carola: En algunos aspectos. Para nosotros, en este país que no tiene que gastar en presupuestos militares,[4] las cosas deberían ser diferentes.

Pasa un rato. Entra Estela nuevamente.

Estela: Ya me voy para casa. Compré una carne excelente a tres kilos por cincuenta colones.[5] Pero quería contarles lo que dice la gente por la Avenida Central. Comentan muy preocupados lo que está sucediendo en San Salvador.

Carola: ¿Por qué no lo explicas mejor, para que pueda entenderte?

Estela: Es que no tengo tiempo para eso. Esta tarde te llamo por teléfono y te cuento.

Dueño: Sí, Estela es un ciclón, pero de los que no causan desastres.

---

ventas *sales*   **lo implementarán** *they will put it into effect*   **autoridad** *authority*
monja *nun*   **ciclón** *cyclone*   **Asamblea Legislativa** *Legislative Assembly*   **presupuestos militares** *military budgets*

Preguntas _____

1. ¿Qué acaba de escuchar Carola? ¿Cuál fue su reacción?   **2.** ¿Qué consejo le da el dueño?   **3.** Según el dueño, ¿para quiénes va a ser bueno el nuevo plan económico?

4. ¿Por cuántos meses tendrán todavía el plan viejo? **5.** ¿Qué quiere decirles Estela?
6. ¿Qué opinión tiene el dueño de la política? ¿Está de acuerdo Carola? Y usted ¿está de acuerdo? **7.** ¿Para dónde va Estela? ¿Para qué va a llamar a Carola por teléfono? **8.** ¿Cree usted que es una obligación estar al tanto de las noticias en un país con sistema democrático?

NOTAS CULTURALES

1. San José, the capital city of **Costa Rica,** is situated in a central valley surrounded by high mountains. The city houses the **Universidad de Costa Rica,** one of the most important universities in Latin America.

2. The **Teatro Nacional** building, a Paris Opera-Comique look-alike, was inaugurated in 1897. It is a treasure chest of turn-of-the-century art work. Its marvelously preserved interior glitters with gold, shines with alabaster and sparkles with mirrors. It stages more than 300 performances a year.

3. The **province of Limón** extends along the entire Caribbean coastland of Costa Rica. The capital of the province is the city of Limón, an important port on the Caribbean handling more freight yearly than any other Costa Rican port. There is a narrow-gauge railroad going from San José to Limón (95 miles), which makes 52 stops while rising some 5,000 feet.

4. In Costa Rica, there is no army at all but only a noncoscripted civil guard of 7,000 people that has police duties. The army has been unconstitutional since 1949.

5. The **colón** is the currency of Costa Rica. It is named after Cristóbal Colón (*Christopher Colombus*) and it is worth about $0.12 in U.S. currency.

ACTIVIDADES

El mundo, los acontecimientos y las noticias

una huelga de conductores
de autobús para protestar
por las condiciones de trabajo

hombres pobres
roban una tienda
de comestibles

una manifestación organizada
por estudiantes

una guerra de guerrillas
ha empezado en las montañas
de un país del Tercer
Mundo

el asesinato del dictador
de Isla Chica fue cometido por
unos soldados (*soldiers*)

un gran aumento del
costo de vida

Many say that news reporting is slanted. After reading through the illustrated news items above, answer the following questions.

1. ¿Cuál de los siguientes titulares (*headlines*) corresponde a cada uno de los acontecimientos ilustrados?
2. ¿Puede usted decir, en cada caso, si el/la periodista que lo escribió estaba a favor o en contra del acontecimiento?

Titulares

1. ISLA CHICA LIBERADA POR MILITARES
2. ¿HASTA CUÁNDO VAN A SUBIR LOS PRECIOS?

3. PROTESTA IRRESPONSABLE EN LA UNIVERSIDAD
4. VIOLENCIA EN LAS MONTAÑAS: OTRA VEZ EL DESORDEN
5. 200 EMPLEADOS DEL SERVICIO DE TRANSPORTE FALTAN AL TRABAJO
6. ¡LO HICIERON POR HAMBRE!

Entrevista

Ask a classmate the following questions. Then report the information to the class.

1. ¿Qué tipo de noticias te interesan más: las políticas, las deportivas, las culturales?
2. ¿Lees un periódico todos los días o sólo a veces? ¿Cuál?
3. ¿Cuál de las revistas norteamericanas te gusta más? ¿Por qué?
4. ¿Qué noticias acabas de oír hoy?
5. ¿Cuál de los políticos norteamericanos te parece más interesante e inteligente?
6. ¿Crees que ciertos acontecimientos reciben demasiada atención en los medios (*means*) de comunicación? ¿Cuáles?

Situación

Las noticias de hoy

Imagínese usted que el periódico de esta mañana trae estos titulares:
HUELGA DECLARADA POR PROFESORES DE LA UNIVERSIDAD
PRIMER CONTACTO CON «PERSONAS» DE OTRO PLANETA
TORMENTA (*STORM*) DE NIEVE EN FLORIDA
«ATLANTIS» DESCUBIERTA EN EL CARIBE POR ARQUEÓLOGOS
Un miembro de la clase será el periodista y entrevistará a cinco personas, preguntándoles qué piensan de alguna de las noticias del día. Luego otro periodista preguntará sobre otra noticia, etc.

VOCABULARIO ACTIVO

Verbos útiles

acabar de + inf. *to have just; (imperfect) had just*
aceptar *to accept*
aparecer(zc) *to appear*
comunicarse *to communicate*
conducir(zc) *to drive, conduct*
conseguir(i) *to obtain, get*
conversar *to converse*
cumplir *to fulfill*
enterarse *to find out*
entrevistar *to interview*

exagerar *to exaggerate*
filmar *to film*
informarse *to become informed, inform oneself*
prender *to turn on*
traducir(zc) *to translate*
transmitir *to transmit*

Los medios de comunicación y las noticias

el acontecimiento *event*
el asesinato *assassination, murder*
el aumento *rise, increase*

el canal *channel*
la cuestión *issue, question*
el discurso *speech*
la entrevista *interview*
la estación (de radio, televisión)
  (radio, television) station
la huelga *strike*
el impuesto *tax*
la manifestación *demonstration*
el noticiero *newscast*
la novedad *novelty, something new*
la (película) documental *documentary*
la prensa *press*
la reforma *reform*
el reportaje *report*
el, la reportero *reporter*
el secuestro *kidnapping*
el triunfo *victory, triumph*

Otras palabras útiles

el alquiler *rent*
el conductor (la conductora) *driver*
el, la diplomático *diplomat*
doblar *to turn*
e *(to replace* **y** *before* **i** *or* **hi**) *and*
el kilómetro *kilometer*
mientras tanto *in the meantime*
principal *main*
señalar *to signal*
sino *but, but rather*
la taza *cup*
la telenovela *soap opera*
el tránsito *traffic*
u *(to replace* **o** *before* **o** *or* **ho**) *or*

La Vida Cotidiana

El extranjero que visita un país hispano frecuentemente tiene la impresión de que la gente vive en la calle. El ritmo de vida es muy diferente al norteamericano. Normalmente, *a eso de las ocho* se toma   at about 8:00 un pequeño desayuno que puede ser té o café con leche y pan con mantequilla o mermelada. Después, la gente va a trabajar. Es común que las horas de trabajo sean de nueve a doce y de tres a seis o siete, con una interrupción de tres horas para almorzar y descansar o dormir la siesta. Al mediodía, cuando los trabajadores vuelven a sus casas o van a algún restaurante a comer, las calles *se llenan de* gente,   are filled with y naturalmente la escena se repite a las tres cuando regresan al trabajo. Más tarde, después de salir del trabajo, muchos empleados acostumbran dar un paseo, mirar *vidrieras* o reunirse con algún   store windows amigo a *charlar* y tomar un cafecito antes de volver a casa a cenar.   to chat Después de volver a casa y descansar unos minutos se cena. La cena se sirve generalmente a eso de las diez en España y un poco más temprano, entre las ocho y las nueve, en Hispanoamérica. Después de la cena, las calles se llenan otra vez. Como la gente ha descansado durante el mediodía, no es raro ver familias enteras que van al cine o niños que juegan en la calle *a altas horas de la noche*.   very late at night

En general, la familia es *más unida* y tiene un papel más importante — closer
en la sociedad hispana que en la anglosajona. En la misma casa o
apartamento, con el *matrimonio* y sus hijos, es muy común que vivan — couple
uno o dos abuelos, una tía soltera o algún otro pariente. Aunque
esta numerosa familia no les ofrezca a los esposos mucha oportunidad de comunicación privada, no hay duda de que les ayuda mucho
en el cuidado de los niños y de la casa. *En cuanto* a los abuelos y — as far
personas mayores de esta gran familia, pasan su *vejez* en compañía — older people / old age
de hijos y nietos, bajo el cuidado de *seres queridos*, sin sentir la — loved ones
soledad y el abandono que probablemente sienten *quienes* pasan sus — loneliness / those who
últimos años en «*hogares de ancianos*», lejos de parientes y amigos. — old-age homes

Los varios miembros de la familia pasan mucho tiempo juntos.
Generalmente, tanto el padre como los niños regresan a casa al
mediodía a almorzar. El almuerzo es la comida principal del día y
consta, casi siempre, *de* tres o cuatro platos, incluyendo entre ellos — consists of
una sopa y alguna ensalada. Después, la familia se queda en la mesa
conversando o jugando a las *cartas* o a algún otro juego. Esta cos- — cards
tumbre se llama «sobremesa».

En los pueblos y comunidades pequeñas, la vida de la mujer
todavía *se limita* principalmente a la casa, a los hijos y a un pequeño — is limited
grupo de amigas y parientes. Entre los jóvenes, la separación de los
sexos es aún grande. Como consecuencia, el *noviazgo* avanza lenta-
mente y *según etapas fijadas por la costumbre*. Por lo general, los fu- — according to stages
turos novios se conocen en lugares públicos—la plaza, el mercado, — established by custom
la iglesia, alguna fiesta del pueblo—o en *reuniones* privadas. Las *citas* — get-together / dates
iniciales son generalmente públicas: el «pretendiente» (muchacho

interesado en una muchacha) encuentra «*casualmente*» a la muchacha en la calle o en algún otro lugar público y la acompaña por unas cuadras. Sólo cuando la relación está ya avanzada hacia el matrimonio, el pretendiente visita a su futura esposa en su casa y es recibido allí como novio oficial.

by chance

La situación de los jóvenes que viven en ciudades más grandes es diferente. En ciudades como Buenos Aires, Lima, México o Caracas las escuelas *mixtas* y las universidades han contribuido a *crear un ambiente* de informalidad y mayor libertad en las relaciones entre los sexos. Muy frecuente entre los jóvenes de hoy es formar grupos de amigos y salir a divertirse juntos. Estos grupos tienen un valor social relativamente importante ya que de allí nacen muchos noviazgos.

co-ed / create an atmosphere

Los amigos son una parte importante de la vida hispana. Aunque con los *desconocidos* el hispano *se comporta* con más formalidad que el norteamericano, con los amigos es probable que se comporte con más *intimidad*. Una de las manifestaciones más obvias de esta intimidad es el contacto físico. Es común ver a dos o más muchachas o señoras que van por la calle *tomadas del brazo*. También se puede ver a hombres o muchachos que caminan *abrazados* sin que esto indique ninguna anormalidad.

strangers / conducts himself

intimacy, closeness

arm in arm
with their arms over each other's shoulders

Una costumbre hispana muy extendida es la *tertulia* o reunión *amistosa* donde un grupo de amigos se reúne regularmente por la tarde o por la noche a charlar. A veces juegan a las cartas o al dominó, pero la mayor parte del tiempo la dedican a la conversación, ingrediente básico de toda tertulia.

regular get-together of friends / friendly, of friends

Hoy día muchas costumbres antiguas están cambiando, *sobre todo* en las grandes ciudades. Aquí no hay tiempo para hacer la siesta. En muchos empleos comerciales y públicos existen los *horarios corridos*; entonces, se trabaja de ocho a cuatro o de nueve a cinco y sólo hay una breve interrupción para almorzar. Ahora más mujeres tra-

especially

uninterrupted work schedule

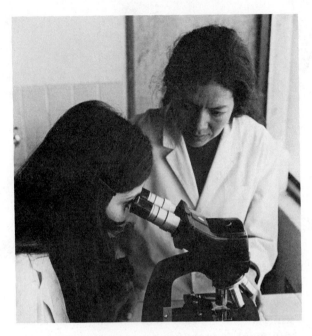

bajan fuera de casa y, como consecuencia, el número de mujeres que
sólo se dedican al *hogar* y a los hijos *está disminuyendo*. Muchos   home / is diminishing
empleados de grandes compañías tienen que mudarse de ciudad con
frecuencia y por eso no les es posible mantener relaciones muy ínti-
mas con los amigos. Por estas razones, hoy día la vida en ciertas
ciudades hispanas—especialmente en ciudades industrializadas como
Buenos Aires o Madrid—tiene mucho en común con ciudades de los
Estados Unidos. Algunos anticipan el día en que las costumbres
serán *las mismas* en todos los centros urbanos del mundo; otros dicen   the same
que ese día no llegará jamás. Pero lo cierto es que si en un país
hispano, uno *se aleja unos cuantos* kilómetros de una gran ciudad,   goes outside / a few
se puede encontrar todavía la rica variedad de costumbres hispanas.

Preguntas

1. ¿Qué impresión tiene frecuentemente el extranjero que visita un país hispano?
2. ¿Qué hacen los empleados después de salir de su trabajo? ¿A qué hora se cena en
España? ¿en Latinoamérica?   **3.** ¿Cuáles son los miembros de la familia, aparte de padres
e hijos, que viven en la misma casa? ¿Qué le parece a usted este modo de vivir?   **4.** ¿De
cuántos platos consta un almuerzo? ¿Cómo llaman el momento de conversación después
de la comida?   **5.** ¿Cuál es la posición de la mujer en los pueblos y ciudades
pequeñas?   **6.** ¿Cómo es la situación de los jóvenes que viven en ciudades grandes?
7. ¿Con quiénes es formal el hispano? ¿Cómo se comporta con los amigos? ¿Cuál es una
de las manifestaciones obvias de la intimidad?   **8.** ¿Qué es la tertulia?   **9.** ¿Por qué están
cambiando las costumbres antiguas en las grandes ciudades? ¿Cuáles son los horarios de
trabajo?   **10.** ¿Cree usted que en el futuro las costumbres serán las mismas en todos los
centros urbanos del mundo? ¿Le gusta esa idea de uniformidad?

COMPRA Y VENTA

—¿Cuánto cuesta?
—¿Y . . . no puede rebajármelo?

—Treinta pesos.
—Este . . . bueno, son cinco pesos.

OBJECTIVES

LANGUAGE: In this chapter we introduce, discuss, and practice:

1. the imperfect subjunctive
2. *if*-clauses
3. the present and past perfect subjunctive, two compound past subjunctive tenses

You will also learn vocabulary related to buying and selling.

CULTURE: The dialogue takes place in a small town in Venezuela. A group of middle-aged people are discussing a recent visit to Caracas, Venezuela's modern and cosmopolitan capital city. In another room their children are also discussing the trip— but with a very different point of view! You will learn something about the city of Caracas and about the changing system of values and social mores in the Hispanic world.

EXPLICACIÓN

I. THE IMPERFECT SUBJUNCTIVE

(1)	**El viejecito:**	¿Dónde has estado, Marta?
(2)	**La viejecita:**	Ana me pidió que *fuera* de compras con ella y la *ayudara* a escoger unos zapatos.
(3)	**El viejecito:**	¿Encontraron algo que les *gustara?*
(4)	**La viejecita:**	No, no compramos nada. Pero vimos a Angelita Pérez, la hija de Ramón y Celia. ¿La recuerdas? Nos sorprendió muchísimo que *estuviera* con un joven y que *se besaran* en público.
(5)	**El viejecito:**	¡No me digas!
(6)	**La viejecita:**	Sí, y eso no es todo. Me pareció extraño que no nos *hablara*—y que *llevara* una falda cortísima.
(7)	**El viejecito:**	¡Los jóvenes de hoy son tan descorteses! Nuestra generación nunca fue así. Pero no sabía que los Pérez permitían que su hija *saliera* con muchachos.
(8)	**La viejecita:**	Dudo que lo sepan. ¡Qué escándalo!

1. ¿Qué le pidió Ana a Marta?   **2.** ¿Por qué no compraron nada?   **3.** ¿A quién vieron ellas? ¿Qué les sorprendió?   **4.** ¿Qué les pareció extraño?   **5.** ¿Qué piensa el viejecito de los jóvenes de hoy? ¿Qué dice de su generación? ¿Y de los Pérez?   **6.** ¿Cree usted que los jóvenes de hoy son realmente más descorteses que los de antes?

A. To form the imperfect subjunctive of *all* verbs, remove the **-ron** ending from the third person plural of the preterite indicative and add the imperfect subjunctive endings: **-ra, -ras, -ra, -ramos, -rais, -ran.** Notice that the **nosotros** form requires a written accent.

(1) Where have you been, Marta? (2) Ana asked me to go shopping with her and help her choose some shoes. (3) Did you find anything you liked? (4) No, we didn't buy anything. But we saw Angelita Pérez, Ramón and Celia's daughter. Do you remember her? We were very surprised that she was with a young man and that they were kissing in public. (5) No! (6) Yes, and that's not all. It seemed strange to me that she didn't speak to us—and that she was wearing a very short skirt. (7) The young people of today are so impolite! Our generation was never like that. But I didn't know the Perezes allowed their daughter to go out with young men. (8) I doubt that they know (about) it. What a scandal!

hablar		comer		vivir	
hablara	habláramos	comiera	comiéramos	viviera	viviéramos
hablaras	hablarais	comieras	comierais	vivieras	vivierais
hablara	hablaran	comiera	comieran	viviera	vivieran

The imperfect subjunctive forms of all stem-changing verbs are regular:

pensar		volver		pedir	
pensara	pensáramos	volviera	volviéramos	pidiera	pidiéramos
pensaras	pensarais	volvieras	volvierais	pidieras	pidierais
pensara	pensaran	volviera	volvieran	pidiera	pidieran

The stems for the imperfect subjunctive of some verbs that have irregular third-person preterites are:

andar	**anduvie-**	poder	**pudie-**
construir	**construye-**	poner	**pusie-**
creer	**creye-**	querer	**quisie-**
dar	**die-**	saber	**supie-**
decir	**dije-**	tener	**tuvie-**
estar	**estuvie-**	traer	**traje-**
haber	**hubie-**	venir	**vinie-**
hacer	**hicie-**	ver	**vie-**
ir, ser	**fue-**		
leer	**leye-**		
morir	**murie-**		

B. The imperfect subjunctive is used in the same cases as the present subjunctive, except that the verb in the main clause is usually in some past tense rather than in the present. Compare the following examples:

No quiero que usted pague la cuenta.	*I don't want you to pay the bill.*
No quería que usted pagara la cuenta.	*I didn't want you to pay the bill.*
Es mejor que ahorres parte de tu salario.	*It's better that you save part of your salary.*
Era mejor que ahorraras parte de tu salario.	*It was better that you saved part of your salary.*
Es importante que no nos equivoquemos.	*It's important that we not make mistakes.*
Era importante que no nos equivocáramos.	*It was important that we not make mistakes.*
El dependiente dice el precio claramente para que los turistas lo puedan entender.	*The salesclerk is saying the price clearly, so the tourists can understand it.*
El dependiente dijo el precio claramente para que los turistas lo pudieran entender.	*The salesclerk said the price clearly so that the tourists could understand it.*

Sometimes the verb in the main clause is in the present, but the imperfect subjunctive is used in the dependent clause to refer to something in the past.

¿Es posible que la casa valiera* tanto?   *Is it possible that the house was worth that much?*

No, no es posible que costara 200.000 pesos.   *No, it's not possible that it cost 200,000 pesos.*

C. The imperfect subjunctive is used in the same cases where the present subjunctive is used.

1. In noun clauses where the main clause expresses will, desire, doubt, emotion, necessity, approval, prohibition, and so forth.

Esperábamos que el precio no subiera.   *We were hoping that the price would not go up.*

El gerente mandó que estuviéramos allí.   *The manager ordered us to be there.*

Dudaba que él tuviera el dinero.   *I doubted that he had the money.*

No creí que su padre fuera tan estricto.   *I didn't believe that their father was so strict.*

Necesitábamos que alguien nos prestara dinero.   *We needed someone to loan us money.*

El comerciante permitió que todos entraran a las nueve.   *The businessman permitted everyone to come in at nine o'clock.*

2. In adjective clauses where the main clause refers to something indefinite or negative.

Buscaba a alguien que supiera regatear.   *I was looking for someone who knew how to bargain.*

No había nadie allí que pudiera hacerlo.   *There was no one there who could do it.*

No vi nada que me gustara y que fuera barato.   *I didn't see anything that I liked and that was inexpensive.*

3. In adverbial clauses with **antes (de) que, a menos que, con tal (de) que, en caso (de) que, para que, sin que,** and with other adverbial conjunctions to express an indefinite time or action.

Le compraron el regalo sin que ella lo supiera.   *They bought the gift without her knowing it.*

Eduardo no iría a menos que la compañía pagara el viaje.   *Eduardo wouldn't go unless the company paid for the trip.*

Hablé con la vendedora antes de que se fuera.   *I spoke with the saleslady before she left.*

4. With certain impersonal expressions which express doubt, emotion, expectation, or personal judgment.

* The verb **valer,** *to be worth,* is conjugated like **salir**—see the appendix.

¿Era verdad que él fuera rico?	*Was it true that he was rich?*
Era importante que volviéramos para el sábado.	*It was important that we return by Saturday.*
Era necesario que usted nos lo dijera.	*It was necessary for you to tell us.*

D. The imperfect subjunctives of **querer** and **deber** are sometimes used to indicate politeness, to soften a statement or question.

Yo quisiera hablar con el gerente.	*I would like to speak to the manager (wish)*
Quiero hablar con el gerente.	*I want to speak to the manager (will).*
Debiéramos esperar.	*We should wait (no strong obligation).*
Debemos esperar.	*We should (must) wait (stronger obligation).*

E. There is an alternate set of endings for the imperfect subjunctive that are often used in Spain and are found in many literary works. These endings are used with the same stem (the third-person plural preterite without the **-ron** ending): **-se, -ses, -se, -semos, -seis, -sen.** You should learn to recognize these forms; they are used just as the other forms are except that they are not used to indicate politeness. The **-ra** forms, however, are preferred for conversation in Latin America.

| Me alegraba de que tú regateases. | *I was happy that you bargained.* |
| Ella tenía miedo de que su esposo comprase el nuevo coche. | *She was afraid her husband would buy the new car.* |

Ejercicios

A. Create new sentences, substituting the words in the lists for those in italics.

1. Querían que *usted* lo comprara.
   a. tú **b.** mis amigos **c.** yo **d.** nosotros **e.** los estudiantes
2. No creí que *tú* vinieras.
   a. Ricardo **b.** tú y tu novio **c.** las chicas **d.** Susana **e.** usted
3. Era importante que *nosotros* lo hiciéramos.
   a. él **b.** ustedes **c.** las maestras **d.** yo **e.** tú
4. Era necesario que *yo* fuera al mercado.
   a. usted **b.** tú **c.** nosotros **d.** ellos **e.** Paco

B. Complete the following sentences with the appropriate imperfect subjunctive forms of the verbs in parentheses.

1. (hacer) ¿Esperaba que Enrique lo _____?
2. (acostarse) ¡Te dije que te _____!

3. (salir) Quería que nosotros _____ temprano.
4. (gustar) Teníamos miedo que a él no le _____ el auto que escogimos.
5. (poder) ¿No había nadie que _____ decirte el precio de la casa?
6. (saber) Fueron al mercado sin que ella lo _____.
7. (ir) Pepe te pidió que _____ de compras con él, ¿no?
8. (estar) Te llamé a la oficina en caso de que todavía _____ allí, pero ya no estabas.

C. Restate the following sentences, using the imperfect subjunctive.

Modelo: Es importante que Ramón venga.   **Era importante que Ramón viniera.**

1. Sus padres no permiten que ella salga sola de noche.
2. No creo que Juan quiera vender sus libros.
3. Es importante que compremos un televisor de buena calidad.
4. ¡No es posible que tú me digas eso!
5. ¿Dudan que el señor García se equivoque?
6. ¿Hay alguien en la clase que sepa escribir latín?
7. Te doy el dinero para que pagues la cuenta.
8. Tengo miedo que no me guste ese mercado.

D. Following the example, combine one item from each of the three columns to form five sentences. Make sure that each sentence makes sense.

Modelo: mi padre (no) quería que   yo   decir la verdad   **Mi padre quería que yo dijera la verdad.**

mi padre (no) quería que	los trabajadores	ser dentista(s)
los profesores (no) querían que	yo	fumar marihuana
mis abuelos (no) querían que	Conchita	pedir mejores salarios
el presidente (no) quería que	los (las) estudiantes	ir de compras con Silvana
los políticos (no) querían que	las mujeres	decir la verdad
	los periódicos	tener más libertad
	mamá	llegar tarde a clase

Preguntas

1. ¿Cuando usted era niño(a), querían sus padres que usted se acostara temprano? ¿que terminara toda la comida de su plato?   2. ¿Le prohibían ellos que fuera al cine a ver películas violentas?   3. ¿Le permitían que organizara fiestas en su casa?   4. ¿Hacía usted muchas cosas sin que sus padres lo supieran? ¿Qué cosas?

II. *IF*-CLAUSES

En el mercado.

(1)	**La señorita:**	¿Cuánto cuesta este poncho, señora?
(2)	**La vendedora:**	Doscientos pesos, señorita. Es de pura lana, sabe . . .
(3)	**La señorita:**	¿Doscientos pesos? No los tengo . . . y si los *tuviera* no lo compraría. ¡Es demasiado caro!
(4)	**La vendedora:**	¿Y si se lo *vendiera* por ciento ochenta?
(5)	**La señorita:**	Pues . . . lo preferiría en otro color.
(6)	**La vendedora:**	Es el último que tengo. Hace sólo unos diez minutos vendí uno rojo muy bonito . . . Pero, llévelo por ciento cincuenta, señorita.
(7)	**La señorita:**	Si me lo *diera* por ciento veinte, lo llevaría.
(8)	**La vendedora:**	Está bien. Se lo doy por ciento veinte.
(9)	**La señorita:**	¡De acuerdo! Muchas gracias.*

1. ¿Cuánto cuesta el poncho?   **2.** ¿Cree la señorita que el poncho es muy caro o muy barato?   **3.** Si ella tuviera doscientos pesos, ¿compraría el poncho?   **4.** Si la señora le vendiera el poncho por ciento ochenta pesos, ¿lo compraría?   **5.** ¿De qué color era el poncho que la señora había vendido unos minutos antes?   **6.** ¿Compraría ella el poncho si la señora se lo diera por ciento veinte pesos?

A. When an *if*-clause expresses a situation that the speaker or writer thinks of as true or definite, or makes a simple assumption, the indicative is used.

Si llueve, Carlos no va de compras.	*If it is raining, Carlos is not going shopping.*
Si llovió ayer, Carlos no fue de compras.	*If it rained yesterday, Carlos didn't go shopping.*
Si Manuel va al mercado, yo voy también.	*If Manuel goes to the market, I will go too.*
Si llegan hoy, vamos al aeropuerto.	*If they arrive today, we'll go to the airport.*

At the Marketplace.
(1) How much is this poncho, ma'am? (2) Two hundred pesos, miss. It's pure wool, you know . . . (3) Two hundred pesos? I don't have them . . . and if I had them I wouldn't buy it. It's too expensive! (4) And if I gave it to you for 180? (5) Well . . . I'd prefer it in another color. (6) It's the last one I have. Just some ten minutes ago I sold a very pretty red one . . . But, take it for 150, miss. (7) If you gave it to me for 120 I would take it. (8) Okay, I'll give it to you for 120. (9) Agreed! Thank you very much.

---

* When shopping at marketplaces **(mercados)** it's common to hear people bargaining **(regateando)** for goods. However, this should never be done in stores where the prices are marked.

B. However, when the *if*-clause expresses something that is hypothetical or contrary to fact and the main clause is in the conditional, the *if*-clause is in the imperfect subjunctive.

Esa cámara es fabulosa; si tuviera dinero, la compraría.
That camera is fabulous; if I had money, I would buy it.

Luis y Mirta irían con nosotros si estuvieran aquí.
Luis and Mirta would go with us if they were here.

Si las frazadas fueran de mejor calidad, las compraríamos.
If the blankets were of better quality, we would buy them.

Si fueras más cuidadoso, no romperías las cosas.
If you were more careful, you would not break things.

C. The expression **como si** (*as if*) implies a hypothetical, or untrue, situation. It requires the imperfect subjunctive.

¡Regateas como si fueras un experto!
You are bargaining as if you were an expert!

Se besaban como si estuvieran solos en el mundo.
They were kissing as if they were alone in the world.

Elena vive como si tuviera una fortuna.
Elena lives as if she had a fortune (were a millionaire).

Ejercicios

A. Create new sentences, substituting the words in the lists for those in italics.

1. Hablas como si (*estar triste*) *estuvieras triste.*
   a. ser un experto   **b.** tener razón   **c.** querer llorar   **d.** leer algo   **e.** saber la respuesta

2. Si *ustedes* llegaran hoy, mañana iríamos a Caracas.
   a. tú   **b.** Alicia   **c.** los muchachos   **d.** nosotros   **e.** mis padres

3. Si *sus amigos* pensaran vivir aquí, no venderían esas cosas.
   a. Marta **b.** nosotros **c.** los Gómez **d.** tu hermano **e.** yo

4. Si el auto no fuera tan caro, *nosotros* lo compraríamos.
   a. yo **b.** Elsa y Carlos **c.** Felipe **d.** ustedes **e.** tú

B.   Complete the sentences with the appropriate form of the verbs in parentheses.

1. (comprar) Si yo tuviera dinero, _____ aquel piano.
2. (poder) Si usted me lo _____ dar por veinte pesos, lo llevaré inmediatamente.
3. (trabajar) Si yo fuera rico, no _____ nunca.
4. (volver) Si Sofía _____ temprano, vamos a ir al mercado.
5. (regresar) Pero si ella _____ tarde, no iríamos de compras.
6. (ser) Si tú _____ más cuidadoso, no perderías tus cosas.
7. (costar) Si ese poncho fuera de pura lana, _____ más.
8. (estar) Si yo pudiera, _____ viajando siempre.
9. (tener) Juana compra ropa como si _____ una fortuna.
10. (ir) Ella dice que si él _____ ella iría también.

C.   Complete the following sentences using your imagination. For example:

Modelo: Si hoy fuera domingo, . . . **Si hoy fuera domingo, no estaríamos en clase.**

1. Si tú no tuvieras dinero, . . .
2. Si ustedes . . . , les dolería la cabeza.
3. Si yo . . . , (yo) viajaría por todo el mundo.
4. Si las mujeres se liberaran (*became liberated*) completamente, los hombres...
5. Si yo fuera hombre (mujer), . . .
6. Si los países ricos dieran toda su riqueza (*wealth*) a los países pobres, . . .

D.   Give the Spanish equivalent of the following sentences.

1. I didn't see anything that I liked.
2. It wasn't true that they wanted to sell their house.
3. If you (*usted*) gave it to me for 100 pesos, I would buy it.
4. If it is raining, Mario is not going to class.
5. What would you (*tú*) do and where would you go if you were rich?

Preguntas

1. Si usted tuviera mucho dinero, ¿qué compraría? **2.** Si pudiera dar un millón de dólares a alguien o a alguna organización, ¿a quién o a qué organización se los daría? ¿Por qué? **3.** Si el médico le dijera que sólo tiene un año de vida, ¿qué haría? **4.** Si estuviera en una isla desierta, ¿con quién le gustaría estar? ¿qué le gustaría hacer? **5.** Si hiciera un viaje por un año y sólo pudiera llevar tres libros, qué libros llevaría?

III. THE PRESENT AND PAST PERFECT SUBJUNCTIVE

En el aeropuerto.

(1) **Tía Sonia:** ¡Hola, José Luis! Espero que *hayas tenido* unas lindas vacaciones.

(2) **José Luis:** Excelentes, tía Sonia. Los países sudamericanos que visité me gustaron muchísimo.

(3) **Tía Sonia:** Me alegro de que *hayas llegado* tan puntualmente.

(4) **José Luis:** Y yo me alegro de que tú *hayas venido* a esperarme. ¿Por qué no está aquí mi querida prima Leticia?

(5) **Tía Sonia:** ¡Leticia y Rubén se casaron la semana pasada! Ellos creían que tú los llamarías . . . Esperaban que ya *hubieras recibido* la carta que te mandaron.

(6) **José Luis:** ¡Pero no he recibido nada! . . . Sin embargo . . . ¡parecería que lo *hubiera adivinado!* Tengo un regalo de bodas fabuloso para ellos . . . una frazada indígena que compré en el Perú.

(7) **Tía Sonia:** ¡Les va a encantar! Ojalá no te *haya costado* muy caro . . .

---

1. ¿Dónde ha estado José Luis? **2.** ¿Quién fue a esperarlo al aeropuerto? ¿Qué le sorprendió a José Luis? ¿Por qué Leticia no había podido ir? **3.** ¿Qué esperaban ella y Rubén? **4.** ¿Tiene José Luis un regalo de bodas para ellos? ¿Qué es?

A. The present perfect subjunctive is formed with the present subjunctive of **haber (haya, hayas, haya, hayamos, hayáis, hayan)** plus a past participle. It is used in a dependent clause that expresses an action that happened (or was supposed to have happened) before the time indicated by the verb in the main clause. Compare the following examples.

Espero que te paguen el sueldo.   *I hope they pay you your salary.*
Espero que te hayan pagado el   *I hope they have paid you your salary.*
    sueldo.

At the airport.
(1) Hi, José Luis! I hope you have had a nice vacation. (2) Fantastic, Aunt Sonia. I very much liked the South American countries that I visited. (3) I'm glad you arrived so punctually. (4) And I'm glad that you have come to wait for me. Why isn't my dear cousin Leticia here? (5) Leticia and Rubén got married last week! They thought that you'd call them . . . They hoped that you had already received the letter that they sent to you. (6) But I haven't received anything! . . . However . . . it would seem as if I had guessed it! I have a fabulous wedding present for them . . . an Indian blanket that I bought in Peru. (7) They are going to love it! I hope it didn't cost you too much . . .

Es probable que no vendan todos los boletos.	*It's probable that they aren't selling all the tickets.*
Es probable que no hayan vendido todos los boletos.	*It's probable that they haven't sold all the tickets.*
Dudo que adivines qué compramos.	*I doubt that you will guess what we bought.*
Dudo que hayas adivinado qué compramos.	*I doubt that you have guessed what we bought.*
Es una lástima que paguen tanto.	*It's a shame they are paying so much.*
Es una lástima que hayan pagado tanto.	*It's a shame they've paid so much.*

B. The past perfect subjunctive is formed with the past subjunctive of **haber (hubiera, hubieras, hubiera, hubiéramos, hubierais, hubieran)** plus a past participle.* Compare the following examples:

Esperaba que rebajaran el precio.	*I was hoping they might lower the price (were going to lower the price).*
Esperaba que hubieran rebajado el precio.	*I was hoping they had lowered the price.*
Ella dudaba que tuvieras tiempo.	*She doubted that you had time.*
Ella dudaba que hubieras tenido tiempo.	*She doubted that you had had time.*
Fue una lástima que José perdiera dinero en el negocio.	*It was a shame that José lost money in the business.*
Fue una lástima que José hubiera perdido dinero en el negocio.	*It was a shame José had lost money in the business.*
Preferiría que él me lo dijera.	*I would prefer that he told it to me.*
Preferiría que él me lo hubiera dicho.	*I would prefer that he had told it to me.*

* The **-iese** variant (**hubiese, hubieses, hubiese, hubiésemos, hubieseis, hubiesen**) is commonly used in Spain, but the **-iera** form is more frequent in Latin America.

Ejercicios

A. Create new sentences, substituting the words in the lists for those in italics.

1. ¿Es posible que *Lidia* ya haya adivinado cuánto pagamos?
   a. los vecinos **b.** el señor Ortiz **c.** tú **d.** su hija **e.** ustedes

2. Isabel dudaba que *Víctor* hubiera vendido eso.
   a. nosotros **b.** yo **c.** los Fernández **d.** tú **e.** Elsa

B. Mrs. Torres has just come back from shopping and is going through her mail when her husband arrives. She tells him the news. Complete Mr. Torres' comments, as in the example.

Modelo: Pamela y Daniel han pagado veinte mil dólares por un auto. **Dudo que ellos hayan pagado veinte mil dólares por un auto.**

1. Yo he ido de compras sola.
   Es una lástima que tú _____.
2. Los Gutiérrez le han vendido su casa a un doctor.
   Es difícil que ellos _____.
3. El precio de la electricidad ha aumentado otra vez.
   No es posible que el precio de la electricidad _____.
4. He pagado doscientos dólares por este poncho.
   Es ridículo que tú _____.
5. Irene todavía no ha recibido nuestra carta.
   Me parece extraño que ella _____.
6. Tú y yo hemos gastado todo tu sueldo de este mes.
   No creo que nosotros _____.

C. María Luisa is telling her friend Martín what had happened in her neighborhood and in her family while she was away at college. She's also commenting to him how she felt about those events at the time. Complete her comments using the past perfect subjunctive, as in the example.

Modelo: Mis mejores amigos se habían divorciado. **Era una lástima que ellos se hubieran divorciado.**

1. Mi hermana se había casado con Jorge.
   Me alegré de que ella _____.
2. Los vecinos habían comprado dos casas en el centro.
   No creía que ellos _____.
3. Luisa había escrito dos novelas buenísimas.
   Me gustó mucho que ella _____.
4. Mis padres habían vendido su viejo Mercedes.
   Era una lástima que ellos _____.
5. Alguien había robado mi bicicleta.
   Me parecía extraño que alguien _____.
6. Yo no había comido carne por más de dos años.
   Parecía imposible que yo _____.

D. Restate the following sentences using the present or the past perfect subjunctive, as in the examples.

> **Modelos:** Espero que ellos reciban mi regalo. **Espero que ellos hayan recibido mi regalo.**
>
> Esperaba que ellos recibieran mi regalo. **Esperaba que ellos hubieran recibido mi regalo.**

1. Es probable que Patricia venga.
2. Fue una lástima que usted no estuviera presente.
3. Miguel espera que lleguen a las seis.
4. Tus padres temían que compraras algo muy caro.
5. No creo que Jorge pueda ir.
6. La vendedora dudaba que nosotros encontráramos un poncho más barato.

Preguntas

1. ¿Es bueno que se haya inventado el automóvil? ¿el televisor? ¿la bomba atómica? ¿Por qué? **2.** ¿Es posible que sus antepasados (*ancestors*) hayan sido más felices sin estas cosas? ¿Por qué? **3.** ¿Cree usted que algunos habitantes de otros planetas hayan visitado la tierra en el pasado? ¿Para qué? **4.** ¿No cree usted que hayamos vivido otra vida antes de la presente? **5.** ¿Preferiría usted que sus padres le hubieran dado otro nombre? ¿Cuál?

DIFERENCIAS ENTRE PADRES E HIJOS

Un matrimonio venezolano de un pueblo pequeño toma café con sus vecinos.

La señora: Coman más arepas,[1] si quieren.

La vecina: Gracias. Están sabrosísimas.

El vecino: No nos han dicho nada de su viaje a Caracas. ¿Qué les pareció la capital?

La señora: ¡Horrible!

El señor: Una gran desilusión. Todo era muy caro y de mala calidad. Además, las cosas tenían precios fijos y no se podía regatear. Nosotros hicimos el viaje principalmente para que los muchachos vieran los sitios importantes: los museos, la casa de Bolívar[2]...

La señora: Pero también vieron otras cosas sin que lo quisiéramos nosotros.

Los vecinos: ¿Qué cosas?

El señor: Fuimos al Parque del Este[3] y vimos novios que se besaban en público como si estuvieran solos en el mundo.

El vecino: ¡Qué escándalo! Si no fuera usted quien me lo cuenta, no lo creería.

El señor: Había muchachos de once o doce años que fumaban en la calle y, si no me equivoco, tomaban drogas.

La señora: ¡Y si hubieran oído las palabrotas que decían!

La vecina: ¡Qué falta de vergüenza!

El señor: Por eso regresamos pronto. Queríamos volver antes de que los muchachos empezaran a imitar las malas costumbres.

La vecina: Pues me alegro que no hayan pasado más tiempo en esa ciudad.

En otra parte de la casa, el hijo de catorce años y la hija de dieciséis toman refrescos con sus amigos.

El amigo:	¿Y el viaje a Caracas? ¿Qué les pareció la ciudad?
El hijo:	¡Fabulosa! Allí todo es muy barato y de buena calidad. En los mercados se venden miles de cosas. El único problema es escoger.
La hija:	Sí, es un sueño. Los jóvenes se visten a la moda y andan con toda libertad.
El hijo:	Los edificios son bellos y modernos.[4] Nos pareció una lástima que ustedes no hubieran venido.
La amiga:	¿Vieron la Rinconada?[5]
El hijo:	Sí, por fuera. Yo quería que entráramos, pero mi padre dijo que no.
La hija:	Es una lástima que no pudiéramos pasar más tiempo en las playas.[6] Conocimos allá a un grupo de jóvenes caraqueños que nos invitaron a una fiesta.
El hijo:	Mientras ellos fueron a comprar unos helados, vino mamá y nos prohibió que aceptáramos la invitación.
El amigo:	¡Qué injusticia!
La hija:	Le pedimos que por lo menos esperara hasta que regresaran los jóvenes. Queríamos explicarles que no podíamos ir y darles las gracias.
El hijo:	Pero mamá insistió en que nos fuéramos inmediatamente.
La amiga:	Es una lástima que ustedes hayan tenido que ir a Caracas con sus padres.
El hijo:	Sí. Si yo pudiera vivir en esa ciudad, sería el muchacho más feliz del mundo.

desilusión *disappointment*   **drogas** *drugs*   **injusticia** *injustice*   **por lo menos** *at least*

Preguntas

1. ¿A qué ciudad viajó el matrimonio venezolano? ¿Para qué hicieron el viaje? **2.** ¿Qué vieron en el Parque del Este? **3.** ¿Por qué querían volver los padres? **4.** ¿Qué les pareció la ciudad a los jóvenes? ¿Por qué les gustó hacer compras allí? **5.** ¿A quiénes conocieron en la playa? **6.** ¿Por qué no aceptaron la invitación que les hicieron? **7.** ¿Cómo se sentiría el hijo si pudiera vivir en Caracas? **8.** ¿Hay muchas diferencias de opinión entre usted y sus padres? ¿Le gustaría a usted viajar con ellos?

NOTAS CULTURALES

1. Arepas, the national bread of Venezuela, are of Indian origin. They are flat cakes made of corn, water, and salt and prepared so that they are crisp on the outside and soft on the inside. They are always served hot and are frequently stuffed with cheese, meat, or other fillings.

2. Caracas is the birthplace of Simón Bolívar, one of South America's greatest heroes, and the site of the Bolívar Museum, which houses his personal effects and documents. Bolívar was born in 1783 and became a major figure in the movement for independence from Spain. He was a brilliant general and a greatly admired politician who dreamed of uniting the countries of South America as one nation. He died brokenhearted in 1830 without realizing his dream.

3. El Parque del Este in Caracas is a large park with artificial lakes, a zoo, playgrounds, and a surrey-topped train. A great variety of orchids can be seen in its gardens, and in its excellent aviary there are specimens of the many tropical birds for which Venezuela is famous, including 120 different types of hummingbirds.

4. Caracas is a city of modern and ultramodern architecture. In the last several decades the government has sponsored many low-rent apartment complexes. The money for such projects comes from Venezuela's oil industry.

5. La Rinconada is one of the world's most luxurious racetracks, complete with escalators, an air-conditioned box for the president, and a swimming pool for the horses.

6. Several beautiful ocean beaches are less than an hour from Caracas by car via **la autopista**/(*freeway*) **Caracas-La Guaira,** one of the most modern highways in the world.

ACTIVIDADES

De compras en el pueblo

En la tienda de ropa
hay blusas, faldas,
pantalones, calcetines

En la tienda de comestibles
hay verduras, carne, queso,
frutas. . . .

En la panadería
hay pan, galletas, bizcochos. . . .

En la farmacia
se venden aspirinas,
medicinas, cosméticos . . .

En la estación de tren
(o autobús) se pueden
comprar boletos

En el banco
se pueden comprar
cheques del viajero,
cambiar dinero . . .

En el mercado
los indios muestran
su artesanía: alfarería,
(pottery), tapices (wall-hangings)

Imagine that you are traveling through South America and have stopped in a small town (*pueblo*). Then answer the following questions in original sentences.

Modelo: —Si usted necesitara un sombrero nuevo ¿adónde iría?
—Si yo necesitara un sombrero nuevo iría a la tienda de ropa.

1. Si usted necesitara comprar unos boletos de autobús ¿adónde iría?
2. Si usted se sintiera mal ¿adónde iría y qué compraría allí?
3. Si usted hubiera ganado 1.000 dólares en la lotería ¿adónde iría a gastarlos?
4. Si usted y sus amigos hicieran planes de ir de picnic al río ¿qué comprarían primero? ¿Dónde?
5. Si usted quisiera comprar muchos regalos para sus parientes ¿adónde iría y qué buscaría allí?
6. Si usted necesitara cambiar un cheque ¿adónde iría?
7. ¿Adónde iría usted si quisiera regatear?

Entrevista

Ask a classmate the following questions. Then report the information to the class.

1. ¿Qué te gustaría comprar si tuvieras mucho dinero?
2. ¿Cuándo regateas el precio de lo que compras?
3. Si hicieras un viaje a Sudamérica, ¿qué cosas te gustaría comprar allá?
4. ¿Te gusta gastar dinero, o prefieres ahorrarlo? ¿Por qué?
5. Si no hubieran inventado el dinero, ¿cómo sería el mundo? ¿Qué diferencias tendría con el mundo que conocemos?

Situación

¡Adivine qué compré!

Un estudiante debe hacer de cuenta (*pretend*) que ha comprado algo en una tienda, y dar un indicio (*clue*) a la clase, diciendo «Acabo de comprar algo y . . .». El resto de la clase tratará de adivinar dónde ha ido y qué ha comprado, usando el presente perfecto del subjuntivo: «Es probable que hayas ido a _____ y que hayas comprado _____.» La primera persona que adivina la respuesta correcta empieza el juego otra vez.

Modelo: A. Acabo de comprar algo y ahora no tengo hambre.
B. Es probable que hayas ido a la tienda de comestibles y que hayas comprado comida.
A. No.
B. Es probable que hayas ido a la panadería y que hayas comprado dulces.
A. Sí.

VOCABULARIO ACTIVO

Verbos útiles

adivinar to guess
ahorrar to save (as money or time)
equivocarse to be mistaken, make a
    mistake
escoger to choose, select
imitar to imitate
inventar to invent
prestar to loan; **pedir prestado** to
    borrow
rebajar to lower
regatear to bargain, haggle over prices
valer to be worth

Compra y venta

barato(a) cheap, inexpensive
la calidad quality
el, la dependiente salesperson, clerk in a
    store
fijo(a) fixed; **precio fijo** fixed price

el salario salary (hourly wage)
el sueldo salary

Otras palabras útiles

cuidadoso(a) careful
descortés impolite
el escándalo scandal
estricto(a) strict
fabuloso(a) fabulous
la frazada blanket
fuera outside: **por fuera** from the
    outside
la generación generation
indígena native, indigenous
la lana wool
la palabrota swearword, bad word
el poncho poncho
¡Qué falta de vergüenza! What
    shamelessness!
el refresco soft drink

CAPÍTULO 22

VALORES MORALES Y RELIGIOSOS

OBJECTIVES

LANGUAGE: In this chapter we introduce, discuss, and practice:

1. the future and conditional perfect tenses (corresponding to *will have* or *would have* + past participle)
2. the sequence of tenses with the subjunctive, a review of when to use each subjunctive tense
3. the passive voice

You will learn vocabulary related to religion and religious values and also some words you might need in a post office when mailing a letter or package.

CULTURE: The dialogue takes place in Guatemala shortly after Easter. An elderly Guatemalan man is receiving some visitors from the United States, and they are discussing religious customs and values. You will learn something about Guatemala and its traditions.

EXPLICACIÓN

I. THE FUTURE AND CONDITIONAL PERFECT

(1) **Pepe:** Te *habrán contado* que Delia se ha ido de viaje . . . ¡La pobre! Creo que todavía no puede aceptar el divorcio de nuestra hija.

(2) **Paco:** ¿No *habrás hecho* mal en dejarla viajar sola?

(3) **Pepe:** Espero que no. ¿Crees que ella ya *habrá llegado* a Montevideo?

(4) **Paco:** Lo dudo, Pepe. Te *habría llamado* desde allí, ¿no?

(5) **Pepe:** Tienes razón. Si hubiera llegado, me *habría llamado* desde el aeropuerto.

(6) **Paco:** No te preocupes. Para el próximo sábado ya *habrá vuelto* y la tendrás contigo otra vez. Pero Delia tiene que comprender que *habría sido* peor para los niños si Lolita y Tomás hubieran seguido juntos.

(7) **Pepe:** Eso mismo se lo *habré dicho* unas cien veces . . . ¡Pero ella está convencida de lo contrario!

---

1. ¿Qué cree Pepe que Delia todavía no puede aceptar?   **2.** ¿Ya habrá llegado a Montevideo?   **3.** ¿Qué habría hecho ella si ya hubiera llegado?   **4.** ¿Habrá vuelto ella a casa para el próximo viernes? ¿Para cuándo habrá vuelto?   **5.** ¿Cree Paco que habría sido mejor para los niños si Lolita y Tomás hubieran seguido juntos?   **6.** En general, si una pareja tiene problemas en su matrimonio, ¿cree usted que los esposos deben tratar de seguir juntos por el bien de sus hijos? ¿Por qué sí o por qué no?

(1) They must have told you Delia has gone traveling. Poor thing! I believe that she still can't accept our daughter's divorce. (2) Might you not have done wrong in letting her travel alone? (3) I hope not. Do you think that she must have already arrived in Montevideo? (4) I doubt it, Pepe. She would have called you from there, right? (5) You are right. If she had arrived, she would have called me from the airport. (6) Don't worry. By next Saturday she will have returned already and you'll have her with you again. But Delia has to understand that it would have been worse for the children if Lolita and Tomás had stayed together. (7) I must have told her that very same thing about one hundred times . . . But she is convinced of the contrary!

A. The future perfect tense is formed with the future tense of the auxiliary verb **haber** plus a past participle. Remember that the past participle always ends in **-o** when used to form a perfect tense.

haber

habré	habremos		
habrás	habréis	+	past participle
habrá	habrán		

It expresses a future action with a past perspective—that is, an action that *will have taken place* (*or may have taken place*) by some future time. It can also express probability, an action that *must have or might have taken place.*

En unos meses habremos celebrado nuestro aniversario de casados.	*In a few months we will have celebrated our wedding anniversary*
Mañana a esta hora me habré ido a la boda de Ana.	*Tomorrow at this time I will have gone to Ana's wedding.*
Para entonces, se habrán puesto de acuerdo, ¿no?	*By then, you will have agreed, won't you?*
¡Habrás estado muy contento!	*You must have been very happy!*
No sé si habrán ido a un consejero matrimonial.	*I don't know whether they might have gone to a marriage counselor.*

B. The conditional perfect tense is formed with the conditional tense of the auxiliary verb **haber** plus a past participle. It often corresponds to the English *would have* plus past participle.

haber

habría	habríamos		
habrías	habríais	+	past participle
habría	habrían		

Habrían dejado de llamar.	*They would have stopped calling.*
¿Qué habría hecho usted?	*What would you have done?*
Habría sido interesante visitar la iglesia.	*It would have been interesting to visit the church.*
El cura habría estado en contra del aborto y del control de la natalidad.	*The priest would have been against abortion and birth control.*

C. The conditional perfect is often used to express something that *would have or might have taken place if.* . . . Such sentences require the use of the past perfect subjunctive in the *if*-clause and the conditional perfect in the main clause.

Si hubiera sabido que querías venir, te habría llamado.	*If I had known you wanted to come, I would have called you.*
¿Cómo habría sido su vida si hubiera nacido en el siglo diecinueve?	*What would your life have been like if you had been born in the nineteenth century?*

Habría celebrado mi cumpleaños si no hubiera celebrado el día de mi santo.	*I would have celebrated my birthday if I hadn't celebrated my saint's day.*

Ejercicios

A. Create new sentences, substituting the words or phrases in the lists for those in italics.

1. Para el lunes, *nosotros* ya habremos dejado de trabajar.
    a. yo   **b.** Claudia   **c.** tú   **d.** los dependientes   **e.** Inés y yo

2. *Marcelo* habrá ido a la iglesia, ¿no?
    a. Elena y Mónica   **b.** Nosotros   **c.** Abuela   **d.** Tú   **e.** Ustedes

3. ¿Qué habría hecho *usted* en esa situación?
    a. tú   **b.** Manuel   **c.** Sandra y yo   **d.** Toño y Paco   **e.** yo

4. *Yo* lo habría llamado si hubiera tenido tiempo.
    a. mi hija y yo   **b.** ustedes   **c.** Miguel   **d.** tú   **e.** nuestros vecinos.

B. It's Easter Sunday (**domingo de Pascua**) of 1981. The Aquinos are enjoying dinner when young Ramón asks, "I wonder what will have happened to all of us by Christmas of 1991." His sister makes the predictions that follow. Form sentences using the future perfect, as she would.

Modelo: tú / terminar tus estudios   **Tú habrás terminado tus estudios.**

1. abuelito / cumplir ochenta años
2. mamá y papá / celebrar su aniversario número veinticinco
3. yo / casarse con Germán
4. él y yo / tener dos o tres hijos
5. yo / graduarse de la universidad.
6. ustedes y yo / pasar juntos otros diez domingos de Pascua
7. tú / comprar tu primer auto
8. abuelito y abuelita / asistir a tu boda y a la mía

C. Had they had more money and/or time to spend as they pleased, here is a list of what each of the Villalbas would have done last year. Form sentences using the conditional perfect, as Mrs. Villalba would when reading her list to her husband.

Modelo: mamá y papá / ir a Antigua en Semana Santa   **Mamá y papá habrían ido a Antigua en Semana Santa.**

1. nosotros / viajar a Europa
2. yo / hacer una fiesta para celebrar nuestro aniversario
3. Susanita / pasar Semana Santa con sus tíos
4. ellos / ver a Ramón.
5. tus padres / venir a visitarnos en las vacaciones
6. mamá / visitar todas las iglesias de México
7. Isabel y Rogelio / hablar con un consejero matrimonial
8. tú y Pedrito / divertirse mucho jugando al fútbol todo el verano

D. Give the Spanish equivalent of the following sentences.

1. Mario is against birth control.
2. The Núñezes will have arrived there by 11:00 p.m.
3. Your grandmother must have been in church.
4. What would you (*usted*) have said to him?
5. If Sonia and Raúl had divorced, their children would have been happier.
6. By 1990 her daughter will have gotten married.
7. If you (*tú*) had read this book, you would have agreed with me.
8. They would have helped us if they could have.

Preguntas

1. ¿Cree que habremos terminado este capítulo para mañana? **2.** ¿Piensa usted que para el año 2000 la religión habrá desaparecido del planeta? ¿que la tercera guerra mundial habrá destruido la tierra? ¿Qué cree usted que habrá pasado en el mundo para ese año? ¿en los Estados Unidos? ¿en su vida personal? **3.** ¿Qué habría hecho usted hoy si no hubiera tenido que venir a clase? **4.** ¿Cómo cree usted que habría sido su vida si hubiera nacido en 1790? ¿en 1865? ¿en 1915? ¿en 1945? **5.** ¿Habría creído usted en Dios si hubiera nacido en España durante la Edad Media (*Middle Ages*)? ¿en qué Dios? ¿Por qué? **6.** ¿Habría sido mejor para el ser humano si no se hubieran inventado las doctrinas religiosas? ¿Por qué?

II. SEQUENCE OF TENSES WITH THE SUBJUNCTIVE

En el correo.

(1)	**El empleado:**	Buenas tardes, señor. *Perdone que lo haya hecho esperar.* ¿En qué puedo servirle?
(2)	**El señor:**	Quiero mandar esta carta certificada.
(3)	**El empleado:**	¿Por correo aéreo?
(4)	**El señor:**	Sí, por favor. *Quiero que llegue lo antes posible.* El próximo lunes es el día del santo de mi hija, y . . .
(5)	**El empleado:**	Pues *si usted quiere que su hija la reciba pronto, sería mejor que la mandara expreso.* Las cartas certificadas a los Estados Unidos tardan unos diez días.
(6)	**El señor:**	*No creí que tardaran tanto.* Entonces *la mandaré expreso para que llegue más rápido.*
(7)	**El empleado:**	Muy bien. Son quince pesos. ¿Algo más, señor?
(8)	**El señor:**	Sí, *un amigo me ha pedido que le compre estampillas navideñas y aerogramas.*
(9)	**El empleado:**	Estampillas, aerogramas y tarjetas postales pueden comprarse en el mostrador de enfrente.
(10)	**El señor:**	Muchas gracias, señor. ¡Y feliz Navidad!

At the Post Office.
(1) Good afternoon, sir. Sorry to have kept you waiting. What can I do for you? (2) I want to send this letter by certified (registered) mail. (3) By air mail? (4) Yes, please. I want it to arrive as soon as possible. Next Monday is my daughter's saint's day, and . . . (5) Well, if you want your daughter to get it soon, it would be better if you sent it by express mail. Registered letters to the United States take about ten days. (6) I didn't think they took so long. Then I'll send it by express mail so that it will get there faster. (7) All right. Fifteen pesos. Anything else, sir? (8) Yes, a friend asked me to buy him Christmas stamps and aerograms. (9) Stamps, aerograms, and post-cards can be bought at the counter across the hall. (10) Thank you very much, sir. And Merry Christmas!

1. ¿Qué quiere el señor? **2.** ¿Por qué quiere mandar la carta por correo aéreo? **3.** ¿Cómo llegaría más rápido? ¿Por qué? **4.** ¿Qué le ha pedido un amigo al señor? **5.** ¿Dónde puede comprar las estampillas y los aerogramas?

A. It is sometimes difficult to know whether to use a present or a past form of the subjunctive. Remember that in sentences requiring the subjunctive, the *present* or the *present perfect subjunctive* is generally used in the dependent clause when the verb in the main clause is:

1. In the present

Ramón quiere que vaya con él a la ceremonia.	*Ramón wants me to go with him to the ceremony.*
Es imposible que el cura haya afirmado que no creía en Dios.	*It is impossible for the priest to have affirmed that he didn't believe in God.*

2. in the present perfect

Ella me ha pedido que le compre unas tarjetas postales.	*She has asked me to buy her some postcards.*

3. in the future

Comeremos aquí después que regresen de la iglesia.	*We'll eat here after they return from church.*
Hablaremos con alguien que haya visto la procesión.	*We will talk with someone who has seen the procession.*

4. a command

Mande la carta tan pronto como pueda.	*Send the letter as soon as you can.*
Tráeme el periódico cuando hayas terminado de leerlo.	*Bring me the newspaper when you have finished reading it.*

In general, a compound tense is used in Spanish in the same way that a compound is used in English, as you can see from the examples. For instance, if you want to say, *I am happy that they are winning,* you would say in Spanish, **Me alegro de que ganen.** If you want to say, *I am happy that they have won,* you would say, **Me alegro de que hayan ganado.**

B. A dependent clause usually takes the *imperfect* or the *past perfect subjunctive* when the verb in the main clause is:

1. in the preterite

Le dije que la mandara por correo aéreo, pero que no la certificara.	*I told her to send it air mail, but not to certify it.*
Dudé que tú te hubieras hecho miembro de esa organización.	*I doubted that you had become a member of that organization.*

2. in the imperfect

Siempre le pedía a su hijo que asistiera a misa.	*She was always asking her son to attend mass.*
Esperaba que me hubieras traído las estampillas.	*I was hoping you had brought me the stamps.*

3. in the past perfect

Su madre no había permitido que nos casáramos por civil.	*His mother had not permitted us to get married in a civil ceremony.*

4. in the conditional

No sabíamos que hubiera existido un templo pagano en ese lugar.	*We didn't know a pagan temple had existed in that place.*
Me sorprendería que estuvieran equivocados.	*It would surprise me if they were wrong.*

Again, a compound subjunctive is used in Spanish when it would be used in English, as you can see from the examples.

Ejercicios

A. Create new sentences, substituting the words in the lists for those in italics and changing the verbs to the imperfect subjunctive as required.

1. *Quiero* que compren estampillas.
   a. quería **b.** les pedí **c.** espero **d.** dudo

2. La *mandarán* hoy para que llegue antes de Navidad.
   a. mandaron **b.** van a mandar **c.** mandan **d.** mandarían

B. Create new sentences, substituting the words in the lists for those in italics and changing the verbs to the past perfect subjunctive as required.

1. *Me alegro* que no te hayas equivocado.
   a. me alegré **b.** no creía **c.** esperaba **d.** es bueno

2. *No es cierto* que Juan haya afirmado eso.
   a. me sorprende **b.** es mejor **c.** era imposible **d.** no esperábamos

C Complete each sentence with the correct form of the verb in parentheses.

1. (ir)
   a. Sería bueno que usted _____ a la iglesia.
   b. Es mejor que usted _____ a la iglesia.
   c. No esperaba que usted _____ a la iglesia.

2. (llegar)
   a. Irán al correo antes de que _____ sus amigos.
   b. Fueron al correo antes de que _____ sus amigos.
   c. Vayan al correo antes de que _____ sus amigos.

3. (creer)
   a. No es necesario que usted _____ que Dios existe.
   b. Me gustaría que usted _____ que Dios existe.
   c. Prefería que usted _____ que Dios existe.

4. (ser)
   a. No creían que el aborto _____ un crimen.
   b. Dudan que el aborto _____ un crimen.
   c. No pensaron que el aborto _____ un crimen.

D.   Give the Spanish equivalent of the following sentences.

   1. Grandma will ask me to go to church with her.
   2. Miguel and Irma divorced before I got married.
   3. Nora and her children will wait here until Pedro returns from the post office.
   4. I have told Luis to send me a postcard from Guatemala.
   5. Were you looking for someone who had been to Antigua?
   6. Lorenzo used to give me stamps without my asking him for them.

Preguntas

1. ¿Espera que alguien le haya escrito hoy? ¿Quién?   **2.** Para que una carta llegue más rápido, ¿cómo hay que mandarla?   **3.** ¿Viviría usted en América del Sur aunque no supiera hablar español? ¿Por qué?   **4.** ¿Negaría usted que la religión fuera más necesaria para los viejos que para los jóvenes? ¿para los pobres que para los ricos? ¿para los enfermos que para los sanos? ¿Por qué?   **5.** ¿Estaría usted a favor o en contra del divorcio si fuera abogado? ¿sacerdote católico? ¿infeliz en su matrimonio? ¿Por qué?   **6.** ¿Votaría usted a favor o en contra del aborto si fuera católico(a)? ¿comunista? ¿doctor(a)? ¿Por qué?

III. THE PASSIVE VOICE

(1) **Enrique:** Si quieres vivir más de cien años, debes dejar de comer carne, Carlos.

(2) **Carlos:** ¡No me pidas lo imposible! Mamá sólo desea que no coma carne durante Semana Santa . . . ¡y ni eso puedo!

(3) **Enrique:** Pues esto de vivir más tiempo lo leí anoche, antes de ir a una cena que *fue organizada* por el Club de los Vegetarianos.

(4) **Carlos:** Claro, eso *fue escrito* por uno de ustedes.

(5) **Enrique:** Estás equivocado. Son dos artículos y *fueron escritos* por dos médicos muy famosos. Te traeré la revista donde *fueron publicados* para que tú también los leas.

---

1. Según Enrique, ¿qué es necesario hacer para vivir más de cien años? **2.** ¿Es eso fácil o difícil para Carlos? **3.** ¿Por quién fue organizada la cena? **4.** ¿Por quiénes fueron escritos los dos artículos? ¿Dónde fueron publicados? **5.** ¿Qué va a hacer Enrique? ¿Para qué?

A. The passive voice is formed as follows:

subject + **ser** + past·participle + **por** + agent

Las catedrales magníficas de Antigua, Guatemala, fueron contruidas en el siglo dieciséis.	*The magnificent cathedrals of Antigua, Guatemala, were built in the sixteenth century.*
Una misa especial fue celebrada ayer.	*A special mass was celebrated yesterday.*
Esa revista es publicada en Madrid.	*That magazine is published in Madrid.*
Ese libro sobre el cristianismo fue escrito por un sacerdote.	*That book about Christianity was written by a priest.*
El aborto y el control de la natalidad han sido condenados por la Iglesia Católica.	*Abortion and birth control have been condemned by the Catholic Church.*

(1) If you want to live for more than a hundred years, you ought to stop eating meat, Carlos. (2) Don't ask the impossible of me! Mom only wants me not to eat meat during Holy Week . . . and I can't even do that! (3) Well, I read this thing about living longer last night, before going to a dinner that was organized by the Vegetarians' Club. (4) Of course—that was written by one of you. (5) You're wrong. It's two articles and they were written by two very famous physicians. I'll bring you the magazine where they were published so that you can read them too.

Notice that the verb **ser** must be in a conjugated form and the past participle must agree with the subject in gender and number. The agent or doer of the action is not always expressed, but when it is, it is generally introduced by the preposition **por**.

The passive voice is used less frequently in Spanish than in English because many sentences that are passive in English are translated in Spanish with the construction **se** plus a verb in the third person (see Chapter 13).

B. Remember that **estar** is used to express or describe a state or condition resulting from an action. This is not the same as the passive voice, which expresses the action itself.

La comida está preparada.	*The food is prepared (ready).*
La comida fue preparada por los miembros de la iglesia.	*The food was prepared by the members of the church.*
Miriam y Fernando están casados.	*Miriam and Fernando are married.*
Miriam y Fernando fueron casados por el cura.	*Miriam and Fernando were married by the priest.*

Ejercicios

A. Create new sentences, substituting the words in the lists for those in italics.

1. *Ese artículo* fue escrito hace dos años.
   a. la composición   **b.** esos cuentos   **c.** este poema   **d.** las cartas
2. *La cena* será organizada por el club estudiantil.
   a. el concierto   **b.** las fiestas   **c.** la excursión   **d.** los bailes
3. Allí *el aborto* es condenado por la sociedad.
   a. la superstición   **b.** el control de la natalidad   **c.** los alcohólicos   **d.** las mujeres divorciadas

B. Doña Rosa's church had a special mass followed by a big party in honor of Father Domínguez, who turned eighty last Sunday. To find out how the members of her church were involved in this celebration, form sentences using the passive voice, as Doña Rosa would. Use the preterite throughout.

Modelo: la misa/celebrar/el Padre Domínguez   **La misa fue celebrada por el Padre Domínguez.**

1. el programa/escribir/varios miembros de la iglesia
2. la fiesta/organizar/el club «Amigos de Cristo»
3. los bizcochos/hacer/doña Catalina
4. el vino/traer/Tomás
5. las bebidas no alcohólicas/comprar/la asociación de padres
6. las piñatas/romper/los niños
7. los miembros del club/ayudar/los sacerdotes
8. la descripción del programa/publicar/el periódico local

C. The dictator of a South American country has just been overthrown. Members of the new government are answering some questions about how certain problems will be dealt with in the future, how they are presently being handled, and how they were dealt with in the past. Complete their answers in the affirmative or negative, as indicated. Use the passive voice in your answers.

Modelos: ¿Se permitirá el aborto?   **Sí, el aborto será permitido.**
¿Se permitía el aborto antes?   **No, el aborto no era permitido antes.**

1. ¿Se prohibe ahora la educación sexual en las escuelas?
   No, _____
2. ¿Se prohibía la educación sexual en las escuelas antes?
   Sí, _____
3. ¿Se ayudará económica y psicológicamente a los alcohólicos?
   Sí, _____
4. ¿Se ayuda económica y psicológicamente a los alcohólicos ahora?
   Sí, _____
5. ¿Se están construyendo muchas escuelas en el campo?
   Sí, _____
6. ¿Se construirán más escuelas en el campo?
   Sí, _____
7. ¿Se permitirá el divorcio?
   Sí, _____
8. ¿Se permitía el divorcio antes?
   No, _____
9. ¿Se practica actualmente el control de la natalidad?
   Sí, _____
10. ¿Se practicará el control de la natalidad en el futuro?
    Sí, _____

D. Give the Spanish equivalent of the following sentences.

1. The party was organized by members of the church.
2. My book was published last year.
3. These short stories were written by a famous writer.
4. The post office is open now.
5. The meat will be bought tomorrow.
6. Those two churches were built before 1850.

Preguntas

1. ¿Cómo se llama su novela favorita? ¿Por quién fue escrita? ¿Recuerda cuándo fue escrita?   2. ¿Por quién fue descubierta América? ¿Por quién(es) fueron conquistados los aztecas? ¿los incas?   3. ¿En qué año fue asesinado John Kennedy? ¿Por quién? ¿Y Abraham Lincoln? ¿Por quién?   4. ¿Cómo es visto el divorcio por la iglesia católica? ¿como un mal necesario o como un pecado (sin) muy grave? ¿Cómo es visto por su familia?

LOS VALORES RELIGIOSOS

Don Pepe, un viudo guatemalteco que vive en la capital,[1] *recibe en su casa a unos amigos de los Estados Unidos.*

Don Pepe: ¡Cómo me alegro de verlos! Tenía miedo de que hubieran perdido el avión.

Leslie: Perdone que hayamos tardado, don Pepe. Nuestras maletas fueron perdidas en el aeropuerto. Si hubiéramos sabido que íbamos a tener que esperar tanto, lo habríamos llamado por teléfono.

Don Pepe: Ustedes se habrán puesto muy nerviosos.

Alan: No tanto como los muchachos que trabajan en el aeropuerto. Las buscaron por todas partes hasta que finalmente fueron encontradas detrás de un mostrador.

Don Pepe: Bueno, siéntense, por favor, y descansen.

Alan: Gracias, don Pepe.

Don Pepe: Pensé en ustedes durante la Semana Santa cuando fui a Antigua.[2] Fue una lástima que no hubieran podido acompañarme.

Leslie: Me imagino que las celebraciones fueron muy pintorescas.

Alan: Hace unos años pasamos la Semana Santa en un pueblo pequeño y allí vimos las ceremonias del Maximón.[3] No he visto jamás una costumbre que me haya fascinado tanto como esa extraña combinación de elementos paganos y cristianos.

Leslie: Pero es triste que los indios sean tan ignorantes, ¿no cree, don Pepe?

Don Pepe: ¿Por qué los llama ignorantes? Ellos creen en el Dios cristiano y en los ídolos antiguos al mismo tiempo. Pero eso no significa para ellos ninguna contradicción. Su religión refleja el doble aspecto de su cultura: lo maya y lo moderno. Después de que hayan visitado Tikal,[(4)] lo comprenderán mejor y quizás nos pongamos de acuerdo.

Alan: Dudo que en eso nos pongamos de acuerdo porque nosotros no creemos en Dios. En el mundo de hoy la religión no es necesaria.

Don Pepe: Eso depende de la cultura. Los indios encuentran en la religión un gran consuelo y una manera de afirmar su identidad cultural.

Leslie: ¿Pero no cree usted que la Iglesia haya hecho mal al prohibir el aborto y el control de la natalidad?

Don Pepe: No. Creo que ha hecho bien. Para mí, el aborto es un verdadero asesinato.

Leslie: Pero el aborto es a veces necesario para la salud física de la mujer.

Alan: Y el control de la natalidad podría evitar el peligro de la explosión demográfica.

Don Pepe: Es posible que los expertos hayan exagerado ese peligro por razones económicas.

Alan: ¿Y el divorcio?

Don Pepe: Hace unos años mi hija quería divorciarse. El sacerdote y yo la convencimos de que esperara. Después ella nos lo agradeció.

Leslie: Pero muchas veces el divorcio es la mejor solución.

Don Pepe: Es siempre difícil para los niños . . . Pero tengo amigos que piensan como ustedes.

Alan: Y nosotros tenemos amigos que piensan como usted. La verdad es que la vida sería muy monótona y aburrida si todos pensáramos igual, ¿no?

Don Pepe: Así es. En esta casa sólo hay una verdad absoluta: que el café de Guatemala es el mejor del mundo. ¿Quieren probarlo ahora?

guatemalteco *From Guatemala* **doble** *double*

Preguntas

1. ¿Qué problema tuvieron Leslie y Alan en el aeropuerto? **2.** ¿Quién fue a Antigua durante la Semana Santa? **3.** ¿Qué fue una lástima, según él? **4.** ¿En qué creen los indios? **5.** ¿Qué encuentran los indios en la religión? **6.** ¿Qué opina don Pepe sobre el aborto? **7.** ¿Quién se quería divorciar? ¿Por qué no lo hizo? **8.** ¿Está usted de acuerdo con Alan en que la explosión demográfica es un peligro? Explique. ¿Qué se debe hacer para controlarla?

NOTAS CULTURALES

1. Guatemala City is the largest city in Central America and the political, social, cultural, and economic heart of Guatemala. Founded in 1776 to replace Antigua, the older capital which had been ruined in an earthquake, Guatemala City itself was subsequently destroyed by earthquakes in 1917 and 1918 and was largely rebuilt.

2. Antigua, founded in 1543, was a city of such splendor that it rivaled Mexico to the north and Lima to the south. In 1717 and 1773 it was leveled by earthquakes. The ruins of the beautiful old convents, churches, and government buildings still stand, only partially restored. During **Semana Santa** (Holy Week, the week before Easter), hundreds of men dress in purple with lances in their hands and saints' pictures over their hearts and march through the decorated streets in a reenactment of Christ's passion. Others march dressed as Roman centurions. Each year three prisoners are released from jail to walk in the procession carrying logs heavy with chains as an act of penitence; then they are given their freedom.

3. The **Maximón** is an idol honored during Holy Week by the Mayan Indian inhabitants of the village of **Santiago Atitlán.** It is composed of many layers of clothing bundled around a mysterious core which may be a Mayan statue; its face in public is a wooden mask which always appears with a large cigar in its mouth. Though prayers and gifts are offered to it, **Maximón** is publicly hanged at the height of the celebration. Later it is brought down and hidden until the next year. Some think there may be a connection between the **Maximón** and the effigies of Judas that are hanged in many towns of Guatemala during Holy Week, except that the **Maximón** is the object of devotion, not derision. The **Maximón** is thought to have been derived from ancient Mayan religious practices.

4. Tikal is a partially restored ancient Mayan city of the classical period located in the **Petén,** the northern area of Guatemala. It florished until around 900 A.D and then it was mysteriously abandoned, as were other great Mayan cities, for unknown reasons.

ACTIVIDADES

La Religión y Los Dichos Populares

Una pausa en la conversación. Nadie sabe qué decir.

Un clima extremo: hace mucho frío o mucho calor.

Alguien estornuda una vez, dos veces, ¡tres veces!

Una persona sufre una gran desilusión.

Alguien que explica con gran autoridad algo, a gente que es especialista en el tema.

Alguien que está en una situación difícil y no sabe cómo salir.

Try to guess which of the following common sayings might be used by Hispanic people for each of the above situations:

1. Seis meses de invierno, seis meses de infierno.
2. Pasó un ángel.
3. Se le cayó el alma a los pies.
4. Jesús . . . María . . . ¡y José!
5. Estaba como el diablo con San Miguel.
6. Enseñar el credo a los apóstoles.

La Religión En El Idioma

To see if your answers are correct, read through the following exercises, filling in the blanks with the appropriate form of the indicated verbs.

Históricamente, los hispanos (*have been considered*-considerar) _____ por el resto del mundo un pueblo muy religioso. Entonces, no es sorprendente que el vocabulario religioso (*have had*-tener) _____ influencia en la lengua y en los dichos (*sayings*) populares. Por ejemplo, el clima de Madrid (*is explained*-explicar) _____ por los españoles como «Seis meses de invierno, seis meses de infierno.» Si alguien estornuda (*sneezes*), es común que otro le diga «Jesús»; pero si la persona hubiera estornudado tres veces, el otro le (*would have said*-decir) _____ «Jesús, María . . . ¡y José!» Cuando hay una pausa en la conversación entre amigos, uno de ellos podrá decir «Pasó un ángel» como si un espíritu del otro mundo (*had caused*-producir) _____ el silencio al pasar.

Con frecuencia, se hace uso de los dichos que tienen referencias religiosas para describir ciertos estados emocionales. Para hablar de un individuo que acaba de sufrir una gran desilusión, se dice que «Se le cayó el alma a los pies,» como si el alma (*were*-ser) _____ una parte visible de su cuerpo. O si una persona se encuentra en una situación muy difícil, se dice que está «como el diablo con San Miguel.» La alusión es a la historia popular del diablo que, en forma de serpiente, (*serpent was crushed*-aplastar) _____ por el pie de San Miguel. A veces, cuando se comenta una fiesta se oye decir que cierto individuo «estaba enseñando el credo a los apóstoles.» Esto significa que fue ridículo que el individuo (*should have talked*-hablar) _____ con tanta autoridad a personas que sabían mucho más que él sobre el tema (*topic*).

Es evidente que sin la influencia religiosa, la lengua de los Hispanos (*would have turned out*-resultar) _____ muy diferente.

Entrevista

Ask a classmate the following questions. Then report the information to the class.

1. ¿Crees que la religión tiene una influencia positiva o negativa en la sociedad de hoy? ¿Por qué?
2. ¿Debería permitirse que los sacerdotes católicos se casaran?
3. ¿Qué tienen en común las principales religiones del mundo? ¿Son un gran consuelo? ¿Cumplen un papel importante en la educación moral de los hijos? ¿Enseñan ideales universales?
4. ¿Es mejor que un matrimonio con hijos no se divorcie bajo ninguna circunstancia? Explica.
5. ¿Eres vegetariano? ¿Crees que es mejor que no comamos carne?

VOCABULARIO ACTIVO

Verbos útiles

afirmar to affirm
certificar to register (mail)
condenar to condemn
construir to build
dejar de + inf. to stop (doing something)
depender de to depend on
enviar to send
evitar to avoid
existir to exist
hacer bien (mal) to do well (badly)
mandar to send
ponerse de acuerdo to agree
reflejar to reflect
tardar to take a long time, delay

Los valores y la religión

el aborto abortion
el alma (f) soul
el ángel angel
el apóstol apostle
la ceremonia ceremony
**el consejero (la consejera)
    matrimonial** marriage counselor
el consuelo consolation
la contradicción contradiction
el control de la natalidad birth control
el credo creed
el cristianismo Christianity
el cura priest
el diablo devil
el dios god

el divorcio divorce
equivocado(a) mistaken
la explosión demográfica population
    explosion
el ídolo idol
el infierno hell
pagano(a) pagan
Pascua Easter
la procesión procession
la religión religion
religioso(a) religious
la Semana Santa Holy Week, Easter week
el viudo (la viuda) widower (widow)

El correo

aéreo(a) air
el aerograma aerogram
certificado(a) registered
el correo post office; mail
expreso express mail, special delivery
la estampilla stamp
la tarjeta postal postcard

Otras palabras útiles

el aniversario anniversary
en contra against
ignorante ignorant
el miembro member
monótono(a) monotonous
el mostrador counter
el peligro danger
pintoresco(a) picturesque

CUARTO REPASO

I. ADDITIONAL TENSES IN SPANISH

A. The following are some additional tenses and forms of Spanish verbs.

1. The progressive

   a. Present progressive (**salir**): **estoy saliendo, estás saliendo, está saliendo, estamos saliendo, estáis saliendo, están saliendo**
   b. Past progressive (**pintar**): **estaba pintando, estabas pintando, estaba pintando, estábamos pintando, estabais pintando, estaban pintando**
   c. Present participles with a stem-change: **diciendo, divirtiendo, pidiendo, prefiriendo, siguiendo, sirviendo, durmiendo, muriendo, pudiendo**

2. The future

   a. Regular **-ar, -er,** and **-ir** verbs (**viajar**): **viajaré, viajarás, viajará, viajaremos, viajaréis, viajarán**
   b. Irregular future stems (with regular future endings): **diré, habré, harás, podrás, pondrá, querrá, sabremos, saldremos, tendréis, valdrán, vendrán**

3. The conditional

   a. Regular **-ar, -er,** and **-ir** verbs (**discutir**): **discutiría, discutirías, discutiría, discutiríamos, discutiríais, discutirían**
   b. Irregular stems (with regular conditional endings): **diría, habría, harías, podrías, pondría, querría, sabríamos, saldríamos, tendríais, valdrían, vendrían**

B. Change the verbs in the following sentences to the tense indicated in parentheses.

(Present progressive)
   1. Escucho las noticias.
   2. Ahora miramos televisión.
   3. ¿Piensas en Juanita?
   4. El canal seis transmite un programa religioso.

(Past progressive)
   5. ¿Escribías una carta?
   6. Mis padres querían ir al correo.
   7. ¿Qué hacían mientras yo leía el periódico?
   8. Probablemente dormíamos, ¿Por qué?

(Future)
9. El abogado y la periodista van a la conferencia de prensa.
10. ¿A quién le hacen la entrevista?
11. Ana y yo vamos de compras esta tarde. ¿Puedes llevarnos en tu coche?
12. Mis abuelos quieren visitar las iglesias más antiguas.

(Conditional)
13. Tenemos que llevar a Andrés al doctor.
14. ¿Dices que el aborto es un verdadero asesinato?
15. ¿Duermen? . . . ¿Por qué no contestan el teléfono?
16. Realmente no puedo pagar tanto por esa casa.

C. Change the following verbs from the present to the future tense.

1. yo soy
2. él sabe
3. nosotros viajamos
4. tú haces
5. ellos traducen
6. ella va
7. nosotros pedimos
8. tú dices
9. yo me levanto
10. él puede

D. Now change these same verbs to the conditional tense.

II. POR AND PARA

A. Review the following uses of **por** and **para**.

1. **Por** is generally used to express:

    a. cause or motive: **Lo hice por ti.**
    b. duration or time: **Duermo por la noche.**
    c. exchange: **Yo no haría ese viaje por nada del mundo.**
    d. equivalent of *through, around, by* or *along*: **Tomás miraba por la ventana.**
    e. object: **Pepito salió por pan.**
    f. equivalent of *per*: **¿Cuánto dinero te pagan por semana?**

2. **Para** is generally used to express:

    a. destination: **He comprado esta planta para mi madre.**
    b. direction: **¿Cuándo sales para Cuernavaca?**
    c. purpose or use: **Este alcohol no es para beber.**
    d. lack of correspondence: **Él es muy joven para ella.**
    e. point in time: **Para el lunes, ya estarán en Nueva York.**

B. Complete the following sentences with either **por** or **para**. State the reasons for your choices.

1. Siempre camino _____ la Avenida Independencia.
2. El arquitecto Ramírez conduce a 70 millas _____ hora.
3. Mamá dice que los chocolates son _____ mí.
4. Me gustaría viajar _____ las montañas de Sudamérica.
5. ¿Es verdad que usted estará en Europa _____ más de dos meses?
6. Fue a la playa _____ tomar sol.
7. ¿_____ qué estás triste?
8. Eduardo fue a la panadería _____ pan.
9. _____ republicano, el senador Díaz es muy liberal.
10. Voy a prender la radio _____ escuchar el noticiero.
11. ¿Cuánto pagaste _____ el poncho que compraste _____ Isabel?
12. Papá dice que _____ 1990 yo ya tendré mi título de oculista.

III. ADDITIONAL TENSES OF THE SUBJUNCTIVE MOOD

A. There are three tenses of the subjunctive mood besides the present: the imperfect, present perfect, and past perfect.

1. The imperfect subjunctive

To form the imperfect subjunctive, drop the **-ron** ending of the third person plural preterite and add the endings **-ra, -ras, -ra, -ramos, -rais, -ran**; (**sentir**): **sintiera, sintieras, sintiera, sintiéramos, sintierais, sintieran**

2. The present perfect subjunctive

To form this tense, combine the verb **haber** in the present subjunctive with the past participle (**tomar**): **haya tomado, hayas tomado, haya tomado, hayamos tomado, hayáis tomado, hayan tomado**

3. The past perfect subjunctive

This tense is formed with the imperfect subjunctive of **haber** and the past participle (**poner**): **hubiera puesto, hubieras puesto, hubiera puesto, hubiéramos puesto, hubierais puesto, hubieran puesto**

B. Complete the sentences following the example, using the tense indicated in parentheses.

Modelo: (Imperfect subjunctive)
Tú conoces a Juan. Quería que   **Quería que tú conocieras a Juan.**

(Present subjunctive)
1. Me lo muestran. Les pido que . . .
2. Abrimos la puerta. Siempre nos mandan que . . .

3. Ella se enoja conmigo. No quiero que . . .
4. Duermo mucho. Dudan que . . .
5. Soy puntual. Tampoco creen que . . .

(Imperfect subjunctive)
6. Los estudiantes imitan a su profesor. Era mejor que . . .
7. Vamos a misa. Mamá insistió en que . . .
8. Tienes que ir de compras con Inés. Fue una lástima que . . .

(Present perfect subjunctive)
9. Tomamos esa decisión. Me alegro que . . .
10. El jefe vuelve a su oficina. No creo que . . .
11. Te sirven un rico tinto. Espero que . . .

(Past perfect subjunctive)
12. No podemos ver el programa. Ana tenía miedo que . . .
13. Tienes fiebre. Yo dudaba que . . .
14. Él te lo dice. ¿Podías creer que . . . ?

IV. SEQUENCE OF TENSES AND *IF* CLAUSES

A. Review eight uses of the subjunctive mood in Spanish.

1. After verbs that express desire, necessity, or approval: **Mamá insistió en que yo fuera con ellos a Caracas.**

2. After verbs that express emotion: **Me alegro que hayan tenido tanto éxito.**

3. After verbs that express doubt or uncertainty: **No creo que Marta esté en casa.**

4. After certain impersonal expressions that express necessity, emotion, or a personal judgment: **No es verdad que Javier sea detective.**

5. In adjective clauses that refer to negative or indefinite nouns or pronouns: **No hay otra ciudad de México que me guste tanto como Morelia.**

6. After certain conjunctions (**antes que, a menos que, con tal (de) que, en caso (de) que, para que, sin que**) in all cases: **Mi tía Elena fue a Madrid sin que nadie lo supiera.**

7. **After certain conjunctions when referring to an indefinite time or to a time in the future. These conjunctions are: aunque, como, cuando, después (de) que, donde, adonde, en cuanto, hasta que, luego que, mientras (que), tan pronto como: Tan pronto como termine aquí, te llamaré.**

8. The imperfect or past perfect subjunctive is used in *if*-clauses that are hypothetical or contrary-to-fact, when the main clause is in the conditional or conditional perfect: **Si pudiéramos quedarnos aquí, nos invitarían a la fiesta. Si hubiéramos podido quedarnos, nos habrían invitado a la fiesta.**

B. Complete the following sentences with the indicative or the subjunctive, as required. If the subjunctive is required, state which one of the eight preceding uses of the subjunctive the sentence exemplifies.

(Present indicative or present subjunctive)

1. Necesito que tú me (traer) _____ leche del mercado.
2. Me dicen que el profesor de historia (estar) _____ en México.
3. Se cree que esta costumbre (venir) _____ de la época de los aztecas.
4. Es ridículo que usteden (perder) _____ el tiempo así.
5. Sé que nosotros (ir) _____ a tener que vender la casa.
6. Cuando el señor Álvarez nos (quitar) _____ el rancho, no tendremos nada.
7. Si los compadres (venir) _____ a vivir con nosotros, la vida será más fácil para todos.
8. No creo que mi hermano (querer) _____ casarse todavía.

(Past indicative or imperfect subjunctive)

9. En cuanto su marido (saber) _____ la noticia, se alegró mucho.
10. Si tú (tener) _____ dinero, ¿qué harías?
11. Olga se encontró con una persona que la (tratar) _____ muy bien.
12. Las chicas van a pasar por casa para que yo (ir) _____ de compras con ellas.
13. No vi a ninguna joven que (llevar) _____ ropa decente.
14. Tenía miedo que ellos (perder) _____ el avión.
15. Yo ya sabía que ustedes (ir) _____ a tener ese problema.

V. QUESTIONS FOR CONVERSATION

1. ¿Qué piensas hacer cuando terminen las clases? ¿Por qué? ¿Qué es lo más interesante de la vida de estudiante? ¿de las clases de español? ¿Qué es lo más atractivo de las vacaciones?
2. ¿Qué te gustaría ser en el futuro? ¿Por qué? ¿Te gustaría que tu esposo(a) fuera alguien muy conocido(a) o preferirías que él (ella) se dedicara totalmente a la familia? Por qué?
3. Si tuvieras que escoger entre la vida en Caracas o en un rancho de la costa del Caribe, ¿cuál escogerías? ¿Por qué?
4. Los habitantes de Caracas se llaman «caraqueños». ¿Cómo se llaman las siguientes personas?:
   a. los antiguos «cowboys» de Argentina
   b. la persona mezcla de europeo y de indio
   c. los habitantes de Puerto Rico
   d. los habitantes de Venezuela
5. ¿Es necesaria la religión en el mundo de hoy? ¿Por qué sí o por qué no? ¿Era más necesaria en el pasado? ¿Por qué?

VI. SUPPLEMENTARY TRANSLATION EXERCISE

1. The Garcías will buy the house that has five bedrooms and three bathrooms. Would you (*tú*) buy such a big and expensive house?
2. I wasn't asleep . . . I was thinking with my eyes shut.
3. Mr. Álvarez wants us to work for him on his ranch.
4. If you (*usted*) listened to the news, you would know who is winning and who is losing.
5. We saw couples who were kissing as if it were the end of the world.
6. I wanted for us to go in, but my father told us to stay outside.
7. If they had looked for the suitcases behind the counter, they'd have found them right there.
8. I hope you haven't become nervous because of these sentences.

APPENDIX

IRREGULAR, ORTHOGRAPHIC, AND STEM-CHANGING VERBS

(The numbers refer to verbs conjugated in the charts on pages 434–445.)

acostar(se) o>ue
  (*see* contar)
analizar z>c[1]
andar (1)
almorzar o>ue; z>c[1]
  (*see* contar)
atacar c>qu[2]
atender e>ie
  (*see* perder)
buscar c>qu[2]
cerrar e>ie
  (*see* pensar)
comenzar e>ie; z>c[1]
  (*see* pensar)
conducir (2) c>zc, j
conocer (3) c>zc
construir i>y[3]
contar (4) o>ue
costar o>ue
  (*see* contar)
creer (5)
criticar c>qu[2]
dar (6)
decir (7)
defender e>ie
  (*see* perder)
despertar e>ie
  (*see* pensar)
destruir i>y[3]

divertirse e>ie, i
  (*see* sentir)
doler o>ue
  (*see* volver)
dormir (8) o>ue, u
empezar e>ie, z>c[1]
  (*see* pensar)
encontrar o>ue
  (*see* contar)
entender e>ie
  (*see* perder)
establecer c>zc
  (*see* conocer)
estar (9)
extender e>ie
  (*see* perder)
haber (10)
hacer (11)
herir e>ie; e>i
  (*see* sentir)
ir (12)
jugar (13)
leer i>y[4]
llegar g>gu[5]
llover o>ue
  (*see* volver)
mantener
  (*see* tener)

mentir e>ie, i
  (*see* sentir)
morir o>ue, u
  (*see* dormir)
obtener
  (*see* tener)
oír (14)
oponer(se)
  (*see* poner)
pagar g>gu[5]
parecer c>zc
  (*see* conocer)
pedir (15) e>i
pensar (16) e>ie
perder (17) e>ie
poder (18)
poner (19)
preferir e>ie, i
  (*see* sentir)
probar o>ue
  (*see* contar)
provocar c>qu[2]
querer (20)
recordar o>ue
  (*see* contar)
repetir e>i
  (*see* pedir)
rezar z>c[1]

resolver o>ue
  (*see* volver)
rogar o>ue; g>gu[5]
  (*see* contar)
saber (21)
salir (22)
seguir e>i; gu>g[6]
  (*see* pedir)
sembrar e>ie
  (*see* pensar)
sentar(se) e>ie
  (*see* pensar)
sentir(se) (23) e>ie, i
ser (24)
servir e>i
  (*see* pedir)
tener (25)
teñir e>i
  (*see* pedir)
tocar c>qu[2]
traducir c>zc, j
  (*see* conducir)
traer (26)
valer (27)
venir (28)
ver (29)
vestir(se) e>i
  (*see* pedir)
volver (30) o>ue

---

[1] In verbs ending in **-zar** the **z** changes to **c** before an **e: analicé, almorcé, comencé, empecé, recé.**

[2] In verbs ending in **-car** the **c** changes to **qu** before an **e: ataqué, busqué, critiqué, provoqué, toqué.**

[3] In **construir** and **destruir** a **y** is inserted before any ending that does not begin with **i: construyo, destruyo,** etc. An **i** changes to **y** between two vowels: **construyó, destruyó.**

[4] The **i** changes to **y** between two vowels: **leyó, leyeron.**

[5] In verbs ending in **-gar** the **g** changes to **gu** before an **e: llegué, pagué, rogué.**

[6] In verbs ending in **-guir** the **gu** changes to **g** before **a** and **o: sigo, siga.**

REGULAR VERBS

Simple tenses

Infinitive	Indicative				
	Present	Imperfect	Preterite	Future	Conditional
hablar	hablo	hablaba	hablé	hablaré	hablaría
	hablas	hablabas	hablaste	hablarás	hablarías
	habla	hablaba	habló	hablará	hablaría
	hablamos	hablábamos	hablamos	hablaremos	hablaríamos
	habláis	hablabais	hablasteis	hablaréis	hablaríais
	hablan	hablaban	hablaron	hablarán	hablarían
comer	como	comía	comí	comeré	comería
	comes	comías	comiste	comerás	comerías
	come	comía	comió	comerá	comería
	comemos	comíamos	comimos	comeremos	comeríamos
	coméis	comíais	comisteis	comeréis	comeríais
	comen	comían	comieron	comerán	comerían
vivir	vivo	vivía	viví	viviré	viviría
	vives	vivías	viviste	vivirás	vivirías
	vive	vivía	vivió	vivirá	viviría
	vivimos	vivíamos	vivimos	viviremos	viviríamos
	vivís	vivíais	vivisteis	viviréis	viviríais
	viven	vivían	vivieron	vivirán	vivirían

Perfect tenses

Past Participle	Indicative			
	Present perfect	Past perfect	Future perfect	Conditional perfect
hablado	he hablado	había hablado	habré hablado	habría hablado
	has hablado	habías hablado	habrás hablado	habrías hablado
	ha hablado	había hablado	habrá hablado	habría hablado
	hemos hablado	habíamos hablado	habremos hablado	habríamos hablado
	habéis hablado	habíais hablado	habréis hablado	habríais hablado
	han hablado	habían hablado	habrán hablado	habrían hablado
comido	he comido	había comido	habré comido	habría comido
	has comido	habías comido	habrás comido	habrías comido
	ha comido	había comido	habrá comido	habría comido
	hemos comido	habíamos comido	habremos comido	habríamos comido
	habéis comido	habíais comido	habréis comido	habríais comido
	han comido	habían comido	habrán comido	habrían comido

Simple tenses

	Subjunctive		Commands
Present	**Imperfect**		
hable	hablara (-se)		—
hables	hablaras (-ses)		habla (no hables)
hable	hablara (-se)		hable
hablemos	habláramos (-semos)		hablemos
habléis	hablarais (-seis)		hablad (no habléis)
hablen	hablaran (-sen)		hablen
coma	comiera (-se)		—
comas	comieras (-ses)		come (no comas)
coma	comiera (-se)		coma
comamos	comiéramos (-semos)		comamos
comáis	comierais (-seis)		comed (no comáis)
coman	comieran (-sen)		coman
viva	viviera (-se)		—
vivas	vivieras (-ses)		vive (no vivas)
viva	viviera (-se)		viva
vivamos	viviéramos (-semos)		vivamos
viváis	vivierais (-seis)		vivid (no viváis)
vivan	vivieran (-sen)		vivan

Perfect tenses

Subjunctive	
Present perfect	**Past perfect**
haya hablado	hubiera (-se) hablado
hayas hablado	hubieras (-ses) hablado
haya hablado	hubiera (-se) hablado
hayamos hablado	hubiéramos (-semos) hablado
hayáis hablado	hubierais (-seis) hablado
hayan hablado	hubieran (-sen) hablado
haya comido	hubiera (-se) comido
hayas comido	hubieras (-ses) comido
haya comido	hubiera (-se) comido
hayamos comido	hubiéramos (-semos) comido
hayáis comido	hubierais (-seis) comido
hayan comido	hubieran (-sen) comido

Perfect tenses

Past Participle	Indicative			
	Present perfect	Past perfect	Future perfect	Conditional perfect
vivido	he vivido	había vivido	habré vivido	habría vivido
	has vivido	habías vivido	habrás vivido	habrías vivido
	ha vivido	había vivido	habrá vivido	habría vivido
	hemos vivido	habíamos vivido	habremos vivido	habríamos vivido
	habéis vivido	habíais vivido	habréis vivido	habríais vivido
	han vivido	habían vivido	habrán vivido	habrían vivido

Progressive tenses

Present Participle	Indicative		Present Participle	
	Present progressive	Past progressive		Present
hablando	estoy hablando	estaba hablando	comiendo	estoy comiendo
	estás hablando	estabas hablando		estás comiendo
	está hablando	estaba hablando		está comiendo
	estamos hablando	estábamos hablando		estamos comiendo
	estáis hablando	estabais hablando		estáis comiendo
	están hablando	estaban hablando		están comiendo

IRREGULAR VERBS

Infinitive	Indicative				
	Present	Imperfect	Preterite	Future	Conditional
1. **andar**	ando	andaba	anduve	andaré	andaría
	andas	andabas	anduviste	andarás	andarías
	anda	andaba	anduvo	andará	andaría
	andamos	andábamos	anduvimos	andaremos	andaríamos
	andáis	andabais	anduvisteis	andaréis	andaríais
	andan	andaban	anduvieron	andarán	andarían
2. **conducir**	conduzco	conducía	conduje	conduciré	conduciría
	conduces	conducías	condujiste	conducirás	conducirías
	conduce	conducía	condujo	conducirá	conduciría
	conducimos	conducíamos	condujimos	conduciremos	conduciríamos
	conducís	conducíais	condujisteis	conduciréis	conduciríais
	conducen	conducían	condujeron	conducirán	conducirían

Perfect tenses

Subjunctive

Present perfect	Past perfect
haya vivido	hubiera (-se) vivido
hayas vivido	hubieras (-ses) vivido
haya vivido	hubiera (-se) vivido
hayamos vivido	hubiéramos (-semos) vivido
hayáis vivido	hubierais (-seis) vivido
hayan vivido	hubieran (-sen) vivido

Progressive tenses

Past	Present Participle	Indicative Present	Past
estaba comiendo	viviendo	estoy viviendo	estaba viviendo
estabas comiendo		estás viviendo	estaba viviendo
estaba comiendo		está viviendo	estaba viviendo
estábamos comiendo		estamos viviendo	estábamos viviendo
estábais comiendo		estáis viviendo	estábais viviendo
estaban comiendo		están viviendo	estaban viviendo

Subjunctive Present	Imperfect	Commands	Participles Present	Past
ande	anduviera (-se)	—	andando	andado
andes	anduvieras (-ses)	anda (no andes)		
ande	anduviera (-se)	ande		
andemos	anduviéramos (-semos)	andemos		
andéis	anduviérais (-seis)	andad (no andéis)		
anden	anduvieran (-sen)	anden		
conduzca	condujera (-se)	—	conduciendo	conducido
conduzcas	condujeras (-ses)	conduce (no conduzcas)		
conduzca	condujera (-se)	conduzca		
conduzcamos	condujéramos (-semos)	conduzcamos		
conduzcáis	condujerais (-seis)	conducid (no conduzcáis)		
conduzcan	condujeran (-sen)	conduzcan		

Infinitive	Indicative				
	Present	Imperfect	Preterite	Future	Conditional
3. **conocer**	conozco	conocía	conocí	conoceré	conocería
	conoces	conocías	conociste	conocerás	conocerías
	conoce	conocía	conoció	conocerá	conocería
	conocemos	conocíamos	conocimos	conoceremos	conoceríamos
	conocéis	conocíais	conocisteis	conoceréis	conoceríais
	conocen	conocían	conocieron	conocerán	conocerían
4. **contar**	cuento	contaba	conté	contaré	contaría
	cuentas	contabas	contaste	contarás	contarías
	cuenta	contaba	contó	contará	contaría
	contamos	contábamos	contamos	contaremos	contaríamos
	contáis	contabais	contasteis	contaréis	contaríais
	cuentan	contaban	contaron	contarán	contarían
5. **creer**	creo	creía	creí	creeré	creería
	crees	creías	creíste	creerás	creerías
	cree	creía	creyó	creerá	creería
	creemos	creíamos	creímos	creeremos	creeríamos
	creéis	creíais	creísteis	creeréis	creeríais
	creen	creían	creyeron	creerán	creerían
6. **dar**	doy	daba	di	daré	daría
	das	dabas	diste	darás	darías
	da	daba	dio	dará	daría
	damos	dábamos	dimos	daremos	daríamos
	dais	dabais	disteis	daréis	daríais
	dan	daban	dieron	darán	darían
7. **decir**	digo	decía	dije	diré	diría
	dices	decías	dijiste	dirás	dirías
	dice	decía	dijo	dirá	diría
	decimos	decíamos	dijimos	diremos	diríamos
	decís	decíais	dijisteis	diréis	diríais
	dicen	decían	dijeron	dirán	dirían
8. **dormir**	duermo	dormía	dormí	dormiré	dormiría
	duermes	dormías	dormiste	dormirás	dormirías
	duerme	dormía	durmió	dormirá	dormiría
	dormimos	dormíamos	dormimos	dormiremos	dormiríamos
	dormís	dormíais	dormisteis	dormiréis	dormiríais
	duermen	dormían	durmieron	dormirán	dormirían

	Subjunctive	Commands		Participles	
Present	Imperfect			Present	Past
conozca	conociera (-se)	—		conociendo	conocido
conozcas	conocieras (-ses)	conoce (no conozcas)			
conozca	conociera (-se)	conozca			
conozcamos	conociéramos (-semos)	conozcamos			
conozcáis	conocierais (-seis)	conoced (no conozcáis)			
conozcan	conocieran (-sen)	conozcan			
cuente	contara (-se)	—		contando	contado
cuentes	contaras (-ses)	cuenta (no cuentes)			
cuente	contara (-se)	cuente			
contemos	contáramos (-semos)	contemos			
contéis	contarais (-semos)	contad (no contéis)			
cuenten	contaran (-sen)	cuenten			
crea	creyera (-se)	—		creyendo	creído
creas	creyeras (-ses)	cree (no creas)			
crea	creyera (-se)	crea			
creamos	creyéramos (-semos)	creamos			
creáis	creyerais (-seis)	creed (no creáis)			
crean	creveran (-sen)	crean			
dé	diera (-se)	—		dando	dado
des	dieras (-ses)	da (no des)			
dé	diera (-se)	dé			
demos	diéramos (-semos)	demos			
deis	dierais (-seis)	dad (no deis)			
den	dieran (-sen)	den			
diga	dijera (-se)	—		diciendo	dicho
digas	dijeras (-ses)	di (no digas)			
diga	dijera (-se)	diga			
digamos	dijéramos (-semos)	diga			
digáis	dijerais (-seis)	decid (no digáis)			
digan	dijeran (-sen)	digan			
duerma	durmiera (-se)	—		durmiendo	dormido
duermas	durmieras (-ses)	duerme (no duermas)			
duerma	durmiera (-se)	duerma			
durmamos	durmiéramos (-semos)	durmamos			
durmáis	durmierais (-seis)	dormid (no durmáis)			
duerman	durmieran (-sen)	duerman			

Infinitive	Indicative				
	Present	Imperfect	Preterite	Future	Conditional
9. **estar**	estoy	estaba	estuve	estaré	estaría
	estás	estabas	estuviste	estarás	estarías
	está	estaba	estuvo	estará	estaría
	estamos	estábamos	estuvimos	estaremos	estaríamos
	estáis	estabais	estuvisteis	estaréis	estaríais
	están	estaban	estuvieron	estarán	estarían
10. **haber**	he	había	hube	habré	habría
	has	habías	hubiste	habrás	habrías
	ha	había	hubo	habrá	habría
	hemos	habíamos	hubimos	habremos	habríamos
	habéis	habíais	hubisteis	habréis	habríais
	han	habían	hubieron	habrán	habrían
11. **hacer**	hago	hacía	hice	haré	haría
	haces	hacías	hiciste	harás	harías
	hace	hacía	hizo	hará	haría
	hacemos	hacíamos	hicimos	haremos	haríamos
	hacéis	hacíais	hicisteis	haréis	haríais
	hacen	hacían	hicieron	harán	harían
12. **ir**	voy	iba	fui	iré	iría
	vas	ibas	fuiste	irás	irías
	va	iba	fue	irá	iría
	vamos	íbamos	fuimos	iremos	iríamos
	vais	ibais	fuisteis	iréis	iríais
	van	iban	fueron	irán	irían
13. **jugar**	juego	jugaba	jugué	jugaré	jugaría
	juegas	jugabas	jugaste	jugarás	jugarías
	juega	jugaba	jugó	jugará	jugaría
	jugamos	jugábamos	jugamos	jugaremos	jugaríamos
	jugais	jugábais	jugasteis	jugaréis	jugaríais
	juegan	jugaban	jugaron	jugarán	jugarían
14. **oír**	oigo	oía	oí	oiré	oiría
	oyes	oías	oíste	oirás	oirías
	oye	oía	oyó	oirá	oiría
	oímos	oíamos	oímos	oiremos	oiríamos
	oís	oíais	oísteis	oiréis	oiríais
	oyen	oían	oyeron	oirán	oirían

	Subjunctive		Commands	Participles	
Present	Imperfect			Present	Past
esté	estuviera (-se)		—	estando	estado
estés	estuvieras (-ses)		está (no estés)		
esté	estuviera (-se)		esté		
estemos	estuviéramos (-semos)		estemos		
estéis	estuvierais (-seis)		estad (no estéis)		
estén	estuvieran (-sen)		estén		
haya	hubiera (-se)		—	habiendo	habido
hayas	hubieras (-ses)		he (no hayas)		
haya	hubiera (-se)		haya		
hayamos	hubiéramos (-semos)		hayamos		
hayáis	hubierais (-seis)		habed (no hayáis)		
hayan	hubieran (-sen)		hayan		
haga	hiciera (-se)		—	haciendo	hecho
hagas	hicieras (-ses)		haz (no hagas)		
haga	hiciera (-se)		haga		
hagamos	hiciéramos (-semos)		hagamos		
hagáis	hicierais (-seis)		haced (no hagáis)		
hagan	hicieran (-sen)		hagan		
vaya	fuera (-se)		—	yendo	ido
vayas	fueras (-ses)		ve (no vayas)		
vaya	fuera (-se)		vaya		
vayamos	fuéramos (-semos)		vayamos		
vayáis	fuerais (-seis)		id (no vayáis)		
vayan	fueran (-sen)		vayan		
juegue	jugara (-se)		—	jugando	jugado
juegues	jugaras (-ses)		juega (no juegues)		
juegue	jugara (-se)		juegue		
juguemos	jugáramos (-semos)		juguemos		
juguéis	jugarais (-seis)		jugad (no juguéis)		
jueguen	jugaran (-sen)		jueguen		
oiga	oyera (-se)		—	oyendo	oído
oigas	oyeras (-ses)		oye (no oigas)		
oiga	oyera (-se)		oiga		
oigamos	oyéramos (-semos)		oigamos		
oigáis	oyerais (-seis)		oíd (no oigáis)		
oigan	oyeran (-sen)		oigan		

Infinitive	Indicative				
	Present	Imperfect	Preterite	Future	Conditional
15. **pedir**	pido	pedía	pedí	pediré	pediría
	pides	pedías	pediste	pedirás	pedirías
	pide	pedía	pidió	pedirá	pediría
	pedimos	pedíamos	pedimos	pediremos	pediríamos
	pedís	pedíais	pedisteis	pediréis	pediríais
	piden	pedían	pidieron	pedirán	pedirían
16. **pensar**	pienso	pensaba	pensé	pensaré	pensaría
	piensas	pensabas	pensaste	pensarás	pensarías
	piensa	pensaba	pensó	pensará	pensaría
	pensamos	pensábamos	pensamos	pensaremos	pensaríamos
	pensáis	pensabais	pensasteis	pensaréis	pensaríais
	piensan	pensaban	pensaron	pensarán	pensarían
17. **perder**	pierdo	perdía	perdí	perderé	perdería
	pierdes	perdías	perdiste	perderás	perderías
	pierde	perdía	perdió	perderá	perdería
	perdemos	perdíamos	perdimos	perderemos	perderíamos
	perdéis	perdíais	perdisteis	perderéis	perderíais
	pierden	perdían	perdieron	perderán	perderían
18. **poder**	puedo	podía	pude	podré	podría
	puedes	podías	pudiste	podrás	podrías
	puede	podía	pudo	podrá	podría
	podemos	podíamos	pudimos	podremos	podríamos
	podéis	podíais	pudisteis	podréis	podríais
	pueden	podían	pudieron	podrán	podrían
19. **poner**	pongo	ponía	puse	pondré	pondría
	pones	ponías	pusiste	pondrás	pondrías
	pone	ponía	puso	pondrá	pondría
	ponemos	poníamos	pusimos	pondremos	pondríamos
	ponéis	poníais	pusisteis	pondréis	pondríais
	ponen	ponían	pusieron	pondrán	pondrían
20. **querer**	quiero	quería	quise	querré	querría
	quieres	querías	quisiste	querrás	querrías
	quiere	quería	quiso	querrá	querría
	queremos	queríamos	quisimos	querremos	querríamos
	queréis	queríais	quisisteis	querréis	querríais
	quieren	querían	quisieron	querrán	querrían

	Subjunctive	Commands	Participles	
Present	Imperfect		Present	Past
pida	pidiera (-se)	—	pidiendo	pedido
pidas	pidieras (-ses)	pide (no pidas)		
pida	pidiera (-se)	pida		
pidamos	pidiéramos (-semos)	pidamos		
pidáis	pidierais (-seis)	pedid (no pidáis)		
pidan	pidieran (-sen)	pidan		
piense	pensara (-se)	—	pensando	pensado
pienses	pensaras (-ses)	piensa (no pienses)		
piense	pensara (-se)	piense		
pensemos	pensáramos (-semos)	pensemos		
penséis	pensarais (-seis)	pensad (no penséis)		
piensen	pensaran (-sen)	piensen		
pierda	perdiera (-se)	pierde (no pierdas)	perdiendo	perdido
pierdas	perdieras (-ses)	pierda		
pierda	perdiera (-se)	perdamos		
perdamos	perdiéramos (-semos)	perded (no perdáis)		
perdáis	perdierais (-seis)	pierdan		
pierdan	perdieran (-sen)			
pueda	pudiera (-se)		pudiendo	podido
puedas	pudieras (-ses)			
pueda	pudiera (-se)			
podamos	pudiéramos (-semos)			
podáis	pudierais (-seis)			
puedan	pudieran (-sen)			
ponga	pusiera (-se)	—	poniendo	puesto
pongas	pusieras (-ses)	pon (no pongas)		
ponga	pusiera (-se)	ponga		
pongamos	pusiéramos (-semos)	pongamos		
pongáis	pusierais (-seis)	poned (no pongáis)		
pongan	pusieran (-sen)	pongan		
quiera	quisiera (-se)	—	queriendo	querido
quieras	quisieras (-ses)	quiere (no quieras)		
quiera	quisiera (-se)	quiera		
queramos	quisiéramos (-semos)	queramos		
queráis	quisierais (-seis)	quered (no queráis)		
quieran	quisieran (-sen)	quieran		

Infinitive	Indicative				
	Present	Imperfect	Preterite	Future	Conditional
21. **saber**	sé	sabía	supe	sabré	sabría
	sabes	sabías	supiste	sabrás	sabrías
	sabe	sabía	supo	sabrá	sabría
	sabemos	sabíamos	supimos	sabremos	sabríamos
	sabéis	sabíais	supisteis	sabréis	sabríais
	saben	sabían	supieron	sabrán	sabrían
22. **salir**	salgo	salía	salí	saldré	saldría
	sales	salías	saliste	saldrás	saldrías
	sale	salía	salió	saldrá	saldría
	salimos	salíamos	salimos	saldremos	saldríamos
	salís	salíais	salisteis	saldréis	saldríais
	salen	salían	salieron	saldrán	saldrían
23. **sentir**	siento	sentía	sentí	sentiré	sentiría
	sientes	sentías	sentiste	sentirás	sentirías
	siente	sentía	sintió	sentirá	sentiría
	sentimos	sentíamos	sentimos	sentiremos	sentiríamos
	sentís	sentíais	sentisteis	sentiréis	sentiríais
	sienten	sentían	sintieron	sentirán	sentirían
24. **ser**	soy	era	fui	seré	sería
	eres	eras	fuiste	serás	serías
	es	era	fue	será	sería
	somos	éramos	fuimos	seremos	seríamos
	sois	erais	fuisteis	seréis	seríais
	son	eran	fueron	serán	serían
25. **tener**	tengo	tenía	tuve	tendré	tendría
	tienes	tenías	tuviste	tendrás	tendrías
	tiene	tenía	tuvo	tendrá	tendría
	tenemos	teníamos	tuvimos	tendremos	tendríamos
	tenéis	teníais	tuvisteis	tendréis	tendríais
	tienen	tenían	tuvieron	tendrán	tendrían
26. **traer**	traigo	traía	traje	traeré	traería
	traes	traías	trajiste	traerás	traerías
	trae	traía	trajo	traerá	traería
	traemos	traíamos	trajimos	traeremos	traeríamos
	traéis	traíais	trajisteis	traeréis	traeríais
	traen	traían	trajeron	traerán	traerían

Subjunctive		Commands	Participles	
Present	Imperfect		Present	Past
sepa	supiera (-se)	—	sabiendo	sabido
sepas	supieras (-ses)	sabe (no sepas)		
sepa	supiera (-se)	sepa		
sepamos	supiéramos (-semos)	sepamos		
sepáis	supierais (-seis)	sabed (no sepáis)		
sepan	supieran (-sen)	sepan		
salga	saliera (-se)	—	saliendo	salido
salgas	salieras (-ses)	sal (no salgas)		
salga	saliera (-se)	salga		
salgamos	saliéramos (-semos)	salgamos		
salgáis	salierais (-seis)	salid (no salgáis)		
salgan	salieran (-sen)	salgan		
sienta	sintiera (-se)	—	sintiendo	sentido
sientas	sintieras (-ses)	siente (no sientas)		
sienta	sintiera (-se)	sienta		
sintamos	sintiéramos (-semos)	sintamos		
sintáis	sintierais (-sies)	sentid (no sintáis)		
sientan	sintieran (-sen)	sientan		
sea	fuera (-se)	—	siendo	sido
seas	fueras (-ses)	sé (no seas)		
sea	fuera (-se)	sea		
seamos	fuéramos (-semos)	seamos		
seáis	fuerais (-seis)	sed (no seáis)		
sean	fueran (-sen)	sean		
tenga	tuviera (-se)	—	teniendo	tenido
tengas	tuvieras (-ses)	ten (no tengas)		
tenga	tuviera (-se)	tenga		
tengamos	tuviéramos (-semos)	tengamos		
tengáis	tuvierais (-seis)	tened (no tengáis)		
tengan	tuvieran (-sen)	tengan		
traiga	trajera (-se)	—	trayendo	traído
traigas	trajeras (-ses)	trae (no traigas)		
traiga	trajera (-se)	traiga		
traigamos	trajéramos (-semos)	traigamos		
tragáis	trajerais (-seis)	traed (no traigáis)		
traigan	trajeran (-sen)	traigan		

Infinitive	Indicative				
	Present	Imperfect	Preterite	Future	Conditional
27. **valer**	valgo	valía	valí	valdré	valdría
	vales	valías	valiste	valdrás	valdrías
	vale	valía	valió	valdrá	valdría
	valemos	valíamos	valimos	valdremos	valdríamos
	valéis	valíais	valisteis	valdréis	valdríais
	valen	valían	valieron	valdrán	valdrían
28. **venir**	vengo	venía	vine	vendré	vendría
	vienes	venías	viniste	vendrás	vendrías
	viene	venía	vino	vendrá	vendría
	venimos	veníamos	vinimos	vendremos	vendríamos
	venís	veníais	vinisteis	vendréis	vendríais
	vienen	venían	vinieron	vendrán	vendrían
29. **ver**	veo	veía	vi	veré	vería
	ves	veías	viste	verás	verías
	ve	veía	vio	verá	vería
	vemos	veíamos	vimos	veremos	veríamos
	veis	veíais	visteis	veréis	veríais
	ven	veían	vieron	verán	verían
30. **volver**	vuelvo	volvía	volví	volveré	volvería
	vuelves	volvías	volviste	volverás	volverías
	vuelve	volvía	volvió	volverá	volvería
	volvemos	volvíamos	volvimos	volveremos	volveríamos
	volvéis	volvíais	volvisteis	volveréis	volveríais
	vuelven	volvían	volvieron	volverán	volverían

	Subjunctive		Commands	Participles	
Present	Imperfect			Present	Past
valga	valiera (-se)		—	valiendo	valido
valgas	valieras (-ses)		val (no valgas)		
valga	valiera (-se)		valga		
valgamos	valiéramos (-semos)		valgamos		
valgáis	valierais (-seis)		valed (no valgáis)		
valgan	valieran (-sen)		valgan		
venga	viniera (-se)		—	viniendo	venido
vengas	vinieras (-ses)		ven (no vengas)		
venga	viniera (-se)		venga		
vengamos	viniéramos (-semos)		vengamos		
vengáis	vinierais (-seis)		venid (no vengáis)		
vengan	vinieran (-sen)		vengan		
vea	viera (-se)		—	viendo	visto
veas	vieras (-ses)		ve (no veas)		
vea	viera (-se)		vea		
veamos	viéramos (-semos)		veamos		
veáis	vierais (-seis)		ved (no veáis)		
vean	vieran (-sen)		vean		
vuelva	volviera (-se)		—	volviendo	vuelto
vuelvas	volvieras (-ses)		vuelve (no vuelvas)		
vuelva	volviera (-se)		vuelva		
volvamos	volviéramos (-semos)		volvamos		
volváis	volvierais (-seis)		volved (no volváis)		
vuelvan	volvieran (-sen)		vuelvan		

SPANISH-ENGLISH VOCABULARY

This vocabulary includes contextual meanings of all words and idiomatic expressions used in the book except most proper nouns, adjectives that are exact cognates, and most conjugated verb forms. The Spanish style of alphabetization is followed, with **ch** occurring after **c**, **ll** after **l**, **rr** after **r** and **ñ** after **n**. Stem-changing verbs are indicated by **(ie)**, **(ue)** or **(i)** following the infinitive. A **(zc)** after an infinitive indicates this irregularity in the **yo** form of the present tense (**conozco, produzco**).

The following abbreviations are used:

abbr. abbreviation
adj. adjective
adv. adverb
coll. colloquial
conj. conjunction
contr. contraction
dim. diminutive
dir. obj. direct object of a verb
f. feminine noun; feminine form
fam. familiar (the familiar
  you: **tú** or **vosotros**)
fut. future tense
imperf. imperfect tense
indir. obj. indirect object of a
  verb
inf. infinitive
interj. interjection
m. masculine noun;
  masculine form
n. noun
obj. of prep. object of a
  preposition

obj. pron. object pronoun
  (pronoun used as the object of
  a verb)
pers. person
pl. plural
p. part. past participle of a
  verb
prep. preposition
pres. present tense
pron. pronoun
refl. pron. reflexive pronoun
  (pronoun used reflexively
  with a verb)
rel. pron. relative pronoun
sing. singular
subj. subject
subj. pron. subject pronoun
  (pronoun used as the subject
  of a verb)
subjunc. subjunctive form of a
  verb

A

a to; at; for; from; at a distance of; **a casa** home; **¿A cuánto están. . . ?** How much are . . . ?; **a la** (+ time expression) per; **a menos que** unless; **a eso de** at around (time of day); **a tiempo** on time; **a veces** at times, sometimes; **A ver.** Let's see.
abandonar to abandon
el **abandono** abandonment

abierto open
el **abogado** lawyer
el **aborto** abortion
abrazar to put one's arm around someone's shoulder, hug, embrace

el **abrigo** overcoat; **Ponte el abrigo.** Put on your coat.

abril April

abrir to open

absoluto absolute

abstracto abstract

la **abuela** grandmother

el **abuelo** grandfather; *pl.* grandparents

abundante abundant, ample

aburrido bored; boring

el **aburrimiento** boredom

A.C. **(antes de Cristo)** B.C.

acá here

acabar to finish, end; **acabar bien (mal)** to have a happy (an unhappy) ending; **acabar de** (+ *inf.*) to have just (done something); **acabar por** to end up (by)

el **accidente** accident

la **acción** action

el **aceite** oil

el **acento** accent

aceptar to accept

acerca de about, concerning

acompañar to go with, accompany; **acompañado de** accompanied by

el **acontecimiento** event

acordarse (ue) de to remember

acostar (ue) to put to bed; **acostarse** to go to bed

acostumbrar: acostumbran dar un paseo they usually take a walk;

acostumbrarse (a) to get used to, become accustomed to

la **actividad** activity

activo active

el **acto** act

el **actor** actor

la **actriz** actress

actual of the present

actualmente presently

actuar to act

el **acueducto** aqueduct

el **acuerdo** agreement; **De acuerdo.** Agreed, Okay; **de acuerdo con** in agreement with; **estar (ponerse) de acuerdo (con)** to agree (with)

adelante ahead, forward; **pasar adelante** to come in (to another's home)

además besides, moreover, **además de** in addition to

adicto addicted

adiós goodby

la **administración** administration

admirable admirable

el **admirador (la admiradora)** admirer

admirar to admire

admitir to admit

adonde (to) where, wherever

¿adónde? (to) where?

adorar to adore, love

adornar to adorn, decorate

el **adorno** decoration

adquirir (ie) to acquire

la **aduana** customs, customs office

el **adulto (la adulta)** adult

aéreo *adj.* air; **correo aéreo** air mail; **estampilla aérea** air-mail stamp

el **aerograma** aerogram

el **aeropuerto** airport

afectar to affect

el **aficionado (la aficionada)** fan, devotee; **aficionado a** a fan of

afirmar to affirm

afortunadamente fortunately

africano African

la **agencia** agency; **agencia de viajes** travel agency

el la **agente** agent; **agente de viajes** travel agent

la **agitación** agitation, movement

agitar to agitate

agosto August

agradable pleasant

agradecer (zc) to thank

agrario agrarian, agricultural

la **agricultura** agriculture

el **agua** *f.* water

ahora now; **ahora mismo** right now; **por ahora** for now

ahorita *coll.* right now, right away

ahorrar to save (money, time, etc.)

el **aire** air; look, appearance; **al aire libre** in the open air

al *contr. of* **a** + **el**; **al** + *inf.* on, upon . . . -ing; **al** (+ time expression) per; **¡Al contrario!** On the contrary!

Alá Allah
alargar to elongate
alcanzar to reach, attain
el **alcázar** Moorish palace or castle
alegrarse (de) to be glad, happy (to)
alegremente happily
la **alegría** joy, happiness
alemán German
la **alergia** allergy
alerto alert
la **alfombra** rug
algo something, anything; **¿Algo más?** Anything else?
alguien someone
algún, alguno some, any; some sort of; *pl.* some, a few; some people; **alguna vez** ever, at some time
la **alianza** alliance
el **alimento** food (generally *pl.*)
el **alivio** relief; **¡Qué alivio!** What a relief!
el **alma** *f.* soul, spirit
el **almacén** store
almorzar (ue) to have lunch
el **almuerzo** lunch (the main meal in most Hispanic countries)
el **alpinismo** mountain climbing
alquiler to rent
el **alquiler** rent
alrededor de around
Altamira location of prehistoric cave paintings in Spanish province of Santander

el **altar** altar
la **altitud** altitude
alto high; tall; upper; loud; **altas horas** very late; **clase alta** upper class; **en la más alto** at the top; **en voz alta** aloud
la **altura** altitude, height
la **alusión** reference, allusion
allá there
allí there
la **amabilidad** kindness
amable kind, nice, friendly
amado beloved
el **amanecer** dawn, daybreak
el, la **amante** lover
amar to love
amarillo yellow
ambicioso ambitious
el **ambiente** atmosphere, ambiance
América America (North and South America); la **América Central** Central America; la **América del Sur** South America; la **América Latina** Latin America
americano American; **fútbol americano** football; **méxico-americano** Mexican-American
el **amigo (la amiga)** friend
la **amistad** friendship
amistoso friendly
el **amor** love
amoroso amorous, loving, romantic
anarajado orange (color)

el **anciano (la anciana); hogar de ancianos** old-age home
Andalucía Andalusia (southernmost province of Spain)
andaluz Andalusian
andar to walk; to go about; to run, work; **¿Ándale! (¿Ándele!)** Come on! Go ahead!
andino Andean
el **ángel** angel
anglosajón Anglo-Saxon
el **ángulo** angle
el **anillo** ring
el **aniversario** anniversary
animado lively, animated
el **animal** animal
anoche last night
la **anormalidad** abnormality
ansioso anxious, nervous
anterior former, previous; **anterior a** before; **muy anterior a** much earlier than
antes before; first; **antes de** before; **antes (de) que** before; **lo antes posible** as soon as possible
anticipar to anticipate
Antigua capital of Guatemala in colonial times
antiguo old, ancient
la **antropología** anthropology
el **antropólogo (la antropóloga)** anthropologist

anualmente yearly

el año year; **Año Nuevo** New Year's; **el año que viene** next year; **tener . . . años** to be . . . years old; **todos los años** every year

aparecer (zc) to appear

aparentar to feign, pretend

el **apartamento** apartment

aparte apart, separate; **aparte de** aside from

el **apellido** surname, last name

aplicar to apply

el **apóstel** apostle

apoyar to support

el **apoyo** support

aprender (a) to learn (to)

aprovechar to use

aproximadamente approximately

apurarse to hurry

aquel, aquella *adj.* that; **aquél, aquélla** *pron.* that (one)

aquellos, aquellas *adj.* those; **aquéllos, aquéllas** *pron.* those

aquí here; **por aquí** this way, over here, around here

árabe Arab; Arabic

Aragón province in northern Spain

el **árbol** tree

la **arepa** flat corn cake

el **arete** earring

argentino Argentine, Argentinean

el **arma** *f.* arm, weapon

armado: fuerzas **armadas** armed forces

el **armario** cupboard, armoire

el **arpa** *f.* harp

la **arqueología** archeology

el, la **arqueólogo** archeologist

el, la **arquitecto** architect

la **arquitectura** architecture

arreglar to fix; to arrange; **arreglarse** to be okay, turn out all right

arriba above, over, upstairs; **¡Arriba las manos!** Hands up!

el **arroz** rice

el **arrozal** rice field

el **arte** *(pl.* las **artes)** art; **bellas artes** fine arts; **obra de arte** work of art

el **artículo** article

artificial: fuegos **artificiales** fireworks

el, la **artista** artist

artístico artistic

asado roasted, barbecued

la **asamblea** assembly

el **ascenso** promotion

el **asesinato** murder

así thus, so, in this way, like that; **Así es.** That's right. That's the way it is; **Así es** *(+ n.)* That's . . . ; **así que** so

asistir (a) to attend

el **aspecto** aspect; appearance

la **aspirina** aspirin

Asturias province in northern Spain

asustado frightened, startled

atacar to attack

el **ataque** attack

atemorizar to terrify

la **atención: prestar atención** to pay attention, give heed

atender (ie) to take care of, wait on

atento alert

atlántico: Océano **Atlántico** Atlantic Ocean

el, la **atleta** athlete

atlético athletic

el **atletismo** athletics

atraer to attract

atrapar to catch, trap

atrás backwards; **de atrás** in the back

aumentar to gain (weight)

el **aumento** rise, increase

aún even, still

aunque although, even though

auténtico authentic

el **auto** auto; **en auto** by car

el **autobús** bus; **en autobús** by bus

el **automóvil** automobile

autónomo autonomous

el **autor** (la **autora**) author

la **autoridad** authority

avanzar to advance

la **avenida** avenue

la **aventura** adventure

el **avión** airplane; **en avión** by plane

¡Ay! Oh!

ayer yesterday

la **ayuda** help

el, la **ayudante** helper, assistant

ayudar (a) to help (to), assist

la **azafata** airline
   stewardess
azteca Aztec
Aztlán southwestern
   U.S., real and
   spiritual home of
   many Mexican-
   Americans
azul blue

B

el **bailador** (la **bailadora**)
   dancer
bailar to dance
el **baile** dance
bajar (de) to get off
bajo *adj.* low; short;
   prep. under; **cayó
   bajo** fell to
el **ballet** ballet
la **banana** banana
el **banco** bench, bank
la **bandera** flag, banner
el **banderillero** (la
   banderillera)
   bullfighter who
   places pairs of
   barbed sticks in
   bull's withers
el **bandido** bandit
el **banquete** banquet
el **baño** bath; bathroom
barato cheap,
   inexpensive
la **barba** beard
la **barbaridad** barbarism;
   ¡Qué barbaridad!
   Good Lord!
el **barco** ship, boat
el **barrio** neighborhood,
   district, community
la **base** base
básico basic
el **basquetbol** basketball
el, la **basquetbolista**
   basketball player

bastante *adj.* enough;
   quite a bit; *adv.*
   rather, quite
bastar: Basta de . . .
   Enough . . . **¡Basta
   ya!** That's enough!
la **basura** garbage, trash;
   canasto de basura
   wastebasket
la **batalla** battle
el **bebé** baby
beber to drink
la **bebida** drink,
   beverage
el **beisbol** baseball
la **belleza** beauty
bello beautiful; **bellas
   artes** fine arts;
   bellísimo very
   beautiful
benévolo benevolent,
   kind
besar to kiss
el **beso** kiss
la **biblioteca** library
la **bicicleta** bicycle; **en
   bicicleta** by bicycle
el **bien** good
bien well, fine, all
   right, okay; good;
   acabar bien to have
   a happy ending;
   ¡Qué bien! Great!
la **bienvenida** welcome;
   dar la bienvenida to
   welcome
bienvenido *adj.*
   welcome
bilingüe bilingual
la **biología** biology
el, la **biólogo** biologist
el **bistec** (beef)steak
el **bizcocho** cookie,
   biscuit
blanco white;
   Caucasian
la **blusa** blouse

la **boca** mouth; **callarse
   la boca** to keep
   one's mouth shut
la **boda** wedding
el **boleto** ticket
boliviano Bolivian
el **bolso** purse
la **bondad** goodness
bonito pretty
el **bosque** forest
la **bota** leather wine bag;
   boot
el **bote** boat
la **botella** bottle
el **boticario** pharmacist
el **boxeo** boxing
bravo grand, valiant;
   toro bravo fighting
   bull
el **brazo** arm; **tomadas
   del brazo** arm in
   arm
Bredá city in Holland
breve brief, short
brillante brilliant,
   bright,
   brillantísimo very
   bright
brillar to shine
bromear to joke
el **bruto** (la **bruta**) brute,
   ignoramus
buen, bueno good,
   kind; well, okay, all
   right; **Buenas
   noches.** Good
   evening. Good
   night.; **Buenas
   tardes.** Good
   afternoon. Good
   evening.; **Buenos
   días,** Good
   morning. Good
   day.; **¡Buen
   provecho!** Happy
   eating! Enjoy your
   meal! **Muy buenas.**

Good afternoon.
Good evening.;
¡Qué bueno! Great!
How nice!

el **burro** donkey, burro
buscar to look (for),
search

el **buzón** mailbox

C

el **caballero** gentleman
el **caballo** horse
la **cabeza** head; **dolor de
cabeza** headache
cada each, every
el **cadáver** corpse
caer to fall; **cayó bajo**
fell to
el **café** coffee; café; **café
con leche** coffee
with hot milk
la **cafetería** cafeteria
el **calcetín** sock
la **calculadora** calculator
el **calendario** calendar
calentar to heat
calentarse (ie) to warm
oneself, warm up
la **calidad** quality
caliente hot
(temperature)
la **calma** calm; **Calma.**
Compose yourself.
calmarse to calm
oneself; **¡Cálmate!**
Calm down! Relax!
el **calor** heat, warmth,
hacer calor to be hot
(weather); **¡Qué
calor!** It sure is hot!;
tener calor to be
(feel) hot
callarse to be silent,
keep quiet;
¡Cállate! Be quiet!;

**nunca se calla la
boca** he never shuts
up
la **calle** street
la **cama** bed
la **cama: coche-cama**
Pullman (sleeping,
car)
la **cámara** camera
el **camarero (la camarera)**
waiter (waitress)
el **camarón** shrimp
cambiar to change; to
exchange
el **cambio** change; **en
cambio** on the other
hand
caminar to walk
la **caminata** walk, stroll
el **camino** road, way; **el
camino de** the road
to; **por este camino**
on this street
la **camisa** shirt
la **campaña** campaign
el **campesino (la
campesina)** peasant,
country person
el **campo** field;
countryside
el **canal** channel
el **canasto** basket;
canasto de basura
watebasket
la **canción** song
el **candidato (la
candidata)**
candidate
la **canoa** canoe
cansado tired
cantar to sing
la **capa** cape
la **capital** capital
el **capitán** captain
el **capítulo** chapter
captar to capture,
portray

la **captura** capture
capturar to capture
la **cara** face
el **carácter** character
la **característica**
characteristic
característico
characteristic
caracterizarse por to
be characterized by
¡Caramba! Wow!
Good grief!
caraqueño from
Caracas
cargar to carry
el **(Mar) Caribe**
Caribbean (Sea)
el **cariño** affection
cariñoso loving,
affecionate
la **carne** meat; **carne
asada** roast beef
la **carnicería** butcher shop
caro expensive
el, la **carpintero** carpenter
la **carrera** race; career
la **carta** letter; playing
card; **carta
certificada** certified
letter
cartaginés
Carthaginian
la **cartera** wallet
la **casa** house, home; **a
casa** home; **en casa**
at home; **en casa de**
at (someone's)
house
casado married; **tener
un mes de casados**
to be married a
month
casarse (con) to marry,
get married (to)
casi almost
el **caso** case; **en case (de)
que** in case

castaño chestnut-colored
castañuela castanet
el castellano Spanish (language)
el castigo punishment
Castilla Castile (province in central Spain)
la casualidad coincidence, chance; por casualidad by coincidence; ¡Qué casualidad! What a coincidence!
casualmente by chance
el catalán (la catalana) Catalan (language or person from Spanish province of Cataluña)
Cataluña Catalonia (northeasternmost province of Spain)
la catedral cathedral
católico Catholic
catorce fourteen
la causa cause; a causa de because of
causar to cause
la caza hunting
la cazuela stew, earthen pot in which a stew is cooked
la cebolla onion
la celebración celebration
celebrar to celebrate; celebrarse to be celebrated; to take place
celoso jealous
celta Celt
céltico Celtic
la cena dinner, supper
cenar to dine, have dinner

el centavo cent
central central, main; la América Central Central America
el centro center; downtown
Centroamérica Central America
cerca near, nearby; cerca de near, close to
el cerebro brain
la ceremonia ceremony
certificar to certify, register (mail); sin certificar uncertified
la cervecería brewery; beer bar
la cerveza beer
cerrado closed
cerrar (ie) to close
la cesta basketlike racket used in jai alai
el ciclismo cycling
cielito dim. of cielo
el cielo sky, heaven; "darling"
cien, ciento 100; por ciento percent
la ciencia science; ciencias de computación computer science; ciencias políticas political science; ciencias sociales social science
el, la científico scientist
cierto true; (a) certain
el cigarrillo cigarette
el cigarro cigar
cinco five
cincuenta fifty
el cine movies; movie theatre
la cinta tape
circular to circulate

la circunstancia circumstance
la cita date, appointment
la ciudad city
el ciudadano (la ciudadana) citizen
cívico civic
la civilización civilization
civilizado civilized; civilizadísimo very civilized
claro clear; Claro. Of course.; Claro que . . . Of course . . .
claramente clearly
la clase class; kind; clase alta upper class; clase media middle class; de primera clase first-class, first-rate; (de) toda clase (of) every kind
clásico classical
el clima climate
el club club
la coca coke (Coca-cola)
el cocido stew
la cocina kitchen, cuisine
cocinar to cook
el cocinero (la cocinera) cook, chef
el coctel cocktail
el coche-cama Pullman (sleeping car)
coexistir to coexist
la colección collection
colectivo collective
colombiano Columbian
Colón Columbus
la colonización colonization
el colonizador (la colonizadora) colonist

el **color** color
colorado colored; red
la **comadre** godmother of
one's child, close
family friend
la **combinación**
combination
combinar to combine
la **comedia** comedy
el **comedor** dining room
comentar to comment
comenzar (ie) to
begin, commence
comer to eat
comercial commercial
el, la **comerciante**
businessperson
el **comercio** business
los **comestibles** groceries
cómico comical, funny
la **comida** food; meal;
dinner
como *adv*, as; like,
such as; how; *conj.*
since, as long as;
cómo how (to);
como sí as if; **tan
. . . como** as . . . as;
tanto (. . .) como
as much (. . .) as
¿cómo? (¡cómo!) how?
(how!); what? what
did you say? what
is it?; **¿Cómo es
(son) . . . ?** What is
(are) . . . like?;
¡Cómo no! Of
course!; **¿Cómo se
dice . . . ?** How do
you say . . . ?;
**¿Cómo se llama
usted?** What is your
name?
la **cómoda** chest of
drawers
cómodo comfortable

el **compadre** godfather of
one's child, close
family friend
el **compañero (la
compañera)** mate,
companion
la **compañía** company
compararse con to be
compared with
la **competencia**
competition
completamente
completely
componer to compose;
componerse de to
be composed of
comportarse to
conduct oneself,
behave
la **composición**
composition
comprar to buy
la **compra** purchase;
**hacer las compras,
ir de compras** to go
shopping
comprender to
understand; to
comprise, include
común common,
usual, ordinary; **en
común** in common
la **comunicación**
communication
comunicarse to
communicate
la **comunidad**
community
el, la **comunista**
communist; *adj.*
communist
con with; **con cuidado**
carefully; **con el
nombre de** by the
name of; **con
permiso** excuse me;

con razón no
wonder; **con tal (de)
que** provided that
el **concepto** concept
el **concierto** concert
condenar to condemn
la **condición** condition;
circumstance
conducir (zc) to drive
el **conductor (la
conductora)** driver
la **conferencia**
conference; lecture
confesar (ie) to confess
conmemorar to
commemorate
conmigo with me
conocer (zc) to know,
be acquainted with;
to meet, get
acquainted with
conocido known, well-
known; **más
conocido** better
known
el **conocimiento**
(*generally pl.*)
discovery,
knowledge
la **conquista** conquest
el **conquistador**
conqueror, Spanish
conquistador
conquistar to conquer
la **consecuencia**
consequence
conseguir (i) to bring
about; to obtain, get
el **consejero (la
consejera)**
counselor;
**consejero(a)
matrimonial**
marriage counselor
el **consejo** advice, piece
of advice; **dar**

consejos to give advice

conservar to conserve; to preserve, to keep; **se conserva intacto** is still intact

considerar to consider

constar de to consist of

la **constitución** constitution

la **construcción** construction

construido built, constructed

construir to build, construct

el **consuelo** consolation; joy, comfort

consultar to consult

el **consultorio** doctor's office

el **contacto** contact

la **contaminación** pollution

contaminado polluted

contar (ue) to tell, relate

contemporáneo contemporary

contento happy, content

contestar to answer

contigo with you (fam. sing.)

el **continente** continent

la **continuación** continuation

continuar to continue

contra against; **en contra** against

la **contradicción** contradiction

contrario: ¡Al contrario! On the contrary!; **por el contrario** in contrast

el **contraste** contrast

la **contribución** contribution

contribuir to contribute

el **control: control de la natalidad** birth control

controlar to control

convencer (de) to convince (to)

la **conversación** conversation

conversar to converse, chat

convertir (ie) (a, en) to convert (to) (into)

la **copa: tomar una copa** to have a drink

el **corazón** heart; **de todo corazón** wholeheartedly

la **corbata** tie

Córdoba city in southern Spain

cortar to cut, cut off

la **corte** royal court

cortés polite

corto short, brief

correctamente correctly

el **corredor** hallway

el **correo** mail; post office; **correo aéreo** air mail

correr to run

corresponder a to correspond to

la **corrida (de toros)** bullfight; bullfighting

corrido: horario corrido continuous hours (on a job)

la **cosa** thing

los **cosméticos** cosmetics

cosmopolita cosmopolitan

la **costa** coast

costar (ue) to cost

la **costumbre** custom, habit; **es costumbre** it's the custom

cotidiano daily

crear to create

crecer (zc) to grow

el **credo** creed

creer to believe, think; **Creo que sí.** I think so; **¡Ya lo creo!** Yes, indeed!

la **crema** cream

el **crimen** (pl. los **crimenes**) crime

criollo creole (born in the Americas of European ancestry)

el **cristianismo** Christianity

cristiano Christian

Cristo Christ

criticar to criticize

crítico critical

el **crucigrama** crossword puzzle

la **cruz** cross

cruzar to cross

el **cuaderno** notebook

la **cuadra** city block

el **cuadro** picture, painting

cual, cuales: el (la) **cual, los** (las) **cuales** which, whom; **lo cual** which

¿cuál? ¿cuáles? which? which one(s)? what?

la **cualidad** quality, characteristic

cualquier, cualquiera any

cuando when, whenever

¿cuándo? when?

cuanto: en cuanto as soon as; **en cuanto a** as far; **unos cuantos** a few

¿cuánto? how much?; **¿A cuánto están . . . ?** How much are . . . ?; **¿(por) cuánto tiempo?** how long?

¿cuántos? how many? **¿Cuántos años tiene . . . ?** How old is . . . ?

cuarenta forty

el **cuarto** room; quarter; *adj.* fourth; quarter; **las seis y cuarto** 6:15

cuatro four

cuatrocientos 400

cubano Cuban

cubierto (de) covered (with, by)

el **cubismo** cubism

cubista cubist

cubrir to cover

la **cuchara** spoon

el **cuchillo** knife

el **cuello** neck

la **cuenta** bill, check; **darse cuenta de** to realize

el **cuento** story

la **cuerda: instrumento de cuerda** stringed instrument

el **cuerpo** body

la **cuestión** question, issue

la **cueva** cave; flamenco night spot

el **cuidado** care; **con cuidado** carefully;

¡Cuidado (con . . .)!; Look out (for . . .)!; **tener cuidado (con)** to be careful (of, about)

cuidadosamente carefully

cuidadoso careful

cuidar to take care of, be careful

la **culpa** fault, blame

la **cultura** culture

el **culto** form of worship

la **cumbia** Latin American dance

el **cumpleaños** birthday

el **cumplido** compliment

cumplir to fulfill

el **cura** priest

curar to cure

curioso curious

el **curso** course; **curso de inglés** English class

cuyo whose, of which

CH

el **cha-cha-chá** dance of Cuban origin

el **champú** shampoo

la **chaqueta** jacket

el **charango** guitar-like instrument

charlar to chat

el **cheque** check; **cheque de viajero** traveler's check

la **chica** girl

chicano chicano. Mexican-American

el **chico** boy, guy; *pl.* kids

chileno Chilean

chino Chinese

el **chiste** joke

chistoso funny; **¡Qué chistoso!** How funny!

el **chocolate** chocolate

el **chorizo** spicy smoked pork sausage

D

la **dama** lady

dar to give; **dar a** to face, be facing; **dar hambre (sed, sueño)** to be hungry (thirsty, sleepy); **dar de comer** to feed; **dar las gracias** to thank; **dar un paseo** to take a walk; **darse cuenta de** to realize

datar de to date from

D.C. **(después de Cristo)** A.D.

de of; from; about; in; on (after a superlative); by; made of; as; with; **de ida y vuelta** round-trip; **De nada.** You're welcome; **de veras** really; **de vez en cuando** from time to time; **más de** more than (before a number)

deber must, have to, ought to, should; to be supposed to

el **deber** duty; **los deberes** homework

débil weak

la **decadencia** decadence

decaer to decay

decidir to decide

décimo tenth

decir (i) to say, tell; **¿Cómo se dice . . . ?** How

does one say . . . ?;
¡No me digas! You
don't say!; **querer
decir** to mean
la **decoración** decoration
decorar to decorate
dedicar to dedicate,
devote; **dedicarse a**
to devote oneself to
el **defecto** fault, defect
defender (ie) to defend
deformado deformed,
misshapen
dejar to leave, leave
behind; to let,
allow; **dejar de** +
inf. to stop, cease;
dejar tranquilo to
leave alone
del *contr. of* **de** + **el**
delante de in front of
delicioso delicious
demás: todo lo demás
everything else
demasiado too, too
much; *pl.* too many
el, la **demócrata**
Democrat; *adj.*
Democratic
democrático
democratic
demográfico:
explosión
demográfica
population
explosion
el **demonio** demon, devil
el, la **dentista** dentist
dentro de in, within,
inside (of)
depender de to
depend on
el, la **dependiente**
salesperson, clerk
el **deporte** sport;
practicar un deporte
to play a sport

el **depósito** warehouse
depravado depraved
deprimente
depressing
deprimido depressed
deprimir to depress
la **derecha** right; **a la
derecha** to (on) the
right
el **derecho** right;
privilege; *adj.*
straight
derrotar to defeat
desaparecer (zc) to
disappear
**desarrolar,
desarrollarse** to
develop
el **desastre** disaster
desayunar to have
(for) breakfast
el **desayuno** breakfast;
tomar el desayuno
to have breakfast
descansar to rest
el, la **descendiente**
descendent
la **descomposición** decay
el, la **desconforme**
dissenter, non-
conformist
el **desconocido (la
desconocida)**
stranger
descortés
discourteous,
impolite
describir to describe
descrito described
descubrir to discover,
uncover
desde from; since;
¿desde cuándo?
how long? since
when?; **desde hace
(hacía)** for; **desde
hace años** for years;

desde . . . hasta
from . . . to
desear to wish (for),
want, desire
el **desempleo**
unemployment
el **deseo** wish, desire
el **desfile** parade
deshacer to take apart,
undo
deshonesto dishonest
el **desierto** desert; *adj.*
desert
la **desilusión**
disappointment
desilusionado
disappointed,
disillusioned
desintegrarse to
disintegrate
el **desorden** disorder
despacio slowly
la **despedida** farewell,
leave-taking
despertarse to wake
up
despertar (ie) to
awaken (someone)
despreciar to look
down on, scorn
despierto awake, alert
después afterwards,
then, later; **después
de** after; **después
(de) que** after; **poco
después** a short
time after(wards)
destruido destroyed
destruir to destroy
el **detalle** detail
el, la **detective** detective
detener to stop
detestar to hate, detest
detrás de behind
la **deuda** debt
devorar to devour
devoto devout

el **día** day; **al día** per day; **Buenos días.** Good morning. Good day.; **de día** by day; **día a día** day by day; **día de fiesta** holiday; **Día de Gracias** Thanksgiving; **Día del Año Nuevo** New Year's Day; **Día de los Reyes** Epiphany (Jan. 6); **día de semana** weekday; **hoy día** nowadays; **todos los días** every day

la **diablada** *coll.* Bolivian Indian dance depicting the triumph of angels over devils

el **diablo** devil

el **diálogo** dialogue

el **dibujo** drawing

el **diccionario** dictionary

diciembre December

el **dictador (la dictadora)** dictator

dicho said, told

la **dieta** diet; **estar a dieta** to be on a diet

diez ten

la **diferencia** difference

diferente (a) different (from)

difícil hard, difficult; not likely

la **dificultad** difficulty

el **dinero** money

el **dios** god; **Dios** God; **¡Dios mío!** My goodness! Good grief!

diplomático diplomatic

la **dirección** direction; address

directamente directly

directo direct

la **disciplina** discipline

la **discoteca** discotheque

la **discriminación** discrimination

el **discurso** speech

la **discusión** discussion

discutir to discuss

la **disensión** dissension

la **disputa** dispute, controversy

distinguir to distinguish

distinto different

diverso diverse

divertido amusing, enjoyable

divertir (ie) to amuse, entertain; **divertirse** to have a good time, enjoy oneself

divinar to guess

divorciarse to get a divorce

el **divorcio** divorce

doblar to turn

doble double

doce twelve

la **docena** dozen

el **doctor (la doctora)** doctor

el **dólar** dollar

doler (ue) to ache, pain, hurt; **Me duele la cabeza.** My head aches.

el **dolor** pain, ache; suffering; sorrow; **dolor de cabeza** headache; **dolor de estómago** stomach ache

dominar to dominate, overlook

domingo Sunday; **domingo de Pascua** Easter Sunday

el **dominó** dominoes

don, doña titles of respect or affection used before a first name

donde where, wherever

¿dónde? where?

dormido asleep

dormir (ue) to sleep; **dormir la siesta** to take a nap after lunch; **dormirse** to go to sleep

el **dormitorio** dormitory, bedroom

dos two

doscientos 200

el **drama** drama

dramático dramatic

la **droga** drug

la **duda** doubt

dudar to doubt

el **duelo** grief, sorrow; duel

el **dueño (la dueña)** owner, master (mistress)

el **dulce** sweet, candy

durante during; for

durar to last

duro hard, harsh; **huevos duros** hard-boiled eggs

E

e and (replaces **y** before words beginning with **i** or **hi**)

la **ecología** ecology

el, la **ecólogo** ecologist

la **economía** economy

económico economic

la **edad** age; **¿Qué edad**

tiene . . ? How old is . . . ?

el **edificio** building

la **educación** education; upbringing

egoísta selfish

la **ejecución** execution

el **ejemplo** example; **por ejemplo** for example

el **ejercicio** exercise; **hacer ejercicios** to exercise

el **ejército** army

el the (*m. sing.*); **el de** that of; **el que** the one that

él *subj.* he; *obj. of prep.* him, it; **de él** (of) his

la **elección** election

el **elefante** elephant

la **elegancia** elegance

elegante elegant; stylish

el **elemento** element

elevarse to rise

ella *subj.* she; *obj. of prep.* her, it; **de ella** her, (of) hers

ellos, ellas *subj.* they; *obj. of prep.* them; **de ellos (ellas)** their, (of) theirs

embarazada pregnant

embargo: sin embargo however

la **emoción** emotion; excitement; **¡Qué emoción!** How exciting!

emocionante exciting

la **empanada** meat pie

el **emperador** emperor

empezar (ie) (a) to start (to), begin (to)

empinado steep, high

el **empleado** (la **empleada**) employee

el **empleo** employment, job

en in; into; on; at; **en casa** at home; **en caso (de) que** in case; **en cuanto** as soon as; **en cuanto a** as for; **en punto** on the dot; **en realidad** in reality, actually; **en seguida** at once; **en serio** seriously; **en vez de** instead of; **pensar en** to think about

enamorarse de to fall in love with

encabezar to lead

encantado delighted

encantar to enchant, delight; **me encanta** I love (it)

encargado de in charge of

encarnar to embody

encima: por encima de above

encontrar (ue) to find, encounter; to meet; **encontrarse (con)** to meet, come across

la **enchilada** enchilada

el **enemigo** enemy

la **energía** energy

enero January

enfermarse to get sick

la **enfermedad** disease, illness

el **enfermero** (la **enfermera**) nurse

el **enfermo** (la **enferma**) patient; sick person; *adj.* sick, ill

enfrentarse con to confront

enfrente (de) in front (of) opposite; **de enfrente** across the way

engañar to deceive

enojado angry

enojarse (con) to get mad (at), become angry (with)

enorme enormous

la **ensalada** salad

enseñar to teach; to show

entender (ie) to understand; to hear

enterarse to find out

entero entire

entonces then; in that case

la **entrada** admission ticket

entrar (a) (en) to enter, go in

entre between; among; **entre tanto** in the meantime

entregar to give, hand over

la **entrevista** interview

entrevistar to interview

entusiasmadamente enthusiastically

el **entusiasmo** enthusiasm

enviar to send

épico epic

la **época** period, era, epoch, time

el **equilibrio** balance

el **equipaje** luggage

el **equipo** team; **equipo femenino** women's team

equivocado wrong, mistaken

equivocarse to be

mistaken, make a mistake
la **escalera** stairway
el **escándalo** scandal, disgrace
escandinavo Scandinavian
la **escena** scene
escoger to choose, select
escosés Scotch, Scottish
escribir to write; **escribir a máquina** to type
escrito written
el **escritor** (la **escritora**) writer
el **escritorio** desk
la **escritura: escritura pictográfica** picture writing
escuchar to listen (to)
la **escuela** school
el **escultor** (la **escultora**) sculptor
la **escultura** sculpture
ese, esa *adj.* that; **ése, ésa** *pron.* that (one)
eso *pron.* that; **a eso de** at around (time of day); **por eso** that's why, for that reason
esos, esas *adj.* those; **ésos, ésas** *pron.* those
el **espacio** space
la **espada** sword
la **espalda** back
España Spain
español Spanish; Spaniard
especial special
el, la **especialista** specialist
especialmente especially

espectacular spectacular
el **espectáculo** spectacle, pageant, show
el **espectador** (la **espectadora**) spectator
el **espejo** mirror
la **esperanza** hope
esperar to wait (for); to hope; to expect
el **espíritu** spirit
espiritual spiritual
espléndido splendid
la **esposa** wife
el **esposo** husband; *pl.* husband and wife
el **esquí** skiing
esquiar to ski
la **esquina** street corner
establecer (zc) to establish; to plant
el **establecimiento** settlement
la **estación (de radio, televisión)** (radio, television) station
el **estadio** stadium
el **estado** state; **en estado de** in a state of; **los Estados Unidos** the United States
la **estampilla** postage stamp; **estampilla aérea** air-mail stamp
la **estancia** Argentine or Uruguayan cattle ranch
estar to be (in a certain place, condition or position); to be in (at home, in the office, etc.); **estar de vacaciones** to be on vacation; **estar para** to be about to

la **estatua** statue
este, esta *adj.* this; **éste, ésta** *pron.* this (one)
el **este** east
estético esthetic
estilizado stylized
el **estilo** style, fashion; **al estilo de** in the style of
esto *pron.* this
el **estómago** stomach; **dolor de estómago** stomach ache
estos, estas *adj.* these; **éstos, éstas** *pron.* these
estricto strict
la **estructura** structure
el, la **estudiante** student
estudiantil *adj. student*
estudiar to study; **estudiar para** to study to be
el **estudio** study
estudioso studious
estupendo wonderful, great
estúpido stupid, ridiculous
la **etapa** stage
etcétera *et cetera*
eterno eternal
Europa Europe
europeo European
evadir to escape
evidente evident, obvious
evitar to avoid
exacto exact; **Exacto.** That's right. Exactly.
exagerar to exaggerate
la **exaltación** exaltation
el **examen** (*pl.* los **exámenes**) examination, test

examinar to examine
excelente excellent
excepto except
excluir to exclude
el exilado (la exilada)
   exile (person)
la existencia existence
existir to exist
el éxito success
exótico exotic
la experiencia experience
experimentado
   experienced
el experto (la experta)
   expert
la explicación
   explanation
explicar to explain
la explosión: explosión
   demográfica
   population explosion
la explotación
   exploitation
explotar to exploit; to
   work (a mine)
exportar to export
la exposición exhibition
expresar to express
la expresión expression
expresionista
   expressionistic
la expresividad
   expressiveness
el expreso express (train,
   mail)
extender (ie) to
   extend, continue
extendido widespread
la extensión extent, size
externo external
el extranjero (la
   extranjera)
   foreigner
extraño strange
extraordinariamente
   extraordinarily
extremo extreme

F

fabuloso fabulous
fácil easy
el factor factor
la falda skirt
la falta lack; ¡Qué falta
   de vergüenza! What
   shamelessness!
faltar: ¡No faltaba
   más! That's all we
   needed! What
   nonsense!
la familia family
famoso famous
fanático fanatical
fantástico fantastic
el, la farmacéutico druggist,
   pharmacist
la farmacia drugstore,
   pharmacy
fascinante fascinating
fascinar to fascinate
la fatiga fatigue
el favor favor; a favor de
   in favor of; Hágame
   el favor de . . .
   Please . . .; por
   favor please
favorito favorite
la fe faith
febrero February
la fecha date; day
la felicidad happiness
¡Felicitaciones!
   Congratulations!
feliz happy
felizmente happily
femenino: equipo
   femenino women's
   team
fenicio Phoenician
¡Fenómeno!
   Phenomenal! Great!
la feria fair; holiday
feriado: día feriado
   holiday

fértil fertile; moho
   fertil rich mould
el ferrocarril railroad
la festividad festivity;
   holiday
la fiebre fever
fiel faithful
la fiesta feast; party;
   holiday; día de
   fiesta holiday; fiesta
   brava bullfighting;
   fiesta popular
   country gathering,
   general holiday
la figura figure
fijar to fix, establish,
   fijarse (en) to
   notice, look (at)
fijo fixed; precio fijo
   fixed price
filmar to film
la filosofía philosophy
el filósofo (la filósofa)
   philosopher
el fin end; a fines de
   toward the end of;
   al fin finally; fin de
   semana weekend;
   por fin finally
el final: al final at the end
finalmente finally
firmar to sign
la física physics
físico physical
flamenco Andalusian
   gypsy music, song
   and dance
el flan flan, custard with
   caramel sauce
la flauta flute
la flor flower
florecer (zc) to flourish
el folklore folklore
folklórico folk,
   folkloric
el fondo: al fondo in the
   background

la **forma** form
la **formación** formation
la **formalidad** formality
formar to form
formidable superb
el **formulario** form, application form
la **fortaleza** fortress
el **fósil** fossil
la **foto** photo
la **fotografía** photography; photograph
fracturar to fracture, break
francamente frankly
francés French; Frenchman
Francia France
la **frazada** blanket
la **frecuencia: con frecuencia** frequently
frecuente frequent
la **frente** forehead
fresco cool; **hacer fresco** to be cool (weather)
el **frijol: frijoles refritos** refried beans
el **frío** cold; **hacer frío** to be cold (weather); **morirse de frío** to be dying of cold; **tener frío** to be (feel) cold
frito fried
la **frontera** border
el **frontón** jai alai court
la **fruta** fruit; *pl.* fruit
la **frutería** fruit market, store
el **fuego** fire; **fuegos artificiales** fireworks
fuera: fuera de outside; **por fuera** from the outside

fuerte strong
la **fuerza** *pl.* forces; **fuerzas armadas** armed forces
fumar to smoke
funcionar to function, work, run
fundar to found; **fundada por** founded by
el **fútbol** soccer; **fútbol americano** football
el, la **futbolista** soccer player
el **futuro** future; *adj.* future

G

la **gaita** bagpipes
Galicia northwesternmost province of Spain
el **galón** gallon
el **gallego** Galician (language of the Spanish province of Galicia)
la **galleta** cracker, cookie
el **gallo** rooster, cock
la **gana: tener ganas de** to feel like, want
ganar to earn; to win; to gain; **ganar el pan** to earn a living
la **garganta** throat
la **gaseosa** soft drink (carbonated)
gastar to spend; to waste
el **gato** cat
el **gaucho** herdsmen of the pampas, Argentine cowboy
el **gazpacho** a cold, spicy vegetable soup from

the Spanish province of Andalusia
la **generación** generation
el **general** general; *adj.* general, usual; **en general (por lo general)** in general, generally
generoso generous
el **genio** genius
la **gente** people
gentil nice
la **geografía** geography
geográfico geographic
la **geología** geology
la **geometría** geometry
el **gerente** manager
germánico Germanic
el **gesto** expression; gesture
el **gimnasio** gymnasium
el **gitano** (la **gitana**) gypsy
gobernar (ie) to govern
el **gobierno** government
gordo fat
gracias thanks, thank you; **dar las gracias** to thank; **Día de Gracias** Thanksgiving; **gracias a** thanks to; **Muchas gracias.** Thank you very much.
gracioso funny; **¡Qué gracioso!** How funny!
graduarse to graduate
gran (*apocope of* **grande**) great, large; **gran parte** a great part
grande big, large, great
la **grandeza** greatness, grandeur

gratis free, gratis
griego Greek
el **gringo** (la **gringa**) nickname given to foreigners, especially Americans (generally pejorative)
gris gray
gritar to shout
el **grupo** group
el **guacamole** spicy Mexican sauce or dip made from crushed avocados
guapo good-looking
guardar to keep
guatemalteco Guatemalan
la **guerra** war
guerrero warlike
el, la **guía** guide
la **guitarra** guitar
el **guitarrón** large guitar-shaped bass used by Mexican mariachis
gustar to please, be pleasing; **me gusta más** I like best; **me gustan todas** I like all (the girls)
el **gusto** pleasure, delight; **Mucho gusto.** Glad to meet you.

H

haber to have (auxiliary verb to form compound tenses); *see also* **había, habido, habrá, hay, haya**

había (frequent past tense of **hay**) there was (were)
habido *p. part. of* **haber: ha habido** there has (have) been
la **habitación** room
el **habitante** inhabitant
hablar to speak, talk
habrá (*fut. of* **hay**) there will be; **¿habrá?** could there be?
hace (with a verb in the past tense) ago; **hace dos años** two years ago; **hace un rato** a while ago; **¿Cuánto tiempo hace (hacía) que . . .** (+ *pres. or imperf.*)? How long has (had) . . . been-ing?; **hace . . . que** (+ *pres.*) something has been -ing for . . . (length of time)
hacer to make; to do; **hacer** + *inf.* to have something done; **hacer buen tiempo** to be nice; weather; **hacer calor** to be hot (weather); **hacer deportes** to play sports; **hacer ejercicios** to do exercises; **hacer el favor de** to do the favor of; **hacer el papel de** to take the role of; **hacer fresco** to be cool (weather); **hacer frío** to be cold (weather); **¿Qué**

tiempo hace? How's the weather?; **hacer sol** to be sunny; **hacer un viaje** to take a trip; **hacer viento** to be windy
hacia toward
hacía: hacía . . . que (+ *imperf.*) something *had been -ing* for . . . (length of time)
la **hacienda** farm, estate
hallar to find
el **hambre** hunger; **dar hambre** to make hungry; **tener hambre** to be hungry
la **hamburguesa** hamburger
hasta until; as far as; **desde . . . hasta** from . . . to; **hasta cierto punto** up to a point; **Hasta luego.** See you later. So long.; **hasta que** until
hay (a form of the verb **haber**) there is (are); **hay que** one must, it is necessary to
haya *pres. subjunc. of* **hay: prohibe que haya** forbids that there be
el **hecho: hecho que** an event that
el **helado** ice cream, ice cream cone
la **herencia** heritage
herirse (i) to get hurt, become injured
la **hermana** sister
el **hermano** brother; *pl.* brother(s) and sister(s)

hermoso beautiful
el héroe hero
el hierro iron
la hija daughter
el hijo son; *pl.* children,
  son(s) and
  daughter(s)
hinchado swollen
hispánico Hispanic
hispano Hispanic
  (person)
Hispanoamérica
  Spanish America
hispanoamericano
  Spanish-American
la historia history
histórico historic,
  historical
el hogar home; hogar de
  ancianos old-age
  home
¡Hola! Hello! Hi!
holandés Dutch
el hombre man;
  ¡Hombre! Wow! Hey!
honesto honest
el honor honor, en honor
  de in honor of
honrar to honor
la hora hour; time; a
  estas horas at this
  hour; altas horas
  very late; ¿A qué
  hora? At what
  time?; hora de time
  to; ¿Qué hora es?
  What time is it?
el horario: horario
  corrido continuous
  hours (on a job)
el horno oven
el horror: ¡Qué horror!
  How awful!
el hospital hospital
el hotel hotel
hoy today; hoy en día
  nowadays, presently

la huelga strike
el hueso bone
el huésped guest
el huevo egg; huevos
  rancheros fried eggs
  in a tomato, onion
  and chili sauce
la humanidad mankind,
  humanity
humano human; ser
  humano human
  being
humilde humble
el humor: sentido del
  humor sense of
  humor
hundirse to sink

I

ibérico: Península
  Ibérica Iberian
  Peninsula
ibero Iberian (original
  settlers of the
  Iberian Peninsula)
la ida: ida y vuelta
  round-trip
la idea idea
el ideal ideal; *adj.* ideal
el idealismo idealism
la identidad identity
identificarse con to
  identify (oneself)
  with
el idioma language
el ídolo idol
la iglesia church
ignorante ignorant
ignorar to not know,
  be unaware of
igual the same
la igualdad equality
la ilusión illusion
la imaginación
  imagination

imaginario imaginary
imaginarse to imagine
imitar to imitate
el impacto impact
el imperio empire;
  Imperio Romano
  Roman Empire
el impermeable raincoat
implementar to put
  into effect
imponente majestic,
  impressive
la importancia
  importance
importante important
importar to matter, be
  important; ¿le
  importa . . . ? do
  you care
  about . . . ?; no
  (me) importa it
  doesn't matter, I
  don't care
imposible impossible
la impresión impression
impresionante
  impressive
impresionar to impress
improvisar to
  improvise
el impuesto tax
inca Inca (the people);
  Inca Inca (emperor)
incaico *adj.* Inca, Incan
incluir to include
increíble incredible
la independencia
  independence
independiente
  independent
indicar to indicate
indiferenciado
  undifferentiated
indiferentemente
  indifferently
indígena indigenous,
  native

el **indio** (la **india**) Indian; *adj.* Indian

individuo individual

industrializar to industrialize

infeliz unhappy, miserable

el **infierno** hell

infinitamente infinitely

infinito infinite

la **influencia** influence

influir en to influence

la **información** information

la **informalidad** informality

informarse to become informed, inform oneself

el **informe** report

la **ingeniería** engineering

el, la **ingeniero** engineer

Inglaterra England

inglés English; Englishman

el **ingrediente** ingredient

la **injusticia: ¡Qué injusticia!** How unfair!

inmediato immediate

el, la **inmigrante** immigrant

inocente innocent

inofensivo harmless

insistir (en) to insist (on)

la **insolencia** insolence

la **inspiración** inspiration

inspirar to inspire

la **instrucción** instruction; **instrucción primaria** elementary education; **sin instrucción** uneducated

el **instrumento** instrument; **instrumento de cuerda** stringed instrument

insultar to insult

integrar to compose, make up; **integrarse a** to get into

intelectual intellectual

inteligente smart, intelligent

la **intensidad** intensity

el **interés** interest

interesante interesting

interesar to interest

interior inner

internacional international

interno internal

interrumpir to interrupt

la **interrupción** interruption

la **intimidad** intimacy, closeness

íntimo intimate, close

introducir (zc) to introduce

invadir to invade

inventar to invent

el **invierno** winter

la **invitación** invitation

el **invitado** (la **invitada**) guest

invitar to invite

ir to go; **ir a** + *inf.* to be going to + *inf.*; **ir del brazo (de la mano)** to go (walk) arm in arm (hand in hand); **ir en auto (autobús, avión)** to go by car (bus, plane); **ir de paseo** to take a walk, go out; **irse** to go

(away), leave; **ir y venir** coming and going; **Que le vaya bien.** May all go well with you.; **Vamos.** Let's go.; **Vamos a** + *inf.* Let's . . . ; **No vayamos.** Let's not go.; **No vayamos a** + *inf.* Let's not . . .

Irlanda Ireland

irlandés Irish

la **ironía** irony

irónicamente ironically

la **isla** island

Italia Italy

italiano Italian

la **izquierda** left; **a la izquierda** to (on) the left

J

el **jai alai** jai alai (Basque sport)

jamás never, (not) ever

el **jamón** ham

Janucá Chanukah

el **Japón** Japan

japonés Japanese

el **jardín** garden

el, la **jefe** chief; boss

el **jerez** sherry

Jesucristo Jesus Christ

Jesús Jesus; **¡Jesús!** Gee whiz! Golly!

la **jota** popular dance in Spanish provinces of Aragón and Valencia

el, la **joven** young man, young lady; *pl.* young people; *adj.* young

la **joya** jewel; *pl.* jewelry
la **joyería** jewelry store
judío Jew; Jewish
el **juego** game
jueves Thursday
el **jugador** (la **jugadora**) player
jugar (ue) (a) to play (a game)
el **juglar** minstrel
el **jugo** juice
el **juguete** toy
la **juguetería** toy shop
julio July
junio June
junto together; close
el, la **jurado** juror
la **justicia** justice

K

el **kilo** kilo, kilogram (2.2 pounds)
el **kilómetro** kilometer (a little over six-tenths of a mile)

L

la the *(f. sing.); dir. obj.* her, it, you (**Ud.**); **la de** that of; **la que** the one that
el **labio** lip
el **laboratorio** laboratory
el **lado** side; **al lado de** beside, next to; **a tu lado** next to you
el **lago** lake
la **lámpara** lamp, street lamp
la **lana** wool
la **lanza** lance
lanzar to throw, hurl
el **lápiz** pencil

largo long
las the *(f. pl.); dir. obj.* them, you (**Uds.**); **las de** those of; **las que** the ones (those) that
la **lástima** misfortune; pity; **¡Qué lástima!** What a shame!
el **latín** Latin (language); **latin vulgar** vernacular or spoken Latin
el **latino** (la **latina**) Latin (person); *adj.* Latin
latinoamericano Latin American
el **lavadero** laundry room
lavar to wash; **lavarse** to wash (oneself), get washed
le *indir. obj.* (to, for, from) him, her, it, you (**Ud.**)
la **lección** lesson
la **lectura** reading
la **leche** milk; **café con leche** coffee prepared with hot milk
la **lechuga** lettuce
leer to read
el **legado** legacy
legislativo legislative
la **legumbre** vegetable
lejos far, far away; **lejos de** far from
la **lengua** language; **lengua romance** Romance language
lento slow
la **leña** firewood
les *indir. obj.* (to, for, from) them, you (**Uds.**)
la **letra** lyrics
el **letrero** sign

levantarse to get up, stand up
la **ley** law
la **leyenda** legend
la **liberación** liberation
liberar to liberate
la **libertad** liberty, freedom
la **libra** pound
libre free; **al aire libre** in the open air
la **librería** bookstore
el **libro** book
limitarse a to limit onself, be limited to
limpiar to clean, neaten
lindo pretty, beautiful; nice
la **línea** line
la **liquidación** sale
listo ready
la **literatura** literature
el **litro** liter (a little more than a quart)
lo *dir. obj.* him, it, you (**Ud.**); the (neuter); **en lo más alto** at the top; **lo antes posible** as soon as possible; **lo cierto** what is certain; **lo cual** which; **lo maravilloso de** the wonderful thing about; **lo más** + *adv.* + **posible** as . . . as possible; **lo más . . . que** (+ expression of possibility) as . . . as, **lo mismo** the same (thing); **lo que** what, that which; **por lo tanto** therefore, **todo lo que** everything that

el **loco** (la **loca**) madman
(madwoman); *adj.*
crazy
lograr to bring about
los the *(m. pl.); dir.*
obj. them, you
(**Uds.**); **los de** those
of; **los que** the ones
(those) that
la **lucha** struggle, fight
luchar (por) to fight
(for)
luego then; **Hasta**
luego. See you
later. So long ;
luego que as soon as
el **lugar** place; **en lugar**
de instead of
lujoso of luxury
lunes Monday
la **luz** light

LL

llamar to call; **llamar**
por teléfono to
phone; **llamarse** to
be called, named;
¿Cómo se
llama . . . ? What
is . . .'s name?; **me**
llamo my name is
la **llave** key
la **llegada** arrival
llegar (a) to arrive (in),
get to, reach; **aquí**
llegan here come;
llegar a ser to
become
llenar to fill; **llenarse**
(**de**) to fill up (with)
lleno de full of
llevar to carry, bear; to
take; to lead; to
wear; **llevarse bien**
to get along well

llorar to cry, weep
llover (ue) to rain
la **lluvia** rain

M

la **madera** wood
la **madre** mother; **Madre-**
Tierra Mother Earth
(Indian deity)
la **madrina** godmother
el **maestro** (la **maestra**)
teacher; master
magnífico wonderful,
magnificent
el **maíz** corn
mal *adv.* badly,
poorly; **acabar mal**
to have an unhappy
ending
el **mal** evil
mal, malo *adj.* bad,
naughty
la **maleta** suitcase
la **mamá** mom, mother
el **mambo** dance of Afro-
Cuban origin
mandar to order; to
give orders; to send
el **mando** command
manejar to drive
la **manera** way, manner,
fashion; **de manera**
diferente in a
different way; **de**
ninguna manera in
no way, not at all;
de otra manera
differently; **de una**
manera . . . in a . . .
way
la **manifestación**
demonstration
la **manipulación**
manipulation
el **maniquí** manikin

la **mano** hand; **¡Arriba**
las manos! Hands
up!; **Dame la mano.**
Give me your
hand.; **en (a) manos**
de in (into) the
hands of; **¡Manos a**
la obra! Let's get to
work!
mantener to keep,
maintain
la **mantequilla** butter
la **manzana** apple
la **mañana** morning; *adv.*
tomorrow; **de la**
mañana A.M.:
mañana temprano
early tomorrow
morning; **por la**
mañana in the
morning
el **mapa** map
la **máquina** machine
el, la **mar: Mar Caribe**
Caribbean Sea
la **maravilla** marvel,
wonder
maravilloso
wonderful,
marvelous; **lo**
maravilloso de the
wonderful thing
about
marchar to run, work;
marcharse to leave,
go away
el **mariachi** Mexican
musical group
el **marido** husband
el **marisco** shellfish
martes Tuesday
marxista Marxist
marzo March
marrón brown
más *adv.* more, any
more; most; *prep.*
plus; **¿algo más?**

anything else?, **más conocido** better known; **más de** (+ number) more than; **más o menos** more or less; **más . . . que** more . . . than; **más vale** it is better; **me gusta más** I like best; **otro más** one more, another; **¡Qué idea más ridícula!** What a ridiculous idea!

la **masa** mass

la **máscara** mask

el **matador** (la **matadora**) matador

matar to kill

las **matemáticas** mathematics

la **materia** subject

el **matrimonio** marriage; married couple

maya Maya; Mayan

mayo May

mayor older, oldest; greater, greatest; **la mayor parte** the major part

la **mayoría** majority

me (to, for, from) me, myself

el **mecánico** (la **mecánica**) mechanic

el **mecanógrafo** (la **mecanógrafa**) typist

la **medicina** medicine

médico medical

el, la **médico** doctor

el **medio** middle; environment; *adj.* middle; half; **clase media** middle class; **en medio de** in the middle of; **las doce y media** 12:30;

media hora a half hour; **por medio de** by means of, through

mediodía noon; midday break; **al mediodía** at noon; for the midday meal

la **medianoche** midnight

el **Mediterráneo** Mediterranean Sea

mejor better, best

mejorar to improve

melancólico melancholy

la **melodía** melody

mencionar to mention

el, la **menor** minor; *adj.* younger, youngest

menos less, least; **a menos que** unless; **más o menos** more or less; **menos de** (+ number) less than; **menos . . . que** less . . . than; **por lo menos** at least

mentir (ie) to lie

la **mentira** lie

el **mercado** market, marketplace

el **merengue** popular dance of Caribbean origin

la **merienda** afternoon snack

la **mermelada** jam, marmalade

el **mes** month

la **mesa** table

la **meseta** mesa, plateau

mestizo of mixed race

mexicano Mexican

México Mexico; Mexico City

méxico-americano Mexican-American

la **mezcla** mixture, mixing

mezclarse con to mix with

la **mezquita** mosque

mi, mis my

mí *obj. of prep.* me, myself

el **miedo** fear; **tener miedo (de)** to be afraid (of, to)

el **miembro** member

mientras (que) while; whereas; **mientras tanto** in the meantime

miércoles Wednesday

mil 1000; **miles** thousands

el **milagro** miracle

el **militar** military man, soldier; *adj.* military

la **milla** mile

el **millón** million; **un millón de . . .** a million . . .

la **mina** mine

la **minoría** minority

el **minuto** minute

mío(s), mía(s) *adj.* my, (of) mine; **el mío** (**la mia, los míos, las mías**) *pron.* mine; **¡Dios mío!** My goodness!

mirar to look (at), watch; **mirar el aceite** to check the oil

la **misa** mass (church)

la **miseria** misery; poverty

la **misión** mission

mismo same; very, just, right; **ahora mismo** right now;

al mismo tiempo at the same time; allí mismo right there; lo mismo (que) the same (thing) (as); por eso mismo that's just it

misterioso mysterious

el misticismo mysticism

místico mystical

mixto co-ed

la moda fashion

moderado mild

moderno modern

modesto modest

el modo: modo de ser nature, way of being; de modo que so that

la mola Panamanian needlework panel of quilted or appliqued fabric

molestar to bother, annoy

el momento moment

la moneda coin, currency

la monja nun

monótono monotonous

el monstruo monster

la montaña mountain

montar to mount

moreno dark-haired, brunette

morir (ue) to die; morirse (de) to die, be dying (of)

el mostrador counter

mostrar (ue) to show

el motor motor, engine

mover (ue) to move

el movimiento movement

la muchacha girl

el muchacho boy; pl. children, boy(s) and girl(s)

muchísimo very much; pl. very many

mucho adj. much, a lot of; very; too much; pl. many; adv. very much; Muchas gracias. Thank you very much.; Mucho gusto. Glad to meet you.; mucho que hacer a lot to do; mucho tiempo a long time

mudarse to move (change residence)

mueble: los muebles furniture

la muerte death

el muerto (la muerta) dead person, corpse; adj. dead

la mujer woman; wife; nombre de mujer woman's name

mulato mulatto (of African and Caucasian blood)

mundial adj. world, worldwide

el mundo world; Nuevo Mundo New World (America); todo el mundo everyone; the whole world

la muñeca doll

la muñeira dance from the province of Galicia in northern Spain

el mural mural

el muro wall

el músculo muscle

el museo museum

la música music; música folklórica folk music

el músico (la música) musician

musulmán Moslem

muy very

N

nacer (zc) to be born

nacido born

el nacimiento birth; crèche, Nativity scene

la nación nation

nacional national

la nacionalidad nationality

nada nothing, not anything; de nada you're welcome; por nada del mundo (not) for anything in the world

nadar to swim

nadie no one, nobody, not anyone

napoleónico Napoleonic

la naranja orange

la nariz nose

la natación swimming

la natalidad: el control de la natalidad birth control

la natilla custard

la naturaleza nature; natural setting; naturaleza muerta still life

naturalmente naturally

Navarra Navarre (province in northern Spain)

la Navidad Christmas; pl. Christmas holidays

necesario necessary

la **necesidad** necessity

necesitar to need

el **negocio** business; **viaje de negocios** business trip

negro black; Negro

el **neoyorquino** (la **neoyorquina**) New Yorker

nervioso nervous

nevado snow-covered

ni nor, or; **ni . . . ni** neither . . . nor

la **niebla** fog

la **nieta** granddaughter

el **nieto** grandson; *pl.* grandchildren

la **nieve** snow

ningún, ninguno none, not any, no , not one, neither (of them); **de ninguna manera** in no way, not at all

la **niña** girl, child

el **niño** boy, child; *pl.* children, kids

el **nivel** level

no, no, not; **¿no?** right? true?

el **noble** noble

la **noche** night, evening; **de la noche** P.M. (at night); **de noche** at night; **esta noche** tonight, this evening; **por la noche** at night, in the evening; **todas las noches** every night

la **Nochebuena** Christmas Eve

el **nombre** name; **a (en) nombre de** in the name of; **nombre de**

mujer woman's name

el **noreste** northeast

el **noroeste** northwest

el **norte** north

norteamericano North American; American (U.S.)

nos (to, for, from) us, ourselves

nosotros, nosotras *subj. pron.* we; *obj. of prep.* us, ourselves

la **nota** note; grade

notar to notice

la **noticia** (piece of) news; *pl.* news

el **noticiero** newscast

novecientos 900

la **novedad** novelty, something new

la **novela** novel

noveno ninth

noventa ninety

la **novia** girlfriend; fiancée

el **noviazgo** courtship; engagement

noviembre November

el **novio** boyfriend; suitor; fiancé; *pl.* sweethearts

la **nube** cloud; **por las nubes** sky-high (prices)

nublado blurry

nuestro *adj.* our, of ours; **el nuestro** *pron.* ours

nueve nine

nuevo new; **Año Nuevo** New Year's; **Nuevo Mundo** New World (America); **¿Qué hay de nuevo?** What's new?

la **nuez** nut, walnut

el **número** number

numeroso numerous

nunca never, not ever

O

o or; **o . . . o** either . . . or

obedecer (zc) to obey

el **objeto** object; **objeto de arte** art object

obligado (a) obligated (to)

la **obra** work; body of work; **¡Manos a la obra!** Let's get to work! **obra de arte** work of art; **obra de teatro** play

observar to observe

obsesionar to obsess

obtener to get, gain, obtain

obvio obvious

la **ocasión** occasion

occidental western

el **océano** ocean; **Océano Atlántico** Atlantic Ocean

octavo eighth

octubre October

el, la **oculista** oculist

ocupado busy

ocupar to take, occupy

ocurrir to occur, happen

ochenta eighty

ocho eight

ochocientos 800

odiar to hate

el **oeste** west

ofender (ie) to offend, be offensive; **ofenderse** to become offended

oficial official

la **oficina** office

ofrecer (zc) to offer

el **oído** hearing, ear

oír to hear

ojalá que I hope

el **ojo** eye

olvidar to forget; **olvidarse (de)** to forget (about)

once eleven

la **ópera** opera

opinar to believe, hold an opinion

la **opinión** opinion; **según su opinión** in your opinion

oponerse (a) to oppose, be against (it; each other)

la **oportunidad** opportunity, chance

el **opresor (la opresora)** oppressor

el **orden** order; **a sus órdenes** at your service

la **oreja** ear

organizar to organize; **organizarse** to get organized

el **orgullo** pride

orgulloso proud

el **origen** origin

originarse to originate

el **oro** gold

la **orquesta** orchestra

os (to, for, from) you, yourselves (*fam. pl.*)

oscuro dark

el **otoño** autumn

otro other, another; **otro más** one more; **otra vez** again

P

la **paciencia** patience

el, la **paciente** patient

el **padre** father; priest; *pl.* parents

el **padrino** godfather; los **padrinos** godparents

la **paella** Spanish dish of seafood and saffroned rice

el **paganismo** paganism

pagano pagan

pagar to pay

la **página** page

el **país** country

la **palabra** word

la **palabrota** swear word

pálido pale

el **pan** bread; **ganar el pan** to earn a living; **pan tostado** toast

la **panadería** bakery

panameño Panamanian

el **pantalón:** los **pantalones** pants

el **papá** dad, father; *pl.* parents

la **papaya** papaya (tropical fruit)

el **papel** paper; role; **hacer el papel de** to take the role of

el **paquete** package

el **par** pair

para for; in order to; by (a certain time); **estar para** to be about to; **estudiar para** to study to be; **para que** so that; **¿para qué?** why? for what purpose?; **para siempre** forever

la **parada** stop

el **paraguas** umbrella

paraguayo Paraguayan

parar(se) to stop, halt

parecer (zc) to seem, appear, look like; **¿Qué le(s) parece si . . . ?** How about if . . . ?

la **pared** wall

la **pareja** couple, pair, set

el, la **pariente** relative

el **parque** park

la **parte** part; portion, section; **de parte de** on behalf of; **¿De parte de quién?** Who is calling?; **en parte** partly; **gran parte** a great part; **la mayor parte** the major part; **por otra parte** on the other hand; **por (a, en) todas partes** everywhere

la **participación** participation

participar (en) to participate (in)

particular special, particular

la **partida** departure

el **partido** game, match; political party

partir to leave, depart

el **pasado** past; *adj.* past, last; **el verano pasado** last summer

el **pasaje** ticket

el **pasajero (la pasajera)** passenger

el **pasaporte** passport

pasar to pass, get by; to spend (time); to happen; **pasar (adelante)** to come in (to one's home); **pasar a ser** to become; **pasar por** to drop by; to pass by; **¿Qué le pasa a . . . ?** What's the matter with . . . ?; **¿Qué pasa?** What's wrong? What's going on?

la **Pascua** Easter

pasear to take a walk, a drive

el **paseo** walk; ride; **dar un paseo** to take a walk, a ride

la **pasión** passion; Passion

el **paso** step; religious float carried during Holy Week processions

patear to kick

patinar to skate

el **patio** patio

la **patria** native land

el **pavo** turkey

la **payada** improvisational competition among gaucho singers

el **payador** gaucho singer

la **paz** peace

el **pecado** sin

el **pedazo** piece

pedir (i) to ask (for), request, order (in a restaurant); **pedir perdón** to beg one's pardon

el **peinado** hairdo

la **pelea** fight, argument

la **película** film, movie; **película documental** documentary (film)

el **peligro** danger

peligroso dangerous

el **pelo** hair

la **pelota** ball; jai alai (Basque sport)

la **peluquería** beauty salon; barber shop

el **peluquero (la peluquera)** beautician; barber

la **pena: valer la pena** to be worth the trouble

penetrar to penetrate

la **península** peninsula; **Península Ibérica** Iberian Peninsula

el, la **peninsular** person born in Spain

el, la **penitente** penitent

pensar (ie) to think; to plan, intend, think of, about (followed by *inf.*); **pensar de** to think of, about (an opinion); **pensar en** to think about, concerning (followed by *n.* or *pron.*)

la **pensión** boarding house

peor worse, worst

el **pepino** cucumber

pequeño little, small

la **percusión** percussion

perder (ie) to lose; to miss (train, plane); **perder (el) tiempo** to waste (one's time); **perderse** to get lost

perdido lost

el **perdón** pardon; **¡Perdón!** Excuse me!

perdonar to pardon, forgive; **¡Perdone!** Excuse me!

perezoso lazy

perfecto perfect, fine

el **periódico** newspaper

el, la **periodista** journalist

el **permiso: Con permiso.** Excuse me.

permitir to permit, allow

pero but

la **persona** person

el **personaje** character (as in a literary work)

la **personalidad** personality

la **perspectiva** perspective, outlook

pertenecer (zc) a to belong to

peruano Peruvian

pesado boring, heavy

el **pesar: a pesar de (que)** in spite of (the fact that)

el **pescado** fish

pescar to fish; **ir a pescar** to go fishing

la **peseta** monetary unit of Spain

pesimista pessimistic

el **peso** monetary unit of several Latin American countries

el **picador** mounted bullfighter who prods the bull with a lance

picante hot (spicy)

el **pico** peak

pictográfico: escritura pictográfica picture writing

el **pie** foot; **a pie** on foot

la **piedad** pity

la **piedra** stone, rock

la **piel** skin

la **pierna** leg

la **píldora** pill

la **pimienta** pepper (spice)

el **pimiento** green pepper
pintar to paint

el **pintor** (la **pintora**) painter

pintoresco picturesque

la **pintura** painting

la **pipa** pipe

piramidal pyramidal

la **pirámide** pyramid

los **Pirineos** the Pyrenees (mountain range)

el **piropo** compliment

el **piso** floor

la **pizarra** blackboard

el **plan** plan

la **planta: planta baja** ground floor

la **plata** silve

el **plátano** banana

el **plato** fish, plate

la **playa** beach

la **plaza** plaza, square; bullring

la **pluma** pen, fountain pen

la **población** population

pobre poor; los **pobres** the poor (people)

la **pobreza** poverty

poco little (in amount); *pl.* few; **poco a poco** little by little; **poco después** a short time after(wards); **poquísimo** very little; **un poco** a little (bit)

poder (ue) to be able, can, may; **puede ser** (it) may be; **se puede** one can

el **poder** power

poderoso powerful

el **poema** poem

la **poesía** poetry

el **poeta** poet

el **policía** policeman

la **policía** police; policewoman

la **política** politics; policy; politician (*f.*)

el **político** politician (*m.*); *adj.* political

el **pollo** chicken

el **poncho** poncho

poner to put, place; **poner la mesa** to set the table; **ponerse** to get, become; to put on (clothing); **ponerse de acuerdo** to agree

popular popular; **fiesta popular** country gathering, general holiday

por for; because of, on account of; for the sake of; by; per; along; through; throughout; around (in the vicinity of); in; during; in place of; in exchange for; **por aquí** this way, over here, around here; **por casualidad** by coincidence; **por ciento** percent; **por ejemplo** for example; **por eso** that's why, for that reason; **por favor** please; **por fin** finally; **por la mañana** in the morning; **por la noche** in the evening, at night; **por las nubes** sky-high (prices); **por la tarde** in the afternoon, evening; **por lo general** generally; **por lo menos** at least; **por lo tanto** therefore; **por medio de** by means of, through; **por nada del mundo** (not) for anything in the world; **por otra parte** on the other hand; **por supuesto** of course; **por teléfono** on the telephone; **por televisión (radio)** on TV (radio); **por todas partes** everywhere

¿**por qué**? why?

el **porcentaje** percentage

porque because

el **porteño** (la **porteña**) a person from Buenos Aires

portugués Portuguese

la **posada** lodging; Mexican Christmas celebration

la **posibilidad** possibility

posible possible

postal: tarjeta postal postcard

el **postre** dessert

practicar to practice; to play (a sport); **se practica** is played

práctico practical

el **precio** price; ¿**A qué precio**? What's the price?; ¿**Qué precio tiene . . . ?** What's the price of . . . ?

precioso precious; lovely; darling

precisamente precisely

preciso precise

precolombino pre-Columbian

predominar to predominate

preferible preferable

preferir (ie) to prefer

la **pregunta** question

preguntar to ask; **preguntarse** to wonder

prehistórico prehistoric

el **premio** prize

la **prenda** article (clothing); **la prenda de vestir** article of clothing

prender to turn on

la **prensa** press

la **preocupación** worry

preocuparse (por) to worry (about)

preparar to prepare

la **presencia** presence

presentar to present, show; to introduce

presente present

el **presidente** president

prestar to loan; **pedir prestado** to borrow; **prestar atención** to pay attention, give heed

el **presupuesto** budget

el **pretendiente** suitor

la **primavera** spring

primer, primero first; **de primera clase** first-class; first-rate

el **primo** (la **prima**) cousin

principal main, principal

el **príncipe** prince

el **principio** beginning; **a principios de** around the beginning of

la **prisa: tener prisa** to be in a hurry

privado private

privilegiado privileged

probar (ue) to try out; to try, taste; **probarse** to try on

el **problema** problem

la **procesión** procession

proclamado proclaimed

producir (zc) to produce

el **producto** product

la **profecía** prophecy

la **profesión** profession

el **profesor** (la **profesora**) teacher, professor

profundo deep, profound

el **programa** program

prohibir to prohibit, forbid

la **promesa** promise

prometer to promise

el **promotor** (la **promotora**) promoter, champion

pronto soon; fast, quickly; **lo más pronto posible** as soon a possible; **prontísimo** very soon; **tan pronto como** as soon as

la **propiedad** property

propio own

propósito: a propósito by the way

próspero prosperous

la **protesta** protest

el, la **protestante** Protestant

protestar to protest

la **provincia** province

provocar to provoke

próximo next, coming

prudente prudent

la **psicología** psychology

psicológico psychological

publicar to publish

el **público** public; spectators; *adj.* public; **en público** in public

el **pueblo** people; village, town

el **puente** bridge

la **puerta** door

el **puerto** port, harbor

puertorriqueño Puerto Rican

pues *interj.* well . . . ; *conj.* for, because

puesto put

el **puesto** job, position

el **pulso** pulse

la **punctualidad** punctuality

el **punto** point, dot; **en punto** on the dot, exactly; **hasta cierto punto** up to a point

puntual punctual

puro pure; all

Q

que *rel, pron.* that, which, who, whom; *adv.* than; **el (la, los, las) que** which, who(m), the one(s) that, those who; **lo que** what, that which; **mucho que hacer** a lot to do; **Que le vaya bien.**

May all go well with you.

¿qué? what?, which?; **¿para qué?** why?, for what purpose?; **¿por qué?** why?; **¿Qué hay de nuevo?** What's new?; **¿Qué tal . . . ?** How about . . . ?

¡qué . . . ! What (a) . . . ! How . . . !; **¡Qué alivio!** What a relief! **¡Qué barbaridad!** Good grief! **¡Qué casualidad!** What a coincidence! **¡Qué emoción!** How exciting! **¡Qué falta de vergüenza!** What shamelessness! **¡Qué gracioso!** How funny! **¡Qué idea más ridícula!** What a ridiculous idea!; **¡Qué lástima!** What a shame! **¡Qué va!** Oh, come now!

quedar to remain, be left; to fit; **quedarse** to stay, remain; **quedar tiempo** to have time left

la **quena** Indian flute (Peru)

querer (ie) to want, wish; to love; **querer decir** to mean

querido dear; **seres queridos** loved ones

quien, quienes who, whom; the one who, those who

¿quién? who?, whom?; **¿de quién?** whose?

la **química** chemistry

el, la **químico** chemist

quince fifteen

quinientos 500

quinto fifth

quitar to take away; **quitarse** to take off (clothing)

quizás maybe, perhaps

R

la **rabia** anger; **¡Qué rabia!** What anger! How angry I am!

el, la **radio** radio; **por radio** on the radio

la **ranchera** type of Mexican song

el **rancho** ranch; in Venezuela and Colombia, a small house

rápidamente quickly, rapidly

rápido *adj.* rapid, fast; *adv.* fast, quickly

la **raqueta** racket

raro rare

el **rato** short time; **hace un rato** a while ago

la **raza** race; people of Spanish or Indian origin; **Día de la Raza** Columbus Day

la **razón** reason; **con razón** no wonder; **tener razón** to be right

razonable reasonable

la **reacción** reaction

real royal; el **Real Madrid** Spanish soccer team

la **realidad** reality; **en realidad** in reality, actually

el **realismo** realism

realista realistic

realizarse to become reality

realmente really, actually

rebajar to lower

rebelde rebel

la **rebelión** rebellion

el **recado** message

el, la **recepcionista** desk clerk; receptionist

la **receta** recipe

recibir to receive

reciente recent

recientemente recently

la **Reconquista** Reconquest (of Moorish Spain by the Christians)

recordar (ue) to remember

recrear to re-create

el **recurso: recursos naturales** natural resources

la **referencia** reference

reflejar to reflect

la **reforma** reform

el **refrán** proverb, saying

el **refresco** soft drink

el **refrigerador** refrigerator

refrito: frijoles refritos refried beans

refugiarse to take refuse

regalar to give (as a gift)

el **regalo** gift, present

regatear to bargain, haggle over prices

el **régimen** (*pl.* **regímenes**) regime

la **región** region

regresar to return, go (come) back

la **reina** queen

el **reino** kingdom

reírse to laugh

la **relación** relation, relationship

relativamente relatively

la **religión** religion

la **religiosidad** religiousness

religioso religious

el **reloj** clock; watch

el **remedio** cure, remedy

remoto remote

la **rendición** surrender

rendir (i) to produce; **rendirse** to surrender, give up

repetir (i) to repeat; **Repita(n), por favor.** Please repeat.

el **reportaje** report

el, la **reportero** reporter

la **representación** representation; portrayal

representar to represent; to portray, show

reproducir (zc) to reproduce

la **república** republic; **República Dominicana** Dominican Republic

republicano Republican

requerir (ie) to require

resentir (ie) to resent

la **reserva** reservation

reservar to reserve

el **resfriado** cold

la **residencia: residencia estudiantil** dorm

la **resistencia** resistance

resolver (ue) to solve, resolve

respectivamente respectively

respetar to respect

el **respeto** respect

la **responsabilidad** responsibility

responsable responsible

la **respuesta** answer

el **restaurante** restaurant

el **resto** rest, remainder

resuelto solved, resolved

el **resultado** score

la **resurrección** resurrection

el **retrato** portrait

la **reunión** meeting, gathering, get-together

reunirse (a) to meet, gather (to); **reunirse con** to get together with

revelar to reveal

el **revés** reverse, opposite; **al revés** the opposite, backwards

la **revista** magazine

la **revolución** revolution

revolucionario revolutionary

revuelto scrambled

el **rey** king; *pl.* king and queen; **Día de los Reyes** Epiphany (Jan. 6); **Reyes Católicos** Catholic Monarchs (Ferdinand and Isabella); **Reyes Magos** Three Kings (Wise Men)

rezar to pray

rico rich; delicious

ridículo ridiculous

el **río** river

la **risa** laughter

el **ritmo** rhythm

el **rito** rite

robar to steal

el **robo** theft, robbery

rodear to surround; **rodeado de** surrounded by

rogar (ue) to beg

rojo red

romance: lengua romance Romance language

romano Roman

romper to break; **romper con** to break up with

la **ropa** clothes, clothing; **ropa vieja** Caribbean dish

el **rostro** face

roto broken

rubio blond

el **ruido** noise

la **ruina** ruin

la **rumba** dance of Afro-Cuban origin

S

sábado Saturday

saber to know; to find out; **saber** + *inf.* to know how to

el **sabio** (la **sabia**) learned person, scholar

sabroso delicious

sacar to take out; **sacar una nota** to get a grade

el **sacerdote** priest

el **sacrificado** (la **sacrificada**) sacrificial victim

sacrificar to sacrifice

el **sacrificio** sacrifice

la **sal** salt

la **sala** large room; living room; **sala de clase** classroom

el **salario** salary (hourly wage)

la **salchicha** sausage

salir (de) to leave, go out, come out; **salir con** to go out with; **salir para** to leave for; **Todo saldrá bien.** Everything will turn out fine.

la **salud** health; **¡Salud!** To your health! Cheers!

saludar to greet

la **samba** dance of Brazilian origin

san (apocope of **santo**) saint

la **sandalia** sandal

el **sándwich** sandwich

la **sangre** blood; heritage

la **sangría** wine and fruit punch

sanguinario bloody

san (apocope of **santo**) saint; **San Juan** capital of Puerto Rico

sano healthy

el **santo** (la **santa**) saint; saint's day; *adj.* holy; **santo patrón (santa patrona)** patron saint; **Semana Santa** Holy Week

la **sardana** dance from province of

Cataluña in northeastern Spain

la **sátira** satire

el, la **satirista** satirist

satisfactorio satisfactory

se *indir. obj.* (to, for, from) him, her, it, you (**Ud., Uds.**), them; *refl. pron.* (to, for, from) himself, herself, itself, yourself (**Ud.**), themselves, yourselves (**Uds.**)

sé *first person sing. pres.* of **saber**; *second person sing. imperative* of **ser**

la **sección** section

el **secretario** (la **secretaria**) secretary

el **secuestro** kidnapping

el **secreto** secret; *adj.* secret

el **secundario** secondary school, high school

la **sed: tener sed** to be thirsty

sefardí Sephardic

seguida: en seguida right away, at once

seguido consecutive

seguir (i) to follow; to continue, keep on, still be; **seguir cursos** to take courses

según according to; **según su opinión** in your opinion

segundo second

seguro sure, certain

seis six

seiscientos 600

la **semana** week; **día de semana** weekday;

fin de semana weekend; **la semana que viene** next week, this coming week; **Semana Santa** Holy Week

semejante similar

el **semestre** semester

sencillo simple, easy

sensacional sensational

sentado seated, sitting

sentarse (ie) to sit down

el **sentido** sense; **sentido de humor** sense of humor

sentir (ie) to feel; to be sorry; **sentirse** to feel

el **señal de tránsito** traffic signal

señalar to signal

el **señor** (*abbr.* **Sr.**) man, gentleman; sir; mister, Mr.

la **señora** (*abbr.* **Sra.**) lady; wife; ma'am; Mrs.

los **señores** (*abbr.* **Sres.**) Mr. & Mrs.; ladies and gentlemen

la **señorita** (*abbr.* **Srta.**) young lady; miss; Miss

la **separación** separation

separado separate; separated

separar to separate

septiembre September

séptimo seventh

el **ser: ser humano** human being; **seres queridos** loved ones

ser to be (someone or something; description or characteristics);

¿Cómo es (son) . . . ? What is (are) . . . like?; Es que . . . That's because . . .; llegar (pasar) a ser to become; ser de to be from (somewhere); to be (someone's); ¿De dónde será? I wonder where she's from.; El libro es de Felipe. The book is Phillip's.

la serenidad serenity, calm

la serie series

serio serious; en serio seriously

el servicio service

la servilleta napkin

servir (i) to serve; ¿En qué puedo servirle? What can I do for you?

sesenta sixty

setecientos 700

setenta seventy

severo severe

sexista sexist

el sexo sex

sexto sixth

si if; como si as if

sí yes

sicológicamente psychologically

siempre always; para siempre forever

la sierra mountain range

la siesta midday break for lunch and rest; dormir la siesta to take a nap after lunch

siete seven

el siglo century

el significado meaning, significance

significar to signify, mean

silencioso silent

la silla chair

el sillón armchair

simbólico symbolic

simbolizar to symbolize

el símbolo symbol

simpático nice

simplemente simply

simultáneamente simultaneously

sin without; sin certificar uncertified; sin embargo however; sin que without

la sinagoga synagogue

sincero sincere

sino but, but rather

sinónimo synonymous

el síntoma symptom

el, la sirviente servant

el sistema system

el sitio place, site, location

la situación situation

situado situated, located

situar to place, locate

sobre on, about, concerning; on, upon; over; sobre todo especially

la sobremesa after-dinner conversation

la sobriedad moderation

la sobrina niece

el sobrino nephew

el, la socialista socialist; adj. socialist

la sociedad society

el sofá sofa

el sol sun; hacer sol to be sunny

solamente only

el soldado soldier

la soledad loneliness

solitario lonely

solo alone; single

sólo only, just

soltero single, unmarried

la solución solution

la sombra shadow

el sombrero hat

sonoro sonorous

soñar con to dream of

la sopa soup

sorprender to surprise

la sorpresa surprise

su, sus his, her, its, their, your (Ud., Uds.)

la subconsciencia subconscious

la subida ascent, climb

subir to go up, climb

el subjuntivo subjunctive

subordinar to subordinate

suceder to happen

el sucesor (la sucesora) successor

sucio dirty

Sudamérica South America

la suegra mother-in-law

el suegro father-in-law; pl. in-laws

el sueldo salary

el suelo floor, ground

el sueño dream; tener sueño to be sleepy

la suerte luck

el suéter sweater

suficiente enough, sufficient

el sufrimiento suffering

sufrir to suffer

el, la superintendente supervisor

superior higher

la **superioridad** superiority

el **supermercado** supermarket

la **superstición** superstition

supersticioso superstitious

suponer to suppose

supremo supreme

supesto: por supuesto of course

el **sur** south; **al sur de** south of; **la América del Sur** South America

el **suroeste** southwest

el **surrealismo** surrealism

el, la **surrealista** surrealist

el **susto** fright

suyo(s), suya(s) *adj.* (of) his, her, of hers, your, of yours **(Uds., Uds.)**, their, of theirs; **el suyo (la suya, los suyos, las suyas)** *pron.* his, hers, yours **(Uds., Uds.)**, theirs

T

el **taco** taco

tal such (a); **con tal (de) que** provided that; **¿Qué tal . . . ?** How about . . . ?; **tal vez** perhaps

el **talento** talent

el **Talgo** deluxe Spanish train

también also, too

tampoco neither, (not) either; **Tampoco.** Not that either.

tan so; such; **tan . . . como** as . . . as

el **tango** popular music and dance of Argentina and Uruguay

tanto so much, as much; *pl.* so many, as many; **entre tanto** meanwhile **No es para tanto.** It's not that important.; **por lo tanto** therefore; **tanto como** as much as; as well as; *pl.* as many as; **tanto(s) . . . como** as much (many) . . . as; both . . . and

la **tardanza** delay, lateness

tardar to take a long time, delay

tarde *adv.* late; **más tarde** later; **tardísimo** very late

la **tarde** afternoon; **Buenas tardes.** Good afternoon. Good evening; **de la tarde** P.M. (afternoon or early evening); **por la tarde** in the afternoon

la **tarjeta** car; **tarjeta postal** postcard

el **taxi** taxi

la **taza** cup

te *ojb. pron.* (to, for, from) you, yourself *(fam. sing.)*

el **té** tea

el **teatro** theatre

técnico technical

el **techo** roof

el **teléfono** telephone; **hablar por teléfono** to talk on the phone; **llamar por teléfono** to phone

la **telenovela** soap opera, t.v. series

la **televisión** television; **por televisión** on television

el **televisor** television set

el **tema** subject, theme

la **temperatura** temperature

el **templo** temple

temprano early; **mañana temprano** early tomorrow morning

el **tenedor** fork

tener to have; **¿Quê tiene . . . ?** What's wrong with . . . ?; **tener . . . años** to be . . . years old; **tener calor** to be (feel) hot; **tener celos** to be jealous; **tener cuidado (con)** to be careful (of, about); **tener dolor de cabeza** to have a headache; **tener fiebre** to have a fever; **tener frío** to be (feel) cold; **tener ganas de** to feel like, want; **tener hambre** to be hungry; **tener mareos** to be dizzy; **tener miedo** to be afraid; **tener prisa** to be in a hurry; **tener que** to have to, must; **tener razón** to be right;

tener sed to be thirsty; **tener sueño** to be sleepy; **tener suerte** to be lucky; **tener tos** to have a cough

el **tenis** tennis

la **tensión** tension

teñir (i) to color, dye

la **teoría** theory

tercer, tercero third

la **terminación** end, termination

terminar to end, finish

la **tertulia** regular get-together of friends

el **terreno: ganar terreno** to gain ground

el **territorio** territory

el **tesoro** treasure; **¡Mi tesoro!** My darling!

el **testamento: Nuevo Testamento** New Testament

el **testimonio** evidence

ti *obj. of prep.* you, yourself

la **tía** aunt

el **tiempo** time; weather; **al mismo tiempo** at the same time; **a tiempo** on time; **con el tiempo** in time, eventually; **hace buen tiempo** it's nice weather; **mucho tiempo** a long time; **perder (el) tiempo** to waste (one's) time; **¿(por) cuánto tiempo?** how long?; **¿Qué tiempo hace?** How's the weather?

la **tienda** store, shop; **tienda de comestibles** grocery store

la **tierra** earth, land; **Madre-Tierra** Mother Earth (Indian deity)

tinto: vino tinto red wine; in Colombia, black coffee

el **tío** uncle; *pl.* aunt(s) and uncle(s)

típico typical; traditional

el **tipo** type, kind; guy

el **título** title

la **tiza** chalk

tocar to touch; to play (music or musical instrument)

todavía still, yet; **todavía no** not yet

todo *adj.* all, entire, whole; complete; every; *m. n.* everything; **a (en, por) todas partes** everywhere; **sobre todo** especially; **todo el mundo** everyone; the whole world; **todo lo demás** everything else

todos *adj.* all, every; *n.* all, everyone; **a (en, por) todas partes** everywhere; **de todas maneras** anyhow, anyway; **todos los días** every day

tolerar to tolerate

tolteca Toltec

tomar to take; to drink; to have (a meal); **Toma.** Take it; **tomadas del brazo** arm in arm

el **tomate** tomato

el **tono** tone

la **tontería** nonsense

tonto silly, foolish

el **torero** (la **torera**) bullfighter

el **toro** bull; **corrida de toros** bullfight; **toro bravo** fighting bull

la **tortilla** in Spain, omelette; in Mexico, tortilla (flat, pancake-shaped corn bread)

la **torre** tower

la **tos** cough

la **tostada** piece of toast

totalmente totally

el **trabajador** (la **trabajadora**) worker; *adj.* hard-working

trabajar to work

el **trabajo** work, job

la **tradición** tradition

tradicional traditional

traducir (zc) to translate

el **traductor** (la **traductora**) translator

traer to bring

el **tráfico** traffic

trágico tragic

el **traje** suit; costume; uniform

el **tranquilizante** tranquilizer

tranquilo: dejar tranquilo to leave alone

transformar to transform; **transformarse** to be transformed

el **tránsito** traffic

transmitir to transmit

trasladar to transfer

tratar to treat; **tratar de** to try to
trece thirteen
treinta thirty
el **tren** train; **en tren** by train
tres three
trescientos 300
la **tribu** tribe
el **trimestre** quarter (in a school year)
triste sad
la **tristeza** sadness
triunfar to win, triumph
el **triunfo** triumph
el **trovador** troubadour
tu, tus your
tú *subj. pron.* you *(fam. sing.)*
la **tumba** grave, tomb
la **tuna** group of student musicians (Spain)
el **turismo** tourism
el, la **turista** tourist
turnarse to take turns
tuyo(s), tuya(s) *adj.* your, of yours; **el tuyo (la tuya, los tuyos, las tuyas)** *pron.* yours *(fam. sing.)*

U

u or (replaces **o** before a word beginning with *o* or *ho*)
último last, latest
único unique; only one
unido: Estados Unidos United States
unificarse to become united
la **unión** union

unir, unirse to unite
la **universidad** university
universitario *adj.* university
el **universo** universe
uno (un), una one; a, an
unos, unas some, a few, several; **unos + *a number*** about
urbano urban
urgente urgent, pressing
usar to use
usted (*abbr.* **Uds., Vd.**) you (formal); *pl.* **ustedes** (*abbr.* **Uds., Vds.**) you (fam. & formal); **de usted (ustedes)** your, (of) yours
útil useful
utilizar to utilize

V

las **vacaciones** vacation; **(estar) de vacaciones** (to be) on vacation; **ir de vacaciones** to go for a vacation
la **vainilla** vanilla
valer to be worth; **más vale** it is better; **valer la pena** to be worth the trouble, worthwhile
valiente brave
el **valor** value, worth, merit ¡**Vamos!** Come on, now!
vanidoso vain, conceited
variado varied
variar to vary

la **variedad** variety
varios several
vasco Basque
el **vaso** glass (drinking)
vasto vast
las **veces:** *pl. of* la **vez**
el **vecino** (la **vecina**) neighbor
la **vega** fertile lowland
el **vegetariano** (la **vegetariana**) vegetarian
veinte twenty
la **vejez** old age
la **velocidad** speed
el **vencedor** (la **vencedora**) victor
el **vendedor** (la **vendedora**) vendor, salesperson
vender to sell
Venecia Venice
venezolano Venezuelan
la **venganza** revenge
venir to come; **ir y venir** coming and going; **la semana que viene** next week, this coming week; **Ven acá.** Come here.
la **venta** sale
la **ventana** window
ver to see; **A ver.** Let's see; **verse** to be seen; **Ya veremos.** We'll see.
el **verano** summer
veras: de veras really
la **verdad** truth; ¿**verdad?** right? isn't that so? really?
verdadero real, true
verde green
la **verdura** vegetable
la **vergüenza** shame; **darle vergüenza a**

alguien to make someone ashamed; **no tener vergüenza** to be shameless; **¡Qué falta de vergüenza!** What shamelessness!

el **vestido** dress
vestir (i) (de) to dress (as); **vestirse (de)** to dress (as); to get dressed

la **vez** (*pl.* **veces**) time, occasion; **a la vez** at the same time, at once; **alguna vez** ever, at some time; **a veces** at times, sometimes; **en vez de** instead of; **muchas veces** often; **otra vez** again, once more; **por primera vez** for the first time; **tal vez** perhaps
viajar to travel

el **viaje** trip, journey; **¡Buen viaje!** Have a good trip!; **hacer un viaje** to take a trip; **(salir) de viaje** (to leave) on a trip; **viaje de negocios** business trip

el **viajero** (la **viajera**) traveler
vibrante vibrant

la **víctima** victim
la **victoria** victory
victorioso victorious
la **vida** life; **llevar una vida . . .** to lead a . . . life

la **vidriera** store window
el **viejecito** (la **viejecita**) little old man (woman)
viejo old; *n.* old person
el **viento** wind; **hacer viento** to be windy; **instrumento de viento** wind instrument
el **vientre** stomach, abdomen
viernes Friday
la **vihuela** an early guitar
el **vino** wine
Viña del Mar coastal resort town in Chile
violento violent; **violentísimo** very violent
violeta violet, purple
el, la **violinista** violinist
la **virgen** virgin
el **visigodo** (la **visigoda**, Visigoth
la **visión** vision
visitar to visit
la **vista** view
visto seen
la **vitamina** vitamin
el **viudo** (la **viuda**) widower (widow)
vivir to live; **¡Viva . . . !** Hooray for . . . ! Long live . . . !
vivo alive; bright; vivid
el **vocabulario** vocabulary
el **volcán** volcano
el **vólibol** volleyball

volver(ue) to return; **volver a** + *inf.* to do (something) again
vosotros, vosotras *subj. pron.* you (*fam. pl.*); *obj. of prep.* you, yourselves
votar to vote
la **voz** voice; **en voz alta** out loud
la **vuelta: ida y vuelta** round trip
vuelto returned
vuestro *adj.* your; **el vuestro** *pron.* your, (of) yours (*fam. pl.*)
vulgar common; vulgar; vernacular
la **vulnerabilidad** vulnerability

Y

y and
ya already; now; **ya en** by; **ya no** no longer; **ya que** since; **Ya veremos.** We'll see.
el **yerno** son-in-law
yo I

Z

la **zamba** South American dance
la **zampoña** pan-pipes (Bolivian flute)
la **zapatería** shoe store
el **zapato** shoe

ENGLISH-SPANISH VOCABULARY

The following abbreviations are used:

abbrev.	abbreviation	*neut.*	neuter
adj.	adjective	*obj.*	object
adv.	adverb	*pl.*	plural
art.	article	*poss.*	possessive
conj.	conjunction	*prep.*	preposition
dem.	demonstrative	*pres.*	present
dir.	direct	*pron.*	pronoun
f.	feminine	*reflex.*	reflexive
fam.	familiar	*rel.*	relative
indef.	indefinite	*sing.*	singular
ind.	indirect	*subj.*	subject
inf.	infinitive	*vb.*	verb
m.	masculine		

A

a *indef. art.* un, una
A.M. de la mañana
about *(of)* de; *(some)* unos(as); **at about one o'clock** como a la una; **to be about to** *(+inf.)* estar para *(+inf.)*; **to dream about** soñar con; **to think about** pensar en
accept *vb.* aceptar
accident accidente *m.*
address dirrección *f.*
advice consejo *m.*
affect *vb.* afectar
afternoon tarde *f.*
again otra vez
against *prep.* contra
age edad *f.*
agency agencia *f.*
ago: six months ago hace seis meses
agree (with) *vb.* estar de acuerdo con

air mail correo aéreo *m.*
airplane avión *m.*
airport aeropuerto *m.*
all todo(a); **all right** bien; **All Saints Day** Día de Todos los Santos
alone *adj.* solo
already ya
although *conj.* aunque
always siempre
and y; e *(before* i- *or* hi-)
angry: to get angry enojarse
another *adj. + pron.* otro (a)
answer *vb.* contestar
anxious *adj.* ansioso(a)
anymore no . . . más
anything algo; **not anything** nada
application formulario *m.*
April abril *m.*
Argentinean *adj. or noun* argentino(a)

arm brazo *m.*
arrive *vb.* llegar
article artículo *m.* **ask** *vb.* *(to inquire)* preguntar; *(to request)* pedir
asleep dormido(a)
aspirin aspirina *f.*
at a; *(a place)* en; **at last** por fin; **at least** por lo menos
athlete atleta *m. + f.*
attend *vb.* asistir
automobile automóvil *m.*

B

basketball basquetbol *m.*
bathroom baño *m.*
be *vb. (condition or location)* estar; *(characteristic)* ser; *(to remain)* quedar; *(weather)* hacer

(+ *noun*); **be able**
poder; **be cold** tener
frío; **be glad (that)**
alegrarse (de que); **be
named** llamarse; **be
obliged** (*must*) deber;
be sorry (*to regret*)
sentir; **be thirsty** tener
sed; **be . . . years old**
tener . . . años
beach playa *f.*
beard barba *f.* because
adv. porque
become *vb.* llegar a ser
bedroom alcoba *f. prep.*
beer cerveza *f.*
before *adv.* (*time*) antes
(de)
begin *vb.* empezar (ie)
behind *prep.* detrás (de)
believe *vb.* creer, pensar
belong (to) *vb.* ser de
besides *adv.* además;
prep. además de
best mejor
better mejor; (*with* gustar)
más
big gran, grande
birth: birth control
control de la natalidad
m.
birthday cumpleaños *m.
sing.*
boarding house pensión
f.
book libro *m.*
boring *adj.* aburrido(a)
boy muchacho, niño,
chico *m.*
boyfriend novio *m.*
breakfast desayuno *m.*
bring *vb.* traer
brother hermano *m.*
build *vb.* construir
bus autobús *m.*
busy *adj.* ocupado(a)

but *conj., adv.* pero; *prep.*
excepto
buy *vb.* comprar

C

call *vb.* llamar; **to be
called** llamarse
can (*to be able*) poder
car auto *m.*; coche *m.*
careful: to be careful
tener cuidado
carry *vb.* llevar
Catholic *adj. & noun*
católico(a)
center centro *m.*
chapter capítulo *m.*
chicken pollo *m.*
child niño *m.*, niña *f.*;
children niños *m. pl.*;
(*sons and daughters*)
hijos
chocolate chocolate *m.*
Christmas navidad *f.*
church iglesia *f.*
city ciudad *f.*
class clase *f.*
close *vb.* cerrar (ie)
coffee café *m.*
cold frío *m.*; **to be (very)
cold** (*referring to
persons*) tener (mucho)
frío; (*weather*) hacer
(mucho) frío
Colombia Colombia *f.*
come *vb.* venir; **to come
(by)** pasar (por); **to
come in** pasar; **to come
up** subir; **come in!**
¡adelante! *or* ¡pase
usted!
commit: commit suicide
matarse, suicidarse
concert concierto *m.*
conserve *vb.* conservar

cool fresco(-a)
cost *vb.* costar (ue)
counter mostrador *m.*
country (*rural*) campo;
(*nation*) país *m.*
couple matrimonio *m.*
course curso *m.*; (*class*)
clase *f.*; **of course!**
¡claro!, por supuesto,
desde luego, ¡cómo no!;
of course . . . claro
que . . . , por supuesto
que . . .
cry *vb.* gritar
cultural *adj.* cultural
custard flan *m.*

D

dance baile *m.*; *vb.* bailar
daughter hija *f.*
day día *m.*
December diciembre *m.*
decide *vb.* decidir
delicious *adj.* delicioso,
rico
depressing *adj.*
deprimente
die *vb.* morir(se) (ue)
diet dieta *f.*
difficult *adj.* difícil
dinner comida *f.*; cena *f.*
diplomat diplomático *m.*
+ *f.*
divorce *vb.* divorciarse
do *fb.* (*to make, to act*)
hacer
doctor doctor *m.*, doctora
f.
dollar dólar *m.*
door puerta *f.*
doubt duda *f.*; *vb.* dudar
downtown (*in the city*) en
el centro; (*to the city*) al
centro

dozen docena *f.*
dress: to get dressed *vb.* vestirse
drink *vb.* beber
during *prep.* durante

E

each cada **each other** nos, os, se
early *adv.* temprano
earn *vb.* ganar
eat *vb.* comer; **to eat breakfast** desayunar; **to eat lunch** almorzar; **to eat supper, dinner** cenar
eggs huevos *m.*
eight ocho; **eight o'clock** las ocho; **eight hundred** ochocientos(as)
eighteen dieciocho
eighteenth *(in dates)* dieciocho
eighth octavo(a); *(in dates)* ocho
eighty ochenta; **eighty-one** ochenta y uno(a); **eighty-two** ochenta y dos, *etc.*
either o; *(after negative)* tampoco
elegant elegante
eleven once; **eleven o'clock** las once
eleventh *(in dates)* once
employment empleo *m.*
end *vb.* terminar; fin *m.*; **have a happy ending** acabar bien
ending fin *m.*; terminación *f*
energy energía *f.*
English *adj.* inglés
enjoy oneself *vb.* divertirse (ie)
event acontecimiento *m.*

everyone todos(as); todo el mundo
every: everyday todos los días
exchange *vb.* cambiar
excuse (**me**) con permiso; perdón
expensive caro(a)
eye ojo *m.*

F

fall *vb.* caer; **fall** otoño *m.*
family familia *f.*
famous *adj.* famoso(a)
fanatical fanático(a)
fascinate *vb.* fascinar
fast *adj.* rápido
father padre *m.*
favor favor *m.*
February febrero *m.*
feel *vb.* sentirse
fever fiebre *f.*
fifteen quince
fifteenth *(in dates)* quince
fifth quinto(a); *(in dates)* cinco
fifty cincuenta; **fifty-one** cincuenta y uno(a); **fifty-two** cincuenta y dos, *etc.*
film película *f.*
finally por fin
find *vb.* encontrar (ue)
first primer, primero(a)
fish pescado *m.*
five cinco; **five hundred** quinientos(as)
follow *vb.* seguir
food comida *f.*
for *prep.* para; por; **for the (second) time** por (segunda) vez
forbid *vb.* prohibir, no dejar

foreigner extranjero(a)
forget *vb.* olvidar
fork tenedor *m.*
form formulario *m.*
forty cuaranta; **forty-one** cuarenta y uno(a); **forty-two** cuarenta y dos, *etc.*
four cuatro **four o'clock** las cuatro; **four hundred** cuatrocientos(as)
fourteen catorce
fourteenth *(in dates)* catorce
fourth cuarto(a); *(in dates)* cuatro
French *(language)* (el) francés *m.;* **French, Frenchman, Frenchwoman** *adj. or noun* francés, francesa
Friday viernes *m.*
friend amigo *m.*, amiga *f.*
from de, desde; **far from** lejos de; **to be from** *(a place)* ser de; **to leave from** salir de
front: in front of enfrende de, delante de
fruit fruta *f.*
furniture muebles *m. pl.*
future *adj.* futuro(a)

G

game juego *m.;* partido *m.*
geography geografía *f.*
get *(to obtain)* conseguir; *(to take out)* sacar; **to get up** levantarse
gift regalo *m.*
girl niña, chica, muchacha *f.*

girlfriend novia *f.*
give *vb.* dar
glass *(drinking)* vaso *m.*
go ir; **to go away** irse; **to go back** volver (ue); **to go in** pasar, entrar; to go out salir; **to go shopping** ir de compras; **to go to bed** acostarse (ue); **to be going to** (do something) ir a + *inf.*; **to go up** subir; **to go with** *(accompany)* acompañar: **how's it going?** ¿qué tal?
good buen, bueno(a); **good afternoon** buenas tardes; **good evening or good night** buenas noches; **good morning** buenos días; **to have a good time** divertirse (ie)
good-by adiós
grandfather abuelo *m.*
grandmother abuela *f.*
grandparents abuelos *m. pl.*
guitar guitarra *f.*
guest invitado(a), huésped *m. + f.*

H

half *or* **a half** medio(a); **half past one** la una y media
hand mano *f.*
happy contento(a); feliz
hardworking *adj.* trabajador(a)
have *vb.* tener; *(in compound tenses)* haber; *(food or drink)* tomar; **have fun** *(or a good*

time) divertirse (ie); **have just** *(done something)* acabar de (+ *inf.*) **have to** *(do something)* tener que (+ *inf.*)
he *subj. pron.* él
hear *vb.* oír
hello *(good morning)* buenos días; *(good afternoon)* buenas tardes *(good evening)* buenas noches; **hello** *(hey! hi!)* ¡hola!
help *vb.* ayudar
her *poss. adj.* su, sus, *or* el (la los, las) . . . de ella; *dir. obj.* la; *ind. obj.* le, se *(before lo, la, los, las); obj. of prep.* ella
here aquí; **here is** *or* **here are** aquí tiene usted *or* tome usted
hers *poss. adj.* suyo(a) (os) (as) *or* de ella; *pron.* el suyo, el de ella, *etc.*
herself *reflex. pron.* se
hi! ¡hola!
himself *reflex pron.* se
his *poss. adj.* su, sus, *or* el (la, los, las) . . . de él; suyo(a) (os) (as) *or* de él *(in stressed position); pron.* el suyo, el de él, *etc.*
history historia *f.*
home casa *f.*; **at home** en casa; **to arrive home** llegar a casa; **to leave home** salir de casa; **to return home** volver a casa
hope *vb.* esperar; **I hope** . . . ojalá que
hospital hospital *m.*
hot: to be (very) hot *(referring to persons)*

tener (mucho) calor; *(weather)* hacer (mucho) calor
hour hora *f.*
house casa *f.*
how? ¿cómo?; **how goes it?** ¿qué tal?; **how is the weather?** ¿qué tiempo hace?; **how many?** ¿cuántos(as)?; **how much?** ¿cuánto(a)?; **how old (is he)?** ¿cuántos años (tiene)?
how! ¡qué!; **how many!** ¡cuántos(as)!; **how much!** ¡cuánto(a)!
hundred: a *(or)* **one hundred** cien, ciento
hungry: to be (very) hungry tener (mucha) hambre
hurry: to be in a hurry tener prisa
hurt *vb.* doler (ue)
husband esposo *m.*, marido *m.*

I

I *subj. pron.* yo
if si; **as if** como si; **even if** aunque
immigrant inmigrante *m. or f.*
important importante
in en; *(after superlative)* de; **in the afternoon** por la tarde; **ten o'clock in the morning** las diez de la mañana; **in order that** para que; **in order to** para
inform (oneself) *vb.* informarse
in-law suegros; **father-in-law** suegro *m.*; **mother-in-law** suegra *f.*

instead of *adv.* en lugar de, en vez de
intelligent *adj.* inteligente
interesting interesante
interview entrevista *f.*
invite *vb.* invitar
it *subj. pron., not expressed in Spanish; dir. obj.* lo, la; *ind. obj.* le; *obj. of prep.* él, ella
Italian *adj.* italiano

J

January enero *m.*
jealous celosa(a); **to be jealous** tener celos
jewel joya *f. (pl* **jewelry)**
job empleo *m.;* trabajo *m.*
July julio *m.*
June junio *m.*
just: to have just *(done something)* acabar de *(+ inf.)*

K

key llave *m.*
kill *vb.* matar
kiss *vb.* besar
kitchen cocina *f.*
knife cuchillo *m.*
know *(a fact)* saber; *(to be acquainted with)* conocer; **I don't know** no (lo) sé

L

lady señora *f.;* **lady and gentleman** señores *m. pl;* **ladies and gentlemen** damas y caballeros; **young lady** señorita *f.*

language idioma *m.,* lengua *f.*
last *(latest)* último(a); *(past)* pasado(a)
late *adv.* tarde; **lately** *adv.* últimamente; **later** más tarde, *(afterwards)* después; **see you later** hasta luego
laugh *vb.* reír
learn *vb.* aprender
least *adj.* mínimo(a)
leave *vb.* salir de
lecture conferencia *f.*
less menos
let *vb.* dejar
letter carta *f.*
library biblioteca *f.*
like: what's (she) like? ¿cómo es?; **I like (it)** me gusta
listen *vb.* escuchar
literature literatura *f.*
live *vb.* vivir
look: to look at mirar; **to look for** buscar
lose *vb.* perder
love amor *m.; vb.* querer, amar

M

ma'am señora *f. (abbrev:* Sra.)
magnificent magnífico(a)
mail *vb.* mandar, enviar por correo
make *vb.* hacer
man hombre *m.*
many muchos(as); **as many** tantos(as) . . . como; **how many?** ¿cuántos (as)?; **how many!** ¡cuántos (a)!; **so many** tantos
map mapa *m.*

March marzo *m.*
marry *vb.* casarse con
mathematics matemáticas *f. pl.*
matter *vb.* importar
may *(can)* poder (ue)
me *dir. or indir. obj.* me; *obj. of prep.* mí; **with me** conmigo
meat carne *f.*
meet *vb.* conocer
member miembro *m.*
Mexican mexicano(a)
milk leche *f.*
million millón *m.;* **a million . . .** un millón de . . .
mine *poss. adj.* mío(a) (os) (as); *pron.* el mío, *etc.*
minute minuto *m.*
Miss (la) señorita *(abbrev.* Srta.)
Monday lunes *m.*
money dinero *m.*
month mes *m.*
more más
morning mañana *f.;* **good morning** buenos días; **in the morning** por la mañana; **ten o'clock in the morning** las diez de la mañana
mother madre *f.; (mama)* mamá *f.*
mountain montaña *f.*
mouth boca *f.*
movie película *f.;* **movies** *(cinema)* cine *m. sing.*
Mr. (el) señor *(abbrev.* Sr.); **Mr. and Mrs.** (los) señores *(abbrev.* Sres.)
much *adv.* mucho; *adj.* mucho (a); **as much** *adv.* tanto, *adj.* tanto(a); **as much . . . as** tanto (a) . . . como; **how much?** ¿cuánto(a)?;

so much tanto(a); **very much** mucho
murder asesinato *m.*
museum museo *m.*
music música *f.*
must *(to be obliged)* deber; **one must** *(do something)* hay que *(+ inf.)*; **must, must have** *expressed by future or conditional*
my *poss. adj.* mi, mis
myself *reflex pron., dir. or indir. obj.* me; *obj. of prep.* mí; **with myself** conmigo

N

name: my name is me llamo; **what is your name?** ¿cómo se llama usted?
natural natural
near *adv.* cerca; *prep.* cerca de
necessary *adj.* necesario(a)
need *vb.* necesitar
neighborhood barrio *m.*
neither tampoco; **neither . . . nor** ni . . . ni
nervous nervioso(a)
never nunca, jamás
new nuevo(a); **what's new?** ¿Qué hay de nuevo?
news noticias *f.*
newscaster noticiero *m.* + *f.*
newspaper periódico *m.*
next próximo(a); **next week** la semana próxima, la semana que viene
nice *(likeable)* simpático(a), amable

night noche *f.* **at night** de noche, por la noche; **good night** buenas noches; **last night** anoche
nine nueve; **nine o'clock** las nueve; **nine hundred** novecientos(as)
nineteen diecinueve
nineteenth *(in dates)* diecinueve
ninety noventa; **ninety-one** novienta y uno(a); **ninety-two** novienta y dos, *etc.*
no no; *adj.* ningún, ninguno(a)
nobody nadie
no one nadie
nor ni
not no; **to believe not** *or* **to think not** creer que no
November noviembre *m.*
now ahora; **right now** ahora mismo
number número *m.*

O

o'clock: at three o'clock a las (tres); **it is (three) o'clock** son las (tres)
October octubre *m.*
of de; **a quarter of three** las tres menos cuarto
offer *vb.* ofrecer
office oficina *f.*
often muchas veces
old viejo(a); *(ancient)* antiguo(a); **to be . . . years old** tener . . . años; **how old (is he)?** ¿cuantos años (tiene)?
omelette tortilla (de huevos) *f.*

on *(doing something)* al (+ *inf.*); **on (Wednesday)** *adv.* el (miércoles), *adj.* del (miércoles); **on the dot** en punto; **to put on** *(clothes)* ponerse
one un, uno(a); *pron.* uno(a), se; **one another** nos, os, se; **one o'clock** la una; **one hundred** cien, ciento; **one must** *(do something)* hay que (+ *inf.*); **which one?** ¿cuál?
open abierto(a); *vb.* abrir
or o; u *(before o- or ho-)*
orange naranja *f.*
orchestra orquesta *f.*
order orden *f.*; **in order that** para que; **in order to** para; *vb. (request)* pedir; *(command)* mandar
organize *vb.* organizar
other otro(a); *(remaining)* demás; **each other** nos, os, se; **on the other hand** en cambio
our *poss. adj.* nuestro (a) (os) (as)
ours *poss. adj.* nuestro (a) (os) (as); *pron.* el nuestro, *etc.*
ourselves *reflex. pron., dir. or indir. obj.* nos; *obj. of prep.* nosotros(as)
outside afuera

P

P.M.: **(two) P.M. (las dos) de la tarde; (ten) P.M. (las diez) de la noche**
painting pintura *f.*, cuadro *m.*

parents padres *m.*
party fiesta *f.*
passenger pasajero *m.*
passport pasaporte *m.*
pay (for) *vb.* pagar
pencil lápiz *m.*
people gente *f. sing.*
phone teléfono *m.*
plan (on) *vb.* pensar en
play obra de teatro *f.; vb.*
  (music) tocar; *(a game)*
  jugar; **to play (tennis)**
  jugar (al tenis)
player jugador(a)
please *(to be pleasing)*
  gustar; *(as a favor)* por
  favor; **to please** *(do*
  something) hacer el
  favor de *(+ inf.)*
police policía *f.* **police**
  (man, woman) policía
  m. + f.
politician político *m, + f.*
poor pobre
postcard tarjeta postal *f.*
post office correo *m.*
practice práctica *f.; vb.*
  practicar
prepare *vb.* preparar
present regalo *m.*
president presidente *m.*
  + f.
press con ference
  conferencia de prensa
  f.
probably probablemente;
  often expressed by future
  or conditional
professor profesor *m.,*
  profesora *f.*
prohibit *vb.* prohibir
promise *vb.* prometer
Protestant *adj. + noun*
  protestante *m. + f.*
publish *vb.* publicar
put poner; **to put on**
  (clothes) ponerse

Q

quarter: a quarter to (two)
  (las dos) menos cuarto
quiet tranquilo(a),
  silencioso(a); **to keep**
  quiet, quiet down
  callarse

R

rain lluvia *f.; vb.* llover
  (ue)
ranch rancho *m.*
realize *vb.* darse cuenta
  de
receive *vb.* recibir
refuse *vb.* no querer
region región *f.*
remain (stay) *vb.*
  quedarse
reporter reportero *m. + f.*
request *vb.* pedir
restaurant restaurante *m.*
return *vb.* volver (ue),
  regresar
rice arroz *m.*
rich rico(a)
right derecho(a); *adv.*
  mismo; **right?** ¿eh?,
  ¿verdad?; **right now**
  ahora mismo; **(to be)** all
  right (estar) bien; **on**
  the right, to the right a
  la derecha; **right away**
  ahora mismo; **to be**
  right tener razón
ring anillo *m.*
robbery robo *m.*
run *vb.* correr

S

Saturday sábado *m;* **on**
  Saturday *adv.* el
  sábado, *adj.* del sábado

sausage chorizo *m.*
say *vb.* decir
school escuela *f.*
second segundo (a); *(in*
  dates) dos
see *vb.* ver; **see you**
  (tomorrow) hasta
  mañana
sell *vb.* vender
semester semestre *m.*
senator senador *m.*
send *vb.* enviar, mandar
sentence frase *f.*
September septiembre *m.*
serve *vb.* servir
seven siete; **seven**
  hundred setecientos(as)
seventeen diecisiete
seventeenth *(in dates)*
  diecisiete
seventh séptimo(a); *(in*
  dates) siete
she *subj. pron.* ella
shoe zapato *m.*
short *adj.* corto(a)
should *(ought to)* deber
shut cerrado(a)
sir señor *m.*
sister hermana *f.;*
  brother(s) and sister(s)
  hermanos *m. pl.*
sit down *vb.* sentarse (ie)
six seis; **six hundred**
  seiscientos(as)
sixteen dieciseis
sixth sexto(a); *(in dates)*
  seis
sixty sesenta; **sixty-one**
  sesenta y uno(a); **sixty-**
  two sesenta y dos, *etc.*
sleep *vb.* dormir (ue); **to**
  go to sleep dormirse
sleepy; to be sleepy tener
  sueño
small pequeño(a)
so tan; *(it)* lo; *(thus)* así;
  (therefore) luego; *(and*

so) de modo que; **I should say so!** ¡ya lo creo!; **so long** (*good-by*) hasta luego, hasta la vista; **so-so** (*fair*) así así; **so many** tantos(as); **so much** tanto(a); **so that** para que, de modo que; **to believe so** *or* **to think so** creer que sí

soap opera telenovela *f*.

socialist socialista *m*.

some *adv.* algo; *adj.* algún, alguno(a), *pl.* unos(as), algunos(as); *pron.* algunos(as)

someone alguno(a); alguien

son hijo *m*.

soon pronto; (*then*) luego; **as soon as** *conj.* en cuanto; **as soon as possible** lo más pronto posible

Spain España *f*.

Spaniard español *m*., española *f*.; **he is a Spaniard** es español

Spanish (*language*) (el) español; *adj.* español, española

speak *vb.* hablar

special especial

spend (*time*) *vb.* pasar

sport deporte *m*.

spring primavera *f*.

stamp estampilla *f*.

stand up levantarse

start *vb.* empezar (ie)

stay *vb.* quedarse

store tienda *f*.

story cuento *m*. historia *f*.

street calle *f*.

student estudiante *m*. or *f*.

study *vb.* estudiar

suitcase maleta *f*.

summer verano *m*.

sun sol *m*. **sunbathe** *vb.* tomar el sol

Sunday domingo *m*.

sunny: to be sunny haber sol

T

table mesa *f*.

take tomar; **take a trip** hacer un viaje; **take off** (*clothing*) quitarse

talk *vb.* hablar

tall alto(a)

teach *vb.* enseñar

teacher profesor(a), maestro(a)

telephone teléfono *m*.

television televisión *f*.; **television set** televisor *m*.

tell *vb.* decir

ten diez

tennis tenis *m*.

test *vb.* probar (ue), examinar; examen *m*.

than que; (*before a numeral*) de

thanks gracias *f. pl.*; **thank you** gracias

that *conj.* que; *rel. pron.* que; *dem. adj.* ese, esa; (*over there*) aquel, aquella; **that (one)** *pron.* ése, ésa, aquél, aquélla; **that** (*idea, fact, etc.*) *pron.* eso, aquello

the el, la, los, las; **lo** (*neut.*); **of the** del (= de + el), de la, de los, de las; **to the** al (= a + el), a la, a los, a las

theater teatro *m*.; (*movies*) cine *m*.

their *poss. adj.* su, sus, *or* el (la, los, las) . . . de ellos(as)

them *dir. obj.* los, las; *ind. obj.* les, se (*before* lo, la los, las); *obj. of prep.* ellos(as); **with them** con ellos(as)

themselves *reflex. pron.*, *dir. or ind. obj.* se

then entonces; (*soon*) luego; **well, then** pues

there allí; (*over there*) ahí; **therefore** luego, por eso **there is** *or* **there are** hay

they *subj. pron.* ellos(as)

thing: the (good) thing lo (bueno)

think *vb.* pensar; (*to believe*) creer; **to think of** *or* **about** pensar en; **to think not** creer que no; **to think so** creer que sí

third tercer, tercero(a); (*in dates*) tres

thirsty: to be thirsty tener sed

thirteen trece

thirteenth (*in datea*) trece

thirty treinta; **thirty-one** treinta y uno(a); **thirty-two** treinta y dos, *etc.*; **thirty-first** (*in dates*) treinta y uno

this *dem. adj.* este, esta; **this (one)** *pron.* éste, ésta; **this** (*idea, fact, etc.*) *pron.* esto

those *dem. adj.* esos, esas; (*over there*) aquello, aquellas; *pron.* ésos, ésas

thousand: a (*or* **one**) **thousand** mil

three tres

Thursday jueves *m*.

ticket pasaje *m*., billete *m*.

time (*duration*) tiempo *m*.; (*sequence*) vez *f*.; (*hour*) hora *f*.; **at times** a veces; **to have a good time** divertirse (ie)

tired cansado(a)

to a, para; **according to** según; **in order to** para; **a quarter to (two)** (las dos) menos cuarto

today hoy
tomato tomate *m.*
tomorrow mañana
tonight esta noche
too *(also)* también; **too much** demasiado
town pueblo *m.; (business district)* centro *m.;* **in town** en el centro; **to town** al centro
transmit *vb.* transmitir
travel *vb.* viajar
trip viaje *m.;* **to take a trip** hacer un viaje
truth verdad *f.*
try on *vb.* probarse
Tuesday martes *m.*
twelfth *(in dates)* doce
twelve doce
twentieth *(in dates)* veinte
twenty veinte; **twenty-one** veintiún; veintiuno(a); **twenty-two** veintidós; *etc.;* **twenty-first,** *etc. (in dates)* veintiuno, etc.
two dos; **two hundred** doscientos(as)

U

uncle tío *m.;* **uncle(s) and aunt(s)** tíos *m.pl.*
understand *vb.* entender, comprender
united: the United States los Estados Unidos
university universidad *f.*
unless *conj.* a menos que
until *prep.* hasta; *conj.* hasta que
us *dir. or indir. obj.* nos; *obj. of prep.* nosotros(as)
use *vb.* usar
used to: *expressed by imperfect tense*

usually *adv.* usualmente, generalmente

V

vain vanidoso(a)
very muy; *(extremely)* muchísimo; **very much** *(a lot)* mucho
visit *vb.* visitar

W

wait *vb.* esperar
wake up *vb.* despertar (ie)
want *vb.* querer, desear, tener ganas de
warm: to be (very) warm *(referring to persons)* tener (mucho) calor; *(weather)* hacer (mucho) calor
we *subj. pron.* nosotros(as)
weather tiempo *m.;* **to be (good, bad) weather** hacer (buen, mal) tiempo; **how's the weather?** ¿qué tiempo hace?; **the weather is bad** hace mal tiempo
Wednesday miércoles *m.*
week semana *f.*
weekend fin de semana *m*
well bien; **well . . .** bueno . . .; **well (then) . . .** pues . . .
what! ¡qué! **what a (pretty house)** ¡qué (casa) más (linda)!
what? ¿qué?; **what is (she) like?** ¿cómo es?; **what is your name?** ¿cómo se llama usted?

when? ¿cuándo?, ¿a qué hora?
whenever *conj.* cuando
where? ¿dónde?; *(to what place?)* ¿adónde?
who? ¿quién?, *pl.* ¿quiénes?
whose cuyo(a)
why? ¿por qué?
wife esposa *f.*
win *vb.* ganar
wind viento *m.*
window ventana *f.*
windy: it is (very) windy hace (mucho) viento
wine vino *m.,* **red wine** vino tinto, **white white** vino blanco
wish *vb.* desear
with con
without sin
woman mujer *f.*
wonder *vb.* preguntarse
word palabra *f.*
work *(artistic)* obra *f.; vb.* trabajar
world mundo *m.*
world *adj.* mundial
worse *or* **worst** peor
write *vb.* escribir
writer escritor *m.,* escritora *f.*

Y

year año *m.;* **to be . . . years old** tener ... años
yellow amarillo(a)
yesterday *adv.* ayer
you *subj. pron. (fam.)* tú, vosotros(as), *(polite)* usted, ustedes, *(indef.)* se; *dir. obj. (fam.)* te, os, *(polite)* lo, la, los, las; *ind. obj. (fam.)* te, os, *(polite)* le, les, se *(before*

lo, la, los, las); *obj. of prep. (fam.)* ti, vosotros(as), *(polite)* usted, ustedes; **with you** *(fam.)* contigo, con vosotros(as), *(polite)* con usted, con ustedes

young joven; **young lady** señorita *f.*

younger menor, más jóven

your *poss. adj. (fam.)* tu, tus, vuestro(a), (os), (as), *(polite)* su, sus, *or* el (la, los las) . . . de usted *or* de ustedes

yours *poss. adj. (fam.)* tuyo, (a), (os), (as), vuestro, (a), (os), (as), *(polite)* suyo, (a), (os), (as) *or* de usted, de ustedes; *pron. (fam.)* el tuyo, el vuestro, *etc.*, *(polite)* el suyo, el de usted, *etc.*

yourself, yourselves *reflex. pron., dir. or indir. (fam.)* te, os, *(polite)* se; *obj. of prep. (fam.)* ti, vosotros(as); **with yourself, with yourselves** *(fam.)* contigo, con vosotros(as)

GLOSSARY OF GRAMMATICAL TERMS

As you learn Spanish, you may come across grammatical terms in English with which you are not familiar. The following glossary is a reference list of grammatical terms and definitions with examples. You will find that these terms are used in the grammatical explanations of this book. If the terms are unfamiliar to you, it will be helpful to refer to this list.

adjective   a word used to modify, qualify, define, or specify a noun or noun equivalent. (*intricate* design, *volcanic* ash, *medical* examination)
demonstrative adjective designates or points out a specific item (*this* area)
descriptive adjective provides description (*narrow* street)
interrogative adjective asks or questions (*Which* page?)
possessive adjective indicates possession (*our* house)
predicate adjective forms part of the predicate, complements a verb phrase (His chances are *excellent*.)
    In Spanish, the adjective form must agree with or show the same gender and number as the noun it modifies.
    See **clause, adjective.**

adverb   a word used to qualify or modify a verb, adjective, another adverb, or some other modifying phrase or clause (soared *gracefully, rapidly* approaching train)
See **clause, adverbial.**

agreement   the accordance of forms between subject and verb, in terms of person and number, or between tenses of verbs (The *bystander witnessed* the accident but *failed* to report it.)
    In Spanish, the form of the adjective must also conform in gender and number with the modified noun or noun equivalent.

antecedent   the noun or noun equivalent referred to by a pronoun (The *book* is interesting, but it is difficult to read.)

article   a determining or nondetermining word used before a noun
definite article limits, defines, or specifies (*the* village)
indefinite article refers to a nonspecific member of a group or class (*a* village, *an* arrangement)
    In Spanish, the article takes different forms to indicate the gender and number of a noun.

auxiliary   a verb or verb form used with other verbs to construct certain tenses, voices, or moods (He *is* leaving. She *has* arrived. You *must* listen.)

clause   a group of words consisting of a subject and a predicate and functioning as part of a complex or compound sentence rather than as a complete sentence.
adjective clause functions as an adjective (The ad calls for someone *who can speak Spanish.*)
adverbial clause functions as an adverb (*Clearly aware of what he was saying,* he answered our questions.)
dependent clause modifies and is dependent upon another clause (*Since the rain has stopped,* we can have a picnic.)
main clause is capable of standing independently as a complete sentence (If all goes well, *the plane will depart in twenty minutes.*)
noun clause functions as subject or object (I think *the traffic will be heavy.*)

cognate   a word having a common root or being of the same or similar origin and meaning as a word in another language (*university* and *universidad* in Spanish)

command   See **mood (imperative).**

comparative   level of comparison used to show an increase or decrease of quantity or quality or to compare or show inequality between two items (*higher* prices, the *more* beautiful of the two mirrors, *less* diligently, *better than*)

comparison   the forms an adjective or adverb takes to express change in the quantity or quality of an item or the relation, equal or unequal, between items

conditional   a verb construction used in a contrary-to-fact statement consisting of a condition or an *if*-clause and a conclision (If you had told me you were sick, *I would have offered* to help.)
    See **mood (subjunctive).**

conjugation   the set of forms a verb takes to indicate changes of person, number, tense, mood, and voice

conjunction   a word used to link or connect sentences or parts of sentences

contraction   an abbreviated or shortened form of a word or word group (*can't, we'll*)

diminutive   a form of a word, usually a suffix added to the original word, used to indicate a smaller or younger version or variety and often expressive of endearment (duck*ling,* pup*py,* novel*lette*)

diphthong   in speech, two vowel sounds changing from one to the other within one syllable (*soil*, b*oy*)

gender   the class of a word by sex, either biological or linguistic. In English, almost all nouns are classified as masculine, feminine, or neuter according to the biological sex of the thing named; in Spanish, however, a word is classified as feminine or masculine (there is no neuter classification) on the basis of grammatical form or spelling.

idiom   an expression that is grammatically or semantically unique to a particular language (*I caught a cold. Happy birthday.*)

imperative   See **mood.**

indicative   See **mood.**

infinitive   the basic form of the verb, and the one listed in dictionaries, with no indication of person or number; it is often used in verb constructions and as a verbal noun, usually with "to" in English or with "-ar," "-er" or "-ir" in Spanish.

inversion   See **word order (inverted).**

mood   the form and construction a verb assumes to express the manner in which the action or state takes place
imperative mood used to express commands (*Walk* to the park with me.)
indicative mood the form most frequently used, usually expressive of certainty and fact (My neighbor *walks* to the park every afternoon.)
subjunctive mood used in expression of possibility, doubt, or hypothetical situations (If I *were* thin, I'd be happier.)

noun   a word that names something and usually functions as a subject or an object (*lady, country, family*)
    See **clause, noun.**

number   the form a word or phrase assumes to indicate singular or plural (*light/lights, mouse/mice, he has/they have*)
cardinal number used in counting or expressing quantity (*one, twenty-three, 6,825*)
ordinal number refers to sequence (*second, fifteenth, thirty-first*)

object   a noun or noun equivalent
direct objective receives the action of the verb (The boy caught a *fish*.)
indirect object affected by the action of the verb (Please do *me* a favor.)
prepositional object completes the relationship expressed by the preposition (The cup is on the *table*.)

orthographic   See **verb (orthographic-changing).**

participle   a verb form used as an adjective or adverb and in forming tenses
past participle relates to the past or a perfect tense and takes the appropriate ending (*written* proof, the door has been *locked*)
present participle assumes the progressive "-ing" ending in English (*protesting* loudly; will be *seeing*)
   In Spanish, a participle used as an adjective or in an adjectival phrase must agree in gender and number with the modified noun or noun equivalent.

passive   See **voice (passive).**

person   designated by the personal pronoun and/or by the verb form
first person the speaker or writer (*I, we*)
second person the person(s) addressed (*you*)
   In Spanish, there are two forms of address: the familiar and the polite.
third person the person or thing spoken about (*she, he, it, they*)

phrase   a word group that forms a unit of expression, often named after the part of speech it contains or forms
prepositional phrase contains a preposition (*in the room, between the window and the door*)

predicate   the verb or that portion of a statement that contains the verb and gives information about the subject (He *laughed.* My brother *commutes to the university by train.*)

prefix   a letter or letter group added at the beginning of a word to alter the meaning (*non*committal, *re*discover)

preposition   a connecting word used to indicate a spatial, temporal, causal, affective, directional, or some other relation between a noun or pronoun and the sentence or a portion of it (We waited *for* six hours. The article was written *by* a famous journalist.)

pronoun   a word used in place of a noun
demonstrative pronoun refers to something previously mentioned in context (If you need hiking boots, I recommend *these.*)
indefinite pronoun denotes a nonspecific class or item (*Nothing* has changed.)
interrogative pronoun asks about a person or thing (*Whose* is this?)
object pronoun functions as a direct, an indirect, or a prepositional object (Three persons saw *her.* Write *me* a letter. The flowers are for *you.*)
possessive pronoun indicates possession (The blue car is *ours.*)
reciprocal pronoun refers to two or more persons or things equally involved (María and Juan saw *each other* today.)

reflexive pronoun refers back to the subject (They introduced *themselves.*)
subject pronoun functions as the subject of a clause or sentence (*He* departed a while ago.)

radical   See **verb (radical-changing).**

reciprocal construction   See **pronoun (reciprocal).**

reflexive construction   See **pronoun (reflexive).**

sentence   a word group, or even a single word, that forms a meaningful complete expression
declarative sentence states something and is followed by a period (*The museum contains many fine examples of folk art.*)
exclamatory sentence exhibits force or passion and is followed by an exclamation point (*I want to be left alone!*)
interrogative sentence asks a question and is followed by a question mark (*Who are you?*)

subject   a noun or noun equivalent acting as the agent of the action or the person, place, thing, or abstraction spoken about (*The fishermen* drew in their nets. *The nets* were filled with the day's catch.)

suffix   a letter or letter group added to the end of a word to alter the meaning or function (like*ness*, transport*ation*, joy*ous*, love*ly*)

superlative   level of comparison used to express the utmost or lowest level or to indicate the highest or lowest relation in comparing more than two items (*highest* prices, the *most* beautiful, *least* diligently)
absolute superlative when a very high level is expressed without reference to comparison (the *very beautiful* mirror, *most diligent*, *extremely well*)

tense   the form a verb takes to express the time of the action, state, or condition in relation to the time of speaking or writing
future tense relates something that has not yet occurred (It *will* exist. We *will* learn.)
future perfect tense relates something that has not yet occurred but will have taken place and be complete by some future time (It *will have* existed. We *will have* learned.)
past tense relates to something that occurred in the past, distinguished as **preterite** (It *existed.* We *learned.*) and **imperfect** (It *was existing.* We *were learning.*)
past perfect tense relates to an occurrence which began and ended before or by a past event or time spoken or written of (It *had existed. We had learned.*)
present tense relates to now, the time of speaking or writing, or to a general, timeless fact (It *exists.* We *learn.* Fish *swim.*)

present perfect tense relates to an occurrence that began at some point in the past but was finished by the time of speaking or writing (It *has existed.* We *have learned.*)

progressive tense relates an action that is, was, or will be in progress or continuance (It *is*happening. It *was happening.* It *will be happening.*)

triphthong   in speech, three vowel sounds changing from one to another within one syllable (*wire, hour*)

verb   a word that expresses action or a state or condition (*walk, be, feel*)
intransitive verb no receiver is necessary (The light *shines.*)
orthographic-changing verb undergoes spelling changes in conjugation (infinitive: buy; past indicative: *bought*)
radical-changing verb undergoes a stem-vowel change in conjugation (infinite: draw; past indicative: dr*e*w)
transitive verb requires a receiver or an object to complete the predicate (He *kicks* the ball.)

voice   the form a verb takes to indicate the relation between the expressed action or state and the subject
active voice indicates that the subject is the agent of the action (The child *sleeps.* The professor *lectures.*)
passive voice indicates that the subject does not initiate the action but that the action is directed toward the subject (I *was contacted* by my attorney. The road *got slippery* from the rain. He *became* tired.)

word order   the sequence of words in a clause or sentence
inverted word order an element other than the subject appears first (*If the weather permits,* we plan to vacation in the country. *Please* be on time. *Have* you met my parents?)
normal word order the subject comes first followed by the predicate (*The people celebrated the holiday.*)

GRAMMATICAL INDEX

ILLUSTRATION CREDITS

Black and white by page numbers

Peter Menzel: 1, 9, 26, 31, 44, 54, 66, 67, 74, 87, 117, 127 *(top)*, 153, 158 *(bottom)*, 160, 174, 187, 188, 195, 231, 261, 279, 285, 297, 319, 340, 351 *(right)*, 371, 388, 403, 415. Dorka Raynor: 16, 23, 53, 85 *(right)*, 139, 154, 158 *(top)*, 203, 219, 238, 299, 307 *(top)*, 314 *(left)*, 385, 401, 407, 411. Editorial Photocolor Archives: 71 (Alain Keler), 122 (Andrew Sacks), 128 (Arthur Sirdofsky), 161 *(center)*, 168, 175 (Andrew Sacks), 245 (Alain Keler), 248, 250 (Carlos Hernández), 254, 267, 269, 270, 271 *(both)*, 273 (Sotheby Parke-Bernet), 300 (Steve Dunwell), 343 (Alain Keler), 347 (Robert Rapelye), 348, 350 (Robert Rapelye), 362 (Alain Keler), 379, 387 (Carlos Hernández), 396 (Alain Keler), 418 (Peter R. Dickerson), 421. Monkmeyer Press Photo Service: 81, 86 (Silberstein), 91 (Sybil Shelton), 100 (Fujihira), 127 *(bottom)*, (Elizabeth Hibbs), 134 (Sybil Shelton), 159 (Hans Mann), 161 *(left)*, (Mimi Forsyth), 304 (Fujihira), 308 (Linares), 330 (Fujihira), 333 (Pat Morin), 349 *(top)*, (Fujihira), 349 *(bottom)*, (Grabitzsky), 399 (Sybil Shelton). Beryl Goldberg: 85 *(left)*, 161 *(right)*, 196, 224, 386. Robert Frerck: 206. Taurus Photos: 226 (Eric Kroll). Spanish National Tourist Office: 230, 232 *(top)*, 233, 307 *(bottom)*. Bettmann Archive: 232 *(bottom)*. Photo Researchers: 263 (Fritz Henle), 286 (Carl Frank). Marga Clark: 265, 314 *(right)*, 373. Museum of Modern Art: 272. Kay Reese and Associates: 306, 381. Andrew Rakoczy: 342. Organization of American States: 351 *(left)*. Wendy Hilty Studio: 356.

Color by illustration number

Editorial Photocolor Archives: 1, 6 (Albert Moldvay). Robert Frerck: 2, 4, 5, 7, 8, 9, 16, 17, 18. Magnum: 3 (Burri). Rapho Guillumette: 10 (Silverster). Taurus Photos: 11 (L.L.T. Rhodes), 12 (Allan Price). AAA Photo: 13 (Ricatto). William Harris: 14. SCALA: 15 (Bencini). The Metropolitan Museum of Art: 19 (Isaac D. Fletcher Fund, Jacob S. Rogers Fund and Bequest of Adelaide Milton de Groot (1876–1967), Bequest of Joseph H. Durkee, by exchange, supplemented by Gifts from Friends of the Museum, 1971). The Metropolitan Museum of Art: 20 (Bequest of Mrs. H. O. Havemeyer, 1929, the H. O. Havemeyer Collection). Sotheby Park—Bernet. Agent, Editorial Photocolor Archives: 21.